URBAN BLUE SPACES

This book presents an evidence-based approach to landscape planning and design for urban blue spaces that maximises the benefits to human health and well-being while minimising the risks. Based on applied research and evidence from primary and secondary data sources stemming from the EU-funded BlueHealth project, the book presents nature-based solutions to promote sustainable and resilient cities.

Numerous cities around the world are located alongside bodies of water in the form of coastlines, lakes, rivers and canals, but the relationship between city inhabitants and these water sources has often been ambivalent. In many cities, water has been polluted, engineered or ignored completely. But, due to an increasing awareness of the strong connections between city, people, nature and water and health, this paradigm is shifting.

The international editorial team, consisting of researchers and professionals across several disciplines, leads the reader through theoretical aspects, evidence, illustrated case studies, risk assessment and a series of validated tools to aid planning and design before finishing with overarching planning and design principles for a range of blue-space types.

Over 200 full-colour illustrations accompany the case-study examples from geographic locations all over the world, including Portugal, the United Kingdom, China, Canada, the US, South Korea, Singapore, Norway and Estonia. With green and blue infrastructure now at the forefront of current policies and trends to promote healthy, sustainable cities, *Urban Blue Spaces* is a must-have for professionals and students in landscape planning, urban design and environmental design.

Simon Bell is a professor of landscape architecture at the Estonian University of Life Sciences, Estonia, and Associate Director of the OPENspace Research Centre at the University of Edinburgh, UK.

Lora E. Fleming is a professor and Chair of Epidemiology, Oceans and Human Health and Director of the European Centre for Environment and Human Health at the University of Exeter Medical School, UK.

James Grellier is a research fellow at the European Centre for Environment and Human Health at the University of Exeter Medical School, UK, and a senior scientific fellow at the Institute of Psychology at the Jagiellonian University, Poland.

Friedrich Kuhlmann is a chief specialist in landscape architecture at the Estonian University of Life Sciences, Estonia.

Mark J. Nieuwenhuijsen is a research professor in environmental epidemiology at ISGlobal, Spain.

Mathew P. White is a senior scientist in environmental psychology at the University of Vienna, Austria.

URBAN BLUE SPACES

Planning and Design for Water, Health and Well-Being

Edited by Simon Bell, Lora E. Fleming, James Grellier, Friedrich Kuhlmann,
Mark J. Nieuwenhuijsen, and Mathew P. White

LONDON AND NEW YORK

First published 2022
by Routledge
2 Park Square, Milton Park, Abingdon, Oxon OX14 4RN

and by Routledge
605 Third Avenue, New York, NY 10158

Routledge is an imprint of the Taylor & Francis Group, an informa business

British Library Cataloguing-in-Publication Data
A catalogue record for this book is available from the British Library

Library of Congress Cataloging-in-Publication Data
Names: Bell, Simon, 1957 May 24– editor. | Kuhlmann, Friedrich, editor. | White, Mathew P., editor.
Title: Urban blue spaces : planning and design for water, health and well-being / edited by Simon Bell, Friedrich Kuhlmann, Mathew P. White, Mark J. Nieuwenhuijsen, James Grellier and Lora E. Fleming.
Description: New York, NY : Routledge, 2022. | Includes bibliographical references and index.
Identifiers: LCCN 2021016588 (print) | LCCN 2021016589 (ebook) | ISBN 9780367173180 (paperback) | ISBN 9780367173173 (hardback) | ISBN 9780429056161 (ebook)
Subjects: LCSH: Land use—Europe—Planning—Case studies. | Sustainable development—Europe—Case studies. | Ecological landscape design—Europe—Case studies. | Landscape protection—Europe—Case studies.
Classification: LCC HD108.6 .U727 2022 (print) | LCC HD108.6 (ebook) | DDC 712.094—dc23
LC record available at https://lccn.loc.gov/2021016588
LC ebook record available at https://lccn.loc.gov/2021016589

ISBN: 978-0-367-17317-3 (hbk)
ISBN: 978-0-367-17318-0 (pbk)
ISBN: 978-0-429-05616-1 (ebk)

DOI: 10.4324/9780429056161

Typeset in Univers
by Apex CoVantage, LLC

Contents

Contents

Acknowledgements

Support for the writing of this book was provided by the BlueHealth project, funded by the European Union's Horizon 2020 research and innovation programme under grant agreement no. 666773.

Figures

Figures

Figures

Tables

Author short biographies

Jekaterina Balicka has an MSc in landscape architecture and also a professional university degree in landscape architecture and planning. She is a researcher and teacher at the Chair of Landscape Architecture, Estonian University of Life Sciences. Her interests are connected with the topics of urban nature and human health in the city: urban wilderness and wastelands as informal green spaces, urban acupuncture and temporary projects. In BlueHealth, her tasks were mainly connected with project review, the public involvement and design of Estonian small-scale interventions, virtual spatial interventions design and the BlueHealth book.

Simon Bell, PhD, CMLI, is Chair Professor of Landscape Architecture at the Estonian University of Life Sciences and Associate Director of the OPENspace Research Centre at the University of Edinburgh. His research interests focus on the role of landscape in promoting human health and well-being, among other aspects. He was a principal investigator in the BlueHeath project, leading the Estonian team, and worked primarily on planning and design for BlueHealth. He was chief editor of the book.

Matthias F.W. Braubach, MPH/MSc, is an urban geographer and environmental health expert. He works as Technical Officer Urban Health and Equity in the European Centre for Environment and Health of the WHO Regional Office for Europe. His work priorities address health impacts of environmental risks in urban settings, with a focus on urban nature and the unequal distribution of environmental risks and benefits across urban populations. In the BlueHealth project, he coordinated the development of the BlueHealth Decision Support Tool.

Marina Cervera Alonso de Medina, MLA, is an architect and landscape architect with a masters in landscape architecture and a master in research towards urbanism. Besides planning and projects on green infrastructure and public spaces developed through her professional practice based in Barcelona, she is adjunct lecturer for the Universitat Politècnica de Catalunya UPC-BarcelonaTech, related to both the Architectural and Landscape Architecture Schools.

Giovanni Coppini holds a PhD in environmental sciences from the University of Bologna. Since 2003, he has worked as a technologist at INGV in the operational oceanography division. Since 2012, he has worked at the Euro-Mediterranean Centre on Climate Change Foundation where he is Director of the Ocean Predictions and Applications Division. Since May 2015, he has led the European Copernicus Marine Service for the Mediterranean Sea, providing ocean forecasting and reanalysis products at the basin scale. He coordinates the development of marine pollution and marine safety applications at CMCC.

Arnt Diener, MSc, is an environmental scientist and public health professional. He works as a consulting specialist for WHO's European Centre for Environment and Health. As policy advisor and topical trainer, his focus lies on the risk-based management of environmental hazards through regulation and targeted programmes. He has a particular interest in evidence-based and realistic approaches to ensuring water safety for consumption and recreation. For the BlueHealth project, he served as lead advisor for the BlueHealth Decision Support Tool.

Lewis R. Elliott, PhD, is an environmental psychologist and lecturer at the European Centre for Environment and Human Health at the University of Exeter. His research focuses on the impact of natural environments on the physical and mental health of humans and behaviour change, particularly in relation to promoting outdoor physical activity through persuasive communication. In the BlueHealth project, he was responsible for all aspects of the BlueHealth International Survey.

Lora E. Fleming, MD, PhD, is a professor, chair and director of the European Centre for Environment and Human Health at the University of Exeter Medical School. As a physician and epidemiologist, she is interested in promoting interdisciplinary and trans-sector research and training in environment and human health, particularly ocean(s) and human health. She was the Principal Investigator and Project Coordinator of the H2020 BlueHealth Project.

Mireia Gascon, PhD, is Assistant Research Professor at the Barcelona Institute for Global Health (ISGlobal). As an environmental epidemiologist, she is interested in improving scientific understanding of the health impacts of the built environment and transport planning. In the BlueHealth project, she coordinated case studies, especially the case study at Rubi near Barcelona, and led a systematic review on outdoor blue spaces and health.

James Grellier, PhD, is a research fellow at the European Centre for Environment and Human Health (University of Exeter Medical School, UK) and a senior scientific fellow at the Institute of Psychology at the Jagiellonian University (Krakow, Poland). As an epidemiologist and environmental scientist, he is interested in modelling the impacts on human health of various aspects of the environment. He worked as a researcher in various aspects of the BlueHealth project while also providing overall coordination in his role as project manager.

Judith Hin, PhD, is a human geographer and a researcher on healthy living and the environment at the National Institute for Public Health and the Environment (RIVM) in the Netherlands. Previously, she worked as a strategic advisor in local government on integral issues and trends in neighbourhoods. Her field of expertise is in the area of multi-party governance processes, stakeholder analysis, multi-party/multi-sectoral cooperation, public-private partnership innovation, citizen participation and strategic integral policy advice.

Friedrich Kuhlmann, Dipl-Ing, is a landscape architect, a researcher and a doctoral student at the Estonian University of Life Sciences. His teaching and research interests focus on the fields of urban landscape design, contemporary landscape architecture theory and go-along assessment methods. In the BlueHealth project, he worked primarily on planning and design of the case studies and local interventions in Spain, Portugal and Estonia.

Mart Külvik, PhD, is a professor of biodiversity planning and management in the chairs of landscape management and nature conservation and landscape architecture at the Estonian University of Life Sciences. His main current research focuses on conservation planning and policies with an emphasis on participation in interaction with spatial planning, especially regarding blue-green infrastructure, ecosystem services and nature-based solutions.

Laura Mancini has an MSc in environmental economics and sustainable development tools. She is currently the Director of the Ecosystems Health Unit of the Italian National Institute of Health and professor of general and applied hygiene. Her scientific activity has developed inside the environment–human health interactions wider research area following its evolution and adopting its technological innovations. Research interests focus on health and climate change, environmental and global change and ecosystems health characterised by an integration between basic and applied research for promoting human health and well-being. She was a principal investigator in the BlueHeath project.

Marco Martuzzi is currently the Head of the Asia-Pacific Centre for Environment and Health of the World Health Organization Regional Office for the Western Pacific, in Seoul, Republic of Korea. He is an epidemiologist with experience in environmental and occupational studies. His current work is concerned with the impacts of environmental risk factors and determinants on health and health equity. While working at the WHO European Centre for Environment and Health, in Bonn, Germany, he coordinated WHO's participation in the BlueHealth Project.

Frederico Meireles Rodrigues, PhD, is Professor in Landscape Architecture at the Universidade de Trás-os-Montes e Alto Douro (UTAD), Portugal, and a chartered landscape architect. His teaching and research interests are in the fields of evaluation and critique of open space and in landscape design, health and inclusion. He was responsible for the Guimarães City Park case study in the BlueHealth Project.

Himansu S. Mishra, MSc, is an architect, landscape architect and urban planner. He is currently a researcher at the Finnish Environmental Institute (SYKE) and a doctoral student at the Estonian University of Life Sciences. His research focuses on sustainable urban design, environmental justice and benefits of nature-based solutions, environmental support for health and benefits of blue spaces in particular. In BlueHealth, he worked primarily on the health and well-being benefits of improving accessibility to urban blue spaces using evidence-based approaches. He also contributed to the development of case studies in the UK and Spain.

George P. Morris, PhD, FFPH, is Honorary Visiting Professor in the European Centre for Environment and Human Health at the University of Exeter. He has had a career-long interest in the role of environment in human health, initially in a regulatory role in local government and subsequently in an academic position. Later, he worked as an adviser and consultant on environment and health to the National Health Service in Scotland and the Scottish government.

Mark J Nieuwenhuijsen, PhD, is a research professor and a director of the Urban Planning, Environment and Health initiative and the Air Pollution and Urban Environment research programme at ISGlobal Barcelona, Spain. He is a world-leading expert in environmental exposure assessment, epidemiology and health impact assessment, with a strong focus on and interest in healthy urban living. In 2018, he was awarded the ISEE John Goldsmith Award for Outstanding Contributions to Environmental Epidemiology. He participated in the BlueHealth project as principal investigator for the ISGlobal team.

Gloria Niin, MSc, is a junior researcher at the Chair of Landscape Architecture, Estonian University of Life Sciences. Her research focuses on urban forest recreation and management in Estonia. She also has interests in art and community activism. In the BlueHealth project, she conducted online map-based surveys using the participatory GIS approach to understand how local residents use blue spaces in their cities and how they feel in those places.

Francesco Palermo, B.Eng, is a software engineer at Centro Euro-Mediterraneo per i Cambiamenti Climatici (CMCC), where he is in charge of the development and monitoring of software and services for the production and visualisation of oceanographic data, through customised web applications and decision support system (DSS) tools. In BlueHealth, he was responsible for the design and development of the BlueHealth Decision Support Tool (DST) web application.

Tiina Rinne, DSc, is a postdoctoral researcher at the Department of Built Environment, Aalto University. Her research focuses on health-promoting aspects of the built environment, human–environment interactions primarily from the active living perspective and particularly the endless possibilities of participatory mapping methods. She advised on the PPGIS part in the BlueHealth Project.

Bethany Roberts, PhD, is a postdoctoral research associate at the European Centre for Environment and Human Health at the University of Exeter. Her research focuses on the links between interactions with the marine environment and the impacts this has on individual health and well-being. On the BlueHealth project, her role was to combine data from the BIS, BCLS and PPGIS to explore the impacts of blue space visits across multiple spatial scales.

Katrin Saar, MSc, is a hydro-biologist and now works at the Estonian Research Council. Before that, she was a junior researcher in the chair of Fisheries and Hydrobiology at the Estonian University of Life Sciences. She has carried out research on the evaluation of the ecological quality of Estonian lakes and has worked on several applied projects concerning lake ecology and restoration. In The BlueHealth project, she worked on the development of the aquatic part of the BlueHealth Environmental Assessment Tool.

Joanna Tamar Storie, PhD, is a researcher at the Chair of Landscape Architecture, Estonian University of Life Sciences. Her research interests are focused on rural landscapes and their role in society, particularly in the current northern and eastern European context. She has examined sense of place and identities connected to these rural spaces with a focus on participation. Within the BlueHealth project, she helped to assemble the BlueProfiles database.

Monika Suškevičs, PhD, is a junior professor at the Chair of Environmental Protection and Landscape Management, Estonian University of Life Sciences. Her research focuses on qualitative methodologies and participatory environmental governance, in particular in the context of Eastern European countries. She has expertise on public and stakeholder participation related to spatial planning and nature conservation governance.

Peeter Vassiljev, MSc, is a lecturer in the Chair of Landscape Architecture at the Estonian University of Life Sciences. As a PhD student, he has a particular interest in use of virtual reality in landscape assessment. In BlueHealth, he coordinated the construction of the two experimental interventions in Tallin and Tartu as well as the behaviour observation work on the case studies and also in the work on Virtual BlueHealth.

Cristina Vert, PhD, is an environmental epidemiologist. Her PhD was developed at the Barcelona Institute for Global Health (ISGlobal). She is interested in promoting health through urban regeneration projects. Her research is mainly focused on the evaluation of urban blue infrastructure and its effects on human health and well-being. In the BlueHealth project, she contributed to the development of case studies in the area of Barcelona.

Mathew P. White, PhD, is an environmental psychologist at the University of Vienna, Austria, and Honorary Associate Professor at the University of Exeter. His research focuses on the impact of natural environments on people's mental health and well-being, and from 2011–2020 he co-ordinated the UK's Blue Gym project, which focused on improving our understanding of the benefits of Blue Space environments in particular. He led the BlueHealth project work looking at survey data from a range of sources.

Anna Wilczyńska, MSc, is a junior researcher and PhD student in the Chair of Landscape Architecture at the Estonian University of Life Sciences and the Warsaw University of Life Sciences. She has an interest in blue spaces and health and well-being in Warsaw where she has been carrying out parallel work. Her main role in BlueHealth was in creating the illustrations, especially those of the projects presented in Chapters 11–15.

Susanne Wuijts, PhD, is a hydrologist with expertise in environmental engineering and a doctorate in water quality governance. Currently she is a senior researcher and policy advisor at the National Institute for Public Health and the Environment (RIVM) based in Bilthoven, The Netherlands. Her field of expertise is within water management (water quality and quantity) embedded in the policy context. She was one of the principal investigators of BlueHealth (as well as the other EU-funded projects SOPHIE and Fairway), working on the BlueHealth Scenarios, and the coordinator of a project on emerging contaminants and drinking water.

Wilma Zijlema, PhD, is an epidemiologist and a postdoctoral researcher at the Barcelona Institute for Global Health (ISGlobal). Within BlueHealth, she contributed to the work on improving understanding of how blue environments can affect health and disease and was involved in collecting and analysing data related to the community-level surveys and interventions carried out in Catalonia.

Foreword

Throughout history, stories abound of human interactions with rivers, lakes, seas and oceans. Many tell of catastrophes associated with great floods, horrendous storms and episodes of water-borne disease, while others recount tales of exciting journeys along major rivers or across oceans to new lands, rich in novel resources and unexpected benefits. Finding the right balance in this dance of "risk" and "opportunity" still challenges us today. Over 50% of the world's population lives closer than 3 km to a freshwater body. As for living near seas and oceans, there was a ca. 35% increase in coastal residents between 1995 and 2005, involving more than a third of the global population, some 2.75 billion people. This trend continues today. Australians, Asians and Europeans live closest to water and are constantly faced with balancing the benefits on offer with the dangers posed.

The diversity of links between so-called "blue environments" and human health have emerged gradually over many years. Human dependence on fishing stretches far back into early human evolution, bringing people into close contact with aquatic ecosystems, both marine and freshwater. But over the last 100 years, many other lines of connection have been cast. For example, since the early 1900s, scientists have found ways of using a wide range of aquatic organisms to advance medical science. By the 1950s, they had expanded their interests to address threats to humans arising from water pollution and loss of aquatic biodiversity. They have focused not only on microbial pathogens but also on toxic environmental chemicals such as pesticides, fertilisers, industrial compounds and pharmaceuticals. The early indications of climate change that emerged during the 1970s warned us of another threat: an increase in the number and severity of once-in-a-lifetime floods in most regions across Europe, further highlighting dangers for those living by water. Fortunately, the other side to the human–water relationship also began to take form by the 1990s, when nascent research started to explore the potential for using aquatic environments, especially coastal environments, for fostering improvements in health and well-being. This opportunity was first alluded to as the "coastal effect" in Australia and then explored more broadly in the "Blue Gym" research programme in the United Kingdom. By 2009 researchers were asking whether blue space (coastal areas, lakes, rivers and canals) might have significant positive effects on health and well-being and whether the public could be encouraged, through the use of blue space, to become more active in preserving and protecting these environments.

We have come a long way since these early beginnings. The findings of the BlueHealth programme, reported in this book, represent a step change in our knowledge of past and present interactions between humans and aquatic environments. The transdisciplinary approach used has created a synthesis of the key elements that generate and maintain public health in "blue communities" (those living by or near water bodies – rivers, canals, lakes, estuaries and seas). In particular, the programme explored how urban blue infrastructure can be used to address cultural issues, as well as socioeconomic, ethnic and gender inequalities in health and well-being. The implications for policymakers regarding the importance of developing and maintaining blue infrastructure are made abundantly clear.

The methodological strategy of the BlueHealth team has been to base their work on the "good practice" that has come to the fore increasingly in recent years, namely to be evidence based, employing systematic review, co-design of studies with local stakeholders, the use of indicators to chart progress and the development of decision support processes and standardised tools to ensure consistency and comparability.

Several blue infrastructure case studies and experimental interventions have permitted the creation and fine-tuning of the research and assessment tools, assembled in the programme from diverse disciplines, ranging from toxicology to virtual reality and on to environmental economics, a truly transdisciplinary approach. The perspectives of team members from seven European countries, as well as the WHO Regional Office for the Environment, add an especially rich perspective to the analysis of the findings.

Urban aquatic ecosystems provide an especially wide range of benefits, including opportunities for recreation, cooling of urban heat islands, flood alleviation and urban nature. The BlueHealth programme set out to determine whether the careful design and implementation of urban blue infrastructure can capitalise on these benefits while helping to reduce threats, as well as the stress and anxiety created by living in highly urbanised settings. The use of scenarios to establish healthy blue cities provides important guidance for critical future planning, as many predict that in the decades ahead, we will move beyond having just ca. 50% of the global population living in cities, to a much higher proportion – perhaps as much as 70% by 2050, according to the United Nations. As alluded to earlier, many of these urban enclaves will be close to water bodies.

As we look to the future, there is no doubt that we will have to reinvigorate our efforts to avoid causing further damage to our aquatic environments and also take much greater care over the types of settings we build for people to live in. Unattractive, oppressive, lifeless, urban ecosystems themselves continue to threaten physical and mental health. This once again highlights the need to remember the unbreakable interconnections between nature, ecosystems, human health and well-being. The findings of the BlueHealth programme reported in this valuable book are precisely of the kind necessary to guide planners in making progress towards helping us live healthy, sustainable lives close to our rivers, lakes, seas and oceans.

Michael Depledge CBE FRCP
Emeritus Professor of Environment and Human Health,
University of Exeter Medical School.
February, 2021.

Introduction

Simon Bell, Lora E. Fleming and James Grellier

This book came about as a major dissemination output of the BlueHealth Project (https://bluehealth2020.eu), a large, integrated interdisciplinary research project carried out under the European Union Horizon 2020 Research Framework Programme between 2016 and 2020. The project took an international and innovative, interdisciplinary and cross-sectoral approach to health promotion and disease prevention by exploring how to use Europe's aquatic 'blue' infrastructure to reduce threats and particularly to foster improvements in the health and well-being of its citizens (and beyond into the wider world), now and into the future.

Most urban areas in Europe (where the majority of people live) are strongly associated with inland waterways, lakes, or sea coasts (see the following). BlueHealth focused on blue infrastructure primarily in urban contexts, and this will be a key feature throughout the book. Much of Europe's blue infrastructure spans national boundaries (for example, rivers such as the Rhine or Danube or certain lakes and substantial coastline), making the international recognition of the issues and cross-border cooperation essential.

Dealing with the health implications of the growing importance of blue infrastructure is key to the European Union's 'Health in All Policies' Agenda. European blue infrastructure offers not only significant but relatively unexplored health- and well-being–related opportunities and benefits (e.g. urban cooling, increased recreational opportunities) but also a means of mitigating threats (e.g. from flooding and microbial and chemical pollution). The project investigated these synergies and trade-offs, with the aim of developing targeted environmental, health and well-being assessment indicators, illustrative case studies, best practices, decision support tools and guidelines to inform and improve decision-making for current blue infrastructure as well as future blue infrastructure interventions in light of climate and other environmental change.

In addition, there are many blue infrastructure-related policies at the European level, such as the EU Water Framework Directive and Marine Strategy Framework Directive, as well as the EU Blue Growth strategy together with contributions to international policies such as the Rio+20 agenda, the United Nations Sustainable Development Goals (SDGs), and the World Health Organization Parma Declaration 2010, to which the work carried out by this project adds considerable value.

The BlueHealth project brought together interdisciplinary teams of experts in a broad consortium to apply mixed-methods research in fields including public and environmental health, ecosystems management, epidemiology, landscape and urban planning and design, environmental psychology, climate change modelling, social geography, virtual reality, health and environmental economics and policy. The Partners in the project came from seven EU member states together with the World Health Organisation (WHO) Regional Office for Environment and Health in Europe. A lot of the work of this wide-ranging group, although not all, is represented here.

At the heart of the project was the detailed and systematic consideration of blue infrastructure case studies and experimental interventions which, together with a set of research and assessment tools, form the heart of this book. Blue infrastructure initiatives were evaluated systematically and from different perspectives.

DOI: 10.4324/9780429056161-1

The diverse case studies presented a range of interventions and locations for the exploration of varying climatic and environmental conditions, examining challenges at multiple levels from individual behaviour, through communities to cultural aspects at the population level. Important challenges such as how urban blue infrastructure can be used to address socioeconomic, ethnic and gender inequalities in health and well-being were explored. The integration of urban blue infrastructure into spatial design and local policy was also addressed. Finally, the innovation potential for reducing health and well-being risks and the gain in benefits through modifying the ways people interact with the environment and climate were explored, assessed and quantified in terms of economic and social costs.

The importance of blue space

With 91,000 km of coastline, Europe has considerable access to very different marine and other blue environments, including the Atlantic Ocean, the North Sea, the Irish Sea, the Mediterranean Sea, the Black Sea and the Baltic Sea. Approximately 50% of the European population lives within 50 km of a coastline, while the average urban European lives only 2.5 km from a freshwater source such as a river, lake or canal.

Although Europe's blue infrastructure is sometimes considered a subset of its 'green' infrastructure, this conception ignores blue infrastructure's unique cross-sectoral roles (e.g. river and marine transport, trade, fisheries and aquaculture, tourism and health). Moreover, growing evidence shows that the health promotion and disease prevention opportunities of blue infrastructure are distinct from, and in some cases synergistic with, those provided by 'green' and 'grey' infrastructure. Blue infrastructure may also be more vulnerable to short- and long-term climate and other environmental change and stressors (e.g. rivers drying up, sea levels rising, pollution), as well as becoming of increasing global importance with regard to water availability and quality.

Urban blue spaces are ubiquitous across Europe. They have been and continue to be exploited for many functions, including the transport of people and goods and the provision of water for industry, fisheries and aquaculture, building and energy generation. They are also crucial pillars of urban public health, providing direct benefits to health through the provision of drinking water and by aiding waste and sewage treatment. What is far less well understood is whether and how urban blue spaces can also play a role in tackling the major public health challenges of the 21st century, such as obesity, physical inactivity, chronic diseases and mental health disorders.

The aim of BlueHealth was to explore these possibilities systematically and to investigate whether the careful design and implementation of urban blue infrastructure can promote benefits to public health and prevent disease by, for instance, encouraging people to take more exercise or by helping to reduce the stress and anxiety known to be created by living in highly urbanised settings. When we initiated BlueHealth, initial evidence suggested that these benefits could be substantial and widespread (White et al. 2013a, 2014; MacKerron and Mourato 2013; Wheeler et al. 2015) and could be especially important for vulnerable populations such as children (Amoly 2014), those with underlying poor health (Weimann et al. 2015) and those in deprived communities (Wheeler et al. 2012). BlueHealth was the first attempt to characterise or quantify these benefits systematically and to use this information to inform and improve the design of urban blue infrastructure to aid in the promotion of health and prevent disease.

The BlueHealth Consortium brought together for the first time leading research, public health and policy institutes at the forefront of understanding the relationships between the environment and human health across Europe in order to address opportunities for BlueHealth interventions with interactive cross-sector stakeholder engagement.

Key questions to be addressed (and included in this book) were:

- How are the unexplored benefits of urban blue infrastructure (e.g. promotion of physical activity and stress reduction) distributed across the EU, and will these address the public health challenges of the 21st century?
- Which social groups derive the most benefit, and are there pockets of good practice that promote more equitable distribution?

- Can these benefits of blue infrastructure programmes be assessed in ways that inform good design (e.g. through the use of prospective longitudinal evaluation of ongoing and planned environmental interventions)?
- How might different climate and environmental futures influence the ability of urban blue infrastructures to deliver these benefits to public health and well-being?
- How can existing health and environmental planning policies be built upon to best ensure that these benefits to health and well-being are factored into the policies for maintenance and retrofitting of existing, and the development of future, urban blue infrastructures?

The aim of the BlueHealth Project was to quantify the impacts on population health and well-being of existing and novel interventions and policy initiatives connected to urban blue infrastructure and to identify opportunities and obstacles for cross-sectoral collaboration in this area. We recognised that assessments of the health and well-being (and environmental) benefits, risks, trade-offs and costs should improve our understanding of the role of urban blue infrastructures, both positive and negative, on health promotion and disease prevention.

Many of these infrastructures were originally designed for other policy goals (e.g. transport, flood prevention). However, innovative design and planning can promote health by ensuring that the co-benefits are captured. For example, walking and cycle paths can become integrated features of existing and future blue infrastructure; promoting better access to water bodies for recreation can foster better mental health and increases in physical activity. Blue infrastructure can also aid sustainability and connectivity with other transport networks.

Given peoples' preferences for blue spaces and their willingness to visit them (White et al. 2010; Völker and Kistemann 2013), the evidence suggested that the population uptake of blue infrastructure initiatives that encourage, for instance, greater levels of active recreation, should be particularly high and thus important for disease prevention and health promotion at the individual, community and population levels. Conversely, the predicted increased use of water in urban areas introduces new challenges for improving human health and well-being (e.g. as exposures to known and unknown environmental stressors such as flooding, pathogens and chemical pollutants increase), as well as making the attainment of the long-term sustainability of urban blue ecosystems more difficult.

Throughout the project, we developed innovative indicators and other measures to demonstrate the health, economic, environmental and social impacts of the community-level interventions, policies and best practices. The book is structured around these assessment tools, as well as around what we learned from best practices from around the world and our own experimental planning and design interventions.

BlueHealth concept and approach

Although often considered a source of disease and a threat to health (e.g. the stressors of microbial and chemical pollution, flooding, risk of drowning), at the time of beginning BlueHealth, there was growing evidence that blue infrastructures can directly and indirectly promote health and prevent disease (Völker and Kistemann 2011; Wheeler et al. 2015). As with earlier research around green spaces, epidemiological evidence showed that people who live near the coasts are generally healthier than those who live inland (Wheeler et al. 2012) and that mental and physical health can improve following a relocation nearer to water (White et al. 2013b). Furthermore, coastal and inland water bodies are prime leisure and tourism destinations, and homes with water views are significantly more expensive (Luttik 2000), leading to extensive waterside development (as well as growing access equity issues for more deprived individuals and communities) across many European countries.

Mechanisms and pathways appeared to include greater stress reduction (White et al. 2013a), a greater propensity to engage in recommended levels of physical activity (White et al. 2014) and the positive effects from social engagement. Given the very strong associations between these factors, well-designed blue infrastructure that encourages recreation could offer significant health promotion and disease prevention opportunities, as well as direct and indirect cost co-benefits and innovation opportunities (e.g. climate change adaptation measures of urban cooling and flood prevention).

The importance of urban blue space

Partly for historical and economic reasons, many of Europe's urban centres are situated on or near water, including along major rivers (e.g. Danube, Vienna; Elbe, Hamburg; Liffey, Dublin; Rhein, Rotterdam; Po, Turin; Seine, Paris; Thames, London), on the banks of major lakes (e.g. Geneva; Zurich) or on the coast (including 194 cities bordering Europe's five major seas, e.g. the Atlantic, Lisbon; Baltic, Helsinki; Black, Istanbul; Mediterranean, Barcelona; and North, Edinburgh). Furthermore, many of these rivers, lakes and coastal cities are connected by a network of canals and man-made waterways (e.g. Amsterdam, Annecy, Birmingham, Bruges, Stockholm, Utrecht, Venice) and have a broad array of open reservoirs to supply water to these rapidly growing 'blue' urban centres. Importantly for public health, many urban waterfronts have been 'regenerated', starting in the 1980s (Jauhiainen 1995; Breen 1996), transformed from docks and warehouses into housing and open public spaces with major potential implications for the health and well-being of urban populations (Sairinen and Kumpulainen 2006; Völker and Kistemann 2011).

Many of these benefits may also be linked to other sectoral goals such as transport. For instance, a new cycle network along the main riparian and canal arteries in a city, established to reduce car use and associated negative environmental impacts, may also have positive health benefits if it promotes active travel in a less polluted environment (e.g. Toccolini 2006). Importantly, there is also growing development pressure on many urban green spaces, suggesting that urban blue spaces may become increasingly important health- and well-being-promoting pockets of outdoor space in otherwise 'grey' urban settings for tackling the key 21st-century public health challenges.

Although supplies of fresh water (e.g. rivers), food (e.g. fish) and transport (e.g. canals) opportunities were undoubtedly important in the development of these major urban centres, for many modern city dwellers, their relationships with these urban blue spaces are now quite different from those in previous centuries (Van Leeuwen 2013). In particular, where once they were almost exclusively associated with work and industry, today, they are increasingly likely to be associated with leisure, recreation and tourism, supporting the general contention that people like to be and are willing to pay to be near water, even or particularly in urban settings.

What do we mean by blue space?

Early in the project, we defined blue space as outdoor environments – either natural or manmade – that prominently feature water and are accessible to humans either proximally (being in, on or near water) or distally/virtually (being able to see, hear or otherwise sense water) (Grellier et al. 2017). So far a number of different types of such blue spaces have been mentioned – broad and generally easily recognised categories. However, so far, there has been no comprehensive typology of blue spaces available (unlike those for green and public spaces), so for many aspects of the research undertaken in the BlueHealth project where, for example, the specific benefits or threats related to different categories of blue space varied, a blue space typology became necessary. Table 0.1 summarises the comprehensive typology we used, and Appendix 1 presents it in much greater detail.

The blue space typology is represented in the project review chapters in Part Three of the book. There each type is described in detail in terms of the characteristics which define them, the associated blue infrastructure usually associated with them, the health and well-being benefits, the risks associated with them and ecological aspects and sensitivities.

Table 0.1 **Summary of the blue space typology used in BlueHealth**

Main categories	*Types within the category*
Constructed coastal spaces	Promenade, pier
Natural coastal spaces	Sandy beach, stony beach, sand dunes, sea cliffs, salt marsh, estuary
Lakes and other still water bodies	Natural lake, artificial lake, reservoir, pond, wetland, fen, marsh, bog
Rivers, streams and canals	Large river with artificial banks, large river with natural banks, medium-sized river with artificial banks, medium-sized river with natural banks, stream with a mix of artificial or natural banks, urban canal, rural canal, waterfall or rapids
Docks, ports and marinas	Dock, harbour, marina
Other blue infrastructure	Ornamental water feature or fountain, mineral spring, thermal spring, outdoor skating, curling or ice hockey rink, lido/open-air swimming pool

What do we mean by 'exposure' to urban blue space?

For the purposes of our research, we considered three types of exposure to urban blue space (Kenniger et al. 2013):

- *Intentional* (i.e. deliberately chosen direct exposure that could be *in* [e.g. bathing], *on* [e.g. boating] or *by* [e.g. resting, cycling, walking alongside] the water);
- *Indirect* (e.g. a view from a home/office/building window or benefits such as urban cooling even without visual exposure); and
- *Incidental* (e.g. visual exposure during a commute; if the route is chosen specifically because of its proximity to water, this would be considered 'intentional').

For research purposes, 'exposure' may be operationalised as the proximity of home, school or workplace to urban blue space (Amoly 2014); self-reported frequency and duration of visits (White et al. 2013b); and/or monitoring visitor behaviour at selected urban blue sites (Bell 2008).

Of note at the beginning of BlueHealth, evidence in the United Kingdom suggested that only a relatively small number of visits to any aquatic environment (urban or rural) involve actually getting *in*, or *on*, the water. For instance, only 4.1% of the 260 million annual visits to the coast, and as little as 0.6% of visits to inland waters, involve swimming, and water sports (e.g. canoeing, sailing) account for as little as 2.0% of coastal visits and 2.6% of inland water visits (White et al. 2015). Rather, the vast majority of UK leisure visits involved people taking a walk alongside blue spaces (62.6% beaches and 74.5% inland waters). While this may reflect the United Kingdom's relatively cool and wet climate compared to other EU Member States where bathing may be higher (and, indeed, there are some 15,363 designated coastal bathing water sites and 6,473 inland bathing water sites across Europe), it suggests that many of the health-related benefits (discussed in the following and in Chapter 2) may come from being *by* water or through indirect or incidental exposure.

As such, the investigation of the potential opportunities for health can still be explored in situations where no bathing takes place but where, for instance, the banks of major rivers such as the Rhine or Elbe are used as public open spaces (e.g. in Köln or Hamburg; Völker and Kistemann, 2013). In addition, urban water features such as fountains and splash parks to play *in* or pass *by* are more and more common; some health hazards associated with these features had been identified in the Netherlands (De Man 2014) but not in combination with the positive trade-offs of their health benefits.

What are the potential health outcomes and pathways?

At the time of beginning BlueHealth, several authors had developed conceptual frameworks for the ways in which urban green space could affect health and well-being (e.g. Pretty 2011; Lachowycz and Jones 2013; Church et al. 2014; Hartig et al. 2014; Keniger et al. 2013), and we expected that many of the potential benefits to health and well-being from exposure to urban blue space would be the same as those for exposure to urban green space (e.g. lower obesity rates, improved mental health, etc.).

However, there are two important caveats. First, some of the environmental conditions believed to be important for health and well-being in relation to urban green space (e.g. lower air pollution) may be less applicable to urban blue spaces where other factors such the urban cooling effect may be particularly strong for some aquatic environments (i.e. not just through urban tree cover). Second, research suggests that people are particularly motivated to spend time in blue spaces (including urban ones, e.g. Korpela et al. 2010) compared to green, grey or even mixed blue/green spaces and that the experiences in blue spaces may be particularly beneficial, even relative to green or mixed spaces (e.g. White et al. 2013b).

Therefore, it should not be assumed that blue and green spaces are one and the same thing. Our BlueHealth conceptual model developed throughout the project (discussed at the end of Chapter 1) details the different ways to measure the 'blue' exposures (e.g. type, quality [including biodiversity and other ecosystem services] and health and well-being outcomes [e.g. physical, mental, social]), as well as the possible mechanisms underpinning the apparent benefits of interacting with health and well-being (e.g. physical activity, stress reduction, a sense of place).

Contextual issues (e.g. age, gender, socioeconomics/deprivation, cross-sector considerations, etc.) are also very important to understanding the pathways to health and well-being. However, interactions with blue infrastructure are not always inherently positive, since these interactions can also involve risks as already noted (e.g. flooding, poor water quality from microbes and chemicals, biodiversity loss) that have negative impacts on health (e.g. drowning, poor mental health, waterborne diseases). The trade-offs of both positive and negative impacts from interactions with blue infrastructure were taken into account in BlueHealth and are included in this book. Finally, key to this conceptual model from the point of view of behaviour change, health promotion and disease prevention is the potential for a feedback loop from the health outcome(s) to the exposure(s) that can influence future interactions with the blue environment (e.g. if a walk along a canal helps people feel more relaxed, they may be more likely to repeat the visit).

Book structure

This book focuses on the findings of the BlueHealth project, which are especially relevant to the theme of planning and designing blue spaces for health and well-being. The primary aim is to help planners and designers to implement evidence-based design – in effect, how to use the research evidence and the planning tools to create the best blue spaces possible.

To this end, it is structured in three main parts, starting with the historical context of public health and the environment and the main general research evidence supporting the notion that blue space has an important role to play together with a discussion and illustration of co-design principles. The second part follows with a number of planning/research tools which can be used to collect information about a site and its users at different spatial scales as well as to evaluate the effectiveness of a planning or design intervention and finally to assess the risks and benefits associated with such an intervention. Part three, the largest part, focuses on the design of a range of types of blue spaces (from the blue space typology; Appendix 1), bringing evidence from reviews of completed projects to identify key principles which can be used by planners and designers to inform and inspire their own projects.

Part I: water, blue space and health and well-being: the evidence base and how to use it

This section starts the book off with three chapters that explore, in their own ways, a series of overviews of the main evidence bases to be applied later on.

Chapter 1: Blue space as an essential factor in environment and health

In this chapter, George P. Morris, Himansu S. Mishra and Lora E. Fleming locate the growing knowledge about the public health importance of urban blue spaces within a much longer evolution and history of understanding about the environment and human health, including discussion of conceptual models and theoretical frameworks, ending with specific discussion of the use of conceptual models within the BlueHealth project.

Chapter 2: Potential benefits of blue space for human health and well-being

In this chapter, Mathew P. White, Lewis R. Elliott, Mireia Gascon, Bethany Roberts and Lora E. Fleming present an overarching review of the evidence from the current research literature and from the findings of the research carried out in the BlueHealth project in order to provide the best evidence which planners and designers can use to support their policies, plans and projects. It is essentially an overview of the current knowledge, extensively but not exhaustively referenced and presented in a way which is accessible to professional and student readers. It integrates the benefits and risks by showing that the one often come with the other.

Chapter 3: Co-design with local stakeholders

The aim of this chapter by Mart Külvik, Mireia Gascon, Marina Cervera Alonso de Medina, Lewis R. Elliott, Jekaterina Balicka, Frederico Meireles Rodrigues and Monika Suškevičs is to present the ways in which co-design and public participation can be undertaken, with examples of stakeholder and local community involvement using the BlueHealth case studies in Plymouth in the United Kingdom, Rubí near Barcelona in Spain, Guimarães in Portugal and Tallinn in Estonia. It covers the theoretical aspects of co-design and participation with stakeholders, discussing stakeholder identification, different modes of engagement and the specifics of co-design.

Part II: tools, indicators and models for planning and design

This set of chapters is used to present the range of tools developed within the BlueHealth project and demonstrates their application for policy makers, planners and designers and also local communities.

Chapter 4: Generating evidence in support of site planning and design: the BlueHealth toolbox

In this chapter, James Grellier, Himansu S. Mishra, Lewis R. Elliott, Susanne Wuijts and Matthias F.W. Braubach set the scene for the rest of the chapters in Part Two and connect the individual tools into a comprehensive approach or system for assisting in planning, design and management of blue spaces for health and well-being. By applying all of them, it is possible to provide a comprehensive means of establishing a baseline; deciding what to do; assessing the risks and benefits; and, having done a project, evaluating its success and what difference it has made. Many of the tools are also available to download or use via two project websites – the main website (https://bluehealth2020.eu) and a specific one for the tools and project reviews (https://bluehealth.tools/).

Chapter 5: Assessing the land-water environment

This chapter by Himansu S. Mishra, Katrin Saar and Simon Bell presents the development and application of the BlueHealth Environmental Assessment Tool (BEAT), illustrated with examples from the pilot testing and later application. It describes, in a "how to do it" form, the development and application of the BEAT. It also introduces the online tool, which is an output of the project and free to use by readers.

Chapter 6: Observing behaviour for site planning and design
In this chapter, Peeter Vassiljev, Cristina Vert and Simon Bell focus on two tools used to assess behaviour in blue spaces. One is an existing tool – the System for Observing Play and Recreation in Communities (SOPARC) – and the other is a method which was further developed for the project – the BlueHealth Behaviour Assessment Tool (BBAT). The theory, development and application as well as how to apply and analyse the results are presented for both tools, based on the examples of application in BlueHealth case study sites in Barcelona, Spain (for SOPARC) and Tallinn, Estonia (for BBAT). The chapter is illustrated with different approaches to analysis and presentation as well as interpretation of the results using the two case studies.

Chapter 7: Capturing affordances for health and well-being at the city scale
In this chapter, Gloria Niin, Peeter Vassiljev, Tiina Rinne and Simon Bell focus on the application of Public Participatory Geographic Information Systems (PPGIS), sometimes known as "SoftGIS", using the 'Maptionnaire' tool (an existing system originating in Aalto University in Finland and now commercially available to license) for city-level capture of the blue spaces which local people value the most, explaining how to apply it and how to interpret the results for planning purposes, illustrated using the example of Plymouth, United Kingdom.

Chapter 8: Assessing city-wide and local health and well-being benefits
In this chapter, Lewis R. Elliott, Mathew P. White, Cristina Vert, Wilma Zijlema and Peeter Vassiljev summarise the development and application of the two survey tools, the BlueHealth Survey (BIS) (international but could be applied at a national level) and the BlueHealth Community Level Survey (BCLS) – a questionnaire for use in local areas to capture the benefits of the presence of and access to blue spaces (based on a synthesis of a number of existing survey instruments and validated questions), with an overview of the results from Bulgaria (for the BIS) and Plymouth (for the BCLS) as illustrative of the efficacy of the tools, their ease or difficulty of application and the limitations of what they can tell us, together with information on protocols. The idea is that local authorities, communities and others could use the survey tools to gather their own data and interpret their own results.

Chapter 9: A decision support tool for optimising blue space design and management for health
In this final chapter in Part II, Arnt Diener, Marco Martuzzi, Francesco Palermo, Laura Mancini, Giovanni Coppini and Matthias F.W. Braubach introduce the decision support tool (DST) for BlueHealth, explaining the rationale behind it and how it can be used. It introduces the concept of DSTs in general, some background to the development of this particular DST and the way it works, with some demonstration of results from different locations and some discussion of its limits and generalisability.

Part III: inspirational practice for planning and design
The aim of this third part, the largest of the book, is to present, under different major categories from the blue space typology (Appendix 1), a number of principles for designing blue spaces which arose from a detailed and comprehensive review of projects from around the world. The aim is to bring the evidence and tools together with best practice and to help planners and designers use all of these to achieve the best possible solutions at a range of scales. In Chapters 11–15, a number of representative projects are presented in text, together with a short critical analysis and a set of analytical sketches. Jekaterina Balicka and Anna Wilczyńska created the sketches for each project, while different authors wrote the text and interpreted the critical assessment.

Chapter 10: Reviewing the evidence for good planning and design

This chapter by Himansu S. Mishra, Simon Bell, Jekaterina Balicka and Anna Wilczyńska focuses on the project reviews, the methods used and the overall results, leading into the more specific and thematic coverage of the next set of chapters, where key examples from the review will be presented, critiqued and discussed.

Chapter 11: Urban river revitalisation

In this chapter, Friedrich Kuhlmann, Jekaterina Balicka and Anna Wilczyńska cover the aspects related to different types of rivers as found in the project reviews and also through first-hand experience. It starts with an overview of urban rivers, a history of how they have been mistreated, regulated, polluted, buried and rediscovered. The main risks and benefits for health and well-being are described. Some principles being adopted for restoration are presented. Then a selection of inspirational projects is introduced, and each is evaluated and compared with the others against the set of criteria already defined in Chapter 10.

Chapter 12: Seafronts, beaches, lakesides and promenades

This chapter by Simon Bell, Himansu S. Mishra, Anna Wilczyńska and Jekaterina Balicka starts with an overview of seafronts, beaches, lakesides and promenades and a short history of how they have been developed and used for bathing and recreation, highlighting some famous historical and contemporary examples. The main risks and benefits for health and well-being associated with beaches are described. Some principles being adopted for their re-development, management and maintenance are summarised. Then a selection of innovative projects is introduced, and each is evaluated and compared with the others against the set of criteria defined in Chapter 10.

Chapter 13: Urban wetlands and storm water management

In this chapter, Himansu S. Mishra, Simon Bell, Anna Wilczyńska and Jekaterina Balicka look at the growing popularity of combining storm and other ecological water treatment systems with recreational aspects in urban wetland parks. It starts with a review of the problems facing urban areas in terms of storm water management and urban drainage, leading to extensive sustainable urban drainage systems (SUDS) and special storm water wetland parks and how they can be used for recreation. The risks of their use for health (e.g. if using bio-remediation to clean polluted water) are covered, and an inspirational selection of projects are introduced and evaluated using the criteria defined in Chapter 10.

Chapter 14: Docklands, harbours and post-industrial sites

This chapter by Simon Bell, Anna Wilczyńska and Jekaterina Balicka focuses on the recent wave of rejuvenation of docklands and ports, which are often the largest scale of blue space planning and design being undertaken at present, often being part of whole urban regeneration areas. It starts with an overview of docklands and ports, a history of how they developed and how many old port and docklands have been released from industry and made available for redevelopment. The main risks and benefits for health and well-being are described. Some principles being adopted for redevelopment into mixed use urban settings are summarised. Then a selection of iconic projects is introduced, and each is evaluated and compared with the others against the set of criteria already defined in Chapter 10.

Chapter 15: Tactical urbanism, urban acupuncture and small-scale projects

In this chapter, Jekaterina Balicka, Joanna Tamar Storie, Friedrich Kuhlmann, Anna Wilczyńska and Simon Bell deal with the smallest end of the scale, that of small interventions under the concept of "urban acupuncture". It starts with some theory, definitions and examples of urban acupuncture/tactical urbanism from other fields (permanent and temporary) of urban design and then leads to the application of the concept in blue spaces. The selected projects are evaluated and compared with the others against the set of criteria already defined in Chapter 10.

Chapter 16: Future outlook studies: the use of scenarios to create healthy blue cities
This final stand-alone chapter by Judith Hin and Susanne Wuijts look at some scenarios developed in the BlueHealth project and then indicates areas for policy interventions around the challenges and opportunities for blue space urban planning. It starts with some of the major issues facing urban areas, then introduces the concept of scenarios and how to develop them. The examples of city profiles and results of scenario workshops in several of the BlueHealth research cities are summarised. From this analysis, the challenges for urban blue space planning are identified, leading to potential policy interventions and future research areas and the practical challenges associated with blue spaces. The importance of inter/transdisciplinary and trans-sector approaches across groups and institutions is emphasised.

Who should read this book?

As the subject area is already rather topical and as the whole area of the relationship between nature, landscape and human health and well-being is growing in research and practice importance, we believe that the readership is very wide. We consider that urban planners, landscape architects, urban designers, urban ecologists, specialists in health and well-being working in national or regional and local community and governmental organisations (city councils, etc.) and professional companies (architects, planners, landscape architects) should all find the book valuable.

We also hope that students of all these subjects will find the book inspiring in their learning and, for design students especially, in their studio projects and eventual practice.

Links to the evidence, online tools and project database

The book is linked to various online tools and websites, as well as a growing evidence base of peer-reviewed articles (https://bluehealth2020.eu/publications/) prepared by the project researchers which should remain active and available after the book is published. The BlueHealth Toolbox (Grellier et al. 2020) is on the main project website at: https://bluehealth2020.eu/resources/toolbox/. The BlueHealth Tools website (managed by a separate organisation) can be found here: https://bluehealth.tools/, from which readers can gain access to the BEAT, information and materials for the BBAT and the full database of inspiring BlueProfiles. The BlueHealth Decision Support Tool is available here: https://bluehealth2020.eu/projects/decision-support-tool/.

References

Amoly E. Green and blue spaces and behavioral development. *Environmental Health Perspective*, 2014;122(12):1351.
Bell S. *Design for outdooor recreation*. Abingdon: Routledge, 2008.
Breen A. 1996. *The new waterfront: A worldwide urban success story*. New York: McGraw-Hill Professional Publishing, 1996.
Church A, Fish R, Haines-Young R, et al. *UK national ecosystem assessment follow-on phase*. Work Package Report 5: Cultural Ecosystem Services and Indicators. 2014. http://uknea.unep
De Man H. *Best urban water management practices to prevent waterborne infectious diseases under current and future scenarios*. Thesis Utrecht University, 2014.
Grellier J, Mishra HS, Elliott LR, Wuijts S, Braubach MFW, Hall KL, Bell S, White MP, Fleming LE. The BlueHealth Toolbox – Guidance for urban planners and designers. 2020. doi:10.5281/zenodo.3786387

Grellier J, White MP, Albin M, Bell S, Elliott LR, Gascon M, Gualdi S, Mancini L, Nieuwenhuijsen MJ, Sarigiannis DA, van den Bosch M, Wolf T, Wuijts S, Fleming LE. BlueHealth: A study programme protocol for mapping and quantifying the potential benefits to public health and well-being from Europe's blue spaces. *BMJ Open*, 2017;7(e016188):1–10. doi:10.1136/bmjopen-2017-016188

Hartig T, Mitchell R, de Vries S, et al. Nature and health. *Annual Review of Public Health*, 2014;35:207–228.

Jauhiainen JS. Waterfront redevelopment and urban policy: The case of Barcelona, Cardiff and Genoa. *European Planning Studies*, 1995;3:3–23. doi:10.1080/09654319508720287

Keniger LE, Gaston KJ, Irvine KN, et al. What are the benefits of interacting with nature? *International Journal of Environmental Research and Public Health*, 2013;10:913–935. doi:10.3390/ijerph10030913

Korpela KM, Ylén M, Tyrväinen L, et al. Favorite green, waterside and urban environments, restorative experiences and perceived health in Finland. *Health Promotion International*, 2010;25:200–209.

Lachowycz K, Jones AP. Towards a better understanding of the relationship between greenspace and health: Development of a theoretical framework. *Landscape and Urban Planning*, 2013;118:62–69.

Luttik J. The value of trees, water and open space as reflected by house prices in the Netherlands. *Landscape and Urban Planning*, 2000;48(3):161.

MacKerron G, Mourato S. Happiness is greater in natural environments. *Global Environmental Change*, 2013;23:992–1000.

Pretty J. Health values from ecosystems. In: *UK National Ecosystem Assessment: Technical report*. Cambridge, UK: WCMC-UNEP, 2011:1–48.

Sairinen R, Kumpulainen S. Assessing social impacts in urban waterfront regeneration. *Environmental Impact Assessment Review*, 2006;26:120–135.

Toccolini A. Greenways planning in Italy. *Landscape Urban Planning*, 2006;76(1):98.

Van Leeuwen CJ. City blueprints: Baseline assessment for water management. *Water Resources Management*, 2013;27:5191–5206.

Völker S, Kistemann T. The impact of blue space on human health and well-being – Salutogenetic health effects of inland surface waters: A review. *International Journal of Hygiene and Environmental Health*, 2011;214:449–460.

Völker S, Kistemann T. Reprint of: 'I'm always entirely happy when I'm here!' Urban blue enhancing human health and well-being in Cologne and Düsseldorf, Germany. *Social Science & Medicine*, 2013;91:141–152.

Weimann H, Rylander L, Albin M, Skärbäck E, Grahn P, Östergren P-O, et al. Effects of changing exposure to neighbourhood greenness on general and mental health: A longitudinal study. *Health & Place*, 2015;33:48–56.

Wheeler BW, Lovell R, Higgins SL, et al. Beyond greenspace: An ecological study of population general health and indicators of natural environment type and quality. *International Journal of Health Geography*, 2015;14:17.

Wheeler BW, White MP, Stahl-Timmins W, et al. Does living by the coast improve health and wellbeing. *Health Place*, 2012;18:1198–1201.

White MP, Alcock I, Wheeler BW, et al. Coastal proximity, health and well-being: Results from a longitudinal panel survey. *Health Place*, 2013a;23:97–103.

White MP, Pahl S, Ashbullby KJ, et al. Feelings of restoration from recent nature visits. *Journal of Environmental Psychology*, 2013b;35:40–51.

White MP, Pahl S, Ashbullby KJ, et al. The effects of exercising in different natural environments on psycho-physiological outcomes in post-menopausal women: A simulation study. *International Journal of Environmental Research Public Health*, 2015;12:11929–11953.

White MP, Smith A, Humphryes K, et al. Blue space: The importance of water for preference, affect, and restorativeness ratings of natural and built scenes. *Journal of Environmental Psychology*, 2010;30:482–493.

White MP, Wheeler BW, Herbert S, et al. Coastal proximity and physical activity: Is the coast an under-appreciated public health resource? *Preventive Medicine (Baltimore)*, 2014;69:135–140.

Part I

Water, blue space and health and well-being

The evidence base and how to use it

Chapter 1: Blue space as an essential factor in environment and health

George P. Morris, Himansu S. Mishra and Lora E. Fleming

Introduction

In this chapter, we attempt to locate the growing knowledge about the public health importance of urban blue spaces within a much longer evolution and history of understanding about the environment and human health. To begin with, we will briefly review the interest in physical environment as a determinant of human health, which dates back several millennia. Within an environmental frame of reference, we then present a more detailed analysis of the changing perspectives on human health and its determinants, from the beginning of modern public health to the present day – a period of approximately 200 years. With the subject matter of this book in mind, our review concludes that the provision and maintenance of urban blue and green spaces, aligned to the needs of the surrounding community, are wholly consistent with the most modern perspectives on public health. Specifically, the topic of blue space speaks to 21st-century public health aspirations going beyond health protection and promotion. These can be summarised as embracing prevention, equity and the urgent need to reduce damage to the Earth's biophysical systems.

In his 'grand narrative' on the progress of public health from pre-Socratic times to the immediate post-Second World War era, George Rosen observed that humanity's major health problems have always "been concerned with community life", especially the control of transmissible disease, the management and improvement of the physical environment, the provision and safety of the food supply, medical care and the relief of disability and destitution (Rosen, 1958/ 1993). While noting the ever-shifting emphasis among these activities over time, for Rosen, they formed the basis of public health as it was understood in the 1950s.

From a 21st-century perspective, Rosen's and other post-Second World War narratives (e.g. Sands, 1952) sound a rather triumphalist note, tracing progress in 'taming' epidemic and endemic diseases over nearly two centuries powered by science, medicine and improvements to the physical environment (Porter, 1999). Later, Thomas McKeown (1976), in an equally celebrated text, courted some controversy by attributing only a very limited role to clinical medicine in improving health outcomes and related population growth. Instead, he identified improved nutrition and environmental reforms as the major contributors.

Events since the 1980s have demonstrated mid-20th-century optimism over the containment of infectious disease to be misplaced, serving to emphasise the dynamic nature of public health. As Rayner and Lang have observed, "public health is wrapped around the reality of change" (Rayner and Lang, 2012). Rosen, Sands, and even McKeown, wrote at a time before the emergence of HIV, Ebola, SARs and, more recently, COVID 19; before widespread concern over the catastrophic potential of antimicrobial resistance; and, of course, well in advance of today's understanding about the grave health implications of human impact on the natural world in terms of climate and other environmental change. Yet their observations concerning the centrality of environmental factors and implicitly the importance

DOI: 10.4324/9780429056161-3

of towns and cities as crucibles for public health action are enduring. Indeed, these insights have, if anything, been reinforced by the socioecological and planetary perspectives which now dominate the public health discourse.

The classical perspective

Rosen's definitive textbook, *A History of Public Health*, offers conclusive evidence of sanitary/environmental provision in ancient towns and cities, plausibly driven by a concern for community health (Rosen, 1958/ 1993). By drawing on the archaeological record, Rosen cites evidence from excavations covering different civilisations and multiple places dating back over 4000 years. Sites in India, Southern Europe, the Middle East and North America variously reveal evidence of sewer lines; water supply arrangements; and, within buildings themselves, bathrooms, drains and even water-flushing arrangements for toilets. Moreover, the layout of many ancient cities indicates a measure of conscious planning and, putatively, a form of building regulation.

However, the key common early point of reference for commentators on public health and its environmental dimension is the so-called Hippocratic Corpus (Adams, 1891). Set out in 62 books, the Hippocratic Corpus emanated from Greece between 430 and 330 BC. In their original content and their selective assimilation of ideas from others, the books of the Corpus are now considered the bedrock of western medicine. Importantly, they depart from ancient notions of diseases as products of evil spirits and the curative potential of magical incantation and potions (Frumkin, 2005). Of particular relevance to this narrative, these books were the first example of a systematic attempt to present a causal relationship between human disease and the environment.

The Hippocratic treatise, *Airs, Waters and Places* (Adams, 1891) introduced several ideas foreshadowing much later thinking on the environment and health. The book recognises, as we do today, the potential of food, water and wider environmental conditions to be sources of disease and, more generally, that health is unlikely to thrive in poor environmental conditions. By alluding to the health relevance of perturbations in discrete environmental compartments, the text presages a 'compartmentalised' way of thinking about the environment that many would recognise in conventional approaches to environmental management and indeed in environment and health activity (Morris and Saunders, 2017).

The Greek writers inevitably lacked a 'planetary perspective', as we would understand it based on 21st-century knowledge of the Earth's systems, their connectivity and their fragility, yet, in parts, the texts convey acceptance that humans have capacity to damage the natural environment in health-relevant ways. Also consistent with current thinking, they saw humanity as situated in nature, subject to its rules and composed of natural substances – the body, within its environment, as a composite whole. This perspective lies at the core of 21st-century concepts such as ecological public health (Rayner and Lang, 2012), planetary health (Whitmee et al., 2015) and one health (www.onehealthcommission.org/en/why_one_health/what_is_one_health/).

It would be wrong, though, to imply a continuum of enlightened ecological thought stretching from Hippocrates over two millennia to the present day. In his book, *Ecological Transition*, published in the 1970s, the celebrated American anthropologist John Bennett observed that the history of the human species is marked by increasing denial of nature in, and by, humankind. Bennett believed this denial to be strongly stimulated by the Western Renaissance (with its anthropocentric orientation) and subsequently accelerated by later processes of industrialisation (Bennett, 1976; Rayner and Lang, 2012). Nash (2006) goes still further in asserting that the dichotomy that separates human beings from nature "underwrites the very discipline of history".

Modern public health: from miasma to ecological public health

We will now direct an environmental focus on the more recent history of public health and to a period sometimes termed the 'modern public health era' – an interval starting from the early 19th century to the present day. We deliver our narrative in two parts. The first part takes its structure from a chronological framework created by South

African-born, American epidemiologists Susser and Susser to analyse and predict developments in epidemiology (1996). Epidemiology is public health's underpinning science and is the study of the distribution of disease in the population and the determinants of this distribution (Baker and Nieuwenhuijsen, 2008). Given our more specific focus on the environment, in the second part of our narrative, we uncouple and review the mix of ideas, principles, shifting cultural norms and so on which profoundly shape today's perspectives on the environment in public health. We support this where appropriate by the use of conceptual models.

In the Sussers' conceptualisation, the period from the early 19th until the closing decades of the 20th century can be seen as a succession of three 'eras in epidemiology'. They identified, within each era, an underpinning paradigm concerning disease and its causation in which those seeking to understand and control disease adopted particular analytical and preventive approaches. We draw on this conceptualisation to reflect on how the role of environment in health was perceived within each era and whether there is a contemporary legacy.

From the 1990s onwards, conceptual models increasingly featured in the public health literature, including the subdiscipline of environment and health (Morris et al. in Nieuwenhuijsen and Khreis, 2019). Conceptual models are, in essence, simple representations of complex real-world situations. In public health, they are invariably schematic diagrams showing relationships among the broad domains whose interactions generate health, disease and inequity. In an interdisciplinary area like public health, conceptual models can become common points of reference, offering a common language (and visualisation) for discussion and collaboration among different constituencies of policy and practice. Some generic models may be 'populated' to analyse quite specific challenges or outcomes. Equally, they may support health impact assessment, gap analysis or the configuration of information or surveillance systems. However, in their simplest terms, conceptual models might best be understood as tools with which to think and communicate (McIntosh et al., 2007; Reis et al., 2015).

The environment in an Era of Sanitary Statistics

Most accounts of modern public health choose as their starting point the Industrial Revolution, first in Britain and then mirrored closely thereafter in mainland Europe and the United States. In Britain, at least, rapid industrialisation was spawned in the late 18th and early 19th centuries by a convergence of technological innovation, abundant coal supplies and a supportive economic and political context. Notably, industrialisation initiated and accelerated several major societal-level transitions (Morris and Saunders, 2017). The subsequent interactions of urban, energy, nutritional, economic, cultural and other major transitions have shaped the conditions for the pursuit of population health and equity ever since, defining and redefining the public health challenge (Rayner and Lang, 2012).

Industrialisation was famously the source of prosperity for some, but for others (notably the urban poor), life in towns and cities was characterised by poverty, squalor, severe overcrowding and an absence of wholesome water or sanitation. These conditions supported endemic diseases (such as typhus and tuberculosis) and sustained successive waves of epidemic disease (notably cholera) with attendant mortality. Also contributing greatly to chronic diseases and reduced life expectancy, and otherwise compounding the misery of urban life, were appalling working conditions and polluted air.

By choosing the term 'Era of Sanitary Statistics' for a period which endured for much of the 19th century, the Sussers discerned that the launch, and the early success, of the new public health movement was not founded on an intimate understanding of disease processes and causation (Susser and Susser, 1996). Rather, progress came through linking statistics on morbidity and mortality to a developing range of district-level social and environmental data, notably on overcrowding, housing and working conditions. The finding that the worst health was co-located with the most squalid insanitary and overcrowded conditions fuelled a sanitary revolution, which, over a period of several decades, would transform the living conditions of city dwellers, improving health and extending life expectancy. The promotion of sanitary measures – largely a mix of slum clearance and the provision of water-borne sewerage and piped water supplies – was entirely consonant with the prevailing 'miasmic paradigm' which postulated that diseases were spread through noxious vapours in air (Baker and Nieuwenhuijsen, 2008).

Several observations relevant to environment and health can be sustained from an overview of the Era of Sanitary Statistics. The first is that, while biologically flawed, the miasma paradigm suffused the nascent public health movement with an environmental conceptualisation of challenges and solutions but one in which environmental and social variables were interlaced. Second, for sanitary reformers and politicians, aspects of the environment were seen solely as hazardous to health, with little recorded reference to the health-generating potential of good environments. Third, continuing a tradition enshrined in so-called 'bills of mortality' for different locations analysed so compellingly by John Graunt (1662/1939), sanitary reformers were concerned with the health of communities, as opposed to individuals.

The environment in an Era of Infectious Disease Epidemiology

Spanning a period from the late 19th century until the years immediately following the Second World War, the Era of Infectious Disease Epidemiology was founded on the 'germ theory paradigm'. Enabled by developments in microscopy, the existence of micro-organisms was already known, yet the belief that they might be causally linked to disease substantially derived from Jacob Henle's 1840 text, *Miasma and Contagion* (www.worldcat.org/title/jacob-henle-on-miasmata-and-contagia/oclc/31767786); John Snow's work on epidemic cholera in mid-19th-century London; and research on micro-organisms by Louis Pasteur from the late 1850s onwards (Vinten-Johansen et al., 2003; Bynum, 2008). Building on techniques for growing micro-organisms pioneered by Pasteur, in 1882, Robert Koch revealed the bacterial cause of tuberculosis (Foster, 1970; Collard, 1976; Brock, 1999). The capacity to isolate micro-organisms from the human body had transformational diagnostic and the treatment implications, while isolating the same organisms in environmental carriers opened up preventive opportunities, such as the control of water and food supplies and improvements in living and working conditions.

The germ theory actually vindicated the thrust of 19th-century public health reforms and accorded scientific validity to an established environmental, local and community perspective on disease. Nor, for a time, was any contradiction perceived between long-established notions of the human body in constant interaction with, and closely dependent on, its local social and environmental context and the altogether narrower, more reductionist perspectives of laboratory science (Nash, 2006). A combination of sanitary and social measures and scientifically evidenced isolation and immunisation strategies greatly reduced the burden of infectious disease in Western society over a few decades. However, justifiable excitement over bacteriology's explanatory power and the potential for good masked more insidious processes which would negatively and enduringly impact public health as a discipline.

Beguiled by scientific possibility, 19th- and early 20th-century physicians understandably sought microbial explanations for a very broad spectrum of hitherto unexplained diseases. Of greater concern, though, doctors became complicit in forging a narrower definition of 'health' – making it solely an absence of disease. More subtly, but of importance to this narrative, developing diagnostic and therapeutic power shifted the emphasis of medical science towards the maintenance of 'self-contained' human bodies in contrast to the body in its social and environmental context (Nash, 2006).

It is necessary to note the increasingly medical focus of disease in the inter-war years did not, in practice, lead to wholesale abandonment of social and environmental approaches in public health. Conscientious preventive societal-level action, including on the environment, continued, albeit with a lower profile than before. Yet we argue that a previously embedded sense of common cause in pursuit of population and community health between doctors and sanitarians was substantially eroded. Also, while it was an incremental process, by the time society transitioned to a new epidemiological era in the years following the Second World War, a tendency to regard health and disease as the sole property and responsibility of individuals rather than communities and social groups had taken root (Morris and Saunders, 2017).

The environment in an Era of Chronic Disease Epidemiology

Western society emerged from the Second World War to a changed health landscape. Most obviously, the historical preoccupation with infectious disease was being rapidly supplanted by concern over the growth in chronic diseases of presumed non-infectious aetiology. The origin of this 'epidemiological transition' was, in part, a century's progress in understanding and addressing infectious scourges but also wider social, economic and cultural change (Omran, 2005; McKeown, 1976).

In the preceding infectious era, those vulnerable to disease were typically the very young, the old and those whose immune response was in some way compromised. However, heart attacks, strokes, cancers, stomach ulcers and so on targeted those in middle years and, disproportionately, men (Susser and Susser, 1996; Kessel, 2006). Using an approach known as risk factor epidemiology (RFE), a close association was soon demonstrated between the diseases and the lifestyle and individual behaviour of those affected, for example, in relation to diet, smoking and activity levels. Yet RFE has relied in its statistical analyses of data for its precision on its capacity to control, methodologically, for complicating factors in any relationship under investigation. This is despite the real-world co-existence and policy-relevance of such factors. Often these 'complicating factors' are social or environmental and have a profound bearing on outcome. That RFE's outputs are 'abstractions' clearly matters in a complex, multivariate world, particularly where these outputs become the basis for policy (Susser and Susser, 1996; Kessel, 2006)

Although it had proven efficacy in isolating specific influences bearing on a health outcome, where the problem was ultimately driven by societal problems, RFE could not elucidate the point(s) or levels where interventions would be most effective. By extension, the failure to control the epidemics of the late 20th century was significantly rooted in a failure adequately to understand how illness was generated in a social context (Susser and Susser, 1996). Citing the example of HIV transmission, an infection with a demonstrably complex web of causation, Susser and Susser noted that, while all that was known indicated societal behaviours had to change, very little was known about how to change them. There are surprising but striking parallels here with the current climate crisis and its implications for health.

From an environment and health perspective, the decades following the Second World War present something of a mixed picture. Efforts to understand and address new epidemics of chronic disease were unquestionably blunted by reductionism in medicine and epidemiology. Moreover, the progressive individualisation of health status across society was relentless, further divorcing disease and health from its social and environmental context and diminishing the influence of public health. Yet, at the same time, local environmental and public health agencies and their professional staffs continued to strive, within established legal and administrative frameworks, to secure healthy environmental standards. A blend of monitoring, inspection and enforcement was typically directed towards the food chain, water quality and aspects of the housing and occupational environments. These largely successful efforts helped to contain toxic and infectious pressures but had generally low visibility, only attracting attention on rare occasions when the 'protective envelope' was breached, leading to an incident or outbreak.

Importantly, though, the period did witness some very high-profile air pollution incidents which have left a lasting legacy on perceptions of the environment in health. Most infamously, the London Smog of 1952 reminded society that environmental hazards retained the capacity to exert huge tolls in morbidity and mortality, even in the cultural hub of an advanced country (Baker and Nieuwenhuijsen, 2008; Royal College of Physicians and Surgeons, 2016). Alarm over urban air pollution in the 1950s gave rise to much stricter controls on domestic and industrial emissions. Thus, in summary, while interest in the environment as a determinant of health was evident and did inform health protection activity in the decades following the Second World War, it remained within the narrow, hazard-focused and compartmentalised framework defined for it by the laboratory sciences – primarily toxicology and microbiology.

An evolution of 'ideas'

Thus far, the concept of successive eras in public health, each underpinned by a dominant paradigm about health and its determinants, has provided a useful framework in which to describe changing perspectives on the environment in health. However, the utility of the framework diminishes, becoming constraining, when considering the recent history of the environment in health. Since the 1970s, influential ideas about health and its determinants, including the environment; about society's priorities and norms; and about mankind's relationship to nature have emerged or achieved much greater currency. We argue later that not until the last decade have the often distinct and separate trajectories of these 'ideas' coalesced to represent a paradigm of health and its determinants, capable of sustaining a new era. Here we introduce some of these ideas.

A socioecological model

In our analysis to this point, we have plotted an incremental detachment of health and disease, as experienced by the individual, from its social and environmental context, diminishing the influence of public health and blunting the preventive approach. One consequence is that society has placed disproportionate and increasingly unrealistic reliance on curative medicine to maintain a healthy citizenry.

One of the earliest, most influential statements on the paucity of the medical model came in the Canadian white paper *A New Perspective on the Health of Canadians* published in 1974 (Lalonde, 1974). This, often termed the 'Lalonde Report', recognised an impending crisis in Canada's capacity to fulfil a growing and seemingly insatiable demand for healthcare services. Placing emphasis on prevention, Lalonde's core argument was that any health problem could be traced to one or more of four elements: lifestyle, environment (physical and social), human biology and healthcare organisation. Attention to all of these domains could reduce the burden of disease.

Later, citing Lalonde as a precedent, Evans and Stoddart (1990) were to produce an elegant conceptual model of the determinants of health (Figure 1.1). Significantly, they presented the physical environment, alongside the social environment and genetic endowment, as the primary drivers of health outcome, notably relegating behaviour to the status of a dependent variable. Other popular representations of the so-called 'socioecological model' take the form of 'rainbow' images. That produced by Dahlgren and Whitehead (1991) (Figure 1.2) is among the most frequently cited examples and has had particular resonance in efforts to understand inequalities in health and disease and the factors which influence them.

Notwithstanding the many policy, cultural and other difficulties of operationalising a socioecological model of health, it implied a need for environment and health to reach beyond narrow pollutant and infectious boundaries to understand a richer and more subtle contribution to health from the environment. Socioecological perspectives also called for a greater understanding of how environmental factors, especially in the proximal context, helped to create and sustain inequalities and shape health-relevant behaviours. Much of the rhetoric around socioecological complexity hinted, too, at what, for a time, was the largely disregarded potential of health-generating environments.

Health inequalities

A desire to understand and address inequalities in health substantially drove early 19th-century public health, retaining importance, too, for the germ theorists of the late 19th and early 20th centuries. Yet, with the progressive individualisation of health status and the increasing dominance of the medical model, the political and societal profile of health inequalities diminished. That the topic was 'rediscovered' in the 1970s and would, on occasions, be catapulted to the forefront of political debate owes much to socioecological perspectives but also to a number of sentinel analyses and reports.

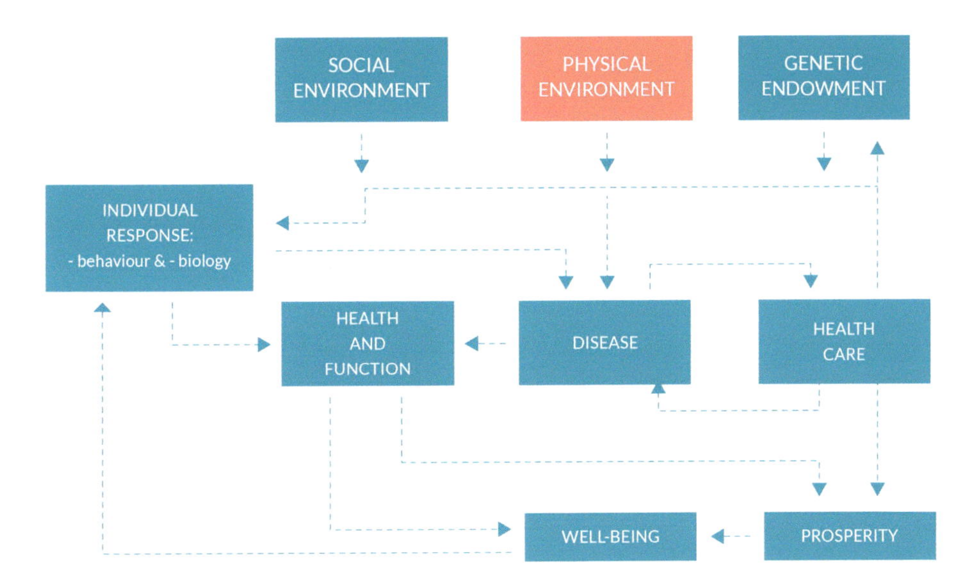

Figure 1.1

The framework of the determinants of health

(*Source*: Anna Wilczynska, based on Evans and Stoddart,1990)

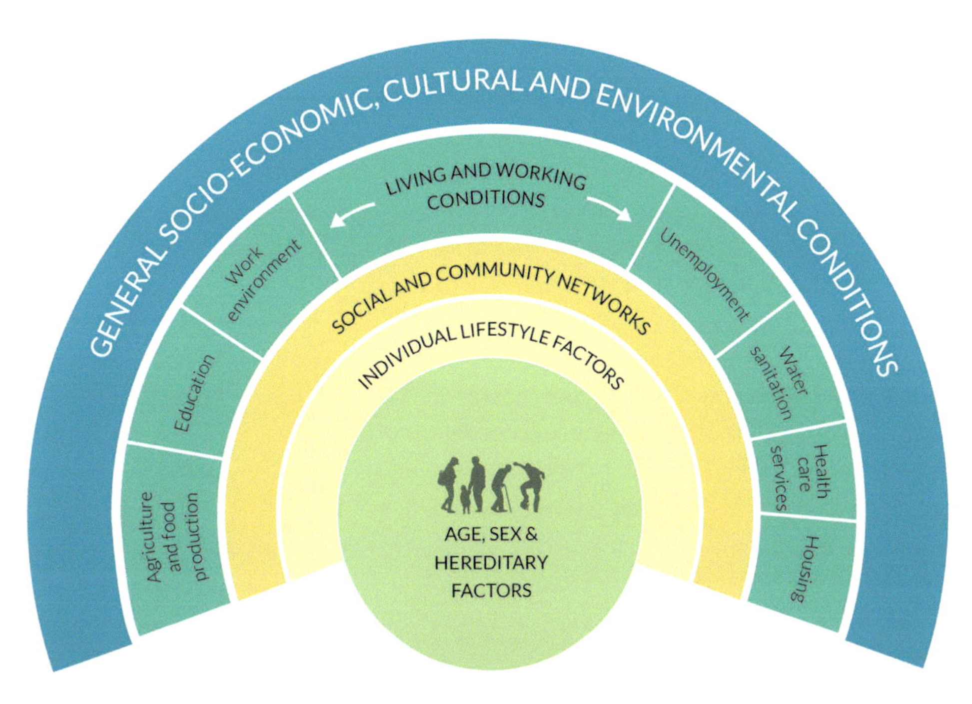

Figure 1.2

The social determinants of health

(*Source*: Anna Wilczyńska, based on Dahlgren and Whitehead 1991)

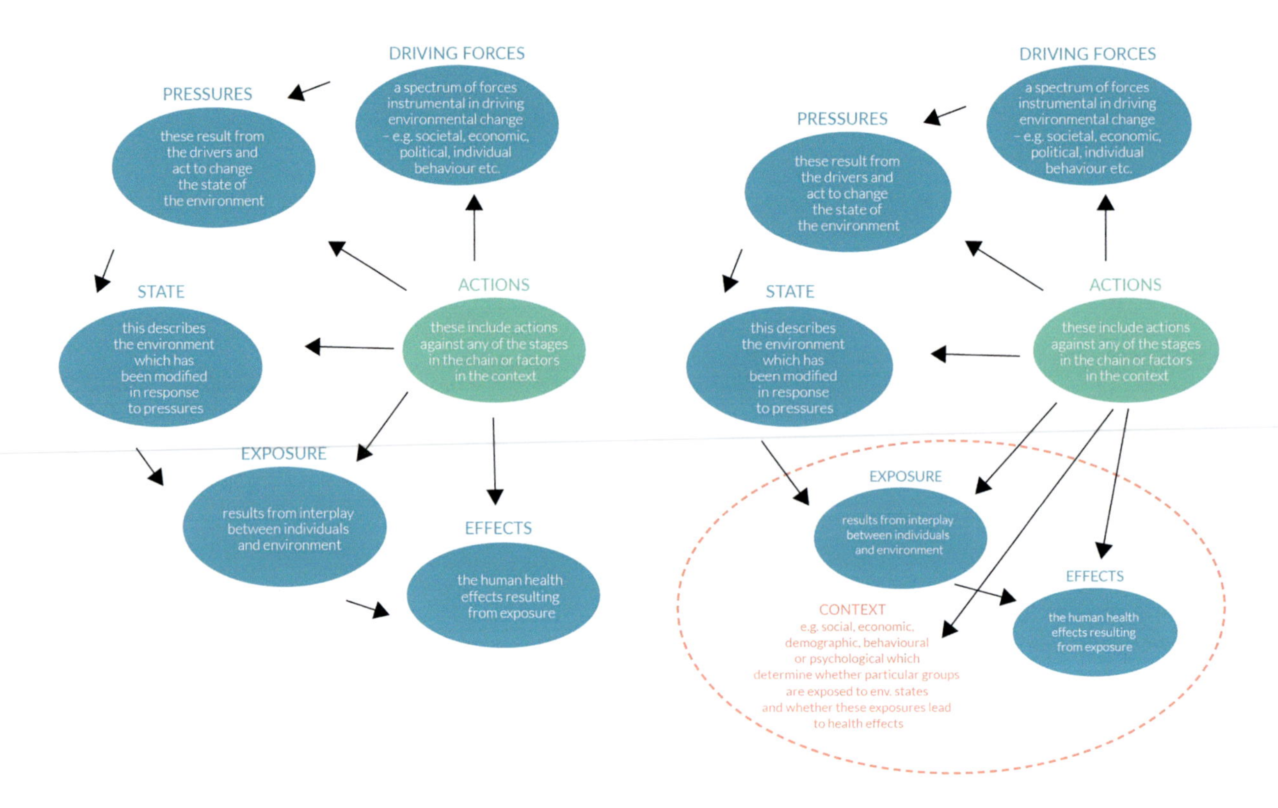

Figure 1.3a and b

a) The original DPSEEA model; b) the modified or mDPSEEA model

(*Sources*: a) Anna Wilczyńska, adapted from Corvalán et al., 2000; b) Anna Wilczyńska, adapted from Morris et al., 2006)

The Black Report (Townsend and Davidson, 1982) had a particular impact in the United Kingdom and internationally (see also Whitehead, 1987; Marmot et al., 1978; Marmot and Davey Smith, 1997). Coming much later, the 2008 final report of the Commission on the Social Determinants of Health (CSDH, 2008) gave a global profile to health inequalities and their roots in the interplay of societal-level influences. The environmental dimension of this has often been discussed under the rubric of 'environmental justice', which focuses on the fair distribution of environmental burdens and benefits. More recently, in a European context, the issue has been developed through the concept of 'environmental inequalities' (WHO, 2012, 2019). A key realisation has been that capturing data which allow spatial/social comparisons of environmental variables within and between different neighbourhoods, cities and countries is central to progress in tackling health inequalities across the world.

A comparison of two related conceptual models (Figures 1.3a and 1.3b) illustrates how socioecological complexity and social patterning can be more expressly considered in the field of environment and health.

The drivers–pressures–state–exposure–effect–action or 'DPSEEA model' (Figure 1.3a) was conceived in the 1990s as an integrated framework for decision-making in environmental health (Kjellstrom et al., 1995). By linking a 'drivers–pressures–state' sequence, used in environmental science, with a classical environmental health approach (in essence, a 'state–exposure–effect' sequence), DPSEEA offered a much more integrated (and policy-relevant) 'full chain' representation of the relationship among human activity, the environment and human health. By elegantly fusing the aspirations of environmental science with those of public health in any location where it is applied, DPSEEA has proved enduringly useful and has generated a family of conceptual models (Morris et al., 2006; Reis et al., 2015; Van der Vliet et al, 2018). In its original form, however, DPSEEA generally supported a traditional environment and health approach without compelling consideration of socioecological perspectives or, necessarily, a divergence from exclusively hazard-focused traditions.

Later, the 'modified DPSEEA', or mDPSEEA, model (Figure 1.3b) was developed as a configuring framework for a Scottish government policy initiative on environment and health (Scottish Government, 2008). Among the aspirations of the *Good Places, Better Health* initiative was a desire to translate into policy a richer understanding of the environmental contribution to health inequalities and to recognise, too, the potential of the environment to impact positively health and well-being. This was achieved by emphasising, first, that a very broad spectrum of interacting driving forces generates and sustains quite different environmental states in different locations and, second, that these environmental states can be hazardous but equally health generating. By incorporating a 'context bubble', the modified DPSEEA model recognises the fact that whether an individual or social group is exposed to or experiences a specific aspect of environmental state in their neighbourhood is influenced by a diverse set of interacting factors which include socioeconomic circumstance, demography, behaviour and even environmental co-exposures. Moreover, whether an individual goes on to experience a health effect (positive or negative) linked to exposure or experience of the environment is dependent on a usually different set of contextual factors which confer individual vulnerability/susceptibility (Morris et al., 2006).

Heightened concern over mental health and well-being

Concern over the effects of modern life on mental health and well-being has rightly gained a much higher profile in recent decades. The idea that health embraces both mental and physical well-being is long established and indeed has very noble provenance in the original WHO definition of health as "a state of complete mental, physical and social well-being and not merely an absence of disease of infirmity" (1946). Yet it is only comparatively recently that the role of the environment in mental health and mental illness been has been properly explored. This research has established the health-generating/promoting (or 'salutogenic') environment as one of the core ideas of modern public health and one with obvious policy relevance. Indeed, this book is motivated in part by a desire to operationalise these ideas in the urban context. Chapter 2 gives an overview of the evidence for the potential health and well-being benefits of urban green, blue and natural spaces and the biophysical and psychological mechanisms which appear to explain these benefits.

The environment and health constituency is not unique in its rather tardy engagement with mental health and well-being issues. A number of factors are contributory. First, although mental health problems may have an organic aspect, they are not always definable in organic terms. Second, the physical environment is only one aspect of the neighbourhood context, which interacts in complex ways with individual characteristics to generate stress (e.g. poorer neighbourhoods are more likely to experience violence, air pollution, etc.). Third, as Rayner and Lang (2012) have observed, an abiding question must be that even where an organic malfunctioning is identified, did this precede or follow the environment stress? Each of these factors is challenging for the traditional reductionist environmental and health approach.

However, what is beyond reasonable challenge is that aspects of the physical environment, whether discernible to the unaided senses or not, can generate stress to the detriment of both mental and physical health. Understanding of stress biology plausibly connects environmentally induced stress to a spectrum of chronic diseases, including cancers and cardiovascular disorders. There is also ample evidence that deprived communities are not only frequently more *exposed* to environmental hazards but also more *susceptible* to their effects (Goodman et al., 2011; Carder et al., 2008; Richardson et al., 2011, 2013; Vinikoor-Imler et al., 2012). It is believed that stress, however generated, at both community and individual levels, can, in the long term, weaken body defences against external insult and influence the internal dose of toxins from environmental sources (Gee and Payne-Sturges, 2004).

Environmentalism and ecologism

While there is ample evidence of environmentalist sentiment dating from much earlier (see, for example, Thoreau, 1854; Darwin, 1859; Wallace, 2003, cited in Smith and Wallace, 2003), Rachel Carson's hugely influential book *Silent Spring* is generally regarded as the origin of modern environmentalism and public interest in ecology (Carson, 1962; Nash, 2006). Ecology is the branch of biology concerned with the relations of organisms both to one another and to their physical surroundings.

Published in 1962, *Silent Spring* is a book about the impact of pesticides on wildlife. Yet its central concern was, in fact, human health (Nash, 2006). It contained, for example, a chapter dealing with the impact of pesticides on cells and genetics and another considering their carcinogenic potential. Perhaps most indicative of Carson's ambitions and prescience lies in her stated intention, revealed in communication with her editor, to set the new threats to human health "within the general framework of disturbances to the basic ecology of all things" (Carson, quoted in Nash, 2006).

Carson died in 1964, well in advance of, for example, today's heightened concerns over shrinking biodiversity or even the coalescence of scientific opinion around the notion of anthropogenic causes of a warming planet. However, *Silent Spring* stands as the seminal text of modern environmentalism. Of specific relevance to our narrative, and contrary to Carson's intention, we believe the environmentalist and public health movements maintained largely distinct and separate trajectories for perhaps three decades post-Carson, only establishing true common cause in this century against a backdrop of the climate crisis, the COVID-19 pandemic, unprecedented biodiversity loss and devastating damage to other Earth systems.

Ecosystem services and well-being

The concept of ecosystem services first appeared in the 1970s, but its transition to standard terminology in the scientific literature is traceable to 1981 (Ehlrich and Ehlrich, 1981). The purpose of 'ecosystem services' is to determine the (measurable economic) services that ecosystems provide to humanity. While unquestionably useful, the ecosystem services concept has proved controversial, not least in the implication that nature exists solely as a resource for humanity. Moreover, the implied dichotomy between humans and the natural world, to any reasoned interpretation, underestimates the importance of humans and integral components of ecosystems and their intimate links (especially through their social and economic activity) to biodiversity and to biological and biophysical processes (Reis et al., 2015).

An important milestone in the evolution of ecosystem services and in its operationalisation in a public health context came with the Millennium Ecosystems Assessment (MEA). Specifically, the MEA explored the links between ecosystems and human well-being (MEA, 2005). The MEA identified four broad categories of ecosystem services. These were *provisioning services* – covering products obtained from the ecosystem such as water, food, timber, fibres and pharmaceuticals; *regulating services* – through which nature controls issues like climate, rainfall, pollination, the spread of disease, the purification of water and the filtration and breakdown of organic waste; *cultural services* – which encompass a spectrum of non-material ways in which people benefit from ecosystems; and, last, *supporting services* – which underpin the production of all other ecosystem services. These include soil formation, which implicitly supports many provisioning services, photosynthesis and primary production (which includes assimilation or accumulation of energy and nutrients by organisms) and nutrient cycling – most importantly, the cycling of nitrogen and phosphorous.

For public health, the MEA made a significant contribution by observing that the interruption of ecosystem services might damage health in five distinct ways: (i) by interruption of the flow of material goods (so-called "material minima"), (ii) through disrupting social relationships, (iii) by reducing security, (iv) by denying freedom of choice and (v), most obviously, through direct damage to mental and physical health. Of direct relevance to the subject matter of this chapter, the MEA articulated very pragmatic reasons for respecting the natural environment in the interests of society, the economy and human health.

Damage to earth's biophysical systems

Through the work of Rachel Carson, and countless other contributions in the intervening years, generations alive today are afforded unprecedented insight into humankind's dramatic and damaging impacts on the natural world and the implications for economies, societies and health everywhere. Indeed, few today doubt that the anthropogenic changes to the Earth's biophysical systems now underway profoundly threaten human existence. Rockström and colleagues encapsulate the gravity of the problem in a much-cited paper (2009), later updated by Steffen and co-workers (2015).

In summary, these researchers nominate nine Earth systems which they define as 'planetary boundaries'. The systems are chosen because, in the absence of urgent corrective action, it will not be possible to maintain a "safe operating space for humanity". Where the evidence supports it, thresholds are proposed for the systems beyond which non-linear, abrupt and potentially catastrophic system changes might occur. The nine systems are inter-related, such that changes in one system may have profound implications for the others. The researchers note that in the preindustrial era, all nine parameters were within the safe operating boundaries but, by the 1950s, changes were discernible, most obviously in the nitrogen cycle. By 2009, according to their analysis, three planetary boundaries had been transgressed, specifically those concerned with climate change, biodiversity loss and the nitrogen cycle. Although, perhaps inevitably, aspects of the planetary boundaries concept have proved controversial, it emphasises that the health and existential threats to humanity from our impacts on the planet extend beyond climate change and biodiversity loss.

In 2015, informed by the MEA's four classifications of ecosystem services and their links to human well-being, Reis and colleagues (2015) developed an 'Ecosystems-Enriched or eDPSEEA Model'. Their intention was to convey, within a DPSEEA format, how, in combination, similar driving forces to those which created health-relevant changes to the proximal or local environment could also damage health in locations throughout the world through damage to global ecosystems and the services they provide for local populations and humanity as a whole.

The health-promoting potential of urban blue green and natural spaces

Just as historical accounts leave no doubt that the health-damaging potential of the environment is long recognised, acceptance that individuals and communities may benefit from experience of a good environment is also evidenced. The ancient Greeks appeared to embrace such notions and, while perhaps not translating into conscious efforts to manipulate the environment, the perceived benefits of contact with nature appear, often, to have influenced the choice of places to live (Carmona, 2018; MacKerron and Mourato, 2013). Similar 'pro-nature' sentiments can be discerned in various guises ever since.

The Romantic Movement – an artistic and intellectual development approximately contemporaneous with the rise of the industrial era in the late 18th century – was characterised by attention to individual sensitivity and emotion as counterpoints to Enlightenment perspectives which presented 'reason' as the foundation of all knowledge. An appreciation of, and desire to connect with, nature in many forms was an inevitable concomitant of Romanticism, yet, simultaneously, the industrial revolution was robbing individuals and communities of access to nature with its attendant benefits. Despite this, and driven by moral rather than evidence-based imperatives, there are countless examples of philanthropic gifting of areas of open and recreational space for use by the working classes. Such provision, and the subsequent development of public parks by local municipalities, was perhaps inevitably inconsistent, patchy and ultimately vulnerable to erosion by ill-conceived development but has left an imprint on many towns and cities (Morris and Saunders, 2017).

Regardless of perspective and in any era, good-quality green, blue and natural spaces make the places in which we live, work and play more attractive, yet not until the late 20th century did robust evidence of the true health benefits begin to build. This affirmed the capacity of green spaces to reduce the incidence of certain diseases (Villeneuve et al.,

2012), extend life expectancy (Faculty of Public Health, 2011), improve mental health (Faculty of Public Health, 2011) and reduce health inequalities (Mitchell and Popham, 2008). Of direct relevance to the subject of this book, the particular importance of blue space has materialised as a key element of public health's evidential landscape (see Chapter 2).

Not only does this call for reflection on what constitutes healthy urban design, it underlines the penalties for health and well-being which have unwittingly accrued through sustained disregard for the rivers, canals and other 'blue' components which have been part of the urban environment for so long. By highlighting the health promoting potential of access to high-quality blue, green and natural spaces as one of the key 'ideas' which can sustain a new epidemiological era, we recognise a special potential of such provision simultaneously to drive the equity, well-being and sustainability agendas so central to modern public health.

Discussion

We have described how, throughout two centuries of modern public health, the perceived contribution and importance of the environment to health has varied. In the immediately preceding section, we identified a number of 'ideas', each with an environmental dimension, which have become prominent in public health and wider society. We argue that in combination, these ideas have a profound bearing on how public health aspirations must now be framed. We have noted that, despite many conspicuous successes and continuing relevance, traditional reductionist approaches in public and environmental health have struggled to respond to these ideas.

A consequence is a failure fully to unmask the environmental contribution to many contemporary public health challenges, including the obesity epidemic, diminishing mental health and well-being, diabetes and, critically, stubborn inequalities in health and environment between social groups. Importantly, traditional environment and health approaches struggle for traction in the face of a health and existential crisis from the human destruction of the natural world.

Eras and paradigms

The term "ecological public health" encapsulates the need to build health and well-being, henceforth, on ecological principles (Rayner and Lang, 2012). Distilled to a simple graphic, the dynamics of ecological public health are illustrated in Figure 1.4.

The image is helpful in reinforcing, first, the inextricable connectivity between human beings and natural systems and humanity's reliance on the natural world for health and well-being. Second, it implies a necessity for those concerned with the environment and human health to think on a vastly extended temporal and spatial scale. Yet,

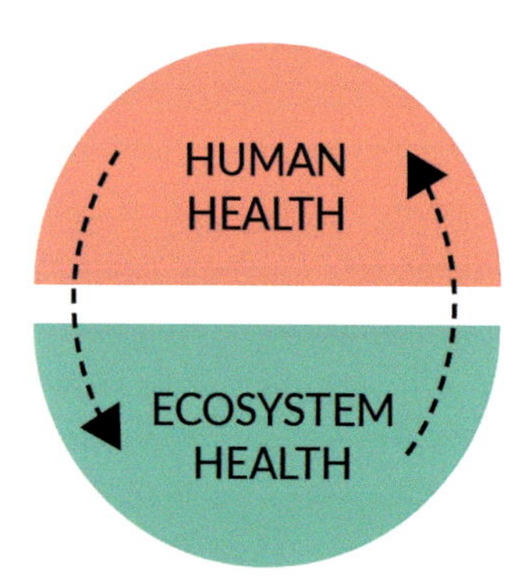

Figure 1.4
The dynamics of ecological public health: a simple model
(*Source*: Anna Wilczyńska, based on Rayner and Lang, 2012)

abstracted from Rayner and Lang's compelling text, the graphic cannot alone convey the true enormity of "reshaping the conditions for good health" now and in the future.

Despite specific differences and separate provenances, the concepts of ecological public health, 'Planetary Health' and 'One Health' convey broadly similar messages about the urgency, complexity, extended scales and need for intersectoral collaboration in confronting the 21st-century public challenge. Of direct relevance to this narrative, all three concepts are 'environmental conceptions of health'.

Drawing on the Sussers' notion of eras in epidemiology, we argue it is now important for the 21st century to become an "Era of Ecological Public Health" if humankind is to confront its pressing challenges. Framed in positive terms, the corresponding paradigm for the pursuit of health and well-being, equity and, necessarily, sustainability in such an era might be *respect for, and the sensitive integration of, the social ecology* (which underpins the socio-ecological model of health) *and the natural ecology.* History portrays a protracted, damaging and wholly perverse disconnect between these "inescapable ecologies" (Nash, 2006). However, if it is to have utility, the Era of Ecological Public Health must have not only an underpinning paradigm but also effective analytical and preventive approaches.

An analytical approach

A core theme throughout this chapter and especially in later sections is complexity. In essence, health and disease are products of multiple factors which interact within a connected whole. This is sometimes called a 'complex systems model of health', and the literature contains frequent calls for a corresponding 'complex systems approach' to analysis (Diez Roux, 2011; Fink and Keyes, 2017). Rutter and colleagues elegantly summarise the case for 'complex systems research' in public health but emphasise the considerable challenge of moving from away from simple linear causal models (2017).

We wholly concur that complex systems research can create a superior evidence base when seeking a step change in health and health and environment equity. Similarly, we support Rutter and colleagues in their view that there is some considerable way to go. Public health lags well behind but in time may learn from other disciplines such as climate change science and economics where complex systems methodologies are already established. However, given the urgency of the challenge, a fundamental question for the present must be, 'what extant analytical approaches and tools are available which may be deployed to progress ecological public health?'

In this chapter, we have expressed enthusiasm for the versatility and operational utility of conceptual models as tools in public health, not the least because human brains are wired for visual images. We recognise that many different models have comparable utility but focused on a 'family' of essentially linear, conceptual models derived from the DPSEEA model (Kjellstrom, 1995), which, in the direct experience of the authors, allow complex issues to be mapped in simple and policy-relevant ways. Even against the unprecedented complexity of the ecological public health challenge, we argue there is currently a role for the enlightened use of more fully articulated versions of the DPSEEA model (Reis et al., 2015; Van der Vliet et al., 2018).

Preventive approaches: a local response

A further theme of our narrative has been the enduring importance of towns and cities as key theatres for public health and environment and health activity. While the current ecological crisis manifestly demands action on an international and global scale, the local and proximal contexts are vital for ecological public health. The concept of the 'triple win' was first articulated in the EU Horizon 2020-funded INHERIT project to encapsulate the shared 21st-century public health policy goal for all local constituencies of policy and practice. A triple-win policy or intervention must have demonstrable capacity to deliver improved health and well-being, greater equity plus environmental sustainability (Van der Vliet et al., 2018). A key benefit of the triple-win concept is that it enables local actors to relate the global challenges of ecological public health to a local scale and to their immediate sphere of influence. This is both motivating and empowering. Not every local intervention or policy has the potential simultaneously to deliver all three dimensions of the triple win. Yet, in delivering one or more of the three elements, it should not prejudice the capacity to achieve the other element(s).

Place and health versus environment and health

In many situations, it is both more inclusive and practical to speak in terms 'healthy places' as opposed to 'healthy environments'. The concept of 'place' integrates the social, economic, physical, cultural and historical aspects of a location. In combination, the characteristics of place generate health outcomes, good and bad, and often reproduce them, generation to generation (Scottish Government, 2011). Notions of place may be particularly useful when planning 'triple win' policies.

Conclusions

Our narrative has charted significant change over time in how the environment is viewed within public health. We have identified the origins of these shifting perspectives in a complex interaction of societal-level transitions with scientific and technological advances and constantly shifting societal norms and values. Looking forward, and consistent with this analysis, we have listed some key influences or 'ideas' which, in our view, militate in favour of an entirely new epidemiological era, one which reinstates the environment at the heart of the public health project but in ways which goes far beyond environmental health's narrow, hazard-focused and compartmentalised traditions.

Acknowledging overlap with other environmental conceptions of health (notably Planetary Health and One Health), we adopt the term 'Ecological Public Health' Rayner and Lang, 2012) as a shorthand for the product and process of achieving meaning change. We submit that an appropriate paradigm for the pursuit of health, equity and environmental sustainability in the 'Era of Ecological Public Health' must be 'respect for, and sensitive integration of, natural ecology with human social ecology'. If embraced, this will terminate a protracted, damaging and wholly perverse disconnect between humanity and the natural world on which we so evidently rely.

Again, consistent with the Sussers' elegant concept of 'eras in epidemiology', there is an implicit need for innovative analytical approaches to secure progress in the new era with its inherent complexity. We concur with the widely stated view that the deployment of complex systems research/approaches in public health holds great promise and is overdue. However, public health's existing analytical toolbox is far from empty and certainly not irrelevant in the context of ecological public health. An array of generic conceptual models, of which the DPSEEA model and its derivatives are only one type, can help frame or map issues in a policy-relevant way with reference to a wide range of issues which bear upon them. Logic modelling approaches are also effective in public health as a means to test and communicate the theories, assumptions and reasoning behind policies or programmes and, in this way, constructively challenge whether a programme and the like can be expected to produce the desired outcome.

Although public health's temporal and spatial scales are now greatly expanded and its goals reframed in terms not just of health, well-being and equity but also global environmental sustainability (a triple win), the importance of the local and proximal is undiminished. The proximal environment of our towns and cities remains the key theatre for environmental health activity for individuals and communities. The concept of the triple win as the goal for local policy is more than simply an aspiration. It can be the basis for evaluating existing or proposed initiatives in the proximal environment.

An output of the Horizon 2020-funded INHERIT project (www.inherit.eu) is a series of case studies where local projects are evaluated in terms of the triple win using qualitative and quantitative methodologies, including cost benefit analysis. INHERIT identified triple-win outcomes as most likely to exist in the domains of: 'living', for example,

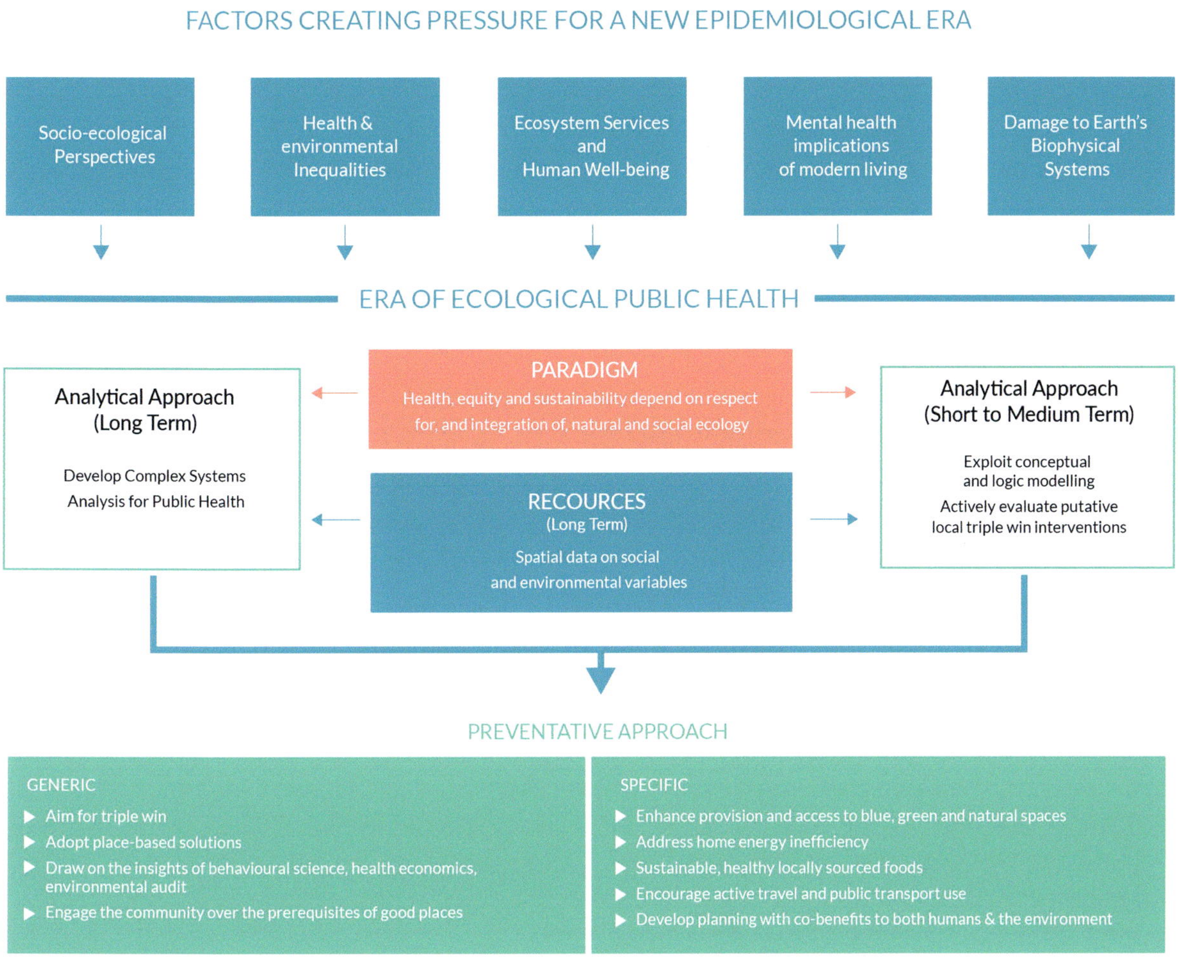

FACTORS CREATING PRESSURE FOR A NEW EPIDEMIOLOGICAL ERA

Socio-ecological Perspectives

Health & environmental Inequalities

Ecosystem Services and Human Well-being

Mental health implications of modern living

Damage to Earth's Biophysical Systems

ERA OF ECOLOGICAL PUBLIC HEALTH

Analytical Approach (Long Term)

Develop Complex Systems Analysis for Public Health

PARADIGM

Health, equity and sustainability depend on respect for, and integration of, natural and social ecology

RECOURCES (Long Term)

Spatial data on social and environmental variables

Analytical Approach (Short to Medium Term)

Exploit conceptual and logic modelling

Actively evaluate putative local triple win interventions

PREVENTATIVE APPROACH

GENERIC

- Aim for triple win
- Adopt place-based solutions
- Draw on the insights of behavioural science, health economics, environmental audit
- Engage the community over the prerequisites of good places

SPECIFIC

- Enhance provision and access to blue, green and natural spaces
- Address home energy inefficiency
- Sustainable, healthy locally sourced foods
- Encourage active travel and public transport use
- Develop planning with co-benefits to both humans & the environment

Figure 1.5

The schematic diagram of the paradigm of the era of ecological public health

(*Source*: The authors and Anna Wilczyńska)

initiatives seeking to improve home energy efficiency or the quality of or access to green and natural spaces; 'consuming', for example, initiatives which promote consumption of locally produced foods; and 'moving', for example, active travel. The goal of a triple win at the local level has the potential to unite in common cause the disparate local actors whose input is essential while being genuinely empowering in the face of global crisis.

Figure 1.5 provides a schematic representation of the concepts introduced above. In summary, the Era of Ecological Public Health is motivated by the need for public health to respond more effectively to six 'Ideas' which, we submit, must profoundly shape the conditions for health and well-being in the 21st century.

As an environmental conception of health, ecological public health demands respect for, and integration of, natural ecology and human social ecology. Complex systems research holds alluring middle- to long-term analytical potential, while there is an enduring role for the active evaluation of interventions in terms of their capacity to deliver the triple win. Temporally and spatially tagged data on environmental and social variables are an important resource for all analysis. A successful preventive approach to delivering the triple win in an Era of Ecological Public Health will exhibit some generic characteristics, which can be reflected in specific preventive interventions.

The immediately succeeding chapter of this book presents a summary of the compelling evidence of the capacity of natural, green and blue spaces in towns and cities to improve population health and well-being though a variety of mechanisms, following different types of exposure. Chapter 2 also points to a small but growing and persuasive body of evidence suggesting a positive impact from access to high-quality blue spaces on health inequalities.

Accordingly, we are confident in saying that the provision and maintenance of urban green, blue and natural spaces aligned to the needs of the local community can plausibly contribute to at least two elements of public health's triple win. This general assertion will invariably be verifiable through evaluation of particular cases in specific localities and communities. The third element of public health's triple win – the contribution to global sustainability – is near impossible to evaluate for specific blue, green and natural spaces, and often the only recourse is to draw on the literature to conduct a general assessment as to the potential to contribute to global sustainability.

Using conceptual models in the BlueHealth project

We have chosen to conclude our deliberations by discussing the use of conceptual models to support the H2020 BlueHealth project (https://bluehealth2020.eu), of which this book is one major output, aimed at helping to operationalise improvements to the potential for better human health and well-being from well-planned and design blue spaces. Although we do not pretend that we have covered the full scope of the uses and applications of conceptual models (Robinson et al., 2015), in our following discussion, we believe that our own journey with conceptual models in BlueHealth may be of interest within the overall theme of this chapter and also set the scene for the rest of the book.

Throughout the project, we used a series of conceptual models at the individual work package and overall project levels, primarily as diagrams/figures, for a variety of purposes:

- A cooperative visualisation process
- Identifying the research pathways and linkages
- Identifying evidence gaps
- Rapid communication of the overall concept of the project

Conceptual models can also be used to involve stakeholder groups in a group understanding of the challenges and towards co-creating approaches to address these challenges (Reis et al., 2015). Probably the most important task of the appropriate use of conceptual models is to identify the specific target group and the question(s) that need to be answered (e.g. just for use within the research group or for use with other external audiences) and to make sure the design and content are suitable for the target audience.

When we began creating the BlueHealth project proposal over a nine-month period in 2014–2015, we were interested primarily in a conceptual model (Figure 1.6) which would communicate to the proposal reviewers (mostly researchers) that we were aware of the complexity of the subject, as well as the potential pathways and linkages. In addition, this model helped the evolving research group to identify the linkages and research gaps which we were proposing to explore in our proposal. We also took pains to base and build this model upon the understanding of the area as evidenced in the existing scientific literature (Hartig et al., 2014).

After the Project was funded and started in 2016, we revisited our conceptual model as part of developing a protocol paper to serve as a consensus road map for our future work. In this case, the conceptual model was an influence diagram (Figure 1.7) describing the causal chain between drivers and impacts under investigation in the BlueHealth project (Grellier et al., 2017). The target audience was the wider scientific community, as well as being useful internally to make sure we were covering all the areas of interest around blue space, human health and well-being and other factors.

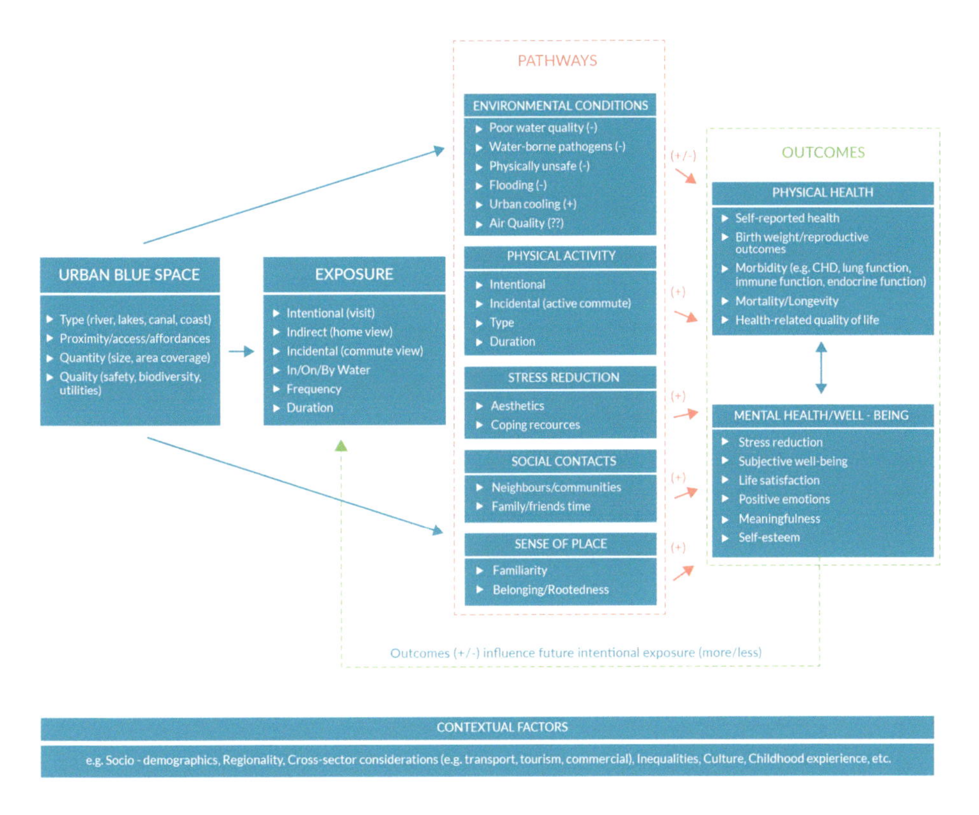

Figure 1.6
Early BlueHealth conceptual model
(*Source*: Anna Wilczyńska and the BlueHealth consortium)

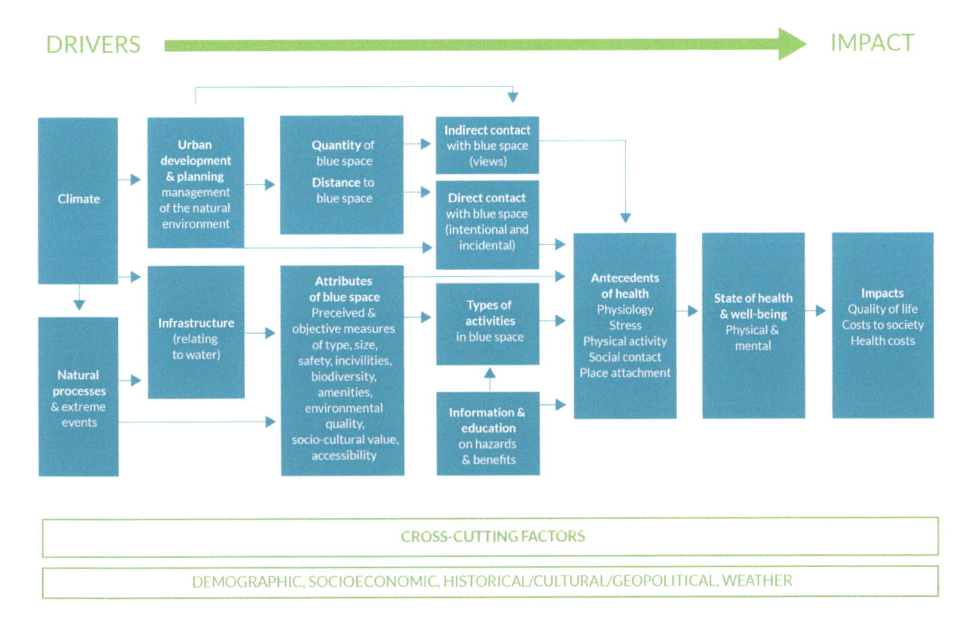

Figure 1.7
Second-generation BlueHealth conceptual model
(*Source*: Anna Wilczyńska based on Grellier et al., 2017)

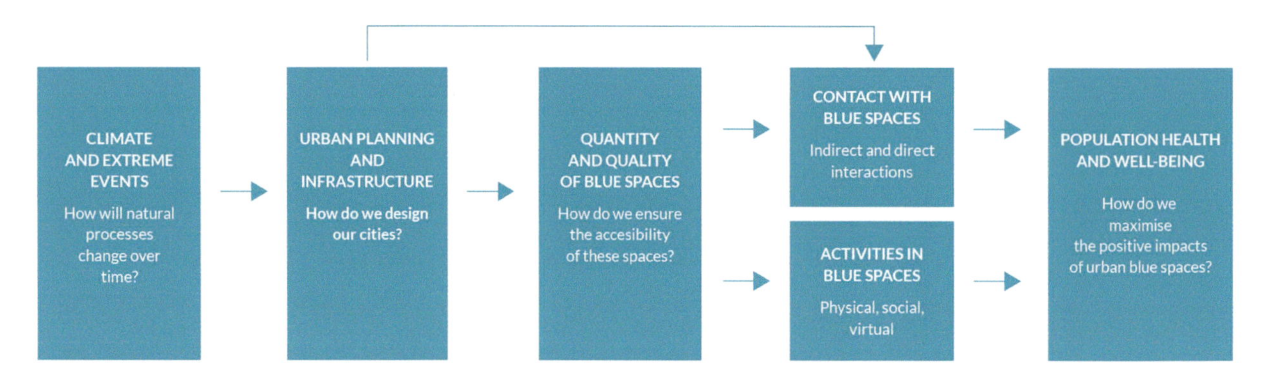

Figure 1.8

The final BlueHealth conceptual model version reading from, or starting from, the left with the environmental context and moving to the impact on population health at the right

(*Source*: Anna Wilczyńska and the BlueHealth consortium)

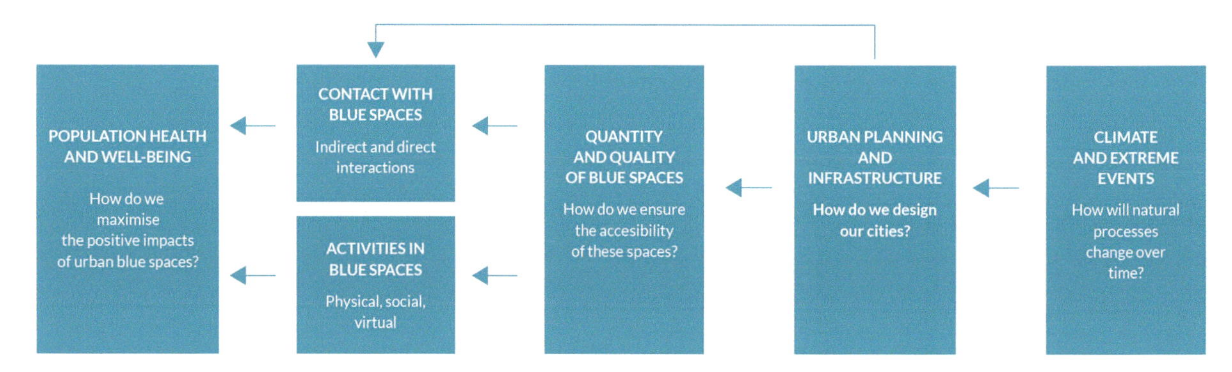

Figure1.9

The final BlueHealth conceptual model version, which starts with the outcome, population health and well-being, at the left side, working back to the determinants towards the right

(*Source*: Anna Wilczyńska and the BlueHealth consortium)

As the BlueHealth project proceeded, it became increasingly important to communicate with diverse audiences; inherently this meant that we needed to simplify the conceptual model both in terms of its concepts and its presentation. We ultimately developed two conceptual models that are interesting from the point of view of the overall development of conceptual models/frameworks in public health described throughout this chapter. For a more scientific audience, we tended to use the conceptual model that "started" on the left with the "exposures" of climate change and blue space leading to the "impacts" on human health on the right of the diagram (Figure 1.8). This was particularly important for experts with an environmental science point of view and background.

However, when communicating with more human-focused audiences, including public health/medical experts, planners and some decision-makers, as well as general audiences, we often used the conceptual model (Figure 1.9) that started with humans on the left side and moved out to the exposures that we wanted to identify and understand

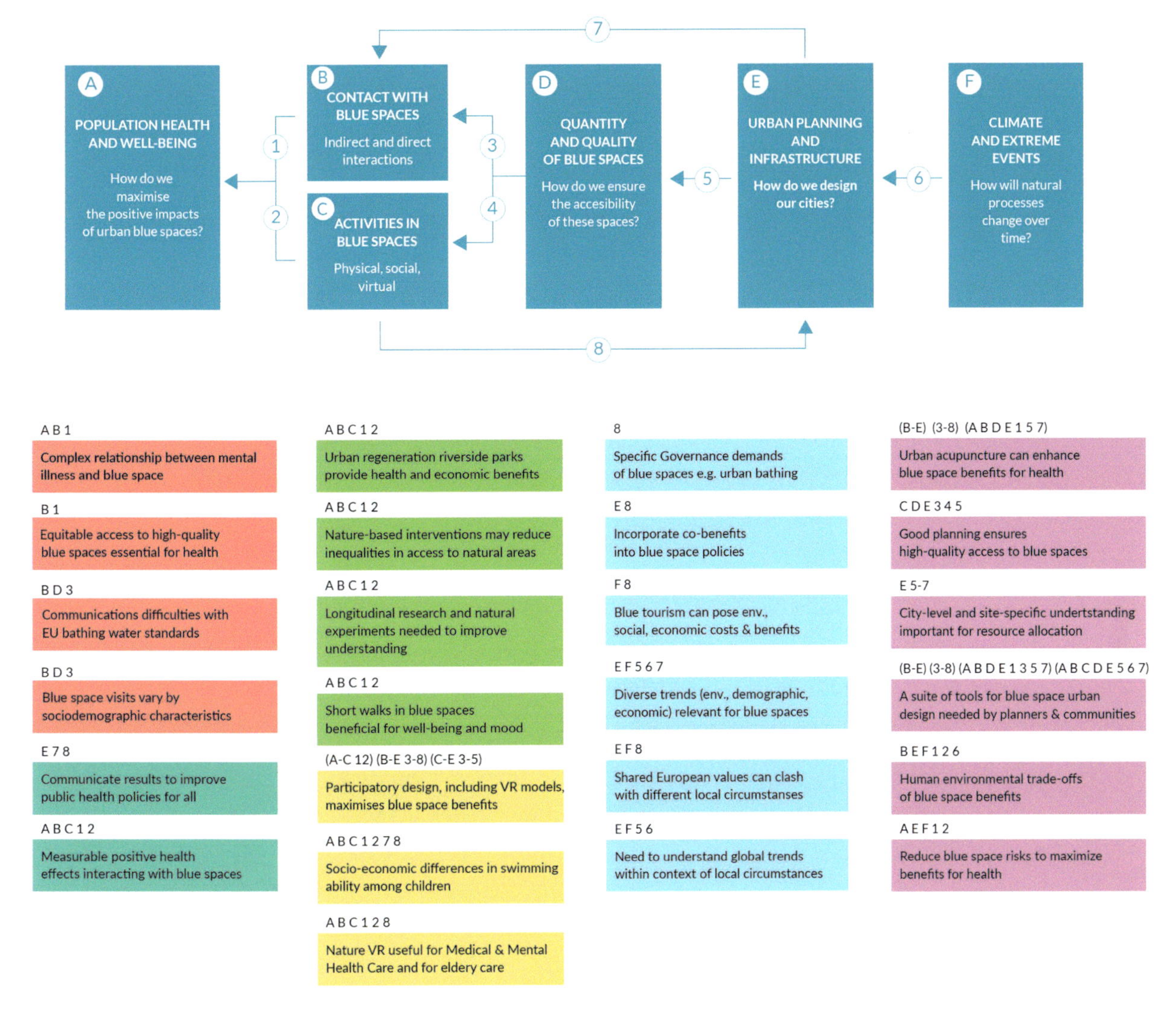

Figure 1.10

The final BlueHealth conceptual model, with a range of project outcomes mapped to each of the steps in the causal chain

(*Source*: Anna Wilczyńska and the BlueHealth Consortium)

on the right side of the diagram. Of note, there was considerable discussion within the BlueHealth project team about all of these conceptual diagrams throughout the project!

Finally, as we neared the end of the project, we wanted to use the conceptual model as part of an overall effort to integrate the evidence and outcomes of the project. We also hoped that this would help us to identify and communicate the major messages of the overall project. Therefore, we used the diagram (Figure 1.10) to map our outcomes relative to the different components of the model.1 This exercise was primarily internal to the BlueHealth team, although it also helped with the development of our final outward communications about the accomplishments of the project (https://bluehealth2020.eu/resources/). Of interest, this mapping exercise also clearly demonstrates where there are still gaps in the evidence for future research and exploration.

Note

1 Susanne Wuijts, Emma Squire, Mare Löhmus Sundström, James Grellier, Simon Bell and Mathew P. White contributed to the H2020 BlueHealth Project research model and integration described at the end of this chapter.

References

Adams F. *The genuine works of Hippocrates*. New York: William Wood and Company, 1891. www.worldcat.org/title/reinventing-hippocrates/oclc/46732640

Baker D, Nieuwenhuijsen M. *Environmental epidemiology: Study methods and application*. Oxford: Oxford University Press, 2008.

Bennett JW. *The ecological transition: Cultural anthropology and human adaptation*. Oxford: Pergamon Press, 1976.

Brock TD. *Robert Koch: A life in medicine and bacteriology*. Washington, DC: ASM Press, 1999.

Bynum WJ. *A history of medicine: A very short introduction*. Oxford: Oxford University Press, 2008.

Carder M, McNamee R, Beverland I, et al. Does deprivation index modify the acute effect of black smoke on cardiorespiratory mortality? *Occupational and Environmental Medicine* 2008;67:104–110.

Carmona M. Place value: Place quality and its impact on health, social, economic and environmental outcomes. *Journal of Urban Design*, 2018; 1–48.

Carson R. *Silent spring*. Boston: Houghton Mifflin, 1962.

Collard P. *The development of microbiology*. Cambridge: Cambridge University Press, 1976.

Commission on Social Determinants of Health. *Closing the gap in a generation: Health equity through action on the social determinants of health*. Final Report of the Commission on Social Determinants of Health, 2008. http://whqlibdoc.who.int/publications/2008/9789241563703_eng.pdf. Accessed 06.12.2020

Corvalán C, Briggs DJ, Zielhuis G. *Decision-making in environmental health: From evidence to action*. New York: Taylor & Francis, 2000.

Dahlgren G, Whitehead M. *Policies and strategies to promote social equity and health: Background document to a WHO Strategy Paper for Europe*, 1991. https://core.ac.uk/download/pdf/6472456.pdf. Accessed 07.11.2020

Darwin C. *On the origin of species by natural selection*. London: John Murray, 1859.

Diez Roux AV. Complex systems thinking and current impasses in health disparities research. *American Journal of Public Health* 2011;101:1627–1634.

Ehrlich PR, Ehrlich A. *Extinction: The causes and consequences of the disappearance of species*. New York: Random House, 1981.

Evans R, Stoddart G. Producing health, consuming health care. *Social Science and Medicine*, 1990;31:1347–1363.

Faculty of Public Health and Natural England. *Great outdoors: How our natural health service uses green space to improve wellbeing briefing statement*. London: FPH, 2011.

Fink DS, Keyes KM. Wrong answers: When simple interpretations create complex problems. In AM El-Sayed, S Galea (eds.), *Systems science and population health*. New York: Oxford University Press, 2017: 25–36.

Foster WD. *A history of medical bacteriology and immunology*. London: Heinemann, 1970.

Frumkin H. (ed.). *Environmental health: From global to local*. San Francisco, CA: Jossey-Bass, 2005.

Gee GC, Payne-Sturges DC. Environmental health disparities: A framework integrating psychosocial and environmental concepts. *Environmental Health Perspectives*, 2004;112(17):1645e53.

Goodman A, Wilkinson P, Stafford M, Tonne C. Characterising socioeconomic inequalities in exposure to air pollution: A comparison of socio-economic markers and scales of measurement. *Health and Place*, 2011;17:767–774.

Graunt J. *Natural and political observations made upon the bills of mortality.* London: T. Roycraft, 1662. Reprinted: Baltimore, MD: The John Hopkins Press, 1939.

Grellier J, White MP, Albin M, Bell S, Elliott LR, Gascon M, Gualdi S, Mancini L, Nieuwenhuijsen MJ, Sarigiannis DA, van den Bosch M, Wolf T, Wuijts S, Fleming LE. BlueHealth: A study programme protocol for mapping and quantifying the potential benefits to public health and well-being from Europe's blue spaces. *BMJ Open*, 2017;7:e016188. doi:10.1136/bmjopen-2017-016188

Hartig T. Mitchel R, de Vries S, Frumkin H. Nature and health. *Annual Review of Public Health*, 2014;35:207–228. doi:10.1146/annurev-publhealth-032013-182443

Kessel A. *Air, the environment and public health.* Cambridge: Cambridge University Press, 2006.

Kjellstrom T, Corvalan C. Framework for the development of environmental health indicators. *World Health Stat Q*, 1995;48:144–154. https://pubmed.ncbi.nlm.nih.gov/8585233/

Lalonde M. A new perspective on the health of Canadians. *Ministry of supply and services Canada.* 1974. www.phac-aspc.gc.ca/ph-sp/pube-pubf/perintrod-eng.php. Accessed 06.12.2020.

MacKerron G, Mourato S. Happiness is greater in natural environments. *Global Environmental Change*, 2013;23(5):992–1000.

Marmot MG, Adelstein AM, Robinson N, Rose G. The changing social class distribution of heart disease. *British Medical Journal*, 1978;2:1109–1112.

Marmot MG, Davey Smith G. Socio-economic differences in health. *Journal of Health Psychology*, 1997; 2(3).

McIntosh BS, Seaton R A, Jeffrey P. Tools to think with? Towards understanding the use of computer-based support tools in policy relevant research. *Environmental Modelling and Software*, 2007;22(5):640–648.

McKeown T. *The modem rise of population.* London, England: Edward Arnold, 1976.

M.E.A. *A report of the millennium ecosystem assessment. Ecosystems and human well-being.* Washington, DC: Island Press, 2005.

Mitchell R, Popham F. Effect of exposure to natural environment on health inequalities: An observational population study. *The Lancet*, 2008;372:1655–1660.

Morris GP, Beck SA, Hanlon P, Robertson R. Getting strategic about the environment and health. *Public Health*, 2006;120:889–907.

Morris GP, Saunders P. The environment in health and well-being. In *Oxford research encyclopedia of environmental science.* 2017. https://doi.org/10.1093/acrefore/9780199389414.013.101. Accessed 04.12.2020.

Morris GP, Staatsen B, van der Vliet N. Using conceptual models to shape healthy sustainable cities. In M Nieuwenhuijsen, H Khreis (eds.), *Integrating human health into urban and transport planning.* Cham: Springer, 2019. https://doi.org/10.1007/978-3-319-74983-9_33

Nash L. *Inescapable ecologies: A history of environment, disease and knowledge.* Berkeley, CA: California University Press, 2006.

Omran AR. The epidemiological transition: A theory of the epidemiology of population change. *The Milbank Quarterly*, 2005;83(4):731–757, doi:10.1111/j.1468-0009.2005.00398.x, PMC 2690264, PMID 16279965,

Porter D. Changing definitions of the history of public health. *The History of Public Health: Current Themes and Approaches*, 1999;1:9–21.

Rayner G, Lang T. *Ecological public health: Reshaping the conditions for good health.* London: Routledge, 2012. doi:10.4324/9780203134801

Reis S, Morris G, Fleming LE, Beck S, Depledge MH, Steinle S, Sabel CE, Cowie H, Hurley F, Dick J, Smith R, Austen M, White M. Integrating health and environmental impact analysis special issue on ecological public health. *Journal of Public Health* (eds. T Lang, G Rayner). 2015;129(10):1383–1389.

Richardson EA, Pearce J, Kingham S. Is particulate air pollution associated with health and health inequalities in New Zealand? *Health and Place*, 2011;17:1137–1143.

Richardson EA, Pearce J, Tunstall H, et al. Particulate air pollution and health inequalities: A Europe-wide ecological analysis. *International Journal of Health Geographics*, 2013;12:34.

Robinson S, Tolk A, Arbez G, Birta LG. Conceptual modeling: Definition, purposes and benefits. In L Yilmaz, WKV Chan, I Moon, TMK Roeder, C Macal, MD Rossetti (eds.), *Proceedings of the 2015 Winter simulation conference*. 2015: 2812–2826.

Rockström J, Steffen W, Noone K, Persson A, Chapin FS, Lambin EF, et al. A safe operating space for humanity. *Nature*, 2009;461:472–475. doi:10.1038/461472a.

Rosen GA. *History of public health* (Expanded ed.). Baltimore, MD: Johns Hopkins University Press, 1993. Originally published 1958.

Royal College of Physicians. *Every breath we take: The lifelong impact of air pollution*. Report of a working party. London, 2016. https://www.rcplondon.ac.uk/projects/outputs/every-breath-we-take-lifelong-impact-air-pollution. Accessed 06.12.2020.

Rutter H, Savona N, Glonti K, Bibby J, Cummins S, et al. The need for a complex systems model of evidence for public health. *Lancet*, 2017;390(10112):2602–2604. doi:10.1016/S0140-6736(17)31267-9. Epub 2017 June 13.

Sands R. *The advance of social medicine*. London: Staples Press, 1952.

Scottish Government. *Good places, better health: A new approach to environment and health in Scotland: Implementation plan*. 2008. https://www2.gov.scot/Publications/2008/12/11090318/13. Accessed 07.11.2020.

Scottish Government. *Good places better health for Scotland's children*. 2011. https://www2.gov.scot/resource/doc/924/0124585.pdf. Accessed 06.11.2020.

Smith C. Alfred Russel Wallace, societal planning and environmental agenda. *Environmental Conservation*, 2003;30(3):215–218.

Steffen W, Richardson K, Rockstrom J, Cornell SE, Fetzer I et al. Planetary boundaries: Guiding human development on a changing planet. *Science*, 2015; 347(6223):1259855. doi:10.1126/science.1259855

Susser M, Susser E. Choosing a future for epidemiology: I. Eras and paradigms. *American Journal of Public Health*, 1996;86(5):668–673. doi:10.2105/ajph.86.5.668

Thoreau HD. *Walden: Life in the woods*. Ticknor and Fiends, 1854.

Townsend P, Davidson N. *Inequalities in health: The Black report*. New Orleans, LA: Pelican, 1982.

Van der Vliet N, Staatsen B, Kruize H, Morris G, Costongs C et al. The INHERIT model: A tool to jointly improve health, environmental sustainability and health equity through behavior and lifestyle change. *IJERP*, 2018;15(7). IJERPH I Free Full-Text I The INHERIT Model: A Tool to Jointly Improve Health, Environmental Sustainability and Health Equity through Behavior and Lifestyle Change (mdpi.com). Accessed 06.12.2020.

Villeneuve PJ, Jerrett M, Su JG, et al. A cohort study relating urban green space with mortality in Ontario, Canada. *Environmental Research*, 2012;115:51–58.

Vinikoor-Imler LC, Gray SC, Edwards SE, et al. The effects of exposure to particulate matter and neighbourhood deprivation on gestational hypertension. *Paediatric and Perinatal Epidemiology*, 2012; 26:91–100.

Vinten-Johansen P, Brody H, Paneth N, et al. *Cholera, chloroform and the science of medicine: A life of John Snow*. New York: Oxford University Press, 2003.

Whitehead M. *The health divide*. Sacramenta, CA: Health Education Council, 1987.

Whitmee S, Haines A, Beyrer C, Boltz F, Capon A, et al. Safeguarding human health in the Anthropocene epoch: Report of The Rockefeller Foundation. *Lancet Commission on Planetary Health*, 2015;386(10007):1973–2028, Published: July 15, 2015. doi:10.1016/S0140-6736(15)60901-1

WHO. *Constitution of the World Health Organization* Geneva: World Health Organization 1946. www. who.int/about/who-we-are/constitution. Accessed 06.12.2020.

World Health Organization Regional Office for Europe. *Environmental health inequalities in Europe assessment report*. Copenhagen: WHO, 2012.

World Health Organisation Regional Office for Europe. *Environmental health inequalities in Europe: Second assessment report*. Copenhagen: WHO, 2019. www.euro.who.int/en/health-topics/environment-and-health/air-quality/publications/2019/environmental-health-inequalities-in-europe.-second-assessment-report-2019. Accessed 06.12.2020.

Chapter 2: Potential benefits of blue space for human health and well-being

Mathew P. White, Lewis R. Elliott, Mireia Gascon, Bethany Roberts and Lora E. Fleming

Introduction[1]

This chapter follows on from the story told in Chapter 1, where the emphasis was on the historical development of and current ideas about the relationship between human health and well-being and the environment. It provided a "big picture" overview to place the subject of this chapter in context, and it also discussed models – especially the general model used in the BlueHealth project. Aquatic environments pose a wide range of threats to human health and well-being. There are an estimated 370,000 drownings globally per year, and water-borne diseases such as cholera account for nearly two million deaths annually, mostly among children under five years (World Health Organisation [WHO], 2014, 2019). Storms and floods exacerbate both issues, especially if drinking water supplies and sanitation facilities are contaminated with polluted floodwaters, events that are expected to increase in many parts of the world under climate change and sea-level rise (Neumann et al., 2015). Chemical pollution from mining, agriculture and industry; harmful algal blooms; and emerging threats such as pharmaceuticals and micro-plastics may all undermine human health and well-being (Borja et al., 2020; Fleming et al., 2019; Depledge et al., 2017).

However, we also need freshwater to live, not only for drinking but for irrigating crops and for livestock, as well as in healthcare, sanitation, industry and commerce. Coastal and marine waters also have considerable value in terms of their "ecosystem services", the beneficial effects they have on human well-being via 'provisioning' services (e.g. fish, shellfish, seaweeds, aggregates, etc.) and 'regulatory' services (e.g. water quality and climate regulation) (Millennium Ecosystem Assessment (MEA), 2005). It is no surprise, therefore, that most large towns and cities are sited on the coast or near large inland water bodies in order to exploit the potential benefits to human well-being they provide. Yet despite general recognition of these benefits, research exploring them in detail has been relatively scarce compared to 'green spaces' such as urban parks, woods and forests and even private gardens (Markevych et al. 2017; van den Bosch & Sang, 2017).

Aims and scope

The aim of this chapter, therefore, is to bridge this gap in the literature and to attempt to provide a narrative overview and synthesis of the potential benefits of aquatic environments, or 'blue spaces', for health and well-being (Depledge & Bird, 2009; Grellier et al., 2017; White et al., 2016a). The aim is not to provide a risk-benefit analysis. It is too early to attempt such an endeavour, not least because the risks are generally far better articulated and documented than the benefits. Rather, the focus is on integrating the emerging research on the potential benefits to health and well-being, in particular research that suggests improved access to, and safe use of, blue spaces could play a role in tackling some of the major public health challenges of middle- to high-income countries in the 21st century.

DOI: 10.4324/9780429056161-4

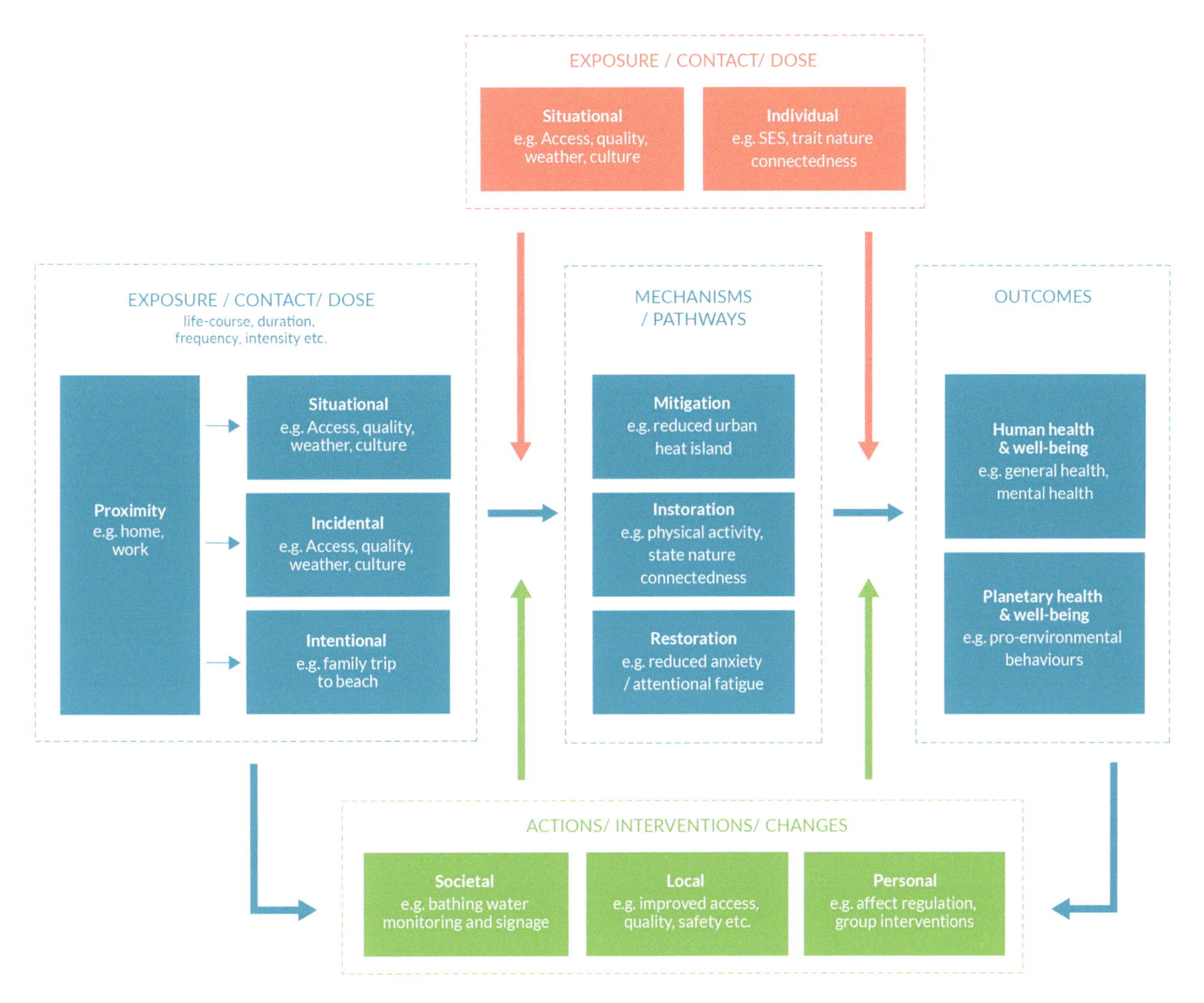

Figure 2.1
A model of BlueHealth – a conceptual diagram of the relationships between blue space and health and well-being
(*Source*: Mathew P. White and Anna Wilczyńska)

These include common mental health disorders such as anxiety and depression (Bloom et al., 2011) and a lack of physical activity that in the long term can increase the risk of cardiovascular disease, dementia and some cancers (WHO, 2018). It also explores evidence suggesting that blue spaces can be used not just to prevent disease but to promote good psychological health and help individuals with chronic health conditions manage their rehabilitation, recovery or ongoing health states. This overview and synthesis draws on a range of research methodologies, including large epidemiological studies, visitor surveys and field and laboratory experiments as well as in-depth qualitative research, as it meant to be representative rather than systematic or authoritative.

Structure

To help structure the evidence, we build on several earlier models of green space and health/well-being to create a bespoke blue space and health/well-being model (Figure 2.1). First, we deconstruct blue space exposure/contact into four types:

1. Home/work proximity; then building on Keniger et al. (2013),
2. Indirect exposure (e.g. window views or TV programmes);
3. Incidental exposure (i.e. exposure that occurs even though the main activity was for a different purpose, e.g. commuting);
4. Intentional exposure (deliberately spending time in aquatic settings, e.g. for work or recreation).

We then extend Markevych et al.'s (2017) three pathways linking green spaces and health to blue spaces and health. Each pathway incorporates several sub-processes:

1. Mitigation (i.e. reduction of harm, e.g. urban heat island effect);
2. Instoration (e.g. promotion of positive outcomes such as improved mood or greater physical activity);
3. Restoration (e.g. recovery from depleted attentional capacity or stress).

We also adopt the two sets of effect modifiers proposed (although not named) by Hartig et al. (2014):

1. Situational (e.g. access, quality, weather, culture, etc.);
2. Individual (e.g. personal characteristics such as age, gender, socio-economic status [SES]).

As well as extending previous models to blue spaces in particular, we make three additional contributions. First, we include 'planetary health and well-being' as an outcome variable. Given the well-established links between planetary health and human health (Whitmee et al., 2015), evidence that blue space exposure might improve pro-environmental behaviours (Alcock et al., 2020) suggests that this can also have positive effects on human health and well-being. Second, we introduce feedback loops from health outcomes to exposure and intermediate pathways reflecting interventions that may result from the outcomes and which ultimately feed back to changes in exposure. Here, we propose three broad types of intervention/action:

1. Societal;
2. Local;
3. Personal.

Finally, we include the psychological concept of nature connectedness in two different ways. First, we include it as a dispositional *trait* (e.g. Mayer & Frantz, 2004) that might moderate linkages between exposure and pathways/outcomes. Second, we include it as a *state*, reflecting short-term changes in attitudes/feelings towards the natural world that might result in immediate benefits (Pritchard et al., 2019). The remainder goes through each section in turn.

Exposure, health and well-being

We begin by exploring issues of exposure (the left of Figure 2.1), including evidence of exposure-outcomes that did not consider intermediate pathways.

Proximity and other exposures

Most people live relatively close to a water body of some kind. In Germany, for instance, the average home distance to a significant piece of water is <1.5km (Wüstemann et al., 2017). Unsurprisingly, people who live closer to blue spaces tend to have greater indirect, intentional and incidental exposure. Having a view of water from home (indirect exposure) is directly associated with proximity, although, as Nutsford et al. (2016) point out, elevation (e.g. living on a hill or in a block of flats) can increase blue space views while not living particularly close. With respect to intentional exposure (deliberately visiting, e.g. for recreation), studies in Denmark (Schipperijn et al., 2010) and England (White et al., 2014b) and across 18 different countries (Elliott et al., 2020) all demonstrate that the closer one lives to blue spaces, the more frequently one visits, with most studies showing an exponential decay function. Of note, visit frequencies may be moderated by socioeconomic and/or ethnic status. In one study, although lower SES/Hispanic individuals often lived nearer to urban waterways than higher-income/white individuals, the latter tended to visit them for recreation more (Haeffner et al., 2017). Finally, a study in Hong Kong (Garrett et al., 2019a), a city dominated by the coast, shows that home proximity to the coast is associated with the likelihood of blue space on one's commute (an incidental exposure).

Proximity and health and well-being outcomes

One of the first studies to show a relationship between living near blue spaces and health and well-being outcomes was Brereton et al. (2008), which found that people who lived within 2 km of the coast in Ireland (but not 2–5 km) were significantly more satisfied with their lives than people living >5 km away. Subsequent research has found that living near the coast or inland water bodies is associated with better mental health, such as in Canada (Pearson et al., 2019), China (Helbich et al. 2019), England (Alcock et al., 2015; Garrett, et al., 2019b) and the Netherlands (de Vries et al., 2016). Several studies have also shown a positive relationship with home proximity to water bodies and self-reported general health, for example, in Belgium (Hooyberg, 2020), England (Wheeler et al., 2012) and Spain (Ballesteros-Olza et al., 2020), as well as mortality (Crouse et al., 2018). A longitudinal study in England found that over time, the same people report better mental and general health in the years when they lived close to the coast (<5 km) versus inland (White et al. 2013a).

A systematic review of 35 different studies around the world by Gascón et al. (2017) rated 22 of the studies to be of 'good quality' and concluded that the balance of evidence suggested

> a positive association between greater exposure to outdoor blue spaces and both benefits to mental health and well-being (N = 12 studies) and levels of physical activity (N = 13 studies). The evidence of an association between outdoor blue space exposure and general health (N = 6 studies), obesity (N = 8 studies) and cardiovascular (N = 4 studies) and related outcomes was less consistent.
>
> (p. 1207)

Further, not all subsequent research has demonstrated a positive effect for mental health (Gascon et al., 2018). The lack of effects seen in some recent studies may be due to evidence suggesting that the effects of living near blue space on health and well-being tend to be significantly stronger for people living in poorer regions (Wheeler et al., 2012) or lower-income households (Garrett et al., 2019b). Studies that have not explored the modifying effect of income may therefore be failing to reveal differences at different levels of income. If these studies are replicated more generally in the future, it would suggest that access to blue spaces may help mitigate chronic socioeconomic-related inequalities in health.

In many developed countries, homes close to inland and coastal waters, especially those with blue space views, tend to be more expensive (Gibbons et al., 2014). Economists assume that people are willing to spend more on accommodation close to blue spaces because buyers derive extra benefit or 'utility'. To the extent this is true, then this 'hedonic pricing' approach would also suggest that well-being is gained from living or staying near water. This is consistent with a range of studies which show that stated preferences for landscapes are higher for those containing water (White et al., 2018).

Indirect and incidental exposure and health and well-being outcomes

Several recent studies have found evidence that having a water view (over and above proximity) may play a role. In New Zealand, Nutsford et al. (2016) showed lower rates of poor mental health among those with a sea view, controlling for proximity (and other factors). In Hong Kong, Garrett et al. (2019b) found general health was significantly higher with a sea view, but there was no association with mental health. Finally, in Ireland, Dempsey et al. (2018) found a lower risk of depression among those with the highest level of sea views, although no effect of coastal proximity. Both of the latter studies were conducted with older aged samples, and it has been argued that blue space views from home may be particularly important to older adults with poorer mobility (Coleman & Kearns, 2015).

We expect more research in this area as innovations in 'viewshed' analysis develop that take into account both elevation and obstruction (Qiang et al., 2019), as well as street view breakdown (Helbich et al., 2019) and even body cameras that film local neighbourhoods from the wearer's perspective (Pearson et al., 2017). As with viewsheds, we suspect that innovations in analysing street views will enable further work exploring incidental contact. For instance, in a study by Helbich et al. (2019), older adults in Beijing were less likely to show signs of depression if their local neighbourhood had both green and blue views at the street level. Crucially, there were no significant effects for satellite estimates, suggesting that the on-the-ground views may be more important than basic amount of land covered.

Intentional exposure and health and well-being outcomes

Although there are now several studies which look at the relationships between intentional blue space visits, most of these focus on the short-term immediate stress reduction potential of specific visits rather than more global mental health. As such, these studies are reviewed in the later section on restoration. In terms of the potential longer-term benefits discussed here, Garrett et al. (2019a) did include a measure of blue space visit frequency and measures of general and mental health in their Hong Kong study. They found that visiting a blue space for recreation at least once a week was associated with better mental health. This is consistent with research documenting positive effects of regular recreational visits to natural environments in general.

One type of repeated intentional visit to blue spaces that is receiving more research attention is outdoor (or wild) swimming. Wild swimming can reduce fatigue (Huttunen et al., 2004) and promote mental health (Foley 2015, 2017; Denton & Aranda, 2020) and may be able to be used in treating major depressive disorder (van Tulleken et al., 2018). There is also evidence that it can promote immune functioning (Tipton et al., 2017) and treatment of inflammation-related conditions (Tipton et al., 2017) and support higher insulin sensitivity (Gibas-Dorna et al., 2016). Individuals who swim outdoors regularly also report experiencing increased connection to place and the natural environment (Foley, 2015, 2017), which may in turn lead to behaviours aimed at protecting the health-promoting aspects of these blue spaces.

Exposure, planetary health and pro-environmental behaviours

Although we know of few studies which have explored exposure to blue spaces and the kind of individual- and community-level pro-environmental behaviours which could be beneficial for planetary health, there are nonetheless some indications. Milfont et al. (2014), for instance, found that New Zealanders who lived closer to the coast had greater belief in climate change and greater support for government regulation of carbon emissions. The authors argued this was because the risks of climate-related events such as storms, floods and sea level rise were more salient for coastal dwellers. A recent English study with over 24,000 participants found that living near the coast (<5 km vs. >20 km) was associated with higher likelihoods of a number of pro-environmental behaviours, including recycling, buying local/seasonal produce, walking/cycling instead of using a car for short journeys and being a member of an environmental organisation (Alcock et al., 2020). Importantly, the associations were mediated not just by the frequency with which the participants visited natural environments such as the coast but also how connected they felt with the natural world. Living near the coast was associated with greater psychological connection to the natural world, and in turn, this greater connection was associated with more pro-environmental behaviours.

Mechanisms/pathways

This section focuses on the centre of Figure 2.1 and the pathways and mechanisms linking exposure to outcomes using Markevych et al.'s (2017) three broad, but inter-related, mechanisms of mitigation, instoration and restoration. Although positive emotional states, which may build creativity and resilience (Fredrickson, 2001), might be included under instoration, for clarity, we reserve discussion of emotional and cognitive states to the restoration pathway.

Mitigation (harm reduction)

Urban heat island

With average global temperatures set to rise, urban settings are particularly vulnerable because they both generate and retain heat more than natural settings. Blue spaces, especially in the urban context, offer important temperature regulation processes, absorbing heat during the day when air temperatures exceed water temperatures and releasing heat during the night when water temperatures exceed air temperatures. In a review of 27 urban blue space versus non-blue comparison sites (mostly in China, Japan and South Korea), Völker et al. (2013) found an average cooling effect of 2.5 Kelvin during May–October. Cooler temperatures were observed across a broad range of aquatic environments, including rivers, lakes, wetlands, ponds and the sea, and across a range of climate zones, including maritime, subtropical and tropical. The capacity of urban blue space to mitigate urban heat islands has also been shown to be connected with positive human health impacts such as reductions in heat-related mortality amongst vulnerable populations in Portugal who live within 4 km of water (Burkart et al., 2015).

Noise

In itself, water can significantly increase the level of sound in an environment, so in that sense, it may have the opposite effect of green space, which may absorb sound (Rådsten-Ekman et al., 2013). The question, however, is whether these aquatic sounds count as 'noise' (i.e. unwanted sound). In a number of experimental studies, water-based sounds, either in isolation (Thoma et al., 2018) or in combination with other natural sounds such as birdsong (Annerstedt et al., 2013), tend to reduce experimentally induced stress faster than either urban sounds, silence or conditions that were specifically designed to reduce stress such as calming music (Thoma et al., 2018). Adding pleasant water sounds (e.g. stream, waterfall, sea) to unpleasant traffic sounds (effectively increasing the overall volume) can also improve positivity ratings (Rådsten-Ekman et al., 2013). Thus, while an advantage of green spaces is that they may mitigate noise, blue spaces may actually increase sound but nonetheless result in more positive health states if these water sounds effectively 'drown out' more unpleasant sounds, such as traffic.

Aerosols and negative ions

Taking the "sea air" for one's health has been recommended by physicians for centuries (e.g. Fortescue Fox and Lloyd, 1938) (see Chapter 12). Recent research in both coastal and inland waters, especially high-force waterfalls, suggests that the mists and sprays created in these settings may help reduce breathing difficulties, for example, among children with asthma, in part through reduced inflammation and improved lung function (Gaisberger et al., 2012). Although the precise mechanisms are still not fully understood, some authors claim that the negative ions produced by crashing water (e.g. Kolarz et al., 2012; Pawar et al., 2012) may also play a role. The direct effects of negative ions on human health are disputed (Perez et al., 2013); however, there is some evidence of lower depression scores at high-density exposure, which is consistent with lower stress reported by participants in Grafstätter et al.'s

(2017) study of exposure to waterfalls (versus similarly attractive alpine settings) in Austria. Given that the benefits to lung function may last for several months post-exposure (Gaisberger et al., 2012), further high-quality research in this area seems warranted.

Aerosolised toxins

A different issue with respect to aerosols concerns aerosolised toxins, such as brevetoxins, that come from 'harmful algal blooms' (Fleming et al., 2011). Natural water bodies contain a wide variety of micro-organisms which can become airborne in water spray at critical places such as waterfalls and ocean shores (Asselman et al., 2019). In some instances, for example, in the Florida red tide caused by the dinoflagellate *Karenia brevis*, the organisms produce potent natural toxins. These toxins can cause or aggravate symptoms among those with asthma (Fleming et al., 2011). However, it has also been argued that at low concentrations, some of these toxins (as well as other substances in marine aerosols) may have positive effects on health. For instance, there is evidence that yessotoxin produced by marine dinoflagellates such as *Protoceratium reticulatum* may reduce inflammation and improve immunoregulation (Asselman et al. 2019; Moore, 2015), but far more research is needed to fully understand these processes.

Solar irradiance

Finally, blue spaces are also associated with higher levels of solar irradiance, leading to higher ultraviolet exposure of those exposed. On the one hand, this can increase the risk of skin cancer (Stenbeck et al., 1990), but it can also lead to higher vitamin D synthesis, which is associated with a reduced risk of certain auto-immune and cardiovascular diseases, some cancers and poor mental health (Cherrie et al., 2015). Clearly, individual behaviours are key with respect to time of day, exposure duration, self-protection measures and so on.

Instoration (capacity building)

In an early review of 36 small-scale survey studies and experiments, Völker and Kistemann (2011) identified four 'dimensions of appropriation' which relate to the way blue spaces are perceived and interacted with to achieve 'salutogenic' (i.e. health-promoting) potential. They labelled these 'activity' space, 'experienced' space, 'social' space and 'symbolic' space, and they correspond respectively to blue spaces as places to engage in physical activity, to build positive emotions/memories, to engage in positive social relations and to form attachment bonds and personal meanings to specific locations.

Encouraging physical activity

Greater levels of physical activity among people who live near the coast or other waterside locations is one of the strongest findings in the blue space literature (Gascón et al., 2017; White et al., 2014a). Nevertheless, most studies are self-reported, and there is emerging evidence that more objective data using accelerometers may not show the effect (e.g. Garrett et al., 2020). What is clear is that much of the activity in blue spaces is not water based but occurs on land, such as beach walks (Elliott et al., 2018; White et al., 2016b), and it is this activity that predominantly explains any link between coastal proximity and health (Pasanen et al., 2019). There is also experimental and survey evidence that when people undertake exercise in blue spaces, they tend to exercise for longer than in green or urban settings (Elliott et al., 2015), in part because perceptions of time are different (White et al., 2015). Attempts have been made to put economic values on blue space activities by calculating how the level of physical activity undertaken there is likely to improve health and well-being (Papathanasopoulou et al., 2016; Vert et al., 2019a). This kind of framing is particularly important for policy makers who have to make budgetary decisions, such as for local urban planners when considering river regeneration interventions (Vert et al., 2019b) or those in charge of marine spatial planning who need to be aware of the 'value' of such recreational activities (Elliott et al., 2018).

Supporting positive social relations

There is growing evidence that compared to green spaces, blue spaces may be particularly important for promoting positive social relationships. Qualitative studies in Germany (Völker & Kistemann, 2015), Iran (Vaeztavakoli et al., 2018), Ireland (Foley, 2015) and the United Kingdom (Ashbullby et al., 2013; Bell et al., 2015) all found evidence suggesting that blue space environments are ideal locations for people to spend high-quality time with friends and family. In the words of a participant in the study of the Niasarm canal in Isfahan, Iran: "When the weather is good, the canal is full of people from the neighbourhood. Women, children, and old people all prefer to socialise together alongside the canal" (Vaeztavakoli, et al., 2018, p. 13). Survey data also suggest that spending time with others is a key motivation for visits to both coastal (Elliott et al., 2018) and inland (de Bell et al., 2017) waters, and a study in Spain suggested that social support was higher for those who had access to blue, but not green, spaces (Triguero-Mas et al., 2015).

Building place/nature connectedness

Although not in Markeyvch et al.'s (2017) original model, we believe place/nature connectedness is nonetheless an important potential instoration pathway. People have a deep innate need to feel connected to other people or something bigger than themselves (Baumeister & Leary, 1995). When interpersonal connections are lacking or attenuated, connections/attachment to places and natural environments in particular may buffer people against the poor mental health that tends to be associated with loneliness (Cartwright et al., 2018). Korpela and colleagues (e.g. Korpela et al., 2020), in particular, have conducted research exploring people's 'favourite places', the places that have particular meaning for them and ones where they often go to 'feel better' or self-regulate their emotional states. Importantly, such emotional states seem to be particularly enhanced in blue space settings (MacKerron & Mourato, 2013; White et al., 2013a), and they are also among many people's favourite places (Vaeztavakoli et al., 2018). Nonetheless, it is also important to recognise that there are sociodemographic inequalities in blue space access (Haeffner et al., 2017), and as such, it may be difficult for marginalised groups (e.g. persons with disabilities) to 'learn to love' blue spaces, especially if historically they have only had access to more dangerous ones (Bell et al., 2019).

Nature connectedness can be considered both an enduring dispositional trait (some people tend to feel more connected to nature than others in general) and a more ephemeral state (the same individual can feel more or less connected depending on context; Capaldi et al., 2014). People who live at the coast tend to have higher trait nature connectedness (or appreciation; Alcock et al., 2020), and visits to blue spaces, especially those of high quality, tend to be associated with higher levels of state nature connectedness (Wyles et al., 2019). We know of only one published study that adapted a standard nature connectedness tool (the Inclusion of Nature in the Self scale; Schultz, 2001) to focus exclusively on blue spaces (Hignett et al., 2018). This study measured children's marine connectedness, as well as health and pro-environmental outcomes, before and after a multi-week surf programme. Although there were benefits for key health outcomes such as resting heart rate and pro-environmental behaviours, these were not mediated by improved marine connectedness. Further studies are needed that explore marine and inland water connectedness in particular as something different from nature connectedness in general.

Restoration (capacity restoration)

In terms of restoration, two influential theories argue that modern urban environments in particular pose demands on our emotional (stress reduction theory, Ulrich et al., 1991) and cognitive/attentional (attention restoration theory, Kaplan & Kaplan, 1989) resources and that we need opportunities to recover and 're-charge'. Both theories argue that non-threatening nature environments (including potentially blue spaces) offer many of the characteristics for supporting such restoration from stressful and cognitively demanding situations.

Stress reduction

As early as 1981, Ulrich (1981) demonstrated that experimental exposure to aquatic versus green space scenes may be particularly relaxing by measuring neural oscillations in the 8–12 Hz spectrum (i.e. alpha waves) using an electroencephalograph (EEG). He suggested that "the fact that alpha during the water exposures was on average lower than during the vegetation scenes may be due to the attention-holding properties of the water views" (p. 546). In a subsequent study, Ulrich and colleagues (1991) showed that watching natural scenes (including an aquatic one) could help participants recover faster (as measured using galvanic skin response, heart rate and frown muscle activation) from a stressful situation than watching urban scenes. However, the green and blue space scenes were collapsed for analysis due to similar effects, so it did not appear that blue space had any marginal advantage.

Since these early studies by Ulrich and colleagues, work in terms of blue space has tended to explore the self-reported mood states of those making intentional recreational visits to a range of urban, green and blue spaces, under the assumption that many recreational visitors to nature are urban residents with habitually high levels of arousal and stress. Comparisons of visits across a range of contexts has repeatedly shown that blue spaces are among the most restorative contexts (Barton & Pretty, 2010; White et al., 2013a), with a study by MacKerron and Mourato (2013) being particularly persuasive. These authors developed an iPhone app (Mappiness) which contacted people at several points during the day over several days to ask how they were feeling, tagging their responses to their geolocations. Results found that people were happiest in marine/coastal settings but that inland waters were more similar to green spaces, such as woodlands and grasslands.

A few experimental studies have also looked at emotions in relation to physical activity in urban, blue and/or green/control settings. Vert et al. (2020) found that subjective well-being and feelings of vitality among office walkers taking an experimentally selected blue space walk during lunchtime were higher than following either an urban walk or seated control condition. However, two similar walking studies (Gidlow et al., 2016; Triguero-Mas et al., 2017) and a simulated cycling study using an indoor bike and large outdoor screen projections (White et al., 2015) found that while blue space walks/cycles were associated with better mood outcomes than an urban walk/cycle, green space activity provided similar benefits. Finally, in-depth qualitative studies (e.g. Bell et al., 2015) have tried to uncover why people report feeling less stressed in aquatic settings, with people reporting that the light, the soundscapes, the quickly changing patterns and/or meaningful histories and personal associations are all potentially important.

Cognitive restoration

Despite the large number of studies that have looked at the potential of green spaces to restore depleted cognitive ability, predominantly attention, there have been very few studies which have looked at blue spaces in particular. Nevertheless, several important experimental studies that compared 'nature' and 'urban' settings actually used predominantly blue space imagery and/or sounds in their 'nature' conditions but systematically (though presumably accidentally) excluded water from their 'urban' conditions (White et al., 2010). Thus, findings that exposure to the 'natural' images/sounds results in better performance on a range of attentional tests might be better framed in terms of blue spaces than nature in general. Although, as with Ulrich et al. (1991), it may be that natural spaces without water may have been as good, we suspect that these researchers chose natural environments containing water because they intuitively felt that the presence of water added to the potentially restorative effects (Kaplan & Kaplan, 1989).

Two experimental studies, one lab based (Emfield & Neider, 2014) and one field based (Gidlow et al., 2016), explored impacts of urban versus specifically blue space exposure on cognitive outcomes. Emfield and Neider (2014) found no improvements on a range of cognitive tasks after viewing blue space images and/or listening to blue space sounds compared to comparable urban (non-blue) stimuli. Gidlow et al. (2016) compared backward digit span (BDS) scores before and after a 30-minute walk in either urban, green or blue space (a river path) settings, as well as employing a delayed post-test 30 minutes after the walk. The pre- to delayed post-test comparison suggests that only in the blue space condition did BDS scores improve significantly. Further research differentiating blue from green spaces with respect to attention restoration is needed to clarify these and other findings.

Effect modifiers

Following Hartig et al. (2014), who identified two types of effect modifier of the relationships between nature in general and health, we identify similar potential modifiers for blue spaces in particular and categorise them as situational (pertaining to environmental circumstances) and individual (pertaining to the individual being exposed to the blue spaces). The role of modifiers is shown at the top of Figure 2.1.

Situational

Blue space type

Much of the blue space and health research has focused on marine/coastal settings (White et al., 2016a). However, there are also studies that focus on rivers (de Bell et al., 2017; Vert et al., 2019a, 2019b; Völker & Kistemann, 2011), canals (Vaeztavakoli, 2018) and lakes (Pearson et al., 2019; Völker & Kistemann, 2015). When looked at independently, it is hard to compare different types of blue space, but a few studies have included both marine and inland waters in the same research. Elliott et al. (2020) found similar distance decay effects for the relationships between home location and visits to coasts and lakes. Both White et al. (2013b) and McKerron and Mourato (2013) found that people reported being more relaxed and happier, respectively, in coastal than inland water settings, at least in England.

Quality

Objective water quality, in both inland and marine waters, is vitally important for a range of health and well-being outcomes (Fleming et al., 2019). One of the chief threats to health comes from human and animal faecal matter in the water, which carries harmful pathogens, including bacteria such as *Escherichia coli* (*E. coli*), which can lead to gastro-intestinal and other illnesses (Prüss, 1998). Further, perceived quality, irrespective of actual quality, is also important because it can influence behaviour, leading to either avoidance of waters that are of good quality (Vert et al., 2019b) or exposure to waters that are of poor quality (Rowles et al., 2018). As early as 1980, the World Health Organization recognised that perceived quality could affect the psychological benefits of interacting with blue spaces (WHO, 1980).

In one of the earliest studies to look at the importance of perceived water quality systematically, Wilson et al. (1995) showed participants photographs of different waterscapes with and without photo-shopped signs of pollution (e.g. foam), algal blooms and so on. As expected, the images with indicators of poor water quality were consistently rated less positively, and people said they would be less likely to use them for recreation purposes, irrespective of the fact that they were given no objective data on water quality. In a similar study, Wyles et al. (2016) experimentally manipulated the amount and type of litter on a beach and showed images of these to participants. Although all forms of litter reduced preference ratings of the scene, visitor generated litter (e.g. food cartons) had a more negative impact than fishing litter (e.g. discarded nets). Therefore, it is necessary to consider perceptions of blue space quality alongside more objective indicators when considering the impacts on health and well-being.

Weather

Blue spaces become especially attractive in hot and sunny conditions, since, as noted, they tend to be cooler, but possibly less attractive in rainy or windy conditions. Supporting this suggestion, landscape preferences in an experimental study using photographs were more affected by the weather for blue spaces than for either green or urban ones (White et al., 2014b). Analysis of over 40,000 visits to different natural settings in England also suggested that people are likely to do more physical activity under warmer temperatures at the coast but not at inland waters (Elliott et al.,

2019). It is also important to take into account the context when considering the weather. In England, temperatures are relatively low compared to California, where lower than mean temperatures at the beach were seen as preferable and more restorative (Hipp & Ogunseitan, 2011), precisely because it was not 'too hot'.

Country/cultural context

Systematic reviews of inland blue spaces (Völker & Kistemann, 2011), home proximity to blue space (Gascón et al., 2017) and blue activity interventions (Britton et al., 2020) suggest that most studies have been conducted in high-income countries, including Europe, the United States, Australia and New Zealand, Japan and China. Similar issues exist in the green space literature, where the vast majority of research has also been conducted in high-income countries. More work is needed in low- to middle-income countries, where water quality may be less regulated (Borja et al., 2020) and threats to health and well-being from water-borne diseases, jellyfish, parasites and predators (e.g. crocodiles), as well as the risk of drowning, may be heightened (WHO, 2014).

Individual

The green space and health literature is replete with papers exploring the moderating role of individual-level differences such as age, gender and ethnicity. One of the most important is socioeconomic status, with a number of studies suggesting that the benefits of green space are greater for poorer than richer individuals (Mitchell & Popham, 2008). As noted earlier, a similar effect has been found with respect to home proximity to the coast, with the relationship to general health being stronger for those in more deprived communities (Wheeler et al., 2012) and the relationship to mental health stronger for those in lower-income households (Garrett et al. 2019b). Less work, however, has been conducted to explore other factors such as age, gender and ethnicity and how these may interact with blue space exposure to affect health and well-being.

Age

Some blue space studies have been conducted with specific age groups. Amoly et al. (2014) explored 7–10-year-old Spanish children's emotional coping and behaviour, as well as symptoms of attention deficit hyperactivity disorder (ADHD, Amoly et al., 2014), as a function of time spent in different settings. The more time the children spent at the beach in the last 12 months, the fewer emotional problems and more pro-social behaviours they exhibited, but there were no associations with ADHD symptoms (Amoly et al., 2014). Crucially, pro-social behaviours were only related to beach, but not green space, time. This finding echoes adult studies suggesting that blue spaces seem to be particularly important for supporting good-quality social relationships.

At the other end of the age spectrum, several blue space studies have focused on older adults. As earlier, Dempsey et al. (2018), Garrett et al. (2019a) and Helbich et al. (2019) all report positive associations between having blue space views from the home or local streets and general and mental health, respectively, among older adults. Coleman and Kearns (2015) have argued that blue space views become increasingly important as people get older and mobility issues emerge. As Finlay et al. (2015) point out, however, although water features are an attractor for older people to public places, other factors such as accessibility, feelings of safety and the presence of facilities (such as toilets and benches) tend to be considered even more important. Although it is often hard to disaggregate the effects of green and blue space, blue spaces do offer certain characteristics, such as heat reduction potential, that may be particularly important in older age (Burkart et al., 2015).

Gender

Elliott et al. (2018) found that females in England were more likely to visit beach settings, while men were more likely to visit inland waterways. Similar findings were reported in Spain, where extensive visitor observations reported more than twice as many men than women using an urban river pathway (Vert et al., 2019b). Nevertheless, the proportion of women increased slightly, and the proportion of men decreased slightly, following extensive renovations, perhaps because the improvements increased perceptions of safety (Vert et al., 2019b). Further, the activities engaged in at blue space settings also show systematic differences: while women are more likely to engage in activities such as paddling and sunbathing, they are less likely to report fishing or water sport activities, with the exception of swimming, which is similar across both genders (Elliott et al., 2018). Differences in activities are important because they are associated with different levels of energy expenditure (Vert et al., 2019a), and since it tends to be the higher-energy activities which are likely to be undertaken by men, women may be missing out on health-related physical activity gains from a more diverse set of activities in blue spaces.

As Britton and colleagues point out (2018) this may, in part, reflect a certain 'masculinity' associated with many water-based activities such as surfing, which may put some women off from engaging with them in the first place or undermine their enjoyment of them. However, apart from these more physically active endeavours, there is little evidence in the broader literature that men and women benefit differently from blue space exposures. Again, the issue is probably about ensuring fair, equitable and respectful access to all rather than trying to conduct lots of further research which sets out to demonstrate that the two genders react differently to blue spaces.

Ethnicity

There is evidence that individuals from minority ethnic backgrounds in the United States tend to visit blue spaces less than their white counterparts (Leeworthy, 2001), even if they live nearer them (Haeffner et al., 2017). There is also evidence that this may have deep historic roots in racial segregation, as opposed to perceptions that the potential benefits to their health and well-being are any less (Bell et al., 2019). In part, the issue may be related to the fact that individuals from minority ethnic groups are less likely to be able to swim than their white counterparts (Pilgaard et al., 2019).

In other contexts, blue spaces may have even deeper historical roots linked to cultural identity and practices. Wheaton et al. (2020), for instance, discuss traditional Māori beliefs and practices with respect to the natural world, and blue spaces in particular, in Aotearoa/New Zealand. While many colonial European settlers see the coastal waters as places of recreation and leisure, Māori communities in have a concept called "kaitiakitanga," which is similar to a sense of guardianship towards the natural world for the good of both future generations but also the natural world in and of itself. Relationships between blue spaces and health/well-being among these traditional marine communities may be quite different from those where most of the research has been conducted to date.

Actions/interventions/changes

Aware of some benefits of blue spaces for the promotion of good health and well-being, policy makers, planners and practitioners have implemented numerous actions, initiatives and changes to improve safe access to high-quality water environments. Although many of these actions operate at several levels, our model (bottom of Figure 2.1) groups them loosely into three types:

1. National/international societal-level interventions;
2. Local/regional infrastructure interventions; and
3. Personal-level interventions with specific groups of people.

We recognise that there are thousands of infrastructure projects to improve water quality as well as regulations to reduce discharge of pollution and so on into inland and marine waters, but these are beyond the scope of the current work because their aim is predominantly to reduce harm rather than promote benefits per se (WHO, 2003).

Societal actions

An excellent example of an international-level intervention that applies to multiple nation states is the EU's Bathing Water Directive (EU, 1976). Before the BWD, there were large quantities of uncontrolled or partially controlled discharges of a range of pollutants into bathing waters across the continent. The directive identified a range of indicators by which bathing water quality could be assessed, with the current focus on levels of microbial pollution, especially *E. coli* and Enterococci emerging after the 2006 revision, based on the best available epidemiological evidence of harm from these bacteria. Although the aim of the directive was mainly to reduce harms (i.e. exposure to faecal matter in the water), it is also consciously trying to promote the use of these settings for active, healthy recreation (EEA, 2019). As a direct consequence of the original and revised directives, bathing water quality in the EU, and similarly monitored countries such as Albania and Switzerland, has improved dramatically and use of these spaces increased (EEA, 2019).

Local/regional actions

A recent review of local blue space interventions that were planned and designed to improve access to coastal and inland waters around the world by Bell (2019) found 172 recent high-profile examples (e.g. they had won awards). These included design interventions such as waterfront promenades, conversion of former docks and improved access to bathing waters. Many of the interventions were designed to improve the aesthetic quality of the area (to make them more attractive for visitors) and/or to explicitly encourage physical activity (e.g. by encouraging walking, cycling and swimming). Several sites where entry into the water was undesirable due to safety (e.g. canalised rivers) were nevertheless designed to improve the visual experience and promote relaxation by building seating and viewing platforms of various types. Many of these were designed to specifically facilitate the kind of social interactions discussed earlier. Further discussion of all these issues can be found elsewhere (Bell et al., 2020) and across the other chapters in the current volume.

Personal actions

A wide range of programmes have been developed to specifically increase people's exposures to safe blue spaces, primarily to engage in water sports or so called 'blue gym' activities (Depledge & Bird, 2009). A recent systematic review of 33 such programs (Britton et al., 2020) suggests they are mainly targeted at people experiencing difficulties of some kind, such as post-traumatic stress disorder (e.g. among army veterans), breast cancer, cognitive impairments and broader mental health issues. The most common intervention activity was surfing, followed by dragon boat racing, sailing, kayaking and fishing. About half of the interventions took place in marine and half in inland waters. As many of the studies were qualitative in nature, or, if quantitative, had relatively small sample sizes, finding clear benefits to health and well-being was difficult. Nonetheless, several suggestive findings emerged, including improvements in self-esteem and social relationships.

A different type of personal blue space intervention for health and well-being has also been investigated in indoor health and care facilities. In practice, many indoor nature-based interventions have used images and sounds of blue spaces (e.g. Kweon et al., 2008). Particularly popular historically have been aquariums, which can help people recover from stress (Cracknell et al., 2017), as well as helping people manage subsequently stressful situations such as electroconvulsive therapy (ECT) (Barker et al., 2003) more effectively. They have also been used in dementia care, where they have been found to help calm older adults, as well as encouraging healthy levels of eating and the promotion of social interactions (Edwards & Beck, 2002).

Summary and limitations

Many of the benefits of blue spaces are obvious, such as the need for freshwater for drinking and irrigation and the existence of food sources (e.g. fish). The aim of the current chapter was not to revisit these already well-documented benefits but to summarise some of the more subtle but potentially no less important benefits, or salutogenic effects, for human health and well-being. To help navigate the literature, we developed a conceptual model (Figure 2.1) to reflect how research into these salutogenic effects is interconnected. The framework drew on several existing frameworks from the green space and health literature to identify types of exposure (e.g. indirect, incidental and intentional; Keniger et al., 2013), pathways linking exposure to outcomes (mitigation, instoration, restoration; Markevych et al., 2017) and situational (e.g. weather) and individual (e.g. age) effect modifiers (Hartig et al., 2014). But it also went beyond these models by recognising the importance of pro-environmental outcomes associated with blue space exposure (e.g. Milfont et al., 2014), nature connectedness (e.g. Martin et al., 2020) and feedback loops from health outcomes to actions, interventions and changes that are undertaken to increase exposure.

A strength of the reviewed literature was the breadth of research methodologies used, including large-scale epidemiological studies, longitudinal work, visitor surveys, experience sampling methods, laboratory experiments, field experiments, randomised controlled trials, infrastructure interventions, behavioural interventions and in-depth qualitative work. The range of methods reflects the highly interdisciplinary nature of the work. Results are not all clear cut, but there is evidence across these mixed methodologies that access to safe, clean and attractive blue spaces has a range of potential health and well-being benefits, due to a variety of mechanisms (e.g. lower temperatures, increased physical activity, lower stress, encouraging quality time with friends and family), for a wide range of people.

Nevertheless, we remain cautious. Because of its breadth, the review lacked depth, and we were unable to conduct the kind of systematic literature searches, thorough quality appraisals or quantitative meta-analyses of specific studies that papers with smaller, more targeted research questions are able to conduct (cf. Britton et al., 2020; Gascón et al., 2017; Völker & Kistemann, 2011). We also recognise that most of the studies reviewed here were conducted in middle- to high-income countries, mainly in North America, Europe and Australasia. Studies such as Vaeztavakoli et al.'s (2018) in Iran are the exception rather than the rule. Given that the majority of the world's population lives in Asia, Africa and South America, further investigation into the potential salutogenic benefits of blue spaces for these populations is crucial, especially when blue space risks such as flooding, drowning and disease may be more pronounced in these countries.

Concluding comments

The aim of this narrative review was to provide an overview of the growing but disparate literature that examines the potential benefits to health and well-being from exposures to aquatic (blue space) environments such as rivers, lakes and the coast. The aim was not to provide definitive answers but rather to outline the breadth of work conducted to date and structure it into a framework that could be used to better identify research gaps and future opportunities. Such a framework, we believe, can also help researchers think more about critical points where risks and benefit trade-offs for health and well-being can occur, considerations of which may be especially important for blue space settings.

Note

1 This chapter is an abridged version of White et al. (2020). Please see the original paper for more complete referencing on all the topics discussed here.

References

Alcock, I., White, M.P., Pahl, S., Duarte-Davidson, R., & Fleming, L.E. (2020). Associations between pro-environmental behaviour and neighbourhood nature, nature visits and nature appreciation: Evidence from a nationally representative survey in England. *Environment International, 136*, 105441.

Alcock, I., White, M.P. Wheeler, B.W., Lovell, R., Higgins, S., Osborne, N., & Depledge, M. (2015). Mental health and land cover in rural England: What accounts for "England's green and pleasant land"? *Landscape & Urban Planning, 142,* 38–46.

Amoly, E., Dadvand, P., Forns, J., López-Vicente, M., Basagaña, X., Julvez, J., . . . Sunyer, J. (2014). Green and blue spaces and behavioral development in Barcelona schoolchildren: The BREATHE project. *Environmental Health Perspectives, 122*(12), 1351–1358.

Annerstedt, M., Jönsson, P., Wallergård, M., Johansson, G., Karlson, B., Grahn, P., . . . Währborg, P. (2013). Inducing physiological stress recovery with sounds of nature in a virtual reality forest – Results from a pilot study. *Physiology & Behavior, 118,* 240–250.

Ashbullby, K.J., Pahl, S., Webley, P., & White, M.P. (2013). The beach as a setting for families' health promotion: A qualitative study with parents and children living in coastal regions in Southwest England. *Health & Place, 23,* 138–147.

Asselman, J., Van Acker, E., De Rijcke, M., Tilleman, L., Van Nieuwerburgh, F., Mees, J., . . . Janssen, C.R. (2019). Marine biogenics in sea spray aerosols interact with the mTOR signaling pathway. *Scientific Reports, 9*(1), 1–10.

Ballesteros-Olza, M., Gracia-de-Rentería, P., & Pérez-Zabaleta, A. (2020). Effects on general health associated with beach proximity in Barcelona (Spain). *Health Promotion International.* https://doi.org/10.1093/heapro/daaa013

Barker, S.B., Rasmussen, K.G., & Best, A.M. (2003). Effect of aquariums on electroconvulsive therapy patients. *Anthrozoös, 16,* 229–240.

Barton, J., & Pretty, J. (2010). What is the best dose of nature and green exercise for improving mental health? A multi-study analysis. *Environmental Science & Technology, 44,* 3947–3955.

Baumeister, R.F., & Leary, M.R. (1995). The need to belong: Desire for interpersonal attachments as a fundamental human motivation. *Psychological Bulletin, 117,* 497–529.

Bell, S. (2019). Health and well-being aspects of urban blue space: The new urban landscape research field. *Landscape Architecture: Special Edition – Resilient Landscapes, 26,* 119–113.

Bell, S.L., Hollenbeck, J., Lovell, R., White, M.P., & Depledge, M.H. (2019). The shadows of risk and inequality within salutogenic coastal waters. In R. Foley, R. Kearns, T. Kistemann & B. Wheeler (Eds.), *Blue space, health and well-being: Hydrophilia Unbounded* (Ch. 10, pp. 133–156). Oxford: Routledge.

Bell, S., Mishra, H.S., Elliott, L.R., Shellock, R., Vassiljev, P., Porter, M., . . . White, M.P. (2020). Urban blue acupuncture: Protocol for evaluating of a complex landscape design intervention to improve health and wellbeing in a coastal community. *Sustainability, 12,* 4084.

Bell, S.L., Phoenix, C., Lovell, R., & Wheeler, B.W. (2015). Seeking everyday well-being: The coast as a therapeutic landscape. *Social Science & Medicine, 142,* 56–67.

Bloom, D., Cafiero, E., Jané-Llopis, E., Abrahams-Gessel, S., Bloom, L., Fathima, S., Feigl, A., Gaziano, T., Mowafi, M., Pandya, A., et al. (2011). *The global economic burden of noncommunicable diseases.* Geneva, Switzerland: WHO.

Borja, A., White, M.P., Berdalet, E., Bock, N., Eatock, E., Kristensen, P., . . . Fleming, L.E. (2020). Moving towards an agenda on ocean health and human health. *Frontiers in Marine Science, 7,* 37.

Brereton, F., Clinch, J.P., & Ferreira, S. (2008). Happiness, geography and the environment. *Ecological Economics, 65*(2), 386–396.

Britton, E., Kindermann, G., Domegan, C., & Carlin, C. (2020). Blue care: A systematic review of blue space interventions for health and well-being. *Health Promotion International, 35,* 50–69.

Britton, E., Olive, R., & Wheaton, B. (2018). Surfer and leisure: Freedom' to surf? Contested spaces on the coast. In M. Brown & K. Peters (Eds.), *Living with the sea: Knowledge, awareness and action* (pp. 147–166). London and New York: Routledge.

Burkart, K., Meier, F., Schneider, A., Breitner, S., Canário, P., Alcoforado, M.J., . . . Endlicher, W. (2015). Modification of heat-related mortality in an elderly urban population by vegetation (urban green) and proximity to water (urban blue): Evidence from Lisbon, Portugal. *Environmental Health Perspectives, 124*, 927–934.

Capaldi, C.A., Dopko, R.L., & Zelenski, J.M. (2014). The relationship between nature connectedness and happiness: A meta-analysis. *Frontiers in Psychology, 5*, 976.

Cartwright, B., White, M.P., & Clitherow, T.J. (2018). Nearby nature 'buffers' the effect of low social connectedness on adult subjective well-being over the last 7 days. *International Journal of Environmental Research & Public Health, 15*, 1238.

Cherrie, M.P.C., Wheeler, B., White, M.P., Sarran, C.E., & Osborne, N.J. (2015). Coastal climate is associated with elevated solar irradiance and higher 25(OH)D level in coastal residents. *Environment International, 77*, 76–84.

Coleman, T., & Kearns, R. (2015). The role of bluespaces in experiencing place, aging and well-being: Insights from Waiheke Island, New Zealand. *Health & Place, 35*, 206–217.

Cracknell, D., White, M.P., Pahl, S., & Depledge, M.H. (2017). Aquariums as restorative environments and the influence of species diversity. *Landscape Research, 42*, 18–32.

Crouse, D.L., Balram, A., Hystad, P., Pinault, L., van den Bosch, M., Chen, H., . . . Villeneuve, P.J. (2018). Associations between living near water and risk of mortality among urban Canadians. *Environmental Health Perspectives, 126*(7), 077008.

de Bell, S., Graham, H., Jarvis, S., & White, P. (2017). The importance of nature in mediating social and psychological benefits associated with visits to freshwater blue space. *Landscape and Urban Planning, 167*, 118–127.

Dempsey, S., Devine, M.T., Gillespie, T., Lyons, S., & Nolan, A. (2018). Coastal blue space and depression in older adults. *Health & Place, 54*, 110–117.

Denton, H., & Aranda, K. (2020). The wellbeing benefits of sea swimming. Is it time to revisit the sea cure? *Qualitative Research in Sport, Exercise and Health, 12*(5), 647–663.

Depledge, M.H., & Bird, W.J. (2009). The blue gym: Health and well-being from our coasts. *Marine Pollution Bulletin, 58*, 947.

Depledge, M.H., Lovell, R., Wheeler, B., Morrissey, K., White, M.P., & Fleming, L.E.F. (2017). *Review of evidence: Health and well-being of coastal communities*. Government Office of Science Foresight 'Future of the Sea' Project. London: GOSF.

de Vries, S., Ten Have, M., van Dorsselaer, S., van Wezep, M., Hermans, T., & de Graaf, R. (2016). Local availability of green and blue space and prevalence of common mental disorders in the Netherlands. *BJPsych Open, 2*, 366–372.

Edwards, N.E., & Beck, A.M. (2002). Animal-assisted therapy and nutrition in Alzheimer's disease. *Western Journal of Nursing Research, 24*, 697–712.

Elliott, L.R. White, M.P., Grellier, J., Garrett, J.K., Cirach, M., Wheeler, B.W., . . . Fleming, L.E. (*2020*). Defining residential blue space distance categories: Modelling distance-decay effects across eighteen countries. *Landscape & Urban Planning, 198*, 103800.

Elliott, L.R., White, M.P., Grellier, J., Rees, S., Waters, R., & Fleming, L.E.F. (2018). Recreational visits to inland and coastal waters in England: Who, where, when, what and why. *Marine Policy, 97*, 305–314.

Elliott, L.R., White, M.P., Smalley, A., Sarran, C., Scoccimarro, E., Grellier, J., . . . Fleming, L.E. (2019). The effects of meteorological conditions and daylight on nature-based recreational physical activity in England. *Urban Forestry & Urban Greening, 42*, 39–50.

Elliott, L.R., White, M.P., Taylor, A.H., & Herbert, S. (2015). Energy expenditure on recreational visits to different natural environments: Implications for public health. *Social Science and Medicine, 139*, 56–60.

Emfield, A.G., & Neider, M.B. (2014). Evaluating visual and auditory contributions to the cognitive restoration effect. *Frontiers in Psychology, 5*, 548.

European Environment Agency (2019). European bathing water quality in 2018. EEA Report No 3/2019.

European Union (EU). (1976). Council Directive 76/160/EEC of 8 December 1975 concerning the quality of bathing water. https://eur-lex.europa.eu/legal-content/EN/ALL/?uri=CELEX:31976L0160 accessed 17 July 2019.

Finlay, J., Franke, T., McKay, H., & Sims-Gould, J. (2015). Therapeutic landscapes and wellbeing in later life: Impacts of blue and green spaces for older adults. *Health & Place, 34*, 97–106.

Fleming, L.E., Kirkpatrick, B., Backer, L.C., et al. (2011). Review of Florida red tide and human health effects. *Harmful Algae, 20*, 224–233.

Fleming, L.E., Maycock, B., White, M.P., & Depledge, M.H. (2019). Sustainable oceans needed to protect and foster human health in the 21st century. *People and Nature*. DOI: 10.1002/pan3.10038

Foley, R. (2015). Swimming in Ireland: Immersions in therapeutic blue space. *Health & Place, 35*, 218–225.

Foley, R. (2017). Swimming as an accretive practice in healthy blue space. *Emotion, Space and Society, 22*, 43–51.

Fortescue Fox, R., Lloyd, W.B. (1938). Convalescence on the coast. *The Lancet, 232*, 37–39.

Fredrickson, B.L. (2001). The role of positive emotions in positive psychology: The broaden-and-build theory of positive emotions. *American Psychologist, 56*, 218.

Gaisberger, M., Šanović, R., Dobias, H., Kolarž, P., Moder, A., Thalhamer, J., . . . Hartl, A. (2012). Effects of ionized waterfall aerosol on pediatric allergic asthma. *Journal of Asthma, 49*, 830–838.

Garrett, J.K., Clitherow, T.J., White, M.P., Elliott, L.R., & Wheeler, B.W., & Fleming, L.E. (2019a). Coastal proximity and mental health among urban adults in England: The moderating effect of household income. *Health & Place, 59*, 102200.

Garrett, J.K., White, M.P., Elliott, L.R., Wheeler, B.W., & Fleming, L.E. (2020). Neighbourhood nature and physical activity: Self-report and accelerometer findings from the Health Survey for England. *Environmental Research*, in press.

Garrett, J.K., White, M.P., Huang, J., Ng, S., Hui, Z., Leung, C., . . . Wong, M.C.S. (2019b). The association between blue space exposure, health and well-being in Hong Kong. *Health & Place, 55*, 100–110.

Gascon, M., Sánchez-Benavides, G., Dadvand, P., Martínez, D., Gramunt, N., Gotsens, X., . . . Nieuwenhuijsen, M. (2018). Long-term exposure to residential green and blue spaces and anxiety and depression in adults: A cross-sectional study. *Environmental Research, 162*, 231–239.

Gascón, M., Zijlema, W., Vert, C., White, M.P., & Nieuwenhuijsen, M.J. (2017). Blue spaces, human health and well-being: A systematic review. *International Journal of Hygiene and Environmental Health*, 1207–1221.

Gibas-Dorna, M., Checinska, Z., Korek, E., Kupsz, J., Sowinska, A., Wojciechowska, M., . . . Piątek, J. (2016). Variations in leptin and insulin levels within one swimming season in non-obese female cold water swimmers. *Scandinavian Journal of Clinical and Laboratory Investigation, 76*, 486–491.

Gibbons, S., Mourato, S., & Resende, G.M. (2014) The amenity value of English nature: A hedonic price approach. *Environmental and Resource Economics, 57*, 175–196.

Gidlow, C.J., Jones, M.V., Hurst, G., Masterson, D., Clark-Carter, D., Tarvainen, M.P., . . . Nieuwenhuijsen, M. (2016). Where to put your best foot forward: Psycho-physiological responses to walking in natural and urban environments. *Journal of Environmental Psychology, 45*, 22–29.

Grafetstätter, C., Gaisberger, M., Prossegger, J., Ritter, M., Kolarž, P., Pichler, C., . . . Hartl, A. (2017). Does waterfall aerosol influence mucosal immunity and chronic stress? A randomized controlled clinical trial. *Journal of Physiological Anthropology, 36*, 10.

Grellier, J., White, M.P., Albin, M., Bell, S., Elliott, L.R., Gascón, M., . . . Fleming, L.E. (2017). BlueHealth: A study programme protocol for mapping and quantifying the potential benefits to public health and well-being from Europe's blue spaces. *BMJ Open, 7*, e016188.

Haeffner, M., Jackson-Smith, D., Buchert, M., & Risley, J. (2017). Accessing blue spaces: Social and geographic factors structuring familiarity with, use of, and appreciation of urban waterways. *Landscape and Urban Planning, 167*, 136–146.

Hartig, T., Mitchell, R., de Vries, S., & Frumkin, H. (2014). Nature and health. *Annual Review of Public Health, 35*, 207–228.

Helbich, M., Yao, Y., Liu, Y., Zhang, J., Liu, P., & Wang, R. (2019). Using deep learning to examine street view green and blue spaces and their associations with geriatric depression in Beijing, China. *Environment International, 126*, 107–117.

Hignett, A., White, M.P., Pahl., S., Jenkin, R., & Lefroy, M. (2018). Can participating in a surfing programme promote young people's well-being and connectedness to the natural environment? *Journal of Adventure Education & Outdoor Learning, 18*, 53–69.

Hipp, J.A., & Ogunseitan, O.A. (2011). Effect of environmental conditions on perceived psychological restorativeness of coastal parks. *Journal of Environmental Psychology, 31*(4), 421–429.

Hooyberg, A., Roose, H., Grellier, J., Elliott, L.R., Lonneville, B., White, M.P., . . . Everaert, G. (*2020*). General health and residential proximity to the coast in Belgium: Results from a cross-sectional health survey. *Environmental Research, 184*, 109225.

Huttunen, P., Kokko, L., & Ylijukuri, V. (2004). Winter swimming improves general well-being. *International Journal of Circumpolar Health, 63*, 140–144.

Kaplan, R., & Kaplan, S. (1989). The experience of nature: A psychological perspective. CUP Archive.

Keniger, L.E., Gaston, K.J., Irvine, K.N., & Fuller, R.A. (2013). What are the benefits of interacting with nature? *International Journal of Environmental Research and Public Health, 10*, 913–935.

Kolarz, P., Gaisberger, M., Madl, P., Hofmann, W., Ritter, M., & Hartl, A. (2012). Characterization of ions at Alpine waterfalls. *Atmospheric Chemistry and Physics, 12*, 3687.

Korpela, K., Korhonen, M., Nummi, T., Martos, T., & Sallay, V. (2020). Environmental self-regulation in favourite places of Finnish and Hungarian adults. *Journal of Environmental Psychology, 67*, 101384.

Kweon, B.S., Ulrich, R.S., Walker, V.D., & Tassinary, L.G. (2008). Anger and stress: The role of landscape posters in an office setting. *Environment and Behavior, 40*(3), 355–381.

Leeworthy, V.R. (2001). *Preliminary estimates from versions 1–6: Coastal recreation participation*. National Survey on Recreation and the Environment (NSRE) 2000. US Department of Commerce.

MacKerron, G., & Mourato, S. (2013). Happiness is greater in natural environments. *Global Environmental Change, 23*(5), 992–1000.

Markevych, I., Schoierer, J., Hartig, T., Chudnovsky, A., Hystad, P., Dzhambov, A.M., . . . Lupp, G. (2017). Exploring pathways linking greenspace to health: Theoretical and methodological guidance. *Environmental Research, 158*, 301–317.

Martin, L., White, M.P., Hunt, A., Richardson, M., Pahl, S., & Burt, J. (2020). Nature contact, nature connectedness and associations with health, well-being and pro-environmental behaviours: Results from a nationally representative survey in England. *Journal of Environmental Psychology, 68*, 101389.

Mayer, F.S., & Frantz, C.M. (2004). The connectedness to nature scale: A measure of individuals' feeling in community with nature. *Journal of Environmental Psychology, 24*, 503–515.

Milfont, T.L., Evans, L., Sibley, C.G., Ries, J., & Cunningham, A. (2014). Proximity to coast is linked to climate change belief. *PLoS One, 9*(7), e103180.

Millennium Ecosystem Assessment, (MEA, 2005). Ecosystems and human well-being. *Synthesis*. www.millenniumassessment.org/en/index.html

Mitchell, R., & Popham, F. (2008). Effect of exposure to natural environment on health inequalities: An observational population study. *The Lancet, 372*(9650), 1655–1660.

Moore, M.N. (2015). Do airborne biogenic chemicals interact with the PI3K/Akt/mTOR cell signalling pathway to benefit human health and well-being in rural and coastal environments? *Environmental Research, 140*, 65–75.

Neumann, B., Vafeidis, A.T., Zimmermann, J., Nicholls, R.J. (2015). Future coastal population growth and exposure to sea-level rise and coastal flooding: A global assessment. *PLoS One*, e0118571.

Nutsford, D., Pearson, A.L., Kingham, S., & Reitsma, F. (2016). Residential exposure to visible blue space (but not green space) associated with lower psychological distress in a capital city. *Health & Place, 39*, 70–78.

Papathanasopoulou, E., White, M.P., Hattam, C., Lannin, A., Harvey, A., & Spencer, A. (2016). Valuing the health benefits of physical activities in the marine environment and their importance for marine spatial planning. *Marine Policy, 63*, 144–152

Pasanen, T., White, M.P., Wheeler, B., Garrett, J., & Elliott, L. (2019). Neighbourhood blue space, health and well-being: The mediating role of different types of physical activity. *Environment International, 131*, 105136.

Pawar, S.D., Meena, G.S., & Jadhav, D.B. (2012). Air ion variation at poultry-farm, coastal, mountain, rural and urban sites in India. *Aerosol and Air Quality Research, 12*(3), 440–451.

Pearson, A.L., Bottomley, R., Chambers, T., Thornton, L., Stanley, J., Smith, M., . . . Signal, L. (2017). Measuring blue space visibility and 'blue recreation' in the everyday lives of children in a capital city. *International Journal of Environmental Research and Public Health, 14*(6), 563.

Pearson, A.L., et al. (2019). Effects of freshwater blue spaces may be beneficial for mental health: A first, ecological study in the North American Great Lakes region. *PloS One, 14*(8), e0221977.

Perez, V., Alexander, D.D., & Bailey, W.H. (2013). Air ions and mood outcomes: A review and meta-analysis. *BMC Psychiatry, 13*(1), 1–20.

Pilgaard, F.I., Östergren, P.O., Olin, A., Kling, S., Albin, M., & Björk, J. (2019). Socioeconomic differences in swimming ability among children in Malmö, southern Sweden: Initial results from a community-level intervention. *Scandinavian Journal of Public Health*, 1403494818821478.

Pritchard, A., Richardson, M., Sheffield, D., & McEwan, K. (2019). The relationship between nature connectedness and eudaimonic well-being: A meta-analysis. *Journal of Happiness Studies, 21*, 1145, 1167.

Prüss, A. (1998). Review of epidemiological studies on health effects from exposure to recreational water. *International Journal of Epidemiology, 27*(1), 1–9.

Qiang, Y., Shen, S., & Chen, Q. (2019). Visibility analysis of oceanic blue space using digital elevation models. *Landscape and Urban Planning, 181*, 92–102.

Rådsten-Ekman, M., Axelsson, Ö., & Nilsson, M.E. (2013). Effects of sounds from water on perception of acoustic environments dominated by road-traffic noise. *Acta Acustica united with Acustica, 99*(2), 218–225.

Rowles III, L.S., Alcalde, R., Bogolasky, F., Kum, S., Diaz-Arriaga, F.A., Ayres, C., . . . Lawler, D.F. (2018). Perceived versus actual water quality: Community studies in rural Oaxaca, Mexico. *Science of the Total Environment, 622*, 626–634.

Schipperijn, J., Ekholm, O., Stigsdotter, U.K., Toftager, M., Bentsen, P., Kamper-Jørgensen, F., & Randrup, T.B. (2010). Factors influencing the use of green space: Results from a Danish national representative survey. *Landscape and Urban Planning, 95*, 130–137.

Schultz, P.W. (2001). Assessing the structure of environmental concern: Concern for self, other people, and the biosphere. *Journal of Environmental Psychology, 21*, 1–13.

Stenbeck, K.D., Balanda, K.P., Williams, M.J., Ring, I.T., MacLennan, R., Chick, J.E., & Morton, A.P. (1990). Patterns of treated non-melanoma skin cancer in Queensland – The region with the highest incidence rates in the world. *Medical Journal of Australia, 153*, 511–515.

Thoma, M.V., Mewes, R., & Nater, U.M. (2018). Preliminary evidence: The stress-reducing effect of listening to water sounds depends on somatic complaints: A randomized trial. *Medicine, 97*(8).

Tipton, M.J., Collier, N., Massey, H., Corbett, J., & Harper, M. (2017). Cold water immersion: Kill or cure? *Experimental Physiology, 102*, 1335–1355.

Triguero-Mas, M., Dadvand, P., Cirach, M., Martínez, D., Medina, A., Mompart, A., . . . Nieuwenhuijsen, M.J. (2015). Natural outdoor environments and mental and physical health: Relationships and mechanisms. *Environment International, 77*, 35–41.

Triguero-Mas, M., Gidlow, C.J., Martínez, D., De Bont, J., Carrasco-Turigas, G., Martínez-Íñiguez, T., . . . Jones, M.V. (2017). The effect of randomised exposure to different types of natural outdoor environments compared to exposure to an urban environment on people with indications of psychological distress in Catalonia. *PloS One, 12*(3), e0172200.

Ulrich, R.S. (1981). Natural versus urban scenes: Some psychophysiological effects. *Environment and Behavior, 13*(5), 523–556.

Ulrich, R.S., Simons, R.F., Losito, B.D., Fiorito, E., Miles, M.A., & Zelson, M. (1991). Stress recovery during exposure to natural and urban environments. *Journal of Environmental Psychology, 11*(3), 201–230.

Vaeztavakoli, A., Lak, A., & Yigitcanlar, T. (2018). Blue and green spaces as therapeutic landscapes: Health effects of urban water canal areas of Isfahan. *Sustainability, 10*(11), 4010.

van den Bosch, M., & Sang, Å.O. (2017). Urban natural environments as nature-based solutions for improved public health – A systematic review of reviews. *Environmental Research, 158*, 373–384.

Van Tulleken, C., Tipton, M., Massey, H., & Harper, C.M. (2018) Open water swimming as a treatment for major depressive disorder. *BMJ Case Reports*. DOI: 10.1136/bcr-2018-225007

Vert, C., Carrasco-Turigas, G., Zijlema, W., Espinosa, A., Cano-Riu, L., Elliott, L.R., . . . Gascon, M. (2019a). Impact of a riverside accessibility intervention on use, physical activity, and well-being: A mixed methods pre-post evaluation. *Landscape and Urban Planning, 190*, 103611.

Vert, C., Gascon, M., Ranzani, O., Márquez, S., Triguero-Mas, M., Carrasco-Turigas, . . . Mark Nieuwenhuijsen, M. (2020). Physical and mental health effects of repeated short walks in a blue space environment: A randomised crossover study. *Environmental Research*, in press.

Vert, C., Nieuwenhuijsen, M., Gascon, M., Grellier, J., Fleming, L.E., White, M.P., & Rojas-Rueda, D. (2019b). Health risk assessment of community riverside regeneration in Barcelona. *International Journal of Environmental Research & Public Health, 16*(3), 01.

Völker, S., Baumeister, H., Classen, T., Hornberg, C., & Kistemann, T. (2013). Evidence for the temperature-mitigating capacity of urban blue space – A health geographic perspective. *Erdkunde*, 355–371.

Völker, S., & Kistemann, T. (2011). The impact of blue space on human health and well-being – Salutogenetic health effects of inland surface waters: A review. *International Journal of Hygiene and Environmental Health, 214*, 449–460.

Völker, S., & Kistemann, T. (2015). Developing the urban blue: Comparative health responses to blue and green urban open spaces in Germany. *Health & Place, 35*, 196–205.

Wheaton, B., Waiti, J., Cosgriff, M., & Burrows, L. (2020). Coastal blue space and well-being research: Looking beyond western tides. *Leisure Studies, 39*(1), 83–95.

Wheeler, B., White, M.P., Stahl-Timmins, W., & Depledge, M.H. (2012). Does living by the coast improve health and well-being? *Health & Place, 18*, 1198–1201.

White, M.P., Alcock, I., Wheeler, B.W., & Depledge, M.H. (2013a). Coastal proximity and health: A fixed effects analysis of longitudinal panel data. *Health & Place*, 23, 97–103.

White, M.P., Bell, S., Elliott, L., Jenkin, R., Wheeler, B.W., & Depledge, M.H. (2016a). The health effects of blue exercise in the UK. In J. Barton, R. Bragg, C. Wood & J. Pretty (Eds.), *Green exercise: Linking nature, health and well-being* (Ch. 7, pp. 69–78). Oxford: Routledge.

White, M.P., Cracknell, D., Corcoran, A., Jenkinson, G., & Depledge, M.H. (2014a). Do preferences for waterscapes persist in inclement weather conditions and extend to sub-aquatic scenes? *Landscape Research, 39*, 339–358.

White, M.P., Elliott, L.R., Gascon, M., Roberts, B., & Fleming, L.E. (2020). Blue space, health and well-being: A narrative overview and synthesis of potential benefits. *Environmental Research, 191, 110169.*

White, M.P., Lovell, R., Wheeler, B., Pahl, S., Völker, S., & Depledge, N.H. (2018). Blue landscapes and public health. In M. van den Bosch & W. Bird (Eds.), *Landscape and public health* (Ch. 5.2, pp154–159). Oxford: Oxford University Press.

White, M.P., Pahl, S., Ashbullby, K.J., Burton, F., & Depledge, M.H. (2015). The effects of exercising in different natural environments on psycho-physiological outcomes in post-menopausal women: A simulation study. *International Journal of Environmental Research and Public Health, 12*, 11929–11953.

White, M.P., Pahl, S., Ashbullby, K.J., Herbert, S., & Depledge, M.H. (2013b). Feelings of restoration from recent nature visits. *Journal of Environmental Psychology, 35*, 40–51.

White, M.P., Pahl, S., Wheeler, B.W., Fleming, L.E.F., & Depledge, M.H. (2016b). The 'blue gym': What can blue space do for you and what can you do for blue space? *Journal of the Marine Biological Association, 96, 5–12.*

White, M.P., Smith, A., Humphryes, K., Pahl, S., Snelling, D., & Depledge, M. (2010) Blue space: The importance of water for preference, affect and restorativeness ratings of natural and built scenes. *Journal of Environmental Psychology, 30*, 482–493.

White, M.P., Wheeler, B.W., Herbert, S., Alcock, I., & Depledge, M.H. (2014b). Coastal proximity and physical activity. Is the coast an underappreciated public health resource? *Preventive Medicine, 69*, 135–140.

Whitmee, C., Haines, A., Beyrer, C., Boltz, F., Capon, A. G., de Souza Dias, B.F., . . . Horton, R. (2015). Safeguarding human health in the Anthropocene epoch: Report of The Rockefeller Foundation – Lancet Commission on planetary health. *The Lancet, 386*, 1973–2028.

Wilson, M.I., Robertson, L.D., Daly, M., & Walton, S.A. (1995). Effects of visual cues on assessment of water quality. *Journal of Environmental Psychology, 15*, 53–63.

World Health Organisation (1980) Environmental sanitation in European tourist areas. Copenhagen, WHO Regional Office for Europe, 33 pp. (EURO Reports and Studies No. 18).

World Health Organisation, (2003). *Guidelines for safe recreational water environments. Volume 1, Coastal and Fresh Waters.* Geneva, Switzerland: World Health Organization.

World Health Organisation (2014). *Global report on drowning: Preventing a leading killer.* Geneva, Switzerland: World Health Organization.

World Health Organisation (2018). *Physical activity [Factsheet].* Geneva, Switzerland: World Health Organization.

World Health Organisation (2019). *Environmental health inequalities in Europe: Second assessment report.* Geneva, Switzerland: World Health Organization.

Wüstemann, H., Kalisch, D., & Kolbe, J. (2017). Accessibility of urban blue in German major cities. *Ecological Indicators, 78*, 125–130.

Wyles, K.J., Pahl, S., Thomas, K., & Thompson, R.C. (2016). Factors that can undermine the psychological benefits of coastal environments: Exploring the effect of tidal state, presence, and type of litter. *Environment and Behavior, 48*(9), 1095–1126.

Wyles, K.J., White, M.P., Hattam, C., Pahl, S., & Austin, M. (2019). Nature connectedness and well-being from recent nature visits: The role of environment type and quality. *Environment & Behaviour, 51*(2), 111–143.

Chapter 3: Co-design with local stakeholders

Mart Külvik, Mireia Gascon, Marina Cervera Alonso de Medina, Lewis R. Elliott, Jekaterina Balicka, Frederico Meireles Rodrigues and Monika Suškevičs

Introduction

This chapter presents the ways in which co-design can be undertaken, with examples of stakeholder and local community involvement in a range of examples of BlueHealth community-level interventions (Barcelona/Rubí, Spain; Plymouth, United Kingdom; Tallinn, Estonia; and Guimarães, Portugal). We introduce the theoretical aspects of co-design and participation with stakeholders and discuss the different modes of engagement that might be used. Subsequently, we present individual case studies and compare the benefits and limitations of the co-design model employed in each.

What is co-design?

Co-design involves developing processes for understanding, developing and supporting mutual learning between multiple participants in collective decision-making and design (The Co-Create Handbook 2019). Co-design is a hybrid concept used in many disciplines and fields, such as service and product development, knowledge co-production in sustainability transformation or collaborative planning and design of urban policies and plans (Evans and Terrey, 2016; Moser, 2016). In urban development, co-design usually refers to participatory approaches in which people play an active role that goes beyond mere information dissemination, consultation or fragmented collaborative workshops (Stelzle et al., 2017).

It is increasingly recognised that people affected by design projects need to have a voice throughout the overall process. In the context of planning and managing urban blue spaces, people affected by design projects typically include citizens as individuals but also stakeholders representing a group or organisation, such as different user groups of green and blue spaces, local residents, landowners, local government and council representatives, investors and local entrepreneurs (Stelzle et al., 2017; Webb et al., 2018). The experts – usually planners, designers, engineers and researchers working in various disciplines (e.g. ecologists, economists, geographers, social scientists) – might also be considered stakeholders, as they have a legitimate stake in the design processes (Enserink and Monnikhof, 2003). However, in co-design practice, participatory approaches vary greatly in terms of the degree of interactivity, the participants that are invited and included and the extent to which a voice is actually given to non-designers (Cruickshank et al., 2016).

An important part of co-design is learning, which takes place in group settings via knowledge exchange and sharing between designers and the public/stakeholders (Cumbula et al., 2013). Ideally, during a co-design process, all stakeholders increase their knowledge and understanding. In effective co-design, it is assumed that citizens do not always speak the same language as experts. Consequently, one of the most important tasks of co-design is to create inclusive activities that aim to boost the participation of all citizens involved. As users are not necessarily

DOI: 10.4324/9780429056161-5

professionals in the field under discussion and are free to ignore the feasibility of aspects of a design (e.g. relating to constraints of engineering, economics, technologies, etc.), those managing of co-design processes must: 1) inform all participants about the possibilities and constraints of any proposed design solutions and 2) envision different possibilities which could meet users' needs. Users benefit from potential options they might otherwise have ignored, and designers obtain experiential knowledge about the users. This should eventually also support the creation of a richer knowledge base for achieving better outcomes of planning and design (Stelzle et al., 2017).

Benefits and challenges of co-design

Co-design processes are intended to achieve three main goals: enhanced legitimacy of expertise (via collaborative knowledge exchange), increased relevance of design outcomes (via a fit better to the needs of citizens, users and other stakeholders) and a wider knowledge basis in support of design solutions (via the integration of multiple knowledge sources) (Moser, 2016). Examples of specific benefits of co-design include (adapted from The Co-Create Handbook, 2019):

- greater opportunities for discussion and reflection with different stakeholders;
- being able to form links and networks more easily, which will enable sharing information better than before;
- some groups and individuals who do not normally have a 'voice' may become included in negotiations and dialogue; and
- different stakeholders can gain greater responsibility for various stages of a project development process, which increases the motivation and commitment of everyone who participates.

Most challenges in co-design relate to working with inter- and transdisciplinary groups (e.g. creating a common language) but also to creating and managing meaningful collaborative platforms (e.g. facilitating the group dynamics) (Lee, 2008; Moser, 2016). Examples of difficulties encountered during co-design (adapted from: The Co-Create Handbook, 2019) include:

- group size complexity: due to the involvement of a large number of stakeholders and design actors;
- social complexity: the personal characteristics of stakeholders and their relationships, as well as social style and differences of culture and knowledge, can limit effective collaboration; and
- resource-intensive management: it may be necessary to expend a lot of effort and time on specific communication with individual actors.

Typical phases of a co-design process and participatory methods used

Commonly, co-design processes include three or four phases (Evans and Terrey, 2016; Lee, 2008; Stelzle et al., 2017), outlined as follows (see Figure 3.1).

1 Initiation: analysis of the situation, priority setting and initiation of the process

This is the phase in which the form of a particular co-design process takes shape and the first steps toward realisation are taken. This phase may involve several sub-steps, such as:

a. Understand the context and set goals, gather information about the issue in question, identify the most relevant stakeholders and spread this information among these potential stakeholders;
b. Clarify the premises for a collaborative process (e.g. legal regulations, deadlines); and
c. Define key structural aspects (e.g. funding, division of responsibilities).

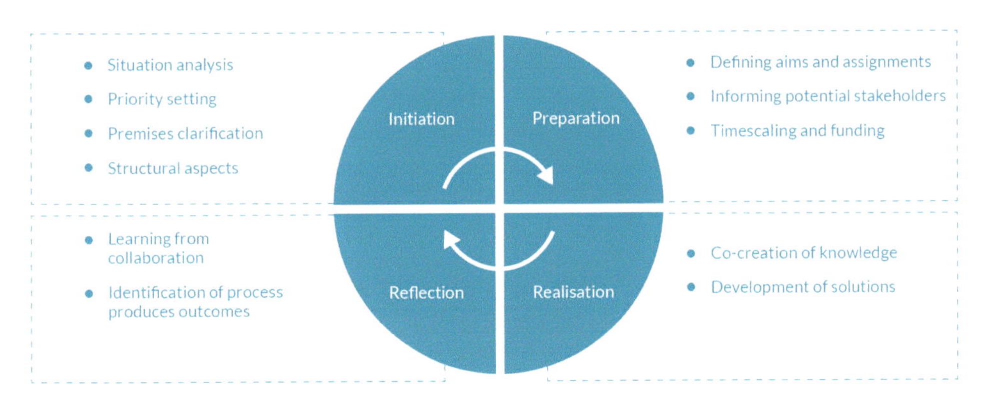

Figure 3.1
Typical phases of the co-design process, which ideally becomes an iterative cycle
(*Source*: Mart Külvik and Anna Wilczyńska)

2 Preparation
Before the actual process of co-design begins, decisions about content and organisation are taken. This phase may include the following:

a. Define aims and assignments;
b. Inform all potential stakeholders; and
c. Clarify and record timescale and financial framework.

3 Realisation of the process: co-creation of knowledge and development of (practice-oriented) solutions
Where stakeholder participation is characterised by clear roles and powers, agreements regarding the sequence of events and rights and duties of participants are achieved democratically. The flow of information between participants is organised, and the general public is kept informed during the implementation. Finally, the ways in which the results achieved together are presented and implemented are clearly and unambiguously established.

4 Reflection on the process and distilling of lessons for the future
This wrap-up phase focuses on answering questions such as: "*What* can be *learned* from the collaboration?", and "For *whom* did the process produce outcomes (e.g. knowledge insights, practical guidance for policy makers/society and integration of co-design outcomes to actual community development)?"

The roles of experts, citizens and stakeholders may be different at each of these phases (Lee, 2008; Stelzle et al., 2017). For instance, in the *realisation* phase, the number and diversity of stakeholders may be the greatest, as well as the intensity needed to collaborate. In contrast, at the *initiation* phase, most of the responsibilities may rely on experts. However, the decisions made in this phase – such as deciding who the key stakeholders are – should set the pre-conditions and tone for all forthcoming phases if the co-design process is to have meaningful outcomes. Best practice guidance suggests that identification and involvement of stakeholders should be iterative; for example, important new actors may be added to an initial list of stakeholders during the process if they become evident and as the co-designed project evolves. Also, co-design processes should encourage iterative learning (Reed, 2008): participants should be able to monitor the progress and outcomes and adapt future co-design projects accordingly from lessons learned in the *reflection* phase.

In the contexts of landscape architecture and urban planning, examples of participatory methods used in co-design include the following.

- Interactive *workshops* with designers, public sector representatives and entrepreneurs (Scott, 2017; Wu and Hou, 2019);
- *Living projects* where designers engage with people and communities to address real-world issues and develop solutions which are implemented (Cruickshank et al., 2016; Stott and Warren, 2017);
- *Games* (e.g. serious or applied games) can be used to create learning environments and may be tailored to include different target groups such as young people, retirees and passers-by in a creative and playful way (Ghibusi and Marchetti, 2018);
- *Intervention-based co-design*, such as installations in public spaces, which use design/engineering tools (like mapping, collage-making, site explorations, sketching) in combination with appropriate participatory tools like "design and development" workshops or go-along interviews (Pawlowski et al., 2017).

BlueHealth co-design case studies

A number of community-level interventions implemented in the BlueHealth project were created through co-design.

Teats Hill, Plymouth, United Kingdom

In 2016, the Plymouth City Council started the Active Neighbourhoods project. Funded by the Big Lottery Reaching Communities programme, it built on similar partnerships for green space projects previously undertaken in the city (Richardson et al., 2013). As a partnership between Plymouth City Council (PCC), Devon Wildlife Trust (DWT) and Public Health's Thrive Plymouth network, over three years, the project aimed to get more people more active and feeling better by using and improving their local natural spaces in five deprived areas of Plymouth. The current case study site, Teats Hill, was identified as an area for improvement within this scheme.

As a public blue/green space in an urban area with direct access to the foreshore, BlueHealth researchers identified Teats Hill as an ideal site for the intervention and together formed a project group with staff from the Active Neighbourhoods team at PCC and DWT to carry out a combined development and research project. The BlueHealth researchers were responsible for evaluating the effects of the Teats Hill development on the health and well-being of the surrounding community and for informing the design of the site through their expertise in evidence-based landscape architecture.

Teats Hill is a small park located in the inner harbour of Plymouth. Until the 1980s, it was set within an area of maritime industry and services, after which a period of urban renewal took place, leading to the establishment of the National Marine Aquarium, some residential development and other facilities such as the University of Plymouth Marine Station. However, since then, there was a deterioration in the quality of the infrastructure (facilities and access) at Teats Hill, and access to the urban beach down a slipway was blocked by parked cars and overgrown vegetation which screened views (Figure 3.2). One half of the site is overseen by social housing due for renovation, while the other side is overseen by new flats in a gated community.

In the first instance, Plymouth City Council chose to convene a group of local stakeholders who would oversee both the renovation of the site itself and the methods proposed by BlueHealth to evaluate the outcomes of the renovation for the local community. The site was characterised by complex land ownership issues, with different tidal sections of the slipway being owned by different organisations (e.g. the council and a local private marina), and in some cases land ownership could not be determined. A team comprising Zoe Sydenham, Jemma Sharman, Kieran Shaw-Flach and Ashley Tod from PCC and Tim Russell from DWT conducted the majority of the engagement activities.

Figure 3.2
A view down the slipway access road partly blocked by parked cars at Teats Hill before renovation
(*Source*: Simon Bell)

A further complication was how to involve the local resident population in overseeing the design and planning of the renovations, together with concurrent research. Anecdotally, some stakeholders (e.g. employees of the social housing organisation) reported that this was a potentially "over-studied" or "over-interviewed" population that might be resistant to further attempts at public engagement or research. As such, engagement methods, as well as recruitment methods for research (see subsequently), were adapted. The overall aim was to co-develop a design for the site which had the support of a diverse array of local stakeholders as well as residents of the local area who were likely to use it for recreation.

Stakeholders were from a variety of backgrounds, including the city council, housing association (who owned the nearby social housing), wildlife trusts, marine biological association, aquarium, local schools and charitable organisations, local universities, conservation groups and local elected representatives. They were tasked with overseeing the development of the intervention and raising issues that might be of concern to the environment and its ecology, the residents living nearby, the parties who owned the land or the surrounding businesses. They were also responsible for the coordination of public engagement events; assisting with data collection for BlueHealth; and seeking further funding for improvements to, and maintenance of, the site.

Plymouth City Council, together with Devon Wildlife Trust, were primarily responsible for recruiting stakeholders to a steering group. Regular stakeholder meetings took the form of an in-person focus group, and activities in these focus groups were sometimes interactive small-group exercises (e.g. drafting visions for the site's renovation) or whole-group feedback exercises (e.g. question-and-answer sessions concerning the research methods employed). As well as focus groups, site visits took place where stakeholders met with developers to discuss the ongoing renovations.

Stakeholders were identified through: 1) previous related projects (e.g. Richardson et al., 2013), 2) because they owned part of the land at the site, 3) because they were involved with adjacent businesses (e.g. the National Marine Aquarium; local marine), 4) because they were involved with local housing (e.g. Plymouth Community Homes), 5) because they were involved with local schools, 6) because they were academic (e.g. Universities of Plymouth and the Marine Biological Association) and could offer research expertise, 7) because they were elected representatives for the area or 8) because they were a local NGO who had contacted PCC about the developments and had expressed an interest in collaborating. Thus, PCC were responsible for contacting most stakeholders and recruiting them to the steering group, but some NGOs 'opted in' to the steering group due to potential opportunities with the site's redevelopment. With only one exception, stakeholders were willing to join the steering group. The one stakeholder who was less willing to contribute constituted one of the landowners at the site, a local marine, and therefore might have been required to provide co-funding; we suspect this may have been the reason for non-participation. In general, PCC tried to maintain a level playing field in terms of stakeholder contributions: to treat all contributions equally. Ultimately, though, PCC and DWT were responsible for submitting planning applications and organising community events (see subsequently) and so had the most responsibility. Given the need for local citizen approval (see subsequently), local housing organisations also had a higher than average amount of interest and responsibility, too.

The main contested issue that arose during stakeholder meetings was the need to attract visitors to the area versus the desire to maintain the area's delicate and biodiverse ecosystem. These were in conflict due to the amount of, for example, seaweed on the beach, seen as an important habitat by some stakeholders but a deterrent to visiting by others. In the end, the concerns about the biodiverse ecosystem were offset by 1) the installation of BIO blocks at the intertidal zone (concrete cubes which replicate rocky intertidal areas and support seaweed and kelp growth as well as habitats for crabs, anemones and sponges) and 2) the installation of a wildflower meadow in the park area to attract pollinators.

Citizen engagement was a crucial part of this case study, as we had to ensure that renovations matched the needs of the local community. However, the steering group was set up prior to citizen engagement in order to give confidence to citizens that there was multi-party support for the developments, especially with the involvement of the local housing organisation with whom the residents of the social housing had a broadly positive relationship. However, it was always clear that no development would go ahead without citizen consultation. Their first consultation was when preliminary site plans had already been developed.

There were concerns that residents local to this area had been over-studied or over-researched and may be resistant to further work of this nature. A series of strategies were therefore developed to involve citizens in the renovation: First, members of the steering group included employees of the local housing association who owned the social housing; these individuals were seen as more accessible than members of the council and knew more than other stakeholders about local contact and the issues affecting citizens. Second, when approached about the renovation or the data collection which formed the concurrent research, a person-centred discussion took place. That is, discussions started from a place of the issues (social, health, etc.) that most affected those citizens rather than the renovation or research itself. Instead, the planned renovations and research were woven in as opportunities arose to raise these issues with individuals and organisations which may be able to positively contribute to addressing them. Third, a series of family "fun" days were organised as part of the wider Active Neighbourhoods Project. Although these days constituted public consultations on the site plans, where various visual representations of the plans (Figure 3.3) were present and feedback sought, they were not advertised to residents in this way. Instead, they were advertised as opportunities to socialise with peers and engage in informal or playful activities by the water, especially appealing to families. Overall, then, citizen engagement events were designed to be citizen centred rather than renovation centred, in an attempt to engage a population who might otherwise have been resistant to these activities.

Events decreased in frequency over time, especially since the renovations were finished, but there was clear steer from stakeholders and citizens as to the final design of the site. While the renovations were originally designed by landscape architects, there were clear objections to some supposed features by both residents and stakeholders (e.g. lowering the fences around the ball court was objected to due to concerns that windows of adjacent properties

Figure 3.3

The Teats Hill site for renovation as presented to local stakeholders and residents as part of the local participatory planning process. Note the open-air theatre located at the junction of the land and beach at the head of the old slipway (number 8) and the renovated play area (number 2) on the plan

(*Source*: Himansu S. Mishra)

Figure 3.4

One of the family "fun" days; this one, held in 2018 after the intervention was finished (the photograph shows part of the open-air theatre structure), is an example of how community involvement continued beyond merely planning consultations

(*Source*: Plymouth City Council)

may end up damaged). On the other hand, some aspects had clear and broad support (e.g. the inclusion of an open-air theatre around the slipway was seen by many local stakeholders as an opportunity for outdoor classes, performances and social activities, with only minor concerns about the noise and anti-social behaviour that may come as a result).

Similarly, the family "fun" days had success in involving the voices of citizens who might otherwise not have engaged with the renovation plans, precisely because these events were not framed as planning consultations but as social events. Preliminary research results suggested that any observed effects of the renovation on the well-being of people in the local community were likely due to increased social cohesion in the surrounding areas; it is plausible that these fun days contributed towards increased social cohesion in the community.

Since the renovations were completed and the Active Neighbourhoods Project ceased, the site has continued to be used for fun days (Figure 3.5) and also for theatrical and musical performances by local performing arts companies. Another impact was the formation of a so-called "Friend's Group". The Friend's Group was the idea of PCC to oversee the site's maintenance after the Active Neighbourhoods Project funding had ceased. It was planned to be a new partnership of citizens and local stakeholders (excluding PCC) who volunteer to maintain Teats Hill, for example, do regular litter-picks, graffiti cleaning and general maintenance. Some individuals involved in this were initially stakeholders on the steering group or residents who had been engaged as part of the series of social events and took a particular interest in the site. In terms of practicalities, the local councillor offered office space for the Friend's Group to meet regularly. A further impact has been spin-off funding the council was able to obtain for a further artistic installation at the site as a result of the success of the Teats Hill renovations.

Reflections on the process

One particular lesson learned in this stakeholder and citizen engagement exercise is the need to find a way to engage those who might otherwise not have a voice in such planning or research exercises. While there was some

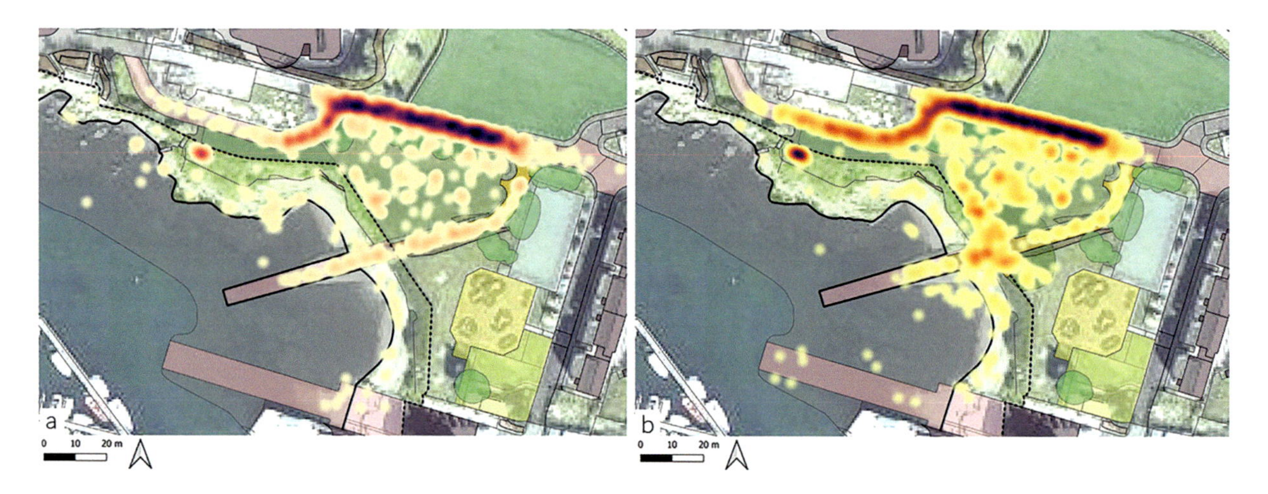

Figure 3.5a and b

Heat maps of Teats Hill, a) before and b) after the intervention. The path leading through the site remains very busy, but there is a clear increase in activity at the open-air theatre and the beach

(*Source*: Himansu S. Mishra)

success with this in the present case study, it was acknowledged that these efforts were not necessarily based on evidence-based models of stakeholder or public engagement. Others have suggested that institutional support for public involvement groups, especially those concerned with environment and health projects, can provide channels for connecting the public with stakeholders and academics.

Furthermore, not all stakeholders that were intended to be included in the steering group participated. For example, individuals in charge of the private marina who had some land ownership over the slipway did not participate in the steering group of stakeholders. While it would be unwise to speculate on the reason for this, it illustrates that if particular issues to do with a renovation are contested, desired engagement, whatever methods are employed, can be made more difficult.

The before and after intervention observation using the BlueHealth Behaviour Assessment Tool (see Chapter 6) show the kind of impact it had – the heat maps in Figure 3.5 show that that Teats Hill experienced an overall absolute increase in users and also that the open-air theatre and the refurbished play area both became hotspots.

Rubí, Barcelona, Spain

Raising civil society's awareness of the complexity of landscape, including ordinary urban landscape as a cultural artefact, has been one of the objectives of the research developed by the masters programme in Landscape Intervention and Heritage Management, led by Professor Francesc Muñoz. The masters programme was established in 2000, the same year the European Landscape Convention (ELC) of the Council of Europe was signed, which proposes training experts capable of developing and designing landscape and heritage management and intervention projects, considering their participation in multidisciplinary teams.

One of the annual workshops of the master's course – the Visual Preference Mapping Workshop led by Marina Cervera Alonso de Medina – addresses landscape identification and active mobilisation of the linked actors and follows the ELC Article 5.c with a view to improve landscape knowledge, analysis and design. It consists of a participatory workshop, where students are commissioned to trigger landscape awareness among a given community, related to a case study. The Visual Preference Mapping Workshop had been previously successful in the city of Barcelona city, developing a particular adoption of Steinitz's visual preference methodology for urban environments (Steinitz, 1990, 2012). More specifically, this methodology had been fine-tuned for the first time to map the visual preference of local inhabitants along the Pere IV street in Barcelona axis and thus detect – through visual preference heat-mapping – where design and intervention were most required. Since the first application, the results of the mapping by the students were presented to the Barcelona Town Council and on some occasions, they were taken into account for subsequent renovation and urbanisation criteria.

For the BlueHealth Project version, the Visual Preference Mapping Workshop aimed to further develop tools to engage a dispersed community of a peri-urban area in Rubí, a city in the metropolitan area of Barcelona, in order to identify their urban landscapes. As opposed to previous case studies, the exercise on landscape identification and qualification was to be done with residents of the local community who had little relation to each other. Thus, the case study in Rubí approached co-design by engaging the neighbours in a comprehensive participatory process integrating analysis and design of the built environment together. The procedure aimed to empower citizens regarding their responsibilities and rights over their everyday landscapes.

The house and land of Can Matarí ("Can" in Catalan means "the house of") – currently in Castellnou district, Rubí – was purchased by Louis Moritz, who used the farmhouse as a summer residence. Moritz came from a bourgeois family who moved to Barcelona in the mid-19th century, where he founded a beer brewing business. After the death of Louis Moritz in 1922, his family built a Modernist house next to the existing farmhouse ("Can Matarí")

Figure 3.6a and b
The Can Moritz spring, Rubí, a) before and b) after the final renovation
(*Source*: Mireia Gascon)

and designed a Modernist style space around a natural spring, which is currently named after Moritz ("Can Moritz"). In the mid-1950s, the family sold the property, and the land was parcelled out, which resulted in the house of Can Moritz remaining private property, currently catalogued as archaeological heritage of Rubí, while the surrounding plots were sold and built-in low-density city garden housing. The spring belonging to Can Moritz happened to end up in public land, as it was located near a stream. The basin of the stream was integrated into the state hydrological area of protection for water systems and thus remained cut off from the summer house area. Scarcely noticed by locals, it fell into a state of disrepair. In December 2014, after a heavy storm, the spring and its art deco-designed recreational basin were rediscovered by neighbouring residents. In 2016, a local NGO, Rubí d'Arrel, undertook the first intervention, with volunteers by cleaning the spring and its surroundings, revealing the original structure dating from 1922 (Figure 3.6).

Design team: experts and important stakeholders

Working in Rubí as a case study was set as a challenge to the ELC conceptual approach to explore the limits of the methodology to address visual preference as basis of landscape identification and landscape awareness raising. The project team had, nevertheless, very good allies among the local authorities and NGOs dealing with environment and forest management.

The local authorities of the Rubí Town Council were on board from the beginning to promote a project within the municipality and were key in the selection of Can Moritz as a potential case study for BlueHealth, as they were concerned by the recent findings of the old spring in ruins. The spring was the perfect catalyst for the process of triggering the opportunity to involve different actors in the whole process: landscape architects, public administration, health researchers (ISGlobal researchers) and the neighbours (through the four neighbourhood associations of Castellnou), who participated in the visual preference mapping. In addition to the solid network linking the administration, neighbours and academia, the project identified three key local NGOs, active in the municipality, though not directly linked to the site, as agents for action. This project would not have been possible without the volunteers from Rubí d'Arrel, Ressò and Centre Excursionista de Rubí. Their engagement with the planned actions was key to organising and making possible the co-design activities of the final project proposal. In fact, the intervention in Rubí was framed as a complex process integrating heritage restoration, training and recreational activities, recovery of a blue space for the enjoyment of the citizenry and their participation through qualitative methodologies and the scientific analysis of the health benefits of blue spaces.

The case study of Rubí started in 2016 and ended in 2020 and displayed different modes of community engagement throughout the period as follows:

1. Through the four neighbourhood associations of Castellnou, we contacted and invited the neighbours of the area to participate in the case study. In addition, the City Council sent letters to all the neighbours inviting them to participate in the Visual Mapping workshop activities led by the master students. After several weeks of research on the social, environmental and landscape conditions, the master students prepared a face-to-face session. This focused on the assessment of a large sample of pictures representative of the nearby landscapes. Based on the Steinitz method (1990, 2012), the degree of preference of those images was rated according to factors developed by Kaplan et al. (1972). The visual preference workshop/session was held in the social and civic centre Ressò in Rubí, with the assistance of the four neighbourhood associations of Castellnou and 17 local participants in total. Recreational activities were offered alongside the workshop, which included semi-structured interviews with some neighbours that were helpful for later participatory stages.
2. Once the results of the first session were analysed, the resulting heat map of visual preference (Figure 3.7a) was used in the following stages of the co-design of the intervention. Throughout the following stakeholder sessions, a draft of the general landscape management and intervention project emerged, with the final aim of producing and animating a public space in the least-preferred area (thus the one needing improvement) and the rediscovered Can Moritz spring. An overall masterplan for the site was co-designed following the inputs of the City Council, the local inhabitants and the recommendations of the local NGOs. Finally, a set of actions and interventions from the vocabulary of the tactical urbanism and "guerrilla" gardening already used by grassroots movements (see also Chapter 15) were developed into an action plan that would enhance the vision: designing a landscape infrastructure to connect fragmented sites and heritage elements with the natural features (blue infrastructure) adding value to the low-density residential areas (e.g. as in the Castellnou area) and its landscape image (Figure 3.7b).
3. The final and main participatory session was organised by all stakeholders, researchers and public administration to produce the public space as agreed at the masterplan level. At this stage, the set of actions were implemented by a range of synchronous and parallel actions to be carried out by the neighbours with assistance of the NGO volunteers and the overall guidance of the masterplan coordinators. The actions were designed to take place during the same weekend, which required a lot of coordination and time management. The total budget was €10,000 to conduct this small-scale intervention. In addition, the City Council assumed the costs of renovating the spring as an architectural structure (the most expensive part of the intervention, costing approximately €80,000).
4. In parallel, a survey of residents of Rubí (over 16 years of age) was conducted, recruited through different strategies: a) online: using a Twitter account specifically created for the project (@FontCanMoritz), b) advertising the study in local media, c) leaflets handed out during the local festivity of Rubí (many people are in the street those days) and d) leaflets distributed to the mailbox of the closest neighbours to the Can Moritz spring. Participants could answer the survey online or fill in a paper version and send it back to us. The survey was based on the BlueHealth Community Level Survey (BCLS) (see Chapter 8) and included demographic questions (gender, age, education level, work status, general health, etc.), frequency of visits to natural environments (in the last 12 months), whether they knew the Can Moritz spring and if they had visited it in the last six months and the last four weeks, their opinion about the quality of the site, the activity conducted there, time spent and so on. The same questions were asked before and after the intervention.

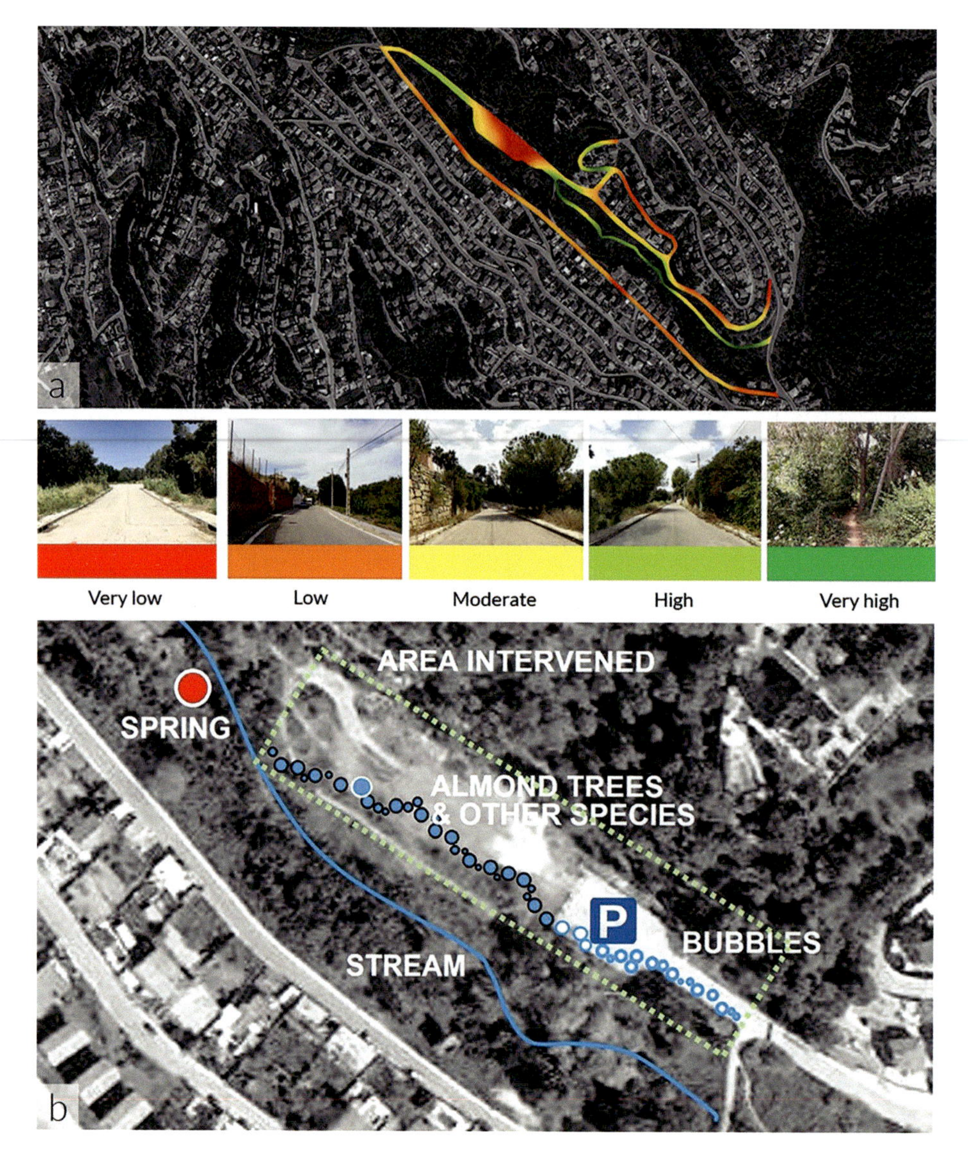

Figure 3.7a and b

a) The visual preference mapping generated during the workshop in September 2017 with the local people (red indicates areas of improvement, and green indicates areas with good quality); b) the main elements of the resulting co-design focusing on the larger red area from the analysis

(*Source*: Marina Cervera Alonso de Medina)

The pre-intervention findings helped to structure the interventions aiming at the development of a continuous route along the river, integrating the Moritz spring as the main recreation area in the valley. The main challenge was to tackle the sizeable red hotspot around a parking lot, which was perceived by the community as having the lowest preference. The pictures and the semi-structured interviews identified illegal activities and nocturnal vandalism, the accumulation of litter and contamination of the stream. The lack of care and stewardship in the flat area next to and within the parking lot was seen as an obstacle along the existing path along the stream. The masterplan developed a series of hands-on actions to emphasise the desired line of the path along the stream

Figure 3.8a and b
Implementing the design in the hotspot area with the participation of local people, a) the line of logs leading through the natural area; b) the line of blue circles being painted on the car park surface (see Figure 3.7)
(*Source*: Mireia Gascon)

through the most fragile section across the parking lot and its immediate surroundings. The purpose of these tactical interventions was to claim back the area by activating the actions and care of the local community. The activities included painting patterns on the car park surface, installing logs, planting trees and bushes and furniture construction (Figure 3.8).

In total, 86 inhabitants of Rubí (not necessarily living nearby the study site) participated in the survey before the intervention. After the intervention, we obtained answers from 43 of these participants. Almost two thirds knew of the existence of the Can Moritz spring, but a third had not visited it in the last six months, and among those who did, only 14 (39%) had visited it in the last four weeks. After the intervention, more than 80% of respondents knew of the spring. Also, participants who had visited the site in the last four weeks reported spending more time in it (from 15.8 minutes on average before the intervention to 32.5 minutes after the intervention). Overall, the quality of the spring and its surroundings was mostly rated as bad or very bad before the intervention (≈40%), whereas after the intervention, more than 50% of the participants rated the site as being of good or excellent quality. When asked for detailed information on how they felt about their visit (in the last four weeks) to the Can Moritz spring area, we found that the levels of satisfaction (rated as totally agree) substantially increased, from less than 20% to more than 60%. After the intervention, participants also reported feeling more a part of nature, very few reported feeling unsafe and the presence of rubbish and litter was less of an issue. Despite the improvements, however, participants felt that facilities (parking, roads, toilets, drinking water fountains, barbecue sites) could be improved.

Reflections on the process

The Can Moritz case study showed that there is a relationship between landscape perception, the use of shared spaces and community well-being. The perceived low quality of the natural environment along the stream in which the Can Moritz spring is located was limiting the use of this common space. The use of the Steinitz method helped to identify the most and least preferred areas in a visual map to inform the strategy for on-site intervention and improved the neighbours' impression of their open spaces. We also demonstrated the importance of collaborative work among different actors and the combination of top-down and bottom-up strategies.

The landscape perception by the local community changed throughout the process triggered by the BlueHealth project. The two-fold strategy of improving site quality through the top-down architectural intervention at the Moritz spring led by the City Council and the bottom-up process of awareness-raising and participatory decision-making and hands-on actions was successful. The surveys made before and after the intervention among the people of Rubí demonstrated the positive impact of the project on the community's perception, sense of belonging and increased use of the space. The "guerrilla" gardening and tactical urbanism actions contributed to the connection of the fragmented community by caring and constructing a new common space around the stream and the spring. Beyond the importance of the action, as a means of triggering a social process, the Can Moritz spring masterplan aimed at establishing the spring as a central feature for the community. Overall, the Can Moritz case study contributes to generating and transmitting tools and knowledge so that community interventions can be implemented to help improve well-being by promoting and improving urban landscapes. For more information on the project, see Cervera et al., 2021.

Guimarães City Park, Portugal

Coincidentally, just as the BlueHealth Project was launched, the municipality of Guimarães had decided to create a new organisation dedicated to the study of landscape and to the engagement of people in new environment-based projects. To do so, the municipality joined efforts with both the Universidade do Minho (UM) and the Universidade de Trás-os-Montes e Alto Douro (UTAD), and the three institutions founded the Landscape Laboratory of Guimarães (LLG). Simultaneously, UTAD was also setting up a new multidisciplinary laboratory to focus on health and inclusion issues related to green spaces, called LOCUS, which develops different types of landscape studies, design and planning projects and is particularly expert in the various methods of open space assessment and post-occupancy evaluation. Also, by this time, the city of Guimarães was already completing its application to be a European Green Capital of 2020, dealing with a list of criteria that led to numerous surveys on a variety of issues related to green and blue infrastructure. On site, attention was focused on building new gardens and parks, looking at connectivity issues and aiming to improve people's access to green space.

One of the most important features of the city's green and blue infrastructure is the Guimarães city park (Figure 3.9). Covering about 30 ha, it is the largest and closest park to the city centre. This park is crossed by the River Costa-Couros, which is one of the most important streams within the hydrological system of the city. Despite this, the water features were, to their users, far from being central elements of the park.

The park reflects the rural landscape background of that valley, which was traditionally occupied by irrigated agriculture. Now it is mostly surrounded by urban settings. The original designer of the park was Aparte (a landscape architecture office), coordinated by Laura Roldão e Costa, and it was built in several phases, starting in 1997 and ending in 2005. As noted earlier, it is very important to the green and blue infrastructure of the city, because it forms one of the main watersheds controlling floods and forms a major green corridor connecting the countryside to the city centre. It also contains a repository of the natural and built heritage linked with the past rural activities of the region. Although the city park was built as a new recreation facility, it still preserves the memory and symbolism of its rural background.

Although close to the centre, the park is located in a relatively quiet part of the city, surrounded by multi-storey housing areas with commercial ground floors; there are also three schools close by and some historic and recreational facilities all around, such as the sports complex of the Vitória Sport Club, occupying a significant area of the

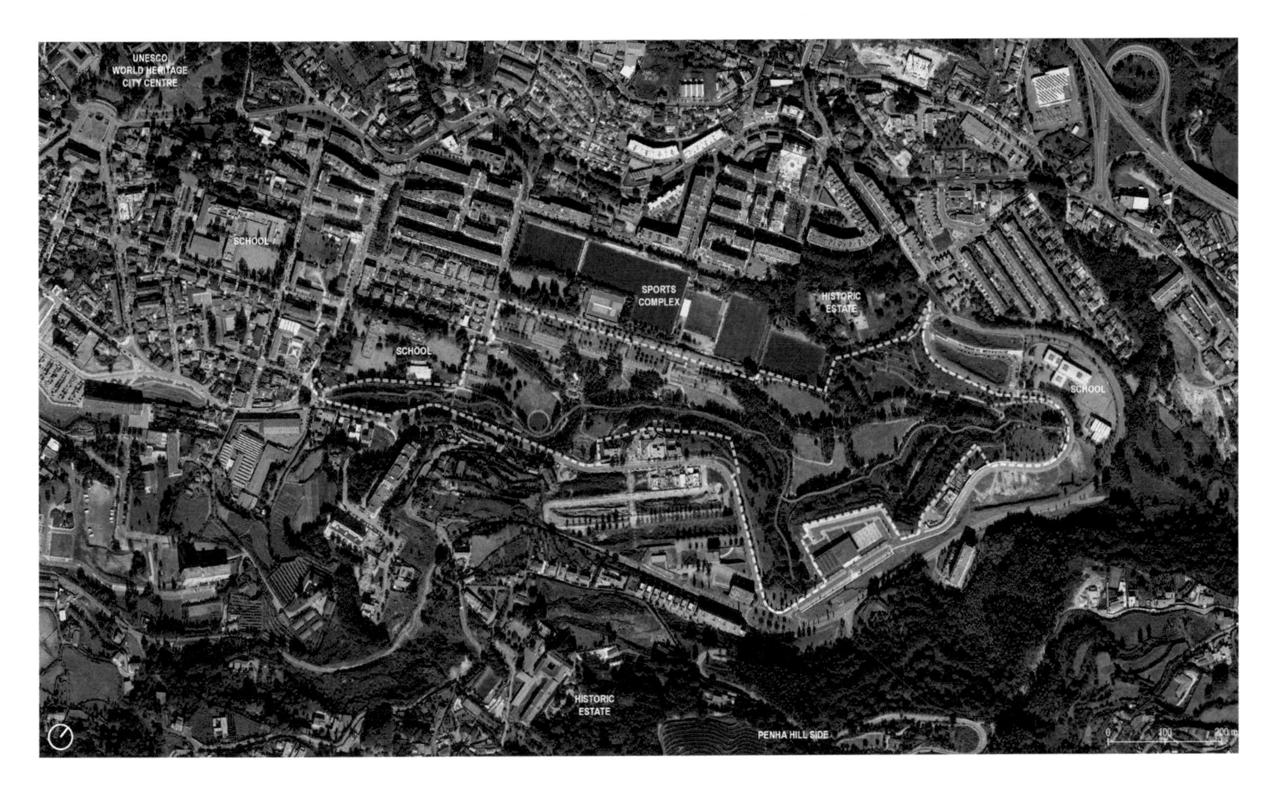

Figure 3.9
The location and extent of the Guimarães city park
(*Source*: Frederico Meireles Rodrigues, Orthophotos 2018 provided by the Portuguese Directorate-General for the Territory)

northwest fringe of the park. An old rural stone house complex was left between the sports complex and the meadows of the park, as a monument and also a useful headquarters for park maintenance. The park is connected to the surrounding areas by nine entrances along its perimeter, at different elevations and connecting different sections of the city, which are either intensively built or still in development, some historic, others more natural or agricultural.

The river is the axial feature of the park. It is contained within stone walls almost all along, as it was to contain soil for the maize fields – a very typical crop of this region, given the fair yearly distribution of water. The once-clipped poplar trees (*Populus nigra*), edging the fields, where vines used to climb, are now naturally growing, as a means of landscape spatial division. In fact, there is not much variety when it comes to vegetation. Trees include *Populus nigra, Fraxinus angustifolia, Alnus glutinosa, Quercus robur* and *Liquidambar styraciflua*. Most of the area is continuous meadow, with a few shrubs close to crossings, entrances and river slopes. Along the park, the river changes depth and width, and there are some small waterfalls. In winter or early spring, the river tends to flood some parts of the park, and, since the recent construction of two retention basins, it has been used as a very effective system of controlling floods threatening central Guimarães. In many points, it is crossed by wooden bridges leading to the gravel path network.

Another major water feature is the circular lake (Figure 3.10), which occupies a rather open and central position at the most used and connected section of the park. This lake is about 30 metres in diameter and is placed down between a continuous surrounding slope, which tends to discourage people from getting close to it. It is often used by ducks and geese.

Figure 3.10
The central lake of the park as it appeared in 2016
(*Source*: Frederico Meireles Rodrigues)

Along the course of the river, from the northeast to the southwest, a variety of sensations can be obtained that also change across the seasons: the upper end is either fresh and shady, covered by trees and benefiting from a small pond, or too open and unfinished, especially along the north slope; there is the warmth and comfort provided by a Bocage-like succession of open meadows enclosed by large hedges covering slopes and lining the network of paths; further downstream, a flatter area consists of large open meadows, only interrupted by the steep natural section of the river; the great open space and sparsely wooded section, which is the most inviting and diverse area, containing the lake; finally, the lower end is a corridor of freshness, shade and relics of past traditions, showing interesting ruins of the old watermill.

The co-design process was kick-started by a core team led by LOCUS and composed of the LLG and technical advisors from the municipality. At this stage, the BlueHealth researchers were also locally involved. After several visits to the different blue spaces of the city, the Guimarães city park was considered the most suitable and interesting choice for a BlueHealth case study. The aim was to implement an intervention resulting from a co-design process. It was considered relevant to the overall concept that the project would enhance the water value and the overall sensory experience provided by the water features in the park as a place people can use to contact with nature, leisure and recreation.

Several objectives were set in order to develop a comprehensive approach to establish the intervention process and to accommodate a variety of participants: augmenting the contact with water and its attractiveness, increasing visibility of the river, naturalising the water margins, improving sensory experiences, adding value to neighbouring recreational areas and promoting diversity of use and place attachment.

After a rather long debate to select the actual site of the intervention, involving several participants (landscape architecture students, the LOCUS, the LLG including its stakeholders, the original park designer and the municipality technical advisors), it was decided to develop an intervention around the central lake. This place was considered to be have been under-designed since the park was completed in 2005 and was showing evident signs of degradation in many of its elements: poor water quality, decayed art elements (fish sculptures), a lack of seating, an irregular grass surface, regular sliding of soil into the water and poor vegetation cover in the surroundings to provide proper screening. On the other hand, this place was also considered to have great potential to meet the objectives because of its good visibility and numerous viewpoints, the freshness of the surroundings, the proximity of the river, the good connection with the network of paths and the diversity of facilities and recreation options.

The process included contributions from the research and teaching institutions, local authorities, local associations and the community, in its various stages, from initial concept development to final execution. The core team was led by LOCUS, the Laboratory of Green Space, Health and Inclusion of UTAD (coordinated by Dr Frederico Meireles Rodrigues) that concluded a partnership agreement with the Environmental Department of the municipality of Guimarães (coordinated by engineer Jorge Fernandes and landscape architect Rita Salgado) and LLG (coordinated by Dr Carlos Ribeiro). The municipality would assist in licensing and supporting execution, and the LLG was to be the local link to other stakeholders and to support public participation and environmental education.

The design team was variously composed of third-year landscape architecture students (concept and exploratory design), LOCUS and the park designer (specification design). The exploratory design was presented to the LLG and the municipality technical advisors before it was discussed by the LLG stakeholders, which included participants from both the UTAD and UM, the municipality, the local environmental NGO, heads of schools and other community representatives. The final design was developed by LOCUS and the park designer (Laura Roldão e Costa). The execution team, composed of LOCUS, the LLG and the municipality, planned the intervention to include participation by the community (local schools and associations), a task managed by the LLG, although most of the preparations and plantings were conducted by the Environmental Department of the municipality.

From the start of this process, the core team considered co-design an exploratory method of public participation in the design process, which could be descriptive, through the use of methods such as surveys; analytical, making use of different quantitative and qualitative methods to find relations among objective variables and opinions; and to develop a comprehensive design programme and general plan as synthesis. It is a real-life situation design methodology, which enables others (beyond the technical designers) to participate in the development of design solutions. The city park of Guimarães, as explained earlier, was seen as the right place to put that view into practice.

This approach was organised into four main stages: 1) site analysis and exploratory design, particularly involving UTAD landscape architecture students; 2) evaluation and site selection, involving discussion of the proposed concepts with the municipality, the LLG, its stakeholders and the general community; 3) specification design and licensing, involving expert landscape architects; and 4) execution by the municipality's Environmental Department green space contractor with the involvement of the local community (schools and associations).

1. One of the key participants at this early stage of the co-design process was the third-year landscape design studio of the bachelor programme in landscape architecture of UTAD. This was implemented by means of an intensive programme of project-based learning (conducted by Professors Frederico Meireles Rodrigues and Luís Loures). This approach is ideal when driven by a real-life challenge. From the point of view of learning, it results in practicable designs and stimulates creativity, commitment and motivation, which is able to engage students in learning of a professional practice.

The participants were asked to think about the urban park as a setting for an intervention that could promote attention to the water features, creating better access and enhancing views of the water. Very much in line with the initially stated objectives, the intervention should also aim to promote a positive impact on the health and well-being of park users and follow the general objectives of the BlueHealth project. Students had to brief themselves on the foundations and the overall organisation of the BlueHealth project. After the initial studio briefing, a site visit was carried out and conducted by the core team, together with the original designer of the park, who explained the concept and design decisions, referring to the initial stage of construction back in 1997; the municipality's technical advisor stressed the issues related to park management and maintenance; the LLG addressed the importance of the park to the community and the numerous environmental education projects going on in Guimarães; and the LOCUS explained how the students' work within the landscape design studio would contribute to a future on-site intervention.

The students developed a complete survey and layout of the site, a case-study review on water in contemporary landscape architecture projects, focused on site analysis (considering four values of the park: the ecological and natural, the cultural and rurally associated, the social and process of intervention and the aesthetic and artistic), which set the basis for programming an intervention and going forward with an exploratory design proposal. The programme aimed to identify the intervention site, within the limits of the park, and its specific objectives, taking into consideration the overall concept of the BlueHealth project. This was developed in groups and resulted in five different programmes, which directed the following individual conceptual design. Sixteen design proposals were selected and collected in a final portfolio BlueHealth – Guimarães Urban Park. This portfolio of ideas was then taken to a more general discussion group.

2. The selection of the proposals was carried out in a discussion group involving the core team and other participants (Figure 3.11). This was led by the LLG and involved the contribution of several representatives from local authorities, universities, schools, local associations and local businesses.

The selected site was the artificial lake at the central section of the park and close to the River Costa-Couros. This is the key water feature, placed by the main central open space meadows. It is an artificial water element, not physically connected to the river but located within the natural curve of the stream. The already known general pattern of occupation, resulting from a programme of pre-intervention observation and behaviour mapping, was also very significant in the decision to focus the intervention at this site. Overall, as discussed in 1, on the aim of the case, the visibility, the concentration of use in its surroundings and the absence of interest at a close range were the main reasons for selecting the central lake site.

3. The specification design was developed by a design team (bringing together LOCUS and the park designer). The Municipality Green Space Services and the Landscape Laboratory acted as consultants throughout the process.

At first, following the student's proposal, the idea was to create a deck structure to connect the surrounding pathway and the meadows to the water. It proved difficult to establish due to the differences of elevation and difficult to build infrastructure able to anchor the deck. The design team then opted to replace the deck with a traditional stone work structure along the edge of the lake, connected to the meadows by a series of stone steps, well integrated with a mixed border of vegetation, with respect to the typical planting style already of the park. This option also proved difficult to execute for budgetary reasons.

The final, and licensed, option proposed to maintain the access over the grass to the margins of the lake while improving integration of the existing muddy margins by planting the mixed border and adding wooden markers as a more visual and structural element of the design. In addition, several sitting areas were placed along the right bank of the river, facing the lake, and a green screen was also planned along the hilly left bank of the river to act as a background to the view over the lake from the great meadow.

Figure 3.11a and b
a) Series of designs produced by the students; b) discussion groups at the LLG where these were evaluated by stakeholders
(*Source*: LLG)

4. The construction was implemented by direct coordination of the green space contractor of the municipality's Environmental Department (which mostly carried out the site preparations and heavy construction works), with participation by the local community (the red-white umbrella day and the school totems, as explained in the following).

The municipality workers started to cultivate the land and prepare for the mixed-border planting. The surveyors set out the placing of the background green screen planting and the placing of all the wooden markers. The work was completed when the mixed border was planted. The municipal environmental agency Vitrus ensured the water cleaning and the removal of the decaying fibreglass artwork (painted fish). These were relocated by the lake, creating another resting area as a sort of happening with the aim of attracting people.

Next, trees and large shrubs for the surroundings of the lake were planted by the local community. An event was organised by the LLG for members of the local community who were willing to participate in the work. The occasion ended up being quite unusual and visually striking, because all the planting was carried out in heavy rain, so every participant was given an umbrella. As a result, the event was later called the red-white umbrella day.

The wooden totem idea was seen as a great opportunity to involve schools at this stage of the process, as well as to promote place attachment. Local schools were asked to design different symbols to be painted on wooden markers by their own students. The idea, as seen in the final proposal plan, was to engage the school community in creating a totem that could reflect the theme of water and the relationship to the BlueHealth project, as well as representing a "tribal interest" of the group of students who created it and their school. A brief instruction sheet was sent to the João de Meira middle school and Santos Simões secondary school. The schools conducted art studios and successfully completed the task.

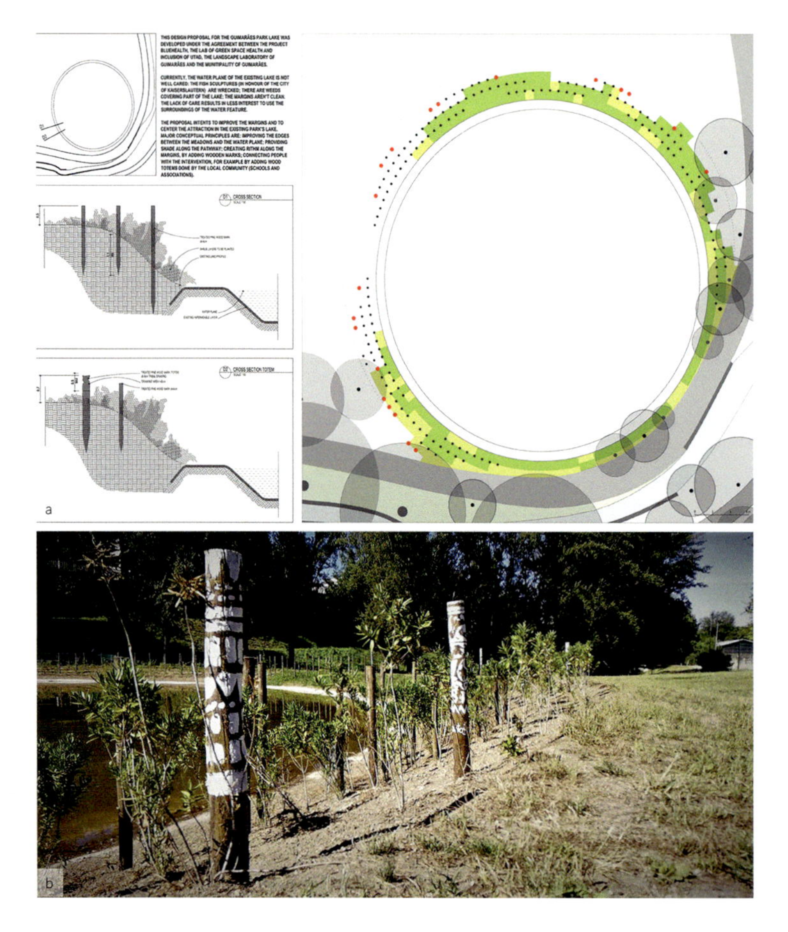

Figure 3.12a and b

a) Final design proposal for the surroundings of the lake; b) the new planting and some of the totem posts painted by school students

(*Source*: Frederico Meireles Rodrigues)

Reflections on the process

Although an event was organised to install the totems on the site, it had to be cancelled due to lockdown restrictions related to the COVID-19 pandemic which started at that time. In fact, all the participatory process planned to the construction phase had to be somewhat adjusted to the circumstances. Nevertheless, the essential objectives of this stage were achieved. The overall design was implemented, and during late spring and summer people were able to use the park with much fewer restrictions.

One of the most visible outcomes is the actual curiosity that the intervention at the lake site has generated. More people are now paying attention to that place and its surroundings. That can be clearly seen when comparing the results of both observation and behaviour mapping campaigns, 2017 (Figure 3.13a) and 2020 (Figure 3.13b).

The area of intervention is now one of the most used areas of the park. People tend to stand on the lakeside just to observe and to look for the various sitting areas around it. At the same time, the seating areas within the viewshed of the lake are quite appealing and now make popular viewpoints of the site. This analysis, however, must be somewhat cautious if taking into consideration the effect of the restrictions caused by the pandemic. In fact, the increase in spread and diversity of use might also be also related to new kinds of behaviour people tend towards when outside. The closing of traditional hotspots, such as the formal sports fields and the playgrounds (which remain closed at the time of writing), has forced people to find other ways of recreation, less plug-and-play and more taking advantage of the multi-functional spaces or finding other means of place appropriation.

A co-design process such as the one developed for the lake intervention at the Guimarães city park can be very interesting in terms of process, offers very valuable insights to the design, contributes to improve the social acceptability of the intervention and infuses specific local knowledge in the design. However, there were challenges associated with the complex and demanding co-design process, including ideas that come from the public are not always technically feasible and always need further discussion; not all of these ideas are possible to adjust or include; the participation of non-designers does not necessarily solve the most important issues and problems of the design; the process of co-design will always have different results which will change every time, because they are based on different values and contemporary references; and, in the end, the co-design process should not be seen as a replacement for designers' decisions.

Nevertheless, when considering the actual intervention, the lake area turned out to be more comfortable and fitting in with the overall layout. Most of the objectives initially identified were achieved: "Augmenting the contact with water and water attractiveness; increasing visibility of the river; naturalising the water margins; improving sensory experience; adding value to adjacent recreational areas; promoting diversity of use and place attachment". In addition, the post-occupational data collection shows a very promising response by the park users, despite the state of emergency due to the pandemic. For instance, the proportion of active adults and senior users actively involved in the park has increased, the overall diversity of activities has also increased and water-related activities are also much more present.

Kopliranna, Tallinn, Estonia

The coastal area of the northern section of the City of Tallinn was once part of a fishing village, re-built for the harbour workers of the harbour during Soviet times. Since the 1990s, it has been a marginal and socially challenged location. Since then, this area of the Kopli peninsula (part of the North Tallinn City District) has been experiencing rapid growth and densification due to the demand for new housing and, as a result, gentrification (Sander and Meikar, 2001). One popular green area, Stroomirand, is located there, providing good access to the sea, but there are also a lot of voids and wastelands, including some by the sea. Tallinn authorities have limited access to the blue-green spaces near the sea in general, partly due to industrial and harbour activities, meaning that places like Stroomirand

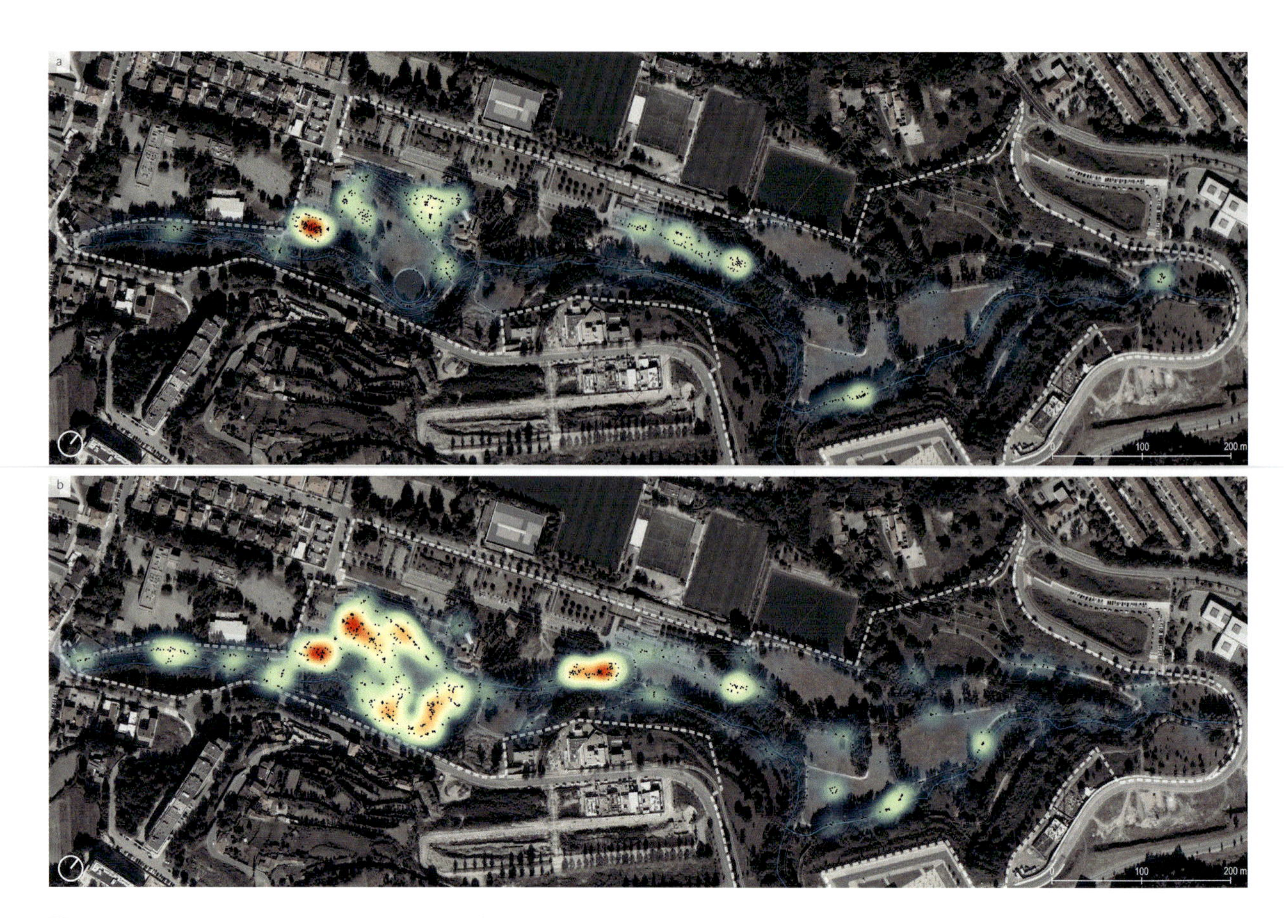

Figure 3.13a and b

Heat maps of the behaviour mapping, a) 34 rounds of observation from the 16th of August to the 18th of November 2017, *N* = 713; b) 34 rounds of observation from the 17th of July to the 16th of November 2020, *N* = 795. Note the new focus around the lake as well as hotspots elsewhere

(*Source*: Frederico Meireles Rodrigues; Orthophotos 2018 provided by the Portuguese Directorate-General for the Territory)

are crowded during good weather. Recreational use also extends to some adjacent wastelands, including waterfront areas. One such site, Koplirand, is popular among a wide range of users despite the deficient management and absence of infrastructure and was chosen as a BlueHealth small-scale intervention site.

The stakeholder and community involvement was organised in order to learn about the needs of the users of the Koplirand area concerning the design and function of the planned small-scale intervention. The stakeholders' role in co-design of the small-scale intervention was the input of knowledge and interests, which later was transferred into and expressed in the design.

The targeted stakeholder knowledge and interests of the case study area included different sectoral plans (like environmental agendas, spatial plans), public initiatives, business initiatives in and around the area and existing studies in relation to the area or any other information which could affect the design process and help to choose the best location and type of design. The local community involvement aimed to obtain knowledge about the use and perception of the site, as well as to identify its main problems from the inhabitants (both users and non-users of the

Figure 3.14
Aerial photo showing the location of the Kopli study area in Tallinn
(*Source*: Peeter Vassiljev and Orthophoto: Estonian Land Board, 2020)

area) in order the choose the best possible types of intervention to address the main problems and meet the needs of the people.

The stakeholder and community involvement was organised by the BlueHealth project team (Estonian University of Life Sciences, EMÜ) consisting of Mart Külvik, Gloria Niin and Jekaterina Balicka. Stakeholders were represented by municipality officials (both at the Tallinn city government planning level and city district level) and specialists representing sectoral authorities like environment, academics in the field of planning and urbanists and local expert activists in related fields.

Engagement was planned at two scales: the expert level and the general public level. The first meeting was with the local stakeholders. Participants were asked to share their knowledge about planning documents which might be important for the Koplirand case study. The meeting included a brainstorming section, where the locations and possible functions of the interventions were discussed. All contributions were documented on a map with notes. Participants were given the task of discussing in a group and providing answers to questions on the existing use, perceived safety/lack of safety, main function of the area, presence/absence of infrastructure and desired vision for the area. The participants documented their answers by marking the place on the area map (if the answer to the question was site related) and writing comments on Post-It notes. The marks were colour-coded in relation to the question. Thus, the EMÜ team was able to gather quite complex information on one map.

The second meeting engaged the local inhabitants. It was organised together with the Linnalabor – a key local NGO for city development issues. The event was promoted with help of printed posters, which were put up in public places around the case-study area, on social media, in local press releases and on the city government website. After

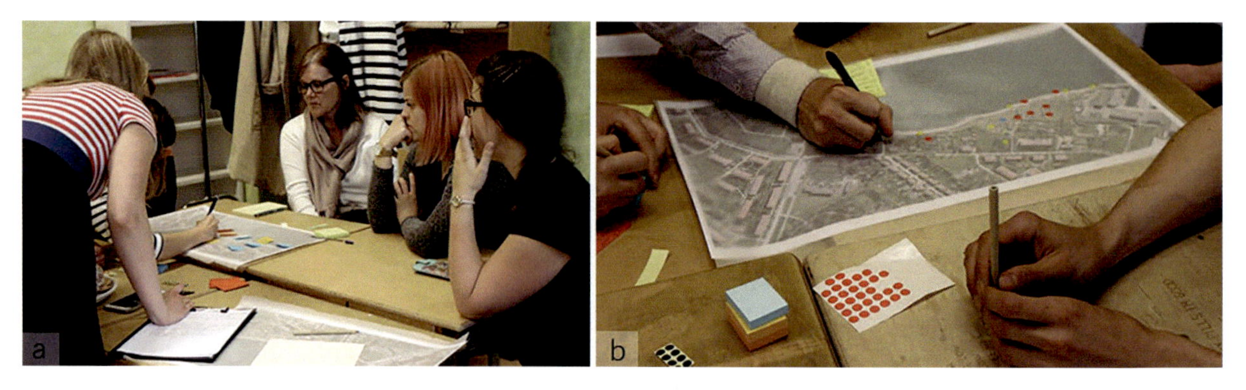

Figure 3.15a and b

Meetings taking place, a) to gather information from local people in the first wave to engagement; b) marking important places on the map and adding Post-It comments. Stickers and Post-Its are colour-coded by topic

(*Source*: Jekaterina Balicka)

an introductory presentation about the BlueHealth project, activities and explanation of small-scale interventions, participants were asked to share their knowledge about current use and practices at the case study site, as well as any conflicts; to suggest the best places to site an intervention in their opinion; to suggest the best function for an intervention in their opinion; and to mark the places on the site which in their opinion should not be changed. Participants of this event were active, but their number was low – therefore it was important to find other engagement methods.

In order to obtain more input from local inhabitants, an on-site communication action was organised during the local Midsummer public festive event. The BlueHealth team made interviews consisting of seven simple questions about the current use of the area and any conflicts, what functions for an intervention the subjects would prefer and what would be the best locations in their opinion. Questionnaire forms were prepared in both Estonian and Russian. Fifty-five people were interviewed, the answers being recorded in the questionnaire form, either by the people themselves or by the BlueHealth team members. There was also an opportunity to leave a comment or to mark particular locations (e.g. suggested sites for an intervention) on a map. Parallel to the event, there was an opportunity to answer the same questionnaire online. The questionnaire was promoted by posters with a QR code. Flyers were distributed around the case-study area.

The first ideas of the design intervention were developed by the BlueHealth team, based on the knowledge gained on the current use of the area, user conflicts and marginal uses, the current state of maintenance, the visions of the inhabitants and their desires in the first phase. Three design ideas were developed based on that information, and these were discussed and developed further with the planning experts of North-Tallinn City authorities.

Next, public involvement events were organised in the local shopping mall, where three design proposals were demonstrated and explained on a poster, and the BlueHealth Community Level Survey was also administered. There was a simple poll with the opportunity to vote for the best design idea and to comment on all proposals (Figure 3.16a). The final versions of the chosen design were discussed with the officials and experts in the North-Tallinn municipality. Then the project was developed into a final design – which involved further detailed design work to ensure it was practical and could be built for the budget after which it was constructed. The final intervention consisted of a steppe deck parallel to an old concrete slipway (Figure 3.16b) with sloping seating for reclining together with a number of benches and wooden surfaces fastened to old concrete blocks to provide more comfortable seating or sunbathing places along the edge of the beach.

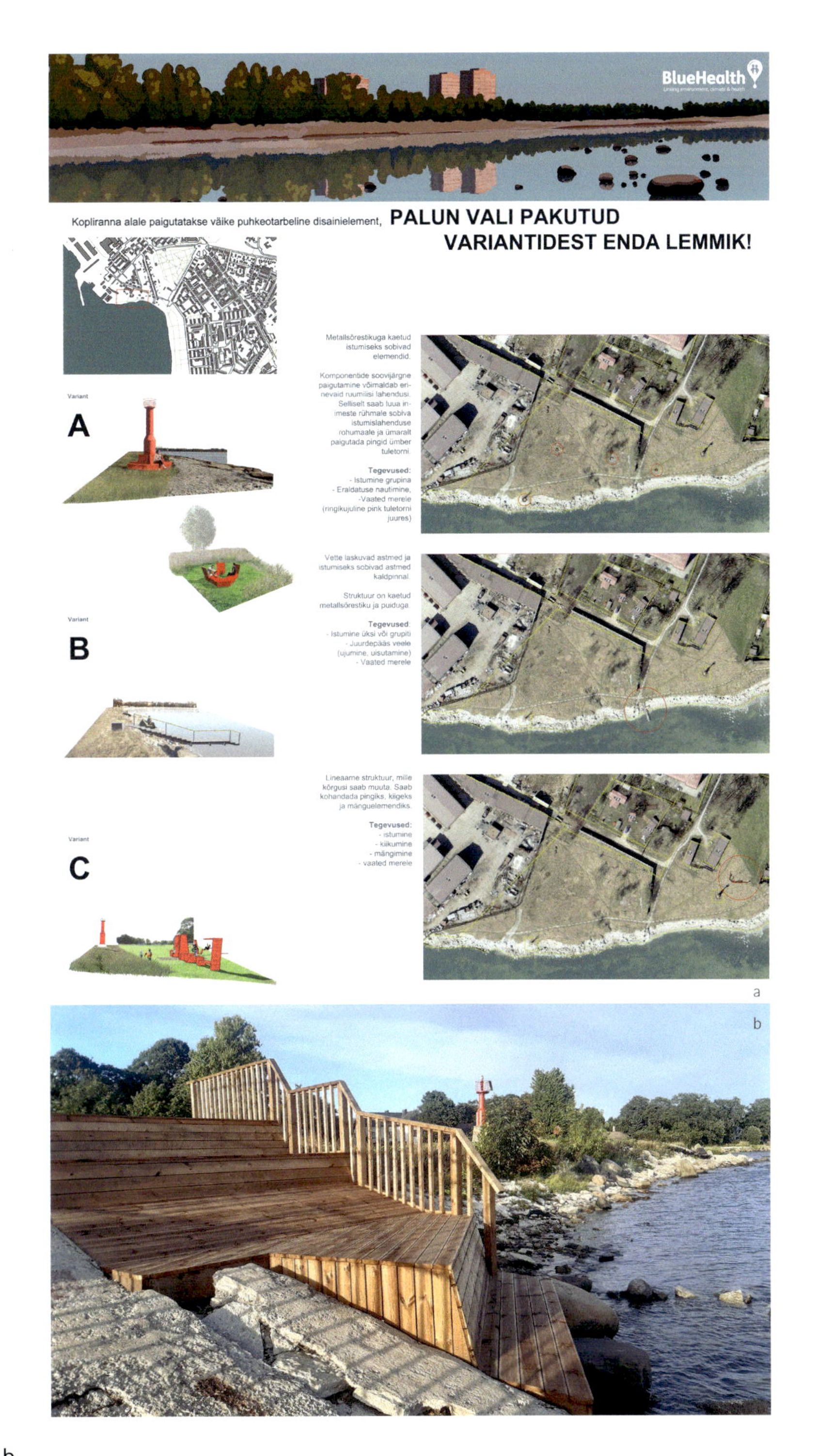

Figure 3.16a and b

a) The poster of design ideas resulting from the workshop which was made available in a local shopping centre where local residents voted for their preferred design (the text says "Please choose your favourite from the options offered"), which was Option B; b) the final constructed intervention structure, following significant development from the original concept

(*Source*: Jekaterina Balicka and Peeter Vassiljev)

Reflections on the process

The BlueHealth team tried a range of methods and formats of public engagement. The meetings with the specialists took place in the format of focus groups, while the engagement of local inhabitants required adopting several methods. First meetings with locals took the form of small groups. There was a pre-developed set of questions and topics, such as current use, use conflicts, general perception of the site, needs for improvement, desired use of the area and missing infrastructure, and the groups gave answers to every topic by both written proposals and mapping the areas using stickers and Post-It comments; therefore, it was possible to gather place-related information.

The format of small-group workshops worked well in the sense that they produced large amounts of information and useful insights regarding the area, but meeting attendance was not very high. The online questionnaire, covering the same questions and topics and discussed during the public meeting, was created, and posters advertising it were spread around the Kopliranna area. An on-site event was also organised, where people in the neighbourhood were invited to answer the same questions as during the first public involvement event. A further set of meetings and events was organised in order to get feedback on the intervention proposal options. The engagement methods were focus group meetings and a questionnaire. Participants were asked to comment on every design option and choose the most suitable.

One of the general goals of the BlueHealth project was to investigate how the benefits of the coastal urban areas could be promoted to those who were unable to benefit from them currently and how new interventions could address this problem. It was not easy to reach many people outside of the circle of the active and engaged, but restricted, group of inhabitants. One of the particular aims of our public involvement was to reach out to less active local inhabitants. Even more important was to meet the people who never visit the case study area or any public space near the sea in order to know why people might *not* visit the area. To reach those who would otherwise not come to the meetings, we had to find alternative methods. We learned that meeting and talking to people in everyday places like shopping centres worked well in elucidating the opinions of non-visitors and non-users of the blue spaces. Another option that worked well was meet such people at festive public events, such as during the local midsummer public bonfire held on the coast.

The preliminary assessment of the before-and-after site observations (Figure 3.17) shows an absolute increase in users and then a distinct focus of use associated with the interventions (shown as red shapes on the second heat map).

Discussion and conclusions

Co-design is a type of participatory design that goes beyond the usual consultative nature of public involvement in participatory planning (Stelzle et al., 2017; Retegi and Predan, 2019). Exemplified by the BlueHealth case studies, one of its core characteristics is that stakeholders are involved from project start and continue to be involved throughout the design process, as contrasted to participation solely in occasional workshops or consultations. In all the case studies presented, potential stakeholders were informed and engaged immediately after the initiation process was completed (see the process cycle Fig 3.2), that is, during the preparation phase. Forming multi-stakeholder expert teams consisting of cross-disciplinary representatives of academia, public authorities and voluntary organisations, as well as local inhabitants and the general public, was a "snowball process" in all case studies. It was a common feature that expert stakeholders and general public engagement took place in different project phases using different communication models. Table 3.1 gives an overview of the characteristics of the projects described in this chapter and some of the main lessons learned.

As demonstrated by the BlueHealth case studies, co-design may give useful input to the design process of public spaces in terms of information on current land use and conflicting uses but also information on the future (e.g. type of desired design elements). Co-design may also increase the social acceptability of the designed area, which has been clearly demonstrated in all the case study locations.

However, some of the co-design challenges reflected in existing scientific literature and guidelines (e.g., Cruickshank et al., 2016; Retegi and Predan, 2019) also arose in our case studies. For instance, some stakeholders and user

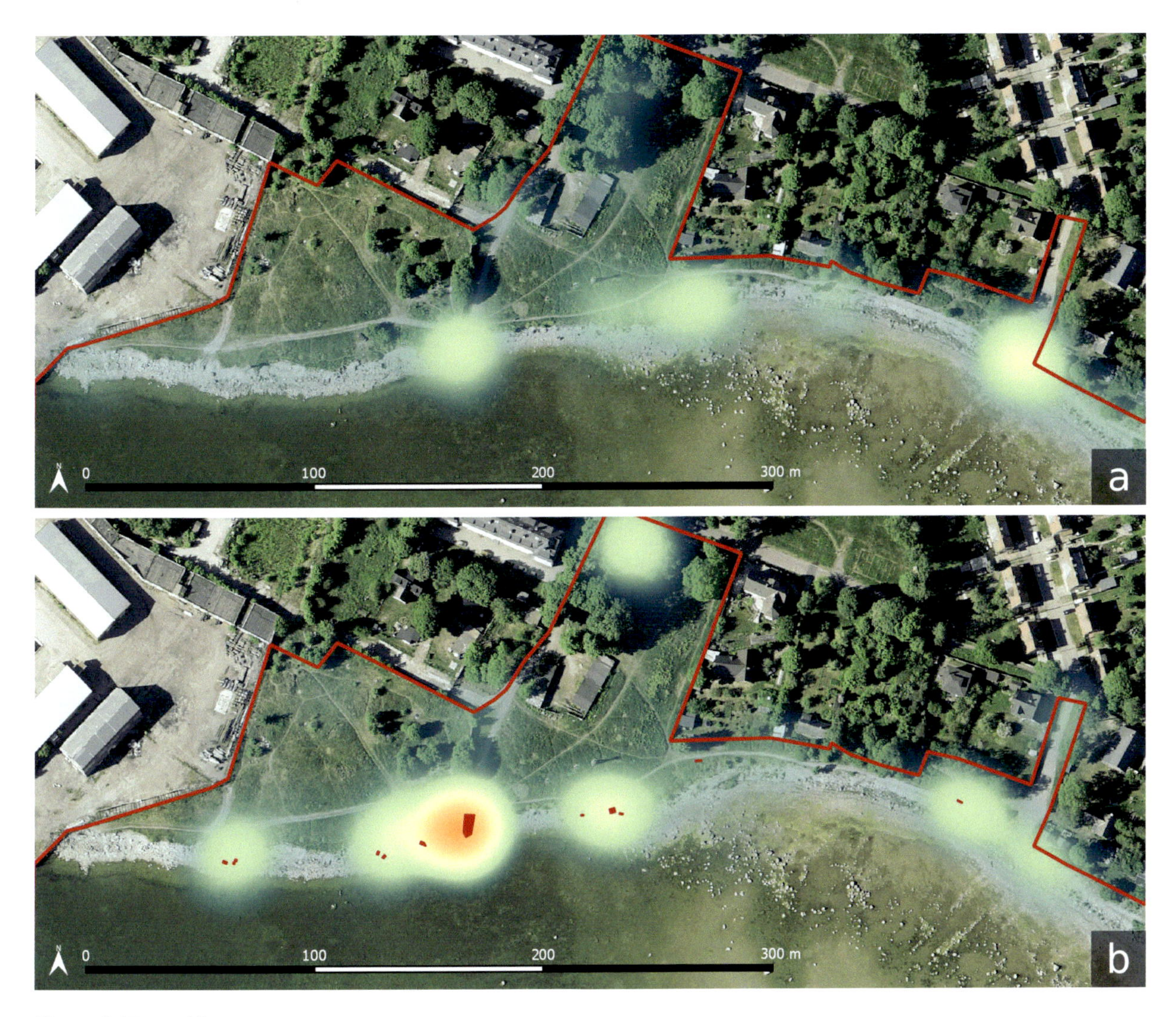

Figure 3.17a and b

Two heat maps to show the use of the site, a) before and b) after the intervention. All user observations are shown; the red marks are the interventions placed on the site – note how the hotter spots clearly coincide with the interventions

(*Source*: Peeter Vassiljev and Orthophoto: Estonian Land Board, 2020)

groups were very difficult to reach. These groups included a sparsely settled neighbourhood (Spain), particular members of a business sector (United Kingdom) and culturally or socially diverse groups of the public (Estonia). Here, living-lab types of activities and the provision of meeting opportunities outside formally organised meeting venues may be useful to engage with hard-to-reach user groups.

It turned out that in all case studies, we met complex and case study-dependent groups of stakeholders, especially among local residents. The hugely varying values of inputs in the co-design process or difficulties in accommodating the non-technical suggestions in the expert design (Portugal) posed challenges for the whole co-design process. How to maintain a balance between different technical planning aspects in a way that is comprehensible to the public and other stakeholders unfamiliar with planning-expert language requires further development. The designer may not only need to be an expert in design but also an effective facilitator able to mediate between different user groups, scientists and decision-makers (Lee et al., 2008).

Table 3.1 **An overview of the characteristics of the projects and some of the main lessons learned**

	Rubí	*Plymouth*	*Guimarães*	*Tallinn*
Aim of the case/ problem addressed	To restore the abandoned historical Can Moritz spring and surroundings to improve the quality and functions of the space	To improve peoples' local natural space in the Teats Hill deprived area	To implement an intervention that could enhance the water value and the overall sensorial experience provided by the water features	To attract people to visit and use the coastal urban areas
Design team: experts and important stakeholders	Landscape architects, environmental epidemiologists, local NGOs (land and heritage conservation), neighbours (local inhabitants)	BlueHealth researchers formed a project group with staff from the Active Neighbourhoods team. Prime stakeholders included city council, housing association, wildlife trusts, marine biological association, aquarium, local schools and charitable organisations, local universities, conservation groups and local elected representatives	The Laboratory of Green Space, Health and Inclusion of UTAD coordinated a team including academic institutions, local authorities, local associations and the community	BlueHealth team of researchers and designers in EMÜ; Tallinn municipality subsections and experts; environmental authorities, urbanistic NGOs and local inhabitants of different cultural backgrounds
Decision-making process/methods used to engage with the stakeholders	Steinitz method, meetings, participation of neighbours in the intervention, survey	Regular in-person focus group meetings with interactive small-group exercises or whole-group feedback exercises; series of carefully prepared citizen engagement events, including person-centred discussions and family "fun" days	A real-life situation design methodology, comprising a) site analysis and exploratory design, b) participative evaluation and site selection, c) expert design and licensing and d) participative execution; case-dependent varying engagement techniques	Step-wise consultation with experts and interviews and questionnaires for the general public, combined with exploratory design and expert design
Outcomes	Renovated spring and surroundings, improved space quality and functions, increase in public visitation	The Teats Hill local natural space renovated in a co-design process in negotiation with stakeholders and residents	Interest in and use of the intervention site (lake area) has been generated; public interest raised for the blue infrastructure of the city	Co-designed interventions have attracted both visitors and area managers

	Rubí	*Plymouth*	*Guimarães*	*Tallinn*
Lessons learned/ success factors	Complicated stakeholder engagement in low-density habitation areas. The collaboration of different actors is important. Inclusion of the neighbours is also important	Any observed effects of the renovation on the well-being of people in the local community were likely due to increased social cohesion in the surrounding areas; further need to find ways to engage particular stakeholders	Co-design is an interesting but complex and demanding process with multiple cons. Public input is non-technical, "never-ending", departing from hugely varying value points	It is complicated to reach beyond the circle of the active and engaged but restricted round of inhabitants, especially those who for different reasons never visit the case-study area

One avenue for further research could be a more systematic stakeholder mapping for each co-design activity (Lee, 2008; Reed, 2008). This might also require a further detailed process and typology analysis in co-design, in particular for landscape intervention design. This might fit the engagement activities more closely as well as methods used according to the stakeholder mapping results.

One common feature of waterfront landscape intervention co-design is the potential for high public interest. In all the case studies, a rise in interest in blue space from public authorities, NGOs and local communities has been observed.

References

Cervera, M., Bell, S., Muñoz, F., Mishra, H.S., Fleming, L.E., Grellier, J., Carrasco-Turigas, G., Nieuwenhuijsen, M.J., Vert, C., Gascon, M.A. (2021). Transdisciplinary approach to recovering natural and cultural landscape and place identification: A case study of Can Moritz Spring (Rubí, Spain). *International Journal of Environmental Research and Public Health*, 18, 1709. doi:10.3390/ijerph18041709

Cruickshank, L., Coupe, G., Hennessy, D. (2016). Co-design: Fundamental issues and guidelines for designers: Beyond the castle case study. *SVID*, 9, 46. doi:10.3384/svid.2000-964X.13248

Cumbula, S.D., Sabiescu, A., Cantoni, L. (2013). Co-design with communities. A reflection on the literature. Unpublished. doi:10.13140/rg.2.1.2309.9365

Enserink, B., Monnikhof, R.A.H. (2003). Information management for public participation in co-design processes: Evaluation of a Dutch example. *Journal of Environmental Planning and Management*, 46, 315–344. doi:10.1080/0964056032000096910

Estonian Land Board. (2020). *Orthophoto.* Summertime forestry flight 28.05.2018. Published under Licence of open data by Estonian Land Board, 1.07.2018

Evans, M., Terrey, N. (2016). Co-design with citizens and stakeholders. In: *Evidence-based policy-making in the social sciences: Methods that matter.* Evans, M. and Terrey, N. (Eds.) Policy Press, University of Bristol, Bristol, pp. 243–261.

Ghibusi, M., Marchetti, F. (Eds.) (2018). *Urban design ecologies: Projects for city environments.* Maggioli S.p.A., Santarcangelo di Romagna.

Kaplan, S., Kaplan, R., Wendt, J.S. (1972). Rated preference and complexity for natural and urban visual material. *Perception & Psychophysics*, 12, 354–356.

Lee, Y. (2008). Design participation tactics: The challenges and new roles for designers in the co-design process. *CoDesign*, 4, 31–50. doi:10.1080/15710880701875613

Moser, S.C. (2016). Can science on transformation transform science? Lessons from co-design. *Current Opinion in Environmental Sustainability*, 20, 106–115. doi:10.1016/j.cosust.2016.10.007

Pawlowski, C.S., Winge, L., Carroll, S., Schmidt, T., Wagner, A.M., Nørtoft, K.P.J., Lamm, B., Kural, R., Schipperijn, J., Troelsen, J. (2017). Move the neighbourhood: Study design of a community-based participatory public open space intervention in a Danish deprived neighbourhood to promote active living. *BMC Public Health*, 17, 481. doi:10.1186/s12889-017-4423-4

Reed, M.S. (2008). Stakeholder participation for environmental management: A literature review. *Biological Conservation*, 141, 2417–2431. doi:10.1016/j.biocon.2008.07.014

Retegi, A., Predan, B. (2019). Co-create handbook for creative professionals. Co-create.

Richardson, J., Goss, Z., Pratt, A., Sharman, J., Tighe, M. (2013). Building HIA approaches into strategies for green space use: An example from Plymouth's (UK) Stepping Stones to Nature project. *Health Promotion International*, 28(4), 502–511.

Sander, H., Meikar, T. (2001). *The history of the Kopli Peninsular in Tallinn*. Forest Research Institute, Tartu.

Scott, I. (2017). Mobility, mood and place – co-designing age-friendly cities: A report on collaborations between older people and students of architecture. *Arts*, 6, 12. doi:10.3390/arts6030012

Steinitz, C.A. (1990). Toward a sustainable landscape with high visual preference and high ecological integrity: The loop road in Acadia National Park, U.S.A. *Landscape and Urban Planning*, 19, 213–250.

Steinitz, C.A. (2012). *Framework for geodesign: Changing geography by design*. Esri Press, Redlands, CA.

Stelzle, B., Jannack, A., Rainer Noennig, J. (2017). Co-design and co-decision: Decision making on collaborative design platforms. *Procedia Computer Science*, 112, 2435–2444. doi:10.1016/j.procs.2017.08.095

Stott, C.R., Warren, S. (2017). Advocating a co-design methodology across academy and community. Presented at the Association of Architectural Educators 2017 Conference; Architecture Connects, 06September 2017–09 September 2017, Oxford Brookes University.

Webb, R., Bai, X., Smith, M.S., Costanza, R., Griggs, D., Moglia, M., Neuman, M., Newman, P., Newton, P., Norman, B., Ryan, C., Schandl, H., Steffen, W., Tapper, N., Thomson, G. (2018). Sustainable urban systems: Co-design and framing for transformation. *Ambio*, 47, 57–77. doi:10.1007/s13280-017-0934-6

Wu, H., Hou, C. (2019). Utilizing co-design approach to identify various stakeholders' roles in the protection of intangible place-making heritage. *Disaster Prevention and Management*. doi:10.1108/DPM-09-2018-0291

Part II
Tools, indicators and models for planning and design

Chapter 4: Generating evidence in support of site planning and design

The BlueHealth toolbox

James Grellier, Himansu S. Mishra, Lewis R. Elliott, Susanne Wuijts and Matthias F. W. Braubach

Facilitating evidence-based planning and design of blue spaces

In the first part of this book, we discussed in detail what we know about the impacts that blue spaces can have on human health and well-being and how changes made in those environments can potentially influence those effects. Faced with the design, repurposing or maintenance of urban blue spaces, decisions are routinely taken that potentially impact health, both positively and negatively. Choices made in other sectors – whether by planners, developers, industrialists, engineers, citizens or other decision-makers involved in the policy-making process – might also impact health and well-being through changes brought about in urban blue spaces.

In the case studies of evidence-based planning we were interested in implementing, testing and developing in the BlueHealth Project, we needed information on which to base the blue space planning and design decisions that would lead to harnessing the benefits to human health and well-being afforded by aquatic natural environments in the urban setting. The evidence-based approach to planning requires that various kinds of data be collected and analysed before and after any intervention is made. This provides the necessary understanding of the balance of risks and benefits associated with changes in an environment, in its usage, in the activities conducted in that space and in the health and well-being of its users and subsequently to plan in a way that maximises benefits and minimises risks. The evidence-based planning paradigm recognises that the prevention of a number of 21st-century public health challenges require that health and well-being be put centre stage in urban planning, creating high-quality environments that afford social interaction, physical activity and restorative recreation.

How do we understand blue spaces and the people in, on and around them in order to create an evidence base of sufficient breadth and depth to inform planning? An overriding aim of the BlueHealth project was to design an integrated set of tools to help facilitate this (Grellier et al. 2017). Part Two of this book provides detailed descriptions of the tools in this BlueHealth Toolbox (https://bluehealth2020.eu/resources/toolbox/), the rationale behind their development and examples of their application. While these tools cannot be used to understand entirely the complexity of an intervention in a blue space – particularly when using them to assess large-scale, multi-faceted interventions – they do represent a consistent means of collecting information on key aspects of environments (including risks and benefits), the status and behaviours of their users and the opinions of all parties potentially affected by an intervention. Furthermore, these tools can be used to assess the changes brought about by intervention in blue spaces by re-applying the tools after intervention has taken place.

Improving our understanding of precisely *how* intentional alteration of urban blue spaces results in concomitant changes in the environment and human health requires the collection and analysis of various kinds of information. In order for this information to be considered *evidence* that serves to support a particular kind of intervention improving human health, it must be collected and analysed using robust tools and methods. Rigour in design, implementation

DOI: 10.4324/9780429056161-7

and application of such tools is essential in ensuring that their findings are good representations of the situations found in the broad palette of urban blue spaces, are consistent and repeatable and are usable by the range of professionals and interested citizens who may need to apply them. The term 'evidence' need not be taken solely to mean quantitative information. Qualitative data are key to understanding people's relationships with their environment and the affordances within it, as well as the impacts that it has on them.

The tools that we developed can be envisaged primarily as a means of understanding the impacts on the environment and human health of any intervention made that affected the use of an urban blue space. However, relatively broad working definitions of the terms 'intervention' and 'site' were kept in mind as the tools were developed. A 'site' is a blue space, defined as an outdoor environment – either natural or manmade – that prominently features water and is accessible to humans either proximally (being in, on or near water) or distally/virtually (being able to see, hear or otherwise sense water) (Grellier et al. 2017). An 'intervention' is anything that has the potential to generate change in a blue space; this could be an alteration to its physical structure or fabric, environmental qualities, accessibility, maintenance, promotion, signposting or provision of information therein or social programmes that result in changes of use or perception of space. Any of these changes might result in change in use of the blue space, which might further impact – positively or negatively – the site's ecosystem or the health and well-being of those visiting it or living nearby. Change in use could also be actuated through the implementation of a policy, the introduction of new regulations or the enactment of new bylaws at local, regional, national or even supra-national levels.

A huge variety of interventions in the built and natural environment might be made that purposely provide people with opportunities to have increased contact with nature. We do not need to imagine such interventions only in the form of newly built structures or physical changes to a landscape but also as changes to the maintenance of an existing site, provision of information about a space or engagement with stakeholders. In BlueHealth, a set of community-level interventions – all aiming to improve health and well-being through altering use of a blue space – were conducted that encompassed a variety of blue spaces, and it was their evaluation that provided the need for bespoke tools. These included so-called 'urban acupuncture' interventions (Lerner 2014), wherein relatively small-scale changes to the landscape were made at underused, inaccessible or negatively perceived sites, with the hypothesis that these changes might confer disproportionately large positive impacts on the use or enjoyment of those places by specific populations (see Chapter 15).

Importantly, even though we developed, tested and validated the tools using a testbed of community-level interventions that had improvement of human health as an ultimate goal, the use of the BlueHealth tools need not be constrained to changes made with such intentions. For example, the tools can be used to assess the effects of the construction of a gated community on a previously accessible coastline and on its local population and visitors. Indeed, from the point of view of applying the BlueHealth tools, an intervention could theoretically even be created by natural processes. Similarly, a section of footpath removed, or a beach swept away, by natural processes such as coastal erosion can be considered an 'intervention' from the point of view of using the BlueHealth tools in order to understand impacts on health and well-being of a population.

Understanding the scale of such impacts could be crucial in determining the value to society and the costs of engineering against similar events in future. Perhaps, somewhat counterintuitively, a lack of action on the part of humanity might even be considered an intervention. For example, where decision-makers have knowledge about potential co-benefits that might result from changing existing urban blue infrastructure but choose not to effect such a change, they have effectively 'intervened', and the impacts of this choice might be estimated indirectly through applying the tools.

The decision-making contexts in which interventions might be made vary considerably, and the objectives of such interventions are even more diverse. An urban site might be developed with the express intention of providing a blue space location for rest, recreation or physical activity. Alternatively, where water infrastructure projects such as storm drains are built to manage storm water or weirs are installed to protect against river flooding, and prevention of risks to human health is foremost in the minds of the decision-makers, the potential health benefits of recreational use of these spaces might additionally be considered a 'co-benefit'.

Additionally, the scale and geographic contexts of these projects can exhibit huge variation. With increases in scale and more urbanised settings, the range of stakeholders involved grows, further adding to the complexities of the governance process. Given these challenges, and since the breadth of situations in which interventions relating to blue spaces might be made is so huge, any tools developed to measure their impact on the health of humans and ecosystems are necessarily widely understandable, scalable and flexible.

Decisions relating to interventions are informed by baseline conditions at a site. However, there is considerable value in conducting an evaluation of the conditions before, during and after an intervention has been instigated and/or completed. Both pre- and post-intervention application of the tools should be considered at several time points. In the case of physical changes to a site, environmental indicators may respond gradually to the intervention, dependent on the nature of those changes and the characteristics of the environmental system, but also be subject to seasonal or climate-dependent variation or human behavioural impacts. Similarly, indicators of impacts of an intervention on health would not generally be anticipated to materialise overnight, unless the health outcome was particularly common and the association with an environmental cause extremely strong (neither of which is typically the case).

Responses to an intervention may also be non-linear through time. For example, the novelty of a new public waterside park may result in greatly increased frequency of visits in the first weeks and months following its construction and then return to baseline levels again once this 'honeymoon period' is over. Alternatively, a stable, increased pattern of use might only be found after a period of 'burn in', perhaps as news of the park spreads through a population. Such changes do not have to be positive, of course, and could also represent decreases in ecological quality at a site, negative effects on neighbouring residents and so on. In short, while the tools described in the following chapters provide measures of the impact that interventions might make on a site and on individual and population health, consideration of the timing of their implementation is paramount to these measures being robust.

The tools have been developed for application at different scales, such as the site and its users, the local neighbourhood and its inhabitants, the city and its population and so on. In planning, their application allows the analysis of how a given intervention affects people and environments with different spatial relationships to the site itself. Additionally, as tools applied in research relating to health/well-being and interventions in built/natural environments, these tools have been used to investigate whether processes that operate at one spatial level are identifiable at others, thereby discerning potentially scalable aspects of a particular intervention.

It is entirely possible to use the tools described in the following chapters individually, at only a single scale. However, they have been carefully designed to work as an integrated toolbox, producing quantitative and qualitative information that can be analysed in parallel or in combination so as to better illuminate potential causal pathways between changes in the environment and human health. Additionally, some of these tools have been designed to elicit the same information at different geographical scales. The incorporation of questionnaire items, for example, in the tools aimed at populations at a given site, close to that site and at some distance to that site, allows for direct comparisons to be made regarding the use of – and the opinions relating to – a site, which may also be used to inform analyses of inequalities of opportunity, economic valuations and so on. Using a particular tool in isolation potentially leads to lost opportunities in terms of understanding the characteristics of a given blue space, the affordances therein and the associated potential for their benefitting the health and well-being of various populations. Similarly, key risks to health related to use of a given environment might not be identified if only one tool is used or if a tool is applied only at a single geographical scale.

From the perspective of the subject of this book, the most obvious application of the BlueHealth tools is in evaluating the impacts a particular planned intervention might make on the environment and/or on human health and well-being. This can be achieved through applying the tools before an intervention – that is, to form a clear picture of baseline conditions – and after an intervention. The change that has been mapped out between the two or more periods of pre-/post-intervention can – with appropriate caveats – be attributed to the changes effected on the ground. In this way, the tools provide information which supports planning and design in the urban landscape specifically geared towards provisioning of health and well-being benefits to a population, with minimal negative impact on the blue space environment.

However, the tools can be applied in other contexts, too, particularly in relation to the timing of the evaluative processes they facilitate. In this sense, it is entirely possible to apply them retrospectively where sufficient data exist elsewhere to inform prior baseline conditions. This might be conducted where a project is planned, is being built or has already been built, without consideration of the evidence-based approach or without any desire to specifically improve health and well-being by the original planners. In such a case, evidence could still be gathered – including retrospectively – using some of the BlueHealth tools, thereby allowing an evaluation of that project in terms of its impact on both the environment and human health. The tools might also be used to evaluate interventions made to achieve different goals. As already mentioned, although it might seem at odds with the overall emphasis of this book, the inter-sectoral applicability of these tools is one of their very important features.

It is apparent that not all tools can be used prospectively. For example, it is not possible to collect data on the patterns of user behaviour in an area of water yet to be reclaimed from the sea for construction of flood defences or a site that was previously private being made publicly accessible. Clearly, these are not limitations of the tool itself but rather constraints imposed by the realities of the sites.

Similarly, where an intervention has already taken place, it may not always be possible reliably to reconstruct information on environmental status or patterns of user behaviours retrospectively. In this case, however, it may be possible to impute information around the pre-intervention environmental status or human uses, provided that some data are either available, perhaps relating to a similar site nearby, or obtainable through interview with local experts or members of the local community. In such circumstances, it is still possible to apply the relevant tools; uncertainties and assumptions related to the information collected should then be detailed and reported.

Interventions and the tools used to evaluate them do not exist in a vacuum. Between identifying a planned intervention, selecting the method of evaluation and choosing the appropriate tools, through to collecting data and interpreting results, there is clearly an extensive interplay with various stakeholders with diverse interests in the planning process, the design of the intervention and in the site itself. The needs and wants of these stakeholders, their resources and their opinions may all shape the evaluation and use of the tools. They might feed into the interpretation of results and the design of any adaptation deemed necessary. It is entirely appropriate that these feedback loops should form a part of the planning, design and evaluative processes and be documented.

Overview of the tools in the BlueHealth Toolbox

The BlueHealth Toolbox comprises six tools that gather data on blue spaces in terms of their physical and ecological qualities (i.e. their environmental characteristics); the behaviours of people within them; and the perceptions, experiences and health and well-being status of the people using them or otherwise affected by them.

All of the tools can be used at any point in the process of changing a blue space site. They are most informative when used pre- and post-intervention, particularly where they are administered at multiple points in time within those phases.

While perhaps the application most relevant to the readers of this book is in purposely maximising the health and well-being benefits associated with a change made to a blue space with that goal in mind, the tools are also more generally applicable to the monitoring and evaluation of changes made to blue spaces with completely divergent goals.

BlueHealth Environmental Assessment Tool

How can we characterise a given blue space, and what is its physical state? What are the qualities that set this site apart from other similar sites? What kind of flora and fauna does the water at the site support? Existing tools assessing outdoor environments in terms of the salutogenic (health-producing) potential have largely examined urban built environmental components, recreational environments, urban green spaces such as parks and urban design qualities related to certain activities (Mishra et al. 2020).

The BlueHealth Environmental Assessment Tool (BEAT) was developed to provide robust, objective measures of the environmental character of blue space sites, including both their terrestrial and aquatic systems. Divided into four steps, the tool guides the user through: (1) a preliminary desk-based study that collects data on a site's location and character; (2) an onsite evaluation of the site's character – a first impression; (3) the main survey, in which aspects of social, aesthetic and physical characteristics of the site are scored; and (4) an evaluation of the aquatic ecosystem.

Two somewhat distinct versions of the tool have been developed. A 'Professional BEAT' is intended for professional users, such as landscape architects, ecologists, recreation planners, urban planners or hydrologists who have expert knowledge of the relevant domains and may have sophisticated methods or instruments for assessing many of the factors. Although the BEAT only requires two assessors, a professional application of the tool might involve a team of experts who can independently collect, moderate and interpret the data; relate data collected on site to existing monitoring data (for example, air or surface water quality); and analyse the factors with one another rather than treating them separately. A 'Community BEAT', on the other hand, is aimed at individuals and community groups with an interest in their local environment that are seeking information on aspects of a blue space, perhaps as a citizen science or educational project or in support of funding applications for other activities. This version of the tool is shorter and less complicated than the professional version.

The BEAT is primarily designed to be used as an online tool, but it is also available for download, which allows for a printed version to be used on sites where assessors are not connected to the internet. There are several opportunities for using BEAT in tandem with the decision support tool (DST). Whereas the BEAT serves chiefly to identify characteristics of the site – some of which may indeed be hazards or potential sources of health benefit – the DST serves to describe risks and benefits to health, contextualise them and provide guidance on design features that might reduce the impacts of health risks and enhance and maximise possible benefits. DST users may benefit from prior application of the BEAT to generate a solid understanding of the environmental character of the blue space, which can then be used as a baseline for identifying potential risks and benefits in the DST. Chapter 5 explains the design and use of the BEAT in detail.

BlueHealth Behavioural Assessment Tool

What do people do at blue spaces? If they are active, what kinds of physical activity are they engaged in, and how much of it are they doing? If they are passive, what is the nature of their passive behaviour? How are their activities in a space associated with characteristics of the space and with aspects of the site status at different points in time? To answer these questions, the BlueHealth Behavioural Assessment Tool (BBAT) was developed.

The starting point for this work was the System for Observing Play and Recreation in Communities (SOPARC) (McKenzie et al. 2006). Whereas SOPARC serves to evaluate the amount of different kinds of physical activity in recreational settings, the BBAT has been designed to systematically capture all kinds of human behaviours and interactions at a site, as well as the weather and water conditions (e.g. tide, waves, etc.) at the time of observation. It captures who is doing what and where and allows researchers to make comparisons between different groups and activities. The BBAT outputs can be presented spatially in geographic point, heat map or hot-spot analysis forms, providing a visual way to assess and discuss results. Interrogation of these outputs allows the identification of affordances in blue spaces and how these relate to specific user groups.

The BBAT is a site-level tool. Background data collection and initial site mapping are comparable and parallel processes to those collected in the application of the BEAT. The outputs may well also prompt decision-makers to identify particular issues using the DST, depending on where the site users congregate and the types of activities they are observed doing. Chapter 6 explains how the BBAT was developed and how it can be used and also compares it with the SOPARC method.

Public Participation Geographic Information System: collaborative mapping of affordances

A blue space located at a particular place in a city might afford or be available for interactions for people living some distance away. Public Participation Geographic Information System (PPGIS; sometimes known, since it collects "soft values", as SoftGIS) is a geographical information system methodology that enables participatory mapping by allowing residents of a city, for example, to share their knowledge about their living environment with urban planners and researchers (Kahila and Kyttä 2009). In the context of BlueHealth, the commercially available Maptionnaire system (https://maptionnaire.com/) was used to understand how local residents used the blue spaces in the cities under study and to gauge what these places meant to them. For example, the system can be used to identify (and to begin to understand why) the favourite blue spaces in a city, those that are avoided, blue spaces that are under- or over-used and opportunities for developing new blue spaces in areas where no natural ones are present.

One limitation of all pre-post intervention work is knowing whether changes observed in behaviours (e.g. visits) are genuinely related to an intervention at a site or in fact reflect general changes in attitudes and behaviours over time unrelated to that intervention. Enabling local residents to comment on their experiences in local blue spaces provides a more complete picture of the importance and relevance of changes made at these sites. The application and illustration of the PPGIS is covered in Chapter 7.

BlueHealth International Survey

The BlueHealth International Survey (BIS) is a bespoke online survey (in the form of a questionnaire) designed to answer the same questions as the BlueHealth Community Level Survey (BCLS; see subsequently) but at a higher spatial scale. The BIS has so far been administered to nationally representative online panels (i.e. to preregistered participants of online surveys) in some 18 countries, mainly in Europe but also in North America, Australia and Hong Kong. It can also be used at the city level by targeting its administration to online panels resident in particular cities.

Used in isolation, the BIS allows the collection and analysis of extremely rich data on how frequently different kinds of blue spaces are visited, how far people travel to reach them and on internationally validated self-reported measures of health and well-being. Cross-sectional analyses provide insights into, for example, the links between health and well-being and the frequencies of visits to blue spaces.

Used as a component of the BlueHealth Toolbox, however, in parallel with other tools, it provides a useful national or regional benchmark of visit frequencies and self-reported health status with which data collected at a city or site level can be compared. Where an intervention is found to work – in the sense that it has net beneficial effects on health of a local population, as measured using the BCLS or BBAT, for example – data from the BIS may prove useful in gauging how representative characteristics and behaviours of that population are of a national population. This information would, for example, potentially lend support to those making the case for scaling up the intervention for application elsewhere in the country. A detailed description of the BIS is provided alongside the BCLS in Chapter 8.

BlueHealth Community Level Survey

How frequently do people visit blue spaces? How do they reach them? What activities do they do there? How do their visits make them feel? How does the state of the environment affect their propensity to visit natural spaces featuring water?

The BlueHealth Community Level Survey is a questionnaire designed to answer these questions. It was designed to serve as a shorter, site-specific version of the BlueHealth International Survey (see previously); the BCLS is particularly suited for administration to communities affected by changes made to a local site. The inclusion of items common to the BIS allows for contextualisation and comparison of findings made locally with those made at a national or city level. Where engagement with people living further afield is desirable, we recommend the use of the PPGIS instead of the BCLS.A full description of how the BCLS was developed and how it can be implemented is presented in Chapter 8.

BlueHealth Decision Support Tool

The BlueHealth Decision Support Tool guides a user through a series of steps to identify the key risks and benefits to health and environment of a given blue space setting. It provides urban planners, architects, policy makers and estate managers with a novel means of approaching the planning, management and maintenance of blue infrastructure, with both health promotion and the management of potential health and environmental risks in mind. It highlights threats and ways to mitigate them, as well as spotting possible opportunities for boosting public health and well-being.

The tool includes information for different blue settings such as marine environments, rivers, lakes, urban water bodies, blue spaces in green settings (parks, etc.) and ornamental blue spaces (e.g. fountains). It features guidance for planning and management on three key elements: (1) health risks related to blue spaces, such as drowning, illnesses, vector-borne diseases, or climate-specific factors (e.g. UV exposure); (2) human health and well-being benefits, such as opportunities for physical activity or improvements in mental and social well-being; and (3) improved ecosystem and environmental benefits, such as improved air and water quality, habitats and biodiversity. Each outcome is described in terms of its relevance to health, identifying the scale of the threat or opportunity and the human populations most likely to be affected.

The DST is an online tool developed to be used at a site, or at least by evaluators with a very good knowledge of the characteristics of a site. The development and application of the DST are described in Chapter 9.

Using the tools together: the BlueHealth Toolbox as an integrated assessment framework

Individually, each tool provides information on a key set of characteristics relating to the site, typically before and after an intervention. Used in combination within a single integrated assessment framework (the BlueHealth Toolbox), these tools have the potential to provide an evaluation team with a very rich dataset on multiple aspects of a blue space and the human populations affected by it before, during and after interventions. It has only been through carefully ensuring that the tools use internally consistent definitions, concepts and questionnaire items that such integration is possible.

All sites have environmental characteristics and qualities that can be evaluated. Similarly, urban blue spaces are all subject to some kind of use, which, alongside behaviours of humans interacting within those spaces, can be assessed. Individuals have a measurable health and well-being status. Collecting data on each of these domains can be done using tools available in the BlueHealth Toolbox, but by no means should a practitioner consider that all tools must be applied to all sites or at multiple points in time.

There are at least three issues, or dimensions, to consider when selecting which tools to employ in assessing a specific intervention and how to employ them. These dimensions relate to: the spatial scale(s) at which the effects of an intervention are considered most relevant, the time scale(s) over which that evaluation should be conducted and the population(s) for whom health and well-being impacts are considered.

Some tools are quite clearly designed to assess characteristics at the site level, such as the BBAT. The evaluator applying the tool can be confident in applying this only at the site, as it is designed specifically to understand use of the blue space itself. Other tools can be used at multiple spatial levels (see Figure 4.1). For example, although it was designed to capture information at the national level, there is no reason the BIS cannot be administered at international, regional and city levels. The only constraint here is whether suitable online panels exist at those levels, that is, whether sufficient numbers of responses would be obtainable. The flexibility of the means of administering the BCLS, which can be printed on paper and posted, delivered as an online survey or used in face-to-face interviews, means that it might be used on- and off-site and with specific populations. BCLS interviewers could approach users of a blue space in the space itself or administer the survey to nearby residents at their doorsteps, for example. The important aspect of both is that they share common questionnaire items, so analyses at different spatial levels are automatically comparable.

The time points at which different tools should be evaluated needs careful consideration (Figure 4.2). Also, there is little value in assessing environmental characteristics of a site multiple times while only evaluating health status once. The combination of these two datasets at the same multiple time points generates far more opportunities for understanding the impacts of an intervention. The characteristics of most environments vary over time, diurnally, seasonally, annually and so on, and so do their usage and the health status of those using them. It is essential that the elucidation of the true impacts of the intervention on health not be obscured by patterns in the data observed

Figure 4.1

Spatial scales at which the tools in the BlueHealth Toolbox are designed to be employed

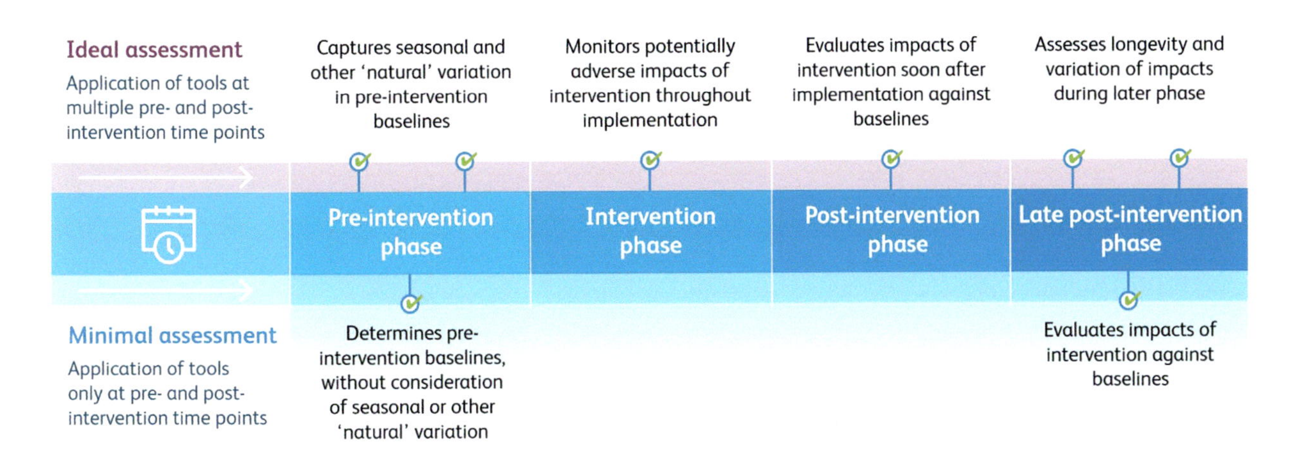

Figure 4.2
Temporal aspects of assessing the impacts of an intervention using the BlueHealth Toolbox

only due to lack of consideration of change affected by factors potentially external to the analysis of interest such as seasonality, for example.

Consideration should be given to assessing several populations when investigating how people use, feel about or are otherwise affected by a site and changes in it. On-site interviews will only ever provide information about current users of an urban blue space and nothing about those who are prevented from visiting by any of several barriers. Doorstep interviews and the like provide useful information about those populations assumed to have a relationship to the site (even if they do not visit it), but some blue spaces are potential destinations for populations spread across whole cities. PPGIS provides a partial solution to this, but it too relies on very partial and potentially unrepresentative sampling as a result of it being an online platform.

The teams that are brought together to work on evaluating an intervention at a given site using the BlueHealth Toolbox can comprise researchers and practitioners representing a wide range of disciplines, and they may also include or be led by stakeholders who have no professional experience in such evaluations. As in any interdisciplinary work, it is essential that methods and results of all the tools be understood sufficiently by all those working on the assessment that they are able to have informed discussions about the overall evaluation of a site.

The BlueHealth Toolbox is a collection of what might be described as 'diagnostic tools'. They can be used to collect a variety of information on the places and the people using or otherwise affected by them; they are not specifically designed to understand the governance processes that facilitate the realisation and management of blue spaces or the city in which they are located. The processes by which such knowledge is obtained are determined by, for example, the participating stakeholders' local ambitions, the instruments and means available and an understanding of the water system and its interactions with the local environment. Because of the complexities of these processes, no single, highly prescriptive method or tool aimed at building such knowledge is appropriate. Numerous existing methodologies are, however, available to analyse governance and to identify gaps and opportunities Wuijts et al. 2020).

Within BlueHealth, stakeholders have been involved in different ways in the implementation and evaluation of all interventions. The specific participatory approaches used to develop long-term planning of BlueHealth interventions are discussed at length in Chapter 16.

References

Grellier, J., White, M.P., Albin, M., Bell, S., Elliott, L.R., Gascon, M., Gualdi, S., et al. (2017). BlueHealth: A Study Programme Protocol for Mapping and Quantifying the Potential Benefits to Public Health and Well-Being from Europe's Blue Spaces. *BMJ Open* 7(e016188): 1–10.

Kahila, M., and Kyttä, M. (2009). SoftGIS as a Bridge-Builder in Collaborative Urban Planning. In *Planning Support Systems Best Practice and New Methods*, edited by Geertman, S. and Stillwell, J.C.H., 389–411. Dordrecht: Springer Netherlands.

Lerner, J. (2014). *Urban Acupuncture*. Washington, DC: Island Press.

McKenzie, T.L., Cohen, D., Sehgal, A., Williamson, S., and Golinelli, D. (2006). System for Observing Play and Recreation in Communities (SOPARC): Reliability and Feasibility Measures. *Journal of Physical Acticity & Health* 3(s1): S208–222.

Mishra, H.S., Bell, S., Vassiljev, P., Kuhlmann, F., Niin, G., and Grellier, J. (2020). The Development of a Tool for Assessing the Environmental Qualities of Urban Blue Spaces. *Urban Forestry & Urban Greening* 49(January): 126575.

Wuijts, S., Friederichs, L., Hin, J.A., Schets, F.M., van Rijswick, H.F.M.W., and Driessen, P.P.J. (2020). Governance Conditions to Overcome the Challenges of Realizing Safe Urban Bathing Water Sites. *International Journal of Water Resources Devlelopment* 00(00): 1–25.

Chapter 5: Assessing the land-water environment

Himansu S. Mishra, Katrin Saar and Simon Bell

Introduction

The BlueHealth project aims to investigate links between environment, climate and health. In order to provide places where people can enjoy access to water and also obtain many of the health and well-being benefits associated with blue spaces, it is important to be able to make effective links from a planning and design perspective. A tool which evaluates a place in a holistic way, through integrating a number of domains (such as the social, physical or ecological), and which enables the positive and negative aspects to be identified is needed. Where some important connections or specific social, spatial, functional, aesthetic, hydrological or ecological aspects are missing or found to be negative, then planners and designers can use this information to improve places and through this contribute to improving the potential for physical and mental health and well-being of target populations.

This chapter presents the background to the development of the BlueHealth Environmental Assessment Tool (or BEAT for short) and describes its structure and how to use it and also illustrates its application in some worked examples. The tool itself is available online at www.beat.bluehealth.tools/.

Objectives for the tool

The BEAT tool presented here aims to provide a comprehensive method of assessing all the relevant domains related to 'blue spaces' (any outdoor space that prominently features water and which individuals may experience, whether by direct contact in, on or by the water or by indirect means such as seeing it). The tool is designed primarily for identifying the extent to which a particular blue space provides opportunities for obtaining exposure to water but also what impacts there might be on the environment itself and what hazards are present (or potentially present) for both environment and people (the tool also makes strong connections with the decision support tool presented in Chapter 9). It can be used as a means of collecting data about blue spaces for monitoring purposes (as an indicator set to be used over time); as a starting point in a planning and design project for upgrading, restoring or providing new access to waterfront landscapes; or for a post-occupancy evaluation of a built project.

The tool is designed to be used by two distinct groups. The first comprises experts, such as landscape architects, ecologists, recreation planners, urban planners or hydrologists. It is expected that these experts know the relevant domains in depth and that they have sophisticated methods or instruments for assessing many of the factors objectively (such as hydrological or ecological aspects), or else they have experience of applying subjective factors in a rational and repeatable way (for example, aesthetic and design factors). A team of experts might be used to collect and interpret the data, to relate data collected on site to that available from monitoring stations (for example, air or water pollution) or from other statistical sources (such as socioeconomic data about local residents) and, most importantly, to relate the factors to one another and not just treat them separately. The second group comprises local

DOI: 10.4324/9780429056161-8

community or citizen groups who have an interest in their local environment and want to be able to check aspects such as how safe it is for their children to go swimming and to educate themselves in urban ecology, as well as to help themselves develop a project for the improvement of a local place. School student use is also a possibility, perhaps for in science projects or in studies of the local environment, its hazards and changing condition.

It is also possible that experts (for example, responsible professional staff in a municipality) might encourage communities to participate in 'citizen science' and work together to collect data and to monitor sites. Such an approach is often employed in the collection of data on urban wildlife (such as counting birds or other animal or plant species). Communities often have members who are themselves rather knowledgeable about some areas, such as bird watchers or fishermen, whose expertise or tacit knowledge might be capitalised upon for the purpose of collecting good quality data.

The tool is therefore designed with these two target groups in mind. The data expectations from the experts are higher than for the community users, and the functional interface of the tool differs. The community-level tool assumes less knowledge, and the interface presents the sections in a simpler and easier-to-follow way which might be suitable for school students or local people with no specific environmental or design background. As such, it also provides a learning platform.

Those elements of the tool that are objective and measurable on site can be administered by a single person. For less objective – or more qualitative – elements where professional experience is required, it is necessary to involve a minimum of two individuals so that the independent assessments of each assessor can be compared prior to agreement or moderation of final scores. This also adds to the overall reliability of the tool.

In developing this tool, we did not intend to create something from scratch or without consideration of other, already developed and tested tools (which, however, in the main, do not cover blue spaces very well). Rather, we conducted a review of existing tools and extracted from these a number of aspects related to content, structure and application methods that were considered most applicable and relevant in terms of blue spaces.

The tool itself covers two linked but separately assessed sections: one for the terrestrial part of a blue space and one for the aquatic part. The conceptual thinking and presentation of the results are different for each, and they were developed by separate teams, one of landscape architects and one of water ecologists. They have been incorporated into one functional tool and user interface, available at www.beat.bluehealth.tools/.

Research informing the development of the BEAT

There are a variety of tools available for assessing the character and uses of places. These have typically been designed for specific aspects or particular kinds of places such as woodlands, parks, residential areas or beaches, for example. Therefore, in developing the BEAT, we searched for existing tools and then reviewed them to see what aspects they covered, how they assessed a place or site, who they were aimed at and how the results were presented. We looked for tools that covered related aspects, were well documented, were applied in practice and/or were developed as part of a project and written up in a scientific journal, as well as being available in English. We found 17 tools which fitted these criteria (see Appendix 1). They are all relatively recent – from the early 2000s usually – reflecting the rise in interest in the field in that period as well as the need to develop means of measuring sustainability and so on following all the Millennium goals and requirements and UN, WHO and EU initiatives and so on.

We found a number of assessment tools, some freely available and well used, others more specific and presented in academic papers but not necessarily widely applied. Many of them make reference to others which they have used to help or guide their development, which accounts for the convergent evolution apparent in many of them. They are all, to some extent at least, intended for use by both professionals and community groups, although some have two versions and are approached a little differently. The type of place or space varies, with no system looking comprehensively at the land-water interface from all possible angles. The scale varies, but most are for use at local spatial levels. There is a great deal of commonality in the factors assessed in each tool, although some aspects are deeper or shallower than others depending on the tool and its intended scope. Tools dealing with water are far fewer than those dealing with land. Most tools are structured with a number of main domains and then a set of factors or aspects within each. This makes them easier and more logical to understand and follow, as well as to compare different domains in order to achieve a full picture of the place under assessment. The use of rating scales of various sorts, together with qualitative descriptions and yes/no answers, are typical ways of assessing the environments and lead to clear ways of presenting comparable results. These have led, too, to the use of spidergrams and other similar diagrams as means of presenting results in easy-to-assimilate forms. Important for successful application of all tools is an accompanying set of instructions, whether provided in a manual, training videos, online resources or games. The tool development is reported in Mishra et al. (2020) for readers interested in this in more detail.

There are gaps in the coverage of environments which the BEAT aims to close. We also provide two versions, one for professionals and one for community groups, fully supported by instruction manuals and worked examples. We also present an online web-based tool for inputting data and producing the results in digestible form.

BEAT conceptual framework

Since the objective of the BEAT is not only to provide a tool for assessing blue spaces but to ensure that such spaces promote health and well-being, it is necessary to ensure that there is a theoretical connection. Therefore, lying behind the practical development and application of the new BEAT is the "person-environment fit" theory (Korpela et al., 2008) which helps us to define the blue space attributes that benefit health and which highlights the importance of key blue space physical environmental features (see Figure 5.1). Physical environments influence human health in

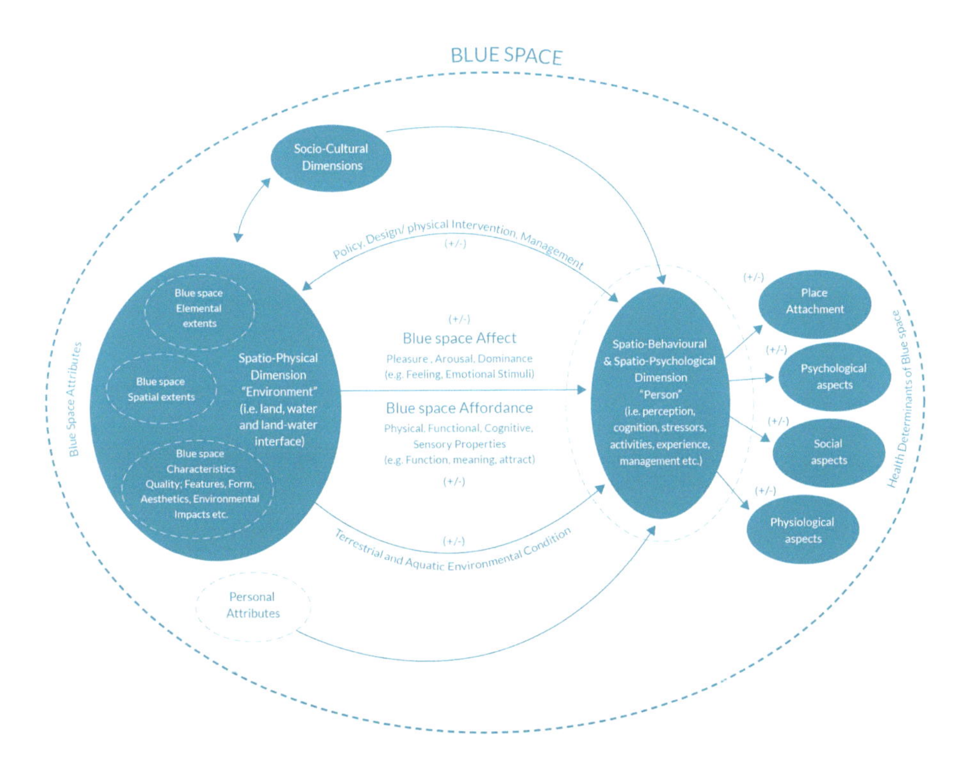

Figure 5.1
The person-environment interaction model for Blue Space and health outcomes which forms the theoretical basis for the BEAT. On the left are the blue space attributes assessed by the tool, and the rest of the model shows the pathways which lead to the expected health outcomes
(*Source*: Himansu Sekhar Mishra and Anna Wilczyńska)

part through psychological and physiological restoration (Berto, 2014) that in turn depends on the capacity of both the people and the place to support various health outcomes (Stokol, 2003). These transactional parameters can be categorised into two ontological dimensions: *environmental affordance* (Hartson, 2003) and *environmental affect* (Bakker et al., 2014) (Figure 5.2).

Figure 5.1 presents the potential relationship between blue space attributes and health determinants. Health determinants are the "active ingredients" in the environment that impact health and well-being positively or negatively. Within this, the properties of the space generate affordances which support a range of potential activities (Gibson, 1979), and in turn, these may promote behavioural and psychological responses. Blue space interventions, policies and management practices that originate from within the "person" dimension tend to improve physical characteristics that in turn enhance the blue space affordances and affects. Conversely, terrestrial and aquatic environmental conditions, qualities and impacts may independently and directly affect a population's exposure to blue space, positively or negatively influencing behaviour and psychology.

Figure 5.2 highlights the importance of physical attributes of the outdoor environment within the nature-health relationship and elaborates on mechanisms that may influence pathways to health (Frumkin et al., 2017; USDA, 2018, Hartig et al., 2014). The relationship between blue space exposure and health determinants is mediated by the perceived affordances and blue space effects. The dimensions of affordances (physical, functional, sensory and cognitive) and dimensions of affect (pleasure, arousal and control and influence) may play a role in reinforcing the link between nature and health.

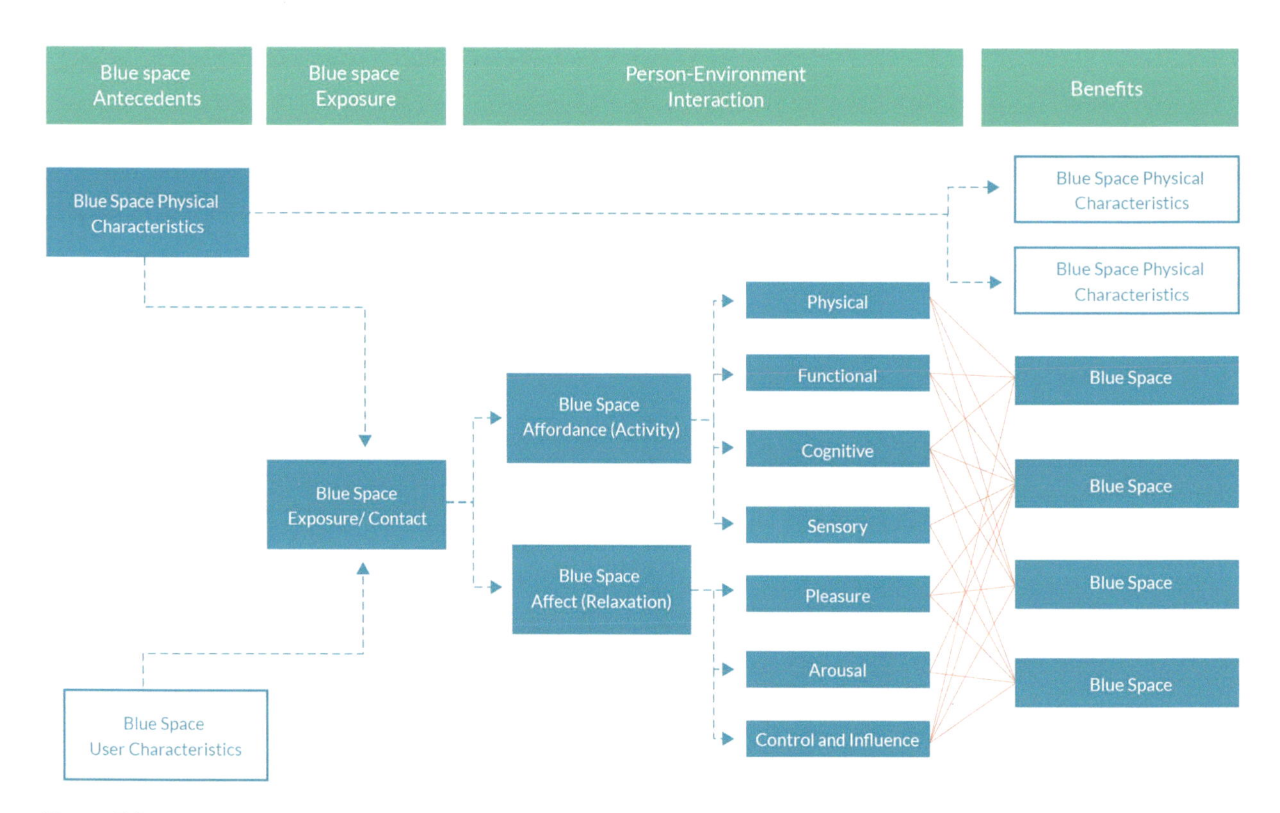

Figure 5.2

An interaction model for Blue Space use for physical activities and relaxation. The unshaded boxes are potential blue space benefits unrelated to the person-environment interaction

(*Source*: Himansu Sekhar Mishra and Anna Wilczyńska)

Development of the BEAT structure

When reviewing and analysing the 17 tools as noted previously, a set of environmental aspects emerged to explain the structure, application and place characteristics and to provide an ontological framework. Generally, tools have a hierarchical structure based on a set of major topic themes or *domains* within which a selection of sub-themes or *aspects* can be found. These vary from tool to tool in how they are grouped and organised. Depending on the focus of a particular tool, some domains and aspects are represented in greater depth than others. The use of an equally weighted domain/aspect structure is one way of enabling the assessment results to be comparable and to be able to see where a site may score higher or lower in different aspects within a single domain and then across different domains. This also helps when making decisions about what to do with a place or space and where to prioritise actions such as physical or social interventions to improve it.

We selected the set of domains and aspects for the BEAT, identifying a number of areas which were weakly represented in the tool review in relation to the land-water interface, this being the focus of our new tool. We set up an overarching structure of *domains* as a relatively simple basis and then ensured, by reference back to the tool review and the categorisation of environment-behaviour interaction dimensions, that all *aspects* were covered.

BEAT structure and content

When considering how tools were applied, there tended to be two or three stages, such as a preliminary desk study to obtain information (maps, data, etc.) and to establish the site boundary to be assessed in context, followed by an initial visit to obtain first impressions and a general overview, followed by a more detailed on-site assessment. The BEAT follows this approach in four steps: 1) preliminary data about the site (macro-level assessment), 2) general site description (for first impressions), 3) on-site survey (micro-level assessment). The separate water/aquatic ecology part of the BEAT (Step 4) is presented separately due to its different origins later in the chapter.

BEAT structure for macro-level assessment

STEP 1: PRELIMINARY DATA ABOUT THE SITE

The preliminary data-gathering step is primarily a desktop study to explore the blue space context, type and surrounding components, including geographical attributes and regional climate, site accessibility and the role of the site in the city or regional level blue space structure. Locational and contextual blue space aspects identified at this stage are:

1. Location
2. Name of site, survey grid reference/GPS coordinates, area (ha)/length (m or km)
3. Blue space type(s) (according to a list used in the BlueHealth project)
4. Site context
    a. Brief description of the site, its current uses and general setting
    b. Historical information about the site
    c. Nature protection status, if any (Natura 2000, etc.)
    d. Symbolism and memory associated with the area, if available
    e. General description of the surrounding landscape and setting (built form, natural elements, etc.)
    f. General description of the water body and its wider connectivity in the hydrological system (character of the water, tidal or flow conditions, general quality)
    g. Accessibility to the site (terrestrial and water-borne)

5. The residential character of the neighbourhood (if relevant)
   a. Property types and ownership
   b. The population within 100 m, 500 m, 1 km (based on different walking times)
   c. Socioeconomic status
   d. Ethnic composition (may be a problem in some locations due to local sensitivities or absence of data – should be checked)
   e. Age structure of the population
6. Other green/blue connectivity (e.g. other green/blue spaces within 100 m, 500 m, 1 km of the site)
7. Tourism and recreational infrastructure and attractions within 1 km of the site

STEP 2: GENERAL SITE DESCRIPTION (FOR FIRST IMPRESSIONS)

This stage records a general description of the site under assessment, comprising a site map marked with different sub-areas or zones and calculated as percentages of the site. For a larger site, it may be necessary to subdivide it into major zones and repeat this for each.

The first impression of the site is recorded based on the condition and activities taking place at the time of the survey. This step is important because for visitors, a first impression says a lot about a place and affects attitudes towards it, and it also helps to put the detailed micro-assessment in context later on. Table 5.1 presents the aspects to be considered in this step.

BEAT structure for micro-level assessment: on-site survey

The main part of the assessment is conducted on-site after the initial walk-around and first impressions have been recorded in Step 2. This survey can be repeated, for example, before and after implementing a new design intervention or at different times of the year when activities may be different (e.g. winter vs. summer). Each domain has a specific set of aspects to be assessed and ways of assessing them.

Table 5.1 **Aspects of the environmental domain**

Aspects	*Assessment criteria*
Open water	Fresh/salt Tidal/non-tidal Running/still Depth
Riparian/water margin structure	Slopes (gradient) Embankments
Water edges	Trees Reeds Shingle Sand Concrete walls Rip-rap (large boulders or concrete blocks piled up to form a breakwater)
Terrestrial land cover	Grass Woodland Shrubs Hard surfaces
Paths and facilities within the site	Paths and benches Water access structures Buildings

SOCIAL DOMAIN

The social domain of the BEAT draws on different environment-behaviour interaction dimensions and includes key aspects of use and activities, safety and security and information and education. Use and activity indicate place support for different behavioural dimensions as well as social activities and cohesion. While perceived community and personal safety and security enhance or inhibit the use of a place, information and education support social benefits and help to promote use. The BEAT social domain aspects are presented in Table 5.2.

AESTHETIC DOMAIN

The spatio-psychological dimension focuses on visual aesthetics, place experience and comfort, as well as such non-visual aesthetics as place attributes that aid psychological restoration. The BEAT aesthetic domain aspects are presented in Table 5.3.

PHYSICAL DOMAIN

The physical domain draws on the spatio-physical, spatio-behavioural and management aspects within the environment-behaviour interaction model. Access and circulation relating to blue space can be enhanced through improving site accessibility, that is, site locations and access points, vehicular access and parking provisions and access and circulation within the site through creating access infrastructure, that is, the walking and cycle path network and accessibility to water and play areas. Ease of access for people with disabilities is an important determinant for place

Table 5.2 **Aspects of the social domain**

Aspects	*Assessment criteria*
Aspect 1: Use of the site and activities	• Activities taking place on land and on or in the water (direct evidence). Negative or anti-social activities, if seen, should also be recorded • Activities taking place from indirect evidence (if there are few or no people on the site at the time of the assessment visit), such as traces left behind or from talking to people on land and on or in the water • An estimate of how many and what kind of people are using the site (age and gender but not ethnicity) NB: Repeated visits across the year will reveal much more about the patterns of use.
Aspect 2: Information and education	• Presence, and usefulness of information such as signs • Presence and functionality of way-marking or directional signs • Presence and clarity of codes of conduct/rules and regulations • Interpretive structures giving information of value to visitors of a cultural, historical or environmental nature • Accessibility of information for people with different types of disability • Presence of information in a range of languages
Aspect 3: Safety and security	• Physical safety and security against traffic and along water edges • Presence of water safety equipment and lifeguards • Presence and functionality of lighting • Sense of general security against crime or anti-social behaviour • Presence of vandalism or damage signalling lack of security • Presence of threatening people • Signs of alcohol or drug use

Table 5.3 **Aspects of the aesthetic domain**

Aspects	*Assessment criteria*
Aspect 1: Visual condition of the surroundings of the site	• Visual quality of buildings and other structures visible along the site boundaries (landside) • Screening of off-site eyesores by trees and vegetation (see guidance for definition of an eyesore) • Quality of views out from the site across the water • Sense of openness and scale of water views • Presence of focal points visible from the site • Visual pollution (such as garish advertising)
Aspect 2: Visual quality of the site	• Quality of views within the site • Quality of views to the site from the water • Visual quality of built structures within the site • Attractiveness of vegetation on the site • Light pollution at night (from outside sources) • Sense of wildness
Aspect 3: Non-visual aesthetic aspects	• Smells and olfactory pollution • Sounds and noise pollution • Sense of atmosphere: wind, moist air, etc. • Feeling of tranquillity or calmness

success, which includes universal design considerations for paths and access routes and access to water, facilities and amenities. The terrestrial and water-based recreation structure aspect assesses all public, recreational and sports amenities and facilities present within the blue space. The management aspect covers site maintenance and sustainable practices. This domain covers the terrestrial part of the site and includes all constructed elements as presented in Table 5.4.

SELECTION OF MEASUREMENT TYPES

For the BEAT measurement and recording system, a 5-point rating scale is used where the quality of an aspect is important, as well as presence/absence and multiple choice checklists. For each aspect, comments and observations can also be added to supplement the scoring. This helps to establish a common means of comparing all aspects within each domain and between sites to make the analysis process simpler and to produce clear comparative graphics.

Aquatic ecology part of the BEAT

This final part of the BEAT – Step 4 – is different in concept and addresses aquatic ecology. It includes a calculation of the condition of the water body as a final output. The main objective of the BEAT aquatic ecology section is to take a snapshot of water quality by assessing the condition of standing, running and marine water body(ies). The water quality assessment can be carried out using online forms and guidance notes that are freely available to be downloaded from the BEAT website (www.beat.bluehealth.tools/).

The tool starts by defining three main water body types: 1) Standing water like lakes, ponds and pools of natural origin containing fresh (i.e. non-saline), brackish or saltwater, including freshwater bodies (i.e. artificially created lakes and reservoirs, provided that they contain semi-natural aquatic communities). 2) Running waters, including springs, streams, rivers, canals and temporary watercourses. 3) Marine ecosystems defined by blue spaces that include marine habitat directly connected to oceans, seas and bays and estuaries. Marine waters may be fully saline,

Table 5.4 **Aspects of the physical domain**

Aspects	*Assessment criteria*
Aspect 1: Access and circulation within the site	• Access roads within the site • On-site car parking and its functional accessibility • Boat launching access and ramps • Footpath network and its functional accessibility (layout, desire lines, etc.) • Cycle path network and its functional accessibility (layout, desire lines, etc.) • Path construction and use of materials • Physical condition of paths (state of surfacing)
Aspect 2: Accessibility for disabled people	• Physical disabilities • Blind and partially sighted • Deaf and hearing impaired • Mental and learning disabilities
Aspect 3: Terrestrial recreation structures (visual quality, functionality, condition)	Presence or absence of: toilets, changing rooms, changing cubicles, cafe/restaurant, fountain, art installation, children's play area, safety equipment store, watchtower, observation deck, food and ice cream stall
Aspect 4: Water access and recreational structures (visual quality functionality, condition)	Presence or absence of: boat slipway, jetty, pier, dock edges, marinas, harbour or other retaining wall, bridge, lock, paddling pool, swimming pool
Aspect 5: Management and maintenance	• Maintenance of hard surfaces • Management of vegetation • Maintenance of street furniture • Site maintenance in general (litter, dog mess) • Maintenance of play areas • Maintenance of safety equipment

brackish or almost fresh. Marine habitats include those below the spring high tide limit (or below the water level in non-tidal waters) and enclosed coastal saline or brackish waters without a permanent surface connection to the sea but either with intermittent surface or sub-surface connections (as in lagoons).

The aspects selected for evaluation provide a snapshot of the ecological status of different aquatic environments. The water quality assessment processes includes monitoring, surveying, and surveillance, all based on data collection. The BEAT aquatic ecology section provides a multi-objective monitoring system based on an inventory of indicators pertaining to aspects such as 1) sedimentation or substrate types, 2) possible impacts of human activities on watercourses, 3) level of ecosystem services and 4) the quality and condition of abiotic and aquatic ecology. This assessment is achieved through a simple monitoring system using an on-site observation method.

The water quality is assessed by determining the physical, chemical and biological attributes of the water (EEA, 2012, 2018; Sivaranjani et al., 2015). The physical attributes can be defined by the shore and littoral conditions, land use and activities surrounding the water body, whereas the chemical and ecological attributes are defined through the abiotic and ecological conditions.

The water quality of a water body is directly dependent on the condition of its basin, its littoral zone or shore zone – its substrate. The substrate types and amount explain the extent of human-induced modifications near to the water and their impact on the water body. The substrate conditions predict possible erosion or anthropogenic activities, and its quantity, quality and characteristics affect the physical, chemical and biological integrity of the aquatic ecosystem.

There are several methods available to assess the human impact (i.e. hydrological, morphological and landscape indicators) on the water quality of surface water bodies, which has been considered an external influence (Zhao et al., 2020), and many indicators have been developed to quantify the human impact on surface water quality, for example, the impact on river systems. The indicators of human impact on water bodies can reflect different types of disturbances which may negatively affect the aquatic ecological status. Changes in surface water levels might depend on climatic factors (i.e. dry periods) or human effects in the case of standing waters (Davraz et al., 2019) and obstruction of watercourses and water extraction in the case of running water, for example. The main threats that aquatic ecosystems face are due to water pollution, biological invasion of exotic species, direct human activities (such as rubbish dumping), land-use changes, the extent of the urban area and socioeconomic developments and agricultural activities that pollute water bodies through point sources (e.g. waste pipes) and non-point sources (e.g. nutrient discharge) (da Silva et al., 2020; Cooke et al., 2020).

Aquatic environments support life systems for many forms of habitat and have historically attracted human settlements and their activities. Aquatic ecosystem services and patterns in ecosystem services differ across aquatic systems. There are multiple factors such as population growth, changes in land use and agricultural and urban expansion that affect the provisioning, regulating, cultural services and human health and well-being benefits (Aznar-Sánchez et al., 2019). There are both positive and negative ecosystem services that, if used or present, could adversely affect the ecological status of a water body.

Aquatic abiotic conditions and outputs that mediate biological services have greater implications for spatial planning, management and decision-making (Teixeira et al., 2019). For example, coastal ecosystems contribute to a substantial proportion of global ecosystem services (Liquete et al., 2013), and a recent EU Member States report suggest that more than 70% of the coastal habitats are assessed as having an unfavourable status (European Union, 2017). Overall, the effect of factors on the aquatic condition such as water temperature (Meshesha et al., 2020) and the fluctuation and the level of water may be connected to the health of the littoral habitat and the whole aquatic biological community (Gownaris et al., 2018). Turbidity explains the reduced water clarity, especially in inland waters, that occurs due to the presence of suspended matter that absorbs or obstructs downwelling light and, as a result, affects phytoplankton productivity and adversely influences zooplankton production and fish feeding (Grobbelaar, 2009). Poor land management alongside water bodies leads to soil erosion, increases water pollution and siltation and degrades water quality by increasing organic matter and nutrients (Issaka & Ashraf, 2017).

Biological indicators are direct measures of the health of the fauna and flora in a water body. Biological and ecological indicators can be useful in evaluating the health status of water bodies (Parmar et al., 2016), and in the EU, biotic ones are prioritised (European Parliament 2000). This may be determined through observation of conditions, for example, domination of emergent plants; floating and floating-leaved plants; presence of invasive species; plants covered with periphyton; floating filamentous algae; dead fish on the shore; presence of waterfowl; submerged plants; presence of amphibians, fish, aquatic mammals, mussels and aquatic insects; and microbiological parameters.

Several established methods assess the ecological and aesthetic quality, and the condition of the riparian zone ascertains the health status of the water body (Saha et al., 2020). Therefore, any promotion of recreational use of coastal or inland waters or building infrastructure requires an assessment of its abiotic and biological condition and the existing ecosystem services of the aquatic environment.

According to how all these factors can be combined into a single, simple-to-administer system, the final part of the BEAT in Step 4 has been developed and tested. It is subdivided into three different aquatic types, with

Table 5.5 **Aspects for assessing the aquatic ecosystem quality for the domain of standing waters**

Domain of standing fresh waters	*Aspects*
Aspect 1: Substrate of the water body	• Substrate of shore zone (lakeside) • Substrate of littoral zone (lakeshore) (The main idea is that there are good, natural substrates and other substrate types that are indicative of moderate or high human impact.)
Aspect 2: Human impact	• Buildings and infrastructure • Agricultural impact • Leisure and recreation • Infrastructure for water management There are some indicators that are positive if present and others that influence a water body negatively if they are present or nearby.
Aspect 3: Ecosystem services (rapid assessment)	• Provisioning services • Regulating and maintaining services • Cultural services
Aspect 4: Biotic and ecological aspects	• Air and water temperature (for background information: if it is not possible to measure these indicators, then they are not needed for assessment) • Water level. For the ecosystem, the average water level is best, because this is natural and usually, in normal conditions, the dominant water level. A higher or lower water level (over or above average) can be an indicator of human impact or weather changes (it can be the influence of climate change, indirectly) • Hydro-physical indicators. This concerns water turbidity, bad smell of water, waste water discharge into water body and erosion • Biological indicators. These mostly concern the different types of plants (emergent, floating and floating-leaved, submerged plants), the presence of wildlife, microbiological parameters and invasive species

parallel assessment criteria and a scoring system which can be used to provide the overall answer as to the current status of the water body and its ecology. Tables 5.5–5.7 present the assessment criteria for each of the three domains.

THE TERRESTRIAL ASSESSMENT PRINCIPLES AND METHOD

As already noted, the assessment method involves a combination of objective and subjective evaluations, many linked to a set of 5-point scales. Some aspects record the presence or absence of an activity; others ask for the relative importance of an activity compared with others taking place, without the need to carry out detailed observations or counts over time. Each aspect within each domain is scored on this scale, and the output is in most cases (where there is a 5-point scale) a spidergraph showing the relative values for the domain as a whole in an easy-to-understand and easily comparable format. On the scale 5, always means that the aspect is in excellent condition, 1 means very poor condition and 3 average condition. A zero means it is not present or not applicable. For the subjective aspects, a set of questions is used to focus on the factors to include in the evaluation, and text comments can be made for all aspects. The use of two (or more) surveyors is a means of achieving more reliable scoring than if a single surveyor

Table 5.6 **Aspects for assessing the aquatic ecosystem quality for the domain of fresh running waters**

Domain of running fresh waters	*Aspects*
Aspect 1: Substrate of the water body	• Substrate of shore zone (riverside) • Substrate of littoral zone (river shore)
Aspect 2: Human impact	• Buildings and infrastructure • Agricultural impact • Leisure and recreation • Infrastructure for water management
Aspect 3: Ecosystem services	• Provisioning services • Regulating and maintaining services • Cultural services
Aspect 4: Biotic and ecological aspects	• Air and water temperature • Water level • Hydro-physical indicators • Biological indicators

Table 5.7 **Aspects for assessing the aquatic ecosystem quality for the domain of marine ecosystems**

Domain of marine ecosystems	*Aspects*
Aspect 1: Substrate of the water body	• Substrate of shore zone (seaside) • Substrate of littoral zone (seashore)
Aspect 2: Human impact	• Buildings and infrastructure • Agricultural impact • Leisure and recreation • Infrastructure for water management • Water traffic
Aspect 3: Ecosystem services	• Provisioning services • Regulating and maintaining services • Cultural services
Aspect 4: Biotic and ecological aspects	• Air and water temperature is for background information, and if there is no possibility to measure these indicators, then these are not needed for assessment • Hydro-physical indicators. This concerns water turbidity and bad smell of water • Biological. Mostly concerning the different type of plants (emergent, floating and floating-leaved, submerged plants), the presence of wildlife, livestock at the seashore, macro-algae and invasive species

carried out the assessment and is strongly recommended. Figure 5.3 shows some examples of spidergraphs generated once the data have been entered for some aspects where the 5-point scale is used.In the terrestrial assessment, there is no attempt to produce a final or average score for the site as a whole: each domain and aspect is kept separate. However, for the water ecosystem assessment, an overall score is achieved by applying the system.

WATER ECOSYSTEM ASSESSMENT PRINCIPLES AND METHOD

For ecosystem health, the assessment principle is that it is good when negative indicators are absent from the assessment site. The assessment methodology is based on scores given by the evaluator for each aspect, using a 3-point scale. The best score is always 1, which means negative indicators are absent, while the lowest score is 3, meaning

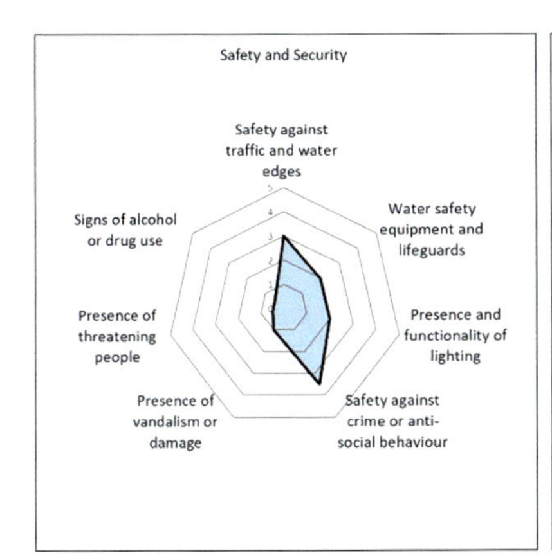

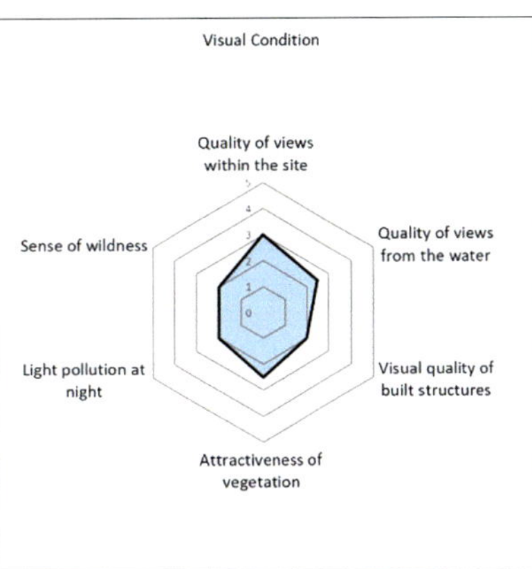

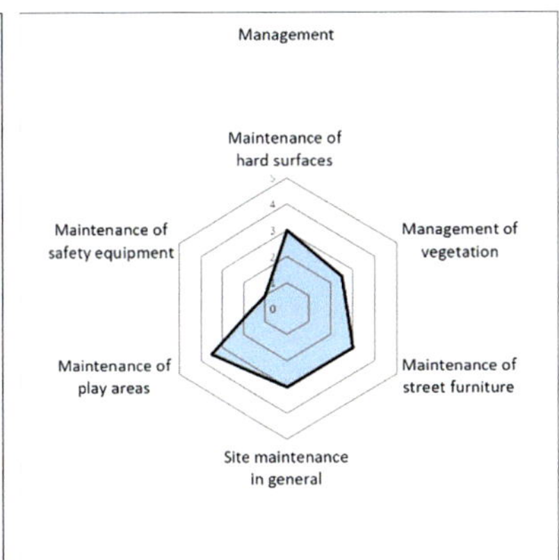

Figure 5.3

Examples of outputs of a site assessment for three aspects – safety and security, visual condition and management. These are clear and easy to understand, showing where a site does well or poorly and thus helping to identify where improvements are needed

(*Source*: Himansu S. Mishra)

negative indicators are present at the evaluation site (up to 200 metres distance from the water edge). The higher score therefore means a greater human impact on the water body.

After every aspect, the evaluator sums up the scores and looks for the corresponding Status Score Point on the scale. At the end of the assessment, the evaluator simply sums up the Status Score Points to find the overall status of the water body. The scale is the same for every aspect: good, moderate and poor.

The Good status indicates that the catchment area near the water body is natural or that there is no or very mild human impact.

The Moderate status indicates that near the water body, there is moderate human impact which can influence the ecosystem negatively (and therefore humans too).

The Poor status indicates that near the water body, there is high human impact which influences the ecosystem negatively.

Expert assessment, guidance and training

Since the BEAT comprises both objective and subjective aspects, it is preferable to involve at least two assessors so that independent assessments can be made and compared. Differences in opinion among the assessment team can then be discussed and final scores agreed on so as to ensure that personal biases do not unduly affect the final assessment.

To ensure a good-quality and replicable assessment, reading the guidance is necessary, followed by some practice and, ideally, training or guidance from people who have used it before. The guidance is essential for anyone using it for the first time, especially for those aspects which tend to be innately more subjective – such as visual aesthetics – where past experience or the assessor's personal standard for beauty, assuming aesthetics or beauty to be an intrinsic physical attribute of that specific environmental setting, may need to be calibrated. It can also be assumed that local experts have knowledge on local culture, social norms and the meanings that local people attach to the place besides their in-depth knowledge of the relevant domain or topic.

It is also possible that planners might encourage communities to participate through "citizen science" and work together to collect data and to monitor sites. This method is used to collect data on urban wildlife by, for example, counting birds or other species. Indeed, some members of local communities are knowledgeable about some areas, such as bird watchers or those engaged in recreational fishing, for example, whose expertise or tacit knowledge might be capitalised upon for the purpose of collecting good-quality data.

The training protocol involves in-office training for two hours, briefing on the detailed BEAT manual and guidance; familiarisation with the assessment items, steps and processes involved in an assessment; operational aspects of the online tool and on-site survey; safety precautions to be taken during the site survey; and illustrative examples of ways of presenting results.

Community assessment, guidance and training

For community groups, it is a good idea if someone with training helps to lead or facilitate the assessment. For Step 1, it may be helpful if the local authority or municipality can provide some of the information, while other materials may be collected or already known by community members. If for Step 2, first unbiased impressions are impossible, due to over-familiarity, then it may be useful to invite people from elsewhere to come and give a fresh opinion. Steps 3 and 4, the on-site assessments, may be done by as many people as would like to do them, and then the results can be compared, for example, in a round-table discussion. From this, an agreed-upon set of scores – or an agreement to differ – should be assembled and used for the stimulation of ideas for, for example, the regeneration of the site, perhaps using the concept of urban acupuncture (see Chapter 15) or for listing management activities which could be carried out by the community. The guidance document downloadable from the website explains what each aspect means.

The online interface for carrying out the survey is available at www.beat.bluehealth.tools/ and at https://bluehealth2020.eu/projects/ – and anyone can use it free of charge. The on-site survey data can be entered online via a tablet or smartphone using mobile data services. A paper version of the survey questions is also available to download and use on-site, allowing the recorded data to be uploaded to the BEAT website later.

Examples of application of the BEAT

In this section, we provide some worked examples of both BEAT assessment systems: Step 3 of the terrestrial BEAT for three key domains to illustrate how the rating scales and scoring work and Step 4. Each project is briefly described, and the results are presented to illustrate the kind of result and how they are presented.

The examples here illustrate three different blue space types: for standing water, a linear urban lake in Tartu, Estonia, with a surrounding green area; for running water, a river and fluvial park and promenade in Barcelona, Spain; and for the marine environment, a coastal tidal beach and marina abutting an open park and children's play area in Plymouth, United Kingdom. The examples represent different geo-climatic regions and different cultural settings. The results presented here are divided into two separate sections 1) BEAT Step 3: terrestrial quality assessment of the blue space and 2) BEAT Step 4: aquatic environmental quality assessment of blue spaces. The terrestrial environmental quality is demonstrated for three blue space domains: physical, social and aesthetic. The aquatic environmental quality domains used for the assessment are substrate quality, human impact, ecosystem services, abiotic factors and water ecology.

Study areas

We present the three study areas first in order to give the context and different conditions, after which the assessment results will be presented as comparisons.

Standing water environment: Anne Kanal, Tartu, Estonia

Anne Kanal is located in the city of Tartu and is an artificial lake constructed during the development of the adjacent Annelinn neighbourhood – an urban extension project – during the 1970s. Today the place offers many outdoor and water-based recreation opportunities for the community living nearby as well for the whole city of Tartu. The site is very accessible by public transport, foot, bicycle and car. It is well connected to the surrounding neighbourhood and city centre shopping district and very well used by large numbers of locals and tourists throughout the year. The place constitutes three distinct geographical units and activity zones. 1) The eastern and northern canal-side recreational zone with a beach, beach facilities and amenities, parking, walking paths, a children's play area, ball game courts and water access infrastructure. 2) The western and southern zone is a strip of land lying between Anne Kanal and the River Emajõgi (to which it is connected) with a walking and cycling path, a vegetated riparian edge and overgrown reed beds, seating spaces and picnic shelters. 3) The lake itself with shallow and deep sections. Figure 5.4 shows the location and setting of Anne Kanal with the three zones.

The water quality of the lake is sufficient for bathing, and it is used for many water-based activities, such as swimming and water sports in summer, and when frozen, it is used for ice-dipping and ice fishing in winter. The area surrounding the lake is extensively used for running, walking, cycling, playing ball games, informal play, children's play,

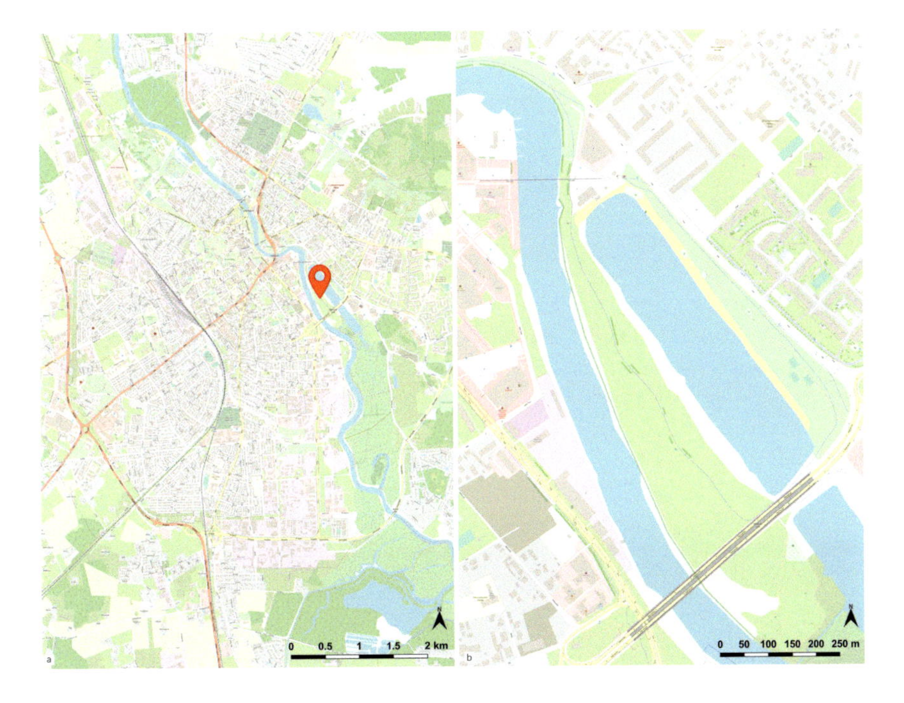

Figure 5.4a and b

a) Location of Anne Kanal in the city of Tartu; b) a close-up of the surveyed area showing the three main zones

(*Source*: © OpenStreetMap CC-BY-SA)

relaxing and fishing and for skiing, skating and other winter activities. Compared to the northern and eastern parts of the lake, the western and southern parts are kept more natural, with dense vegetation patches and a wide reed- and willow-dominated riparian edge. Water accessibility and visibility are higher on the northern and eastern parts of the lake compared to the western and southern sections. Despite the rich natural setting, the site is very urban, with a dominating visual and olfactory experience of urban features and functions.

The water body sedimentation or substrate is mostly sandy and free of mud or the presence of technosol. The major adverse human impacts that can be found are the nearby presence of housing, buildings, maintained landscape, road and parking areas, concrete structures and the presence of rubbish and litter within the site and water. The ecosystem services of the aquatic environment at Anne Kanal can be rated as moderate based on the low level of use in the reed bed areas, a large quantity of water exchange with the river, the presence of some protected species and the water quality being sufficient for bathing and fishing. The majority of the indicators suggest that negative ecosystem services are absent, except for the existence of infrastructure and the presence of recreation facilities. In terms of its hydrological and physical condition, Anne Kanal water is not particularly turbid and does not smell bad or have visible erosion around the water body. Poor biological and ecological indicators were not found to be present, such as invasive species, floating algae or dead fish. The health of water ecology was scored as moderate due to many indicators not being directly present, except for amphibians. Figure 5.5a–d shows some views of Anne Kanal identifying the different parts.

Figure 5.5a–d

Anne Kanal, Tartu, a) Shows the running and cycle path along the edge between the housing public road and lake; b) is the section on either side with the reed and willows along the lake edge; c) shows the swimming facilities; d) is the beach area with play equipment. The photos were taken in October 2019 on a weekday, which is why the site is empty

(*Source*: Himansu S. Mishra)

Northern Besós Fluvial Park, Barcelona

The case study focuses on a canalised stretch of the Besós River, located in the urban context of the Montcada I Reixach municipality, part of the Barcelona metropolitan area. Montcada is a relatively poor municipality which was severely affected by flooding in the 1960s, as a result of which it was canalised and regulated, leading to its present engineered configuration with artificial sloping banks on both sides and a broad bottom to the corridor which allows flood waters to build up without overflowing into nearby areas. The site symbolises the link between the river stretch near Montcada due to its geomorphological configuration. The site is asymmetrical to the river axis. To one side is the urban area, formed of low-cost housing in five- to seven-storey blocks built originally for the workers of the nearby Valentine factory. The other side maintains a somewhat more natural aspect connected to the marine natural park at the river mouth. Until the 1960s, the Besós River was a dynamic, braided river with a bed of shifting gravel deposits and poor water quality due to pollution from industries sited along the upper stretches. The site is now a fluvial park with improved public accessibility, which was developed as a community intervention project. The river is now protected by Natura 2000 and by the ACA (Agència Catalana de l'Aigua), which manages all uses and activities along it. The stretch used for demonstrating the BEAT can be divided into two distinct zones: 1) an upper zone above the retaining embankments with a pathway, urban park, parking and informal and formal play areas and 2) a lower fluvial park within the river basin, containing different biotopes of dense vegetation, grass, a concrete and gravel pathway, concrete steps and ramps which were constructed to allow access into and out of the lower park. The water body is now reduced to a regulated channel managed by a system of dams, with defined grass and riparian vegetated areas on both sides. The water quality is still considered poor, and the place does not offer any water-based activities. The lower fluvial park is primarily used for walking, cycling, dog walking and playing with dogs. The upper zone offers excellent views of the lower fluvial park and the surrounding areas. There is a flood warning system in place in case a flash flood occurs, to allow people in the effluvial park time to escape. Figure 5.6a and b shows the location of the stretch which was assessed within its wider context.

The sedimentation type within the fluvial park is a mix of clay and gravel, suggesting a good substrate type. In terms of human impact on water quality, most of the activities can be found within a distance range of 200 to 1000 m; therefore, the impact of human activities can be considered low according to the criteria. Major human impact concerns spotted during the assessment were the presence of rubbish and pollution, wastewater discharge and the modified river bed. In terms of positive ecosystem services, endangered species have been found at the site and the nearby protected area. Some of the negative ecosystem services identified at the site include the artificial modification of the water body, non-point and point source pollution, wastewater discharge (from a nearby sewage works), construction and obstruction of the watercourse. In terms of hydrological and physical indicators, there were unpleasant smells and visible erosion observed there. Some of the negative biological and ecological indicators suggest poor health of the watercourse through the presence of invasive species. Positive indicators observed at the site include the presence of amphibians, fish, aquatic mammals and insects. Figure 5.7a–d shows some views of the Besós fluvial park.

Teats Hill, Plymouth

Teats Hill in Plymouth, United Kingdom, a waterfront project jointly funded by Plymouth's Active Neighbourhood Project (Plymouth City Council) and the BlueHealth project, was chosen for BEAT testing. As an urban waterfront, Teats Hill has been a long-neglected public space. It is surrounded by institutional and residential land use, exposed to the sea on the southern side, and the site lacked quality and attractiveness. As an experimental project within BlueHealth, it received substantial improvement, before which, and as part of the planning, it was assessed. It is a historically and environmentally rich site situated opposite the famous Mayflower Steps and host to abundant marine wildlife. The site can be divided into four geographical and activity zones: 1) the park with seating facilities, access

Figure 5.6a and b

a) Location of the Besós River within the Barcelona metropolitan area; b) the assessed stretch within its local context

(*Source*: © OpenStreetMap CC-BY-SA)

path and slip road; 2) children's play area, with play equipment, ball court, green informal play areas; 3) the beach, with an old disused boat slipway, gravel beach and shingle; and 4) the water, with the marina. The access to the slipway was blocked with big stones, and aspects of the site had fallen into disrepair, such as the damaged slipway, overgrown vegetation, a degraded beach, excessive seaweed growth and a park environment mainly used by the local community for dog walking and incidental visits. The aquatic space was less used for water-based activities, and the existing marina was the main source of water pollution. The beach collects a huge amount of urban litter and is subject to high tidal variability. The beach can only be accessed via the slip road, as the length of the waterfront has an rocky cliff formation. The site provides excellent views of the old town, marina and bay. Figure 5.8a and b shows the location of Teats Hill within the city of Plymouth and its local context.

The marine substrates were found to be a combination of rock and gravel, which is considered good. Negative human impacts were identified as the presence of buildings, housing, maintained grassland, parking areas, sedimentation, beach activities, boating, drainage disposal, artificial shore protection, artificial objects in the water, rubbish, pollution and water traffic. In terms of positive ecosystem services, the site provides many as a result of the presence of the marine protection zone, natural sedimentation, tidal activity and the water being

Figure 5.7a–d

Views of the Northern Besós Fluvial Park, Barcelona, a) Shows the wide valley park with the river running within, occupying a narrow proportion of the bottom; b) shows the profile of the engineered slopes with a recently added access ramp and steps allowing use of the fluvial park below: c) is a closer view of the river showing the character of the riparian edges, while d) shows the upper linear park on the top of the embanked valley sides in the residential sector

(*Source*: Himansu S. Mishra)

suitable for swimming. Negative ecosystem services were found present at the site, including the presence of concrete structures, boating activities and point and diffuse sources of pollution and wastewater discharge points. The hydrological and physical condition of the site was found to be good. In terms of negative biological and ecological indicators, invasive species were present at the site, and the majority of positive indicators were present, except for a few, such as the absence of amphibians and aquatic mammals (seals visit but were not present at the time of assessment) that suggested good health of the water ecology. Figure 5.9a–d shows some views of Teats Hill.

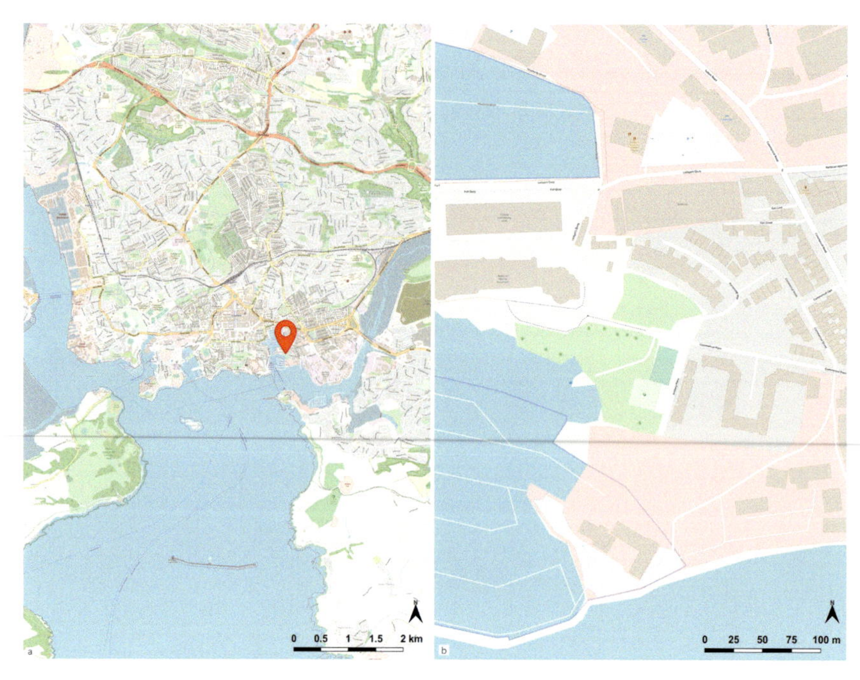

Figure 5.8a and b

a) The site location within the Plymouth urban area; b) the site in its local context

(*Source*: © OpenStreetMap CC-BY-SA)

Figure 5.9a–d

Teats Hill, Plymouth, a) an overview of the site showing the land-water interface with the shore slipway and cliffs; b) the grassy park with picnic tables and trees; c) the slip road leading down to the old slipway, now used for parking; d) the old slipway itself

(*Source*: Himansu S. Mishra)

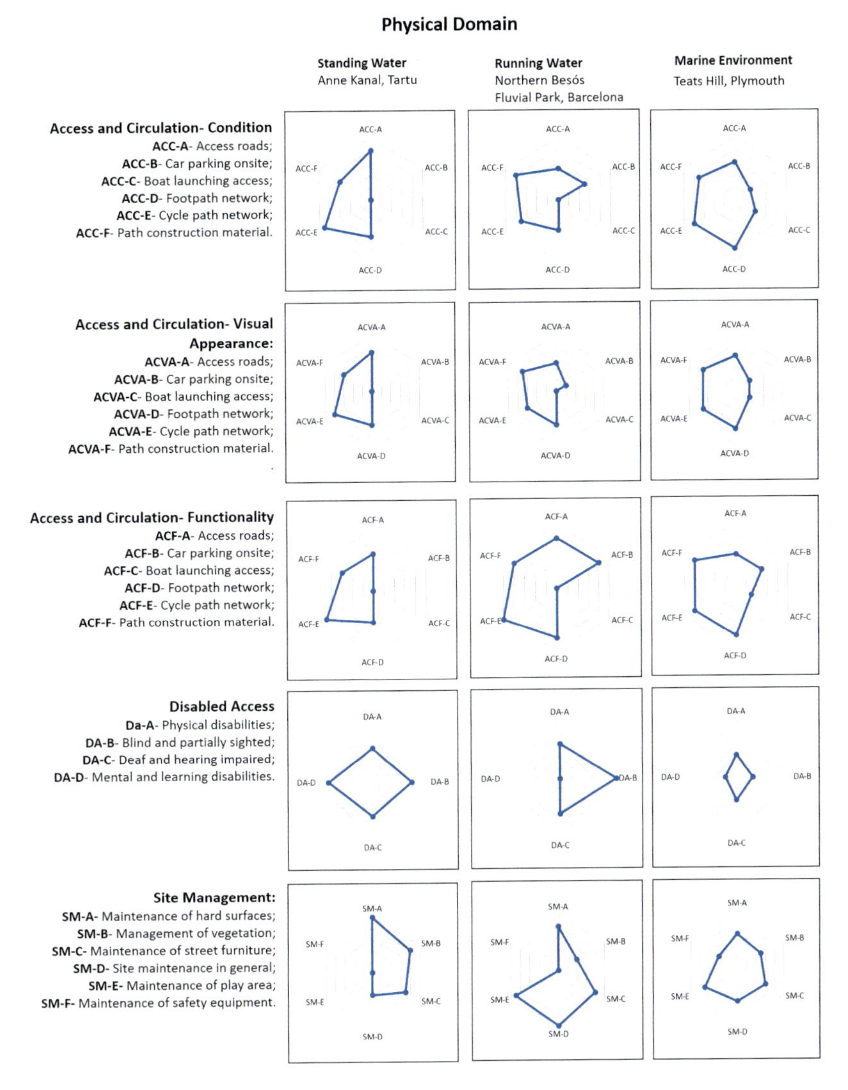

Figure 5.10

Assessment results of aspects of the physical domain of terrestrial blue spaces for the three demonstration sites

(*Source*: Himansu S. Mishra)

Example of results of Step 3: assessment results of the aspects of terrestrial blue space of three domains (physical, social, aesthetic) for each site

The examples here are for the three different water body types presented in the example projects. For standing water, it is Anne Kanal in Tartu; for running water, it is the Besós River in Barcelona; and for the marine environment, it is Teats Hill in Plymouth. Spidergrams presented in Figures 5.10–5.12 show the quality and condition of blue space attributes for different aspects. The aspects are clustered according to the different blue space domains and can be compared by looking at them side by side. The results suggest that even though there are differences in the quality and condition of blue space attributes within each blue space type, there are also similarities that can be observed across blue space types within the three domains: the physical (Figure 5.10), social (Figure 5.11) and aesthetic (Figure 5.12).

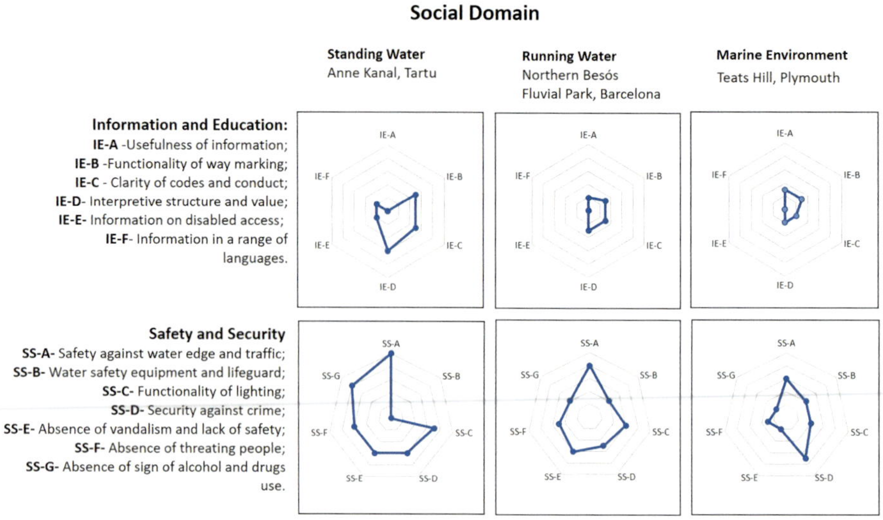

Social Domain

Standing Water
Anne Kanal, Tartu

Running Water
Northern Besós
Fluvial Park, Barcelona

Marine Environment
Teats Hill, Plymouth

Information and Education:
IE-A -Usefulness of information;
IE-B -Functionality of way marking;
IE-C - Clarity of codes and conduct;
IE-D- Interpretive structure and value;
IE-E- Information on disabled access;
IE-F- Information in a range of languages.

IE-A IE-B IE-C IE-D IE-E IE-F

Safety and Security
SS-A- Safety against water edge and traffic;
SS-B- Water safety equipment and lifeguard;
SS-C- Functionality of lighting;
SS-D- Security against crime;
SS-E- Absence of vandalism and lack of safety;
SS-F- Absence of threating people;
SS-G- Absence of sign of alcohol and drugs use.

SS-A SS-B SS-C SS-D SS-E SS-F SS-G

Figure 5.11
Assessment results of aspects of the social domain of terrestrial blue spaces for the three demonstration sites
(*Source*: Himansu S. Mishra)

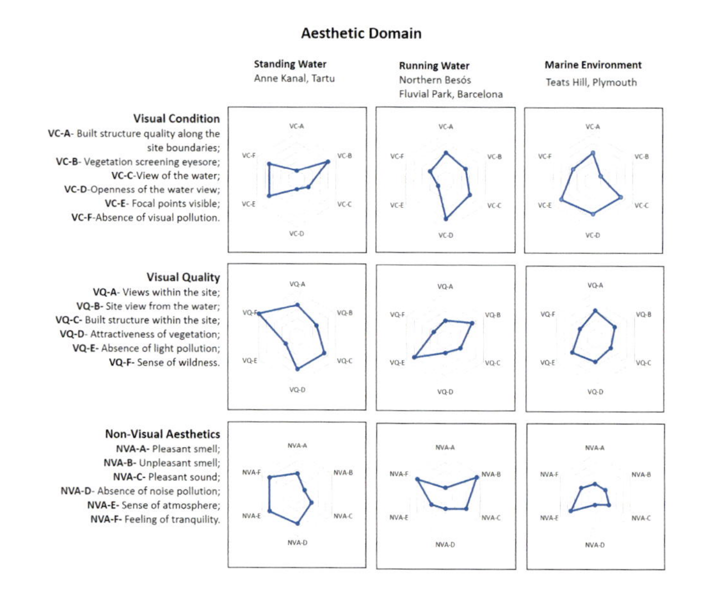

Figure 5.12
Assessment results of aspects of the aesthetic domain of terrestrial blue spaces for the three demonstration sites
(*Source*: Himansu S. Mishra)

Table 5.8 **Results of the assessments of the standing and running water and marine environment demonstration sites**

		Standing water		*Fresh running water*		*Marine environment*	
		Anne Kanal, Tartu		*Northern Besòs Fluvial Park, Barcelona*		*Teats Hill, Plymouth*	
Aspect status score points standing			Points		Points		Points
Substrate	Good	1	2	1	2	1	2
	Moderate	2	4	2	4	2	4
	Poor	3	6	3	6	3	6

Example of results of Step 4: assessment results for three types of water environments

The results for the BEAT Step 4 assessment of aquatic environmental quality of each demonstration site are presented in Table 5.2. The results show a variety of different scores for the input variables and the final results at the time the assessments were made. Of the examples, all sites turned out to be moderate in quality. This is to be expected when all the water bodies are in urban settings with many man-made impacts in their immediate vicinity.

Conclusions

This chapter has presented the need for, the rationale behind and the development and application of a new tool for assessing blue spaces. It has been extensively tested in numerous locations around Europe and beyond, and we have received feedback and reviews from many people. This has helped us to refine the tool and its user-friendliness, as well as helping us ensure that the guidance is comprehensible for users of different types. It has proved versatile and can be used by both professionals and communities.

		Standing water		Fresh running water		Marine environment	
		Anne Kanal, Tartu		Northern Besòs Fluvial Park, Barcelona		Teats Hill, Plymouth	
Human impact	Good	1	29–47	1	30–50	1	31–52
	Moderate	2	48–67	2	51–70	2	53–74
	Poor	3	68–87	3	71–90	3	75–93
Ecosystem services	Good	1	16–26	1	16–26	1	21–35
	Moderate	2	27–37	2	27–37	2	36–50
	Poor	3	38–48	3	38–48	3	51–63
Biological and ecological aspects	Good	1	19–31	1	10–16	1	12–19
	Moderate	2	32–44	2	17–23	2	20–28
	Poor	3	45–57	3	24–30	3	29–36
Sum of Score points and status		7	*Moderate*	7	*Moderate*	8	*Moderate*

Sum of score points present the ecological status of water body (i.e. 4–5 points for Good status, 6–9 points for Moderate status and 10–12 points for Poor status)

References

Aznar-Sánchez, J. A., Velasco-Muñoz, J. F., Belmonte-Ureña, L. J., & Manzano-Agugliaro, F. (2019). The worldwide research trends on water ecosystem services. *Ecological Indicators*, 99, 310–323.

Bakker, I., van der Voordt, T., Vink, P., & de Boon, J. (2014). Pleasure, arousal, dominance: Mehrabian and Russell revisited. In *Current psychology*. New York: Springer Science+Business Media.

Berto, R. (2014). The role of nature in coping with psycho-physiological stress: A literature review on restorativeness, *Behavioral Science*, 4, 394–409.

Cooke, S. J., Bergman, J. N., Nyboer, E. A., Reid, A. J., Gallagher, A. J., Hammerschlag, N., . . . Vermaire, J. C. (2020). Overcoming the concrete conquest of aquatic ecosystems. *Biological Conservation*, 247, 108589.

da Silva, F. L., Stefani, M. S., Smith, W., Schiavone, D. C., da Cunha-Santino, M. B., & Bianchini Jr, I. (2020). An applied ecological approach for the assessment of anthropogenic disturbances in urban wetlands and the contributor river. *Ecological Complexity*, 43, 100852

Davraz, A., Sener, E., & Sener, S. (2019). Evaluation of climate and human effects on the hydrology and water quality of Burdur Lake, Turkey. *Journal of African Earth Sciences*, 158, 103569.

European Union. (2017). *Life and coastal habitats*. Luxembourg: European Commission Environment Directorate General, European Union.

European waters – Assessment of status and pressures. (2012). EEA report. No 8/2012. European Environmental Agency. 100 pp.

European waters. Assessment of status and pressures. (2018). EEA report. No 7/2018. European Environmental Agency. 90 pp.

Frumkin, H., Bratman, G. N., Breslow, S. J., Cochran, B., Kahn Jr, P. H., Lawler, J. J., . . . Wood, S. A. (2017). Nature contact and human health: A research agenda. *Environmental Health Perspectives*, 125(7).

Gibson, J. J. (1979). *The theory of affordances. The ecological approach to visual perception*. Boston: Houghton Mifflin.

Gownaris, N. J., Rountos, K. J., Kaufman, L., Kolding, J., Lwiza, K. M., & Pikitch, E. K. (2018). Water level fluctuations and the ecosystem functioning of lakes. *Journal of Great Lakes Research*, 44(6), 1154–1163.

Grobbelaar, J. U. (2009). Turbidity. In G. Likens, M. E. Benbow, T. M. Burton, E. Van Donk, J. A. Downing, & R. D. Gulati (Eds.), *Encyclopedia of inland waters*. Amsterdam: Elsevier BV.

Hartig, T., Mitchell, R., de Vries, S., & Frumkin, H. (2014). Nature and health. *Annual Review of Public Health*, 35, 207–228.

Hartson, R. (2003). Cognitive, physical, sensory, and functional affordances in interaction design. *Behaviour & Information Technology*, 22(5), 315–338.

Issaka, S., & Ashraf, M. A. (2017). Impact of soil erosion and degradation on water quality: A review. *Geology, Ecology, and Landscapes*, 1(1), 1–11.

Korpela, K. M., Ylén, M., Tyrväinen, L., & Silvennoinen, H. (2008). Determinants of restorative experiences in everyday favourite places. *Health & Place*, 14, 636–652.

Liquete, C., Zulian, G., Delgado, I., Stips, A., & Maes, J. (2013). Assessment of coastal protection as an ecosystem service in Europe. *Ecological Indicators*, 30, 205–217.

Meshesha, T. W., Wang, J., & Melaku, N. D. (2020). Modelling spatiotemporal patterns of water quality and its impacts on aquatic ecosystem in the cold climate region of Alberta, Canada. *Journal of Hydrology*, 124952.

Mishra, H. S., Bell, S., Vassiljev, P., Kuhlmann, F., Niin, G., & Grellier, J. 2020. The development of a tool for assessing the environmental qualities of urban blue spaces. *Urban Forestry & Urban Greening*, 49.

Parmar, T. K., Rawtani, D., & Agrawal, Y. K. (2016). Bioindicators: The natural indicator of environmental pollution. *Frontiers in Life Science*, 9(2), 110–118.

Saha, D., Das, D., Dasgupta, R., & Patel, P. P. (2020). Application of ecological and aesthetic parameters for riparian quality assessment of a small tropical river in eastern India. *Ecological Indicators*, 117, 106627.

Sivaranjani, S., Rakshit, A., & Singh, S. (2015). Water quality assessment with water quality indices. *International Journal of Bioresource Science*, 2(2), 85–94.

Stokols, D. (2003). The ecology of human strengths. In Lisa G. Aspinwall & Ursula M. Staudinger (Eds.), *A psychology of human strengths: Fundamental questions and future directions for a positive psychology*. Washington, DC and London: American Psychological Association.

Teixeira, H., Lillebø, A. I., Culhane, F., Robinson, L., Trauner, D., Borgwardt, F., . . . O'Higgins, T. (2019). Linking biodiversity to ecosystem services supply: Patterns across aquatic ecosystems. *Science of the Total Environment*, 657, 517–534.

USDA. (2018). *Urban nature for human health and well-being, United States department of agriculture*. FS-1096. Washington, DC.

Zhao, Y., Zeng, L., Wei, Y., Liu, J., Deng, J., Deng, Q., . . . Li, J. (2020). An indicator system for assessing the impact of human activities on river structure. *Journal of Hydrology*, 582, 124547.

Appendix 1 Tools used to inform the development of the BEAT

	Tool name	Brief overview
1	Place Standard	**About the tool:** Place Standard, developed by the Scottish government, is an assessment tool developed to evaluate the quality of the place that is well established, undergoing change or still being planned and help evaluators to identify their priorities among interventions to improve the place. **Year:** 2015 **Web reference:** www.placestandard.scot/#/home
2	Green space strategies: a good practice guide	**About the tool:** Developed by the UK Commission on Architecture and the Built Environment (CABE), the tool was designed for public open or green space auditing and aimed to provide more of a snapshot of each space than a detailed analysis. **Year:** 2004 **Web reference:** http://webarchive.nationalarchives.gov.uk/20110118095356/http:/www.cabe.org.uk/files/green-space-strategies.pdf
3	Tools for evaluating impacts of Woodlands In and Around Towns (WIAT) interventions	**About the tool:** This evaluation tool focuses on a community-level evaluation of interventions aimed at improving woodlands to improve people's quality of life. **Year:** 2010 **Web reference:** www.openspace.eca.ed.ac.uk/research-projects/woods-in-and-around-towns/
4	Assessing the Sustainability of Public Space (ASPiS)	**About the tool:** The ASPiS Star Rating Tool originated in a project funded through the Lifelong Learning Programme of the EU to stimulate dialogue between urban citizens and professional architects and planners, with a focus on the sustainability of public open space. **Year:** 2010 **Web reference:** www.aspis-learn.eu/index.php

	Tool name	Brief overview
5	Quality of Public Open Space Tool (POST)	**About the tool:** The Quality of Public Open Space Tool (POST) was developed by the University of Western Australia for conducting environmental audits of public open spaces. **Year:** 2004 **Web reference:** www.see.uwa.edu.au/research/cbeh/projects/post **Reference:** Broomhall M, Giles-Corti B, Lange A (2004). Quality of Public Open Space Tool (POST). Perth, Western Australia: School of Population Health, The University of Western Australia.
6	Green Flag Award Scheme	**About the tool:** The Green Flag Award scheme is the benchmark national standard for parks and green spaces in England and Wales. It aims towards raising standards of green spaces. **Year:** Founded in 1996, updated 2009 **Web reference:** www.greenflagaward.org/about-us/about-green-flag-award/guidance-manual/
7	Blue Flag Award programme	**About the tool:** The Blue Flag programme for beaches and marinas is run by the international, non-governmental, non-profit organisation the Foundation for Environmental Education (FEE). It promotes sustainable development in freshwater and marine areas and aims to achieve high standards in the four categories water quality, environmental management, environmental education and safety. **Year:** 1985 **Web reference:** www.blueflag.global/criteria/
8	Landscape evaluation and quality surveys	**About the tool:** Developed by the Royal Geographical Society, this tool aims to assess people's reactions to and opinion about a particular development, different management strategies, quality of amenity, quality and suitability of services and perception of a place. **Year:** 2015 **Web reference:** www.rgs.org/OurWork/Schools/Fieldwork+and+local+learning/Fieldwork+techniques/Human+impact+studies.htm
9	Neighbourhood green space quality assessment tool	**About the tool:** This tool is published in the journal *Landscape and Urban Planning*. It was developed in Stroke-on-Trent, United Kingdom, for looking at green spaces at the neighbourhood level. **Year:** 2012 **Reference:** Gidlow, C.J., Ellis, N.J., Bostock, S., (2012), Development of the Neighbourhood Green Space Tool (NGST), *Landscape and Urban Planning*, 106, 347–358.
10	Urban stream condition	**About the tool:** This tool was presented in a conference paper as an outcome of research in Brazil. It is designed to provide a rapid evaluation method to assess the condition of a stream by identifying a set of indicators and parameters that may offer appropriate initiative and investment direction for restoration, conservation and protection of urban rivers and streams. **Year:** 2011 **Reference:** Pompêo, C. A., Rigotti, J. A. and Freitas Filho, M.D., (2011), Urban Stream Condition Assessment, 12nd International Conference on Urban Drainage, Porto Alegre/Brazil, 10–15 September 2011.

	Tool name	Brief overview
11	Model for assessment of public space quality in town centres	**About the tool:** This tool was developed by Polish researchers and presented in the journal *European Spatial Research and Policy*. It a model for assessment of the quality of public space in town centres based on studies of methods already used in Poland and abroad and constructs a set of criteria for assessment methods. **Year:** 2016 **Reference:** Wojnarowska, A., (2016), Model for assessment of public space quality in town centres, *European Spatial Research and Policy, 23*(1).
12	NATLAND: Evaluation of public spaces in urban areas	**About the tool:** This tool was developed as part of a master thesis and was itself derived from reviewing other methods. It was applied to the city of New Westminster, British Columbia, Canada. **Year:** 2007 **Reference:** Natland, J. (2007), Urban by Design: An Evaluation of Public Spaces in Downtown New Westminster, Simon Fraser University.
13	What Makes a Successful Place?	**About the tool:** The Project for Public Spaces (PPS) is a non-profit planning, design and educational organisation and developed a public space assessment tool after evaluating thousands of public spaces around the world. **Year:** 2009 **Web reference:** www.pps.org/reference/grplacefeat/
14	Local Action Toolkit: Ecosystem benefit assessment in urban water environments	**About the tool:** The Urban Catchment Partnerships, working with local communities, aims to enhance the value of natural capital in towns, cities and urban spaces. The toolkit was produced by the Westcountry Rivers Trust with funding from DEFRA and the Environment Agency to provide communities with evidence on the impacts, costs and benefits of natural capital/green infrastructure along with the methods to build consensus, facilitate local decision-making and secure funding for opportunities. **Year: 2015** **Web reference:** http://urbanwater-eco.services/project/urban-practitioners-toolbox/
15	Assessing social impacts in urban waterfront regeneration	**About the tool:** This tool, presented in the journal *Environmental Impact Assessment Review*, was developed by researchers in Finland for the purpose of conducting social impact assessments of waterfront developments. **Year:** 2006 **Reference:** Sairinen, R., Kumpulainene, S., (2006), Assessing social impacts in urban waterfront regeneration, *Environmental Impact Assessment Review*, 26, 120–135.
16	SpaceShaper	**About the tool:** Developed by the Commission for Architecture and the Built Environment (CABE), SpaceShaper provides a practical toolkit to measure the quality of a public space before investing time and money in improving it. **Year:**2007 **Web reference:** www.designcouncil.org.uk/resources/guide/spaceshaper-users-guide

	Tool name	Brief overview
17	Facebook 4 Urban Facelifts	**About the tool:** This tool was presented by researchers from Italy in the journal *International Journal of Global Environmental Issues*. It was developed around a case study and aims to assess the attractiveness of urban waterfronts. **Year:** 2015 **Reference:** Gravagnuolo, A., Biancamano, P.F., Angrisano, M. and Cancelliere, A. (2015) 'Assessment of waterfront attractiveness in port cities – Facebook 4 Urban Facelifts', *Int. J. Global Environmental Issues, Vol. 14*, Nos. 1/2, pp. 56–88.

Chapter 6: Observing behaviour for site planning and design

Peeter Vassiljev, Cristina Vert and Simon Bell

Introduction

One of the challenges facing planners and designers of outdoor public spaces is to know exactly for whom the space is being provided and how successful a space is once it has been developed. If a completely new space is being created, for example, at a former dockside to which no one had access, except for the dock workers, then designers must try to predict how and when a place might be used. Once implemented, however, it is possible, through the application of different tools, to measure the success of the project and the design. If, on the other hand, an existing public space is to be the focus of an improvement or regeneration project, it is extremely useful to be able to find out how people already use the site and then use this information alongside the assessment of the site itself, using, for example, the BlueHealth Environmental Assessment Tool (BEAT), which was presented in Chapter 5, to design the layout and programming of the site. Then, as in the previous example, an assessment of the success of the project can be gained.

Of course, when a larger-sized site is the subject of a project, it may be subdivided into different zones (e.g. functional, ecological or aesthetic) where there are different affordances for physical or social activity – places within the site which may also be known as "behaviour settings" (Barker, 1968). In addition, where a location has very pronounced seasonal differences, a site may be used very differently in, for example, summer or winter. Just walking around a site to observe casually what is going on will provide a general picture of its use, but something rather more systematic and reliable can provide valuable evidence for use in planning, design and management. When we add a desire to capture the health and well-being benefits provided by a public space, we must use another tool for this purpose. It needs to be a tool that helps to identify the range and amount of physical or social activities of different types being undertaken by different groups of users and may be able to convert some of this into calories expended by them. This could provide really valuable information. The generic name for this kind of data collection and analysis is "behaviour observation", and it has developed significantly over recent years to become a tool which not only relates well to theory but which has been developed methodologically and technically for both research and practical application in planning, design and management of public open spaces.

This chapter introduces and describes two methods and tools for capturing and mapping of behaviour by users of sites. The first method, the System for Observing Play and Recreation in Communities (SOPARC), is a tool already developed and in use by researchers who want to know how much and what kind of activity is being undertaken in parks (McKenzie et al., 2006). This tool was not developed for the BlueHealth project, but it was applied in one specific study, and the method and this application will be summarised here.

The second tool has different but related aims: to be able to link what people do, who does it, where they do it and when they do it both before and after the introduction of the social or spatial intervention. This approach goes beyond merely recording numbers of users engaged in different levels of physical activity to uncovering spatial,

DOI: 10.4324/9780429056161-9

temporal and weather-related associations between all kinds of passive and active behaviour, social groups and the physical locations or behaviour settings.

Environment–behaviour research using behaviour mapping for understanding the interaction between people and place was initially developed by Ittelson et al. (1970) to record behaviour in a design setting. Bechtel et al. (1987) noted the value of observational methods and behavioural mapping to identify kinds and frequencies of behaviour and to demonstrate their association with particular sites. Cooper Marcus and Francis (1998, p. 346) stated:

> with a very limited investment of time the investigator can achieve considerable insight into the actual use of designed places – a vast improvement over the conjecture and guesswork generated by studying a site plan from the remove of the studio or office.
>
> (1998: 346)

They emphasise its systematic approach, being based on function rather than aesthetics. Work on mapping use of public spaces was advanced by Goličnik and Ward Thompson (2010) in a study of squares and parks in Ljubljana and Edinburgh and also by Unt and Bell (2014) in their use of mapping of a single space in Tallinn at two time periods, before and after a so-called "urban acupuncture" spatial intervention – which was also the inspiration for the BlueHealth intervention case studies. There has also been extensive work by Cosco et al. (2010) on mapping the use of children's play areas, related to specific "behaviour settings" (Barker, 1968). One of the drawbacks of these methods is the fact that they are paper based, points have to be recorded using colours and symbols and analysis has been somewhat limited, especially statistical analysis. One of the strengths is the ability to show spatial patterns.

Some earlier behaviour mapping methods, for example, Project for Public Space (2005), involve dividing the mapped site into zones and using a matrix to record use by people across each zone. This results in large amounts of data, but, because the precise location of individuals is not recorded on the map, it is not good at determining how behaviour relates to the layout of the space. The value of the Cooper Marcus et al., Goličnik and Ward Thompson, Unt and Bell or Cosco et al. techniques is that they take a more detailed approach to behaviour mapping, using techniques that allow detailed recording of each individual's location on a site map. They all stress the importance of time, weather, activity, social interaction and so on in relation to the mapping of individuals' use of a site.

The development, application and utility of SOPARC

General approach

SOPARC is a tool based on systematic observations designed to assess park use in community environments. Although it was primarily designed to assess parks, SOPARC can also be used to assess other types of settings – both indoor and outdoor – such as school campuses or patios, walking/jogging tracks or streets, among others (Mckenzie and Cohen, 2006; McKenzie et al., 2006).

SOPARC is used to quantify the number of people using a predefined area, to assess the observable sociodemographic conditions (mainly gender, age and ethnicity) of these people and to estimate the amount of physical activity that they conduct in the area. Besides this, SOPARC might also be used to evaluate individual aspects of park activity (e.g. accessibility, usability, supervision, equipment of the area, whether there are organised activities, darkness, etc.) to provide contextual information of the site that is being used and assessed (Mckenzie and Cohen 2006; McKenzie et al., 2006). Despite the fact that SOPARC can be adapted for the purpose of each study by including or excluding

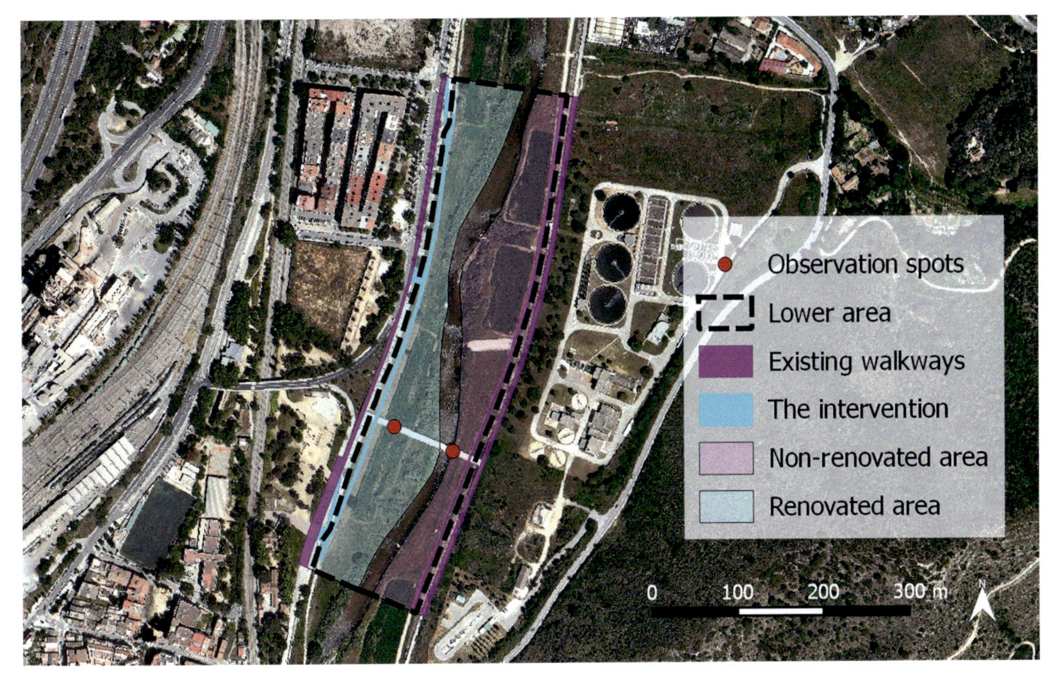

Figure 6.1
Renovated (blue tint) and non-renovated (pink tint) areas of the Besós riverside park in the vicinity of Barcelona. Pink lines denote existing walkways, and the dashed black line indicates the lower part of the area. The intervention (i.e. paved walkway, ramps and stairs) is marked in blue. Red dots indicate the position at which observers made their recordings (further detailed in the following subsections of the chapter) for the pre-post intervention evaluation with the SOPARC tool
(*Source*: Cristina Vert and Orthophoto: Institut Cartogràfic i Geològic de Catalunya, 2020)

characteristics to be recorded and/or by incorporating methodological modifications (Evenson et al., 2017), users are encouraged to follow the existing procedure manual (Mckenzie and Cohen, 2006) as much as possible in order to ensure validity, reliability and feasibility of the tool (Mckenzie and Cohen, 2006; McKenzie et al., 2006). The procedure to be followed when using the SOPARC tool is described in the following section.

The SOPARC tool has been employed in different studies to evaluate the impact of nature-based interventions in urban areas (Cohen et al., 2014, 2015; Evenson et al., 2017; King et al., 2015). It is suitable for this purpose because it is a non-invasive and cost-effective method and observations before and after the intervention can be compared to assess potential changes on the usage of an area. It is useful to evaluate the success of interventions in terms of usability and to identify and assess the target population using the area. As part of the BlueHealth project, SOPARC was used in a pre-post intervention case study of a section of the Besós River in Barcelona (Catalonia, Spain) to evaluate the impact of an urban riverside regeneration project (see Figures 6.1 and 6.2). The aim of the project was to provide access to the riverbanks, facilitating a walkway – for walking, cycling or running – and a resting area. The SOPARC tool was employed before and after the intervention to assess changes on the use of the area and the characteristics of the people using it (Vert et al., 2019).

Figure 6.2

A view of the Besós urban riverside park in the vicinity of Barcelona. The intervention, assessed with the SOPARC tool, included the construction of a paved walkway next to the river (on the left side of the picture)

(*Source*: Cristina Vert).

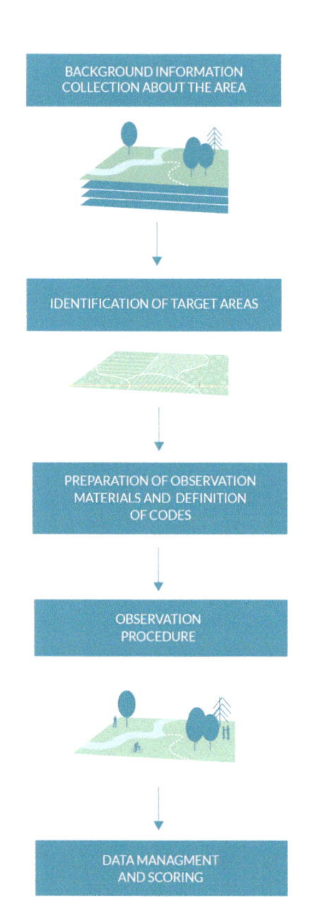

Figure 6.3

Schematic workflow for SOPARC application

Application

SOPARC is an easy tool to use, although suitable preparation before starting the fieldwork for data collection is required. These are the main steps that must be followed when using the SOPARC tool (Figure 6.3):

1. Identification of target areas
2. Preparation of observation materials and definition of codes
3. Observation procedure
4. Data management and scoring

1 Identification of target areas

Target areas are those sections of the setting to be assessed. It is very important to become familiar with the study setting before starting the assessment so as to identify the sections that best represent the study area. This must account for all the locations and spaces likely to be used by people. In each target area, an observation location should also be selected. This needs to be a spot with good visibility, allowing for clear observation of the whole target area. The scale of the target area must be adapted according to the number of people expected to use it. Target areas might also be divided into sub-target areas in order to obtain more accurate measures (Mckenzie and Cohen, 2006).

2 Preparation of observation materials and definition of codes

Observers intending to conduct the observations using the SOPARC tool must be trained in advance using the support materials, including video tutorials and manuals supplied by Active Living Research (2006). Observations may be recorded manually on a paper form or by using the SOPARC app, which allows data collection using a web browser, or an app for Android or iOS (Active Living Research, 2006; Ciafel, 2013). In either case, the coding form needs to be prepared before data collection commences. The original coding form can be found and downloaded from the SOPARC manual (Active Living Research, 2006; Mckenzie and Cohen, 2006), and it can be adapted according to the purpose and characteristics of each study. Either way, the coding form must include at least the following data categories:

a. *Gender.* It is generally categorised into female and male.
b. *Age group.* This is determined according to the following criteria: (i) child = 0 to 12 years old, (ii) teen = 13 to 20 years old, (iii) adult = 21 to 59 years old and (iv) senior ≥60 years old. Since age is assessed by observation, these ranges are designed to be fairly easy to recognise.
c. *Ethnicity.* This is usually categorised into the following (US) categories: (i) Latino, (ii) Black, (iii) white or (iv) other. It might be appropriate to introduce different groups depending on the range of ethnicities expected to be encountered (such as South Asian in the United Kingdom). This data can be important in studies that aim to consider a specific population group characterised as, for example, a minority ethnic group. In some studies, however, this information is not collected due to ethical or practical reasons.
d. *Physical activity.* This is usually classified into three different categories: (i) sedentary, when users are lying down, sitting, crouching or standing in place; (ii) moderate – such as walking at a casual pace; or (iii) vigorous, when users are engaged in a vigorous activity such as running or cycling. When physical activity is categorised as vigorous, the type of physical activity is also specified (e.g. football, skating, jumping, etc.). This is to be used in the scoring step of the SOPARC procedure.

For the case study conducted within the BlueHealth project, in which SOPARC was used to evaluate the Besós River urban riverside regeneration project (Vert et al., 2019), we also included "location" (to indicate whether users were walking, running or doing any other activity in the lower ["L"] or upper ["U"] part of the riverside area – see Figure 6.1) in the coding form (see Figure 6.4), as this was relevant for the study. It is also useful to include a section for taking notes during the fieldwork. This can be helpful for the further steps, in case some of the recordings were not clear. Likewise, it is helpful to include a detailed description of the codes used at the bottom of the form so the observers can easily check them if needed. Observations can be conducted by a single observer, although it is highly recommended to have more than one observer at the same time and location. In this way, the risk of recording incorrect observations is reduced because observers can check and correct each other. The degree of agreement between observers can be assessed, for example, using the intraclass correlation coefficient (ICC) (Hallgren, 2012). A sample of the form used in the urban riverside evaluation study as part of the BlueHealth project is shown in the following.

3 Observation procedure

The duration of each observation, as well as the time sections (i.e. time divisions within each observation), have to be defined in advance. For a walking/jogging track, the duration of a time section is defined as the time a person needs to walk from one side to the other of the track/path (Mckenzie and Cohen, 2006). Thus, for example, if a time section has an observation length of seven minutes, within a one-hour observation, there will be six time sections (7 min × 6 time sections = 42 min), with breaks of approximately three minutes between time sections.

DATE: 23/05/2017 **OBSERVER** (Name): Peter **Time section:** 1 2 3 4 5 6

START TIME: 11:00 **END TIME:** 12:00 **Temperature and weather:** 20°, SUNNY

TARGET AREA: A (La Ribera Neighborhood) B (purifying plant)

# P	Location		Gender		Activity level			Activity (specify)	Age group				Ethnicity	Notes
1	U	L	F	M	S	W	V	WALK	Child	Teen	Adult	Senior	C LA B A O	
2	U	L	F	M	S	W	V	WALK	Child	Teen	Adult	Senior	C LA B A O	
3	U	L	F	M	S	W	V	RUNNING	Child	Teen	Adult	Senior	C LA B A O	
4	U	L	F	M	S	W	V	STANDING	Child	Teen	Adult	Senior	C LA B A O	
5	U	L	F	M	S	W	V	WALK	Child	Teen	Adult	Senior	C LA B A O	
6	U	L	F	M	S	W	V	WALK	Child	Teen	Adult	Senior	C LA B A O	
7	U	L	F	M	S	W	V	RUNNING	Child	Teen	Adult	Senior	C LA B A O	
8	U	L	F	M	S	W	V	CYCLE	Child	Teen	Adult	Senior	C LA B A O	
Etc...	U	L	F	M	S	W	V		Child	Teen	Adult	Senior	C LA B A O	

NOTES:

Time section: each time section will last 7 minutes (in total we will have 6 sections of 7 minutes, so 42 minutes observation time, with breaks of 3 minutes between sections, in total 60 minutes).
Start time: time at which the observation process starts.
End time: time at which the observation process ends.
#P: number of subject observed.
Location: U=upper part of the section (sidewalk), L=lower part of the section (near the river)
Gender: F=female, M=male
Activity level: S=sedentary (lying down, sitting, standing in a place), W=walking, V=vigorous (increasing heart rate, sweating: jogging, biking...)
Activity specify: indicate the specific activity the person is doing.
Age group: Child (<12 years), Teen (13 to 20 years), Adults (21 to 59 years), Seniors (>60 years)
Ethnicity: C=Caucasian, LA=Latin-American, B=Black, A=Asian, O=others
Note: Please indicate any events or observations of interest, including close calls, unlawful behavior, or any other information that may affect your count, or observed behaviors such as significant events or background information, i.e. free zoo day, formal event at park, etc.

Figure 6.4
A sample of a completed SOPARC form used in the urban riverside evaluation study

Figure 6.5
Observer filling in the SOPARC coding form of observations. She does it from a predefined location from which she can observe and assess the target area defined for the study
(*Source*: Glòria Carrasco)

The observation procedure consists of systematically scanning target areas during a specific period of time to quantify the number of people using the area and their characteristics and levels of physical activity (see Figure 6.5). Scans are visual sweeps from left to right across the target area during the established time for each time section. Before each observation, observers need to fill in the heading of the form indicating the date, time, temperature and weather conditions and other information relevant for the study (Figure 6.4). The time length of each time section is measured with a chronometer and, during this time, observers annotate all the observations in the SOPARC form.

Observations must be conducted at different times of the day (e.g. morning, afternoon, evening) and several days per week (including weekdays and weekends) in order to capture the real pattern of use of the area.

This is the recording procedure for walking or jogging tracks, which is the one employed in the BlueHealth project. However, SOPARC can also be used to assess other settings with different characteristics. In this case, the recording procedure has some differences, which are described in the SOPARC manual (Mckenzie and Cohen, 2006).

4 Data management and scoring

All the data recorded in the SOPARC coding forms must be transferred to an Excel spreadsheet and then imported into statistical software to conduct the analysis. First, data must be aggregated according to the variable of interest. This information will be used to conduct descriptive analysis and statistical comparisons between categories (Mckenzie and Cohen, 2006). Second, for the assessment of physical activity levels, physical activity observations must be converted into energy expenditure units, which refers to the amount of energy a person uses. The total number of sedentary, moderate and vigorous users must be summed and then multiplied by the respective metabolic equivalent of task (MET) for each physical activity category according to the compendium of physical activities developed by Ainsworth et al. (2011).

Sample outputs of a BlueHealth case study using SOPARC

The results of the pre-post intervention case study of a stretch of the Besòs River in Barcelona are illustrated in part in the next section of the chapter in order to show how the findings can be presented. The example is drawn from a paper by Vert et al. (2019) and focuses on three main aspects, illustrated by graphs. The first focuses on gender, the second on age and the third on ethnicity.

Generally, for the whole observed sample, the results suggested that interventions developed to facilitate access to blue spaces in socioeconomically deprived urban and peri-urban areas were successful in promoting the use of these natural settings. The number of users significantly increased in the renovated area (30.2% in 2016 vs. 36.1% in 2017, $p < 0.001$), while it significantly decreased in the non-renovated area (69.8% in 2016 vs. 63.9% in 2017, $p < 0.001$). More specifically, in the lower part (riverbank) of the renovated area, we observed a noticeable increase of

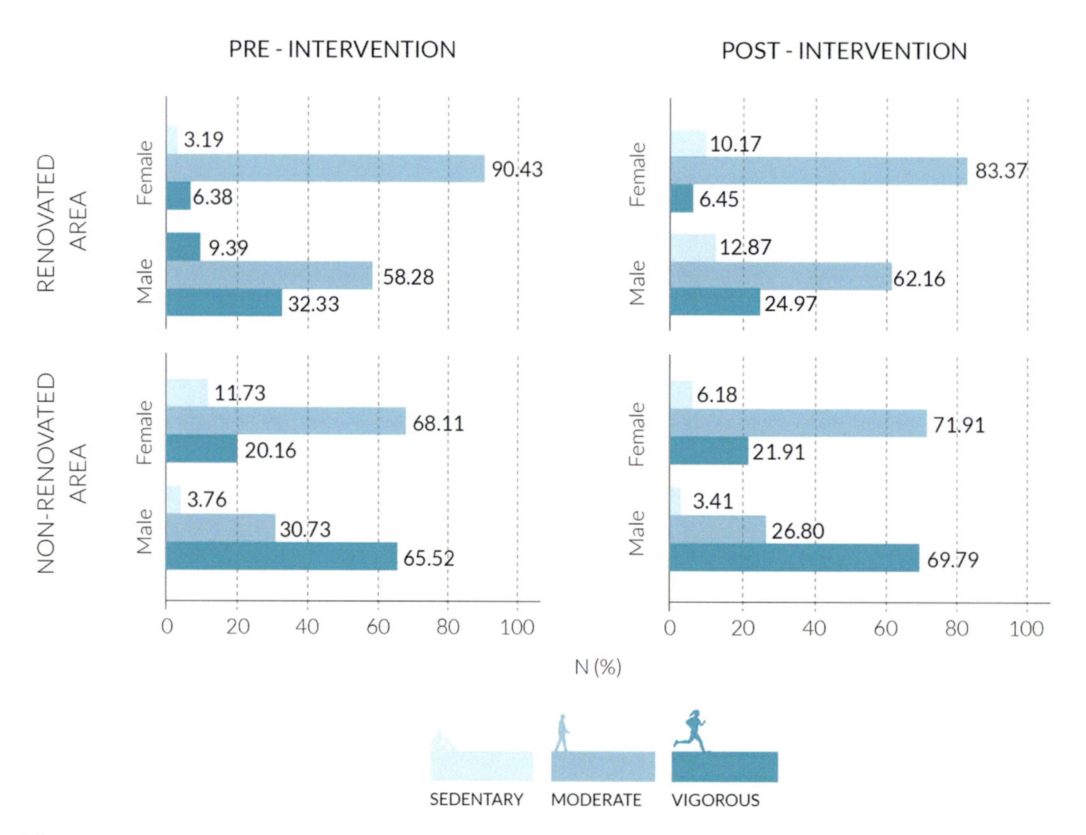

Figure 6.6

Levels of physical activity by target area (i.e. renovated and non-renovated area of the Besòs River) and period of evaluation (i.e. pre/post-evaluation), stratified by gender

(*Source*: Cristina Vert and Anna Wilczyńska)

users (1.7% in 2016 vs. 15.9% in 2017, $p < 0.001$), whereas in the upper part, the number of users decreased, indicating that users employed the stairs and ramps dedicated to facilitate access to the riverbank.

Patterns of physical activity were observed to vary slightly between the different population groups evaluated in this study. First, in the post-intervention evaluation period, sedentary use of the renovated area increased for both females and males (Figure 6.6). Nevertheless, the increase of vigorously active users in the non-renovated area was higher for males (65.5% in 2016 vs. 69.8% in 2017) than for females (20.2% in 2016 vs. 21.9% in 2017) (Figure 6.6). Results showed that females had a significantly higher chance of being sedentary and moderately active both in the renovated and non-renovated area compared with males.

Second, the increase of moderately active users over time in the renovated area was mainly driven by children (38.9% in 2016 vs. 57.7% in 2017) and adults (53.3% in 2016 vs. 60.9% in 2017), although the proportion of moderately active seniors also increased (Figure 6.7). In the non-renovated area, teenagers experienced the highest increase of

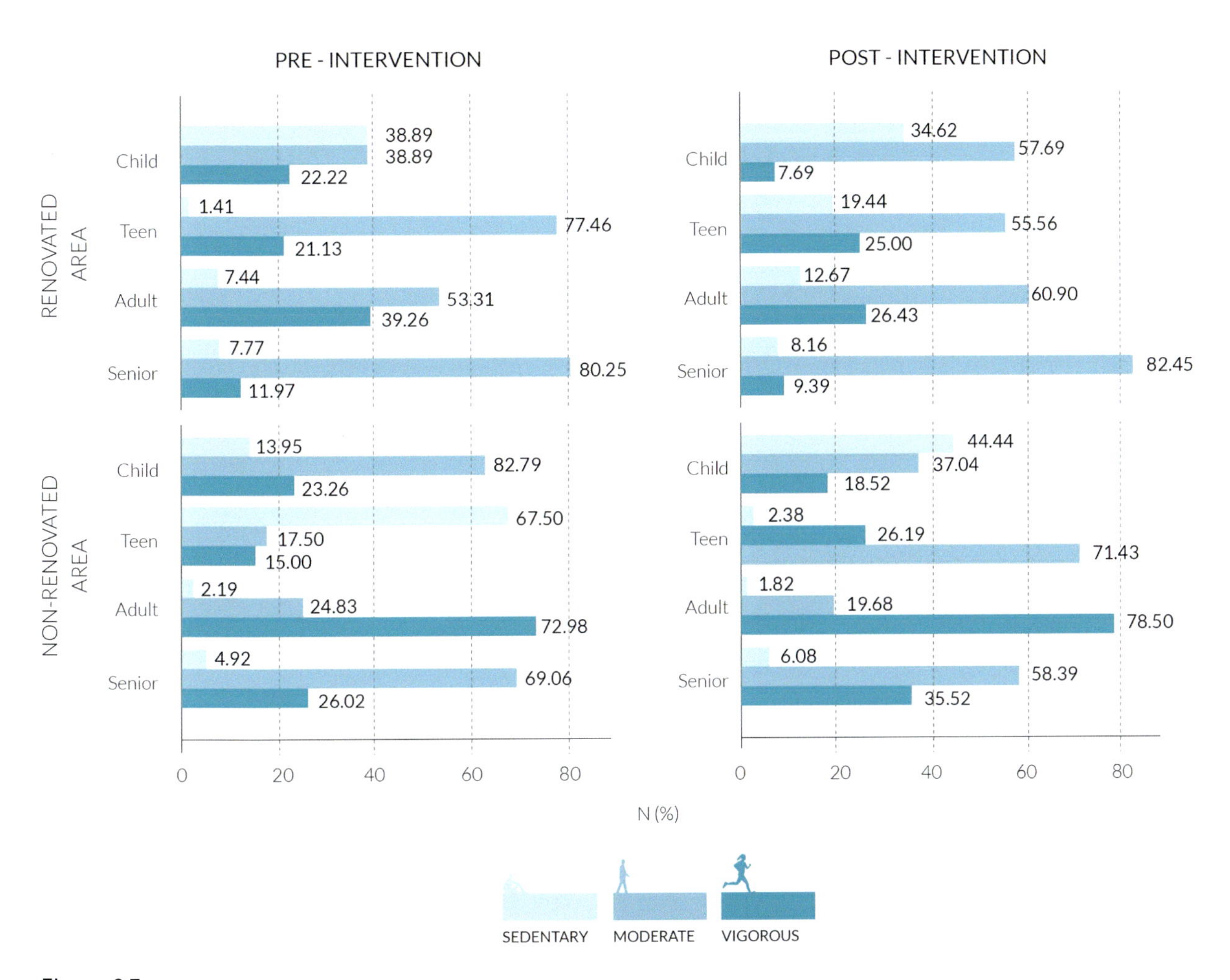

Figure 6.7

Levels of physical activity by target area (i.e. renovated and non-renovated area of the Besòs River) and period of evaluation (i.e. pre/post-evaluation), stratified by age group

(*Source*: Cristina Vert and Anna Wilczyńska)

vigorous physical activity levels (from 15.0% in 2016 to 71.4% in 2017). We also observed an increase of vigorous levels of physical activity for adults and seniors but not for children (Figure 6.7).

Third, non-Caucasians had a significantly higher likelihood of being sedentary and moderately active users than Caucasians. As shown in Figure 6.8, in the post-evaluation, the proportion of sedentary non-Caucasian users increased in both the renovated (from 0% in 2016 to 18.6% in 2017) and non-renovated area (from 2.6% in 2016 to 16.3% in 2017). Likewise, the proportion of Caucasian vigorously active users increased in the non-renovated area (from 56.8% in 2016 to 63.4% in 2017), while the proportion of non-Caucasian vigorously active users decreased (from 35.9% in 2016 to 11.6% in 2017) (Figure 6.8).

Moreover, we observed that the increased use of the riverside area was particularly significant to user groups which are usually underrepresented in such environments (e.g., women, children or migrants). As an example, although more males were observed in the riverside area than females, after the intervention, we observed a 43% increase in females at the renovated area of the river. Furthermore, more than 90% of the users were coded as Caucasians. However, a significant increase of non-Caucasian users was observed in the renovated area after the

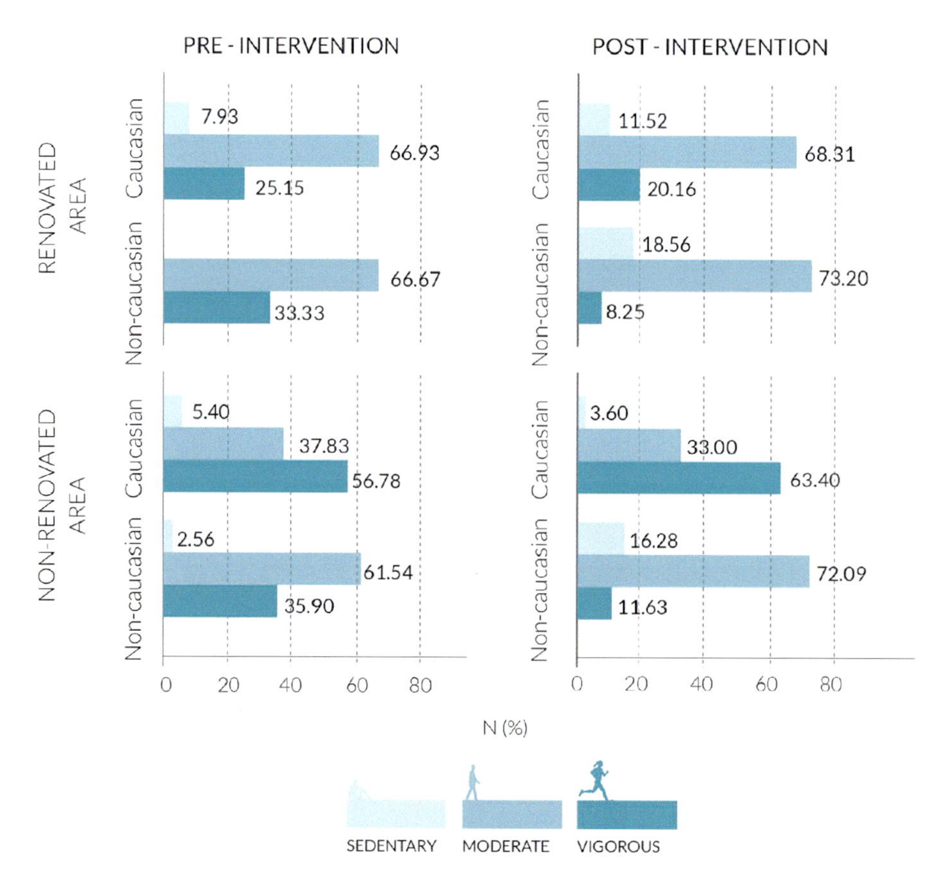

Figure 6.8

Levels of physical activity by target area (i.e. renovated and non-renovated area of the Besòs River) and period of evaluation (i.e. pre/post-evaluation), stratified by ethnicity

(*Source*: Cristina Vert and Anna Wilczyńska)

Table 6.1 **Energy expenditure (in mean METs/observation) by target area for the pre- and post-evaluation SOPARC assessment**

	Renovated area			*Non-renovated area*			*Both areas*		
	Pre (2016)	*Post (2017)*	*Comparison between years (% of change)*	*Pre (2016)*	*Post (2017)*	*Comparison between years (% of change)*	*Pre (2016)*	*Post (2017)*	*Comparison between years (% of change)*
Mean METs/observation									
Upper	4.34	4.12	–5	5.44	5.80	7	5.08	5.21	3
Lower	4.59	3.41	–26	6.79	6.74	–1	6.69	5.29	–21
Total	4.34	4.01	–8	5.64	5.91	5	5.25	5.22	0

intervention (2.6% of non-Caucasian users in 2016 vs. 7.8% in 2017, $p < 0.001$). All this might have a positive impact on the reduction of health inequalities.

Besides using the SOPARC tool to quantify the number of users in the urban riverside park and their sociodemographic characteristics, the tool was also suitable to estimate the physical activity levels of the users of the setting. On average, it was observed that, for the pre- and post-evaluation period and for both areas of the river, 90% of the users of the Besòs Riverside Park were engaged in moderate or vigorous levels of physical activity. However, we found a significant increase of users engaging in sedentary and moderate levels of physical activity in the renovated area (7.7% of sedentary users in 2016 vs. 12.0% in 2017, $p < 0.001$ and 66.9% of moderately active users in 2016 vs. 68.7% in 2017, $p < 0.001$) and a significant increase of users engaging in vigorous levels of physical activity in the non-renovated area (56% in 2016 vs. 62.4% in 2017, $p < 0.001$). Findings from the renovated area of the river were similar to those already reported in other studies (Kramer et al., 2017; Schultz et al., 2017) that suggest that urban regeneration projects might stimulate leisure-time walking (i.e. moderate physical activity) among adults in deprived areas. Nevertheless, residential proximity and access to parks may facilitate physical activity among residents of the area, even if it is only by providing destinations to which people can walk or cycle, although park-based physical activity may account only for a small proportion of the total physical activity people conduct (Cohen et al., 2015; Stewart et al., 2018).

Overall, we did not observe changes in energy expenditure (expressed in METs/observation) after the intervention. However, we observed an 8% decrease of METs/observation in the renovated area and 5% increase in the non-renovated area. This was mainly driven by the decrease of energy expended in the lower part of the river and the increase of energy expended in the upper part of the river in the renovated and non-renovated area, respectively. An example of presenting the METS using a table is presented next (Table 6.1).

The development, application and utility of the BlueHealth Behaviour Assessment Tool

General approach

The BlueHealth Behaviour Assessment Tool takes the basic theory and approach, as described earlier in the introduction, and moves on from paper-based mapping to the application of a geographic information system (GIS)-based recording application on a tablet computer used on site (see Figure 6.9) where all the data are automatically linked to a database. This system is not only more accurate, but it is quicker, enables more points to be collected without the map becoming crowded and allows for primary and secondary activities to be noted simultaneously. The specific GIS program used in the system described in this chapter is Quantum GIS (QGIS) (The QGIS Community at www.qgis.org), which is free,

Figure 6.9
A photo showing how the GIS digital interface is operated on a tablet computer on site. Here the drop-down menu for recording the attributes of someone using the site is open over the map base
(*Source*: Peeter Vassiljev)

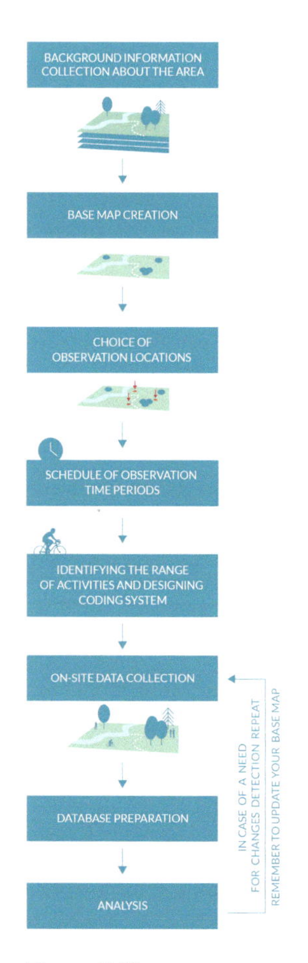

Figure 6.10
Schematic workflow for BBAT application

open-source software. When supplied with some additional scripting (freely available to readers via the BlueHealth Tools website at https://bluehealth.tools), it can easily be set up for use and tailored for activities which might be specific to the site in question. A similar application that served as an inspiration and a basis for us was developed and applied by Frederico Meireles as part of his PhD on assessing the success of a programme of new or restored parks in Portugal (Mereiles Rodrigues, 2015).

Application

The demonstration of the application uses a site of Pelgurand Beach at Kopli in Põhja-Tallinn, Estonia, where an experimental intervention was constructed (see Chapter 3), although we focus only on the pre-intervention state for illustration purposes. The application of the methodology includes several steps (see also Figure 6.10). These are as follows:

1. Background data collection
2. Preparation of site maps divided into specific areas or behaviour settings
3. Planning the observation points or routes
4. Identifying the range of likely activities to be recorded and designing the specific coding system for each
5. Selecting the time periods for sampling
6. On-site data collection
7. Preparation of a spatially explicit database
8. Analysis of results both statistically and visually
9. Repetition of Steps 6–8 for the post-intervention surveys (two phases)

1 Background data collection

Notes and photographs covering the characteristics of the study site should be collected for the initial site survey. This will reveal the character of the area and, if carried out when people are using the site, the likely activities and some of the likely locations within the site where activities are concentrated can be captured, to make planning easier. It will also reveal the condition of the site and help in the preparation of a base plan to be used for the recording. In addition, it will suggest suitable places from where all or significant parts of the site may be observed. If the water element of the site is variable, such as being tidal, or the seasons are significant, such as freezing in winter, these should also be noted, as it may be necessary to include sampling across these variations. Therefore, the site should be visited several times in order to build up a good overview prior to the data collection phases.

2 Preparation of site maps

Site maps should be prepared by simplifying extracts from digital map bases or aerial/satellite photographs in order to accentuate relevant elements and erase unnecessary features that would complicate observation recording. The site map should contain the main features such as boundaries, entrances, paths, water edges, main vegetation zones, specific buildings and landmarks that help with orientation. The digital site map will be used in a GIS data acquisition solution on a tablet computer, but a paper version of the site map will also be required as a fallback solution in case of technical problems (environmental extremes, battery, security). Space on the paper map form should be provided for noting the date, time of day, weather conditions and water conditions. The map should be able to be printed in

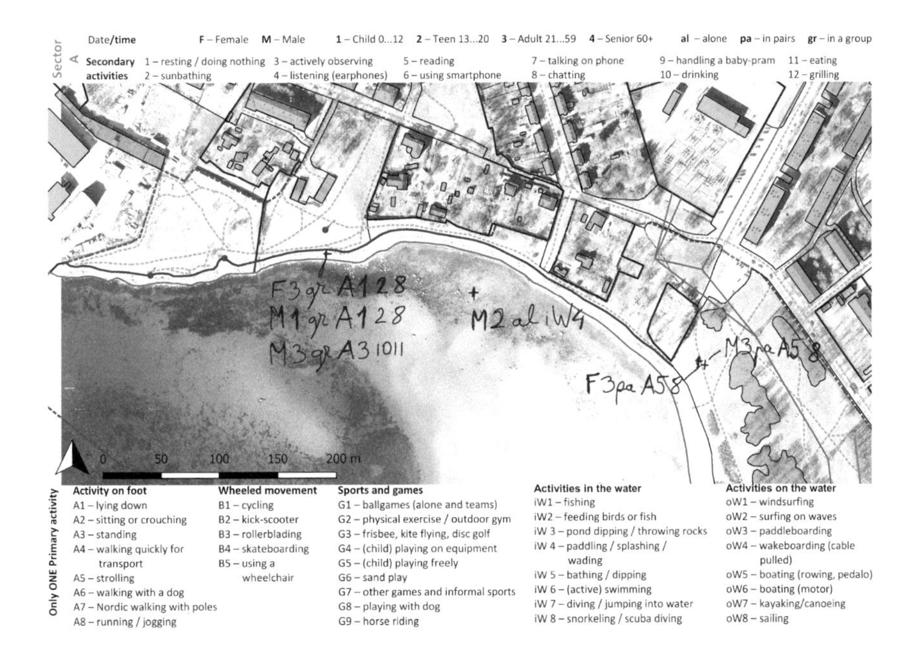

Figure 6.11

An example of a paper form used for BBAT data collection with part of the survey area (sector A) shown on a map (topographic data and orthophoto: Estonian Land Board, 2018) and the coding key to the parameters that should be recorded. For example, the person in the central portion of the map marked with the code "M2aliW4" indicates a male; aged 13. . . 20; alone; paddling, splashing or wading in the water. The western-most point captures a group of three with the last user coded as "M3grA31011" indicating a male, aged 21. . . 59, in a group, standing while also drinking and eating something

(*Source*: Peeter Vassiljev)

black-and-white in A4 format, scaled to fit the paper so that it can be fitted to a clipboard and unobtrusively carried around (see Figure 6.12). Typically, multiple copies are needed for each observation episode to distribute abundant information thematically (usually by gender or age) on the limited form space.

3 Planning the observation points or routes

As the whole idea of the method is to observe the activities of site users, it is necessary to try to be as unobtrusive as possible in the selection of places from which to observe and record without drawing undue attention to the surveyor. If there are single spots such as a high point with an unrestricted view of the entire site, then this is ideal. However, when a site is broken up due to its size, or by tall vegetation or buildings screening parts from the view, it is necessary to find several observation spots and to plan a route between them to enable a systematic repetition of the observation process each time. If the site is very large, it should be subdivided among more than one surveyor to avoid the danger that observations might not fit in the allocated maximal four-hour time slot. In some circumstances, the safety and security of the surveyor may need to be considered in the choice of how the observations are carried out. If the site or part of it is used for children's play, then it may be necessary to take precautions and to carry identification in case of being stopped or suspected of inappropriate behaviour when standing near such places making observations.

4 Identifying the range of likely activities to be recorded and designing the specific coding system for each

The digital BBAT interface consists of a set of drop-down boxes with a number of aspects to be recorded: gender, age group, a selection from a list of main activities, who the person was doing the activity with and what they are doing as a secondary activity (e.g. listening to music, reading, chatting, etc.). Behaviour types to be recorded as the main activity should be predefined, based on past examples when possible, to allow comparison of the results and also new thinking, to capture the specifics of the particular site. The range of main activities used in the BlueHealth experiment sites as well as the range of secondary activities can be seen in the paper form example (see Figure 6.12). The wording

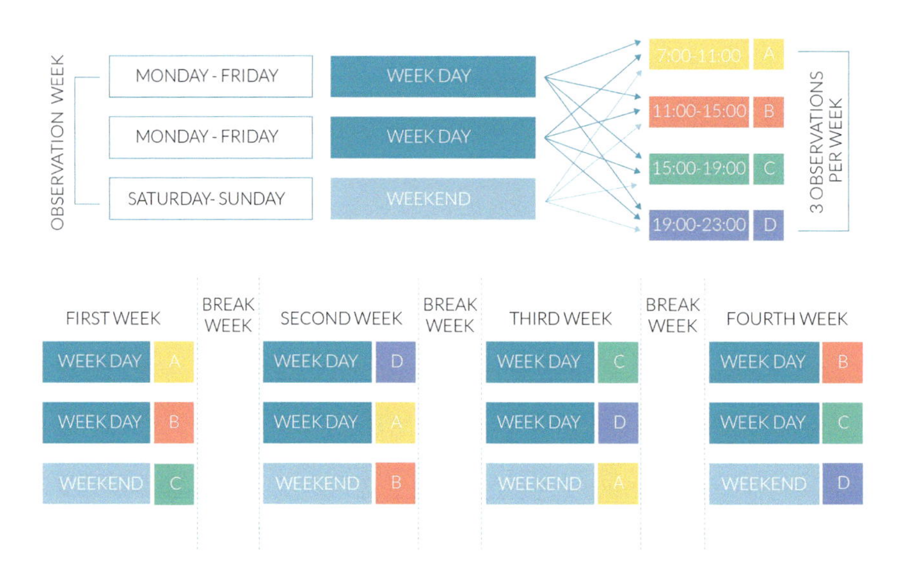

Figure 6.12

Diagram explaining the rotation of observation days and times in the schedule. Notice the cycling of four time slots within the day (marked with A, B, C, D) against the three observation episodes within the week, ensuring all possible time combinations and sufficient time between observations to increase the likelihood of changes in weather

(*Source*: Peeter Vassiljev and Anna Wilczyńska)

of activity types should be concise so that it can be easily and efficiently identified while operating the tablet interface in the field. If the observations are recorded on paper forms, alphanumeric coding can be used (see Figure 6.12).

5 Selecting the time periods for sampling

In general, for many sites in the northern hemisphere, May to September/October is suitable for data collection since blue spaces are more likely to be busy in this period (although, of course, it varies according to climate). However, in cases of strong seasonality and winter use, such as in Estonia, some extra sampling should be carried out in order to capture the differences, and specific winter activity types should also be added to the QGIS menus for this. If the observation is part of a pre- and post-intervention setup, then the repeat observations should follow the same pattern so as to ensure good possibilities for statistically accurate comparison.

During the "on-season" observation period, the behaviour mapping data should be collected at specific time intervals in order to ensure that a good representative sample of all possible times is obtained. For practicality, it has been calculated that to make observations every other week, on two random weekdays (Monday to Friday) and one weekend day (consult Figure 6.11 for a sample schedule) is sufficient. For example, if the first data are collected on three days in the first week of May, then the next observation campaign will be over three days during the third week of May. Following this spread of observations will ensure data will capture the variable weather conditions that represent the whole season, but it is of course possible to compress the observation schedule into a shorter time if less representative results are acceptable. Observing a two weekday/one weekend day schedule will slightly over-sample the weekends, which in principle can be compensated for by omitting some weekend observations or using weighted data in the statistical analysis.

The days of the observation period should be divided into four blocks of morning 7.00–11.00, lunchtime 11.00–15.00, afternoon 15.00–19.00 and evening 19.00–23.00. Four-hour time slots allow for some variation according to the latitude and local patterns of use determined in Step 1. Times for observation are selected rotationally so that consecutive observations cycle through the sequence of morning, lunchtime, afternoon and evening (see last column with letters A to D in Figure 6.11). Adhering to this rotation will ensure that samples are equally spread among times of the day and progression of seasons.

During "off-season" or winter sampling, two or more additional observation weeks can be used. With limited winter daylight, these observation weeks should only use lunchtime and afternoon time periods and double the observations (either one time slot over four weekdays and two weekend days or two time slots over two weekdays and one weekend day). These observation weeks do not have to be separated by one week and instead should try to capture the most characteristic winter conditions according to the weather at the time. If the water body is expected to freeze over sufficiently to be walkable, then such conditions should be targeted, but if, due to climate variability, the freeze is unreliable or there is a sudden thaw, a week with snow cover on the ground should be selected. In milder conditions where only occasional snow cover is expected, that condition should be targeted when it occurs.

6 On-site data collection

Field work is generally safe to undertake, but some sites may be, or feel, a little less safe than others, especially if they are derelict or abandoned or may contain dense vegetation. We usually give the following advice to research assistants:

> Do not put yourself in unnecessary danger. Always let someone know where you are, what you're doing and when you expect to be back. In some circumstances your safety and security may need to be considered in the choice of how the observations are carried out. For example, you may work in pairs, resort to recording data on paper to avoid unwanted attention or leave the site altogether when feeling threatened or in danger.

The observation method should be unobtrusive so that the researcher does not affect how people use the site. Wandering too close to people while making notes might not be very welcome to some, so we also advise research assistants to respect the privacy of people present on-site. Taking photos or recording videos of the subjects present during the behaviour mapping observation with any device is generally an unacceptable invasion of privacy and also runs the risk of affecting the visitors' behaviour. However, in some circumstances when the site is expected to be exceptionally busy and all ethical considerations and regulations have been resolved with the appropriate authorities, then taking sample photos at intervals from a specific viewpoint can be considered (see Sun et al., 2019). All records must be anonymised – there should be no extra information recorded beyond the given data entry forms that would allow identification of a particular individual.

Regardless of whether the data are collected digitally or on paper, observers should always bring:

a. a badge stating who they are and what they're doing and a photo ID (potentially also carrying a letter showing that they are bona fide research assistants and have permission to undertake the work),
b. clipboard (with transparent plastic covering for rain protection),
c. at least two copies of the paper forms (in case the technology fails),
d. set of fine-tipped waterproof markers for manual recording, and
e. larger plastic bag to seal the tablet computer and/or paper forms in case of heavy rain penetrating the backpack or handbag.

Before starting the observations, a set of basic data are noted in the form, which include date, time of day, weather conditions (temperature from the closest available weather station; clear or few clouds/considerably cloudy/almost or completely overcast; dry/light rain/heavy rain/light snow/heavy snow; calm/light breeze/strong winds) and the water conditions (frozen over/calm water/mild waves/strong waves; unknown water level or irrelevant/low tide/average water level/high tide).

The observation protocol involves either sitting/standing in the point or points selected for the complete site overview or else, in case of limited visibility or due to a narrow linear shape to the area, a systematic walk through each site, visiting all sub-areas and taking a visual scan of each sub-area. All visual scans, unless stated otherwise in the specific site instructions, are performed from predetermined observation spots in the direction from left to right. In the case of data collection during a systematic walk-through (done only if stated in site instructions), all users are recorded on the map when closest to the observer (who is only moving on the predetermined track). All users observed in that scan are recorded as point data on the site map using the coding selected or, if the coding does not cover that activity, a note of this is recorded separately (pilot testing of the protocol should hopefully reduce the need to record unique activities). The recording of the points (see Figures 6.12 and 6.9) is accompanied by additional data, including gender (female or male; if gender cannot be identified, record as male), estimated age class (using the same as for the SOPARC – Child 0. . . 12, Teen 13. . . 20, Adult 21. . . 59, Senior 60+; if age cannot be identified, record as adult), social context of the activity (alone, in pairs, in a group; if unknown, then mark as alone), only one main activity and optional multiple secondary activities (doing something, e.g. chatting, using a phone, drinking, eating, etc. while engaged in the main activity), as already noted (see Step 4 and Figure 6.12).

In a case where there are large numbers of users and especially when paper map forms are used for data collection, it is possible to subdivide the visual scan and data entry by gender (recording female users first and male users later) and/or subdivide the observable (sub-)area into yet smaller sub-units. Each person is then recorded in the order of the visual scan from left to right. If a person leaves the sub-area after being counted, the record is still kept; if a person leaves the sub-area before being recorded, the record is not made. The same person may reappear in the next sub-area, and if that happens during the visual scan, that person should be recorded again (because it is the number of activities which are being observed, not the number of people being counted). There is an equal chance of another person moving in the opposite direction and thus never being present in the visual scan and never being recorded. The BlueHealth tools website contains instructions on how to use the QGIS tablet-based data input method.

7 Formatting data after acquisition

The data from every observation episode collected using the BBAT digital interface should be saved in a separate folder (naming convention example: Tallinn_2020_05_17_morning) because programmed forms of the BBAT interface use the same filenames that must be saved in separate folders to avoid overwriting. The data file for every observation session must be checked for consistency and integrity, as each entered point should be accompanied by gender, age, social context, primary and secondary activity information, observation date and time, weather and water condition data. If any of the observation episodes were split between multiple observers (due to the size of the area), these separate files will have to be checked for possible overlaps in observed territory (however unlikely these may be) and reconciled before merging into a single observation file. If the observations were originally mapped on paper, they should be re-coded in the office with the BBAT interface in QGIS. After data for each observation episode have been verified, they need to be merged into a single GIS point shapefile, creating a rich, spatially explicit database of observations ready for visual cartographic, statistical and geostatistical exploration in a number of different ways.

8 Analysis of results using maps and statistics

Once the database is complete, the layer can be examined and interpreted, for example, according to type of activities, estimated age of people observed, weather and water conditions, and so on in GIS, but the database file containing all the attribute data associated with the point shapefile can also be separately imported and analysed in a spreadsheet or a statistics program. Descriptive statistical analysis, such as the production of time series graphs, histograms and bar charts to illustrate activities and behaviour for different segments of the population at different times of day or days of the week can be used to reveal temporal, weather and activity variations. Comparison of the mapped data allows analysis of the different spatial attributes of site use according to different layers of data. Once Steps 6–8 have been repeated, a comparison of pre- and post-intervention surveys can be undertaken. In this section, we will use pre-intervention data from observations made at the experimental intervention site at Pelgurand in Tallinn, Estonia, in order to demonstrate different ways of looking at the data in order to answer certain research questions. We used the high-definition aerial photograph available from the Web Map portal of the Estonian Land Board as the base, as it clearly shows the different landscape features and allows us to make visual associations of uses with specific locations or elements.

ISOLATING PARTS OF THE DATA BY DIFFERENT ATTRIBUTES

First, it is quite useful just to open the GIS and load all the data points in order to see what stands out spatially, if anything, and to obtain the first overall impression – so-called "eyeballing the data". This may produce a very crowded picture depending on the degree of zoom into or out of the site, so it may be best to separate the data between, for example, male and female users. This can be achieved by filtering data by attribute value and/or setting categorised display styles in layer properties. Figure 6.13a and b shows this thematic separation between male and female users for the entire observation period in 2017. The size of the points in combination with the zoom level in the GIS means a lot of data points will overlap, but in general, it can be seen that there are some indicative patterns present, such as a very dense area along the beach to the south, clusters along paths and so on.

This filtering of point data can be explored further by subdividing data according to age, time, social interaction and so on or combining multiple filtering parameters – much more potentially useful analyses and very easy to differentiate. Of course, we also want to see what activities are being undertaken on the site – land- and water-based – where and by whom. We can then visually split the data further and identify the most and least popular locations. Figure 6.14a and b shows active and passive behaviours for a section of the study area. The points are colour coded according to activities, but the gender or age differentiations are not shown. It can be seen that passive use is much more popular and spread over larger territory, with sitting/crouching, lying and standing on the beach and immediate area behind it most preferred, although the grassy places next to and between the trees are also well used. The active uses congregate on the paths (walking, cycling, jogging) and also along the waterline on the beach.

Figure 6.13a and b

a) All the points for the observation period of 2017 for male users and b) for female users

(*Source*: Peeter Vassiljev and Orthophoto: Estonian Land Board, 2020)

Another important variable to explore is time of day. Figure 6.15 shows three maps of all activities involving sunbathing according to the time of day – 1) in the early to mid-morning, 2) in the middle of the day and 3) in the late afternoon/early evening. The pattern is fairly obvious for this type of use – according to the heat and angle of the sun. Yet another observation in the location pattern can be made – contrary to a cliché that sunbathing occurs mainly on the beach, a lot of sunbathing took place away from the beach on the grass in the park. That is especially prominent in the middle of the day, but as the sun sinks to the west, these areas are cast into shadow, so most people use the beach and grassy dunes immediately behind it.

Another variable is that of the weather, especially air temperature. The next set of maps show the level of use (all records) during cooler and warmer periods (Figure 6.16a and b). In the cooler times (14°C and below), the paths are busiest, while in the warmth (20°C and above), it is the beach and grassy areas that are used.

We can also explore the social aspects of site use by differentiating between the users as individuals, in pairs/couples and in groups (and of course by gender and age or activity type if needed). Filtering out data by different variables or combinations of variables and viewing the distribution patterns of the filtered data offers many possibilities, but it also requires considerable time spent in trials, as every site is different and combinations are multiple. It is also worth remembering that besides looking for differences in the data, it is just as valuable to look at similarities between different groups.

COMBINING OBSERVATION DATA WITH SPECIFIC PARTS OF THE LANDSCAPE

It is possible to generate similar maps for many combinations of the variables collected. However, these need to be interpreted in a rather subjective way – for instance, when relating the users/uses to specific parts of the landscape.

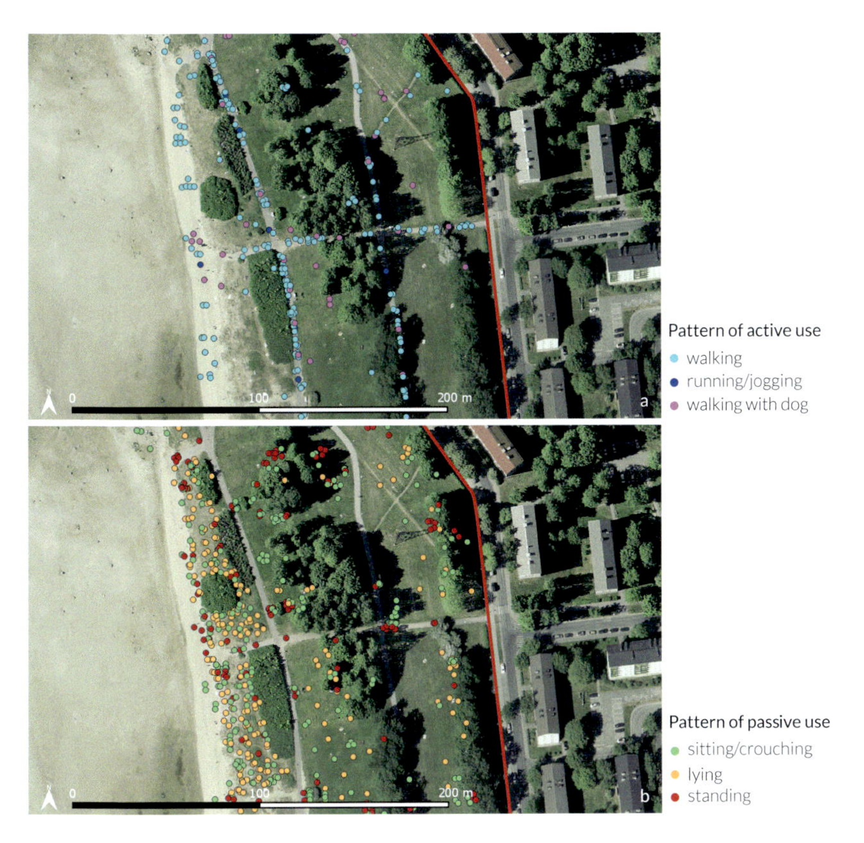

Figure 6.14a and b

a) Pattern of active use in one section of the study area and b) the pattern of passive use (see legend)

(*Source*: Peeter Vassiljev and Orthophoto: Estonian Land Board, 2020)

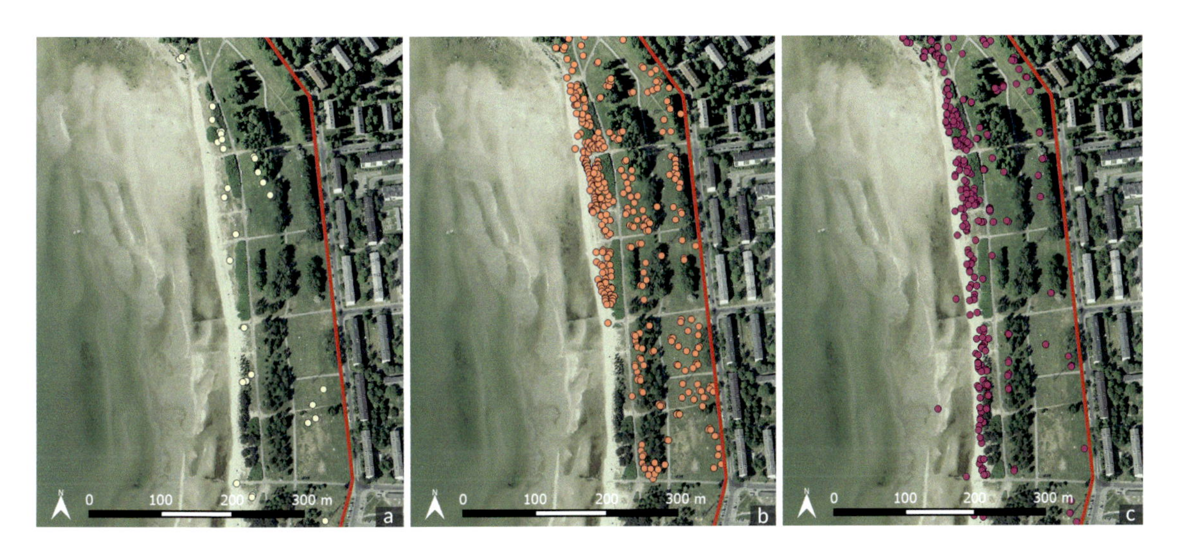

Figure 6.15a–c

Pattern of sunbathing (all records), a) early/mid-morning; b) midday/early afternoon; c) later afternoon/early evening

(*Source*: Peeter Vassiljev and Orthophoto: Estonian Land Board, 2020)

Figure 6.16a and b

a) Usage of the area during the colder periods of the 2017 summer and b) during the warmer periods

(*Source*: Peeter Vassiljev and Orthophoto: Estonian Land Board, 2020)

The next section shows the possibilities when the site has been divided into behaviour settings (Barker, 1968). For this, it is necessary to define the different types of setting based on the physical elements and potential affordances offered by them and then to create a new GIS layer of polygons. Following this, the observation points falling within each behaviour setting can be isolated and analysed to detect the patterns of use and users. This is of value when understanding the actualised affordances offered by each setting and for improving the potential of a site. Figure 6.17 includes a close-up of one section of the behaviour setting map which shows how sunbathing or non-sunbathing can be clearly seen as directly associated with the settings of the beach (more non-sunbathers than sunbathers) and the vegetated sand dunes immediately behind the beach (majority of sunbathers). This difference is also brought out by the percentages of these two sets of activity for each behaviour setting (for the entire site), as shown in the chart in Figure 6.17.

A further interesting example is of bench users. Benches were identified as a specific behaviour setting. The differences in the distribution are not so apparent on a map, while the differences presented as percentages of observations for all benches on the entire area (Figure 6.18) with more occupation by female users, especially older, become apparent.

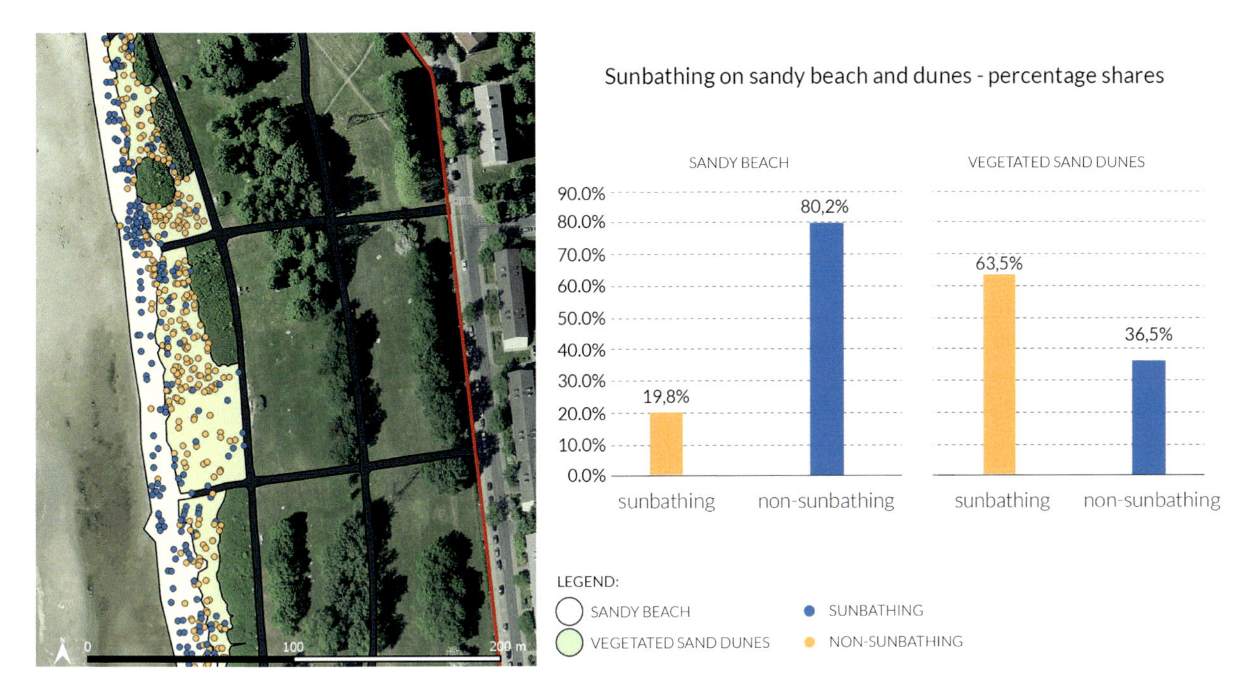

Figure 6.17a and b

The differentiation between two behaviour settings (beach and vegetated dunes) where a clear relationship between sunbathing (orange) and non-sunbathing (blue) stands out visually on the map, (a) (Orthophoto: Estonian Land Board, 2020); b) Percentage shares of sunbathers/non-sunbathers for two behaviour settings at the entire study site confirm the trend

(*Source*: Peeter Vassiljev and Anna Wilczyńska and Orthophoto: Estonian Land Board, 2020)

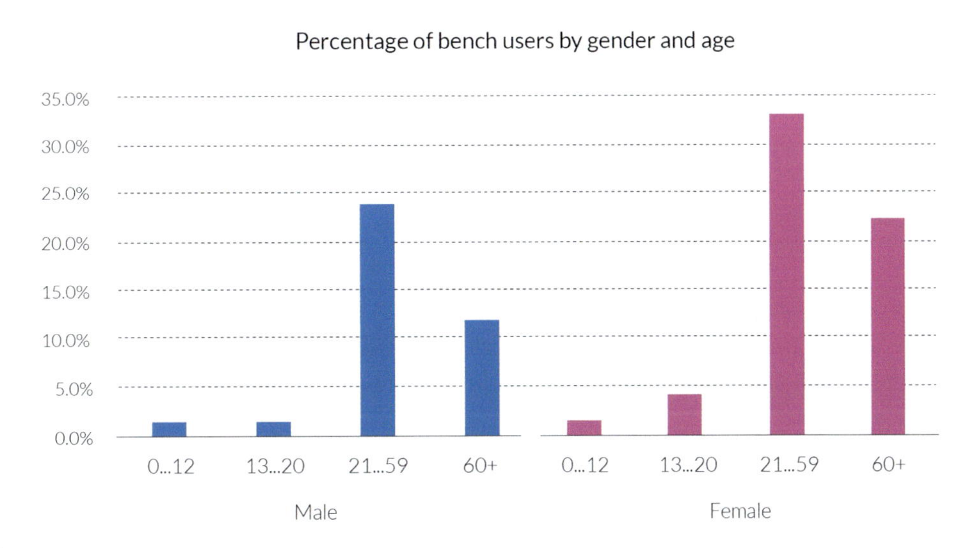

Figure 6.18

Percentages of observations of bench users by age and gender

(*Source*: Peeter Vassiljev and Anna Wilczyńska)

Figure 6.19a–c

a) Standard deviation ellipses for men and women aged 60+ on two comparison areas: b) the rocky beach park; c) the sandy beach park. Centroids for ellipses are also shown along with the radius values of the ellipses in metres

(*Source*: Orthophoto: Estonian Land Board, 2020, photos Peeter Vassiljev)

GEOSTATISTICAL ANALYSIS

The maps so far show points presented over the map base, aerial photo or behaviour settings. It is also possible to examine the data points using geo-statistical approaches such as central tendency measures, some other form of cluster analysis or spatial regression.

A very straightforward way of characterising the distribution within a point cloud is to generate a standard deviation ellipse out from the mean centre of the cloud encompassing locations of roughly two thirds of the points. This can be done for different, such as social groups in the data, to compare distributions in relation to each other and to the boundaries of the site. Figure 6.19 shows an example of ellipses calculated for older visitors to the rocky beach park, the mean centres of which, for both genders, are located in roughly the same place – to the east of the centre of the area itself – indicating that both groups make more use of the eastern part of the beach that is next to the sandy beach park, which has better amenities. We can also see that men are more dispersed over the area compared with women, as indicated by the considerably larger radius values of the ellipse. In the case of the sandy beach park, the radii of the ellipses are very similar for both genders, but the mean centres vary significantly. For women, the standard deviation ellipse fits within the boundaries of the park and is close to its centre, while the location of the ellipse for men is considerably shifted towards the south. The reason for such a shift might be something particular in the landscape that affects this user group and will be investigated further in the following section.

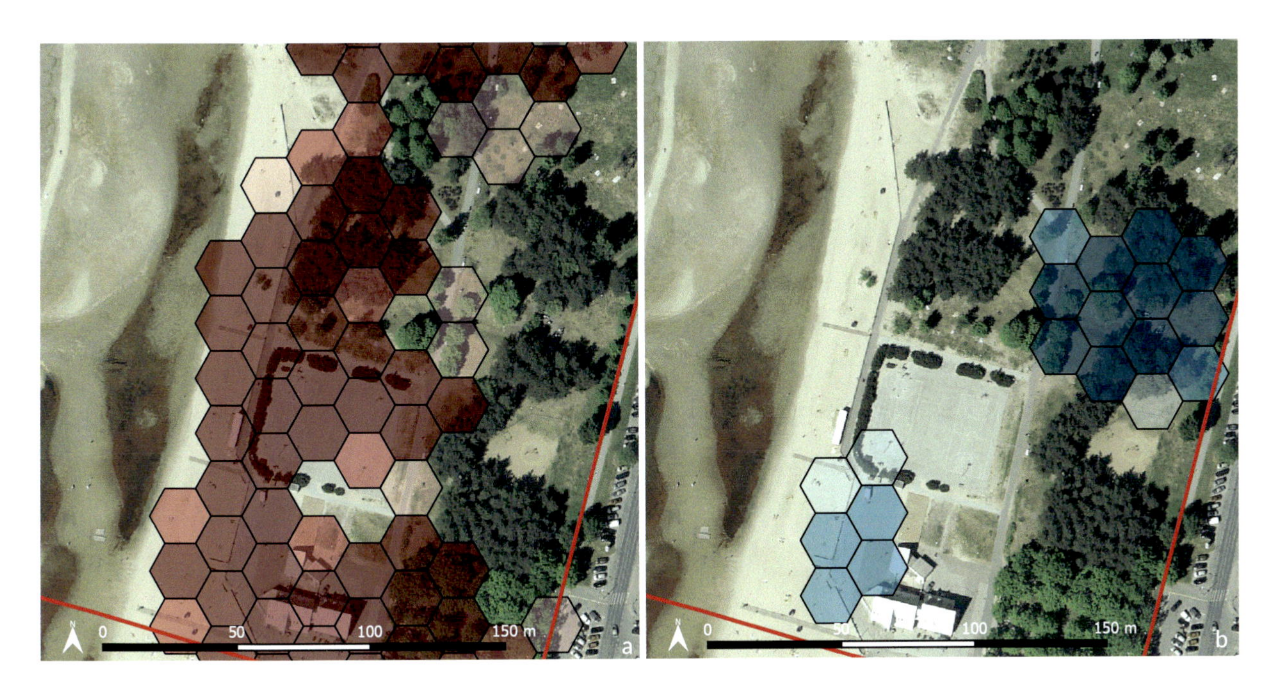

Figure 6.20a and b
a) Hot spot analysis of older women and b) older men overlaid on the aerial image of the southernmost tip of the area
(*Source*: Peeter Vassiljev and Orthophoto: Estonian Land Board, 2020)

A slightly more sophisticated statistical technique to consider is hot spot analysis (not to be confused with heat maps) based on the Getis-Ord Gi* statistic, which uses counts of points within a square or a hexagonal grid of a pre-determined mesh size to determine local regions of higher or lower values. In this way, it is possible to reveal neighbourhoods where the congregation of users (or a subgroup of users) is beyond a random chance with 99%, 95% or 90% statistical confidence. Figure 6.20a and b shows two examples – for older women using the southern part of the site contrasted with older men. These are overlaid on the aerial photograph and can be seen to relate to combined areas of beach and grass in the case of the older women and to two specific spots in the case of the older men. These two specific hot spots are around a cafe and a set of chess tables (Figure 6.21) and are also responsible for the differences in the standard deviation ellipses described earlier (see Figure 6.19a).

NON-SPATIAL ANALYSIS

The maps, as demonstrated so far, are very revealing of how people use the different parts of the site, but so far, we have presented limited quantitative information on the numbers or proportions of users in relation to different attributes. The next set of analyses demonstrate how the data can be analysed non-spatially, taking different sets of attributes associated with the data points to identify trends and patterns associated with the mapped results. Descriptive statistics can be used to explore aspects such as the proportion of gender and age groups compared to the local general population (see Figure 6.22), the relative popularity of different primary activities in general (see Figure 6.23) and by gender or age.

Figure 6.21

A set of chess tables and regular picnic tables that attract a large portion of older male users of the park into a specific, well-defined hot spot – a vivid example of small investment making a large impact

(*Source*: Peeter Vassiljev)

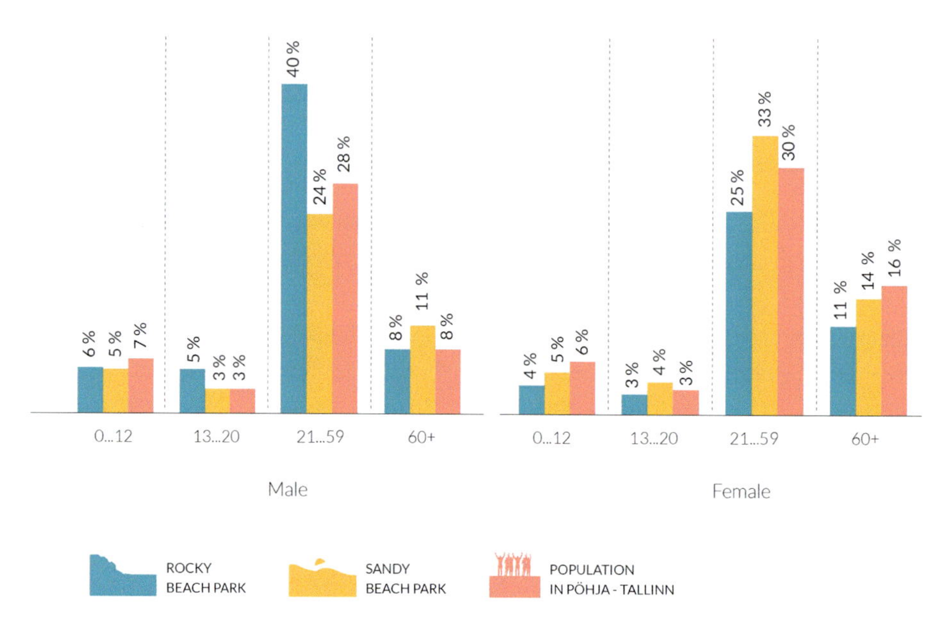

Figure 6.22

Proportions of gender and age groups within observed visitors to the two parts of the study area and comparison with the proportion of these groups in the general population living in the area of Põhja-Tallinn (Statistics Estonia, 2020)

(*Source*: Peeter Vassiljev and Anna Wilczyńska)

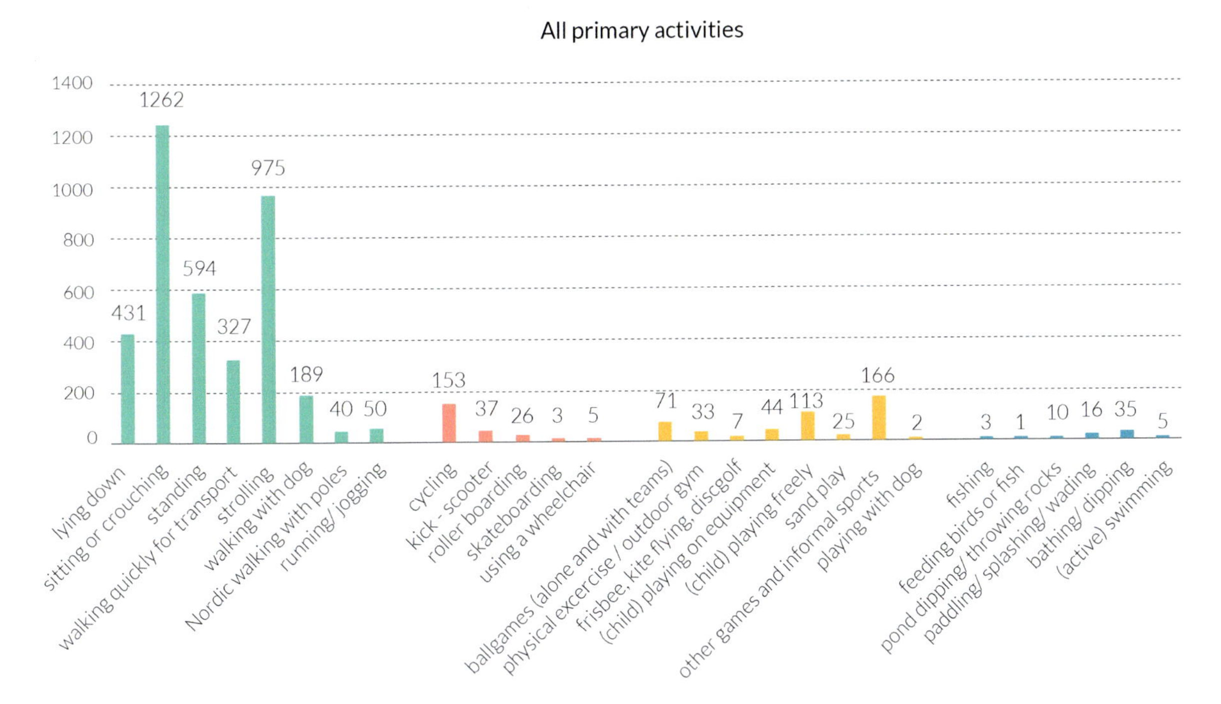

Figure 6.23

Number of users engaged in different primary activities during all observations in 2017

(*Source*: Peeter Vassiljev and Anna Wilczyńska)

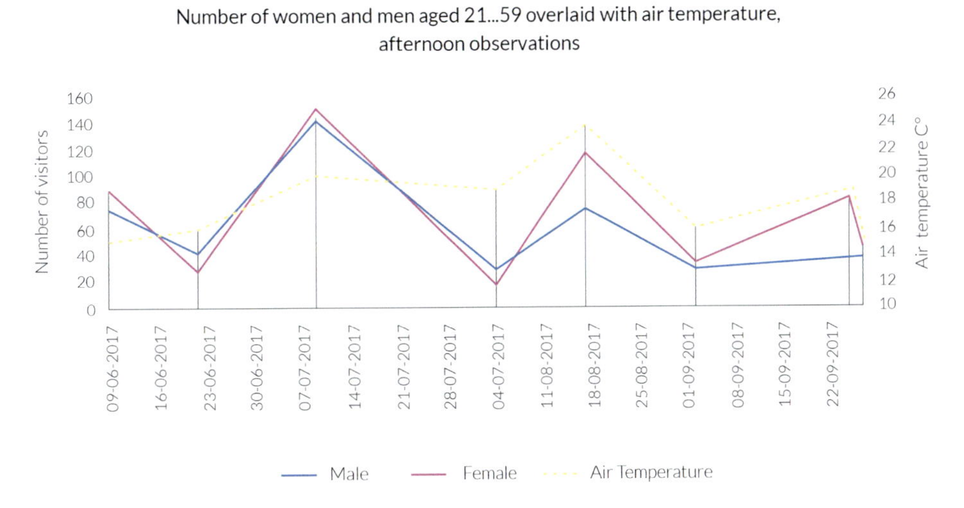

Figure 6.24

The number of observed women and men overlaid with air temperature during the afternoon observations

(*Source*: Peeter Vassiljev and Anna Wilczyńska)

Clearly, there are important findings here which are not apparent from the maps alone. There are also many different attributes which can be explored in this way, depending on what information is needed from the analysis. Another possibility of analysis of the attribute data is to explore changes over time. Figure 6.24 shows a time series graph revealing that visitor numbers tend to follow air temperature fluctuations to some degree. In the second half of the warm season, the number of female visitors appears to become more sensitive to temperature fluctuations, increasing dramatically with warmer periods and returning to the same level as male visitors during cooler spells.

It is also possible to run some inferential or predictive statistics using correlations or regressions. Table 6.2 shows an example of a regression looking at the influence of a range of independent variables such as time of visit or weather conditions "predicting" use of the site by people of different ages. Overall, it can be noted that the regression model performs very well, except for age group 60+, where the *R*-squared value (an indicator of how much variation in visitor numbers the model can explain) is very low. Looking at the particular components in this model, it is possible to observe that air temperature is positively affecting the observed visitor numbers (also confirming the observation presented on the time series graph at Figure 6.24), and the effect is strongest with activities that imply spending a longer time on site – something that seems intuitively logical. However, contrary to what might be expected, the rain does not affect the number of observed visitors. Instead, the level of cloud cover affects the visitor numbers negatively, suggesting a far more sensitive response to even a hint of unfavourable weather. From the temporal perspective, weekends by themselves do not seem to affect the number of observed users, but weekends during summer vacations do seem to cause a reduction in the number of visits. Last, among various age groups, the number of teenagers is affected by the fewest number of factors – air temperature and time of day.

With the ability to model the level of use by different groups in various weather, environmental and temporal conditions, it is possible to identify factors that influence different user groups. This sort of information provides valuable insights into behaviour predictors but also gives hints of possible ways to cater to the needs of specific groups during unfavourable conditions or solutions that could mitigate conflicts between different user groups. Here we demonstrated a regression on the total observed users, but similar modelling applied to a number of users engaged in specific main or secondary activities or social situations could reveal further insights.

Converting BBAT data to the SOPARC format

Sometimes it might be potentially useful to convert BBAT data into the SOPARC format for comparison purposes. Since the data collection rules have the same principles, it is an easy task. First, SOPARC requires counts of visitors by age group, gender and activity level for each sub-area or behaviour setting (McKenzie et al., 2006). Subdividing the BBAT point data to sub-areas that can be determined at a later stage of analysis is a straightforward task of intersecting the point cloud with behaviour-setting polygons in GIS. It is possible to start BBAT observations with less preparation and use the experience gained through the observations to refine the borders of the behaviour settings or sub-areas. Then the BBAT data points can be subdivided between these sub-areas, counted and analysed separately.

Second, BBAT captures a rather specific activity type for each user, while SOPARC observations differentiate between three activity levels (McKenzie et al., 2006): sedentary (lying down, sitting or standing), walking (at a casual pace and other moderate activities) and vigorous (any activity that requires more energy than casual walking). The activities captured in BBAT can obviously be reclassified to calm, moderate and energetic levels – a task that involves creating an extra column in the GIS database and using conditional logic to fill out the values based on other fields in the database. Table 6.3 provides a suggested conversion schema for performing the conversion.

Table 6.2 **Multiple linear regressions of observed visitor counts in various groups with a number of environmental and temporal factors. Green indicates statistically significant results, and the value of beta indicates the direction and magnitude of the influence on visitor numbers**

Dependent variables ->	All users		Age group 0…12		Age group 13…20		Age group 21…59		Age group 60+		All stationary activities	
Adjusted R square ->	0.476		0.383		0.378		0.565		0.181		0.430	
F ->	9.388		6.722		6.614		12.968		3.039		7.955	
p ->	0.000		0.000		0.000		0.000		0.004		0.000	
Independent variables	Beta	p	Beta	p	Beta	p	Beta	p	Beta	p	Beta	p
Influence of vacation on visitor numbers	0.031	0.786	0.092	0.452	0.134	0.278	-0.012	0.906	0.003	0.981	0.058	0.623
Influence of years on visitor numbers	0.089	0.274	0.208	0.021	0.173	0.054	-0.012	0.872	0.225	0.030	0.099	0.247
Influence of weekend on visitor numbers	0.154	0.158	0.151	0.202	-0.047	0.691	0.182	0.069	0.165	0.225	0.132	0.246
Influence of weekends during vacation period on visitor numbers	-0.248	0.043	-0.287	0.031	-0.196	0.139	-0.237	0.035	-0.156	0.304	-0.232	0.069
Influence of time of day on visitor numbers	0.205	0.022	0.074	0.438	0.365	0.000	0.267	0.001	-0.173	0.119	0.127	0.170
Influence of air temperature on visitor numbers	0.469	0.000	0.476	0.000	0.256	0.036	0.496	0.000	0.303	0.031	0.518	0.000
Influence of cloudiness on visitor numbers	-0.273	0.003	-0.208	0.036	-0.143	0.146	-0.290	0.001	-0.269	0.019	-0.219	0.022
Influence of rainy weather on visitor numbers	-0.103	0.257	-0.073	0.464	-0.147	0.140	-0.097	0.246	-0.070	0.541	-0.068	0.478
Influence of windiness on visitor numbers	-0.084	0.307	-0.029	0.741	-0.110	0.219	-0.112	0.135	0.040	0.698	-0.065	0.444

Observations in years 2017, 2018, 2019

statistically significant result

statistically non-significant result

Figure 6.25 shows an example of proportions of activity levels on the study site, grouped by gender and sub-areas, where specific main activities from BBAT observation data have been converted into SOPARC activity intensity levels according to the conversion schema presented in Table 6.3. Comparison of the observation data between Kopli Rand beach in Põhja-Tallinn and Besòs River in Barcelona (see Figure 6.6) becomes possible.

It is possible to assign metabolic energy expenditure rates to every activity and to use average METs per person per observation episode as the analysis unit. Where the BBAT activities are used, the exhaustive list of MET values for various activities in the compendium of physical activities by Ainsworth et al. (2011) can be consulted, while if the activities have been reclassified to the three levels as in Table 6.3, then reference values for these can be used (see Vert et al., 2019). The distribution of the observed points categorised by SOPARC activity levels may be displayed or explored further by intersecting the values with behaviour settings. An example of mean MET values per user per behaviour setting of the Pelgurand demonstration site is shown in Figure 6.26.

A limitation with applying METs in the context of BBAT or SOPARC data is the lack of a duration measurement – it is possible to estimate the potential to expend a certain amount of energy per minute, but it does not take into account the actual duration of visits. Many sedentary activities tend to last longer, so the total calorie budget may be higher than for some vigorous activities. Another limitation of using energy expenditure is that it discounts the quality of the sedentary experience as a source of psychological restoration as opposed to active physical exercise. We must look at these two aspects separately in terms of their respective health benefits.

Table 6.3 **Conversion schema of BBAT main activities into SOPARC activity intensity levels (S – sedentary activities, M – walking and other moderate activities, V – vigorous activities)**

SOPARC intensity	BBAT Activity type: terrestrial	SOPARC intensity	BBAT Activity type: aquatic
Activity on foot		Activities in the water	
<S>	A1 - lying down	<S>	iW1 - fishing
<S>	A2 - sitting or crouching	<S>	iW2 - feeding birds or fish
<S>	A3 - standing	<M>	iW 3 - pond dipping / throwing rocks
<M>	A4 - walking quickly for transport	<M>	iW 4 - paddling / splashing / wading
<M>	A5 - strolling	<V>	iW 5 - bathing / dipping
<M>	A6 - walking with a dog	<V>	iW 6 - (active) swimming
<V>	A7 - Nordic walking with poles	<V>	iW 7 - diving / jumping into water
<V>	A8 - running / jogging	<V>	iW 8 - snorkeling / scuba diving
Sports and games		Activities on the water	
<V>	G1 - ball games (alone and teams)	<V>	oW1 - windsurfing
<V>	G2 - physical exercise / outdoor gym	<V>	oW2 - surfing on waves
<V>	G3 - frisbee, kite flying, disc golf	<V>	oW3 - paddleboarding
<V>	G4 - (child) playing on equipment	<V>	oW4 - wakeboarding (cable pulled)
<V>	G5 - (child) playing freely	<V>	oW5 - boating, rowing, pedalo
<M>	G6 - sand play	<M>	oW6 - boating (motor)
<M>	G7 - other games and informal sports	<V>	oW7 - kayaking/canoeing
<M>	G8 - playing with dog	<M>	oW8 - sailing
<V>	G9 - horse riding		
Wheeled movement			
<V>	B1 - cycling		
<V>	B2 - kick-scooter		
<V>	B3 - rollerblading		
<V>	B4 - skateboarding		
<M>	B5 - using a wheelchair		

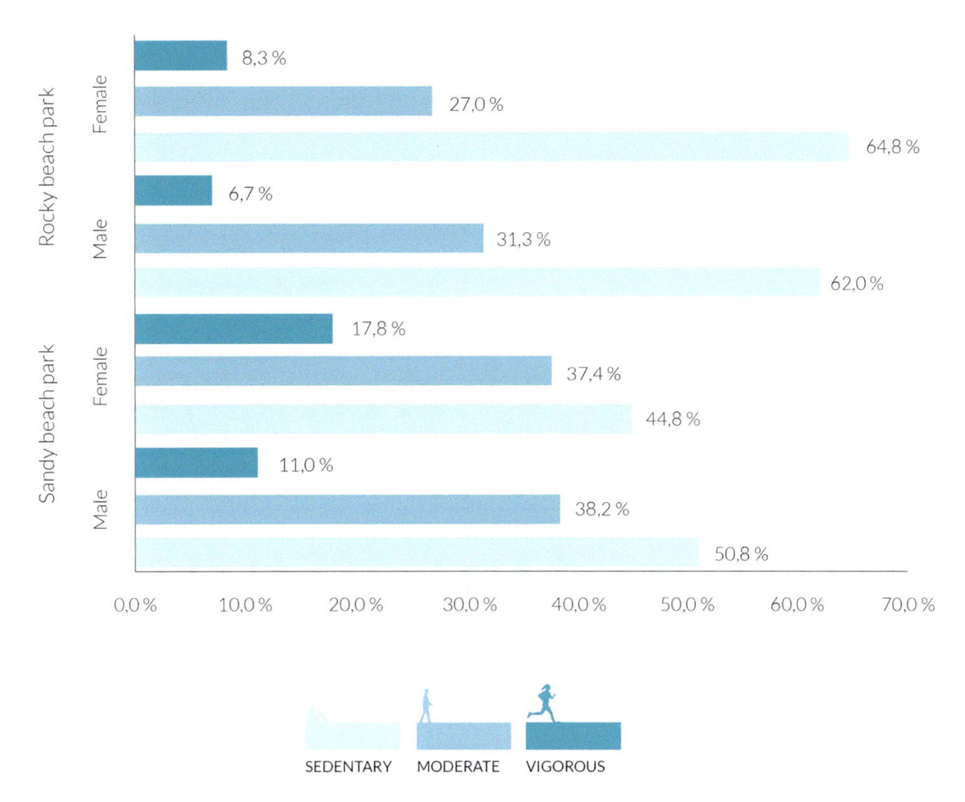

Figure 6.25

Comparison of physical activity levels according to SOPARC activity levels by analysis sub-area (rocky beach and sandy beach of Pelgurand) and by gender

(*Source*: Peeter Vassiljev and Anna Wilczyńska)

Conclusions

This chapter introduced two methods that can be used to conduct observations to capture the use of a blue or green space. Both methods are essentially momentary time sampling techniques which do not give a complete visitor count of an area but rather a series of snapshots of the usage levels taken within a longer period. It is up to the researcher to decide how often this snapshot is taken, but the guiding principle should be to ensure representativeness. Clearly, having observations that cover different time slots only once, for example, one observation per weekday afternoon, will not be enough to draw conclusions as to what people generally like to do on weekday afternoons, but three or four observations will give much greater confidence.

The key difference between the two methods is the spatial resolution and granularity of the activity types recorded (see Figure 6.27). SOPARC looks at user numbers within predetermined sub-areas of the site, while BBAT captures more or less the exact location of every user. Having more specific data allows for significantly more detailed analysis, especially about the question: "Where?" As previously stated, BBAT data can be converted to the SOPARC format, making it possible 1) to compare the new results with observations for the same area that were carried out with SOPARC and 2) to apply the same data analysis techniques so as to be able to compare data from different research teams or from different sites. Converting the data the other way around, however, is impossible.

While the main advantage of BBAT over SOPARC is the finer detail of the data, its main drawbacks are higher requirements for equipment, skills and training. A lightweight tablet computer with a very bright screen running

Figure 6.26

A map showing the mean METs per minute per person calculated for each behaviour setting. Sedentary activities have been assigned 1.3 METs (green), moderate activities 3.5 METs (yellow) and vigorous activities 7.5 METs (red)
(*Source*: Peeter Vassiljev and Orthophoto: Estonian Land Board, 2020)

Windows is required for BBAT, while a simple paper form works fine for SOPARC. Only rudimentary GIS skills, which are well described in the guidance materials, are required to conduct the observations themselves, but preparation of GIS base maps and analysis of the data requires slightly greater skill. Instructions for these tasks have also been provided in the guidance materials (a video on the BlueHealth tools website), but it is yet another set of skills that someone already needs or has to learn. Finally, both methods require observers to be trained so that they can apply the method in a consistent and valid manner and are capable of dealing with data overload scenarios (too many people to be recorded at once). However, BBAT requires slightly greater familiarity with the exhaustive list of activity types and also the ability to pinpoint someone's location on a map in an area that might lack clear landmarks.

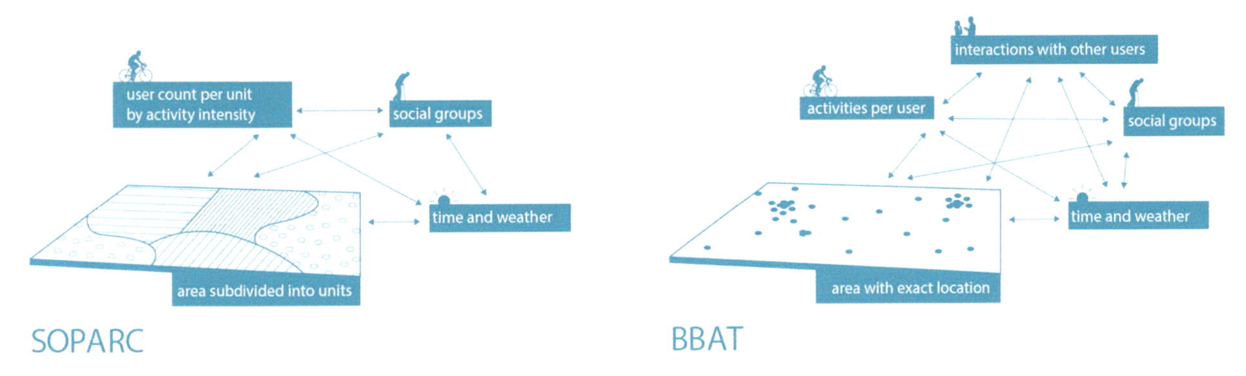

Figure 6.27
Similarities and differences between SOPARC and BBAT
(*Source*: Peeter Vassiljev and Anna Wilczyńska)

Generally, the SOPARC and BBAT methods do not pose major ethical or privacy issues – observations are conducted in public spaces, there is no intentional interaction with the users of the area and the identification of a particular individual from the information being gathered is impossible. Nevertheless, ethical issues must still be considered from the regulatory perspective as well as from the point of perception. For example, standing periodically next to a children's playground might be legal but could be perceived as a potential problem by parents. Another example of a very controversial subject is recording racial, ethnic or religious groups. It is very important to consider if such data are actually needed and even how reliable such a classification can be during observations.

Both methods are labour intensive, so naturally there could be a desire for automation. Using video equipment to reduce the amount of fieldwork is a first option, but the observations could be automated even further with the use of artificial intelligence. From the technical perspective, the biggest challenge is to train the algorithms to understand the context, for example, learning to differentiate between strolling, walking quickly for transport (especially in older visitors) or wading in shallow water (especially in tidal conditions). The biggest challenge, however, would be to ensure the respect for privacy, because the risk of accidental or malicious misuse of the video material and image recognition software is high.

Observation techniques give an objective picture of how visitors use a blue or green space. This can be a powerful tool for building the evidence base to help with planning, design, management and monitoring tasks. What this evidence lacks to some degree is the understanding of values associated with the landscape experience. Short and infrequent activities can supply significant restorative, emotional and spiritual benefits, but these tend to be much less prominent in the count frequency of the observations. A good example of this discrepancy is a person visiting a sandy beach for half a day. If that person were to be asked: "What were you doing?" the most likely reply would be: "I went for a swim." The actual time spent in the water and, subsequently, the probability that the swimming activity would be recorded in the data would be low compared to the time and probability of that person being recorded as lying down or sitting on the sandy beach. The obvious conclusion here is the desirability of using a mixed-methods approach – to combine observations with some form of questionnaire or interview methods so as to be able to attach landscape experience values to the blue and green spaces and to compare these with the observations. This can be achieved using public participation GIS, which will be discussed in the next chapter, Chapter 7.

References

Active Living Research. 2006. *Tools and Measures SOPARC: System for Observing Play and Recreation in Communities*. Available: https://activelivingresearch.org/soparc-system-observing-play-and-recreation-communities [accessed 29 January 2020].

Ainsworth, B.E., Haskell, W.L., Herrmann, S.D., Meckes, N., Bassett, D.R., Tudor-Locke, C., et al. 2011. 2011 compendium of physical activities: A second update of codes and MET values. *Medical & Science in Sports Exercise* 43:1575–1581. doi:10.1249/MSS.0b013e31821ece12.

Barker, R.G. 1968. *Ecological Psychology: Concepts and Methods for Studying the Environment of Human Behaviour*. Palo Alto: Stanford University Press.

Bechtel, R.B., Marans, R., Michelson, W. 1987. *Methods in Environmental and Behavioural Research*. New York: Van Nostrand Reinhold.

Ciafel. 2013. iSOPARC for iPad. CIAFEL iOS Dev. Available: http://ciafel.fade.up.pt/isoparc/ [accessed 18 December 2019].

Cohen, D., Han, B., Isacoff, J., Shulaker, B., Williamson, S., Marsh, T., et al. 2015. Impact of park renovations on park use and park-based physical activity. *Journal of Physical Activity and Health* 12:289–295. doi:10.1016/j.jsr.2014.05.003.A.

Cohen, D., Marsh, T., Williamson, S., Han, B., Derose, K., Golinelli, D., et al. 2014. The potential for pocket parks to increase physical activity. *American Journal of Health Promotion* 28:S19–S26. doi:10.4278/ajhp.130430-QUAN-213.The.

Cooper Marcus, C., Miller Watsky, C., Insley, E., Francis, C. 1998. Neighbourhood parks. In: Cooper Marcus, C., Francis, C. (Eds.), *People Places: Design Guidelines for Urban Open Space, Part 4*. New York: John Wiley & Sons, Inc., pp. 85–148.

Cosco, N.G., Moore, R.C., Islam, M.Z. 2010. Behaviour mapping: A method for linking preschool physical activity and outdoor design. *Medicine and Science in Sports and Exercise* 42(3):513–519.

Estonian Land Board. 2018. Topographic data based on 27.01.2016 ETAK extract and Orthophoto. Low-altitude flight 11.04.2016. Published under Licence of open data by Estonian Land Board, 1.07.2018.

Estonian Land Board. 2020. *Orthophoto*. Summertime forestry flight 28.05.2018. Published under Licence of open data by Estonian Land Board, 1 July 2018.

Evenson, K.R., Jones, S.A., Holliday, K.M., Cohen, D.A., Mckenzie, T.L. 2017. Park characteristics, use, and physical activity: A review of studies using SOPARC (System for Observing Play and Recreation in Communities). *Preventive Medicine (Baltimore)* 86:153–166. doi:10.1016/j.ypmed.2016.02.029.Park.

Goličnik, B., Ward Thompson, C. 2010. Emerging relationships between design and use of urban park spaces. *Landscape and Urban Planning* 94:38–53.

Hallgren, K.A. 2012. Computing inter-rater reliability for observational data: An overview and tutorial. *Tutor Quantitative Methods for Psychology* 8:23–34. doi:10.1080/11035896009449194.

Institut Cartogràfic i Geològic de Catalunya. 2020. May 2019 25cm pixel Orthophoto of Catalonia by the Institut Cartogràfic i Geològic de Catalunya (ICGC). Published under a CC BY 4.0 license.

Ittelson, W.H., Rivlin, L.G., Prohansky, H.M. 1970. The use of behavioural maps in environmental psychology. In: Prohansky, H.M., Ittelson, W.H., Rivlin, L.G. (Eds.), *Environmental Psychology: Man and his Physical Setting*. New York: Holt, Rinehart &Winston, pp. 658–668.

King, D.K., Litt, J., Hale, J., Burniece, K.M., Ross, C. 2015. "The park a tree built": Evaluating how a park development project impacted where people play. Urban For. *Urban Green* 14:293–299. doi:10.1016/j.ufug.2015.02.011.

Kramer, D., Lakerveld, J., Stronks, K., Kunst, A.E. 2017. Uncovering how urban regeneration programs may stimulate leisure-time walking among adults in deprived areas: A realist review. *International Journal of Health. Services* 47:703–724. doi:10.1177/0020731417722087

Mckenzie, T.L., Cohen, D.A. 2006. *System for Observing Play and Recreation in Communities.* York: Description and Procedures Manual. Sci.

McKenzie, T.L., Cohen, D.A., Sehgal, A., Williamson, S., Golinelli, D. 2006. System for observing play and recreation in communities (SOPARC): Reliability and feasibility measures. *Journal of Physical Activity and Health* 1:S203–217.

Meireles Rodrigues, F. 2015. *Da especificidade do parque português contemporâneo – Specifics of the contemporary Portuguese park* (Doctoral thesis in Landscape Architecture, University of Porto), pp. 340. Retrieved from the Scientific Repository (TID N°: 101376057). Available: https://hdl.handle.net/10216/94540.

Schultz, C.L., Wilhelm Stanis, S.A., Sayers, S.P., Thombs, L.A., Thomas, I.M. 2017. A longitudinal examination of improved access on park use and physical activity in a low-income and majority African American neighborhood park. *Preventive Medicine (Baltimore)* 95:S95–S100. doi:10.1016/j.ypmed.2016.08.036.

Statistics Estonia. 2020. *RV0241: Population by sex, age and administrative unit or type of settlement.* 1 January 2017. Available: https://andmed.stat.ee/en/stat/rahvastik__rahvastikunaitajad-ja-koosseis__rahvaarv-ja-rahvastiku-koosseis/RV0241 [accessed 29 November 2020].

Stewart, O.T., Moudon, A.V., Littman, A.J., Seto, E., Saelens, B.E. 2018. Why neighborhood park proximity is not associated with total physical activity. *Health Place* 52:163–169. doi:10.1016/J.HEALTHPLACE.2018.05.011

Sun, Z., Bell, S., Scott, I., Qian, J. 2019. Everyday use of urban street spaces: The spatio-temporal relations between pedestrians and street vendors: A case study in Yuncheng, China, Landscape Research.

Unt, A-L., Bell, S. 2014. The impact of small-scale design interventions on the behaviour patterns of the users of an urban wasteland. *Urban Forestry & Urban Greening* 13:121–135.

Vert, C., Carrasco-Turigas, G., Zijlema, W., Espinosa, A., Cano-Riu, L., Elliott, L.R., et al. 2019. Impact of a riverside accessibility intervention on use, physical activity, and wellbeing: A mixed methods pre-post evaluation. *Landscape and Urban Planning* 190:103611. doi:10.1016/j.landurbplan.2019.103611.

Chapter 7: Capturing affordances for health and well-being at the city scale

Gloria Niin, Peeter Vassiljev, Tiina Rinne and Simon Bell

Introduction

One of the central theories applied throughout this book and in the research within the BlueHealth project has been that of affordances. Environmental affordances are perceived properties of a place which might influence behaviour (Ward Thompson, 2013). For example, a physical element such as a ledge may be a functional signifier for designed or spontaneous activities (sitting, skateboarding), highlighting the importance of understanding the physical environment (Heft, 2010). Affordance as a concept and its role in designing different physical environments has been amply demonstrated, for example, in studies of children's activity in different play settings (Kyttä, 2004). Understanding people's behaviour in outdoor public spaces can provide convincing evidence for urban planning and design aiming to promote more activity. In the case of blue space, for example, wider views of water bodies with spacious and natural characteristics, the presence of bank vegetation, moist atmosphere, rich and diverse wildlife and non-visual sensory stimulation may afford positive perceptions and create fascination (Völker and Kistemann, 2011, 2015).

We focus on urban blue spaces and therefore potentially want to find out what role all blue spaces within a particular city play in providing affordances for obtaining the benefits for health and well-being. Thus it is beneficial if we have the means of collecting information about this from the users themselves. We now have access to detailed and fine-grained geographic information about different land covers or land uses in many larger urban areas through the Urban Atlas vector dataset provided by the European Union's Copernicus Land Monitoring Service (www.eea.europa.eu/data-and-maps/data/copernicus-land-monitoring-service-urban-atlas#tab-data) or, if the city is not included, through Corine Land Cover, also provided through Copernicus (https://land.copernicus.eu/pan-european/corine-land-cover), although this is much coarser grained and raster based. Alternatively, we can also pick up detailed information from high-resolution aerial photographs. These datasets can tell us a lot about what kind of blue spaces are present and what the land cover types and water-land interface are. However, while we can observe what goes on at specific sites (see Chapter 6), we need a way of identifying the key affordances as a city-wide pattern, and for this, we need to capture people-based as opposed to territorially based data related to blue spaces.

We can refer to the kind of geographic information system (GIS) described previously as "hard GIS", as it deals with objective facts about spaces. If we can capture more subjective values which are also spatially related, by asking residents to tell us about, for example, their favourite blue space or the one which they go to in order to de-stress or to carry out a particular activity at or on the water, then we have the means to capture the affordances associated by different people with specific places. This can help a great deal in urban blue space planning. This "SoftGIS", or, as it is also known, public participation GIS (PPGIS), can be applied top down or bottom up and, depending on the system used, can capture highly detailed information from a large number of residents, which has real value for planners as well as researchers (Kahila-Tani et al., 2016; Schmidt-Thomé et al., 2014; Brown and Weber, 2013.

 DOI: 10.4324/9780429056161-10

In the BlueHealth Project, we applied a PPGIS approach to study and collect people-based data related to blue spaces. In this chapter, since we did not develop a tool specifically for the project (unlike the BlueHealth Environmental Assessment Tool [BEAT], BlueHealth Behavioural Assessment Tool [BBAT] or decision support tool [DST]) but used a proprietary tool, we do not spend time on tool development but much more on what can be obtained from applying such approaches and what kind of analyses and outputs are useful for planning purposes. First, we introduce some of concepts behind the PPGIS method and then describe how it can be applied, using the BlueHealth case study of Plymouth to illustrate some of the outputs.

Public participation geographic information systems: concepts

PPGIS refers to methods that use geospatial technology to engage the public in producing spatially related knowledge for land-use planning, decision-making and scientific purposes (Schmidt-Thomé et al., 2014). PPGIS methods offer convenient tools for studying and investigating human behaviour in a context-sensitive way. Localisation of human experiences and behavioural patterns by PPGIS methods attaches them to specific physical contexts, providing geographic coordinates to human behaviour and experiences. PPGIS approaches enable a collection of large datasets with user-friendly online survey applications (Figure 7.1) (Brown and Kyttä, 2014; Fagerholm et al., 2021). Combination of collected PPGIS data with conventional register-based GIS data allows for simultaneous GIS-based analysis of human behaviour in relation to the physical environment.

PPGIS approaches have become one of the most efficient knowledge-based methods gathering new and, in many cases, previously non-existing spatially referenced information from residents for planning, public participation and scientific purposes (Brown and Kyttä, 2014, 2018; Kahila-Tani et al., 2019). One of the earliest examples of an advanced online PPGIS approach is the so-called SoftGIS methodology developed in Aalto University, Finland, since

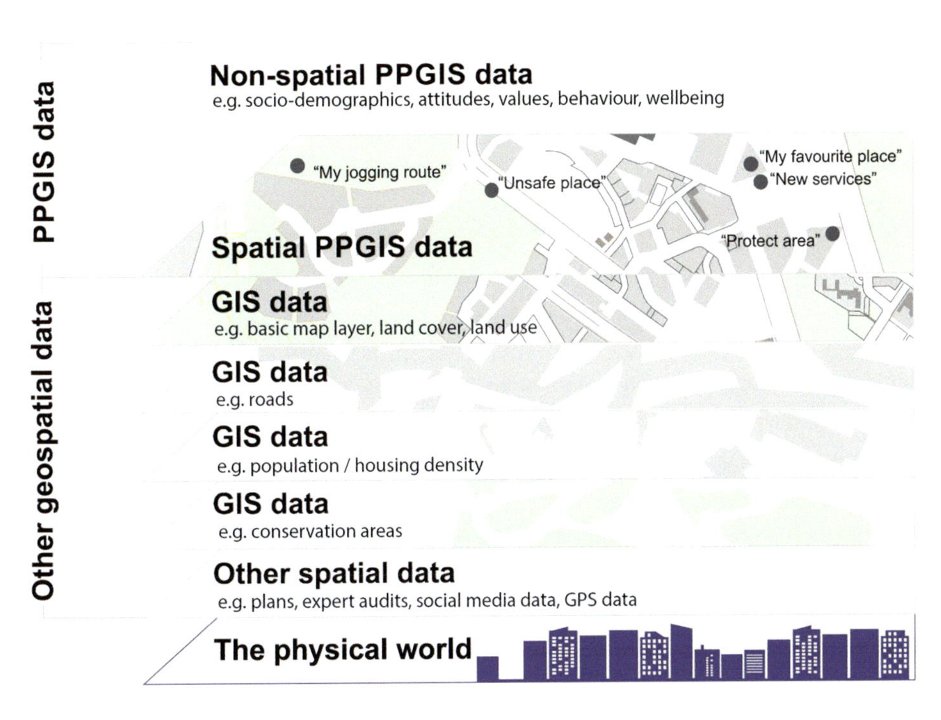

Figure 7.1
The overall concept of PPGIS
(*Source*: Fagerholm et al. 2021)

2005. The development work of SoftGIS methods was later outsourced from Aalto University, and the tool that is based on SoftGIS methodology is nowadays called Maptionnaire. The development of PPGIS tools has accelerated during the last decade, and there are many examples of differing PPGIS tools available (Brown and Kyttä, 2018).

Regardless of the tool used, PPGIS surveys produce two types of data, spatial and non-spatial. In the often self-administered, online PPGIS surveys, individual respondents map various spatial attributes (points, lines or polygons) and answer questions that can be related to both that specific location, such as a park, street or coastline, and information on their sociodemographic background, personal values, attitudes and preferences, personal behaviour intentions and motivations, well-being and health, to name only a few possibilities (Fagerholm et al., 2021). Mapped spatial attributes produce spatial data, and the more traditional survey types of attributes non-spatial data. Spatially explicit data can then be compared with the underlying objective characteristics of the places respondents have marked for further analysis, and both statistical and qualitative, spatial and aspatial analyses can be performed (see the following).

The application of PPGIS in the BlueHealth project

Using PPGIS approaches in BlueHealth Project – specifically, we used the Maptionnaire tool – we were able to study what kind of place-based positive and negative experiences residents have related to blue spaces. The overall aim was, like everything else in the BlueHealth project, to understand the affordances of residents of the cities studied. It was also important to relate many of the questions asked of respondents to the other surveys undertaken at different scales. Thus, as will be explained in more detail in the following, a number of the questions related to health and well-being were taken directly from both the BlueHealth International Survey (BIS) and the BlueHealth Community Level Survey (BCLS) (see Chapters 4 and 8 for details on the relationship of the various surveys), potentially allowing for a comparison of results emerging from surveys at different spatial scales.

Underlying the application was the research objective, which naturally related to the overall aims of the project. We wanted know which the favourite blue spaces in each city were and why; we also wanted to be able to determine how the health benefits of such spaces were experienced by the residents, and we were also interested in relating these preferences and opinions to the physical characteristics of the spaces so identified.

Setting up the survey

The Maptionnaire system is very straightforward to use. It is first necessary to apply for a license from the company, and, once obtained, users can log in to their account and set up their surveys using a wide range of different tools for setting up the questionnaire. Maptionnaire uses OpenStreetMap (© OpenStreetMap contributors) as a base, which allows the user to specify the geographical location for the survey. Some satellite images are also available. It is possible for users to zoom in and out of the map in order to focus on specific places in more detail, for example, for accurately identifying a particular area. The first setup includes choice of language, background images for use in the survey and the style of the appearance, to mention some features. This is important from a usability perspective (Gottwald et al., 2016). An easy-to-use, attractive and welcoming interface can help in persuading respondents to take part.

The questionnaire setup takes place by adding a series of pages – such as a welcome page where the basic information and explanation of the project is presented. There may be a further information page, perhaps explaining anonymity, data protection, consent procedures and other ethical information before the respondent is able to proceed further. Following this, it is useful to identify the general location of the respondent's residence – usually a spot within 300 m of their home, so that while the general district is identifiable (for relating this to, for example, socioeconomic characteristics), the specific address remains completely anonymous. For this, the respondent merely needs to drop a pin to a location. Then is it possible to ask questions which require the respondent to place a point or draw a line or polygon marking a specific location or route or area, for example, and to answer questions about that place – which can be open text questions or include choices, using different tools (rating scales, slider scales, tick boxes, etc.), all very easily added to the question. Non-spatial questions may also be asked, including ones related to preferences, health and well-being and demographic information (gender, age, educational levels, household income, etc.).

The BlueHealth Maptionnaire structure and content

In the surveys for the four BlueHealth case study cities, we wanted to understand what makes a place important for the respondent, asking them to describe why some places are more important to them than others, and then, based on the results of these questions, we wanted explore what sort of topics emerged that could be mapped or measured by looking at the site itself. We wanted to have a combination of place-based insights and also general attitudes/blue space usage habits in each city region (and, of course, this allowed us to compare different geographical regions). We were also interested in the general factors related to the frequency of visitation, the personal importance of blue spaces, perceived health benefits connected with the visitation of blue spaces, region- and user-specific aspects and, finally, what general notions of these topics are over the four European countries.

In the BlueHealth Project, we looked for the blue spaces that users visit in relation to the distance from their home compared with other perceived attributes of the site, such as safety, naturalness and role played by visitation frequency, plus their perceived positive health benefits and habits (such as relaxing after work, resting, sports, physical activity or socialising with friends and family). We were also interested in how important the role of water was in the overall visitation experience.

In order to make the survey interesting and to give it a recognisable title, we named it "My blue Plymouth" (or Tartu, Tallinn or Barcelona). We illustrate this for Plymouth because the survey was in English. The questionnaire structure used in BlueHealth was in several parts, as follows (each illustrated by shots of the appearance of the interface). The survey was pilot tested to ensure that people understood the questions and could answer them easily.

The entry page featured the title, the visual identity of the BlueHealth project, some basic information about what the survey aimed to do, some details about who should fill it in and that it was anonymous. Figure 7.2 shows the appearance of the title page, which has the map in the background.

Figure 7.2
The welcome page of the "My blue Plymouth" Maptionnaire survey
(*Source*: © OpenStreetMap CC-BY-SA)

Following this, the next page asked for personal information so that demographic factors could be taken into account in the subsequent analysis. These factors were exactly the same as in the BIS and BCLS and are fairly standard questions. In this survey, the questions were compulsory, but in others, for reasons of sensitivity, they might not be or might include "prefer not to say" as an option. In this survey, no ethnic data were collected, but they could be included in other versions if deemed particularly relevant. Gender may also need to include additional options such as "other" or "prefer not so say" under certain circumstances. Next, the respondents were asked to note a place close to their home and to give some information about garden access before saving it.

The next set of related questions focused on general use of blue spaces: with a short definition of blue spaces, then recent visit frequency, association with childhood and means of getting to the blue space. Then the respondent was asked to mark the first of up to five blue spaces they liked to visit – the first being the most favourite (Figure 7.3a and b). Each of these locations was then associated with a set of questions about it and about activities and feelings

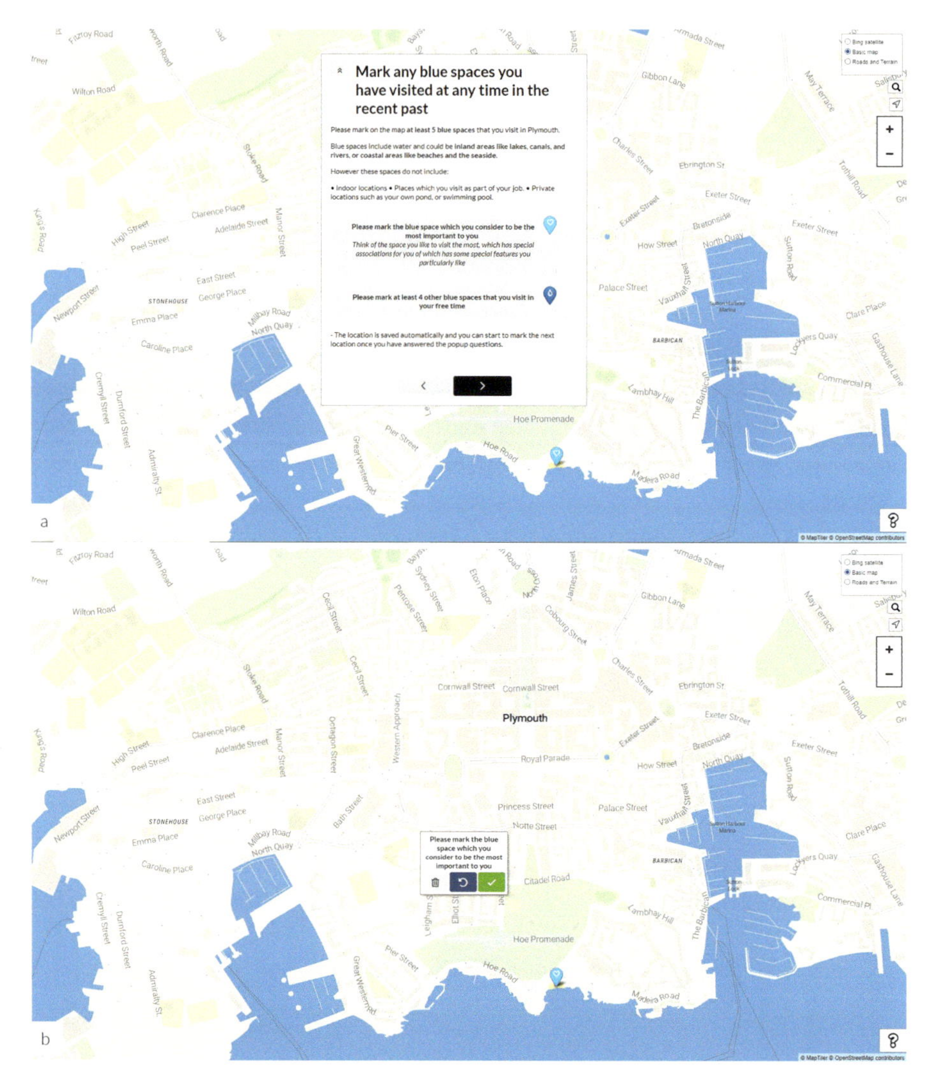

Figure 7.3a and b

The system for identifying points on the map – the most favourite one

(*Source*: © OpenStreetMap CC-BY-SA)

associated with it. It is possible to zoom in closely to be as accurate as possible and also to use the OpenStreetMap imagery instead of a map base.

On identification of the location, a series of questions then appeared, in several sections. These were divided into activities on land or water, the importance of water in the visit, the feelings generated by the visit (using a slider with a range from strongly agree to strongly disagree) and the time spent on the visit (taken from the same list as in the BlueHealth Community Level Survey).

This sequence was then repeated for each of the next four locations. This was followed by a series of questions about health, also using the slider and the range of different answers. Finally, some more personal information questions were asked, including dog ownership, household size, relationship status, employment status and income level (not in absolute terms because of difficulties of comparison but of how comfortable the respondent was financially). Finally, there was a finishing page with thanks and contact details if any respondent wanted to obtain more information.

The data entered to the survey are automatically saved – including those respondents who fail to complete the entire survey – into the servers of the Maptionnaire company, Mapita Ltd., where it is securely held and only accessible by password.

Respondent recruitment and sampling strategy

As an online survey instrument, the Maptionnaire survey is always going to be limited in its ability to reach every segment of a given population, since there is not 100% penetration of the internet or 100% of the population as users. It is also not possible to ensure a representative sample by age, gender or any other demographic trait, as in any other surveys. Given that proviso, and since data are generated about the demographic characteristics, some idea of the bias in the sample can be obtained, and the results can be considered with these limitations in mind.

As a web-based survey, it is important to have a strategy of ensuring it is widely publicised through different media and communication methods. If it is possible to obtain help from the local council or municipality in promoting the survey (especially when the research is undertaken with the cooperation and involvement of such bodies), together with links to relevant organisations such as schools, clubs and societies, local residents' associations and so on, hopefully wide coverage can be obtained.

The sample size obtained in each BlueHealth survey was between 250 and 300 individuals, with up to five sites being recorded per respondent; this meant around 1000 or more specific locations being identified and commented on. These are not large numbers as a proportion of the population but nevertheless give a good picture overall. Figure 7.4 is a map of Plymouth showing the home locations of all respondents. While there is wide distribution, there are also significant areas with few or no respondents, meaning that the results are not completely representative, at least in geographical terms. This is a common challenge in web-based as well as in more traditional social scientific surveys.

Analysis of results

There are various analysis methods that can be applied to PPGIS data. Fagerholm and colleagues (2021) examined the analysis possibilities of PPGIS data and created a PPGIS data analysis framework with three phases. The three analytical phases, *explore, explain* and *predict/model*, proceed from basic to more advanced methods and connect to varying types of knowledge claims as an output of PPGIS data analysis (Fagerholm et al., 2021).

Explore analytics aim, as the name suggests, at exploring spatial patterns and focus mostly on visual representations of spatial PPGIS data. According to Fagerholm and colleagues (2021), one of the main analytical steps included in the *explore* phase is the external and internal validation of collected PPGIS data. Descriptive and visual analysis are listed as the most common explorative PPGIS analysis methods.

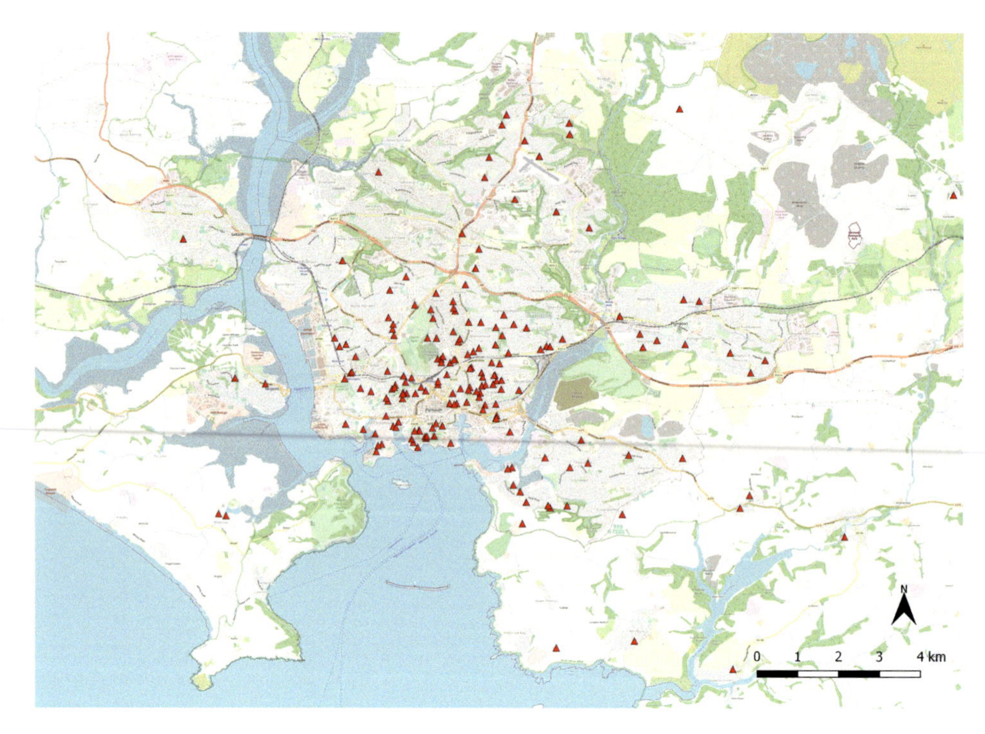

Figure 7.4
All respondents' home locations recorded in the Maptionnaire survey in Plymouth
(*Source*: © OpenStreetMap CC-BY-SA)

The next analytical phase, *explain* analysis, focuses on explaining the spatial patterns of the spatial and non-spatial PPGIS data, and the majority of PPGIS data analysis methods fall into this phase (Fagerholm et al., 2021). There are numerous different possibilities that can be applied for explanatory analysis, such as visual and overlay analysis, proximity analysis, analysis of spatial associations and cluster analysis, to name a few (Fagerholm et al., 2021).

The third analysis phase, *predict/model*, represents advanced PPGIS analytics in its aim to generalise and predict mapped attributes across other places and contexts or produce a representation of a system to make inferences (Fagerholm et al., 2021).

It is worth noting that the analysis framework by Fagerholm and colleagues (2021) presents the three different phases proceeding almost in a linear order, but they also highlight that data analysis is an iterative process where one moves back and forth between the phases. Moreover, not all phases are necessary; it is often the case that the data analysis is focused solely on one of the phases.

The Maptionnaire system itself includes some basic and quite useful analysis tools, especially for exploring the spatial patterns. For example, it is possible to explore the points, lines or polygons on a web browser and to examine the content of the responses, including any text recorded by respondents. Generally, however, the data need to be downloaded as a CSV file, which can then be examined, cleaned and exported into a GIS such as ArcGIS or QGIS or into a statistical package, allowing for various kinds of data analysis to be performed.

Analysing the BlueHealth Maptionnaire data

In this section, we present some examples of the techniques possible for analysing the Plymouth data: first using a range of map approaches and then using the data in a non-spatial way.

Exploring the maps for spatial patterns

Once downloaded, the data are opened in a GIS program, where several simple-to-use exploring possibilities are available. One approach is to use a heat map to show the relative densities and therefore popularities of the different locations. A spatial hot-spot analysis is a more statistically sophisticated approach with a similar aim. These can be used to show the focus of different aspects beyond simple popularity when determined against different variables, such as those in the health and well-being questions. Using the demographic variables can also point to places more popular with men than women, older versus younger and so on. The map base beneath these patterns can simply be the same OpenStreetMap. It is useful to start with a simple look at the data to see what patterns jump out and then to delve into them in more and more detail. Figure 7.5a and b shows the identified favourite places (a) and other visited places (b).

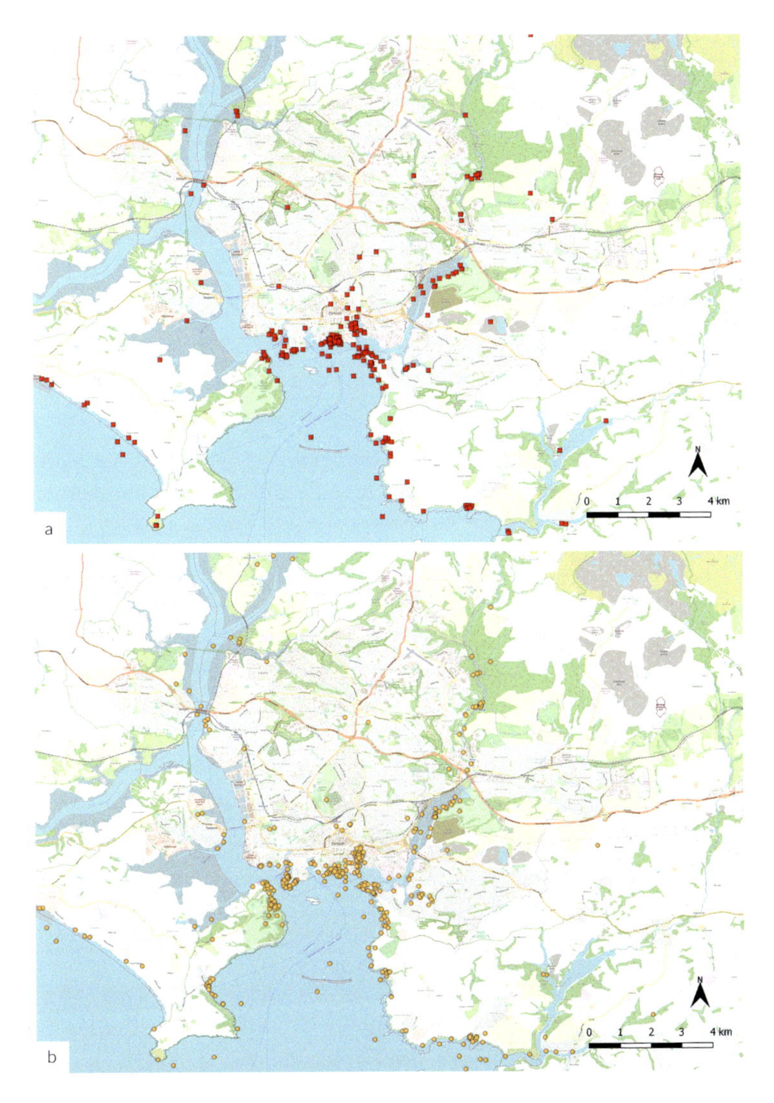

Figure 7.5a and b

The simplest maps showing the distribution of favourite and other spaces already contain some visually clear patterns which deserve further exploration

(*Source*: © OpenStreetMap CC-BY-SA)

Figure 7.6
Visit durations for part of the sampled area: favourite places (darker red means shorter visits) and other places (darker green shows longer visits). Lower intensity colours mean a visit duration somewhere between these extremes
(*Source*: © OpenStreetMap CC-BY-SA)

Taking these maps, it is possible to examine some patterns in more detail by first coming into some clear density clusters and then, for example, looking at variables within them. Visit duration is one aspect. Figure 7.6 shows the locations of favourite visits by visit duration (darker red means shorter visits) and the other locations (darker green shows longer visits). Lower intensity colours mean a visit duration somewhere between these extremes. Some interesting patterns emerge in terms of where these visits take place: for example, the shortest visits are the most frequent ones and to places close to the city centre in the famous Plymouth Hoe area, while longer ones are the less frequent ones and are to places further afield.

Zooming in further, it is easy to select for other variables such as gender or age of visitors (Figure 7.7a and b), although nothing really stands out in this example. What is also apparent when this detail is revealed is the fact that many points are recorded in the water. When checking for activities associated with these points, it becomes clear that not all are actually water based. This means that the points are not necessarily recorded as accurate spots, probably due to the zoom level used by respondents when identifying the points. Therefore, some statistical tools for spatial analysis can be applied to overcome this issue and to provide a clearer picture.

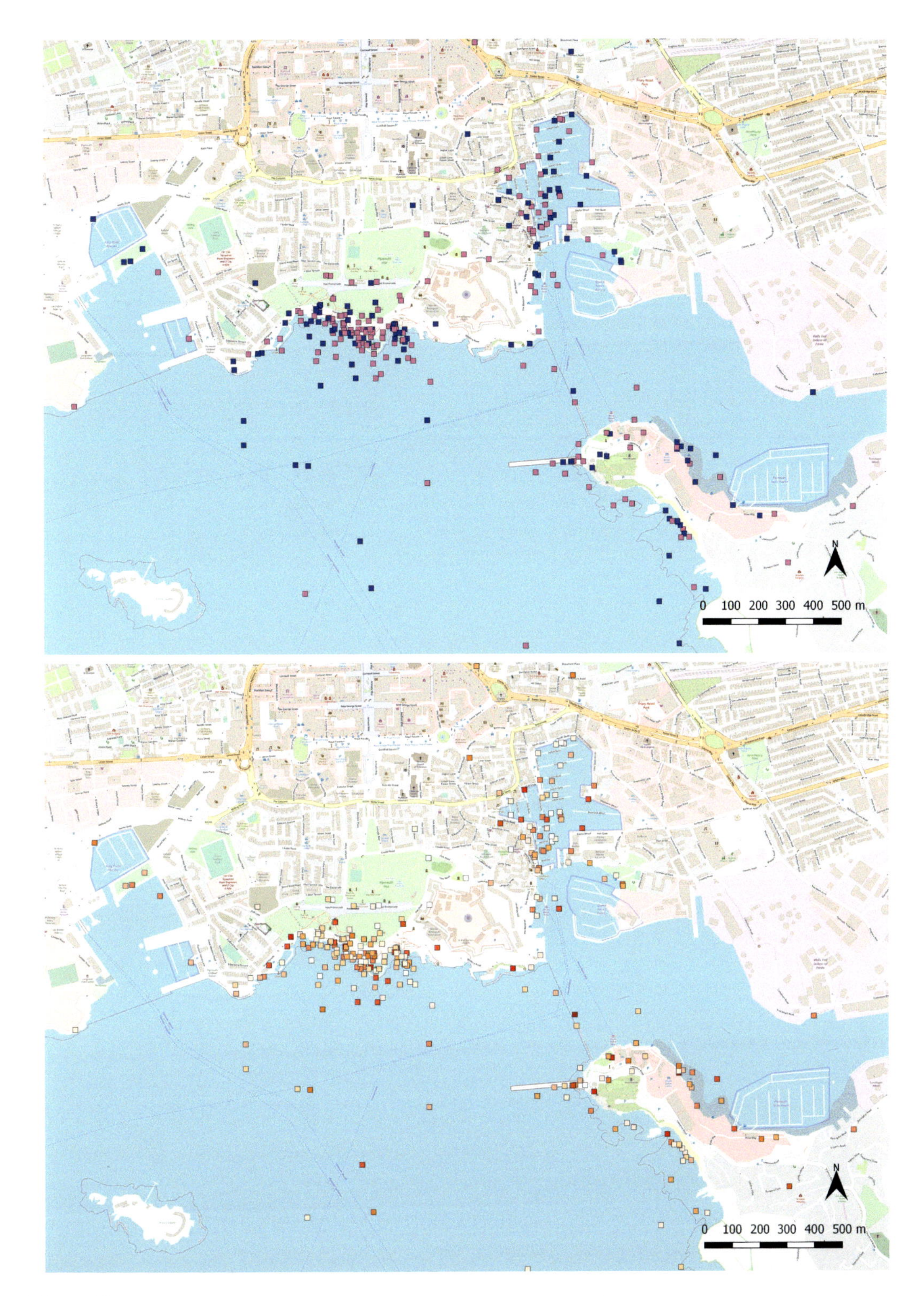

Figure 7.7a and b

a) Breakdown of all visited locations between men (blue dots) and women (pink dots) and b) by age group (darker signifies older people, lighter younger)

(*Source*: © OpenStreetMap CC-BY-SA)

The GIS analysis tools allow for some cluster analyses so that points at varying distances from one another can be identified through statistical distancing parameters to belong to clusters. These can then be analysed as statistical meta-units instead of taking each point separately. Other methods include placing a grid of a suitable interval over the map and assigning points to the grid squares according to the number of points along a range, showing as a

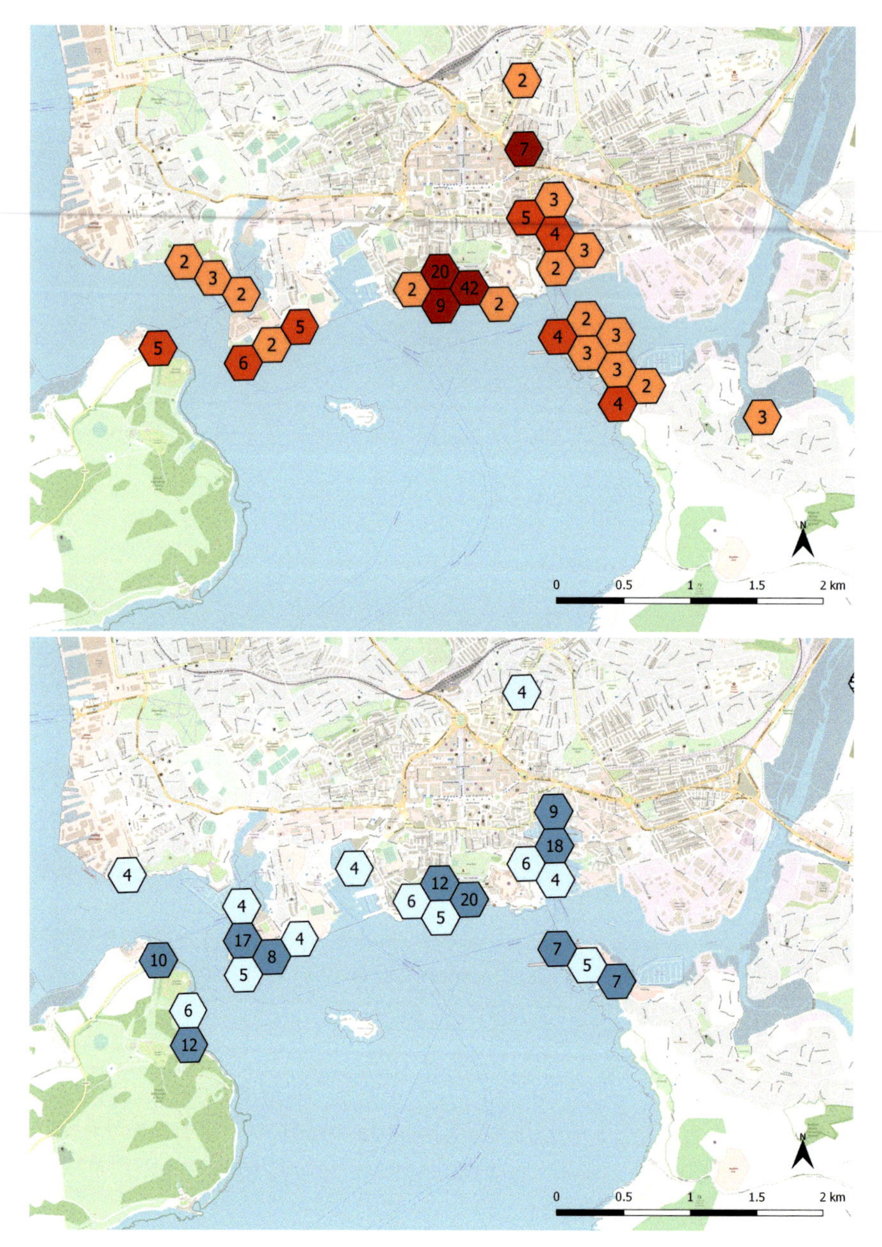

Figure 7.8a and b

a) Cluster analysis of the favourite places and b) of the other locations

(*Source*: © OpenStreetMap CC-BY-SA)

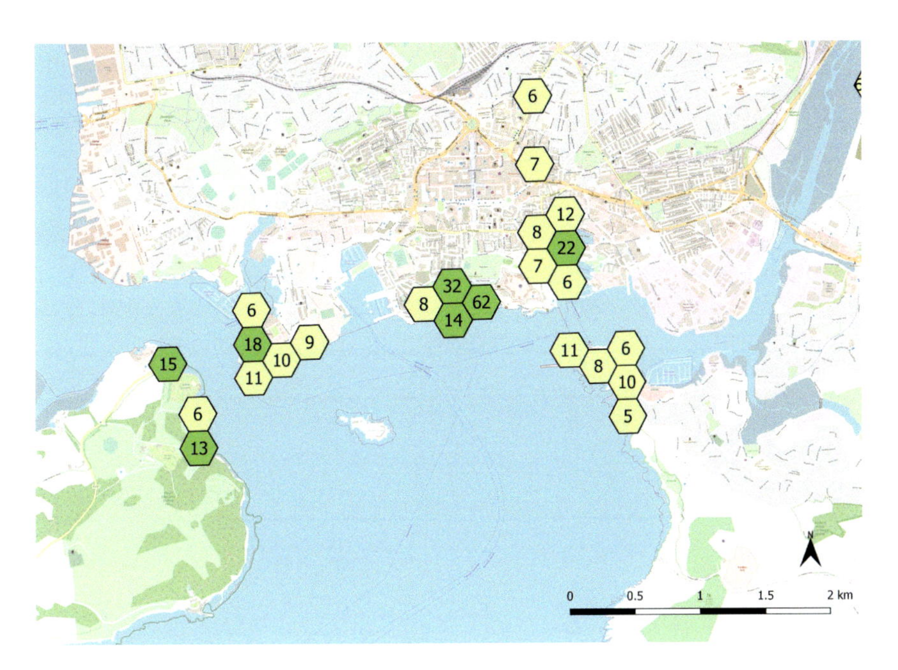

Figure 7.9
Cluster analysis of all visited locations
(*Source*: © OpenStreetMap CC-BY-SA)

result a pattern of density of selected values. Here we demonstrate a hot-spot analysis using a hexagon mesh, with a cut-off for clusters at two recorded points. The diameter of the hexagon grid can be changed to create tighter or looser clusters. Figure 7.8a and b shows two clusters for favourite locations (orange) and other locations (blue). The patterns are much more visible when visualised and analysed like this.

If both sets of locations are pooled and clustered, then, due to the increased total number of points, an even clearer pattern emerges (Figure 7.9), with several distinct visiting zones.

Next, an interesting aspect for us was the most-visited places – what kind of places are they, and what do they have to offer? One approach can be to overlay the hexagons from the clusters over land cover data in GIS, such as from the Urban Atlas, so that the values expressed by survey respondents can be related to land use types, although this is not very revealing in this example due to the resolution of the map data.

Overlaying the same data on a map (an aerial photograph would also be very useful) allows much more of the detailed features of the specific sites to be scrutinised. Figure 7.10 clearly shows what makes the cluster attractive as both favourite and other visited places: the proximity to the Hoe, beaches, open-air swimming pools and the sea itself. Figure 7.11 shows two different locations – the Admiralty Road area and the beaches of Mt Edgecombe Country Park, and Figure 7.12 shows the Barbican area, the most popular city centre place for food, drink, marinas and so on.

Of course, these can then be followed up and checked in the field. A BEAT assessment could also be carried out to capture the physical qualities of the place, too (see Chapter 5).

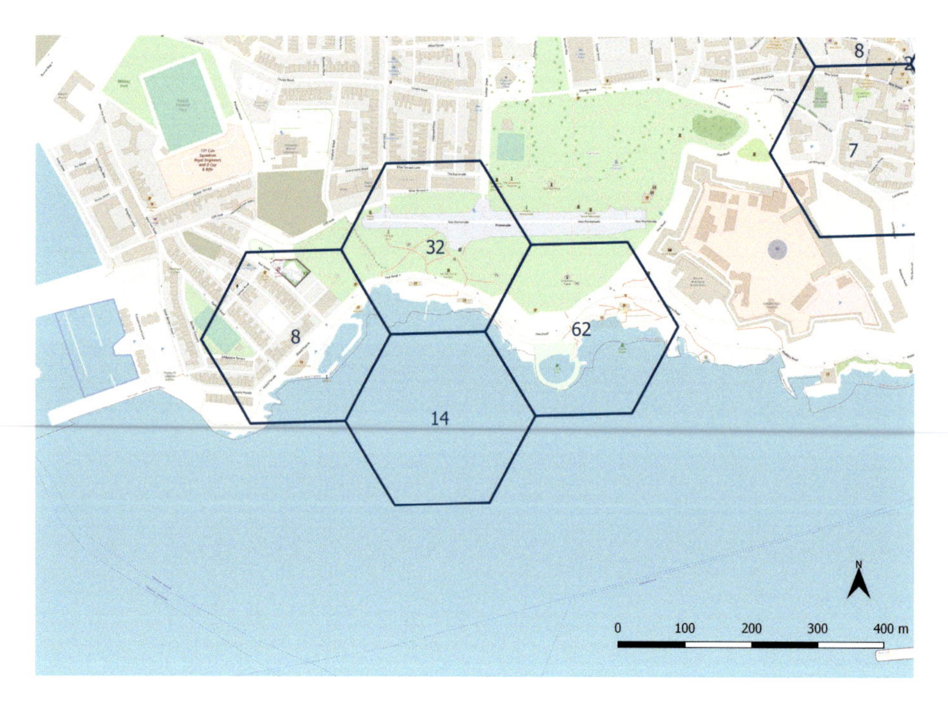

Figure 7.10

Overlaying the cluster hexagons for all visited spots on the map reveals the exact characteristics of the place which attract visitors

(*Source*: © OpenStreetMap CC-BY-SA)

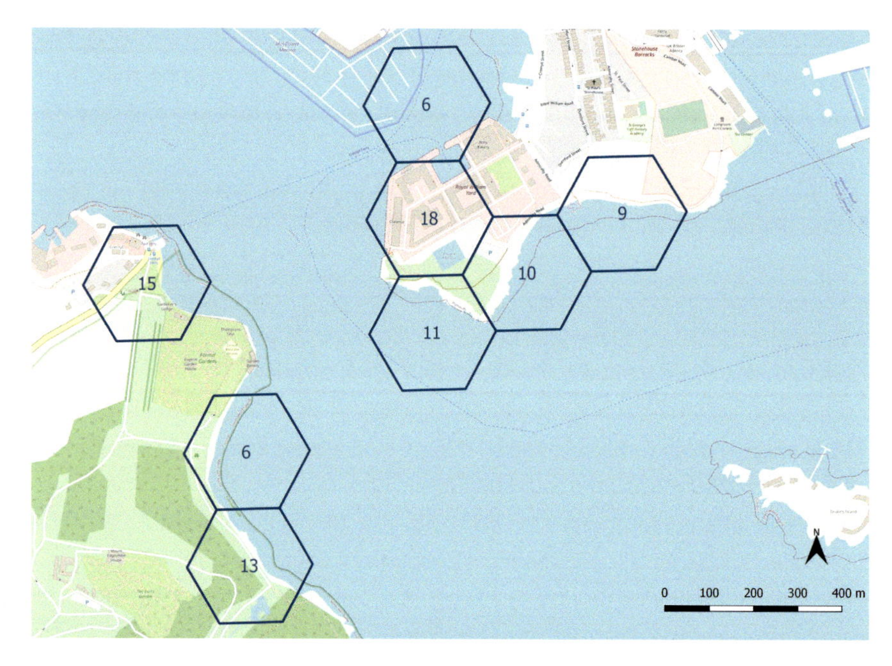

Figure 7.11

The clusters along the Admiralty Road area and the beaches of Mt Edgecombe Country Park, showing the type of popular blue spaces found here

(*Source*: © OpenStreetMap CC-BY-SA)

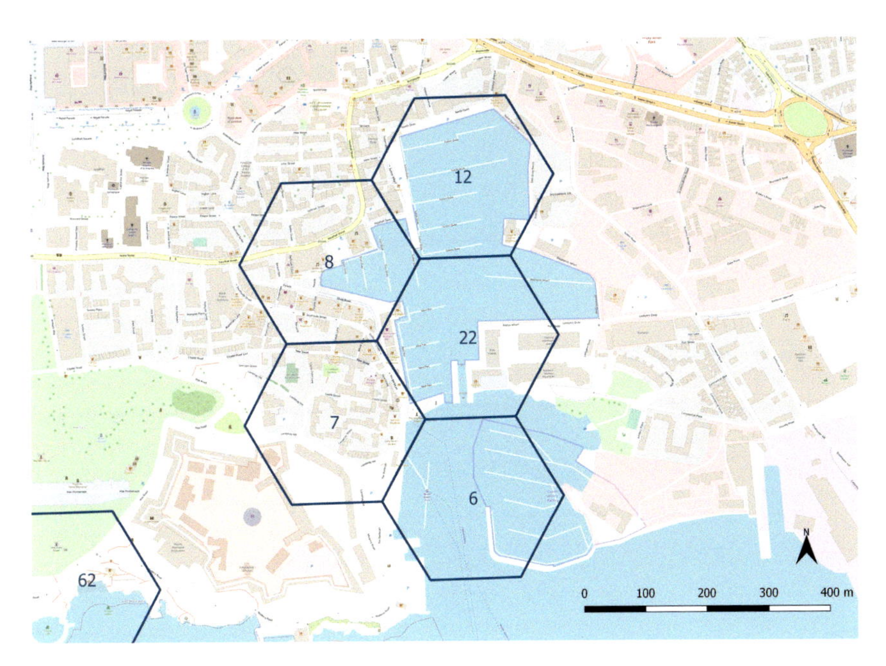

Figure 7.12
The clusters lying over the Barbican area in the city centre
(*Source*: © OpenStreetMap CC-BY-SA)

Explaining the patterns using non-spatial analysis techniques

The collected data contain a lot of variables so that a number of descriptive and inferential statistics can also be found. Associations between the activities, demographics and health and well-being variables can be used to see the main benefits obtained from the blue spaces identified by the respondents. Additional data on the blue space types could be included in the database so that relationships between the well-being outcomes and blue space types could also be identified. As an example, we took the main focal cluster at the Hoe and formulated a question: what characterises the people who use this place? We associated the home locations with the points belonging to the cluster (Figure 7.13), and we interrogated the data for age, employment type, how the respondents reach the site and their frequency of visits to all blue spaces (not just the Hoe – the question did not ask that specifically). We found that visitors are in the young to middle age range, mainly working, and live in a variety of areas but, we infer, commute in (by car in many cases) and then visit in their lunchtimes (on foot), for example. This inference is borne out to some degree by the comments offered by respondents, who stated that it was a great place to go on their lunch breaks. Thus, we can use the statistics to identify one of the main user groups and to see what kinds of health benefits they might receive, such as restoring themselves after a morning or afternoon of day's work. Figure 7.14a–d shows some of the descriptive statistics from this example analysis. When we look at visit outcomes, we can also see some interesting results suggestive of the benefits to health and well-being that such visits to the Hoe provided (Figure 7.15).

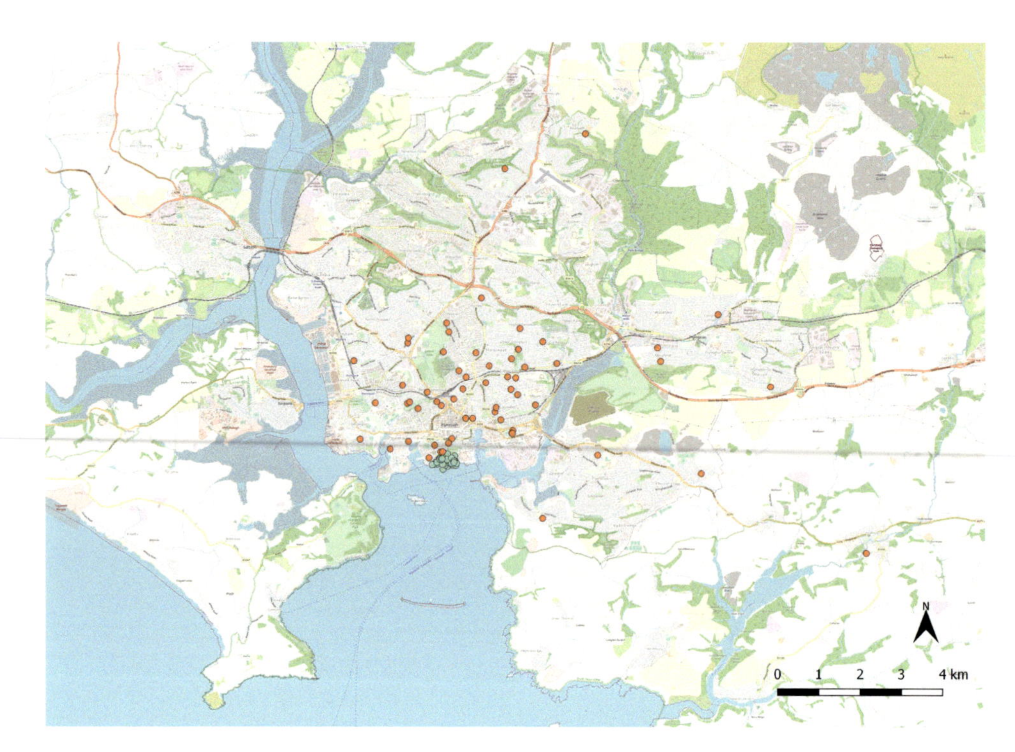

Figure 7.13
The home locations of the respondents belonging to the Hoe cluster – showing a wide distribution around the city
(*Source*: © OpenStreetMap CC-BY-SA)

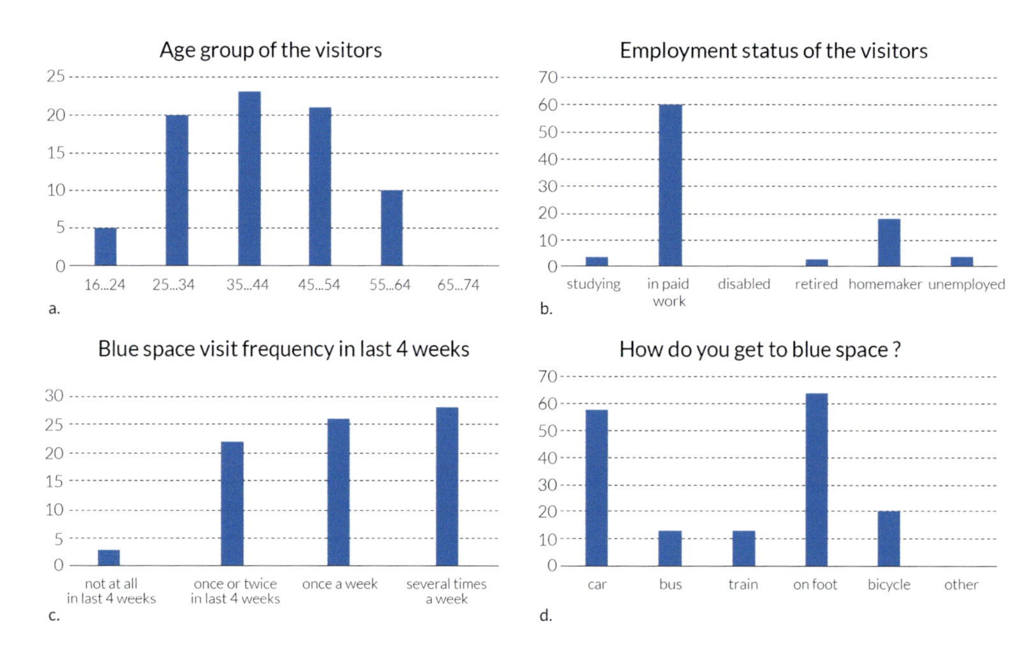

Figure 7.14a–d
a) Age group; b) employment status; c) frequency of visits and d) mode of transport to blue spaces of the respondents who marked points in the Hoe cluster
(*Source*: Peeter Vassiljev and Anna Wilczyńska)

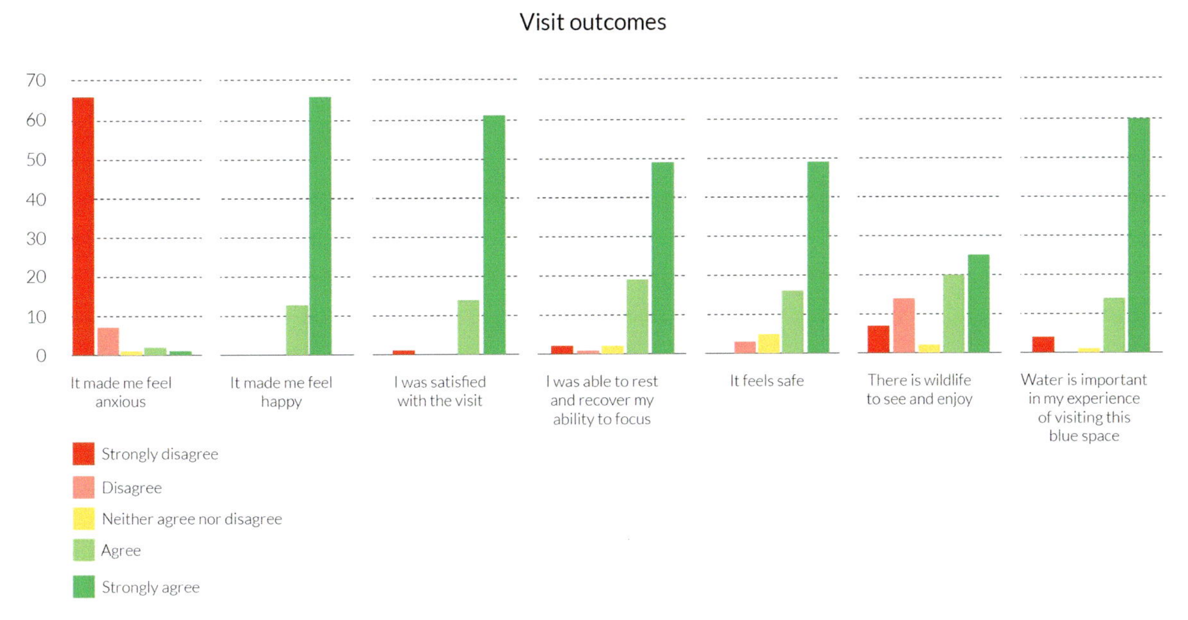

Figure 7.15

Visit outcomes of respondents in the Hoe cluster, showing high levels of agreement for all positive outcomes and a high level of disagreement with the negative outcome, suggesting important benefits to mental health and well-being gained from visiting the Hoe – especially at lunchtime, enabling workers to restore themselves

(*Source*: Peeter Vassiljev and Anna Wilczyńska)

Conclusions

PPGIS, using interfaces such as that provided by Maptionnaire, enables very user-friendly surveys which capture whatever spatially explicit information in, for example, uses, preferences, perceptions or affordances is desired by researchers or planners. There are some practical challenges, such as reaching all segments of the target population, since it requires internet access and familiarity – something which is becoming less of a problem as time goes on but still persists in places. Other challenges include the accuracy of placing points on the map – respondents need to zoom in to identify a specific spot and to place a marker exactly where it is needed. Failure to do so reduces some of the value associated with the aim of spatial explicitness.

It is worth noting that while PPGIS is a highly useful spatial method for both research and practice, to date it has mostly been focused on mobilising knowledge; it has been weaker at contributing for synthesising and translating PPGIS insights across knowledge systems into action more generally (Fagerholm et al., 2021). In particular, there are recognised challenges of communicating and integrating the vast knowledge base gained through these methods into decision-making and planning practices without a broader coupling of the development of advanced analytical methods with knowledge co-creation and deliberative valuation processes (Fagerholm et al., 2021; Raymond et al., 2014). Moreover, the challenge of bringing PPGIS methods that are, arguably, highly useful, for instance, for participatory planning practices, into action lies perhaps not so much in the usability of the method itself but more in the pragmatic and normative motivations for more inclusive planning processes (Kahila-Tani, Kyttä, and Geertman, 2019). However, significant results have been shown for the use of PPGIS methods at various spatial scales and in different phases of planning; PPGIS methods can provide an operational bridge between various sciences and practices, and they offer considerable opportunities for addressing societal challenges and the effective arrangements of public participation (Fagerholm et al., 2021; Kahila-Tani, Kyttä, and Geertman, 2019).

Finally, as we move away from mere public participation into citizen science, then such tools enable large amounts of data to be collected for use in other tasks which are not necessarily directly planning related (although they may have implications for planning) – such as information on how people perceive particular spaces or which are the most beneficial for health and well-being.

References

Brown, G. and Kyttä, M. (2014). Key issues and research priorities for public participation GIS (PPGIS): A synthesis based on empirical research. *Applied Geography*, 46, 122–136.

Brown, G. and Kyttä, M. (2018). Key issues and priorities in participatory mapping: Toward integration or increased specialization. *Applied Geography*, 95, 1–8.

Brown, G. and Weber, D. (2013). A place-based approach to conservation management using public participation GIS (PPGIS). *Journal of Environmental Planning and Management*, 56(4), 455–473.

Fagerholm, N., Raymond, C., Stahl Olafsson, A., Brown, G., Rinne, T., Hasanzadeh, K., Broberg, A. and Kyttä, M. (2021). A methodological framework for analysis of participatory mapping data in research, planning, and management. *International Journal of Geographical Information Science*.

Gottwald, S., Laatikainen, T. E. and Kyttä, M. (2016). Exploring the usability of PPGIS among older adults: Challenges and opportunities. *International Journal of Geographical Information Science*, 30(12), 2321–2338.

Heft, H. (2010). Affordances and the perception of landscape – An inquiry into environmental perception and aesthetics. In C. Ward Thompson, P. Aspinall, and S. Bell (Eds.), *Innovative Approaches to Researching Landscape and Health: Open Space: People Space 2* (pp. 9–32). Abingdon, UK: Routledge.

Kahila-Tani, M., Broberg, A., Kyttä, M. and Tyger, T. (2016). Let the citizens map – Public participation GIS as a planning support system in the Helsinki master plan process. *Planning Practice & Research*, 31(2), 195–214.

Kahila-Tani, M., Kytta, M. and Geertman, S. (2019). Does mapping improve public participation? Exploring the pros and cons of using public participation GIS in urban planning practices. *Landscape and Urban Planning*, 186, 45–55.

Kyttä, M. (2004). The extent of children's independent mobility and the number of actualized affordances as criteria for child-friendly environments. *Journal of Environmental Psychology*, 24(2), 179–198.

Raymond, C. M., Kenter, J. O., Plieninger, T., Turner, N. J. and Alexander, K. A. (2014). Comparing instrumental and deliberative paradigms underpinning the assessment of social values for cultural ecosystem services. *Ecological Economics*, 107, 145–156.

Schmidt-Thomé, K., Wallin, S., Laatikainen, T., Kangasoja, J. and Kyttä, M. (2014). Exploring the use of PPGIS in self-organizing urban development: The case of SoftGIS in Pacific Beach (California). *The Journal of Community Informatics*, 10(3), 131–144.

Völker, S. and Kistemann, T. (2011). The impact of blue space on human health and well-being – Salutogenetic health effects of inland surface waters: A review. *International Journal of Hygiene and Environmental Health*, 214, 449–460.

Völker, S. and Kistemann, T. (2015). Developing the urban blue: Comparative health responses to blue and green urban open spaces in Germany. *Health & Place*, 35, 196–205.

Ward Thompson, C. (2013). Activity, exercise and the planning and design of outdoor spaces. *Journal of Environmental Psychology*, 34, 79–96.

Chapter 8: Assessing city-wide and local health and well-being benefits

Lewis R. Elliott, Mathew P. White, Cristina Vert, Wilma Zijlema and Peeter Vassiljev

Introduction

As noted in Chapter 4, the BlueHealth project (Grellier et al., 2017) developed a range of surveying tools for investigating relationships between residential access to, or recreational contact with, blue spaces and a variety of human health outcomes. Different tools were designed to be applicable at supranational, national and community levels. This chapter outlines two of these tools: the BlueHealth International Survey (BIS) and the BlueHealth Community-Level Survey (BCLS). The former was conceived as an online survey to collect representative national samples of adult participants but could also easily be applicable at a city level. The latter is a concise version of the former, designed to be applicable for surveying communities surrounding a particular site which may be the target of a physical intervention or redesign.

Briefly, this chapter 1) describes the development, sampling, administration and content of the BIS; 2) uses examples from its findings to demonstrate its potential use for planners at a city level; 3) describes the parallel development of the BCLS; and 4) uses findings from a community-level intervention in Plymouth (United Kingdom) to illustrate its potential for planners who are interested in evaluating the impact of a physical intervention on the health and well-being of the local community.

The BlueHealth international survey

The BlueHealth International Survey was conceived as a way of addressing the lack of coordinated and harmonised data across countries on people's recreational visits to natural environments, in particular blue spaces, and their effects on people's physical and psychological health.

Setting

The BIS was administered in 18 countries worldwide. Fourteen of these countries were European Union member states (at the time): the United Kingdom, Ireland, France, Spain, Portugal, Germany, Netherlands, Czech Republic, Italy, Sweden, Finland, Estonia, Greece and Bulgaria. As past research has typically focused on the health benefits of coastal environments as opposed to other blue space environments (Gascon et al., 2017), these countries were chosen for their diversity of blue space geographies. The four other countries where the survey was administered were Hong Kong, Canada, Australia (primarily Queensland) and the United States (state of California only). These were selected based on existing research collaborations and availability of funds to collect data (also the case for Ireland, Finland and Portugal).

National-level sampling was made possible by the online mode of administration used (see subsequently), but equally planners could use regional- or city-level sampling if they wish to contextualise a particular site's surrounding

DOI: 10.4324/9780429056161-11

demography in terms of the wider city or region in which it is situated. Observing similar patterns at different spatial scales (national, regional, city-level) may help illuminate how representative a particular community is of the city, region or country and thus help planners decide where inequalities (e.g. age groups, or disability groups, which may access blue spaces less often) may exist that they then could target with the physical intervention they are planning.

Development, translation and management

The methods associated with the BIS underwent thorough institutional, stakeholder and public consultations to ensure it could address questions that were under-researched in the academic literature and were of interest to national and supranational health and environment policymakers and members of the public, as well as being widely intelligible. The English version of the survey was translated into the primary official language of each territory, with the additions of Russian as well as Estonian in Estonia and French and English in Canada. Official translations of standardised, validated questions and item sets often already existed. For example, many questions were taken or adapted from the European Social Survey, which already undertakes thorough forward- and backward-translation of its items. Otherwise, items were forward-translated. Backward translation would have been ideal, but 1) it would have been costly, and 2) it cannot always overcome problems of conceptual equivalence (i.e. the correct semantic translation of the content). Future iterations of the BIS could address this issue.

It is therefore recommended that if planners intend to adopt an online surveying approach to investigate blue space–health relationships at certain spatial scales, they should consider questions which: 1) are of interest to local stakeholders, 2) are rooted in the public interest and 3) ideally have existing valid translations into the local language. The importance of, and time devoted to, stakeholders and public engagement prior to the development of a novel surveying tool should not be underestimated. Individuals should be mindful that consultation on the BIS took place in 2016 and may require revision if using these items in the future or for other national contexts.

Administration

The survey was administered online by a large market research company based in the United Kingdom that has access to panels of online research participants around the world. This allowed the collection of nationally representative samples according to sex, age and region of residence in most cases: that is, we aimed for the number of participants recruited of each sex, age group and geographical region to match actual proportions of people in the populations of each country. Panel participants from reputable online sources are regularly screened for evidence of systematic response biases which could indicate inattentiveness or automatic completion, increasing the probability of valid responses. They also typically attract diverse demographic samples.

An online surveying methodology using a pre-established panel is recommended if planners wish to target demographically representative samples of adult participants or if they wish to sample residents of a particular region with relative ease. That said, online panels rarely have enough participants to ensure representativeness at finer geographical scales than a region. Nonetheless, online surveying of this kind is a relatively quick and cheap way to gather a large number of responses. It should be noted that online samples do have other limitations in that they only target people with internet access (which could mean that certain demographic groups are under-represented). Furthermore, online panel participants also are usually financially rewarded for participation in surveys, which could lead to socially desirable responding (e.g. responding a certain way because they believe the answer to be a desirable one rather than a truthful one). Planners should also be aware that despite the regular screening of systematic response biases, such biases may still exist in the returned data, and they should be mindful to flag such cases before analysing any data collected. They should also be aware of data loss or ambiguity if "don't know" options are permitted for certain items or if bespoke interactive features (e.g. mapping features) are integrated. As such, if financial resources allow, planners could consider alternative modes of surveying such as face-to-face or telephone interview surveying.

Sampling, design, and recruitment

The BIS used stratified sampling to achieve quasi-representative samples (typically by sex, age group and NUTS1 region of residence in European countries).[1] As the characteristics of visits to blue spaces are susceptible to seasonal variation (Elliott et al., 2018, 2019), we chose to sample across four seasonal, four-week waves of data collection over the course of a year to ensure that we did not bias our analyses by only focusing on one particular season. As such, consideration should be given to particular seasons (e.g. summer/winter holidays) to ensure that responses collected that relate to these periods do not unduly affect findings (if it is the planner's wish to focus on more seasonally representative data). The BIS aimed to collect 250 responses per country/territory per wave from different individuals (i.e. a repeat cross-sectional design), as 1000 responses could be considered an appropriately statistically powerful enough sample to stratify by sex, age and region, based on similar previous pan-European surveying efforts (Gelcich et al., 2014).

Regardless of whether online sampling is chosen, stratified sampling methods are recommended if planners wish to gather representative samples of a particular area. Depending on the behaviour or health outcome of interest, planners should also consider temporally representative sampling if use of a location, or the behaviour or health outcome of interest, is likely to be affected by seasonal variation. A detailed discussion of sample size calculations and power analysis is beyond the remit of this chapter, but these statistical methods refer to the appropriate sample size for answering a particular research question. If planners wish to stratify their sample by more demographic characteristics to achieve a more representative sample of an area (e.g. by sex, age, region, work status, ethnicity, etc.), then they should recruit more participants in order to make valid inferences about the population based on these characteristics.

Content

A detailed description of the BIS and its question content is available online (Elliott & White, 2020). After reading information about what the survey would entail and giving informed consent to participate, participants first proceeded to answer questions concerning their subjective well-being. It is conventional to question subjective well-being at the beginning of a survey so it is not contaminated by responses to other questions (OECD, 2013). These items comprised four questions on life satisfaction, worthwhileness and happiness and anxiety yesterday, as well as a personal well-being index exploring satisfaction with other aspects of one's life. These are commonplace items in international surveys (International Well-being Group, 2013; OECD, 2013).

Participants proceeded to answer questions on their frequency of natural environment visits, a behaviour associated with subjective well-being previously (White et al., 2017). They then answered items on intrinsic motivations for visiting natural environments (Weinstein et al., 2009), nature connectedness (Schultz, 2002), views of blue space from their residence (Dempsey et al., 2018; Nutsford et al., 2016), perceived walking and driving distances from blue spaces, commuting via blue spaces (Zijlema et al., 2018), perceptions of blue space quality (Garrett et al., 2018) and childhood experiences of blue spaces (Calogiuri, 2016). The citations here refer to studies linking these attitudes, behaviours and perceptions to health outcomes.

They were then asked to recall their most recent recreational visit to a blue space and various characteristics associated with this such as the date and time of visit; type of environment visited; time spent at the blue space; perceived water quality; recreational activities undertaken; time spent doing activities; who (if anyone) accompanied them on the visit; psychological outcomes of the visits (e.g. satisfaction happiness; connection with people; connection with nature); perceptions of amenities and qualities of the space; perceived restorative potential; and any accidents, injuries or illnesses associated with the visit. They were also asked detailed questions concerning the journey they took to access the blue space, including geolocation of the blue space on a map. Ultimately, these items were asked in order to identify the characteristics of visits which best predict beneficial health outcomes (White et al., 2013), and items related to travel were to determine valuation using a travel-cost method (Day & Smith, 2016; Sen et al., 2014).

Participants were then asked a series of questions on their general health, including the WHO5 well-being index (Mitchell et al., 2015; Topp et al., 2015), perceived general health (Wheeler et al., 2012), presence of a disability (Boyd et al., 2018), physical activity (White et al., 2014), health behaviours (Martin et al., 2019), use of prescribed medications (Hartig et al., 2007; Helbich et al., 2018; Taylor et al., 2015), use of health services (Maas et al., 2009), sleep (Shin et al., 2020) and BMI (Ying et al., 2015). Again, these citations refer to evidence as to their relationship with blue space exposure (or natural environment exposure more generally).

Last, demographic details were collected on participant's sex, age, work status, ethnicity, dog ownership, car ownership, public transport accessibility, garden access, social contact, household composition, educational attainment, marital status, home location (using an embedded interactive mapping API) and perceived and actual household income. These are all factors that might influence how blue space affects various health outcomes.

Readers are referred to the technical report of the BIS on precise wording and questions included (Elliott & White, 2020). This is not meant as an exhaustive list of useful questions that might be posed when planners decide to survey residents of an area. However, they are meant to illustrate commonly used items, often with established international validity, on a range of health outcomes and environmental factors that may be of interest to the planner. Using such items, a planner can be confident that they are asking questions of potentially meaningful policy interest. Of course, asking all might be time consuming, especially if an online format is not adopted (median completion time of the BIS was 21 minutes), so attention should be paid to which items have most potential utility regarding the physical intervention being proposed or evaluated. For example, if the aim of a physical intervention is to elicit health-enhancing physical activity, they may require more sophisticated physical activity items and may not need to ask items concerning all other aspects of health.

Additional data

After data collection, various data were appended using the respondent's home location, such as the proportion of different land covers surrounding the respondent's home; distances to the nearest coast, water body, or inland waterway; and population density. Such additional data can benefit the planner by identifying areas of a country, city or other area which have relatively better or poorer access to blue spaces. While the BIS used globally consistent land cover data for the purposes of consistent cross-country comparisons, a variety of satellite imagery databases and local land cover maps are available at different spatial resolutions which may better reflect specific land uses at a certain spatial level, and the planner is recommended to seek local sources of such data if it is appropriate to their aims.

Summary

This overview of the content of BIS was intended to demonstrate how a survey might be created, managed, sampled, administered and filled with items of general use to planners. In reality, a variety of options exist for all of these facets of survey design, and the planner interested in health-evidence-based design of blue spaces should first decide on an appropriate question to research (which is of interest to their planning aims) before embarking on how to design, sample or administer a survey or what questions to include. The previous sections were designed to illustrate how BIS was created but also discuss where and why planners might want to consider alternative items and methods. Despite reservations about representativeness of data at a city scale, the following section uses findings from the city of Sofia, Bulgaria, as a means of illustrating how BIS findings (or indeed comparable findings from a bespoke survey in the future) might be useful at a city level for planning purposes.

Application of BIS to Sofia, Bulgaria

As an illustration of how data from the BIS, or a comparable survey, might be beneficial to planners, we outline in the following findings from the city of Sofia, Bulgaria, in terms of resident distances to various types of blue space,

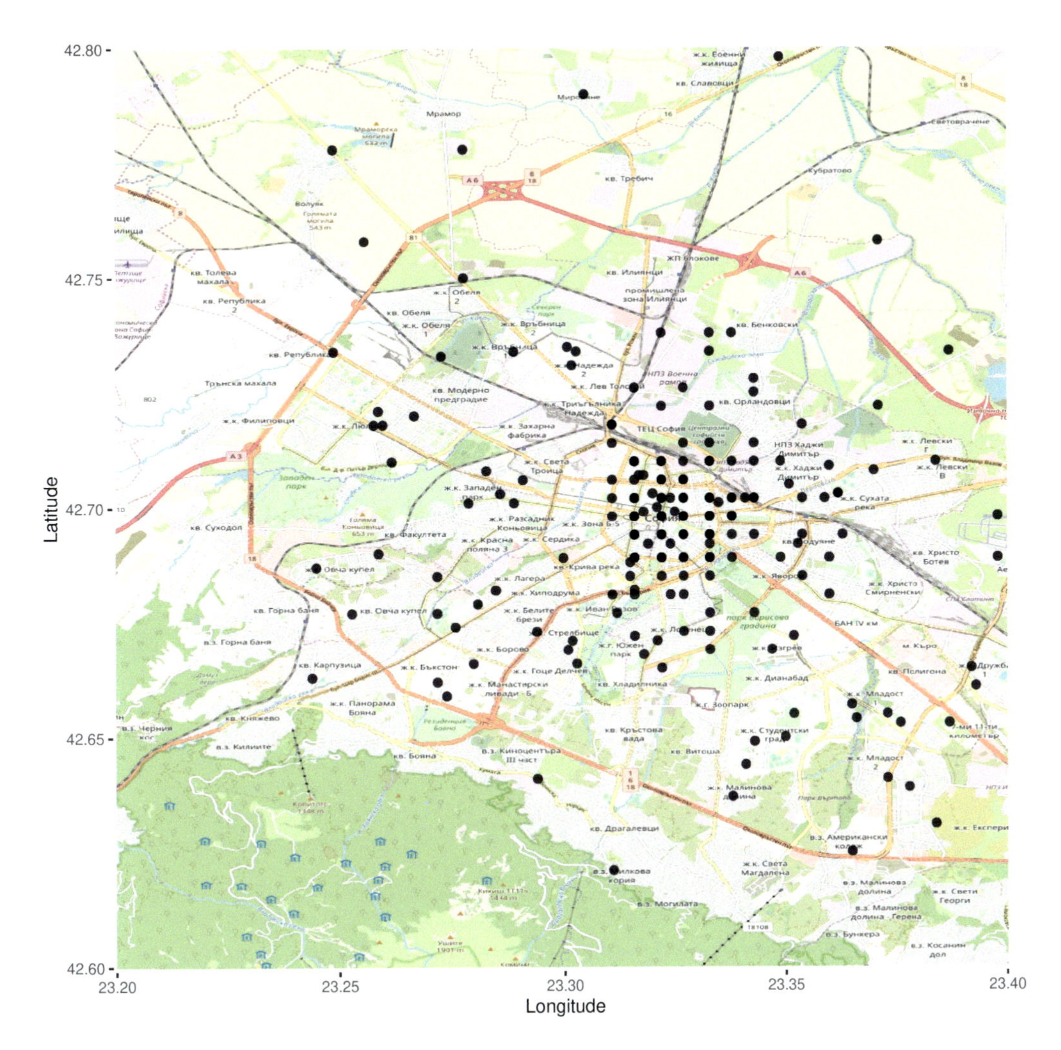

Figure 8.1
Given home locations of the 234 BIS participants who resided in Sofia, Bulgaria
(*Source*: The authors)

inequalities in access and details of their recreational visits to blue spaces. A total of 1054 adults were recruited in Bulgaria, of which 234 with valid home geolocation information were based in the capital Sofia (Figure 8.1).

Residential access to rivers and water bodies in Sofia

Using data from ECRINS (European Environment Agency, 2012), we were able to assign people's residential distance to their nearest river or lake (Figure 8.2).

What is apparent is that those living on the east and west of the city have comparatively poor access to rivers compared to those living in the inner city. However, the reverse is true concerning access to other water bodies (e.g. lakes). By exploring the frequency with which respondents visit natural environments for recreation, for instance, we can also determine the relationship between residential proximity and likely contact with those same environments (Figure 8.3).

These predicted probabilities are derived from a statistical model (specifically, a generalised linear model) which regresses the likelihood of someone visiting a river/lake at least weekly on their residential distance from that same space. For lakes, visits appear to relate reasonably well with distance – the closer you live to one, the more likely you

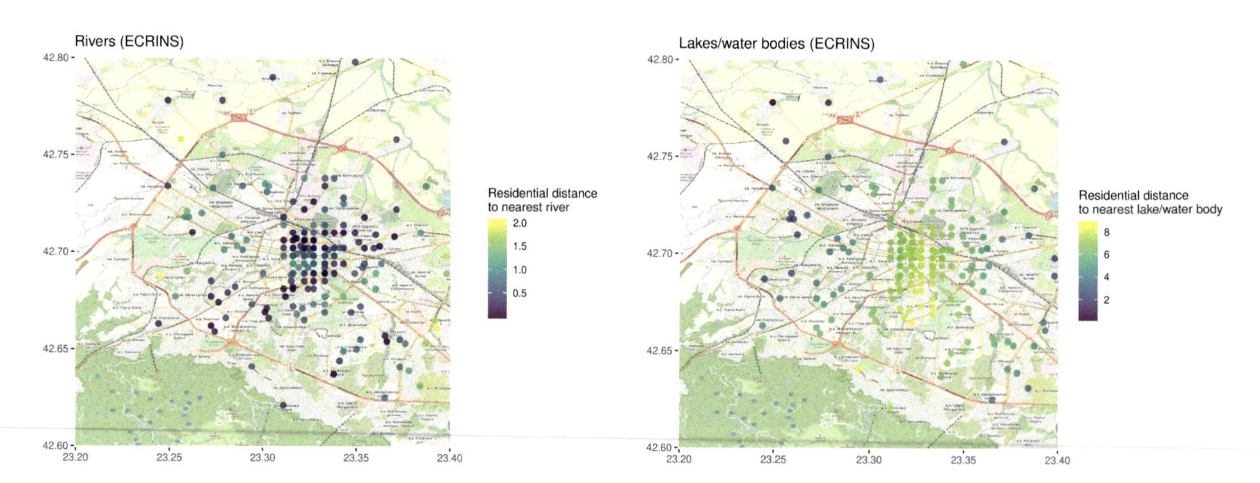

Figure 8.2

Home locations as in Figure 8.1 according to their residential proximity to rivers and inland waterways (left) and lakes and other water bodies (right). Proximity data were taken from the European catchments and Rivers network system dataset

(*Source*: The authors)

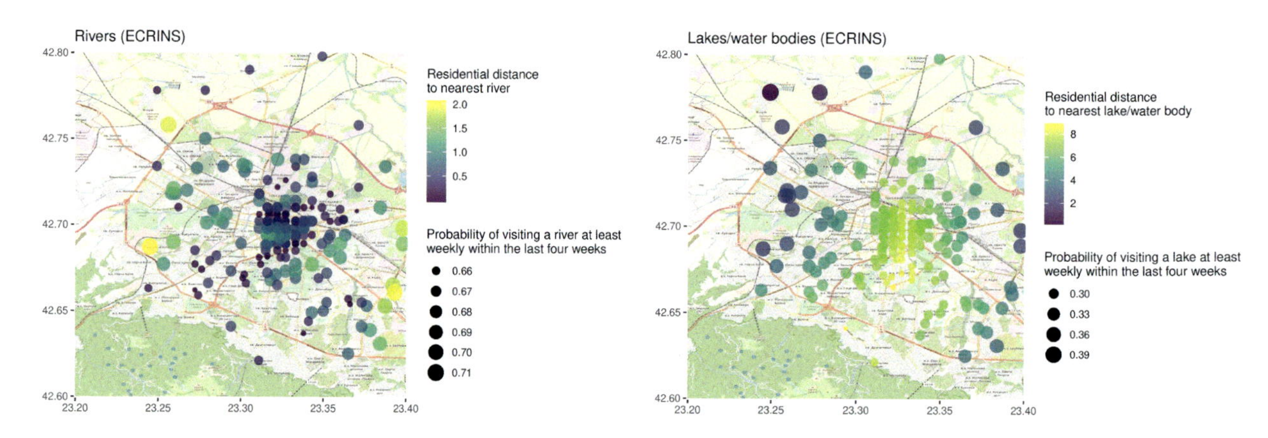

Figure 8.3

Home locations and proximities as in Figure 8.2 according to the predicted probabilities of reporting having visited the corresponding environment type at least weekly in the past four weeks

(*Source*: The authors)

are to visit it. For rivers, however, this is not necessarily the case, with those living further away (i.e. on the outskirts of the city) being no less likely to visit a river at least weekly than those living closer to one.

This simple piece of analysis illustrates that with some GIS and statistical analysis, a planner can begin to identify spatial patterns of where some people in a city may have better access to recreational waters than others, and with the appropriate questions in a city-level survey, they could also identify whether access might be related to actual contact. Such findings could form the basis of siting a physical intervention. Of course, there are likely higher-resolution maps of smaller water bodies and streams at a local level which might explain the patterns seen here (ECRINS is relatively coarse), but nonetheless, local spatial datasets are often freely available.

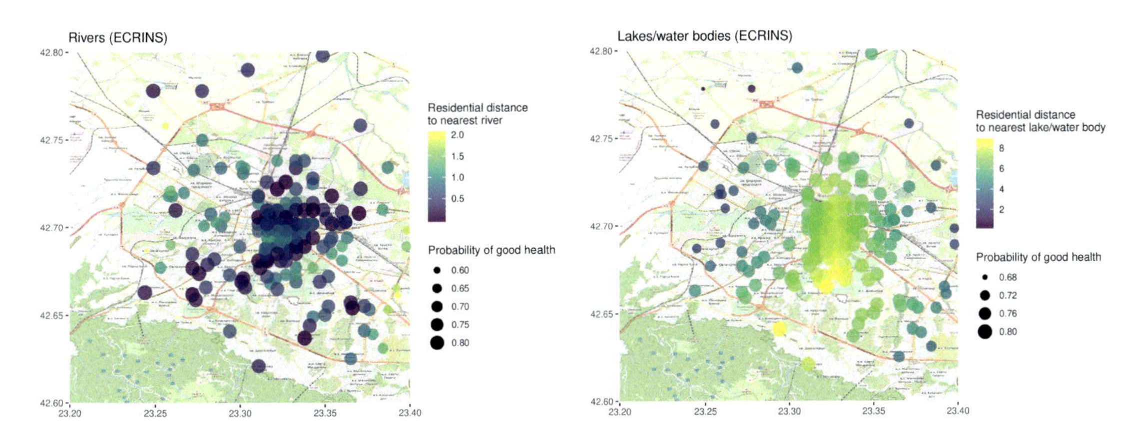

Figure 8.4

Home locations and proximities as in Figure 8.2 according to the predicted probability of reporting 'good' general health

(*Source*: The authors)

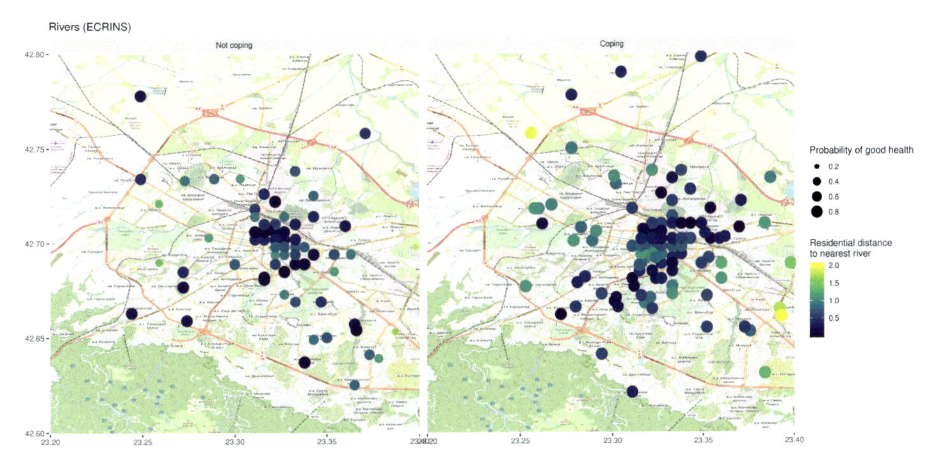

Figure 8.5

Home locations, proximities and predicted probabilities of 'good' health as in Figure 8.4, but for proximity to rivers and inland waterways only and stratified by whether people reported 'coping' or 'not coping' with their present financial situation

(*Source*: The authors)

A key focus of BIS was how access to, and contact with, blue spaces relates to health outcomes. One such question asked about the respondent's overall perception of their own health, a measure that has previously been associated with both physical and mental health indicators, as well as mortality (Gascon et al., 2017). For the planner interested in health-evidence-based design of blue spaces, it may be interesting to view how residential access to blue spaces relates to such a measure of overall health (Figure 8.4).

For the BIS respondents in Sofia, residential distance to lakes does not appear to relate clearly to one's overall health. For rivers, it does appear that those living further away from a river also suffer from slightly worse overall health. This may be accounted for by other unmeasured socioeconomic factors. We could therefore observe patterns by people's perceived financial difficulty (e.g. coping vs not coping with their present income) – another item collected in BIS (Figure 8.5).

This does not reveal a clear pattern – those living further away from a river and suffering worse health do not also appear to be those who report "not coping" with their present income, as one might expect. In other words, in this small sample of participants from Sofia, access to rivers does not appear to be associated with income-related health inequality. Nonetheless, such insights could begin to reveal how health inequalities might be related to access to blue space and therefore help planners decide where a physical intervention will not just bring about better access to water but also potentially address socioeconomic-related health inequality.

Recreational visits to blue spaces in Sofia

BIS also recorded 122 geo-located visits to blue spaces in Sofia (Figure 8.6). Clusters of points can be seen at the fountains in Banski Square and City Garden (Figure 8.7), as well as the Boyanska and Kakach Rivers. Simple questioning of visit characteristics in a survey allows the planner to identify the activities that blue spaces within a city currently afford. The most popular activities recorded at blue spaces in Sofia were walking, socialising and playing with children (Figure 8.8).

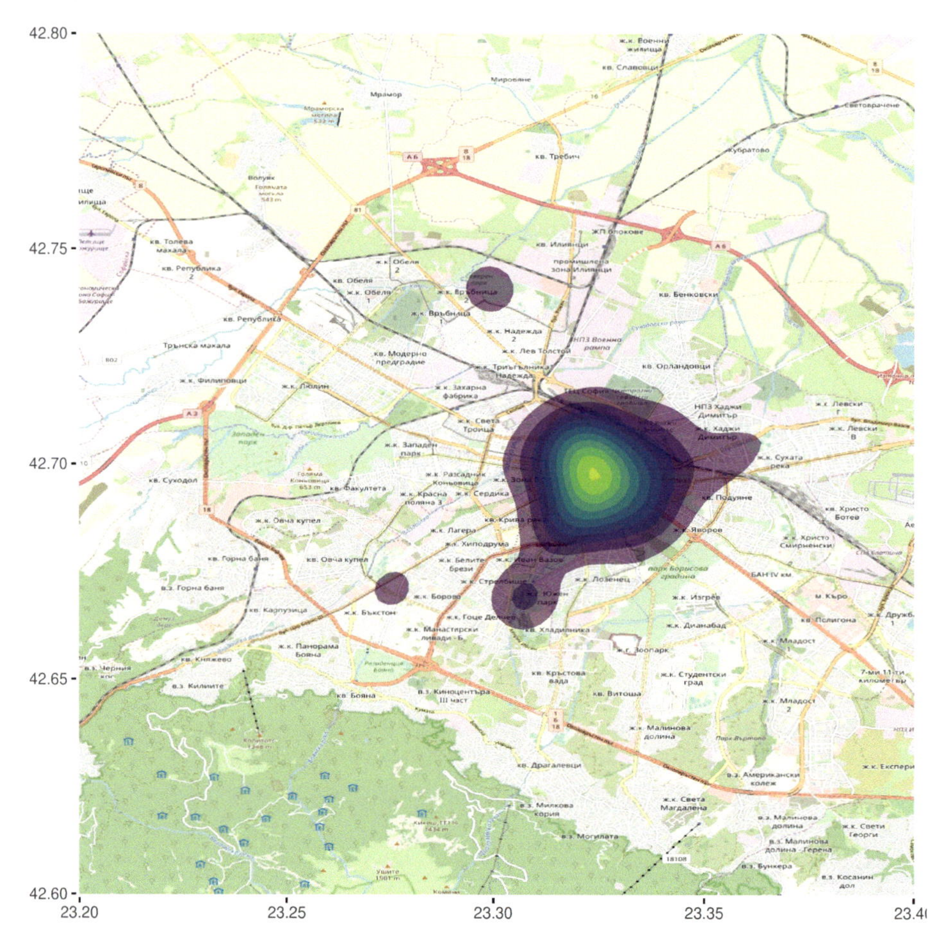

Figure 8.6

Heatmap of the 122 visits to blue spaces recorded in BIS which were reported in Sofia, Bulgaria. Clusters of points at the fountains in Banski Square and City Garden, as well as the Boyanska and Kakach Rivers, can be identified

(*Source*: The authors)

Figure 8.7
The fountains at Banski Square, Sofia; seemingly one of the most popular blue space recreation sites in our sample of respondents from the BIS
(*Source*: Raki_Man, licensed under the Creative Commons Attribution 3.0 Unported license)

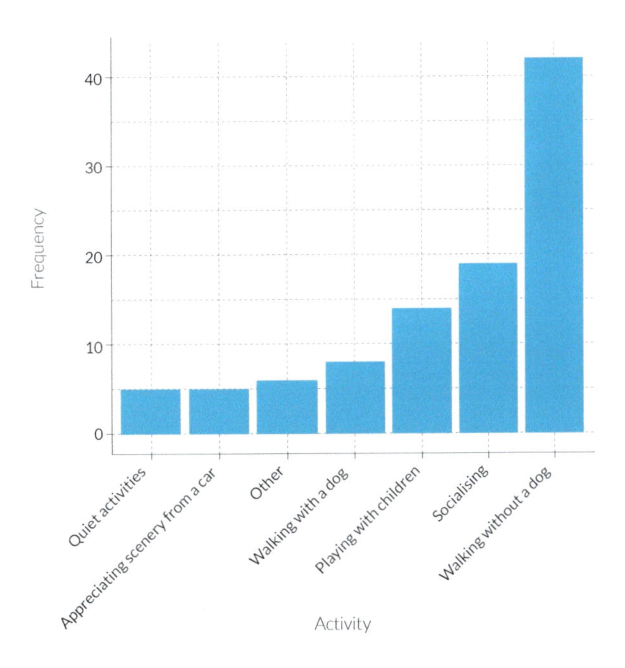

Figure 8.8
Bar chart displaying the frequency with which the most popular recreational activities were reported as the 'main' activity undertaken on a blue space visit recorded in BIS in Sofia, Bulgaria
(*Source*: The authors and Anna Wilczyńska)

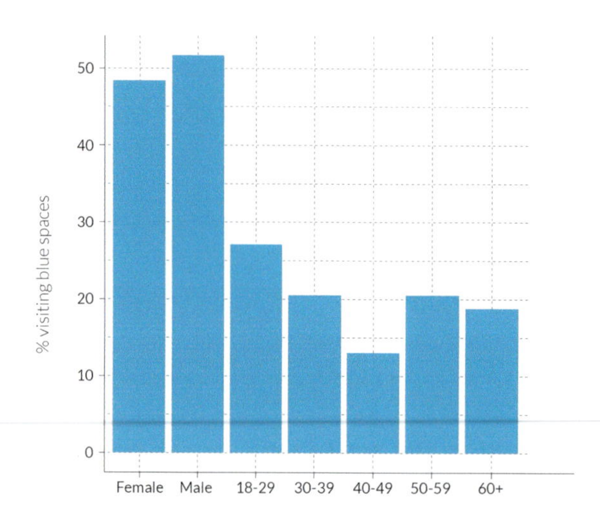

Figure 8.9
Frequency of reported blue space visits recorded in BIS in Sofia, Bulgaria, according to sex and age group
(*Source*: The authors and Anna Wilczyńska)

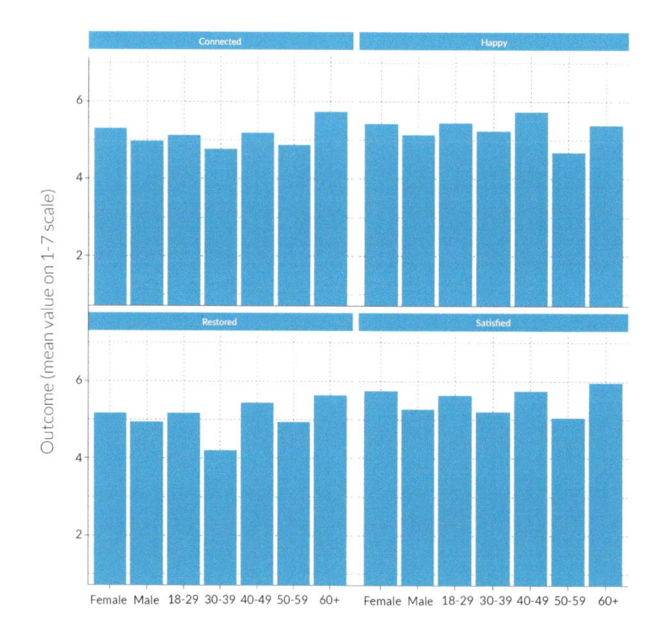

Figure 8.10
Psychological outcomes associated with blue space visits recorded in BIS in Sofia, Bulgaria, according to sex and age group
(*Source*: The authors and Anna Wilczyńska)

By exploring demographic details, the planner can also recognise where inequities in blue space visits may exist across a city and therefore what populations they may wish to target to encourage more demographic parity in visit frequency. In Sofia, for example, slightly more males and younger adults tend to visit blue spaces (Figure 8.9).

These inequalities may not reflect differences in health outcomes associated with those visits, though. BIS also asked a variety of questions concerning the psychological health outcomes of visits to blue spaces. In Sofia, we can see that females often feel happier, more satisfied, more connected to nature and more restored following a visit to a blue space (Figure 8.10). Older people also appear to feel more satisfied, connected and restored. Therefore, the planner may want to design physical interventions that target the psychological outcomes of male, or younger, visitors.

Again, this section is meant to illustrate that with the correct selection of questions, a city-level survey could inform planners on the visits a certain population currently take to blue spaces, the characteristics of these visits and the characteristics of the people making them. Identification of patterns may help inform the siting of an intervention or the population or setting to be selected, especially if the aim is to reduce inequalities in visits or the health outcomes associated with visits.

The BlueHealth community-level survey

The BCLS was conceptualised as a concise version of the BIS, designed to investigate similar relationships at a community level. As such, much of the content of the survey was identical to that of the BIS, allowing some flexibility for questions of local interest. It is impossible to be too prescriptive about the sampling methods or content of the BCLS because of the local context involved in its use, but the following two sections outline the general recommendations for community-level interventions that were given at the outset of BlueHealth. To demonstrate the flexibility of the BCLS in a local context, the following section illustrates how it was applied in a community-level intervention involving the redevelopment of an urban beach site in a deprived part of the city of Plymouth (United Kingdom) (Bell et al., 2020).

Recommendations for development and sampling

In terms of development, the BCLS is designed for use in pre-post studies of the changes to health that might result from interventions to a blue space. Such an intervention could be a promotion intervention (i.e. supporting people to use an existing space more often) or a physical intervention (i.e. altering or adding to the design of a blue space in some way). It could also be used experimentally (i.e. comparing an 'exposed' group of people who experience an intervention to those not experiencing an intervention) and with either repeat cross-sections of a population (i.e. different people over time) or longitudinally (i.e. the same people over time).

It is not prescriptive about a mode of administration; as with the BIS, face-to-face interview surveying may be considered the gold standard, but resources may only allow for different types of recruitment. As such, the BCLS is designed for multiple modes of administration (e.g. online, postal, telephone, face to face). In the same way, it is not prescriptive about sample size or sampling method. Ideally, a census sample (all members of the population of some area) would be surveyed at multiple time points, but often this is not possible. Instead, random samples of households might lead to a less biased sample of respondents, systematic samples of households (e.g. every other house on a street) could lead to a good geographical spread or opportunistic samples of visitors to a site could be used to garner a large response rate efficiently but could also introduce bias to the sample. The method chosen again depends on what resources are available. Sample size will depend on the population you are trying to generalise the results to; a reasonable number of people should be recruited such that 1) there is sufficient variation in responses to questions to analyse meaningful patterns, and 2) the planner can feel confident that they can speak to the behaviour, attitudes and perceptions of their target population.

The length of the survey will also depend on the sampling method chosen. While there are specific recommendations for content (section 4.2), such questions may take more or less time to complete based on how they are presented to participants and via what mode of administration.

Recommendations for content

As stated earlier, the BCLS was intended to be a concise version of the BIS. It queried people's general and more recent visits to natural environments at the outset. It then questioned a person's most recent visit to the blue space site of interest in the last four weeks (if the respondent had made such a visit). It asked about their perception of the site's quality, the date of the visit, the duration of time spent at the blue space, activities undertaken and who accompanied the respondent on the visit. It also asked about visit outcomes such as satisfaction; nature connectedness; and perceptions of safety, litter and facilities. Following this (or if the respondent had not made a visit), they were asked about their life satisfaction, satisfaction with their community, well-being, general health and physical activity. Last, they were asked demographic details, including dog ownership, garden access, household composition, work status, ethnicity, marital status, income, sex and age.

The idea behind this more succinct set of questions is that they are sufficient for examining changes to the characteristics of people's blue space visits before and after an intervention and also any concurrent changes in health that might occur as a result of this. Such a survey lends itself to path models which might illuminate the mechanisms by which intervening with a blue space might result in changes to health.

The Teats Hill intervention, Plymouth, United Kingdom

Plymouth is a city with maritime heritage situated in the county of Devon in the southwest of England. The intervention site, Teats Hill, is a small park and beach area within a relatively socioeconomically deprived district of the city. The city council had received funding to improve various natural environments within the city, and Teats Hill was one such site. Prior to the intervention, there was prominent deterioration in the quality of the infrastructure, blocked access to the urban beach by parked cars and overgrown vegetation. Through coordinated stakeholder involvement and public engagement and consultation, a renovation of the site was designed as part of the BlueHealth project. This involved the improvement of the playground, clearing of overgrown vegetation, regular beach cleans, resurfacing of the slipway to the beach with car access prohibited and, most saliently, the construction of a small open-air theatre where the slipway met the beach (Figure 8.11). As the size of the park and beach at Teats Hill was relatively small, these renovations had a fairly major impact on the overall character of the area. The application

Figure 8.11
View of the main intervention at Teats Hill, Plymouth: the open-air theatre
(*Source*: Lewis R. Elliot)

of the BCLS aimed to explore how this intervention affected the health of the local community, with measurements taken in summer seasons either side of the physical construction of the intervention in winter 2017–2018.

Application of the BCLS to the Teats Hill intervention

In Plymouth, a face-to-face mode of administration of the BCLS was selected, as resources allowed this. In two waves pre- (June–September 2017) and post- (June–September 2018) intervention, systematic samples of the local community were recruited to participate. Specifically, as a primary surveying method, we selected the seven census output areas (a small area geography used in the United Kingdom) that were nearest the Teats Hill site and systematically sampled alternating households in the first wave of data collection and the remaining alternating households in the second wave. We aimed to recruit 300 adults per wave. As this is a relatively high target considering the surrounding area (1000 households in the seven surrounding census areas), we also undertook opportunistic sampling of adults as they were passing through the Teats Hill site once household data collection had been exhausted. All surveys were undertaken by a professional market research company who could sample participants at all times of day to reduce bias in the kinds of people recruited. This demonstrates the flexibility allowed in surveying methods and illustrates that the BCLS can be adapted to the needs and population size of the local setting.

The content of the BCLS was also adapted. While we were keen to keep the duration of the survey to less than 10 minutes because of the need to gain a high response rate, local stakeholders also had priorities in terms of what they wished to find out about the local area and its inhabitants' attitudes and perceptions towards the intervention site. For example, we also asked about people's satisfaction with their safety in general, as this was deemed an important issue for the nearby population. At pre-test, we also presented participants with plans for the site and asked how much they might (in theory) be willing to donate a 'one-off' contribution to a charitable fund to help fund the redevelopment (in practice, we were not seeking donations). This hypothetical exercise was intended to 1) provide a means of assessing the cost-effectiveness of the intervention (i.e. whether the actual cost matched what the surrounding population might have been willing to pay for it), 2) provide an economic way of assessing its benefits (i.e. how does willingness to pay compare with economic valuations of changes in, for example, life satisfaction?) and 3) demonstrate the potential feasibility of crowdfunding to the city council of funding projects like this in the future. Again, this demonstrates that, if time allows, questions of local interest can be added to the survey which enhance and augment the core questions that already exist. This might provide planners with more precise insights that they need to inform specifics of the intended physical intervention.

Illustrative results from the BCLS in Plymouth

In a sample of 640 people, we observed significant improvements in life satisfaction and positive well-being (measured by the WHO5 well-being index) from before until after the intervention (Figure 8.12). Importantly, people's perceptions of the site itself also improved. Our statistical analysis controlled for a series of demographic variables and also how someone was recruited (in their home or at the site), so we know these changes are not due to differences in the measured characteristics of the two samples recruited in each wave.

We can also observe how the outcomes of people's recreational visits to Teats Hill changed from before until after the intervention. We did not observe changes in people's satisfaction with their visit nor how connected to nature they felt (Figure 8.13). There was a marginally significant increase in people's perceptions of the environmental quality of the site on their visit and also a significant increase in how safe people perceived the site to be.

These findings illustrate how a planner can evaluate the effectiveness of their intervention at improving the health of the community or the outcomes of people's visits to the site. Of course, this book presents complementary methods of evaluation of people's interactions with the site itself (Chapter 6), but the BCLS allows surveying of the entire community, whether they visit the site or not, and therefore could allow insights into why people do not choose to visit the site after its renovation as well.

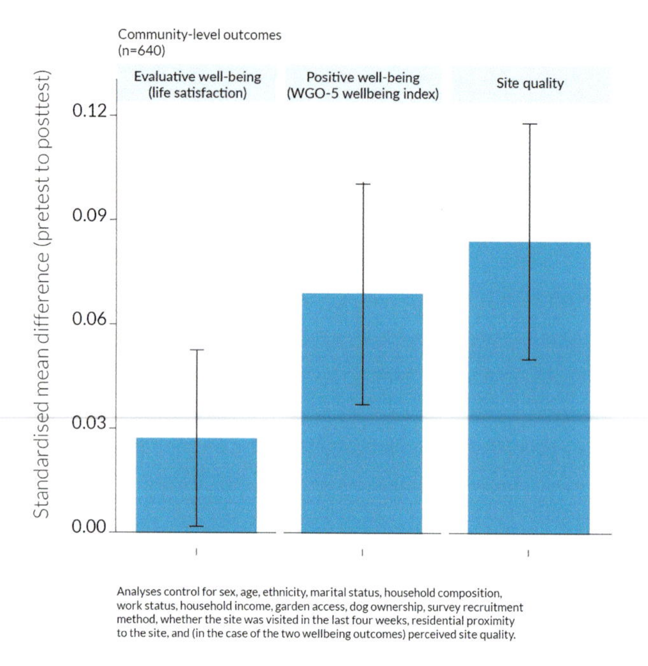

Figure 8.12

Bar chart displaying standardised mean differences between pre-test and post-test measurements according to two psychological outcomes, and perceived site quality. Data are taken from the BCLS results of an intervention conducted in Plymouth, United Kingdom

(*Source*: The authors and Anna Wilczyńska)

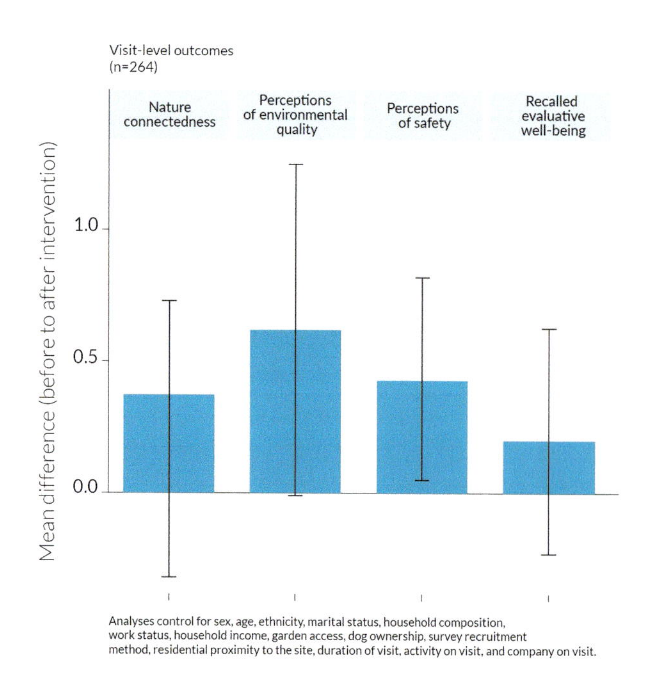

Figure 8.13

Mean changes in visit-related perceptions of nature connectedness, environmental quality, safety, and evaluative well-being from before until after the Teats Hill intervention. Bars represent 95% confidence intervals. Results control for potential confounding variables

(*Source*: The authors and Anna Wilczyńska)

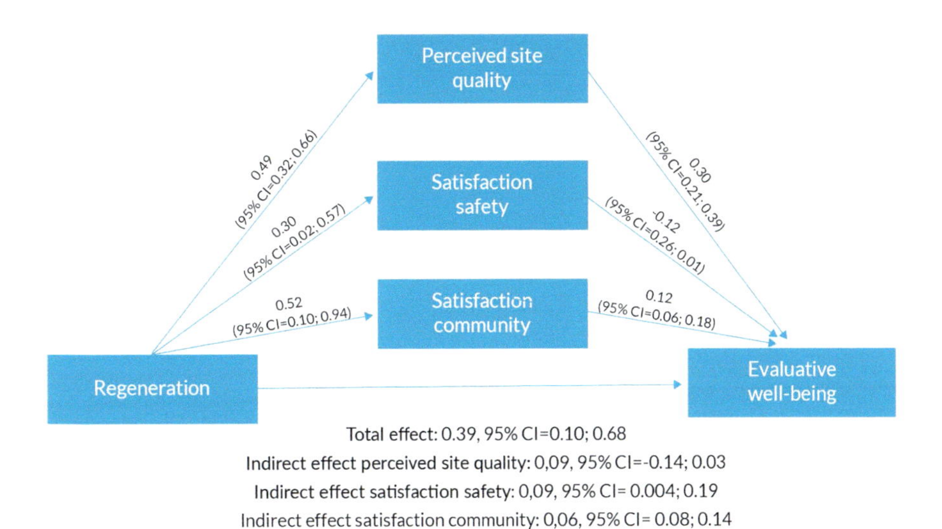

Figure 8.14

A path model for Teats Hill BCLS data, seeking to explain why the regeneration might have impacted life satisfaction (evaluative well-being)

(*Source*: the authors and Anna Wilczyńska).

Why might the intervention improve community health and well-being?

The BCLS also allows 'path modelling'. This means we can investigate not just *whether* the intervention had an effect on people's health and well-being but also *why* it might have had such an effect. Figure 8.14 demonstrates one such proposed path model. This looked at the relationship between the regeneration of Teats Hill and evaluative well-being (life satisfaction). Specifically, it looked at whether the improvements seen in life satisfaction from before until after the intervention could be explained by improvements in the perceived quality of the site, satisfaction with safety and satisfaction with community. The positive numbers at the bottom of the figure (labelled 'indirect effects') indicate that improvements in satisfaction with safety and community *did* account, in part, for why life satisfaction also improved after the intervention. This is important because it illustrates that the Teats Hill intervention may have worked through the mechanisms we proposed (i.e. improving people's satisfaction with their community and their safety). Such path models may provide planners with evidence on why an intervention had the effect it did and justify the planning of future interventions on similar grounds.

Summary of the BCLS

This section is intended to show the development of the BCLS and how it was applied in a community-level intervention in Plymouth. The surveying itself has its limitations. For example, despite our systematic sampling, the people we recruited before and after the intervention had some significantly different characteristics: there were significantly more participants in long-term relationships, households without children, households with access to a garden and dog owners in the post-survey compared to pre-survey. While we attempted to control for these factors, characteristics associated with them may have been responsible for some of the results observed and not the intervention itself. Planners must be mindful, therefore, of the limitations associated with surveying people in this way, especially the fact that observed effects may not always be attributable to the intervention. Ideal evaluations of interventions using the BCLS would have a control group who were not exposed to an intervention in order to assess whether improvements occurred even in the absence of an intervention; therefore, reducing potential problems from unmeasured temporal factors (e.g. better weather in one wave of data collection). They would also ideally recruit the same people before and after the intervention, but this is not always possible. Last, our surveying periods took place a year apart, approximately equidistant from the construction of the intervention itself. This does, however, mean that any effects observed may only be applicable in the short term. If resources allow, planners could assess effects at further, longer-term follow-up periods. To some extent, the other methods presented in this book involving nuanced behavioural assessment, and environmental evaluations, once triangulated with findings from the BCLS, may help to overcome some of these limitations.

Conclusions

This chapter presented the BIS, an international survey of people's recreational contact with blue spaces and health, and how it could be used in a city setting. A comparable survey can inform the siting of an intervention within a city, what demographics are currently 'missing out' on access to blue space, where certain populations might suffer a disproportionate burden of poor health and thus where a blue space intervention might have the potential to contribute to the reduction of health inequalities. It also presented the BCLS, a shortened version of the BIS, designed to be applicable to testing before and after effects of blue space interventions. The BCLS can evaluate whether a blue space intervention can improve the health of a community and explore *why* any changes might occur. The chapter has been brief in outlining the principles of survey design and analysis, and the planner interested in health-evidence-based design of blue space, and evaluation of blue space interventions, might need to better understand these methods if they are to be used in the future. Nonetheless, and especially if triangulated with other methods presented in this book (Chapters 5, 6 and 7), these surveys can better inform the development of blue space interventions and their evaluation.

Note

1 NUTS1 refers to a standard by Eurostat for referencing subdivisions of European countries for statistical purposes.

References

Bell, S., Mishra, H. S., Elliott, L. R., Shellock, R., Vassiljev, P., Porter, M., Sydenham, Z., & White, M. P. (2020). Urban blue acupuncture: A protocol for evaluating a complex landscape design intervention to improve health and wellbeing in a coastal community. *Sustainability, 12*(10), 4084. https://doi.org/10.3390/su12104084

Boyd, F., White, M. P., Bell, S. L., & Burt, J. (2018). Who doesn't visit natural environments for recreation and why: A population representative analysis of spatial, individual and temporal factors among adults in England. *Landscape and Urban Planning, 175*, 102–113. https://doi.org/10.1016/j.landurbplan.2018.03.016

Calogiuri, G. (2016). Natural environments and childhood experiences promoting physical activity, examining the mediational effects of feelings about nature and social networks. *International Journal of Environmental Research and Public Health, 13*(4), 439. https://doi.org/10.3390/ijerph13040439

Day, B., & Smith, G. (2016). *Outdoor recreation valuation ORVal user guide* (p. 27). Department for Environment, Food and Rural Affairs. http://leep.exeter.ac.uk/orval

Dempsey, S., Devine, M. T., Gillespie, T., Lyons, S., & Nolan, A. (2018). Coastal blue space and depression in older adults. *Health & Place, 54*, 110–117. https://doi.org/10.1016/j.healthplace.2018.09.002

Elliott, L. R., & White, M. P. (2020). BlueHealth international survey methodology and technical report. https://doi.org/10.17605/OSF.IO/7AZU2

Elliott, L. R., White, M. P., Grellier, J., Rees, S. E., Waters, R. D., & Fleming, L. E. (2018). Recreational visits to marine and coastal environments in England: Where, what, who, why, and when? *Marine Policy*. https://doi.org/10.1016/j.marpol.2018.03.013

Elliott, L. R., White, M. P., Sarran, C., Grellier, J., Garrett, J. K., Scoccimarro, E., Smalley, A. J., & Fleming, L. E. (2019). The effects of meteorological conditions and daylight on nature-based recreational physical activity in England. *Urban Forestry & Urban Greening, 42*, 39–50. https://doi.org/10.1016/j.ufug.2019.05.005

European Environment Agency. (2012). *European catchments and Rivers network system (ECRINS)* [Data]. www.eea.europa.eu/data-and-maps/data/european-catchments-and-rivers-network

Garrett, J. K., White, M. P., Huang, J., Ng, S., Hui, Z., Leung, C., Tse, L. A., Fung, F., Elliott, L. R., Depledge, M. H., & Wong, M. C. S. (2018). Urban blue space and health and wellbeing in Hong Kong: Results from a survey of older adults. *Health & Place*. https://doi.org/10.1016/j.healthplace.2018.11.003

Gascon, M., Zijlema, W., Vert, C., White, M. P., & Nieuwenhuijsen, M. J. (2017). Outdoor blue spaces, human health and well-being: A systematic review of quantitative studies. *International Journal of Hygiene and Environmental Health, 220*(8), 1207–1221. https://doi.org/10.1016/j.ijheh.2017.08.004

Gelcich, S., Buckley, P., Pinnegar, J. K., Chilvers, J., Lorenzoni, I., Terry, G., Guerrero, M., Castilla, J. C., Valdebenito, A., & Duarte, C. M. (2014). Public awareness, concerns, and priorities about anthropogenic impacts on marine environments. *Proceedings of the National Academy of Sciences, 111*(42), 15042–15047. https://doi.org/10.1073/pnas.1417344111

Grellier, J., White, M. P., Albin, M., Bell, S., Elliott, L. R., Gascón, M., Gualdi, S., Mancini, L., Nieuwenhuijsen, M. J., Sarigiannis, D. A., & others. (2017). BlueHealth: A study programme protocol for mapping and quantifying the potential benefits to public health and well-being from Europe's blue spaces. *BMJ Open, 7*(6), e016188. https://doi.org/10.1136/bmjopen-2017-016188

Hartig, T., Catalano, R., & Ong, M. (2007). Cold summer weather, constrained restoration, and the use of antidepressants in Sweden. *Journal of Environmental Psychology, 27*(2), 107–116. https://doi.org/10.1016/j.jenvp.2007.02.002

Helbich, M., Klein, N., Roberts, H., Hagedoorn, P., & Groenewegen, P. P. (2018). More green space is related to less antidepressant prescription rates in the Netherlands: A Bayesian geoadditive quantile regression approach. *Environmental Research, 166*, 290–297. https://doi.org/10.1016/j.envres.2018.06.010

International Wellbeing Group. (2013). *Personal wellbeing index* (5th ed.). Australian Centre on Quality of Life, Deakin University. www.acqol.com.au/uploads/pwi-a/pwi-a-english.pdf

Maas, J., Verheij, R. A., Vries, S. de, Spreeuwenberg, P., Schellevis, F. G., & Groenewegen, P. P. (2009). Morbidity is related to a green living environment. *Journal of Epidemiology & Community Health, 63*(12), 967–973. https://doi.org/10.1136/jech.2008.079038

Martin, L., Pahl, S., White, M. P., & May, J. (2019). Natural environments and craving: The mediating role of negative affect. *Health & Place, 58*, 102160. https://doi.org/10.1016/j.healthplace.2019.102160

Mitchell, R. J., Richardson, E. A., Shortt, N. K., & Pearce, J. R. (2015). Neighborhood environments and socioeconomic inequalities in mental well-being. *American Journal of Preventive Medicine, 49*(1), 80–84. https://doi.org/10.1016/j.amepre.2015.01.017

Nutsford, D., Pearson, A. L., Kingham, S., & Reitsma, F. (2016). Residential exposure to visible blue space (but not green space) associated with lower psychological distress in a capital city. *Health & Place, 39*, 70–78. https://doi.org/10.1016/j.healthplace.2016.03.002

OECD. (2013). *OECD guidelines on measuring subjective well-being*. OECD Publishing. https://dx.doi.org/10.1787/9789264191655-en

Schultz, P. W. (2002). Inclusion with nature: The psychology of human-nature relations. In P. Schmuck & P. W. Schultz (Eds.), *Psychology of Sustainable Development* (pp. 61–78). Springer. https://doi.org/10.1007/978-1-4615-0995-0_4

Sen, A., Harwood, A. R., Bateman, I. J., Munday, P., Crowe, A., Brander, L., Raychaudhuri, J., Lovett, A. A., Foden, J., & Provins, A. (2014). Economic assessment of the recreational value of ecosystems: Methodological development and national and local application. *Environmental and Resource Economics, 57*(2), 233–249. https://doi.org/10.1007/s10640-013-9666-7

Shin, J. C., Parab, K. V., An, R., & Grigsby-Toussaint, D. S. (2020). Greenspace exposure and sleep: A systematic review. *Environmental Research, 182,* 109081. https://doi.org/10.1016/j.envres.2019.109081

Taylor, M. S., Wheeler, B. W., White, M. P., Economou, T., & Osborne, N. J. (2015). Research note: Urban street tree density and antidepressant prescription rates – A cross-sectional study in London, UK. *Landscape and Urban Planning, 136,* 174–179. https://doi.org/10.1016/j.landurbplan.2014.12.005

Topp, C. W., Østergaard, S. D., Søndergaard, S., & Bech, P. (2015). The WHO-5 well-being index: A systematic review of the literature. *Psychotherapy and Psychosomatics, 84*(3), 167–176. https://doi.org/10.1159/000376585

Weinstein, N., Przybylski, A. K., & Ryan, R. M. (2009). Can nature make us more caring? Effects of immersion in nature on intrinsic aspirations and generosity. *Personality and Social Psychology Bulletin, 35*(10), 1315–1329. https://doi.org/10.1177/0146167209341649

Wheeler, B. W., White, M., Stahl-Timmins, W., & Depledge, M. H. (2012). Does living by the coast improve health and wellbeing? *Health & Place, 18*(5), 1198–1201. https://doi.org/10.1016/j.healthplace.2012.06.015

White, M. P., Pahl, S., Ashbullby, K., Herbert, S., & Depledge, M. H. (2013). Feelings of restoration from recent nature visits. *Journal of Environmental Psychology, 35,* 40–51. https://doi.org/10.1016/j.jenvp.2013.04.002

White, M. P., Pahl, S., Wheeler, B. W., Depledge, M. H., & Fleming, L. E. (2017). Natural environments and subjective wellbeing: Different types of exposure are associated with different aspects of wellbeing. *Health & Place, 45,* 77–84. https://doi.org/10.1016/j.healthplace.2017.03.008

White, M. P., Wheeler, B. W., Herbert, S., Alcock, I., & Depledge, M. H. (2014). Coastal proximity and physical activity: Is the coast an under-appreciated public health resource? *Preventive Medicine, 69,* 135–140. https://doi.org/10.1016/j.ypmed.2014.09.016

Ying, Z., Ning, L. D., & Xin, L. (2015). Relationship between built environment, physical activity, adiposity, and health in adults aged 46–80 in Shanghai, China. *Journal of Physical Activity and Health, 12*(4), 569–578. https://doi.org/10.1123/jpah.2013-0126

Zijlema, W. L., Avila-Palencia, I., Triguero-Mas, M., Gidlow, C., Maas, J., Kruize, H., Andrusaityte, S., Grazuleviciene, R., & Nieuwenhuijsen, M. J. (2018). Active commuting through natural environments is associated with better mental health: Results from the PHENOTYPE project. *Environment International, 121,* 721–727. https://doi.org/10.1016/j.envint.2018.10.002

Chapter 9: A decision support tool for optimising blue space design and management for health

Arnt Diener, Marco Martuzzi, Francesco Palermo, Laura Mancini, Giovanni Coppini and Matthias F.W. Braubach

Introduction

Some urban waterfronts work like a magnet for young and old people alike – for good reasons, as blue spaces can decisively impact our quality of life and have notable effects on physical and mental health (see Gascon et al. 2017; White et al. 2020 and Chapter 1). That is, as long as planners and operators take the right decisions. So, what are the factors that can make or break an urban blue space project?

We translated the reviews of scientific evidence, good practice, case study results and expert insights into a practical tool. The resulting "BlueHealth Decision Support Tool", or BlueHealth DST for short, is a practical guidance and assessment tool for the optimised renovation or new construction of a blue space. In this chapter, we introduce the topic context and the development and piloting process for the tool and provide hands-on instruction for using it. The complete tool is freely available online at www.bluehealth2020-dst.eu.

Demand for guidance on good design and management of blue spaces

The BlueHealth project revealed that many cities still underutilise or jeopardise the potential of blue spaces simply by inexpedient design or management. Only a few of the mechanisms defining the success of a blue space are obvious at first glance. Therefore, decisions on how to design and manage urban water bodies can be complex, as case studies and expert interviews show. We commissioned a survey that revealed unmet demands for design and management guidance among many urban planners and landscape architects. They in turn requested up-to-date orientation and practical guidance in planning, reviewing and optimising urban blue spaces for positive health and environment outcomes. The World Health Organization's (WHO) definition of health comes close to capturing both objectives, as "a state of complete physical, mental and social well-being" that explicitly covers environmental exposures (WHO & Secretariat for the Convention on Biological Diversity 2015). The health effect of blue spaces depends largely on ecosystem status (see e.g. Wood et al. 2018; Marcheggiani et al. 2019).

The outcomes of blue space interventions have been measured from economic, ecological and public health perspectives: with promising results, as shown in Chapter 1 of this book. Blue space interventions can transform neighbourhoods and critically improve social cohesion and both community and individual well-being (e.g. Collins et al. 2020; White et al. 2017). These improvements are of increasing concern, with already over half of the world's population living in urban areas (United Nations 2018). However, securing such benefits from an urban planning project at hand cannot be based on blueprints. Priorities and challenges vary according to locational setting, existing infrastructure, intended activities and user groups. Blue spaces can host a wide variety of activities and benefits – ranging from access to an extensive ocean front to a small pond in an urban park. Thus, the motivations and interests of involved stakeholders are likely to differ, ranging between, for example, enhancing biodiversity and providing for

DOI: 10.4324/9780429056161-12

niche water sports. Good decision-making requires a common understanding of success factors to overcome possibly contradictory interests. A reliable overview of such factors should be derived from the growing body of scientific evidence and good practices (see examples in Part Three of this book). Particularly, as recent reviews and surveys (see Chapter 1) show, health benefits and risks are often insufficiently considered in existing blue space projects.

Evidence and practical guidance are scattered and neither covered by existing guidance tools nor in a comparable format. The idea of decision support for blue space design and management hence holds great potential. Blue spaces are typically public and open-air spaces; thus, anticipatory setup, design and management have to compensate for inherent limitations. These may include limited access control, funding or maintenance – and should not jeopardise the safety of users and thus of the intervention as a whole. Design and management guidance should therefore combine the enhancement of health and environment benefits with the prevention of water- and activity-associated risks.

Added value of the BlueHealth Decision Support Tool

The BlueHealth DST guides the user in on-site assessment and decision-making for optimal design and management. The tool is based on a combination of current scientific evidence, good practices from experienced practitioners and selected reviews of pilot projects. In a nutshell, the BlueHealth DST provides:

1. an overview of typical blue space health benefits and risks, including environmental considerations;
2. distilled background information on the relevance and mechanisms of the most critical health and environment considerations around blue spaces; and
3. a hands-on tool for desk- and field-based blue space assessment based on user choices as a basis for design and management decisions.

The BlueHealth DST guides stakeholders to 1) maximise health benefits, including environmental factors, and 2) reduce and manage associated risks. It is designed first of all to broaden stakeholders' understanding of all the key environmental and health topics around blue spaces before guiding, for example, a team of planners towards a systematic assessment and prioritised intervention. The tool presents the globally evaluated and organised evidence and experience around such benefits and risks. It is set up to help users to understand the health and well-being factors of blue space interventions along examples and effect estimates. The array of possible interventions and focus topics around blue-green infrastructure is enormous, but only a few may be suitable for a given setting and ideal for the local population. The user is thus guided to identify the planning and management factors most relevant for his or her blue space at hand.

The BlueHealth DST is particularly tailored to the needs of practitioners involved in blue space projects, ranging from urban planners or landscape architects to local decision-makers and their stakeholders. The target audiences thus also include professionals in civil engineering, water management, urban ecology, recreation management and related fields. It further caters to policy makers, public health specialists, researchers and other entities with a stake in urban blue spaces. As the practitioner-oriented assessment module can be used separately from the educative module, the BlueHealth DST may generally support:

1. the planning process for a new blue space,
2. the renovation of an existing blue space,
3. the review of an existing blue space and its management and maintenance schemes,
4. blue health policy making (as background information), and
5. research on blue spaces and public health (as topical orientation).

The tool is intended for projects on most kinds of public water bodies, except swimming pools, spas and other types which are typically covered by separate and highly specific regulations.

BlueHealth Decision Support Tool development

The BlueHealth DST is based on proven approaches for guiding decision-makers and practitioners on scientific evidence and good practices. The WHO's European Centre for Environment and Health led the development of the tool in close collaboration with two BlueHealth consortium partners – the Euro-Mediterranean Centre on Climate Change (*Centro Euro-Mediterraneo sui Cambiamenti Climatici*, CMCC) for the programming of the web-based tool and the Italian National Institute of Health (*Instituto Superiore di Sanità*, ISS) for pilot testing. This chapter presents key aspects of the development process:

- the concept and objective of the BlueHealth DST for policy and decision-makers
- an overview of BlueHealth DST components
- an introduction to comparable environmental decision support tools
- an overview of BlueHealth DSTs for urban green and blue space planners
- the knowledge and decision-making demand around blue spaces
- the common blue space types and circumstances in Europe
- a future outlook for blue spaces and trend impacts (politics, climate, etc.)
- the programming behind the BlueHealth DST
- piloting the BlueHealth DST

Background on decision support concepts

Loosely defined, a decision support tool is a way of coherently organising information to support decision-making. It is to inform decisions and ensure that they are robust, transparent, documented and reproducible (Liu et al. 2012). A DST is designed for situations in which problem formulation as well as solution generation and selection are difficult and partially or fully based on complex and possibly conflicting information (McIntosh et al. 2011). It is thus an ideal fit for the topic of environmental health at the complex interface of environmental and human systems.

For environmental-health related DSTs, the HENVINET (Health and Environment Network) project has developed the following definition:

> Any tool based on environmental health knowledge that can be used in different decision-making contexts: from every day operation of health practitioners to strategic long term planning and implementation of policies for reducing the negative effects of environment on health.
>
> (Liu et al. 2012, p. 2)

However, a review of environment and health-specific DSTs carried out by HENVINET indicated that many are limited to single sources, pollutants or health outcomes or to one specific area.

As instruments to support the translation of scientific evidence into decision-making, DSTs facilitate management based on complex and wide-ranging information (Bartonova 2012). The BlueHealth DST guides the screening of interventions on critical factors for health and well-being. Its guidance is based on the insights of a scientific consortium and extensive research reviews. Thus, we promote a concept that is not currently an explicit priority for decision-makers in this area, or at least has not been spelled out as a leading principle. Generally, the need for decision support in public policy is widely recognised, and a large number of DSTs have been developed, with varying degrees of success in their practical use.

Common decision support tool types and basic components

To base the BlueHealth DST on sound methodological principles, we review established concepts in the following section. DSTs aim to provide certain actors with tailored guidance for decision-making. The following elements are almost invariably present in DSTs:

1. The *decision problem*, typically presented as a finite set of alternatives from which a preferred option can be identified to meet the needs of a decision-maker. Those may in turn be representing (nominally or in reality) the preferences or interests of an institution, shareholders, society, etc.
2. The *decision-maker*, as the person, group or institution in charge of deciding on the way forward for the problem considered and thus the customer served by the DST. The decision-maker may choose to involve stakeholders (i.e. those with an interest or concern in the decision at hand).
3. The *decision support framework* is where the elements relevant for the decision and their predictable performance and/or consequences in various areas are organised coherently and systematically. It typically includes some representation of the aspects of importance to the decision-maker or to society. This framework would usually involve some type of user interface.
4. The *decision support outputs* generated by the tool: this may involve anything from a univocal representation of optimal performance of each alternative (e.g. a benefit/cost ratio or a ranking of alternatives) to something much 'fuzzier', such as guidance or identification of critical areas for consideration. Such outputs can include visualisations, quantitative data, text-based guidance or qualitative information and narratives.

For the design of the BlueHealth DST, each of the four elements was addressed and decided upon during a technical workshop and a consortium review. The BlueHealth consortium agreed on two goals for the BlueHealth DST: 1) the promotion and awareness raising of the relevance of planning and maintaining healthy urban blue spaces and 2) the identification of interventions/factors to establish, improve or protect existing blue spaces and to maximise their benefits for health and well-being.

Review of guidance tools for urban and blue space management

To understand the demand for a BlueHealth DST, the consortium carried out a scoping study of existing tools in the specific area. This review identified several tools available or under development for urban green and blue spaces (see also tools reviewed for the BlueHealth Environmental Assessment Tool [BEAT] in Chapter 5). Some tools targeted water-related management issues, but most focused on engineering and technical aspects or on very specific ones such as contamination. Finally, four tools were identified that cover blue spaces or urban water bodies to an extent relevant for planning and management purposes. They may be of added value for interventions with either a strong emphasis on ecosystem service investments, storm water management or urban environmental policy. The products were reviewed as part of the preparatory review for the BlueHealth DST development and are briefly described in the following.

Local Action Toolkit: ecosystem service investments and returns

The Local Action Toolkit provides a framework for the assessment of costs and benefits of catchment management programmes in urban landscapes. The toolkit guides the quantification of benefits of interventions designed to enhance ecosystem service provision. It does not cover direct access to and use of water bodies (e.g. water sports, etc.) or health risks associated with blue spaces. The framework is scalable and can be applied to a broad spectrum of urban situations and guide the measurement of potential benefits (whether directly monetisable or not). The list of interventions is based on green infrastructure components and sustainable drainage systems. It is categorised into 'existing assets' and 'interventions' based on the likelihood of future implementation.

The toolkit covers 12 benefits that influence quality of life. These consider to what extent a green or blue space intervention can help to 1) improve healthy environments, 2) reduce flooding risk and related economic damage, 3) improve habitat provision for biodiversity, 4) stabilise groundwater recharge and improve water quality, 5) support climate regulation and 6) provide social and cultural services and opportunities. The tool mainly aims at city-scale interventions to increase ecosystem services through nature elements and almost exclusively focuses on the provision of benefits (Defra Local Action Project 2017).

Water Sensitive Cities Toolkit: strategic storm water management

For blue spaces with a particular focus on storm water management, the Water Sensitive Cities Toolkit supports strategic planning of related green infrastructure initiatives in urban areas. Its final completion by the Australian Cooperative Research Centre for Water Sensitive Cities was planned for late 2020. The toolkit aims to enable evidence-based quantification of benefits rendered by context-specific planning, design and implementation of ecosystem-based storm water management. The toolkit comprises three functional components: 1) strategic planning and conceptual design, 2) future climate uncertainty and variability (in development) and 3) scenario assessment and multi-benefit evaluation.

The strategic planning and conceptual design component of the toolkit is called "UrbanBEATS". A model combines urban planning information and geospatial data to generate storm-water management options based on a user-defined scenario. The component is based on a GIS and requires four basic input raster maps (elevation, land use, population and soil data), as well as non-spatial data in the form of rainfall and evapotranspiration data and urban design data (Cooperative Research Centre for Water Sensitive Cities 2020).

Green City Tool: sustainable urban environment policy

For urban planners with a broader aim of improving the city's environmental sustainability, the European Commission (DG Environment) developed the Green City Tool. The tool is not explicitly linked to health outcomes but rather assesses overall environmental sustainability. It covers a wide range of urban sustainability topics and is based on a series of steps (assess conditions – view results – explore improvement options).

Guidance focuses on the policy level and helps users to review whether desirable approaches and instruments are in place. The tool reflects the criteria applied in the application process for the European Green Capital Award in 12 topics. Several topics are relevant for green and blue spaces. It does not (yet) provide information on the features of urban environments or how to manage risks and benefits of urban nature elements (European Commission 2019).

Principles for Water Wise Cities: eco-wise urban water policy

The Principles for Water Wise Cities established by the International Water Association (IWA) aim to guide policy makers in improving the urban water management in cities. Particular emphasis is put on eco-system services and the protection and efficient use of water bodies. The 17 principles are structured in five blocks addressing 1) vision, 2) governance, 3) knowledge and capacity, 4) planning tools and 5) implementation tools and feature four levels of actions, covering 1) regenerative water services, 2) water-sensitive urban design, 3) basin-connected cities and 4) water-wise communities. IWA provides implementation tools alongside a focus on financing and investment calculations (International Water Association 2016).

Review of urban landscape assessment tools

In order to understand the guidance needs and good practices for comparable tools, the consortium carried out a review of "tools for assessing places". Seventeen tools fitted the selection criteria, of which most (13) focused on terrestrial assessments, and only 4 included water components (Blue Flag, Local Action Toolkit, Urban Waterfront

Regeneration, Urban Stream Condition). The reviewers pointed out that health and well-being was one of the least considered aspects, while the following categories were most common:

- Quality of landscape/environment (loosely defined);
- Maintenance issues;
- Accessibility to and within space (barriers for people);
- Safety: crime and security perception; and
- Others: transport, ecology, cultural heritage, economic values.

The tools' topical priorities indicate that blue spaces are – often – expected to provide rather general benefits. Thus, access, subjective perceptions of comfort and public safety, as well as maintenance, seem important to ensure active blue space use.

Based on this review, the BlueHealth Environment Assessment Tool presented in Chapter 5 (and in Mishra et al. 2020) was developed by researchers at the Estonian University of Life Sciences. It is limited to environmental dimensions and with a different target audience and output from the BlueHealth DST. It is designed for two groups of users: 1) experts, such as landscape architects, ecologists, recreation planners, urban planners or hydrologists, and 2) local community or citizen groups who have an interest in their local environment.

Needs assessment for blue space guidance in Europe

To assess practitioners' demands for decision-making guidance, the BlueHealth consortium, led by CMCC, carried out a survey among decision-makers and planners in Europe. The survey included questions on the current integration of health and well-being risks into the planning of blue spaces and comparable interventions. It also evaluated current levels of knowledge around public health in urban planning. The analysis served as a critical input for the setup of the BlueHealth DST.

The results showed that, at the time of the survey (2017), blue space projects:

- were planned with a strong consideration of the future implications for maintenance and related management needs;
- were rarely expected to generate improvements related to environmental exposures like noise or air pollution or to reduce disease occurrence; and
- seemed inadequately informed about local environmental conditions and risks, such as revealing a lack of awareness around vector-borne diseases.

Review of existing blue space projects

To identify typical and successful infrastructure and management elements for blue spaces, researchers at the Estonian University of Life Sciences conducted a review of 180 existing interventions (detailed results can be found in Chapter 10). The analysis included, amongst others, the following aspects:

- Potential to increase physical activity and to improve mental health;
- Equitable accessibility to and within the blue space site;
- Facilitation of visitor interaction with water (bodies);
- Day-to-day management and maintenance; and
- Safety and security measures.

Programming of the BlueHealth DST web application

The development of the web application was based on good practice and experiences by the BlueHealth consortium and the CMCC team. It is composed of two main parts: the front-end as the client application for the user's web browser and a back-end as the connection to the BlueHealth DST database.

The front-end component was developed using Ionic, an Angular-based framework. This framework allows the same application to run on both computer and mobile phone browsers. Figure 9.1 shows a diagram of the high-level BlueHealth DST architecture. It illustrates the relation between the user interface on the device (PC, tablet, mobile phone) and the web service on the server to provide the data presented to the user.

The communication between the client and the web service takes place through the HTTP protocol and a RESTful web service which provides data and contents stored in the database to the front-end. The client application connects to the web service and points in a transparent manner for the user. It requests the contents needed to populate the user interface. The data exchange format is JSON. An example of an endpoint is: http://IP_SERVER/blue-health-backend/static/T4_1.

The web service answers to this request by providing the textual content extracted from the database: {“txt”:”<h3>Injuries<\/h3>\r\n<p><strong>Summary<\/strong> <\/p>\r\n<p><em>Facilitating access to a blue space implies exposure to injury risk, including immediate fatality. Many of the. . . ”}

All textual contents associated with the BlueHealth DST entities such as goals, targets and sub-targets are stored in a relational database. The entity-relationship (E-R) model is depicted in Figure 9.2. It describes the entities, their properties and their relations inside the database of the BlueHealth DST.

In order to obtain the implementation schema, the E-R model diagram was converted to a relational model, as shown in Figure 9.3. The model represents the tables and their properties and their relations as they are implemented in the database of the BlueHealth DST. The database instance has been implemented in the MySQL DBMS.

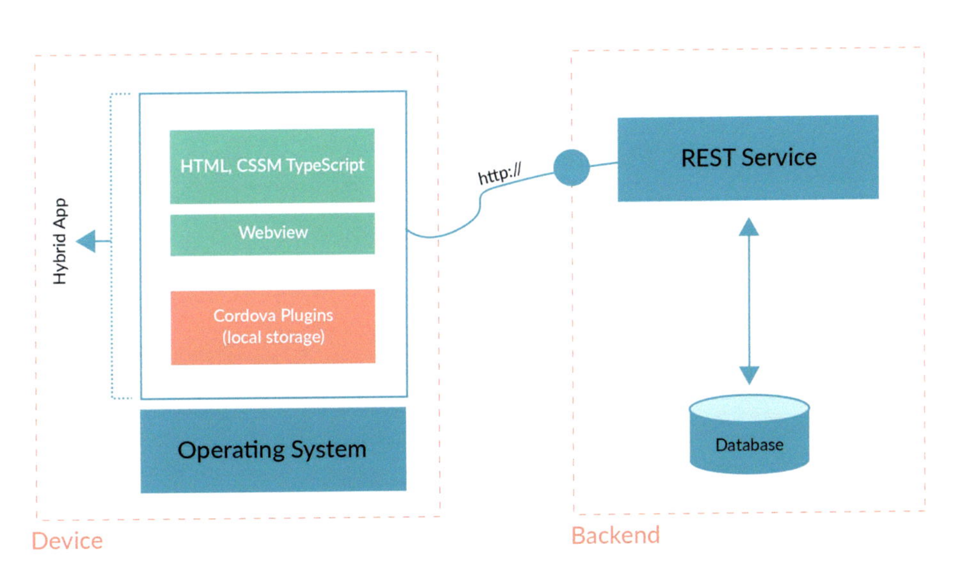

Figure 9.1
Application architecture of the BlueHealth DST: connection between user interface (hybrid app) and backend (database)
(*Source*: CMCC/Anna Wilczyńska)

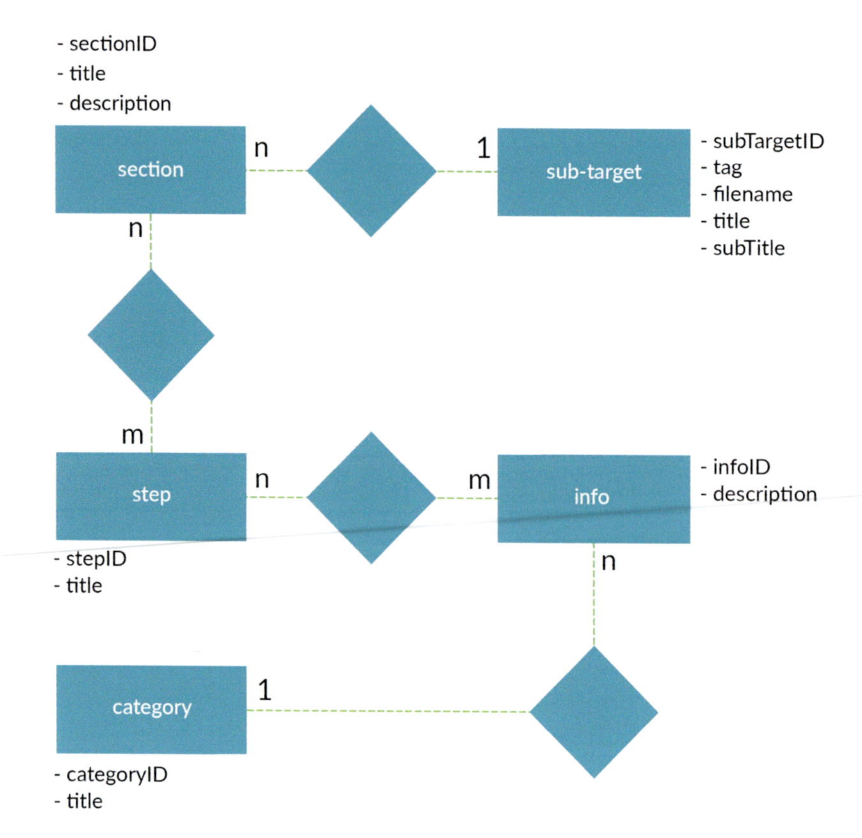

Figure 9.2
A diagram representing the entity-relationship model within the database of the BlueHealth DST
(*Source*: CMCC/Anna Wilczyńska)

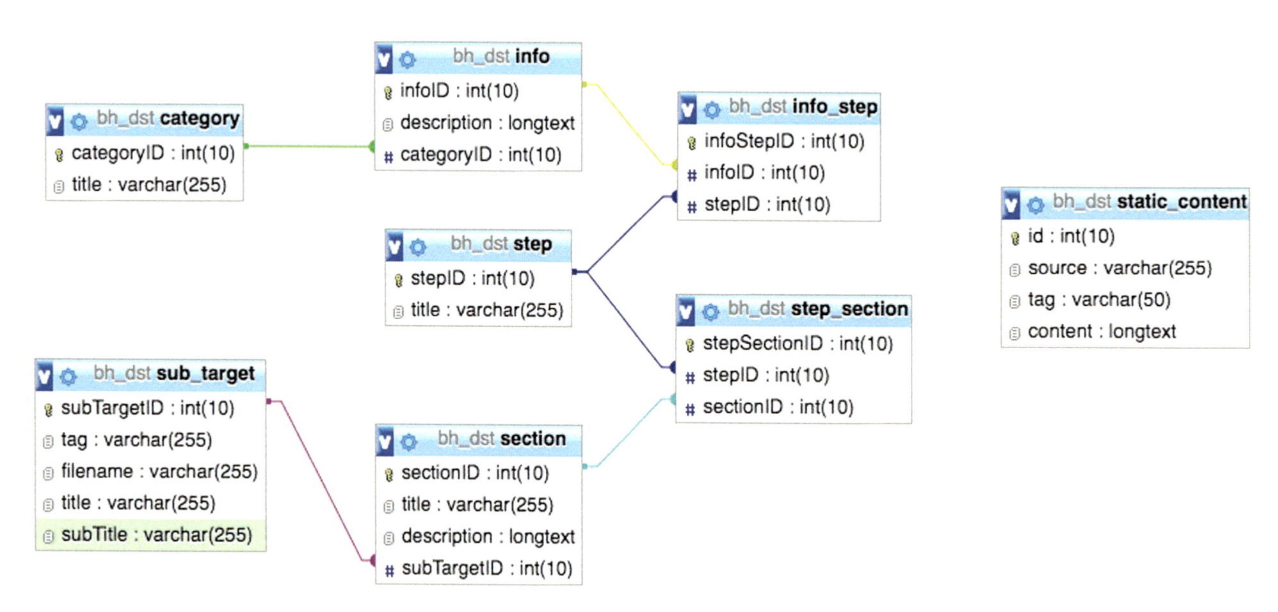

Figure 9.3
A diagram of the relational model within the database of the BlueHealth DST
(*Source*: CMCC)

Piloting of the BlueHealth Decision Support Tool[1]

The development of the BlueHealth DST was supported by several test runs to ensure relevance and applicability in the field. This section provides an insight into the efforts made and shows how the test applications have helped to shape the final tool.

The first pilot version of the BlueHealth DST, produced by CMCC in 2018, was used by ISS for testing in the Appia Antica Park case study in Rome, Italy. A further developed version with improved functionality was then applied and tested at various BlueHealth case studies, led by ISS. The tool was also piloted by all partners during a field exercise at the consortium meeting in spring 2019 in Amersfoort, The Netherlands. The feedback on content and functionality of the tool contributed to the final BlueHealth DST version, which then was confirmed as fit for purpose during a final test application in Plymouth, United Kingdom, in late 2019.

Piloting in Appia Antica Park, Rome

A BlueHealth DST prototype was first piloted in Rome's Appia Antica Park (Figure 9.4a). This park, spanning an area of 4500 ha, contains several blue spaces, comprising both natural and artificial aquatic ecosystems.

The prototype of the web-based BlueHealth DST was applied to guide a project on wetland improvement through the development of a small pond, pathways and benches (see Figure 9.4b and c). The aim of this project was to improve the access and use for local residents who would like to improve their physical and mental well-being. The project team focused on 1) "promotion of human health" and 2) "improvement of ecosystem services", of which the following sub-targets were relevant: "nature experience", "socio-cultural interaction", "noise reduction", "shore activities", "local climate regulation" and "habitat restoration".

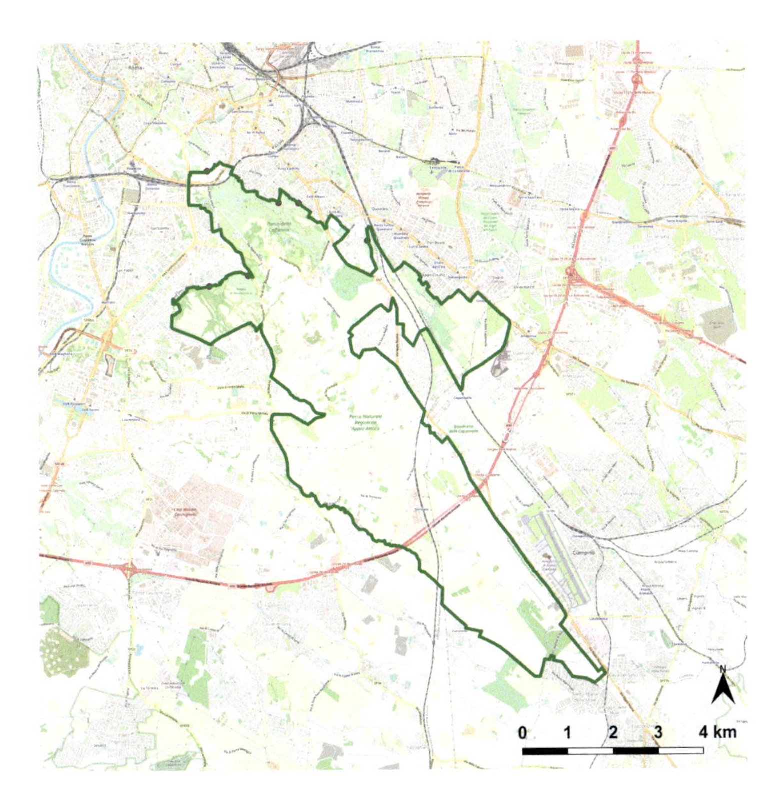

Figure 9.4a–d

a) Location and extent of the Appia Antica Park in Rome; b) the character of the park – the water body is relatively hidden among dense vegetation; c) one wetland to be improved by management; d) screenshot of one page of the DST application outcome following the testing

(*Sources*: a) OpenStreetMap CC-BY-SA; b) and c) ISS; d) BlueHealth DST)

For the selected sub-targets, the tool provided a text output listing a total of 49 factors (Figure 9.4d). For 1) the promotion of human health goal, upon analysis, three key benefits were identified for the project at hand: the reduction

Pooled assessment for the following risk and benefits:

- Nature Experience
- Socialcultural interaction
- Shore activities
- Local climate regulation
- Habitat restoration

The below information provides you with important parameters to consider when planning, assessing, or managing and maintaining public blue spaces, or preparing for interventions and infrastructural measures within the blue space settings.

The pooled guidance document combines the information for the selected health risks and benefits into one document, and thereby provides a resource for structuring information collection and site assessments during field visits to the blue space. For such on-site visits, the pooled guidance lists the blue space features that need to be considered to reduce blue space-specific health risks, and/or to increase related benefits. However, it can also be applied for desktop audits and reviews. The pooled assessment includes a checklist where the need for follow-up action can be documented.

Information and guidance that is applicable for more than one risk or benefit can be identified by the respective label, indicating that the statement can be valid for

- two or more dimensions related to certain risk (▲) or benefit (●) categories
- a variety of different risks (labeled "Risks") or a variety of different benefits (labeled "Benefits"), or
- a variety of both risks and benefits (labeled "General").

Step 1: Review locational and water factors

- ● [Benefits] Are sensitive nature areas protected from human access to avoid environmental degradation (see habitat)?
- ● [Benefits] Does the local infrastructure enable for seating and playing in shaded areas (see UV) to reduce heat stress and provide breaks from recreational activities?
- ● [Climate regulation] Is the blue space surrounded by vegetation, particularly shrubs and trees, which can enhance the blue space climate regulation effect?
- ● [Climate regulation] Does the surrounding infrastructure enhance wind flow (e.g. through low-rise infrastructure or building gaps in wind direction to not block air exchange) to increase climate regulation capacity?
- ● [Climate regulation] Are there fountains or water falls that produce water mist with an additional cooling effect?

Figure 9.4a–d (continued)

of heat stress, which was to be realised by providing shaded areas for seating or shelter; the decrease of noise exposure, to be achieved by enhancing natural water sounds; and the promotion of social interaction through creating easily accessible open spaces. For 2) the improvement of ecosystems services goal, the most relevant factors revolved around the protection of native biota, for instance, by limiting visitor access seasonally or permanently to vulnerable areas and by identifying and managing alien invasive species. Furthermore, the BlueHealth DST-guided analysis revealed the importance of maintenance of the planned infrastructure. Overall, the pilot study confirmed the relevance and usability of the BlueHealth DST and, especially in this case, the benefit of drawing from a complete and exhaustive list of risk and benefit factors to be taken into account for project development, providing guidance on how the site could be managed to maximise its positive impact on public health. This confirmed that the proposed structure and content of the BlueHealth DST was functional and could serve as a baseline for further development and fine-tuning.

Piloting in Amersfoort

In the city of Amersfoort in the Netherlands, the BlueHealth DST was tested in spring 2019 at an urban canal (Figure 9.5).

To make the test run broad and effective, 10 scenarios were prepared, each representing a different type of user with different interests in the blue space and its features (see Table 9.1). For each scenario, four or five targets of the BlueHealth DST were selected for the on-site testing at the urban water canal, checking whether the guidance statements included in the respective risk and benefit targets were applicable and relevant. This setup ensured that each risk or benefit target of the BlueHealth DST was applied several times and tested by groups using the tool with a different perspective in mind.

The test application in Amersfoort provided insights and better understanding of the applicability of the guidance statements on many risks or benefits covered by the BlueHealth DST. The reviewers provided feedback after DST testing about 1) the description, applicability and relevance of risk and benefits; 2) the suitability of the guidance to support assessment of risk and benefits; and 3) its usefulness to provide information for future management of the

Figure 9.5a and b

Amersfoort and its typical canal system, showing some canal edges with barriers and some without, vertical walls rising out of the canal and other aspects which increases risks of, for example, drowning

(*Source*: ISS)

blue space. Most partners considered that the guidance helped to assess risks and benefits, and all of them agreed that the guidance provided useful information for future management of the blue space. As the piloting was done according to various scenarios, it allowed input on the applicability of the DST guidance statements from different perspectives and functional expectations. Based on the feedback of the piloting exercise, content and guidance statements were revised, and the internal consistency between aspects relating to more than one risk or benefit was improved.

Table 9.1 **The ten different scenarios chosen for a BlueHealth DST test application in Amersfoort**

Scenario for DST application	*Goal*	*Target*
1 – Nature conservation/NGO Blue space use: on shore only	Promote human health benefits Promote ecosystem benefits	Nature experience, shore activities Water regulation, habitat restoration
2 – Climate change expert Blue space use: on shore only	Protect human health and minimise risks Promote ecosystem benefits	Temperature, flooding, mosquitoes, snails Local climate regulation
3 – Parents concerned about child safety Blue space use: including swimming and water sports	Protect human health and minimise risks Promote ecosystem benefits	Drowning, injuries in water bodies, injuries around water bodies Water activities, shore activities
4 – Elderly interest group representative Blue space use: on shore only	Protect human health and minimise risks Promote human health benefits Promote ecosystem benefits	Inhalation/*Legionella* Nature experience, sociocultural interaction, noise reduction Local climate regulation
5 – Paediatrician promoting child health Blue space use: including swimming and water sports	Protect human health and minimise risks Promote human health benefits	Drowning, UV Nature experience, water activities
6 – Physical activity promotion network/green gym rep Blue space use: incl. swimming and water sports	Protect human health and minimise risks Promote human health benefits	Injuries around water bodies, water ingestion and contact, UV Water activities, shore activities
7 – Local health department Blue space use: on shore only	Protect human health and minimise risks Promote human health benefits	Water ingestion and contact, inhalation/*Legionella*, temperature, mosquitoes Shore activities
8 – Water expert from local environment department Blue space use: on shore only	Protect human health and minimise risks Promote ecosystem benefits	Water ingestion and contact Local climate regulation, water regulation, habitat restoration
9 – Water sports club president Blue space use: incl. swimming and water sports	Protect human health and minimise risks	Drowning, injuries in water bodies, water ingestion and contact, snails
10 – Urban planner (trying to maximise benefits) Blue space use: on shore only	Protect human health and minimise risks Promote human health benefits Promote ecosystem benefits	Flooding Sociocultural interaction, noise reduction Local climate regulation, water regulation

Piloting in Teats Hill, Plymouth

The further-developed BlueHealth DST was applied in Plymouth, United Kingdom, in November 2019 at Teats Hill, one of the BlueHealth case study sites located at a public section of the Plymouth marina (see Chapter 3). The application of the BlueHealth DST was carried out by members from the South West Coast Path, National Marine Aquarium, Plymouth City Council and local planners who worked on Plymouth's urban beach regeneration project at Teats Hill. The group identified the features and conditions that seemed most relevant for the Teats Hill redevelopment and then visited the site to assess the risks and benefits based on a set of guidance documents provided by the tool (Figure 9.6).

After the test application, the group discussed how they could use the DST in their specific areas of work. They also agreed that the tool's guidance and discussion prompts would be useful when justifying new planning bids.

The feedback showed that the changes implemented after the Amersfoort test run improved the tool significantly, and participants agreed that the BlueHealth DST will be valuable for practitioners when it came to redeveloping and optimising urban blue spaces. After the Plymouth test application, the BlueHealth DST was then edited and finalised in 2020. The final content and structure of the tool is presented in the next section.

The BlueHealth Decision Support Tool: optimisation of blue spaces for health

The growing scientific evidence on the health effects of blue and green spaces encourages the renovation or new development of urban water bodies. For the optimisation of such blue space projects, one needs to understand which factors are precarious versus beneficial for blue space design and management.

The DST is based on scientific evidence, good practice, case studies and expert insights on the mechanisms behind the possible health effects of blue spaces. It covers a total of 18 topics, divided into 10 health risks to be prevented (such as drowning or flooding) and 8 health or environmental benefits to be enhanced (such as nature experience or local climate regulation) (Figure 9.7). The BlueHealth DST presents each of these topics with a guidance document, including insights on typical scenarios and local relevance, and a practical assessment checklist. The checklist is built on the decisive factors identified for blue space success or failure.

Figure 9.6
Members of the group evaluate the redeveloped space at Teats Hill in Plymouth using the BlueHealth DST
(*Source*: Jo Garrett)

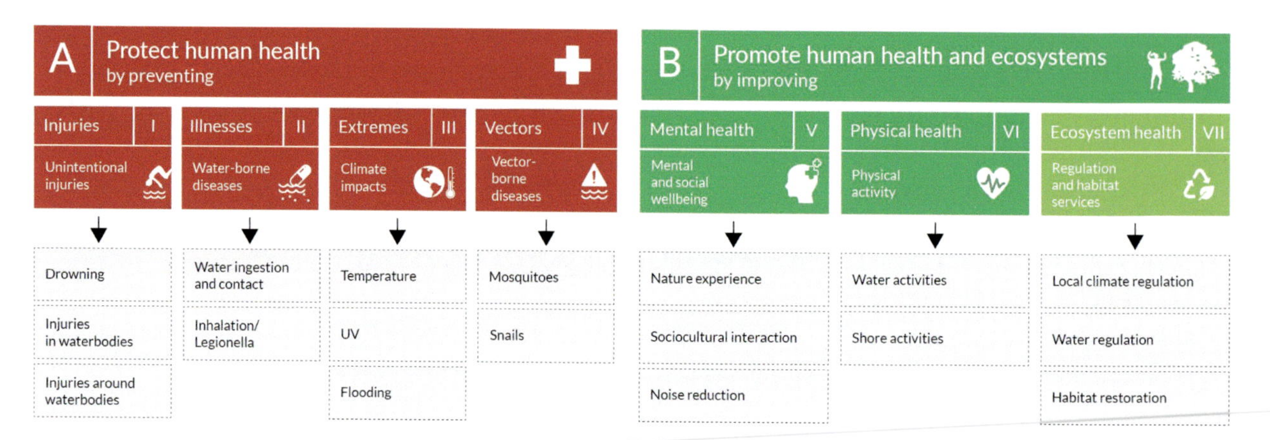

Figure 9.7

Critical topics to address in the optimisation of a blue space

(*Source*: Arnt Diener/Anna Wilczyńska)

The user or project team is guided through the topics to achieve two goals: first, to identify needs for precautionary measures to avoid health risks, and second, to define measures that optimise human health and environmental benefits. The 18 topics were bundled into seven targets (Figure 9.8) that will each be introduced in the following section. For detailed guidance, further references and the customisable assessment checklist, readers may refer to the online tool alongside the instructions provided in the penultimate section of this chapter. Beyond the BlueHealth DST, other tools, particularly the BEAT introduced earlier, can provide additional assessment guidance.

Step 1: Protection of human health and risk minimisation

For any blue space project, the prevention of serious injuries and illnesses should come first. We advise applying a risk-based and anticipatory approach, that is, the integration of infrastructural and managerial measures to prevent those health risks that are found to be most probable and serious in the given circumstances (WHO 2013, 2019).

Figure 9.9 lists the four targets to be reviewed for precautionary measures in blue spaces. In Table 9.2, examples of factors that determine the relevance of a mechanism for a blue space setting at hand are listed.

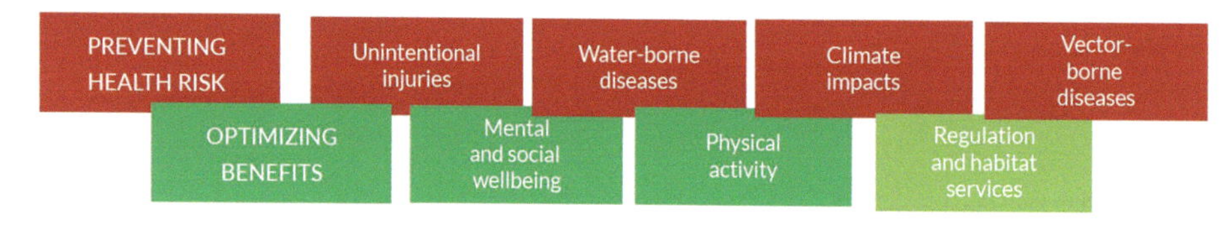

Figure 9.8

The array of assessment and intervention targets used in the BlueHealth DST

(*Source*: WHO)

Figure 9.9

Adverse health risk targets in blue spaces

(*Source*: WHO)

Table 9.2 **Examples of factors for the protection of human health**

Unintentional injuries	• Water-body bottom conditions and depth in water entry zone can affect risk (e.g., underwater objects, steep or shallow relief, slippery surfaces)
Water-borne diseases	• Contamination and nutrient inflows, including from sewage or agricultural runoff, and their seasonal dynamics (e.g. snowmelt or extreme rainfall) can increase health risk
Climate impacts	• Surrounding relief, surface infiltration permeability and water flow patterns can increase flooding risk upon extreme rainfall
Vector-borne diseases	• Corners and edges of the water body with water stagnation, particularly if shaded and shallow, or small water-bearing containers and flooded flower pots can be ideal breeding grounds for certain mosquito genera

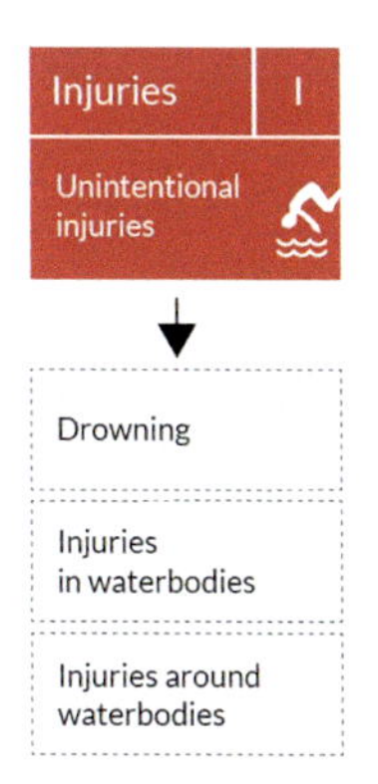

Prevent unintentional injuries

Injury and mortality risk from drowning and unintentional injuries or accidents are associated with most uses and users of blue spaces (Table 9.3). The highest risks are commonly recorded among physically active uses and immersion in water (i.e. all water sports activities). Thus, a particular focus is to be put on drowning as the third deadliest injury in Europe (with five times as many casualties as firearm use). The respective guidance document provides a list of factors to be reviewed based on project documentation and on-site visits. The factors for this category are spread widely: while drowning risk may largely depend on water body features and user behaviour, falls have the highest mortality rates among older people and often occur along slippery or uneven walkways. The example of drowning illustrates the anticipatory design focus that blue spaces typically require in comparison, for example, with swimming pools that inherently allow more control of water depth, visibility, surveillance or access times (WHO 2014; Peden et al. 2018; Hamilton et al. 2018; Patel et al. 2017).

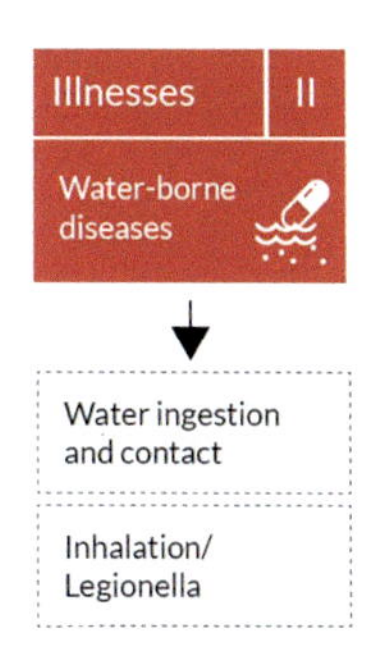

Prevent water-borne diseases

A considerable volume (of roughly 25 ml) of water is ingested during an average swim. Oral ingestion and inhalation, but also skin or mucosal contact, can result in acute and chronic health effects from contaminated water (Table 9.4). Notably, 85% of officially registered bathing-water sites in the European Union were rated at an "excellent" level of recreational water quality in 2019. However, water quality can be highly dynamic in time and space, with particular risk after heavy rain events for open water bodies or prolonged periods of stagnation in water fountains. The oral ingestion of contaminated water mainly risks diarrheal diseases caused by various pathogens. Less likely, contaminated water can also be inhaled and thereby allow certain pathogens, like *Legionella*, to be transmitted through water spray or mist. In warm and nutrient-rich inland and coastal waters, adverse health effects can also be caused by the toxins released during algae or cyanobacteria blooms. Overall, the most susceptible population groups for water-borne illnesses are children, elderly or immune-suppressed persons. In children particularly, disease contraction may also occur through the ingestion of contaminated beach sand or coastal soil (European Environment Agency 2019; WHO Regional Office for Europe 2016; Huisman et al. 2018; Carlson et al. 2020; WHO 2017).

Table 9.3 **Example factors to assess the risk of unintentional injuries**

Drowning	• Offshore winds (a risk for, e.g. flotation devices) and water currents (e.g. rip currents, river currents or tidal currents in maritime waters) can increase risk • Provision of adequate equipment (e.g. lifejackets, lighting, first aid kit) on the shore/for water vessels can help to control risk
Injuries in water bodies	• Water body bottom conditions and depth in water entry zone can affect risk (e.g., underwater objects, steep or shallow relief, slippery surfaces) • Tourists and non-residents are likely to lack local knowledge of blue space risks and require particular attention and guidance (e.g. local currents, steep shores, local water contamination or hazardous aquatic animals)
Injuries around water bodies	• Inadequate/deteriorated conditions of water-related infrastructure (e.g. jetty) and vegetation (e.g., slippery surfaces, risky diving or hangout spots) can increase risk • Provision of medical supplies for injury treatment with provisions for the particular hazards of the area (e.g. removal kit for stingers) can help to control risk

Table 9.4 **Example factors to assess the risk of water-borne illnesses**

Ingestion	• Contamination and nutrient inflows, including sewage, storm-water, solid waste, agricultural runoff or industrial site outflows, and their seasonal dynamics (snowmelt, low-gauge phases or flooding after extreme rainfall) can increase health risk • Monitoring of water quality, particularly upon infrastructural changes within or upstream of the blue space and upon extreme weather events, can help to control risk
Inhalation	• Prolonged periods with water temperatures between 25 and 45°C favour *Legionella* growth in water pipes/reservoirs • Adequacy and maintenance of disinfectant concentration where relevant for artificial ornamental blue spaces such as fountains can help to control risk

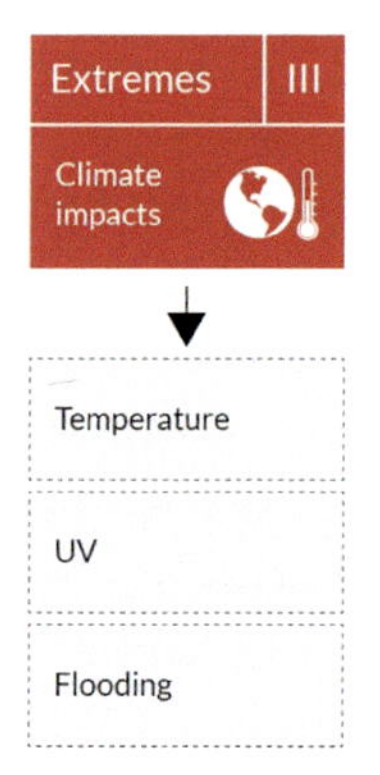

Prevent atmospheric/climate impacts

Facilitating access and promoting the use of blue spaces can increase user exposure to extreme air and water temperatures, UV radiation and extreme weather events. Most of those climate-associated risk factors show apparent seasonal dynamics; in particular, water temperatures typically fluctuate more strongly over time and throughout the water body than expected in swimming pools, for example. Water contamination and injury risk in urban water bodies is adversely affected by extreme events such as flooding or drought. While the provision of UV-shading may be considered common good practice in many places, the monitoring and communication of critical, seasonal water quality dynamics is typically (still) limited to certain water body types. Guidance focuses on three distinct topics (Table 9.5):

1. UV exposure: Exposure to solar UV radiation can cause skin inflammation and adverse long-term health effects. Uses of blue spaces are often associated with prolonged times spent outdoors with reduced clothing and thus an increased exposure of skin surface. Even on cloudy days, up to 75% of UV radiation can still pass through an overcast sky. In blue spaces, exposure to solar UV can be aggravated by surface reflection, with water and sand

Table 9.5 **Example factors to assess the risk of climate-related impacts**

Solar UV	• Risk from UV radiation is higher in locations with a low latitude and high elevation above sea level and also increases with reflection from water, beach sand or snow • Infants under 12 months of age are particularly sensitive to UV radiation
Temperature extremes	• Cool zones or currents within the water body can unexpectedly increase cold water exposure for swimmers • Provision of cold showers near public swimming areas to prepare the body for cold water immersion can control risk
Extreme events/flooding	• Surrounding relief, surface infiltration permeability and water flow patterns may increase flash flooding risk during extreme rainfall • Preservation of local retention areas and reduction of sealed areas can help to mitigate flood risk

reflecting up to 15% and snow up to 80%. Over 20,000 deaths are attributed annually to excessive UV exposure in Europe, mainly caused by cancer (Greinert et al. 2015; Gilbertz et al. 2019).

2. Temperature extremes: Air and water temperature levels not only influence numbers of users of blue spaces but also their health risks. Water temperatures below 15°C can cool down the body around 25 times faster than can comparable air temperatures. The somatic effects can lead to so-called "cold shocks" and premature exhaustion which in turn increases the risk for drowning. Hot weather, on the other hand, is a risk factor, particularly for physically active and for older people. The heat wave in the summer of 2003, for example, caused an estimated 70,000 excess deaths in Europe. Urban water bodies are sought out for recreation and physical activity during hot days; preventative measures like ensuring access to drinking water or providing shading elements then become particularly relevant (Gunawardena et al. 2017; Tipton et al. 2017).
3. Extreme events: Flooding is the most common water-related extreme event. The influx of contaminated water and debris into blue spaces from feeder water bodies or surface water flows typically has adverse effects on water quality and site safety. Facilitating public access to the shores of flood-prone water bodies thus requires consideration for flooding situations, such as signposting, warning systems or physical barriers to prevent exposure. In the WHO European Region, floods affected 3.4 million people in the period from 2000 to 2011. Climate change is projected to increase the occurrence and frequency of flood events in large areas of Europe (Bell et al. 2018; WHO Regional Office for Europe 2013).

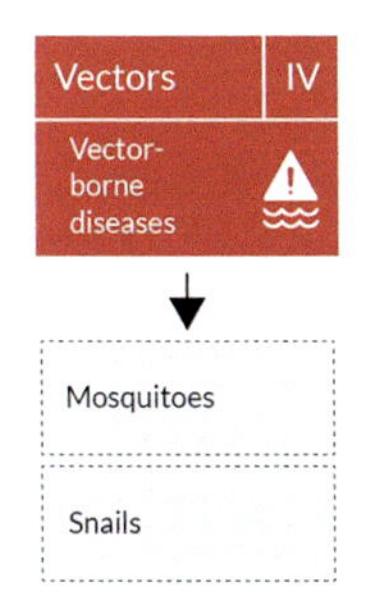

Prevent vector-borne diseases

Vector-borne diseases are caused by pathogens transmitted by host organisms such as mosquitoes, snails or ticks. Mosquito bites are common incidents around water bodies, which can act as breeding sites for them. Under certain conditions, those mosquitoes can also transmit illnesses. Similarly, snails can proliferate along the shorelines of freshwater bodies and carry an illness-causing parasite called *Trichobilharzia*. A review of the vector-borne disease risk can thus be relevant for both blue space users and the adjacent population (Table 9.6).

1. Mosquitoes: Mosquito-borne disease prevalence differs by geographic region, and the current risk for disease transmission in Europe is relatively low. West Nile fever is considered the most relevant disease and is typically associated with a concentrated presence of birds. In 2018, almost 1500 human infections of the West Nile virus and over 150 deaths were reported in the European Union (European Centre for Disease Prevention and Control 2020; Brugueras et al. 2020).

Table 9.6 **Example factors to assess the risk of vector-borne diseases**

Aquatic snails	• Eutrophication, high influx of nutrients and presence of waterfowl can increase the risk of schistosome exposure • Small children may be more vulnerable due to more extended stays in shallow water and near shorelines with potentially higher parasite concentrations
Mosquitoes	• Maintenance of containers and blue space-adjacent areas without water drainage (e.g. by manual drainage or mosquito-proofing with lids) can control risk • Corners and edges of water bodies with water stagnation, particularly if shaded and shallow, or small water-bearing containers and flooded flower pots can increase the risk of mosquito breeding

2. Snails: The most common snail-borne disease is the so-called swimmers' itch upon contact with *Trichobilharzia*-infested water. Outbreaks regularly lead to the closure of lakes for recreational water activities. In the future, global developments are expected to lead to an increase and further extension of vector-borne disease transmission in Europe (Selbach et al. 2016; Soldánová et al. 2013).

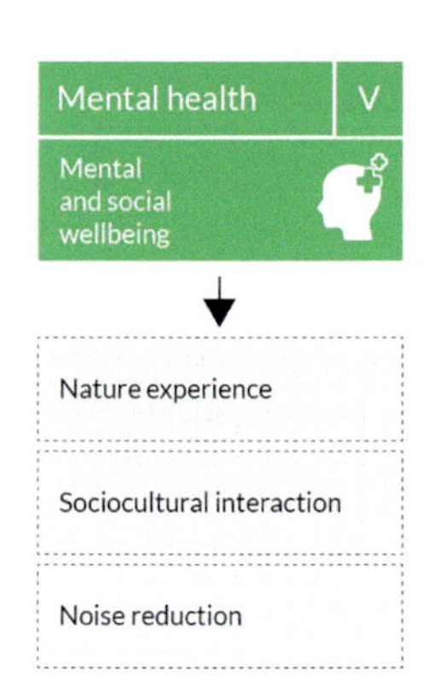

Step 2: Promotion of human and environment benefits

The second goal in optimising any blue space should be the improvement of potential benefits for users, neighbours and local ecosystems. We again encourage an anticipatory and tailored approach, that is, the integration of physical and managerial measures to leverage the benefits that are most prominent and relevant in the local circumstances. Introductions to each of the three targets can complement existing understanding of the topic. Each target consists of several topics that can be selected for reading and analysis for the specific site (Figure 9.10 and Table 9.7).

Improve mental and social well-being

Blue spaces can be ideal locations for both relaxation and social gatherings. The effects of nature experience and social interaction have shown significant influences on human well-being and a sense of belonging (Table 9.8).

Figure 9.10
Health benefit targets in blue spaces
(*Source*: WHO)

Table 9.7 **Example factors for the improvement of health and local ecosystems**

Mental and social well-being	• Space and infrastructure provision for social and group activity without disturbance of user groups sensitive to noise
Physical activity	• Provision and maintenance of opportunities for sport and play activity (e.g. footpaths, fitness and work-out equipment, playgrounds or ping-pong tables)
Ecosystem functions	• (Seasonal) management of vegetation around blue space in balance with desired local climate effects (shading, evaporation) and various user group preferences (e.g. avoiding barren soil with low albedo during dry periods)

Table 9.8 **Example factors to assess mental and social well-being**

Nature experience	• Protection/promotion of biodiversity and visual attractiveness of flora and fauna enhances nature experience (e.g. through habitat restoration) • Space and infrastructure provision for social and group activity without disturbance of user groups sensitive for noise enhances mutual benefits
Social interaction	• Programmes encouraging social interaction ranging from neighbourhood groups for blue space maintenance to exercise groups and social events can enhance benefits • Provision of infrastructure promoting social exchange and participation targeting different groups (e.g. playground for children, soccer fields and BBQ areas for adults and families, or seating and boule lanes for older people) increase benefits
Noise	• Shielding from local noise sources through sound barriers consisting of natural compounds (e.g. trees and vegetation, rocks or landform) or artificial elements (e.g. noise walls) reduces noise exposure and can enhance the positive sound effect of water bodies • People with impaired hearing (higher vulnerability to noise) and persons with high stress levels may benefit the most from calm environments

1. Nature experience: Water elements are recognised as a key factor for mental restoration, particularly in built environments. Living in areas with greater availability of blue space has been associated with a range of mental well-being outcomes, including better mental health, lower odds of mood and anxiety disorders and better quality of life, though these relationships are not always consistent across countries and sub-populations (White et al. 2019; Finlay et al. 2015; Collins et al. 2020).
2. Social interaction: Social interaction in blue space settings may range from spontaneous gatherings of families, friends and acquaintances to organised common interest groups with associated infrastructure, such as running tracks. Participation in urban blue space activity can counteract today's hectic lifestyles, support the maintenance of social networks for older people and promote children's well-being and development. Research suggests that socially disadvantaged people are more likely to underline social interaction and well-being as the key benefit of blue space visits (de Bell et al. 2017; Frantzeskaki et al. 2017).
3. Noise reduction: Blue spaces and surrounding vegetation or green space can buffer noise pollution by pleasant water sounds or absorption. Good blue space design therefore considers the distance and shielding from noise sources like traffic or recreation. Noise is a major environmental health concern, particularly in urban areas, with adverse health effects. Environmental noise mainly include that emitted from traffic and leisure activities. Continuous noise exposure can have severe adverse effects on human health, both physically and mentally. It increases the risk of developing cardiovascular diseases, such as hypertension (high blood pressure) or myocardial infarction and can cause depression and sleep disturbance, reduce cognitive performance and lead to long-term annoyance. Even short-term exposure can increase stress levels and reduce the quality of life. Almost a quarter (23.3%) of the European population living in cities reported problems with traffic or neighbourhood noise in 2016 (Schäffer et al. 2020; WHO 2018; Lacasta et al. 2016).

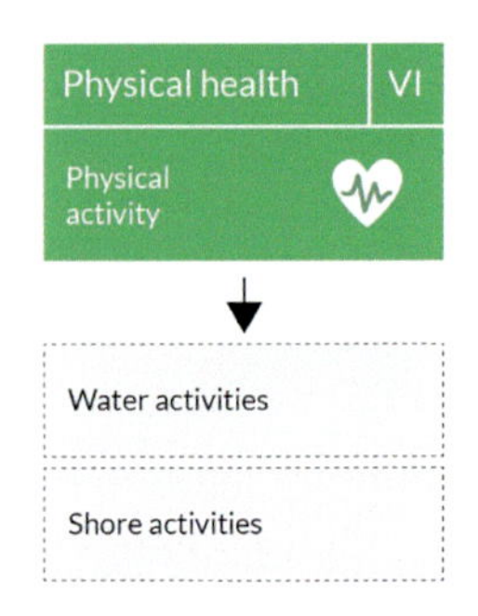

Promote physical activity

Modern lifestyles and increased urbanisation have resulted in higher levels of physical inactivity due to greater use of motorised transport, sedentary work and lifestyle and inadequate provision of and access to activity-promoting public spaces. A lack of physical activity is a leading risk factor for health (contributing to about 10% of mortality in the WHO European Region), and surveys have shown that more than half of the European population is not active enough to meet health recommendations. Physical activity and recreation in blue spaces (swimming, surfing, etc.) and their surroundings (such as taking a walk by a coast/river or around a lake) can represent a major benefit for population health. Swimming is recognised as one of the most beneficial exercise forms. Research has shown that parks and aesthetically pleasing scenes are positively associated with physical activity, which access to water bodies can extend. Onshore, physical activity programmes like running meet-ups, boot camps and yoga classes attract young and old (Table 9.9) (Barnett et al. 2017; WHO Regional Office for Europe 2018).

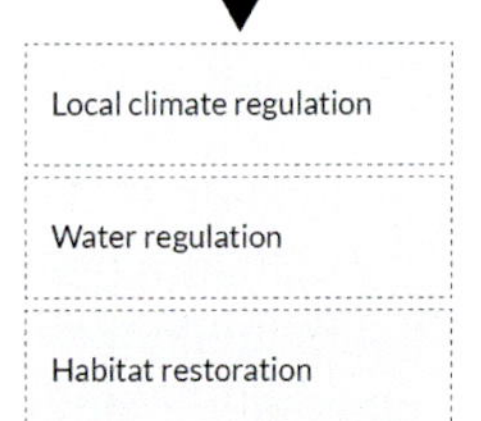

Improve ecosystem functions

Urban blue-green infrastructure can have a regulatory effect on the microclimate through temperature, wind, humidity and precipitation. Furthermore, it can be utilised to provide resilience to flooding at times of water surplus and to drought at times of water shortage (Table 9.10).

1. Climate regulation: Water surfaces and vegetation evaporate water – which in turn creates a cooling effect. They also reflect more solar energy (higher albedo) than dark

Table 9.9 **Example factors to assess physical activity**

Water activities	• Separation of conflicting uses and functions of recreational water (e.g. separate zones for recreational swimming versus other [motorised] water sports) and shore areas (e.g. separate zones for sport activities versus relaxation at the waterfront) • Monitoring of ice thickness and likelihood of suitable ice cover during winter helps to manage risk
Shore activities	• Provision and maintenance of opportunities for sport and play activity (e.g. footpaths, fitness and work-out equipment, playground or ping-pong table)

Table 9.10 **Example factors to assess ecosystem regulation and habitat services**

Local climate regulation	• Surrounding infrastructure with opportunity for wind flow (e.g. low-rise infrastructure or building gaps in wind direction increase climate buffering effect) influences the buffering capacity • (Seasonal) management of vegetation around blue space in balance with desired local climate effects (shading, evaporation) and various user group preferences (e.g. avoid barren soil with low albedo during dry periods)
Water regulation	• Water infiltration rate (e.g. sealing of soil, density of vegetation) of surrounding area or green space enhances water regulation capacity • Clear rules on urban functions permitted or rejected in areas potentially required for water retention or regulation (e.g. recreational infrastructures, commercial functions, gastronomy, playgrounds, campsites, etc.)
Habitat restoration	• Presence of invasive (alien) species may cause risks to biodiversity • Seasonal or permanent limitation of access to certain sensitive water and shore zones to protect wildlife and eco-systems

surfaces like roads or buildings, which contributes to the mitigation of so-called "urban heat islands". The local climate impact of urban water bodies can be remarkable: researchers found air temperature reductions of between 0.5 and 7°C through blue-green infrastructure and so-called "water cooling islands". Findings recommend combining water bodies with complex vegetation, including shrubs and trees, and minimising the extent of impermeable surfaces like pavement (Vieira et al. 2018; Kuttler et al. 2002; Gunawardena et al. 2017).

2. Water regulation: In times of water excess, blue and green spaces can be used as retention areas. This may require (temporary) changes of function and periods without recreational access. Blue and green spaces can facilitate water storage, storm water harvesting and groundwater recharge to supplement urban water resources and provide fire-fighting water or buffer droughts (Voskamp and Van de Ven 2015; Abell et al. 2019).
3. Habitat restoration: The creation or renovation of water bodies can maintain or improve conditions for natural flora and fauna, biodiversity and habitat functionality, while human uses of such water bodies or surrounding green space may need to be restricted. Blue space planners can optimise the habitat and biodiversity value of an urban area in several ways, including by lowering nutrient levels in water or improving the environmental water quality, diversifying the current and depth patterns of the water body or stimulating surrounding natural vegetation growth with a diversity in habitat structure. A healthy aquatic ecosystem with a sound habitat and biodiversity status leads to improvements of related ecosystem services, ranging from water purification to food provision. Certain recreational activities can jeopardise ecological restoration efforts both on land and in the water, such as through the influx of sunscreen products and nutrients from human skin, water disturbance by motorboats or degradation and pollution of vegetation surrounding blue spaces. Investments in local ecosystems are supported by the biodiversity strategy of the European Commission that requires that "by 2020, ecosystems and their services are maintained and enhanced by establishing green infrastructure and restoring at least 15% of degraded ecosystems" (Oertli and Parris 2019; Sutton-Grier and Sandifer 2019).

Hands-on guidance for using the BlueHealth DST

The BlueHealth DST is essentially made up of four work processes: 1) assembly of a team and introduction to the concept of the BlueHealth DST, 2) a desk-based review of the topic summaries to understand key mechanisms in blue spaces and select relevant topics for your case, 3) an analysis of selected topics through on-site visits and information collection and 4) an assessment of identified priorities for interventions before their planning and implementation (Figure 9.11). The web application guides you through the process consecutively, and a demonstration

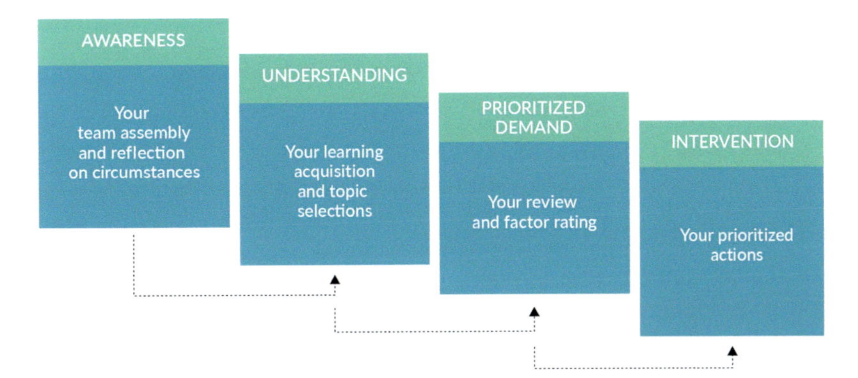

Figure 9.11
Step-wise guidance of the BlueHealth DST along optimisation steps
(*Source*: Arnt Diener/Anna Wilczyńska)

Figure 9.12
Step 1 – Introduction
(*Source*: BlueHealth DST website)

video is also available on the BlueHealth website. The tool starts with an introductory page, which provides general information about the concept of "blue health" and the benefits of the BlueHealth DST (Figure 9.14). For the subsequent guidance, we recommend application of the tool by a blue space project team to bring different perspectives together.

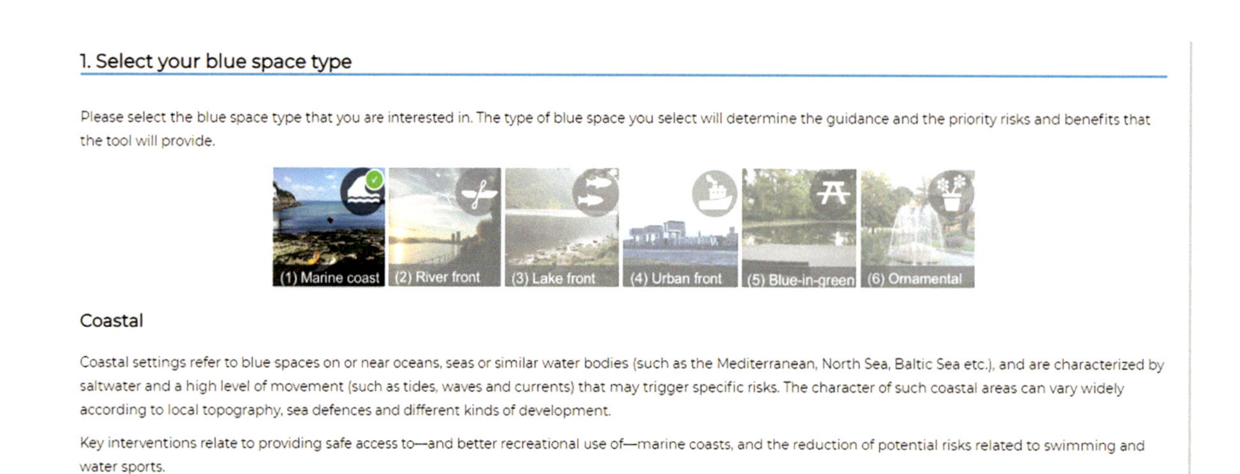

Figure 9.13
Step 2.A – Define your type of blue space
(*Source*: BlueHealth DST website)

2. Describe your blue space

Please provide the tool with information on the ways your blue space is used, and whether you wish to use the tool in connection to future interventions. This information will determine the guidance and the priority risks and benefits that the tool will provide.

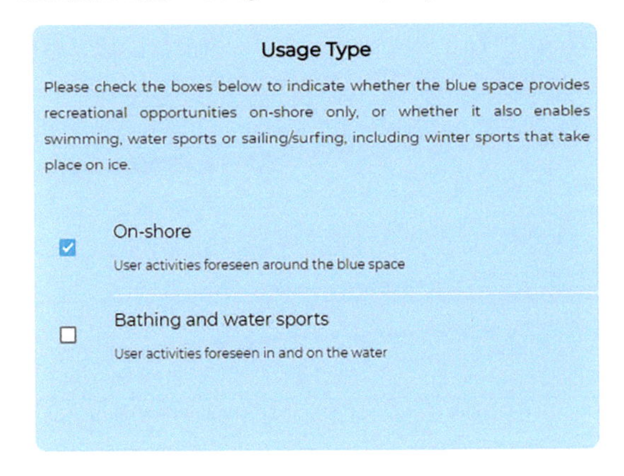

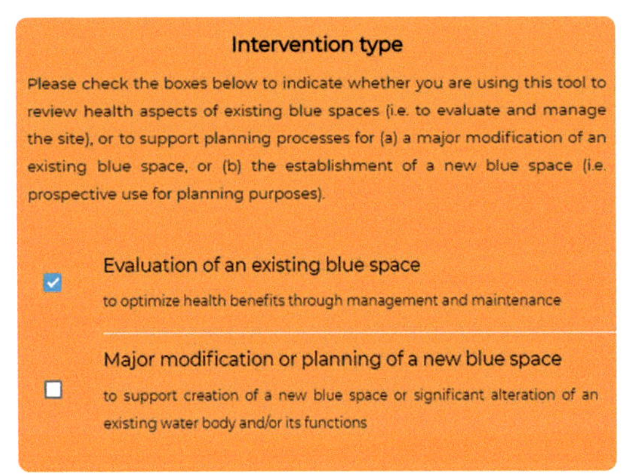

Figure 9.14
Step 2.B – Define your activity and intervention types
(*Source*: BlueHealth DST website)

Step 1: Assemble a team and introduce it to "blue health"

The first step in optimising or developing a blue space should include the definition of a team jointly to complete the BlueHealth DST. Whether your priority is well-being or environmental effects, you will benefit from a multi-disciplinary team. In the process, the team will need to steer the assessment and intervention selection, which will benefit from a clear mandate by decision-makers. One critical step of the assessment is the on-site visits, which will require at least the presence of a core team. Once the team has identified critical topics or even individual factors to focus on, it may make sense to involve additional stakeholders or temporary topic advisors. Experience has shown that the initial grasp of BlueHealth differs greatly between professionals of different disciplines. Thus, a joint introduction to BlueHealth is recommended to ensure a common understanding. Basic introductory information is provided in the first section of the BlueHealth DST, with a number of additional resources available on the BlueHealth project's main webpage.

Step 2: Define your blue space

Following the introduction, you are asked to define the blue space at hand (type, activities, intervention) (Figures 9.13 and 9.14). Based on your selections, the tool highlights some of the 18 topics in subsequent steps as likely to be relevant. These highlights are recommendations only, and regardless of your self-categorisation, all subsequent parts of the tool remain accessible.

The tool only requires a very basic categorisation. Nevertheless, before continuing with the subsequent steps, it is recommended to gather and categorise any existing documentation on your blue space project. This may include maps and descriptions, stakeholder overviews, timelines or budgets.

Step 3: Review topics and choose relevant aspects for your blue space

In this section, your team is introduced to the blue-space specific health and environment topics. To guide selection of topics relevant for your blue space projects, they are grouped into three goals: 1) protect human health, 2) promote human health, 3) promote ecosystem function (see Figure 9.15). Within each goal, the topics are grouped into a total of seven targets. It is recommended to at least read up ("READ MORE") on each of the seven targets before deciding which targets and topics to include or exclude.

The respective guidance (example in Figure 9.16) provided by the BlueHealth DST presents information such as:

- an overview of the topic's health implications and their mechanisms;
- affected or vulnerable user groups;
- figures related to the health relevance and occurrence in Europe; and
- exemplary scenarios for blue spaces.

The team is expected to conclude this step by selecting topics you decide to assess later. A green tick appears above each tile selected. For selected topics, you may download PDFs of the guidance documents with additional sections on resources (as web links) in Step 4.

Step 4: Conduct assessment and prioritise interventions

This is the most important step of the BlueHealth DST. To prepare your assessment, you may now view or download the topical guidance sheets (with further resources as hyperlinks) (Figure 9.19). In addition, the checklist for your on-site and desk-based assessment is provided for download at the bottom of the page ("Pooled Assessment").

Figure 9.15
Step 3 – Gain topical understanding
(*Source*: BlueHealth DST website)

The pooled assessment can be printed as a PDF version for editing with a computer or mobile device and as a hard copy for handwritten notes. It combines the factors for each of the selected topics into one document, supplemented with fill-in tables for your notes. The pooled assessment is grouped into three perspectives on your blue space project:

- Review locational and water factors;
- Consider user group and behavioural factors; and
- Review, establish and maintain safe management and design factors;

The individual factors are marked as benefits and risks with icons, and the downloadable PDF version includes checkboxes to tick (Figure 9.18). You may use these checkboxes during a site visit to highlight the risk and benefits that

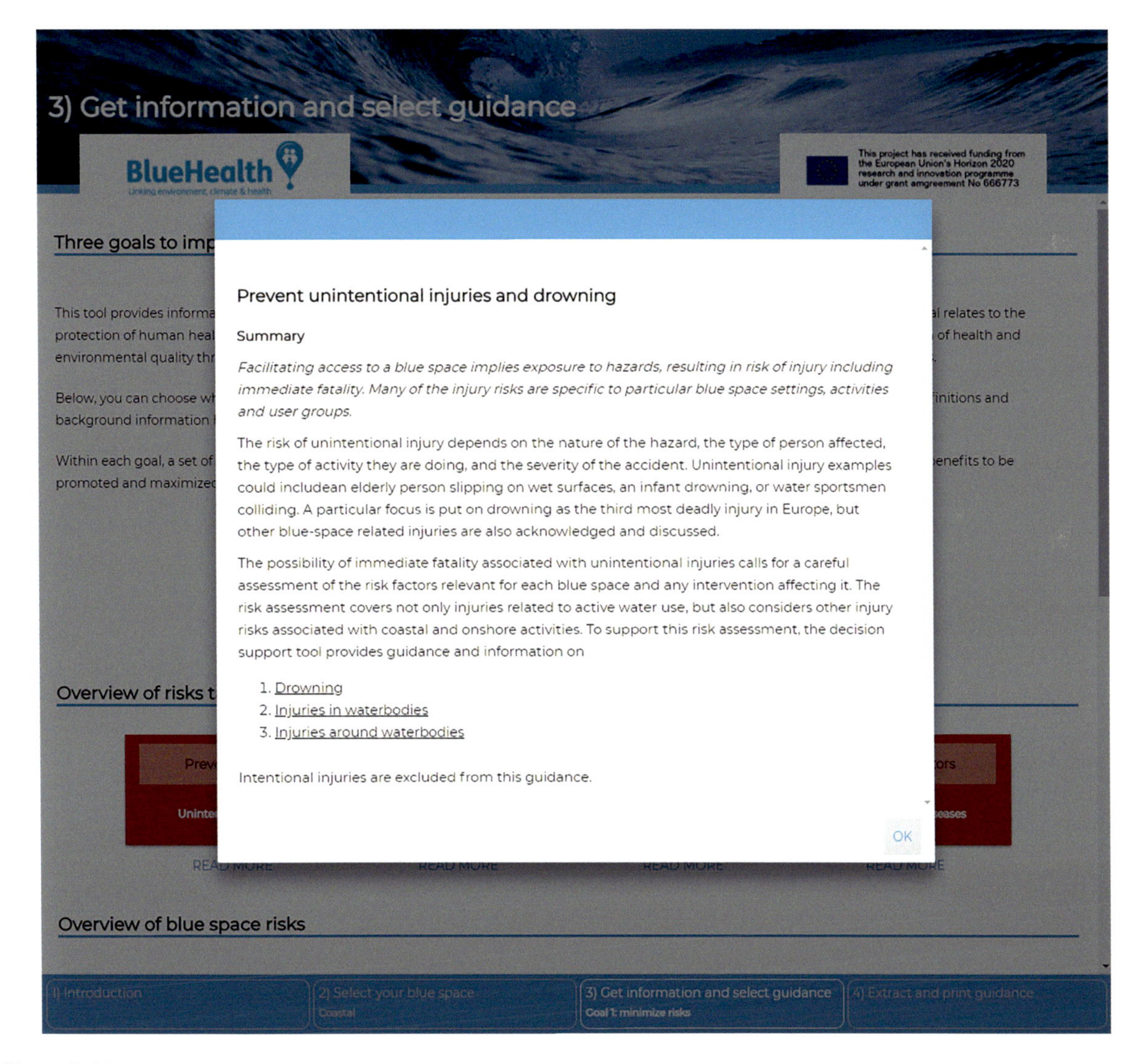

Figure 9.16

Example guidance sheet on the issue of drowning

(*Source*: BlueHealth DST website)

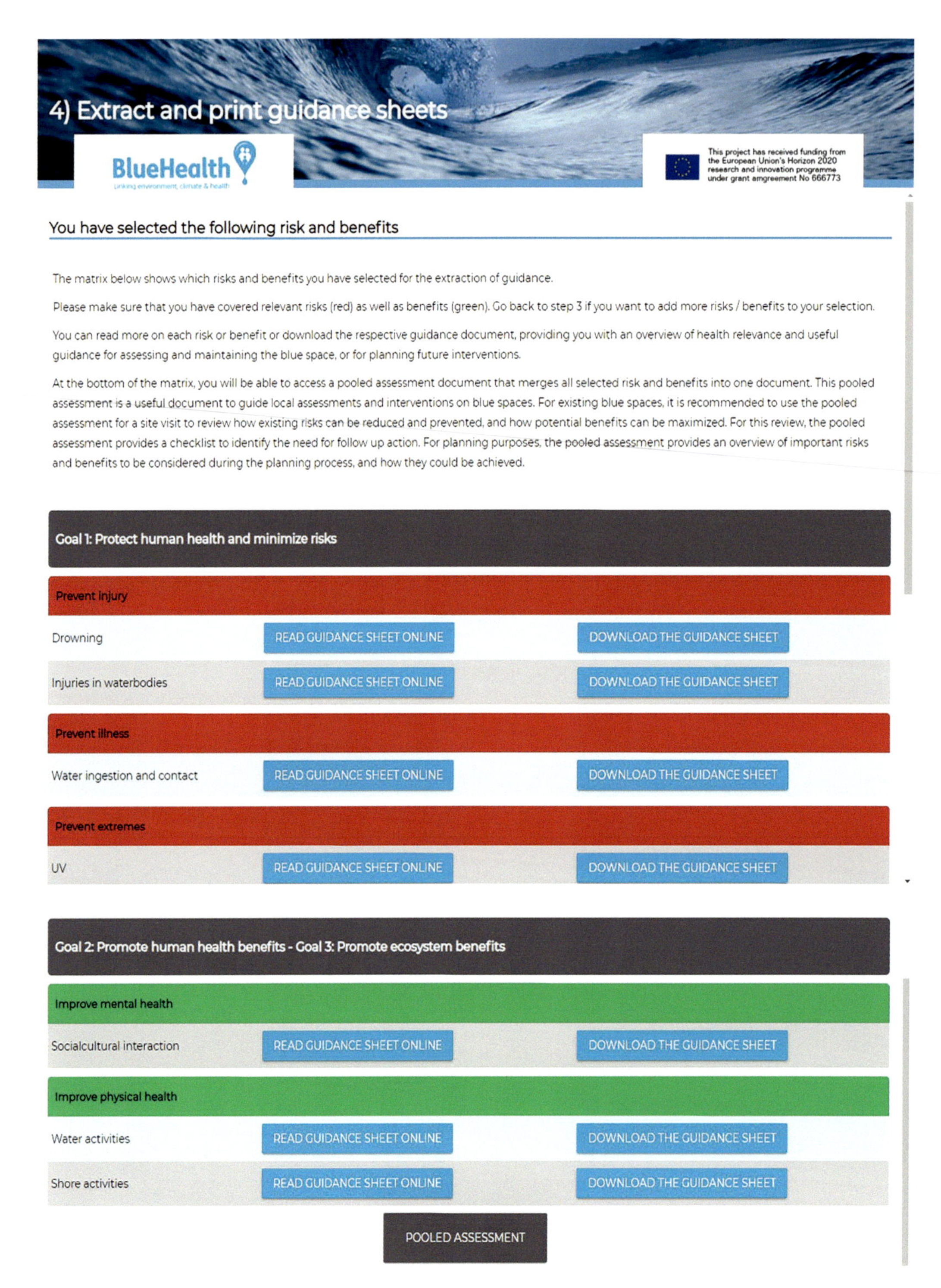

Figure 9.17
List of selected risk/benefits and link to pooled assessment
(*Source*: BlueHealth DST website)

Pooled assessment for the following risk and benefits:

- Drowning
- Injuries in waterbodies
- Water ingestion and contact
- UV
- Socialcultural interaction
- Water activities
- Shore activities

The below information provides you with important parameters to consider when planning, assessing, or managing and maintaining public blue spaces, or preparing for interventions and infrastructural measures within the blue space settings.

The pooled guidance document combines the information for the selected health risks and benefits into one document, and thereby provides a resource for structuring information collection and site assessments during field visits to the blue space. For such on-site visits, the pooled guidance lists the blue space features that need to be considered to reduce blue space-specific health risks, and/or to increase related benefits. However, it can also be applied for desktop audits and reviews. The pooled assessment includes a checklist where the need for follow-up action can be documented.

Information and guidance that is applicable for more than one risk or benefit can be identified by the respective label, indicating that the statement can be valid for

- two or more dimensions related to certain risk (▲) or benefit (●) categories
- a variety of different risks (labeled "Risks") or a variety of different benefits (labeled "Benefits"), or
- a variety of both risks and benefits (labeled "General").

Step 1: Review locational and water factors

- [Benefits] Does the local infrastructure enable for seating and playing in shaded areas (see UV) to reduce heat stress and provide breaks from recreational activities?
- [Benefits] Are sensitive nature areas protected from human access to avoid environmental degradation (see habitat)?
- [Shore activity] Does the surrounding of the blue space provide opportunities and infrastructure for active recreation, sport or play (playground, outdoor gym, sport equipment and play fields, boule lanes, jogging paths etc.)?
- [Shore activity] Are there facilities such as change rooms or showers?
- [Social] Is there accessible open space around the water body that enables social interaction or other forms of gatherings (e.g. group seating areas, children's playground, beach volleyball and BBQ areas for adults and families, or boule lanes for elderly)?

Figure 9.18
Part of the output of a pooled assessment: example of guidance statements on various benefits and risks
(*Source*: BlueHealth DST website)

need further discussion and action, using the follow-up list provided at the end of the document. That list of "action points", with an identification of the proposed action steps for the respective blue space, is your final output of the BlueHealth DST application. For guidance on good practices for design and management, you may then consult the further resources on the main BlueHealth webpage.

Application options

The BlueHealth DST purpose is to support and guide users in optimising their blue space for health and environment outcomes. The specific characteristics of the urban setting, the individual users and the water body itself make every blue space intervention unique. Whether the user is a policy maker, a planner or a member of on-site staff, the guidance is organised to facilitate flexible and prioritised or partial application. Most importantly, the user(s) of the

BlueHealth DST will represent different professions and roles – thus, we want to outline the possible application of the BlueHealth DST for three typical contexts:

1 Guidance for evaluation and revision

In many cities, blue spaces undergo changes of use and accessibility over the years. For such locations, the BlueHealth DST enables a retrospective application for stakeholders to review the health and well-being implications associated with the respective blue space. The tool can be used to assess existing blue spaces and whether and how the (re-)design of the blue space or its management and maintenance could be improved. Such an application of the BlueHealth DST is particularly beneficial in cases where health (and environment) had not been a critical planning factor before. This is often the case, according to our survey (see earlier section on existing tools).

2 Guidance for planners and practitioners

In situations where 1) an existing blue space setting is to be modified or further developed, or 2) a new blue space intervention is planned (adding new blue space dimensions to the local environment), the BlueHealth DST can provide valuable information on the health and well-being risks and benefits of the particular blue space type or intervention. The focus of this application option is to assure that planning, design, construction and maintenance mitigate the local risks and enhance the health and environment benefits. The guidance clearly includes both structural and management factors that guide an optimised management of the blue space.

3 Guidance for decision and policy makers

The tool's decision-making criteria and its structure are aligned to help maximise an urban blue space's positive effects on health and the environment. The information provided is arranged hierarchically. It thus also allows decision- and policy makers at higher levels or their advisors to gain an overview and selected insights on the impacts of their planning decisions on blue space-specific risk profiles and related health and well-being benefits. A critical reflection on the tool's guidance can assist in understanding the situation at a local or regional level, regarding 1) the interface of the respective sectoral circumstances, planning, and health and well-being outcomes; 2) critical challenges related to blue spaces; and 3) potentials to maximise health and well-being benefits through adequate planning and design.

Beyond its main purposes, the BlueHealth DST guidance documents can be used encyclopaedically by students or the interested public.

Conclusions

The BlueHealth DST is the first guidance tool for the optimisation of health and environment outcomes in blue spaces and their surroundings, with partial consideration of green spaces. The successful pilots and extensive consortium-wide reviews illustrate the suitability of the tool. The guidance incorporated within the tool reflects the current scientific understanding, including various recent findings of the consortium's primary and secondary research. The BlueHealth DST is essentially based on a translation of scientific evidence for practical use and thus relies on periodic reviews of this evidence as base for its continued currency. The evidence base is incomplete by nature and the tool's recommendations thus limited in scope and detail. Clearly, any decision and intervention based on the tool can only be as good and targeted as the degree to which the assessment of the blue space at hand was thorough and complete. The related goals of the BlueHealth DST are to widen the stakeholders' view and to ensure that the critical factors are considered for successful blue space projects. The scientific evidence around the benefits of blue spaces keeps increasing – we hope that our tool can help planning teams also to realise those in practice.

Acknowledgements

The authors of this chapter would like to acknowledge the support and contributions to the DST development by Filippo Chiudioni, James Grellier, Vladimir Kendrovski, Gerardo Sanchez Martinez, Dennis Schmiege, Enrico Scoccimarro and Tanja Wolf.

Disclaimer

Arnt Diener, Marco Martuzzi and Matthias F.W. Braubach are staff members of WHO and are themselves alone responsible for the views expressed in the chapter, which do not necessarily represent the views, decisions or policies of WHO or Taylor & Francis Group.

Note

1 The section on DST piloting was authored by Stefania Marcheggiani and Camilla Puccinelli.

References

Abell, R., Vigerstol, K., Higgins, J., Kang, S., Karres, N., Lehner, B., Sridhar, A. and Chapin, E. (2019) 'Freshwater biodiversity conservation through source water protection: Quantifying the potential and addressing the challenges', *Aquatic Conservation: Marine and Freshwater Ecosystems*, 29(7), pp. 1022–1038. doi: 10.1002/aqc.3091.

Barnett, D.W., Barnett, A., Nathan, A. et al. (2017) 'Built environmental correlates of older adults' total physical activity and walking: A systematic review and meta-analysis', *International Journal of Behavioral Nutrition and Physical Activity*. *International Journal of Behavioral Nutrition and Physical Activity*, 14(1), p. 103. doi: 10.1186/s12966-017-0558-z.

Bartonova, A. (2012) 'How can scientists bring research to use: The HENVINET experience', *Environmental Health: A Global Access Science Source*. BioMed Central Ltd, 11(SUPPL.1), p. S2. doi: 10.1186/1476-069X-11-S1-S2.

Bell, J.E., Brown, C.L., Conlon, K., Herring, S., Kunkel, K.E., Lawrimore, J., Luber, G., Schreck, C., Smith, A. and Uejio, C. (2018) 'Changes in extreme events and the potential impacts on human health', *Journal of the Air and Waste Management Association*. Taylor & Francis, 68(4), pp. 265–287. doi: 10.1080/10962247.2017.1401017.

Brugueras, S., Fernández-Martínez, B., Martínez-de la Puente, J., Figuerola, J., Montalvo Porro, T., Rius, C., Larrauri, A. and Gómez-Barroso, D. (2020) 'Environmental drivers, climate change and emergent diseases transmitted by mosquitoes and their vectors in southern Europe: A systematic review', *Environmental Research*, 191. doi: 10.1016/j.envres.2020.110038.

Carlson, K.M., Boczek, L.A., Chae, S. and Ryu, H. (2020) 'Legionellosis and recent advances in technologies for *Legionella* control in premise plumbing systems: A review', *Water (Switzerland)*, 12(3), pp. 1–22. doi: 10.3390/w12030676.

Collins, R.M., Spake, R., Brown, K.A., Ogutu, B.O., Smith, D. and Eigenbrod, F. (2020) 'A systematic map of research exploring the effect of greenspace on mental health', *Landscape and Urban Planning*. Elsevier, 201(February), p. 103823. doi: 10.1016/j.landurbplan.2020.103823.

Cooperative Research Centre for Water Sensitive Cities (2020) *Water Sensitive Cities*. Available at: watersensitivecities.org.au/content/tools-products-tap/#1510192400359-e78d3e29–3f50.

de Bell, S., Graham, H., Jarvis, S. and White, P. (2017) 'The importance of nature in mediating social and psychological benefits associated with visits to freshwater blue space', *Landscape and Urban Planning*, 167, pp. 118–127. doi: 10.1016/j.landurbplan.2017.06.003.

Defra Local Action Project – WT1580 (LAP) (2017) *Local Action Toolkit*. Available at: urbanwater-eco.services/project/local-action-toolkit.

European Centre for Disease Prevention and Control (2020) *Vector Control Practices and Strategies against West Nile Virus*. Available at: ecdc.europa.eu/sites/default/files/documents/Vector-control-practices-and-strategies-against-West-Nile-virus.pdf.

European Commission (2019) *Green City Tool*. Available at: op.europa.eu/en/publication-detail/-/publication/f3b5b718-a44d-11e9–9d01–01aa75ed71a1/language-en/format-PDF/source-104664890.

European Environment Agency (2019) *European Bathing Water Quality in 2019*. Brussels. Available at: eea.europa.eu/publications/european-bathing-water-quality-in-2019.

Finlay, J., Franke, T., McKay, H. and Sims-Gould, J. (2015) 'Therapeutic landscapes and wellbeing in later life: Impacts of blue and green spaces for older adults', *Health and Place*. Elsevier, 34, pp. 97–106. doi: 10.1016/j.healthplace.2015.05.001.

Frantzeskaki, N., Borgström, S., Gorissen, L., Egermann, M. and Ehnert, F. (2017) 'Nature-based solutions accelerating urban sustainability transitions in cities: Lessons from Dresden, Genk and Stockholm cities', pp. 65–88. doi: 10.1007/978-3-319-56091-5_5.

Gascon, M., Zijlema, W., Vert, C., White, M.P. and Nieuwenhuijsen, M.J. (2017) 'Outdoor blue spaces, human health and well-being: A systematic review of quantitative studies', *International Journal of Hygiene and Environmental Health*. Elsevier, 220(8), pp. 1207–1221. doi: 10.1016/j.ijheh.2017.08.004.

Gilbertz, K.P., Placzek, M. and Hotz, M.E. (2019) 'Ultraviolet exposure: Health effects', in Nriagu, J. (ed.) *Encyclopedia of Environmental Health* (2nd Edition). Oxford: Elsevier, pp. 185–194. doi: 10.1016/B978-0-12-409548-9.11267-9.

Greinert, R., de Vries, E., Erdmann, F., Espina, C., Auvinen, A., Kesminiene, A. and Schüz, J. (2015) 'European code against cancer 4th edition: Ultraviolet radiation and cancer', *Cancer Epidemiology*, 39, pp. S75–S83. doi: 10.1016/j.canep.2014.12.014.

Gunawardena, K.R., Wells, M.J. and Kershaw, T. (2017) 'Utilising green and bluespace to mitigate urban heat island intensity', *Science of the Total Environment*, 584–585, pp. 1040–1055. doi: 10.1016/j.scitotenv.2017.01.158.

Hamilton, K., Keech, J.J., Peden, A.E. and Hagger, M.S. (2018) 'Alcohol use, aquatic injury, and unintentional drowning: A systematic literature review', *Drug and Alcohol Review*, 37(6), pp. 752–773. doi: 10.1111/dar.12817.

Huisman, J., Codd, G.A., Paerl, H.W., Ibeling, B.W., Verspagen, J.M.H. and Visser, P.M. (2018) 'Cyanobacterial blooms', *Nature Reviews Microbiology*. Springer, 16(8), pp. 471–483. doi: 10.1038/s41579-018-0040-1.

International Water Association (2016) *Principles for Water Wise Cities*. Available at: iwa-network.org/publications/the-iwa-principles-for-water-wise-cities.

Kuttler, W., Lamp, T. and Weber, K. (2002) 'Summer air quality over an artificial lake', *Atmospheric Environment*, 36 (39–40), pp. 5927–5936. doi: 10.1016/S1352-2310(02)00776-8.

Lacasta, A.M., Penaranda, A., Cantalapiedra, I.R., Auguet, C., Bures, S. and Urrestarazu, M. (2016) 'Acoustic evaluation of modular greenery noise barriers', *Urban Forestry & Urban Greening*, 20, pp. 172–179. doi: 10.1016/j.ufug.2016.08.010.

Liu, H.Y., Bartonova, A., Neofytou, P., Yang, A., Kobernus, M.J. and Negrenti, E. (2012) 'Facilitating knowledge transfer: Decision support tools in environment and health', *Environmental Health: A Global Access Science Source*. BioMed Central Ltd, 11(SUPPL.1), p. S17. doi: 10.1186/1476-069X-11-S1-S17.

Marcheggiani, S., Tinti, D., Puccinelli, C. and Mancini, L. (2019) 'Urban green space and healthy living: An exploratory study among Appia Antica Park users', *Fresenius Environmental Bulletin*, 28(6), pp. 4984–4989. Available at:

researchgate.net/profile/Camilla_Puccinelli/publication/333995950_Urban_Green_space_healthy_living_an_exploratory_study_among_Appia_Antica_Park_users_Rome_Italy/links/5d11efeb92851cf440497d45/Urban-Green-space-healthy-living-an-exploratory-study-among-Appia-Antica-Park-users-Rome-Italy.pdf.

McIntosh, B.S., Ascough, J.C., Twery, M., Chew, J., Elmahdi, A., Haase, D., Harou, J.J., Hepting, D., Cuddy, S., . . . Voinov, A. (2011) 'Environmental decision support systems (EDSS) development – Challenges and best practices', *Environmental Modelling and Software*. Elsevier, 26(12), pp. 1389–1402. doi: 10.1016/j.envsoft.2011.09.009.

Mishra, H.S., Bell, S., Vassiljev, P., Kuhlmann, F., Niin, G. and Grellier, J. (2020) 'The development of a tool for assessing the environmental qualities of urban blue spaces', *Urban Forestry and Urban Greening*. Elsevier, 49(December 2019), p. 126575. doi: 10.1016/j.ufug.2019.126575.

Oertli, B. and Parris, K.M. (2019) 'Review: Toward management of urban ponds for freshwater biodiversity', *Ecosphere*, 10(7). doi: 10.1002/ecs2.2810.

Patel, D., Magnusen, E. and Sandell, J.M. (2017) 'Prevention of unintentional injury in children', *Paediatrics and Child Health*, 27(9), pp. 420–426. doi: 10.1016/j.paed.2017.05.004.

Peden, A.E., Franklin, R.C. and Queiroga, A.C. (2018) 'Epidemiology, risk factors and strategies for the prevention of global unintentional fatal drowning in people aged 50 years and older: A systematic review', *Injury Prevention*, 24(3), pp. 240–247. doi: 10.1136/injuryprev-2017-042351.

Schäffer, B., Brink, M, Schlatter, F., Vienneau, D. and Wunderli, J.M. (2020) 'Residential green is associated with reduced annoyance to road traffic and railway noise but increased annoyance to aircraft noise exposure', *Environment International*. Elsevier, 143(March), p. 105885. doi: 10.1016/j.envint.2020.105885.

Selbach, C., Soldánová, M. and Sures, B. (2016) 'Estimating the risk of swimmer's itch in surface waters – A case study from Lake Baldeney, River Ruhr', *International Journal of Hygiene and Environmental Health*. Elsevier GmbH., 219(7), pp. 693–699. doi: 10.1016/j.ijheh.2015.03.012.

Soldánová, M., Selbach, C., Kalbe, M., Kostadinova, A. and Sures, B. (2013) 'Swimmer's itch: Etiology, impact, and risk factors in Europe', *Trends in Parasitology*, 29(2), pp. 65–74. doi: 10.1016/j.pt.2012.12.002.

Sutton-Grier, A.E. and Sandifer, P.A. (2019) 'Conservation of wetlands and other coastal ecosystems: A commentary on their value to protect biodiversity, reduce disaster impacts, and promote human health and well-being', *Landscape Approaches to Wetland Management*, 39(6), pp. 1295–1302. doi: 10.1007/s13157-018-1039-0.

Tipton, M.J., Collier, N., Massey, H., Corbett, J. and Harper, M. (2017) 'Cold water immersion: Kill or cure?' *Experimental Physiology*, 102(11), pp. 1335–1355. doi: 10.1113/EP086283.

United Nations (UN) (2018) *World Urbanization Prospects: The 2018 Revision, Demographic Research*, New York. Available at: population.un.org/wup/Publications/Files/WUP2018-Report.pdf.

Vieira, J., Matos, P., Mexia, T., Silva, P., Lopes, N., Freitas, C., Correia, O., Santos-Reis, M., Branquinho, C. and Pinho, P. (2018) 'Green spaces are not all the same for the provision of air purification and climate regulation services: The case of urban parks', *Environmental Research*. Elsevier, 160, pp. 306–313. doi: 10.1016/j.envres.2017.10.006.

Voskamp, I.M. and Van de Ven, F.H.M. (2015) 'Planning support system for climate adaptation: Composing effective sets of blue-green measures to reduce urban vulnerability to extreme weather events', *Building and Environment*, 83, pp. 159–167. doi: 10.1016/j.buildenv.2014.07.018.

White, M.P., Pahl, S., Wheeler, B.W., Depledge, M.H. and Fleming, L.E. (2017) 'Natural environments and subjective wellbeing: Different types of exposure are associated with different aspects of wellbeing', *Health and Place*, 45(January), pp. 77–84. doi: 10.1016/j.healthplace.2017.03.008.

White, M.P., Alcock, I., Grellier, J., Wheeler, B.W., Hartig, T., Warber, S.L., Bone, A., Depledge, M.H. and Fleming, L.E. (2019) 'Spending at least 120 minutes a week in nature is associated with good health and wellbeing', *Scientific Reports*, 9(1), p. 7730. doi: 10.1038/s41598-019-44097-3.

White, M.P., Elliott, L.R., Gascon, M., Roberts, B. and Fleming, L.E. (2020) 'Blue space, health and well-being: A narrative overview and synthesis of potential benefits', *Environmental Research*. Elsevier Inc., 191(August), p. 110169. doi: 10.1016/j.envres.2020.110169.

WHO (2013) *Guidelines for Safe Recreational Water Environments*, Geneva. Available at: whqlibdoc.who.int/publications/2003/9241545801.pdf.

WHO (2014) *Global Report on Drowning: Preventing a Leading Killer*, Geneva. Available at: who.int/violence_injury_prevention/global_report_drowning/en.

WHO (2017) *Guidelines for Drinking-Water Quality: Fourth Edition Incorporating the First Addendum*, Geneva. Available at: who.int/publications/i/item/9789241549950.

WHO (2019) *Health Emergency and Disaster Risk Management Framework*, Geneva. Available at: apps.who.int/iris/bitstream/handle/10665/326106/9789241516181-eng.pdf?ua=1.

WHO Regional Office for Europe (2013) *Floods in the WHO European Region: Health Effects and Their Prevention*. Available at: euro.who.int/__data/assets/pdf_file/0020/189020/e96853.pdf.

WHO Regional Office for Europe (2016) *The Situation of Water-Related Infectious Diseases in the Pan-European Region*, Protocol on Water and Health, p. 42. Available at: euro.who.int/__data/assets/pdf_file/0019/322165/Situation-water-related-infectious-diseases.pdf.

WHO Regional Office for Europe (2018) *Environmental Noise Guidelines for the European Region*, Copenhagen. Available at: euro.who.int/__data/assets/pdf_file/0008/383921/noise-guidelines-eng.pdf.

WHO & Secretariat for the Convention on Biological Diversity (2015) 'Connecting global priorities: Biodiversity and human health, a state of knowledge review'. doi: 10.13140/RG.2.1.3679.6565.

Wood, E., Harsant, A., Dallimer, M., Cronin de Chavez, A., McEachan, R.R.C. and Hassall, C. (2018) 'Not all green space is created equal: Biodiversity predicts psychological restorative benefits from urban green space', *Frontiers in Psychology*, 9(November), pp. 1–13. doi: 10.3389/fpsyg.2018.02320.

Part III

Inspirational practice for planning and design

Chapter 10: Reviewing the evidence for good planning and design

Himansu S. Mishra, Simon Bell, Jekaterina Balicka and Anna Wilczyńska

Introduction

Part Three of this book focuses on the character and quality of places and spaces which facilitate and encourage the public to go to and make use of water-related landscapes (blue spaces). As noted in the introduction, we define blue spaces as outdoor environments – either natural or manmade – that prominently feature water and are accessible to people either proximally (being in, on or near water) or distally/virtually (being able to see, hear or otherwise sense water). It is a basic requirement that in order to obtain all of the proximal and some of the distal benefits, people need to be able to get close to or in the water, so the places which allow this most effectively are likely to provide valuable lessons for anyone wishing to plan and design a new blue space. The objective of this chapter is to set the context for the next set of chapters, each of which deals in detail with a selection of specific blue space types. One of the outputs of this review process is a database of projects for use as inspirational examples by planners and designers and, perhaps especially, by students learning how to apply evidence-based design. The database presents nearly 180 projects as a set of "Blue Profiles" which can be found in the https://bluehealth.tools/ website.

The projects selected as examples to illustrate a range of common design aspects were drawn from a wide-ranging search, the process and summaries of results of which are briefly described below (more detailed information is available from the website noted previously). The method and criteria by which the examples which feature in Chapters 11–15 were chosen from the larger sample is also described here so that readers may understand why some were included and some excluded.

The first task for setting inclusion criteria for the wide survey was to identify the key elements of a successful blue space regeneration project. We used the following six categories, with between five and seven aspects within each category (derived from an overview of the tools we reviewed for developing the BlueHealth Environmental Assessment Tool described in Chapter 5). These are reflected in the detailed information and assessment ratings provided for each project in the BlueProfiles database and summarised in text for those featured in Chapters 11–15.

- Accessibility (site visibility, pedestrian bicycle or car access, car parking and inclusive access);
- Design quality (design quality, on-site circulation, views and landmarks, inclusion of cultural heritage values, site furniture fitting the context and cost effective maintenance);
- Facilities (range of facilities, accessibility of facilities, amount of seating, quality of nature, degree of shelter or shade and lighting);
- Health and well-being (genius loci, sense of being away, contact with nature, sensory stimulation, contemplation, safety and security);

DOI: 10.4324/9780429056161-14

- Water connections (land-water connectivity, water visibility, access from and to water, water safety equipment); and
- Physical activities (formal sport activities, informal sports, water sports, children's play and activity zoning).

The review examined a large number and wide range of relatively recent projects which had or have the aim of redeveloping or rejuvenating blue spaces for improved public use. These are projects which have been implemented and, in general, become established and well-used spaces within their local or regional urban setting. We identified a range of types of projects and assessed them critically according to the criteria under the headings listed previously. From this, it was possible to identify the key factors which make such projects successful blue spaces.

The concept of the project review

A systematically undertaken review of evidence from architectural/landscape architectural projects is an unusual but not unheard-of activity (from a scientific perspective). Post-occupancy evaluations are becoming common in architecture and also in landscape architecture, but these are usually of single sites or buildings, not a large selection of projects. While in those scientific disciplines which publish results in peer-reviewed academic papers (e.g. the natural or social sciences), it is relatively easy to carry out a review since the evidence has been quality controlled (through peer-review) during the publication process, what is an equivalent system for reviewing landscape architecture projects? In the art and design disciplines, it is the role of criticism to perform the equivalent of peer review, and in architecture and landscape architecture, this is also the case. In addition, there are design competitions where juries of experts evaluate entries in a completely anonymous way, and, finally, there are annual award schemes where the best projects are also assessed by juries of peers. This is the approach we used in our search for selecting the projects for inclusion and assessment. The detailed method is described in the next sections.

There have been several recent publications – books mainly – which have examined and reviewed certain specific types of blue spaces from different perspectives (e.g. Prominski et al., 2012; Rottle and Yocom, 2011; Macdonald, 2013; Smith and Ferrari, 2012) but none through a health and well-being lens, although they also contain some excellent examples which were, in some cases, included in the review. This is the first attempt at a wider and more comprehensive review of an extensive range of project types.

Project search method

The search included an initial trawl through the internet for projects from anywhere in the world constructed in the last ten or so years. Many projects are presented by the designer's websites and could be found there (in the range of languages noted previously). Professional (and some scientific) landscape architecture journals were searched online or in libraries for projects which featured waterside redevelopments. These included those of the professional organisations in the United States, United Kingdom, Canada, Australia, China and Denmark, as well as several specialised journals published for the profession and which feature critical reviews of projects from around the world. In addition, we consulted some recently published books (in English and German) where some projects were also critically reviewed. Table 10.1 shows the main journals, books and websites and their publishers, country of origin and focus of coverage used for identifying the projects.

An initial search of the internet using terms such as "waterfront regeneration projects", "urban wetland parks" and "river restoration projects" led to the identification of almost 400 potential projects, but further examination in the light of the criteria listed previously allowed us to reduce that number to 180. This number became the database of evidence for the review and all the projects are now available as BlueProfiles in the database at https://bluehealth.tools/.

Table 10.1 **Selected professional magazines and websites used for sourcing projects to be reviewed**

Magazine	*Country*	*Publishers*
Landscape Architecture Magazine, ASLA	United States	American Society of Landscape Architects; www.zinio.com. https://landscapearchitecturemagazine.org/
Landscape Architecture Frontier	China	Higher Education Press and Peking University http://journal.hep.com.cn/laf/EN/column/column13253.shtml
The International Review of Landscape Architecture and Urbanism (TOPOS)	Germany	Georg D.W. Callwey GmbH &Co. KG Streitfeldstrase, Munich www.toposmagazine.com/
Landskab	Denmark	ARKITEKTENS FORLAG http://arkfo.dk/en/shop/product/landskab-denmark
Landscape – The Journal of the Landscape Institute	United Kingdom	Landscape Institute www.landscapethejournal.org/
Landscape Architecture Australia	Australia	Australian Institute of Architects, Australian Garden History Society, Planning Institute Australia https://architecturemedia.com/magazines/landscape-architecture-australia/; http://landscapeaustralia.com/; http://landscapeaustralia.com/reviews/
Landscapes/Paysages – Landscape Architecture in Canada	Canada	Naylor www.csla-aapc.ca/landscapes-paysages-0
Urban Design	United Kingdom	Urban Design Group, United Kingdom www.udg.org.uk/publications/journal
World Landscape Architecture Magazine	China	http://worldlandscapearchitect.com/
Selected websites		
Landezine	Slovenia	www.landezine.com
ArchDaily	Worldwide	www.archdaily.com/
Project for Public Spaces	United States	www.pps.org/
PLANETIZEN	United States	www.planetizen.com/toppublicspaces
Coastal and Waterfront Smart Growth	United States	http://coastalsmartgrowth.noaa.gov/casestudies.html
Waterfront Centre	United States	www.waterfrontcenter.org/
Landscape Performance Series	United States	https://landscapeperformance.org/
ASLA Honours and Awards	United States	www.asla.org/HonorsAwards.aspx
GreenFlag Awards	United Kingdom	www.greenflagaward.org.uk/

Method of critical review

Once a database of projects had been compiled, a detailed questionnaire was developed for the critical assessment of each project based on the six factors and five to seven aspects of each factor listed previously. We then developed a scoring system using a 1–5 scale, where 1 was where the attribute was the least present/lowest quality and 5 the most present/highest quality. A score of 0 meant that the attribute could not be assessed (due to inadequate information) or was not applicable to the project under review. The results for each project under each of the categories were then summarised as a set of spidergrams for each factor, which are presented in detail for each site in the BlueProfiles website.

Conclusions from the initial analysis of the main characteristics

From the analysis of the examples, we could see a clear pattern emerging:

- Waterfront re-development or revitalisation projects are currently a very important part of urban regeneration and include a wide range of types which all have a positive impact on urban life at a range of scales.
- Planners and policy makers have clearly recognised that, whether the motivations are economic regeneration, flood management, water quality improvement, cultural enhancement, provision of recreation and access or restoration of nature (and usually most of these go together in some way), blue space is a critical feature of many urban areas. The de-industrialisation of many cities, the movement of ports to larger sites for container ships, the need to clean up pollution and the recognition that flooding risks and urban microclimate issues are increasingly important are all factors driving these changes.
- The importance given to public access, the creation of waterfront parks, offering visual and physical access to water and enhancing the quality of the landscape by investing in good design has led to the vast majority of projects being given a major role in enhancing quality of life, neighbourhood liveability and the attractiveness of inner urban areas as places to live.
- The brand identity of many cities has been significantly strengthened by the design of iconic waterfront redevelopments including public spaces, and this attracts inward investment and builds tourism. It also means that people want to come to live and work in such environments, and this choice is in part due to the presence of water and the opportunities for engaging with it.
- The climatic zone has no specific impact on whether water is attractive to people – it just affects how much people can use it directly for swimming and recreation and what the degree of seasonality offers for different activities. Even frozen water bodies are attractive for skiing and ice fishing in winter.
- Small-scale interventions can have as big an impact on people as large projects, and if they are all that is possible, then they should take place. Water features which promote playful behaviour in children and adults seem especially attractive, especially for hot weather.

Conclusions of the overview assessment

We also concluded that waterfront developments and water-accessibility projects form a major part of landscape architecture and urban design practice at the moment, and this has been a rising trend since the initial projects were started following de-industrialisation and new port technologies in the 1980s onwards (see Chapter 14), as well as the need to introduce better means of dealing with storm water and other factors (see Chapter 13). Planners and designers are clearly aware of the need to make such places attractive, iconic, accessible, safe and easy to maintain and to offer as close a contact to water as is possible given practical and other constraints. All the sites we reviewed aimed to increase the potential for physical, mental and social health and well-being improvement by offering opportunities for physical activity, for socialising, relaxing, getting closer to nature, soaking up the sun and de-stressing. It is also clear from the evidence that the vast majority of the sites are extremely well used wherever they are located, and that in dense cities with little green space, blue space offers an additional or substitute environment.

Selection of projects for inclusion in Part Three

The following chapters in Part Three focus on a specially selected number of specific types of blue spaces as follows:

- Urban river revitalisation (Chapter 11)
- Seafronts, beaches, lakesides and promenades (Chapter 12)
- Urban wetlands and storm water management (Chapter 13)
- Docklands and ports (Chapter 14)
- Small-scale projects (Chapter 15)

The selection of a limited number of projects to encapsulate the best approaches for planning and design in each category was carried out by applying a number of criteria. As only some 10–12 or so could be included per chapter, it was necessary to try to include a range of size, location, character and different design approaches. We also wanted to present projects with really inspirational and uniquely site-specific characteristics as opposed to very worthy but rather generic solutions.

Project selection using analytical drawing

As well as the ratings used for each project as described and summarised previously, all case study projects from the BlueProfile database were analysed qualitatively using a method of analytical sketching. The essential characteristics of each project were drawn out by hand in order to express the main distinct elements or structures, such as if the project site is divided into different zones, if there are specific landmarks incorporated into it or what the main design elements are, as well as to capture the genius loci. We also focused on the different type of access to water within each project in order to select those with the most distinctive or innovative approaches. While we could of course look at the explanations and descriptions provided by the designers or from the professional review literature or websites, looking at sites with a fresh eye so as to see what stands out before looking at such information is a great way of testing if the design intentions have been achieved. It is another means of critique.

Compared with photographs, which just record everything without discrimination, the analytical sketching/drawing method enables us to be selective when looking at a specific place. Sketching also uses a visual language to support the numerical rating assessment and the verbal description and helps to provide a more rounded, richer appreciation of each project as well as uncovering or revealing aspects which are not captured by the numerical ratings. Figure10.1 shows part of the complete set of drawing laid out on a table for the team to look at and for grouping into categories.

After the sketching phase, we looked at the designers' descriptions of the projects as well as factual information such as:

- Location/context: such as urban core, inner urban area, suburban area/urban fringe, urban periphery, rural hinterland/nature
- Size: such as single object, small site, medium site, large site
- Form: such as multiple interventions, linear, concentrated site
- Design function: such as natural site, urban forest/ruderal plants, ornamental park/plaza, temporary/low cost design
- Also, the subtype of the water body was defined

The main categories were chosen based on the question as to why the particular design strategy was chosen; sub-categories were identified based on the question as to how the design strategy was implemented concerning the relation to water in both questions. Figure 10.1a shows the layout of the sketched projects used for the selection,

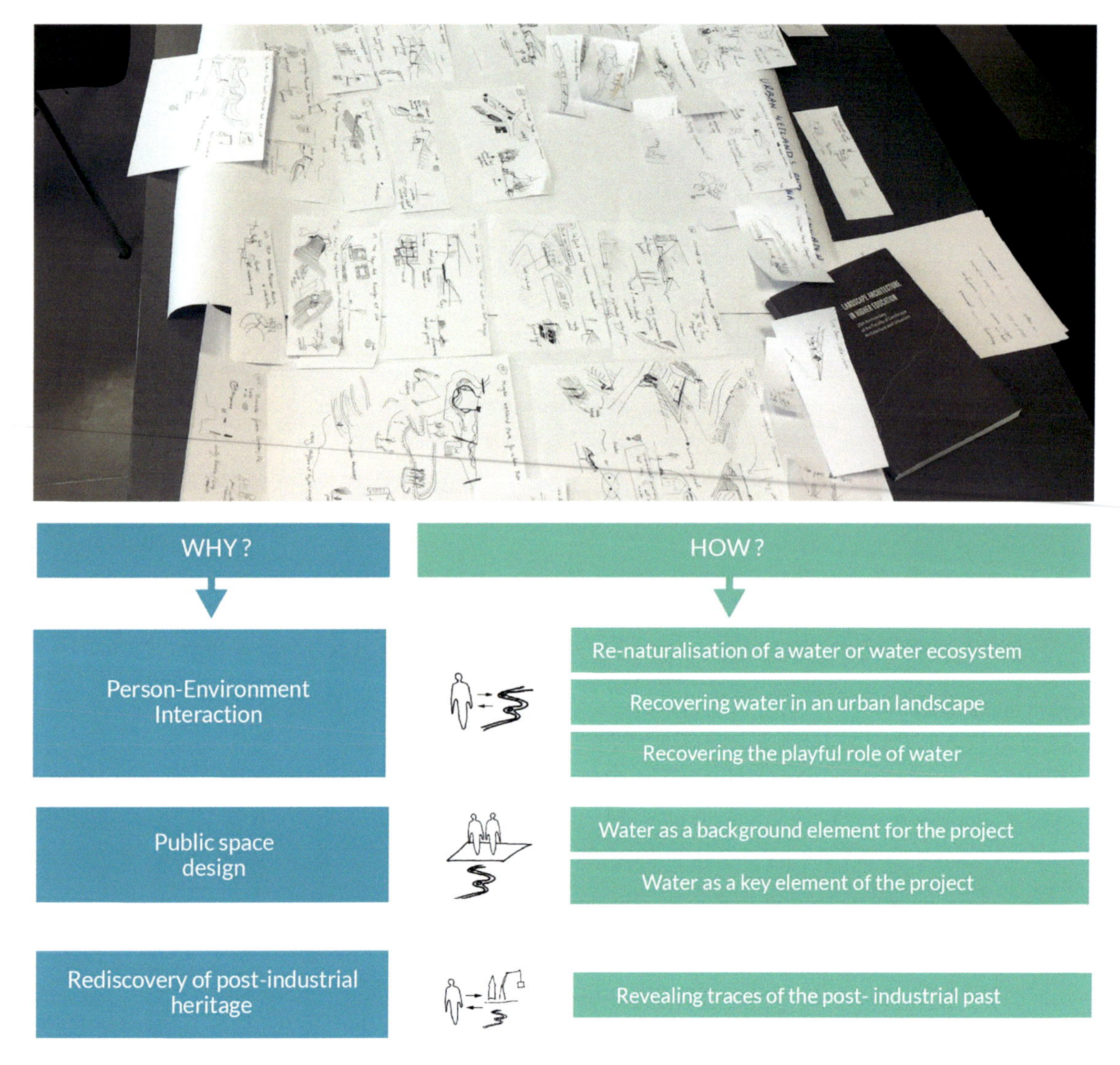

Figure 10.1a and b

a) Many of the sketches of the projects laid out on a table for assessment and classification; b) the typology used in the evaluation and selection process

(*Source*: a) Jekaterina Balicka; b) Jekaterina Balicka and Anna Wilczynska)

and Figure 10.1b shows the typology used to make the final selection. The projects presented in Chapters 11–15 thus represent one or a combination of these types.

Each project was also reviewed, and a summary of the findings in relation to a range of categories (also used and presented as spidergrams with scoring in the BlueProfiles website but not the chapters) is shown in Table 10.2.

Thus, combining the systematic review with analytical sketching and extracting key aspects, we could reflect on both the structural and functional aspect as well as how each project works with the identity of the place in a unique and specific way. The entire team reviewed and discussed the final selection. Please note that while all the projects are considered outstanding examples, for a number of reasons, often practical or functional, not every project can fulfil every criterion to its maximum potential. Thus, some factors may be rated lower for some projects.

Table 10.2 **The factors used for site assessment and the interpretation of the criteria used in the BlueProfiles and in Chapters 11–15**

Theme	*Factor*	*Interpretation of the criteria*
Accessibility	Site visibility	How easy is it to see the site from outside – is it hidden, or can it be seen and does it provide visual access to the water?
	Pedestrian access	How easy is it to gain access to the site on foot (perhaps from public transport)?
	Bicycle access	How easy is it to gain access to the site by bicycle (including connections to a wider network of bicycle paths)?
	Car access	Is car access necessary, such as due to a remoter location, and if so, it is well provided?
	Car parking	If car parking is necessary, is it logically located, and does it provide enough spaces?
	Inclusive access	Is it possible for people with various disabilities to reach the site (e.g. surfaces, street crossings, absence of steps, etc.)?
Design quality	Design quality	An overall judgement on the entire project (sense of unity, organisation of spaces, fit to the context, uniqueness and originality)
	On-site circulation	How well the pedestrian and bicycle circulation works within the site (more important for larger sites than smaller ones, e.g. those in Chapter 15)
	Views and landmarks	The degree to which unique or special views or iconic landmarks have been incorporated into the overall site design
	Inclusion of cultural heritage values	The extent to which, where there are cultural heritage remains or values present on the site, these have been incorporated into the design
	Site furniture fitting the context	The design and appropriateness of materials used in the site furniture
	Cost-effective maintenance	The degree to which the cost effectiveness of maintenance of the site has been incorporated into the design (e.g. the use of materials, technology associated with water features or art installations)
Facilities	Range of facilities	The general breadth of the range of facilities provided which are appropriate for the setting and its size
	Accessibility of facilities	How accessible are all the facilities provided for people with a range of disabilities?
	Amount of seating	How much seating is available – not only formal seats or benches but also other elements which provide sitting affordances?
	Quality of nature	Depending on the character of the site, how well have natural elements been sensitively included in the design?
	Degree of shelter	Where the site is exposed and, in a windy location, how well sheltered it is
	Degree of shade	Where the site is exposed to strong sun (depending on climate and season), how well shaded it is
	Presence of lighting	Depending on the location and use of the site as well as seasonal aspects, the quality and functionality of lighting provided on the site and its impact on the surroundings

(*Continued*)

Theme	Factor	Interpretation of the criteria
Health and well-being	Genius loci	The special qualities of the site, landscape and design, which give a unique and rich aesthetic experience
	Sense of being away	The degree to which, depending on site location and limitations, it is possible to feel away from the normal environment
	Contact with nature	The degree to which it is possible to have direct contact with some aspects of nature on land and on or in water
	Sensory stimulation	The richness of different possibilities for all the senses to be stimulated in a harmonious way
	Contemplation	The potential offered by the site for people to be alone and to be able to sit and think
	Safety and security	The physical safety of the site – especially with regard to water edges – and feeling of security against crime that the design presents (good maintenance, lack of damage, etc.)
Water connections	Land-water connectivity	The degree to which there is direct contact and connection between the terrestrial and aquatic part of the site
	Water visibility	The extent to which water is visible or hidden from all or part of the site
	Access from and to water	Depending on the context and practical possibilities, the degree to which opportunities for providing access to the site from the water have been used
	Water safety equipment	Where appropriate and necessary, how well provided the site is with water safety facilities and equipment (e.g. lifeguards, life-rings, etc.)
Physical activities	Formal sport activities	Depending on the size and context of the site, the degree of provision of fields and pitches for formal sports on land
	Informal sports	The degree to which the site design supports a range of informal games and sports, depending on the size and types of surfaces used
	Water sports	Depending on the nature of the land-water interface and the risk and safety aspects specific to the site, the degree to which water activities and sports are supported
	Children's play	The degree to which children's play – on land or in the water, using formal equipment of just the site affordances – is supported
	Activity zoning	The extent to which, depending on the size of the site and its range of physical activities supported, these are zoned for maximum effectiveness

We leave readers to reflect themselves on the final choices we made and the assessments we made in the next five chapters, together with the more specific lessons we draw from the different thematic foci.

References

Macdonald, M. (2013) *Urban Waterfront Promenades*, Routledge, Abingdon

Prominski, M., Stimberg, D., Stokman, A. and Zeller, S. (2012) *River Space Design*, Birkhaeuser, Basel

Rottle, N. and Yocom, K. (2011) *Basics Landscape Architecture 02: Ecological Design*, AVA Publishing, Lausanne

Smith, H. and Ferrari, M. S. G. (eds.) (2012) *Waterfront Regeneration – Experiences in City-Building*, Routledge, Abingdon

Chapter 11: Urban river revitalisation

Friedrich Kuhlmann, Jekaterina Balicka and Anna Wilczyńska

Introduction

This chapter gives an overview of urban and peri-urban rivers and explains how these water bodies have been regulated, buried and subsequently rediscovered. Using examples from 12 case study projects, we cover aspects related to different types of rivers, as found in the BlueHealth review, and we also draw on our own first-hand experience as landscape architects. We also describe the main risks and benefits for health and well-being associated with rivers and summarise the principles adopted in implementing river restoration.

Why rivers matter

Rivers are connected to flow. The old High German term *fluz* means *to flow* and rivers are linear, naturally flowing water bodies on land surfaces that mostly drain to the sea or occasionally into lakes. They are the main component in a system of different drainage lines within the landscape that gradually collect water from a wide area, with smaller streams converging into larger ones and eventually into rivers.

Rivers are spatially confined by their banks, consisting of different forms of varying slopes and material. Over time, however, the path and character of their flow may change, as they continually eroding higher-lying landscapes and raising the lower-lying river spaces through sedimentation (Prominski et al., 2012). The characteristics of each river depend on several factors within a catchment area, and each river forms the surrounding landscape in diverse ways, while the surrounding environment exerts influence on the shape of the river through the interplay of topography, geology, climatic conditions and the erosive and accumulative activity of the current (Prominski et al., 2012). In the context of this chapter, it is noteworthy that most rivers make a substantial impact on the natural balance of the region through which they run, its cultural history, its transport development and its necessary fresh water supply.

Urban river landscapes

Urban rivers tend to differ from natural, dynamic ones as a result of human activities where they flow through cities, such as regulation, canalisation, burial and rediscovery. These actions are part of a historical urban development process which gradually converted natural water bodies into complex linear infrastructures at multiple scales. Regional awareness towards urban rivers can be enhanced by developing and intertwining three main aspects of sustainability: provision of space for water, for flora and fauna and for people.

Riverside settlements initially developed alongside constantly changing rivers as ideal locations to meet their needs for construction, agriculture, food, hygiene, energy and transport. They were later turned into regulated waterways or even canals with artificial water management (Figure 11.1) in order to try to exert some control over their unpredictable nature – flooding, silting and other factors which interfered with human survival or economic activities. This linear space of flow can be exemplified by the historical presence of the tow-path, where beasts of burden pulled

DOI: 10.4324/9780429056161-15

Figure 11.1
A canalised river in the 1920s. "The Emschergenossenschaft regulated the tributaries of the Emscher with concrete base shells"
(*Source*: Image courtesy of: Archive, Emschergenossenschaft)

boats with heavy loads to their destination, the routes of this hard labour being precursors for today's promenades for strolling along the river banks. Over the last two centuries, recreational aspects such as swimming, boating or walking by the river came to play a significant role connected to aesthetic aspects of rivers, while ecological aspects form the agenda for the more recent development discourses upon which many of the following projects are based.

The contemporary perception of urban river landscapes is thus generated from a contradiction between an image-driven notion of natural flow and its related bucolic setting and an action-driven notion of traffic, trade and necessary maintenance. Urban river landscapes are therefore developed under the condition of conflicts between these different notions, in the sense of a technical, constantly working linear landscape element which buries common differences between nature and culture: a landscape in the making. However, the gap between contemporary life on the river and the idealised images of the past may create a challenge for handling these landscapes today.

A river story

Rivers tell us about both a region and its heritage. One of the main European rivers, the Rhine, has been travelled and described as a trade route since Roman times. The Renaissance brought Francesco Petrarch to the Rhine; Dutch artists followed, and during the 18th century, the river was a regular stop for researchers like Alexander von Humboldt. Of course, the representations of these visitors showed the natural, aesthetic and historical connections, but subsequent descriptions revealed a new landscape experience. Friedrich Schlegel and Victor Hugo (Hugo, 1842) both discovered the untouched, dramatic beauty of the Rhine landscape and created a new field in the European romanticism movement to join natural wilderness and romance (Aversano-Schreiber, 2007), epitomised in Romantic pictures such as that of Tombleson (Figure 11.2).

Later, the symphonic poem *The Moldau* (*Vltava* in Czech) was composed in 1874 as part of the 'My Fatherland/*Má Vlast* cycle' by Bedrich Smetana, with river motifs having an important influence on forming a Czech identity and national heritage in a land-locked region. Smetana used tonal painting to create the sounds and moods that are aroused on a journey on and along the river, describing the course of the river as it grows from two sources merging into a single stream. It then follows its course through woods and meadows through landscapes where a wedding is held, with ruined castles standing on rocky outcrops. Finally, the river widens, flowing towards and through the old capital city Prague before joining another river.

"Life on the Mississippi" is a short story by the American writer Mark Twain about his time as a helmsman on the Mississippi steamboats around the time of the American Civil War. The story tells us about the river, starting with the

Figure 11.2
"Views of the Rhine: Village of Bacharach and ruin of the Werner Chapel" by William Tombleson (1840)
(*Source*: Public domain image courtesy of https://commons.wikimedia.org/wiki/File:Tombleson_Bacharach_Werner.jpg)

first European to see it in 1542, followed by French explorers in the 17th century, to the first settlements, timber rafting and early steam navigation (as pictured in Figure 11.3). Connecting the southern and northern states, which were later in a bloody combat against each other, the river posed a constant flood risk. Twain not only describes the steering of various boats across the constantly changing river course with its risky currents, sandbanks and shallows, he also explains the rivalry of steamships with the railroad. Furthermore, he chronicles the big new cities growing along its banks and the events and tragedies along the river course (Twain, 1883). The river serves as an incubator of progress, technology, poverty and racial conflicts while expanding its cultural influence. It pushes the frontier narrative of the emerging busy waterway and creates a collective memory by exchanging what has been with what is yet to come.

Urban river narratives

As stated, urban rivers are associated with a dense and bustling urban infrastructure, having established the most superimposing context on a region. Accordingly, each urban river landscape not only possesses a certain *genius loci* but also spatial hints to human activities and natural processes happening on land inwards or upstream. In contrast to a natural river environment, we define an urban river landscape not only as a physical artefact but also as a product of our mind and imagination. It contains our collective desires and memories, narrated through different art forms. Being loaded with these desires, the river landscape turns into something whose purpose may have passed. This

Figure 11.3
"The Levee, Vicksburg, Miss.", Detroit Publishing Co. no. 034340 (1900–1906)
(*Source*: Public domain image courtesy of: Library of Congress, Prints and Photographs Washington D.C.)

linear space, however, is not something only to be protected or modified; it has to be constantly thought over and created in order to accommodate new uses and to solve new problems.

Sustainability is achieved when the interaction between people and their environment is visible and therefore negotiable. If people depend on their region or are proud of it, they will tend to contribute to its development. Contemporary dense river landscapes are a product of different actions, common users and stakeholders, by which we ask: How does the landscape design reflect the common and vernacular culture along the urban river? How does the landscape design react to the development of changing trends connected to health and recreation? How does the landscape design maintain natural versus manmade processes, and how does the landscape design handle this complexity and change?

Revitalisation trends

The interest towards urban river reconstruction and associated upgrading practices and their application as a task of landscape architecture has grown internationally. It is connected to the complex background of this seemingly common linear space as well as to urban flood protection, which was until recently focused on discharging the flood wave downstream as fast as possible. This task needs cooperation between hydrologists, landscape architects and urban planners and a systematic understanding of river dynamics with a common language (see Prominski et al., 2012), because owners, space users, governments, planners or traffic authorities often have contradictory goals, interests and ideas about a valuable urban river space. Therefore, there is a growing need for experimental design to encourage and trigger a discussion among all the stakeholders involved, such as the Dutch 'Room for the River Programme'. Part of this was a collaborative project to address flood protection along the Waal River in the Nijmegen area and to create flexible environmental conditions to protect the adjacent region by creating a new channel to hold flood water, the relocation of dikes and removing obstacles to the flow (Ruimte-voor-de-rivieren, 2021).

The following case study projects are connected by a river landscape narrative and are organised to show the impact of these projects on river landscape development. Bringing the projects and their aims into a debate on urban river landscapes in terms of spatial awareness will stimulate social and communal empathy towards river spaces as well as negotiating the quality of recreation and health issues: *There are river spaces all around us, and we can perceive and access them; this is our local river and we share it with other people; we may engage in developing and maintaining it!*

Why the cases were chosen

The selection of cases was chosen to show the range of examples that cover the interface between rivers, canals or streams with the different types of urban, suburban and rural contexts. We looked for originality in concept and design, variety of location and type and something which makes them special. They represent a selection of creative and provocative approaches to river design to provide and strengthen the physical, visual, mental and educational connection of potential users to the river. We also looked for examples which might offer continuity in the tradition of former uses. The types of interventions range in scale from a modest village boardwalk to the rediscovery of a forgotten river once buried under a six-lane highway, offering unique solutions to specific problems. The river projects are linear spatial interventions, typically in an urban or peri-urban environment, which provoke further design action or urban development to the existing context as well as enhancing public access and recreational use.

These projects are significant not just from the point of view of an innovative urban design approach but also to transfer their main principles to other river contexts. There is no typical riverbank: they may be hemmed in by a noisy road or railway where access is the main issue to solve; they may be situated at the edge of the city centre or near a protected landscape which might need careful attention. The protection of significant natural habitats may be required as well as providing facilities to host a large number of users and to take pressure from the sites with limited capacity in case of events.

A relationship between users and the water can be established by recovering a water presence in an urban landscape (Velenje City centre, Chicago Riverwalk), recovering the playful role of the water (Soestbach, Perreux-sur-Marne) or revitalising a water ecosystem (Norges Boardwalk, Recovering Cheonggyecheon). The flowing water can be the key element to a project (Rhone riverbank, Alborg's New Waterfront), can be only a background element for the project (The Red Ribbon, Tagus Linear Park) or can also highlight traces of past uses (Rochetaillée Banks of the Saone, Revitalisation of the River Aire).

Rivers and local identity

We start with streams, the uppermost parts of the river system, which are closely related to the identity of a community and its related region. The projects have all created locally significant places by uncovering and exhibiting traces of past uses. The projects included in this section are:

- Wet Meadow and source of the River Norges, Norges-La-Ville, France
- Aire River Garden, Geneva, Switzerland
- Velenje City Centre Promenada, Velenje, Slovenia
- Discovering Soestbach, Soest, Germany

Rivers and urban life

The next set of projects provides accessible, bustling places for people, by creatively joining the riverbank and its proximity to the existing infrastructure and urban density, forming a new model for the urban public to experience the water. The projects included in this section are:

- Rhone riverbank, Lyon, France
- Chicago Riverwalk, Chicago, United States
- Cheonggyecheon River revitalisation, Seoul, South Korea
- Aalborg's new waterfront, Aalborg, Denmark

Being away at the river

This last category of projects includes cases where proximity to the river and its immediate access create a feeling of being away from everyday life. The built solutions may create challenges for every potential user at certain times but offer possibilities for views of natural and near-natural atmospheres at the waterside. The projects included in this section are:

- Banks of the Sâone, Rochetaillée, France
- River Banks in Perreux-sur-Marne, France
- Red Ribbon Tanghe River Park, Qinhuangdao City, China
- Tagus Linear Park, Vila Franca de Xira, Portugal

Each project is briefly described (based on information from a range of sources, often the designer or articles as well as what the authors have seen). It is then illustrated with a photograph of a typical view, assessed for project quality based on the factors presented in Chapter 10 and then illustrated using a set of sketches designed to bring out the key aspects which make the project special and inspirational. These are presented as annotated images, and they aim to complement the text visually, so there is no additional description in the text, only the captions.

Rivers and local identity: Wet Meadow and Source of the River Norges, Norges-la-Ville, France

This project at Norges-la-Ville in France is a wooden boardwalk system accompanying a small stream on the edge of a village-like peri-urban settlement in the vicinity of Dijon. It was planned and realised by Agence Territoires landscape architects in 2013 as a linear development along quite different water landscape contexts while displaying one

Figure 11.4
A view along the stream and the boardwalk at Norges-la-Ville
(*Source*: Agence Territoires. Photographer: Nicolas Waltefaugle)

unifying character. The path is built modestly for everyday outdoor recreation. While it can be easily accessed, it is at the same time almost immersed into the connected meadow landscape.

Norges-la-Ville has recently developed from different villages along the Norges stream. As more commuters from Dijon have moved to the countryside, the settlements have changed in appearance and identity. This new "rurban" condition asks for a different design approach, which includes the dynamics of water and seasonality. The meadow landscape changes depending on the season and the level of the water, which when high, inhibits the ability to enjoy the beauty of this landscape. The boardwalk crosses a symbolic border into the meadow, moving from the domesticated to the natural. The design respects the natural stream environment and keeps the path above the water level during seasonal overflows, which transforms the whole meadow into a temporary swamp.

This special context demanded a humble material choice, and the landscape architects chose a wooden boardwalk, which flirts with the stream by touching and crossing it and maintaining the contrast between the winding river and the straight lines of the boardwalk, which raises the visitor above the ground to discover the local landscape with minimal human impact (Figure 11.4). An old flax retting pond was converted into a natural pond, and the drainage ditch upstream was developed to diversify the habitats. Shrubs were planted to create soft embankments with water margin plants. The intervention has enlarged the space around the source of the river with a large wooden terrace, and the site maintenance is carried out through mowing or grazing as recommended following an ecological inventory.

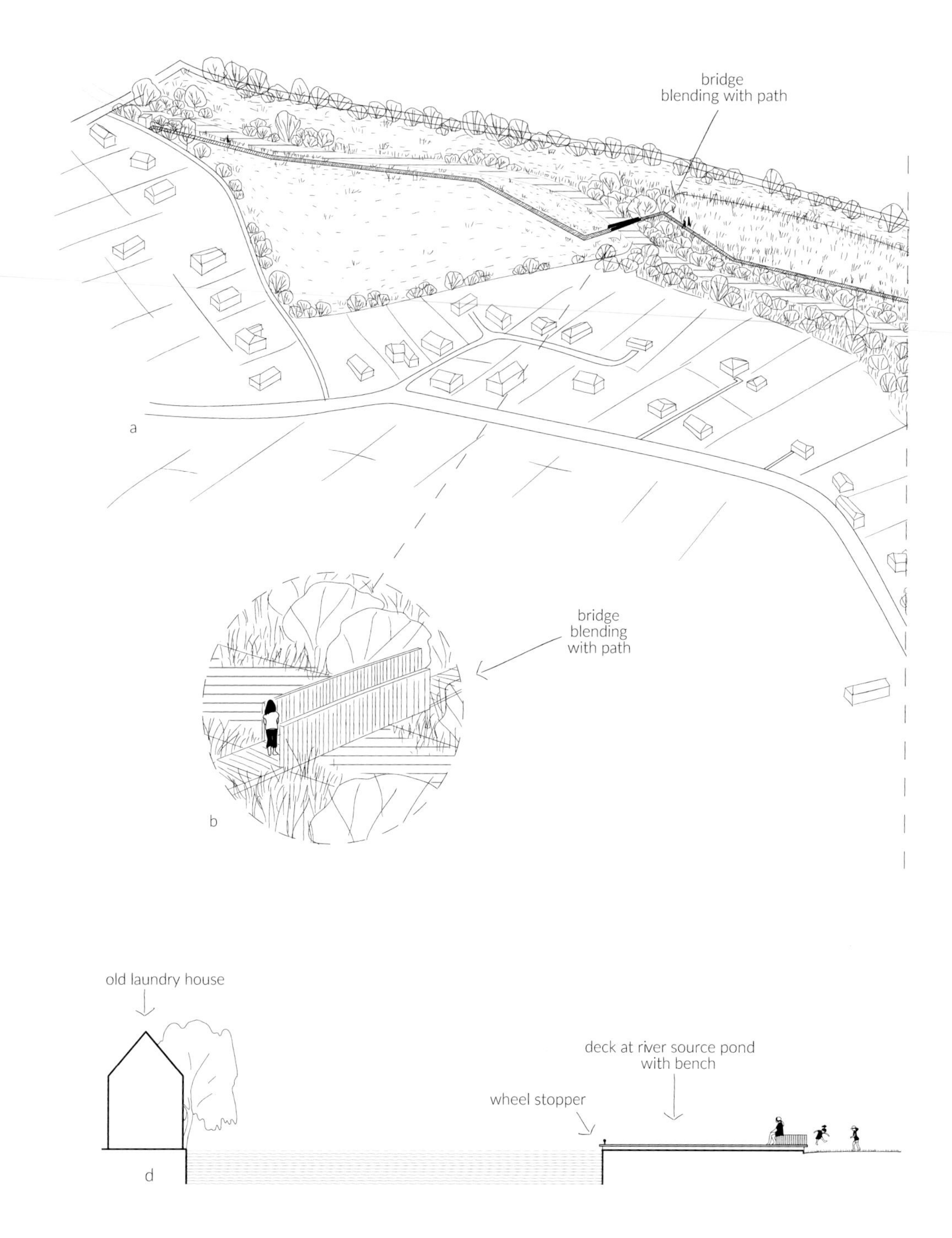

Figure 11.5a–e

a) The complete Norges-la-Ville project with all access points to the boardwalk; b) wooden-framed bridge crossing the stream; c) detailed view of the flax retting pond with the new wooden deck facing the old laundry house; d) cross-section through the flax retting pond with a bench on the deck; e) cross-section through the wet meadow showing the access to the stream-side along the boardwalk

(*Source*: Anna Wilczyńska and Jekaterina Balicka)

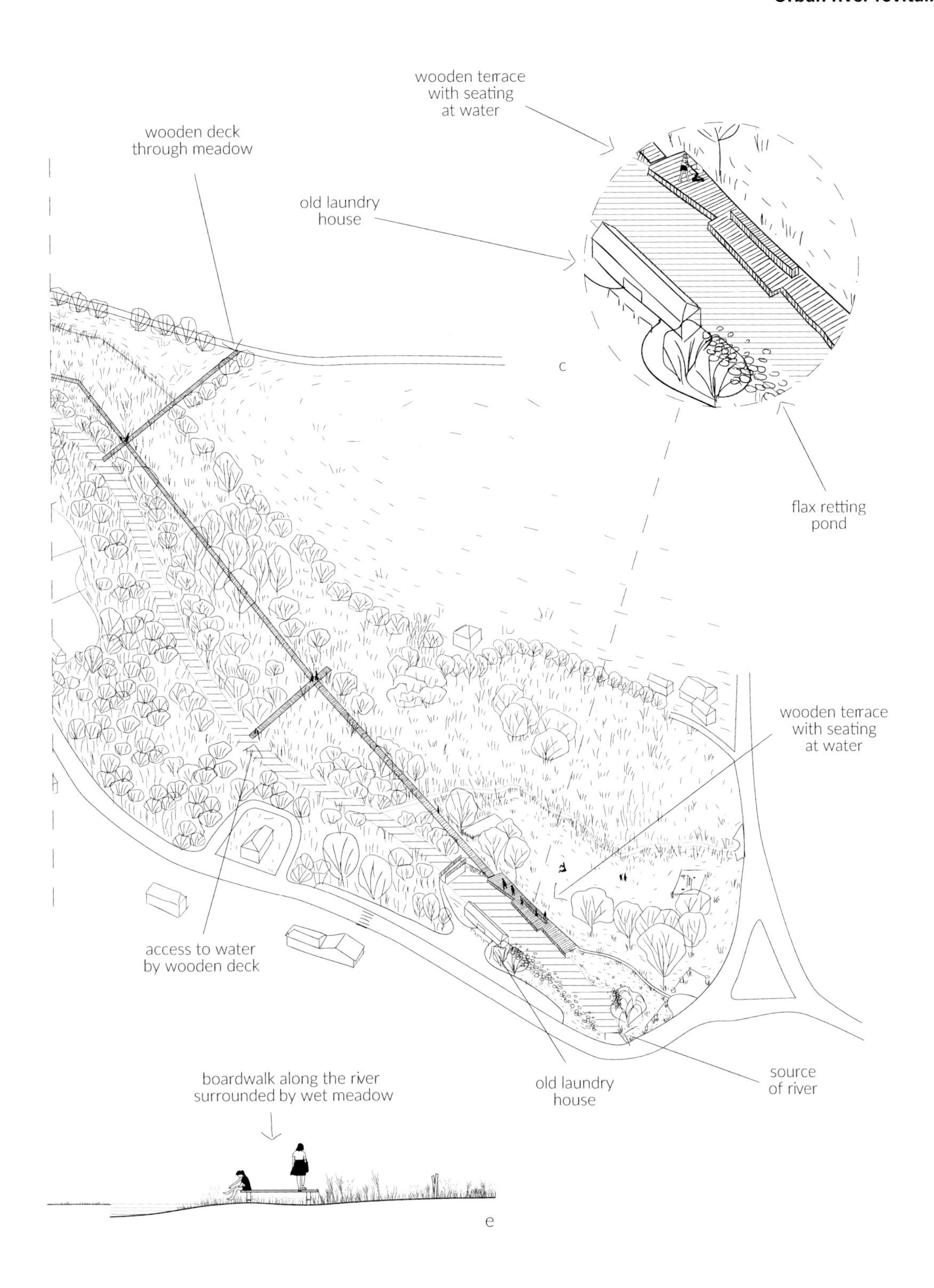

Figure 11.5a–e (continued)

Project quality rating assessment

This project performs well in most of the categories due to its location. The design improves accessibility to the site by a bridge and connects the boardwalk with the village centre and road, but this, of course, is only for pedestrians. From outside of the wetlands, the visibility is limited. The geometrical design is a particular feature and contrasts with the lush appearance of nature. The focus of facilities provided is directed towards the surrounding area rather than equipping the project with functional elements. The local climatic conditions as well as the proximity to the village do not call for an abundant assortment of wind or sun protection or artificial lighting. The visual and symbolic connection to the water landscape is more important than possible activities and immediate access to it. Its naturalness, uniqueness and sense of place make this project a successful waterfront development. Figure 11.5 shows sketches analysing the project.

Aire River Garden, Geneva, Switzerland

The Aire River Garden is a river renaturalisation project that comprises different interventions implemented in four phases on a 5-kilometre length covering almost 50 hectares. It is designed in stages by Atelier Descombes Rampini with Superpositions as a creative collaboration between landscape architects, civil engineers and biologists, with the first three stages completed in 2015.

From the late 19th century, the Aire was gradually canalised as part of the Swiss large-scale drainage projects to turn former wetlands into large-scale agriculture. This canalised river became an iconic element in the local landscape, but in 2001, the canton of Geneva launched a design competition to restore the river to its original shape. The aim was to remove the canal construction while improving the water quality with more effective flood management and providing public access. The landscape architects answered with a challenging response that questioned the established norms of ecological restoration.

Renaturalisation projects often simulate an image of nature, which is not the case here, as the river never existed without any human intervention and has always been a canal. The organisation of the design connects the new river space with a linear series of gardens in the floor of the former canal. The landscape architects did not design a fixed riverbed and instead proposed a diamond-shaped pattern for the new river bed whose form addresses the interplay between the river flow and the prepared terrain (Figure 11.6). This new riverbed does not replace the existing canal but flows alongside it, being fed by rainwater. Channels were excavated to maintain control of the river profile in a near-natural manner and pattern. After opening up the new river space, the river flow has moved sediment downstream, and over a one-year period, the geometrical matrix substantially changed into a new pattern of multiple channels which continue to drift downwards. The canal serves as a reference object for visitors to experience "before and after" and provokes questions about the making of this technical river landscape. In the sense of a pedagogical landscape, it raises awareness about temporality and process (Rosenberg, 2019).

An earlier unrealised regional strategic plan connected sites of natural and cultural value, and each contributed to a sense of place and identity, a typology recalled by the whole river garden. The first phase started with a master plan and a pilot project along a short section of the river to test the aforementioned principles as well as balancing the needs of stakeholders. In the second phase, functional hydraulic work was carried out, which led into the third phase that included the creation of the river and separating it from the canal. The old canal bed was then transformed into a chain of gardens along a continuous promenade, with shelters providing shade and picnicking places, its newly designed bed form deriving from the vernacular language of technical elements, such as weirs, concrete stairs, tree alleys and angular banks (Rosenberg, 2019).

Juxtaposing the river and canal after its restoration respects the historical layers rather than erasing all traces of former use. The Aire River Garden has taken a purely ecological programme and developed it into a

Figure 11.6
A view towards both new Aire River shapes
(*Source*: Superpositions. Photographer Fabio Chironi)

significant regional public space with a complex landscape. Restoration was less about reaching a finished state but more about creating an open process that reconsidered images of nature that we take for granted into an open artwork.

Project quality rating assessment

Good access to the project is provided for most users by most means of transport. The extended area of the project with its comprehensive design approach offers an overall high and original design quality, which also considers the facilities. As this project is on the urban fringe, it requires some lighting to feel safe. In the same way, the design quality also reflects health and well-being needs. The water connectivity is therefore covered, though there is no need for access from the water. By retaining the former canal bed, there is quite a lot of space for physical activity and children's play, but it does not offer space for water sports due to the shallow depth. This project has a unique design which is perfect for creating contact with water in a quite unusual way, but this focus limits other important aspects. Figure 11.7 analyses the project using sketches.

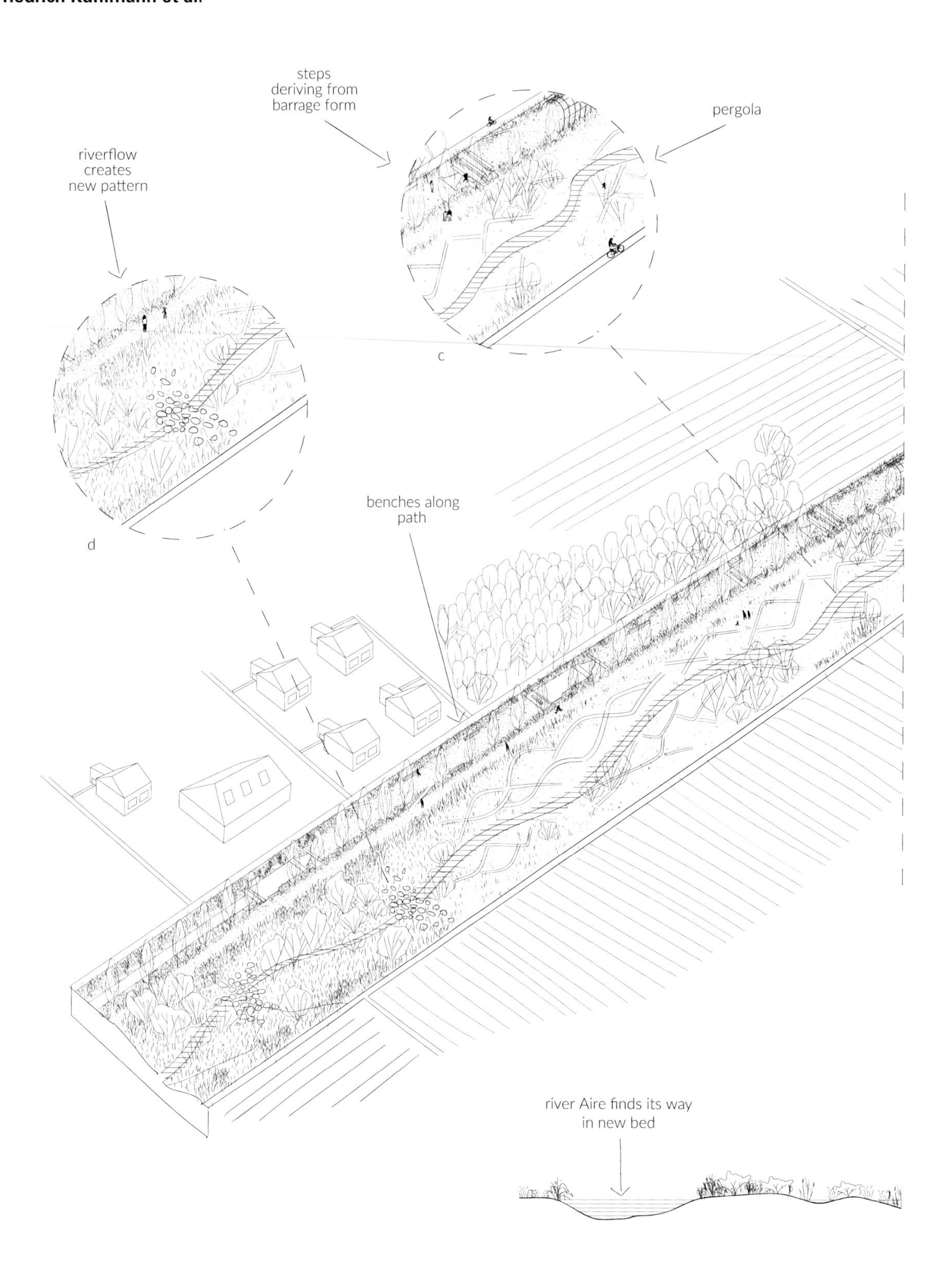

Figure 11.7a–e

a) Both beds of the former canalised Aire River running parallel to each other: the formal river garden in the old bed and the new flow pattern; b) the canalised river converts into the new naturalised flow; c) the old canalised bed has been turned into a linear open space, while the new naturalised river develops alongside; d) the river finds a bed in the new pattern; e) cross-section through both river beds

(*Source*: Anna Wilczyńska and Jekaterina Balicka)

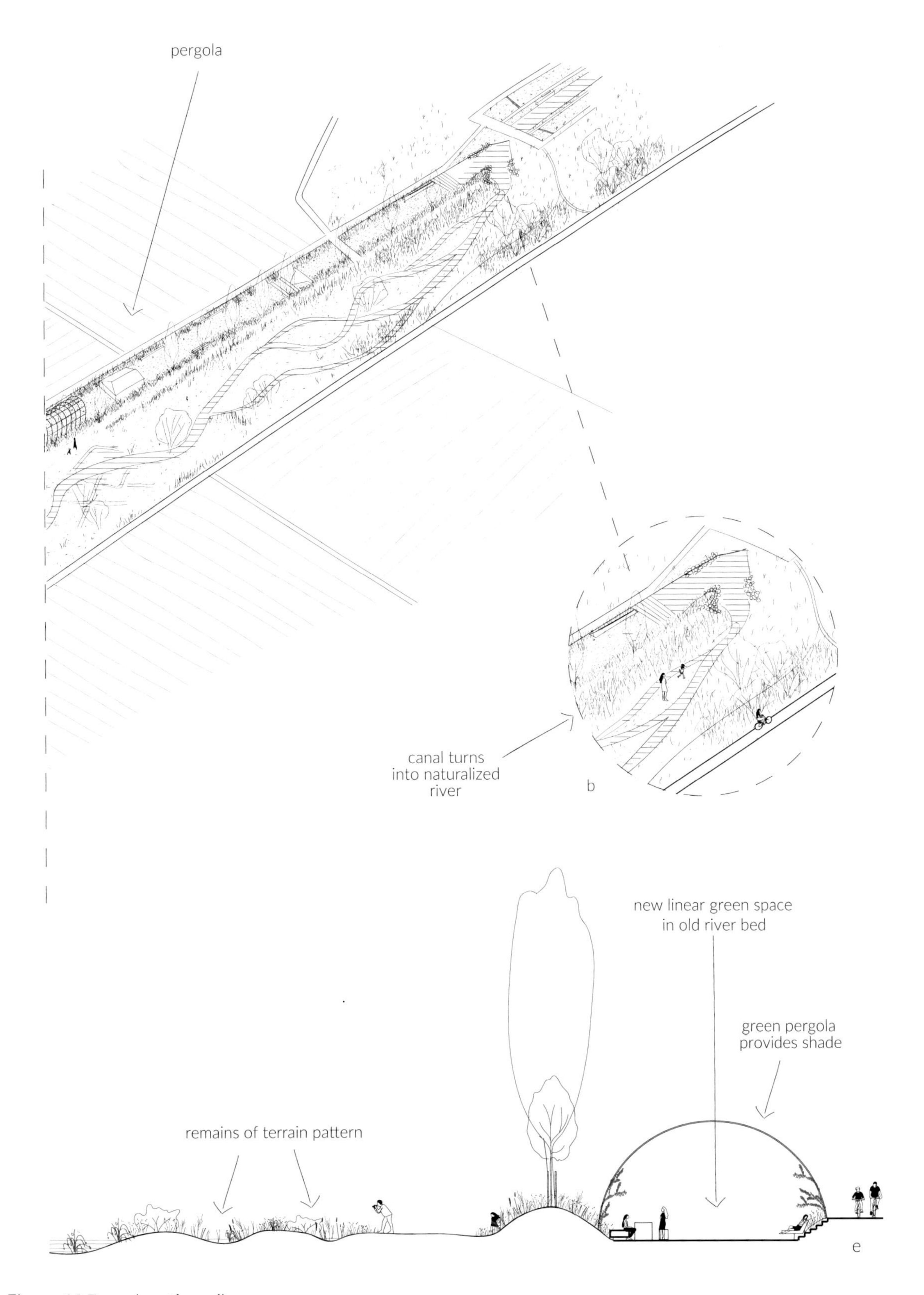

Figure 11.7a–e (continued)

Velenje City Centre Promenada, Velenje, Slovenia

The Velenje "Promenada" is both a public space and a pedestrian connection to the city centre of Velenje, Slovenia, that bridges the River Paka. It was planned and constructed in stages by ENOTA ARCHITECTS starting in 2014 as part of the ongoing revitalisation of the entire city centre. Velenje is an industrial post-war town, laid out on modernistic principles, and its special character and identity needed to be respected while meeting contemporary requests for bringing more life into the city. As a consequence, all foreseen activities needed to be concentrated in the centre to ensure a critical mass and a continuity of activities.

The modernistic urban layout offered sufficient area to accommodate additional programmed activities. These unoccupied grounds, however, had become car parks, despite being labelled as a pedestrian zone, and this affected the quality of open-space uses. This was a problem which increased with more visitors. A pre-condition for the project was therefore to increase the amount of parking to free up space by adding multi-level parking facilities.

Three main linear spaces for pedestrians cross the city centre and visually tie it together: a park, a street and the promenade. While each offers different uses of the space, they needed a distinct visual character. All of the content of the available and foreseen activities was to be concentrated into these linear spaces to prevent the creation of urban voids and to channel people's movement during events. In the first phase, the public spaces were provided with simple surfaces for a range of activities, which only required modest investment. This allowed for future expansion and additional content as required. The water level of the river increases a few times a year but remains low at all other times, generally being invisible. The park was extended across both banks of the river, and footbridges link into the network of paths situated on either bank, giving access to the formerly overgrown river. The street is enhanced by additional cultural and commercial programmes, such as open-air market events, and features concrete elements to frame the space for additional activities.

The first layout of the promenade was created by closing it to traffic, but it retained the character of a road and did not contribute to active public life. Thus, the initial straight connection was transformed into a sequence of widened surfaces, connected by a twisting, narrower path leading towards a new amphitheatre along the river (Figure 11.8).

Figure 11.8
The 'amphitheatre' at the Paka River, Velenje
(*Source*: Enota Arhitekti Velenje 2014. Photographer Miran Kambič)

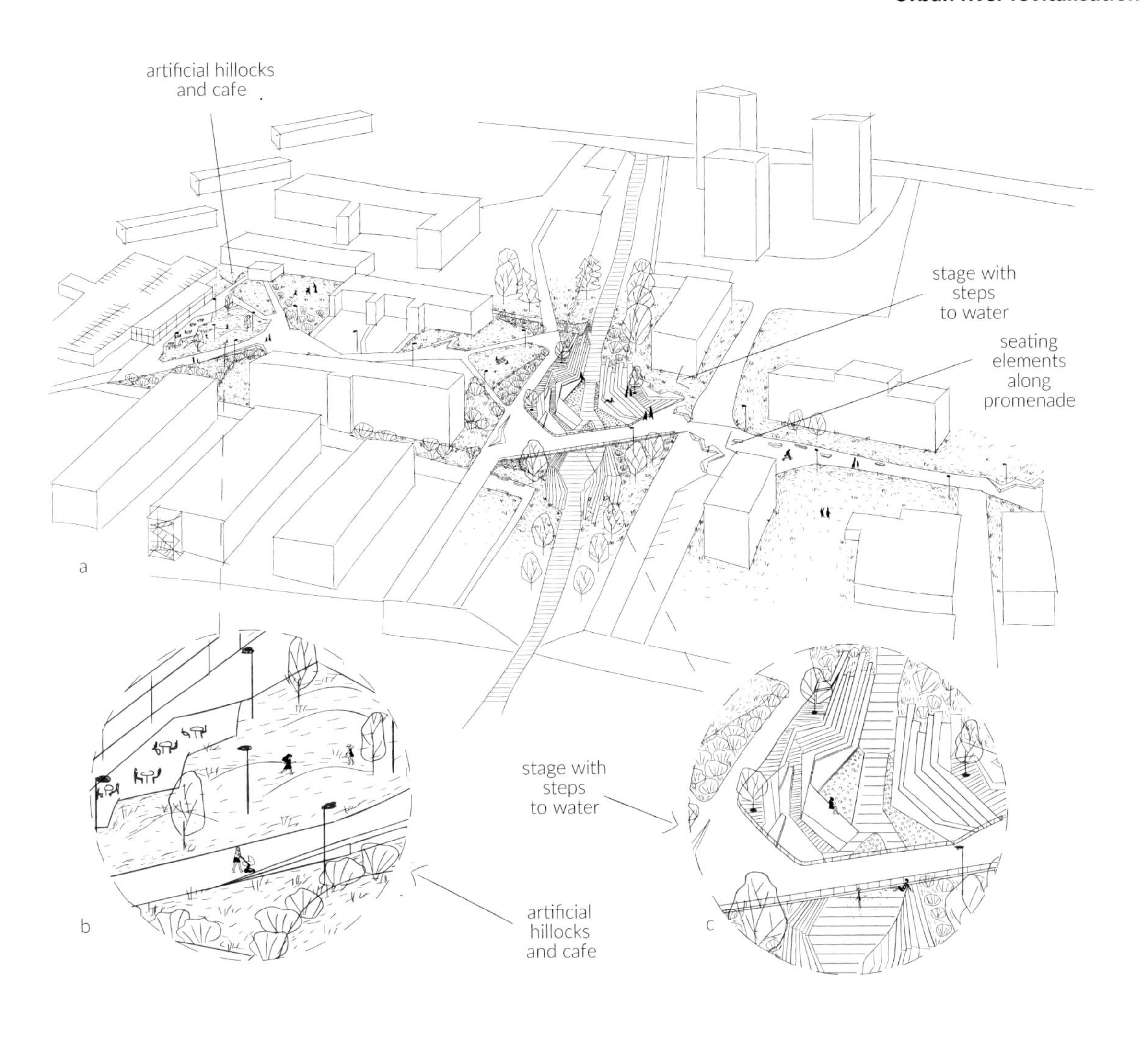

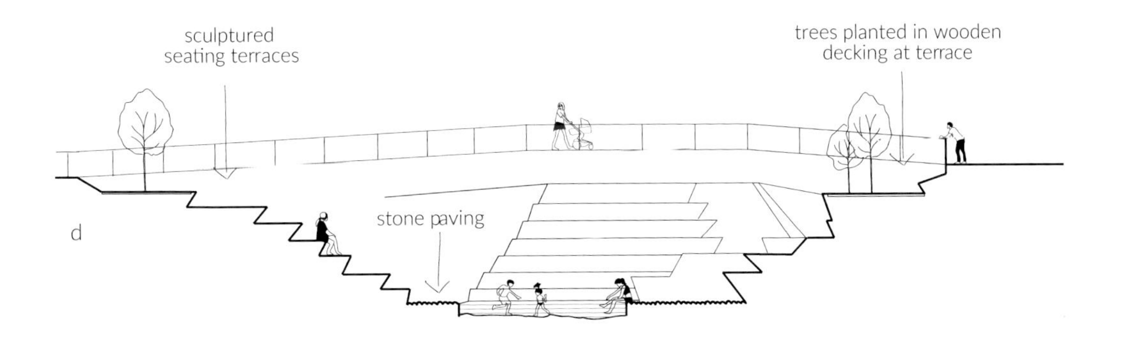

Figure 11.9a–d

a) Design concept of Velenje Promenade, with access to the water at the central stage; b) hilly green and gastronomy area; c) detailed view of the central stage with access to the water; d) cross-section, cutting through the stage area with seating steps at the water

(*Source*: Anna Wilczyńska and Jekaterina Balicka)

Space for the construction of this amphitheatre was gained by narrowing the old road bridge; then terraced surfaces gradually fall towards the river. The riverbed divided the area in half, but by modifying the riverfront and creating terraces towards the water level, it focuses different activities and connects them into a unified whole.

Project quality rating assessment

This project performs well for accessibility. This is a project in a modernist context, so the absence of references to the cultural heritage is different, and there are also almost no landmarks. It is considered modest in terms of maintenance requirements. It is generally well provided with facilities, but the range as well as lack of shade and especially shelter are weaker due to the bridge-like concept and location. The health and well-being aspect lacks potential, except for expressing the genius loci and safety aspects. It also provides a good connection to water but lacks safety equipment and immediate access from the water. This project performs poorly in most activity categories, owing to its location and design, although there are children's play activities available. The project is excellent at achieving formal quality given the location and spatial limitations. Figure 11.9 shows the interpretation of the design using the drawings.

Discovering Soestbach, Soest, Germany

The Soestbach renaturalisation project in Soest, Germany, has rediscovered an urban stream by changing its formerly technical character into an accessible linear public space. It was planned, developed and built in different stages from 1992 by the Büro Stelzig landscape ecology and planning office, initiated by the City of Soest. Previously, the Soestbach was a rather malodorous stream with hostile conditions for the ecology and a high flow velocity. It was a completely technical space while remaining an almost invisible element in the cityscape until the creation of an overall concept to expose it. The construction phases revealed the water flow of the stream and its connected springs. The Soestbach enters the city as a stream meandering through a meadow, mainly fed by more than 20 freshwater and saltwater springs during its course through the centre of Soest. However, it was historically converted into a sewage canal until it was partly redesigned. In the last few decades, though, questions of flood security gained more importance – flooding was always a problem for the city, as the stream flows through the medieval town centre.

The Soestbach saw a major decline in typical floodplain flora and fauna of the key indigenous habitats and an increase in common and alien floristic and faunistic species. It also saw a loss of migratory fish and an impoverishment of the amphibious fauna. The main planning objective was to turn the Soestbach from a eutrophied gutter into an attractive city waterscape. The aim was to utilise all possible spaces for water expansion under the urban planning conditions and to intensify the ecological and morphological diversity within the limited profile of the city stream. The development goal also aimed to achieve a *near-natural urban stream course* using the role model of a gravelly lowland stream, although the actual design is a deviation from the official classification of natural rivers. A precondition for the project was to raise the stream bed by almost 2 metres to ensure varied flow behaviour, as found locally.

By also revealing the feeding streams, they would add to the core flow and different flow velocities to the main stream. These actions changed the stream's behaviour and the flow of its groundwater. It also reduced the bottom shear stresses and eliminated unpleasant smells. Furthermore, the palpable acoustic quality was enhanced by re-establishing the sound of splashing water through the addition of weirs and plant clusters placed to decrease the flow velocity. A combination of stone walls and metal railings forms the basic design material (Figure 11.10).

The quality of the meadow landscape was highlighted by re-establishing references to the local history of Soest, such as historical sculptures indicating flood heights and offering information about the stream landscape and its development. The planning focus was not directed towards aspects such as sports or events, because the visual and symbolic connection to this landscape is more important than direct access. The public space relationship was also improved through the redesign, which not only made the water visible through balconies along the pedestrian routes and ramps or steps leading down to the stream; it furthermore introduced a new public space layer: a natural

Figure 11.10
A view into the 'discovered' Soestbach bed
(*Source*: Jonas Büchel)

stream with artificial banks in the sense of a promenade passing through the city to be constantly experienced by its residents.

Project quality rating assessment

This project performs in a variable way in most of the categories due to its location. The design improves overall inclusive accessibility. The establishment of good design quality, which fits within the context and the cultural heritage of an urban river, has contributed a vital element that is valued in the cityscape. As there are many facilities in the locality, the focus of facilities is more to the display of the new natural character of the stream and providing some lighting rather than providing many elements. The health and well-being potential varies quite a lot, since a sense of being away and contact with nature is not possible in the context. The water connection is mainly visual, with some exceptions, as the river itself is not suitable for activities, and access to and from the water is limited. Physical activity opportunities are fewer due to the location and size of the site. Figure 11.11 shows sketches analysing the project.

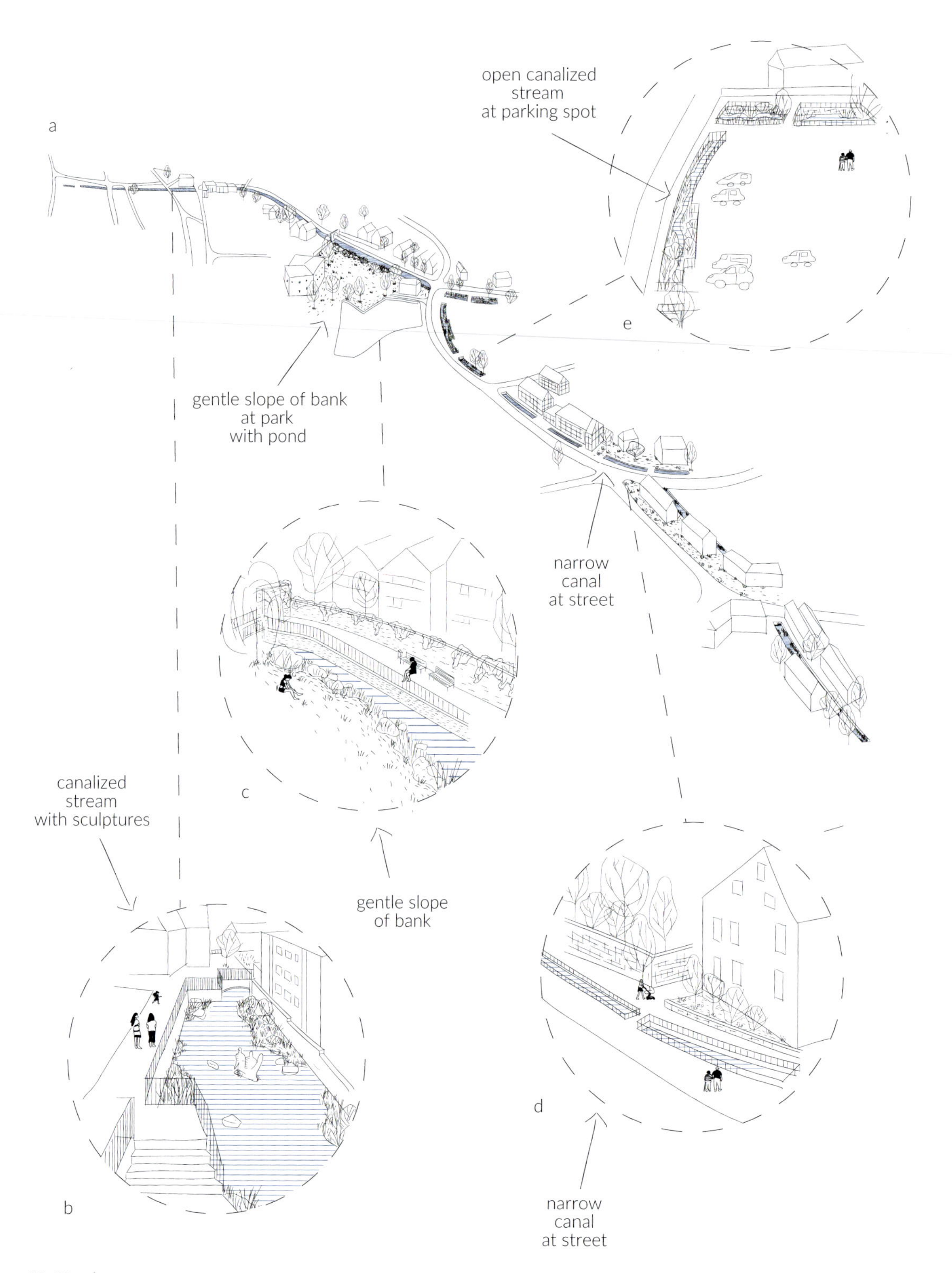

Figure 11.11a–h

a) Sequence of the rediscovered Soestbach within the city texture; b) detail of the stream widening at the square with adjacent vegetation, sculpture and steps to the water; c) the stream with the hard embankment and footpath opposite the gentle green slope; d) the canalised stream is embedded in the sidewalk; e) the widening of the stream with vegetation clusters near the parking; f) cross-section through the stream at the park; g) a section along the widened stream at the parking; h) cross-section through the narrow canalised stream with the sidewalk

(*Source*: Anna Wilczyńska and Jekaterina Balicka)

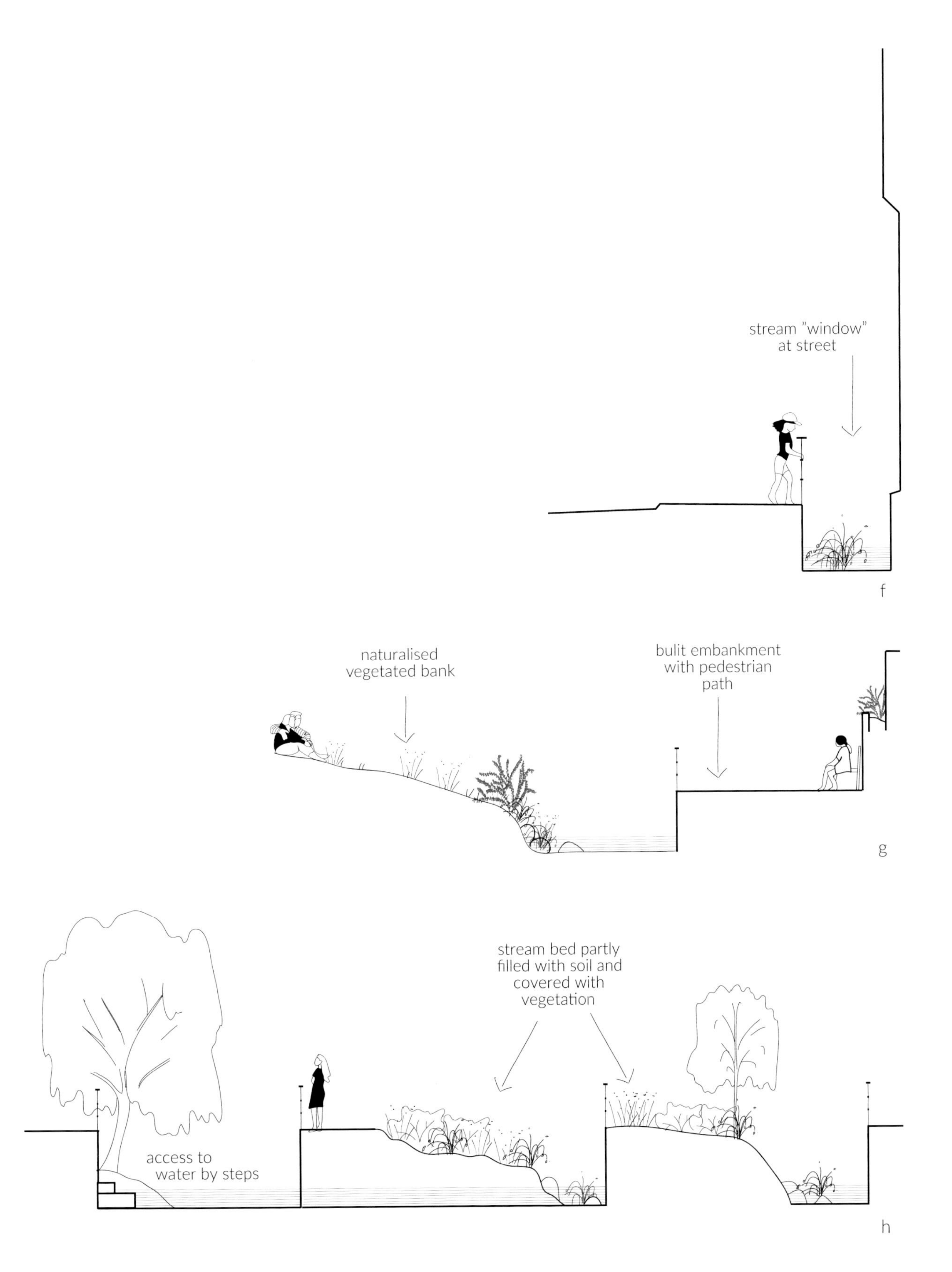

Figure 11.11a–h (continued)

Rivers and urban life: Rhone riverbank, Lyon, France

Historically, the Rhone riverbank in Lyon, France, was a large linear harbour, as in most cities with an industrial past. The so-called 'Berges de Rhône' development is a project undertaken by the city of Lyon, following an architecture competition, which was won by a team of landscape architects from IN SITU Architectes Paysagistes, architect Françoise-Hélène Jourda and lighting designers from Coup d'Éclat. The construction of the winning design was completed in 2007. The result is a transformation from a riverside car park to a multi-functional public space which reconnects the city and its inhabitants with the riverbank. This 5-kilometre-long stretch of riverbank facilitates relaxing and socialising and furthermore encourages local residents and visitors to use public transport or light traffic options. It also facilitates a continuous route along the river for pedestrians and cyclists.

The project was financed through council funding, including the building costs and the provision for spaces for events. It also includes a strategy for maintaining and developing the project in the future. A key component of the design process was applying participatory governance techniques by engaging the local community. A request was made to find out the community's desires and ideas followed by a process to negotiate and merge the expectations of local people and the council to avoid conflicts. The site is also part of a Trans-European bicycle route from Lake Geneva to the Mediterranean coast; upgrading the Lyon section ensures a safe and picturesque experience for cyclists.

The linear route changes in its appearance and thematic content along its course. The width varies between 5 and 75 metres, and this creates a different atmosphere, which is described as being more natural in the upstream and downstream areas and more urban in the centre. A large linear grass area together with an easily accessible linear basin and a terraced open space offers a stage for views over the river and defines the central section. This is accompanied by multiple lines of oak and elm trees on a raised esplanade, while a swimming pool and laid-out sport areas give a functional counterbalance (Figure 11.12). Refreshments, cycle hiring and fishing facilities are

Figure 11.12
A view along the Rhone riverbank
(*Source*: IN SITU. Photographer Karolina Samborska)

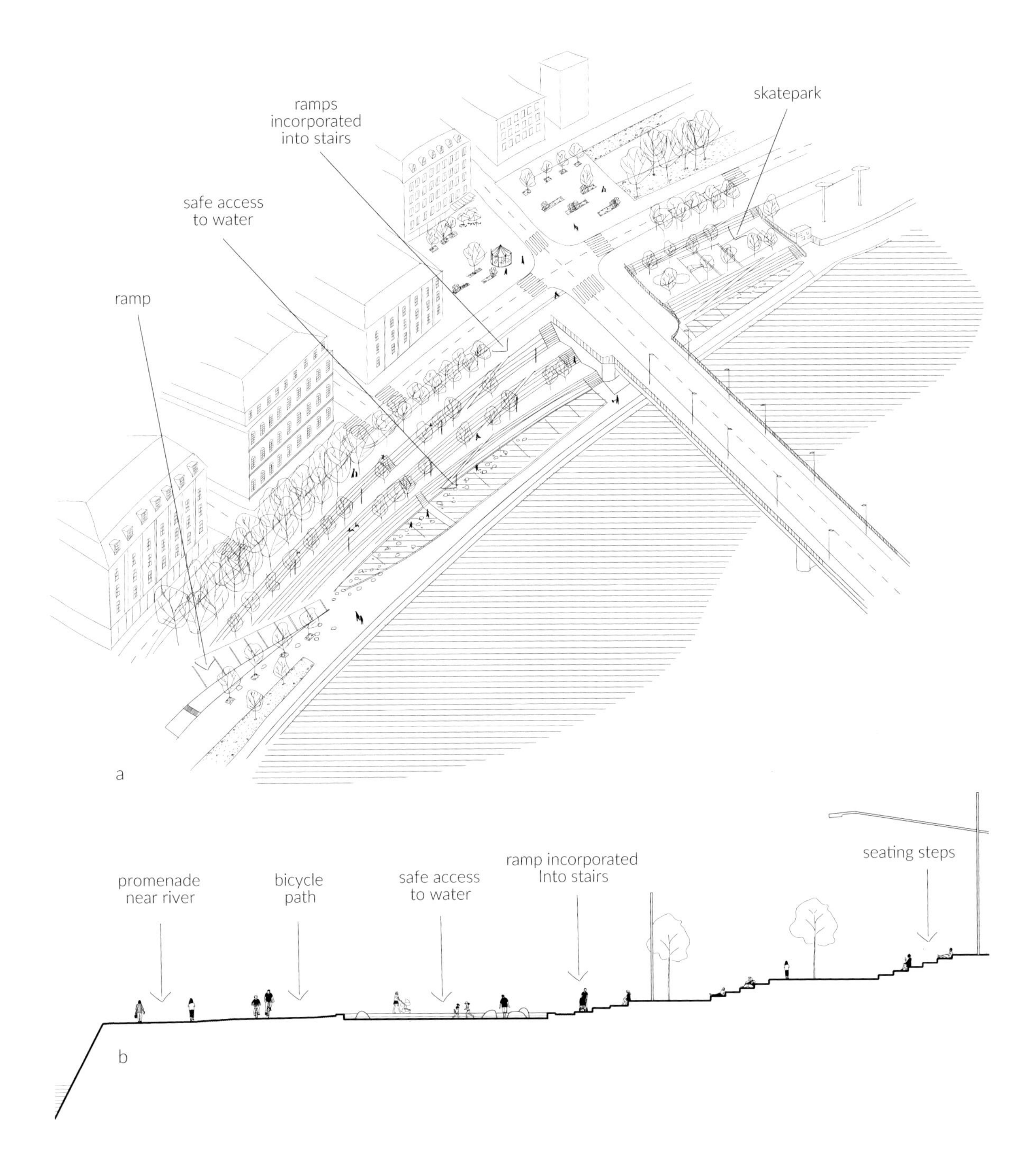

Figure 11.13a and b

a) Design concept of the Rhone riverbank. The sketch brings out how the water was symbolically and functionally made accessible by creating an additional water feature on the promenade; b) a section across the promenade, depicting how the design uses the terrain to create different levels on the promenade, connected with the seating steps allowing a view on the river

(*Source*: Anna Wilczyńska and Jekaterina Balicka)

concentrated in certain points, while in other parts, 'islands of grasses' provide more enclosed spaces for local residents. The intervention also links to the two largest parks and now provides a botanical walk, showcasing local types of vegetation.

The project does not reverse the historical development of the Rhone riverbank but adds a new component of a blue-green public space to the urban setting. It replaces the mono-functional spatial character and non-permeable materials and allows people to reconnect with the water in a quality riverside setting.

Project quality rating assessment

The overall access to the project is limited for public transport, while having improved the car parking, but it is not very visible from the city side. The design quality and diversity are also quite high and reflect the upgraded relationship to cultural heritage. It performs very well for most aspects of facilities, and it rates very highly for all aspects of health and well-being, as well as having excellent water connections. It has plenty of opportunities for physical activity but not for on-water sports. Figure 11.13 shows how it has been analysed using sketches.

Chicago Riverwalk, Chicago, United States

Since the 1990s, busy roads have been reconfigured by the Chicago Department of Transportation to allow greater public access to the river. On the basis of this road reconstruction project, the city worked on the development plan for the Chicago Riverwalk. The construction started in 2001 and was developed by Skidmore, Owings and Merrill. The architects planned four separate sections, each with a specific location and theme. The sections started off at the Confluence as a spatial expansion into the river for more public space and pedestrian access. This was followed by the Arcade, with a more architectural appearance, separating the riverfront from the road. The Civic includes a museum and is the focal point for boat launches, while the *Market* focuses on connecting gastronomy and apartments to the Riverwalk.

The resulting Chicago Riverwalk is a connected pedestrian waterfront. It contains promenades, seating, restaurants, boat rentals and further activities at the river's edge. While the Chicago River was once a busy industrial shipping channel, it is now one of Chicago's main attractions and understood as a second "shoreline" to Lake Michigan. The Chicago Riverwalk was not realised in one project; the different sections were added step by step and have enhanced contemporary opportunities for recreation while merging the new recreational spaces in the city. Each section has a different design and purpose and accommodates activities from dining to fishing, along with their commercial and recreational amenities. It allows people to get closer to the river and actually embrace it as part of big city life (Figure 11.14).

The first phase was completed in 2009, and in 2012, Sasaki and Ross Barney Architects designed an expansion to link six more sections to the Riverwalk. Essentially, these were in a sense a series of rooms, which connected more of the river to the city with floating gardens and piers for more recreational options. These six final new sections were officially opened in 2015 and 2016. The Marina Plaza presents further gastronomy and outdoor seating, while the Cove provides access for docking of individual boats, and the River Theatre links road and river with shaded stairs and seating. A levelled fountain forms the Water Plaza features, whereas Jetty features wetland gardens, which also raises the awareness of river ecology in an interactive learning environment. Finally, the Boardwalk forms an accessible walkway with a vast lawn area.

Chicago is planning further extensions of the Riverwalk, while the oldest section will see improvements following contemporary affordances. The programmes and forms for each section allow for diverse experiences at and on the river. These experiences trigger public social life at the core of the city by removing traffic barriers next to the water edge and encouraging direct contact with the river edge while being less exposed to traffic noise. The design

Figure 11.14
An evening at the Chicago Riverwalk
(*Source*: Sasaki Associates)

provides both continuity and variety for a visitor with materials, details and repeated forms that provide a visual unity along the subsequent sections of the Riverwalk.

Project quality rating assessment

This project is excellent for accessibility and overall design, except for values of cultural heritage. The project has little lighting and is rather exposed to sun and wind, but it is rated highly for most other aspects of the facilities. The health and well-being potential is generally quite high but rated lower for being away, as it is an artificial urban environment, and there is no contact with nature. Water accessibility also performs very well, apart from the range of possible activities in or on the water as well as the fact that water safety equipment is not very evident. There is quite a lot of space for physical activity and children's play, but of course not offering water sports in the centre. It is a versatile project, making good use of the limited space in a very urban context. Figure 11.15 shows the interpretation of the design using drawings.

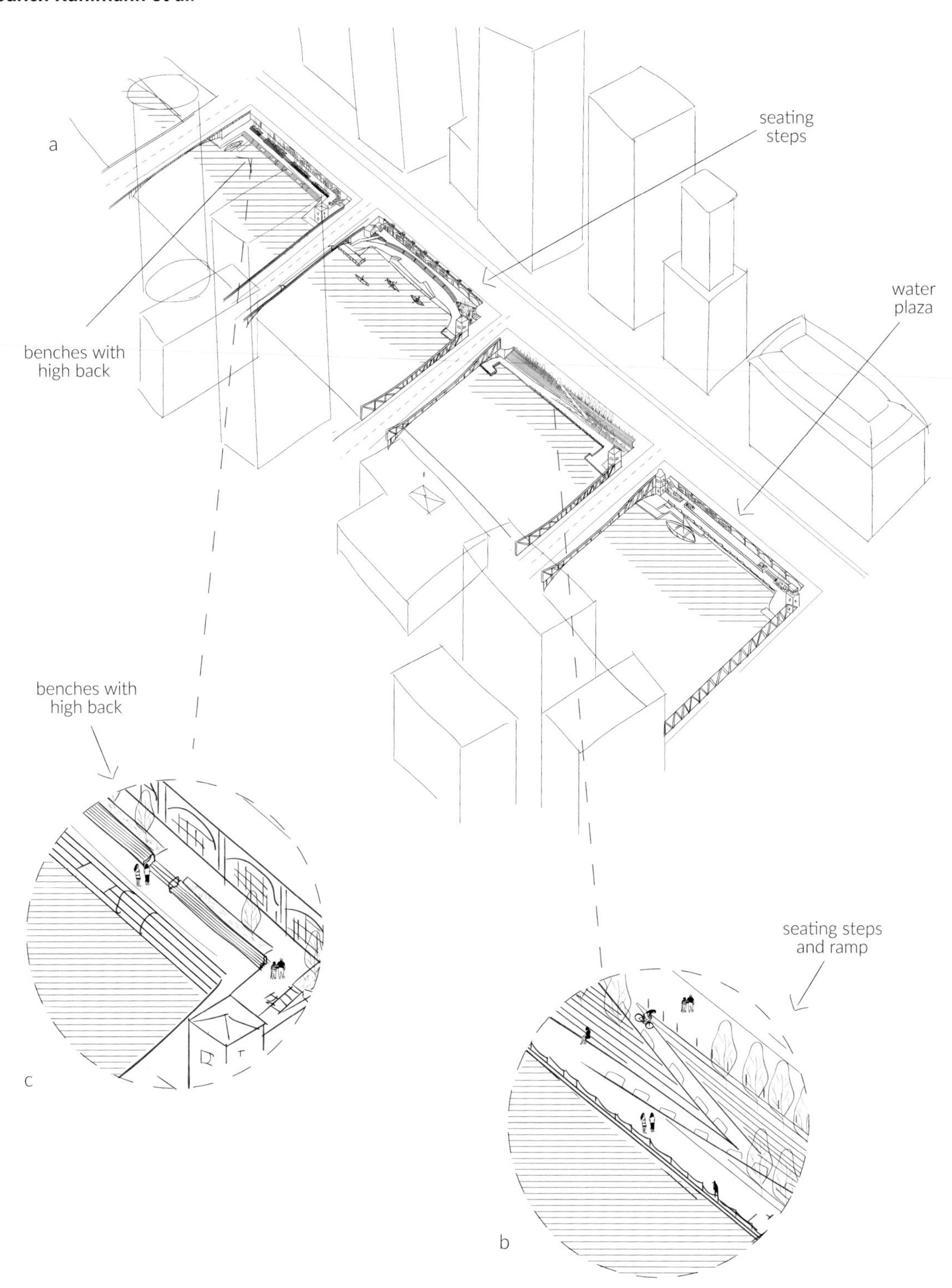

Figure 11.15a–e

a) Overall design concept of the Chicago Riverwalk and how it provides different functional sectors between each bridge; b) the so-called River Theatre, how the design provides seating on steps with the river view and how the lower part is accessed by ramps; c) detail of the Marina section with recreation areas along the water and access to water transport; d) the Jetty section with various decks, allowing people to be close to the water and to see riparian vegetation; e) a section showing how the recreational areas and direct access to the water are offered by the design at the Water Plaza

(*Source*: Anna Wilczyńska and Jekaterina Balicka)

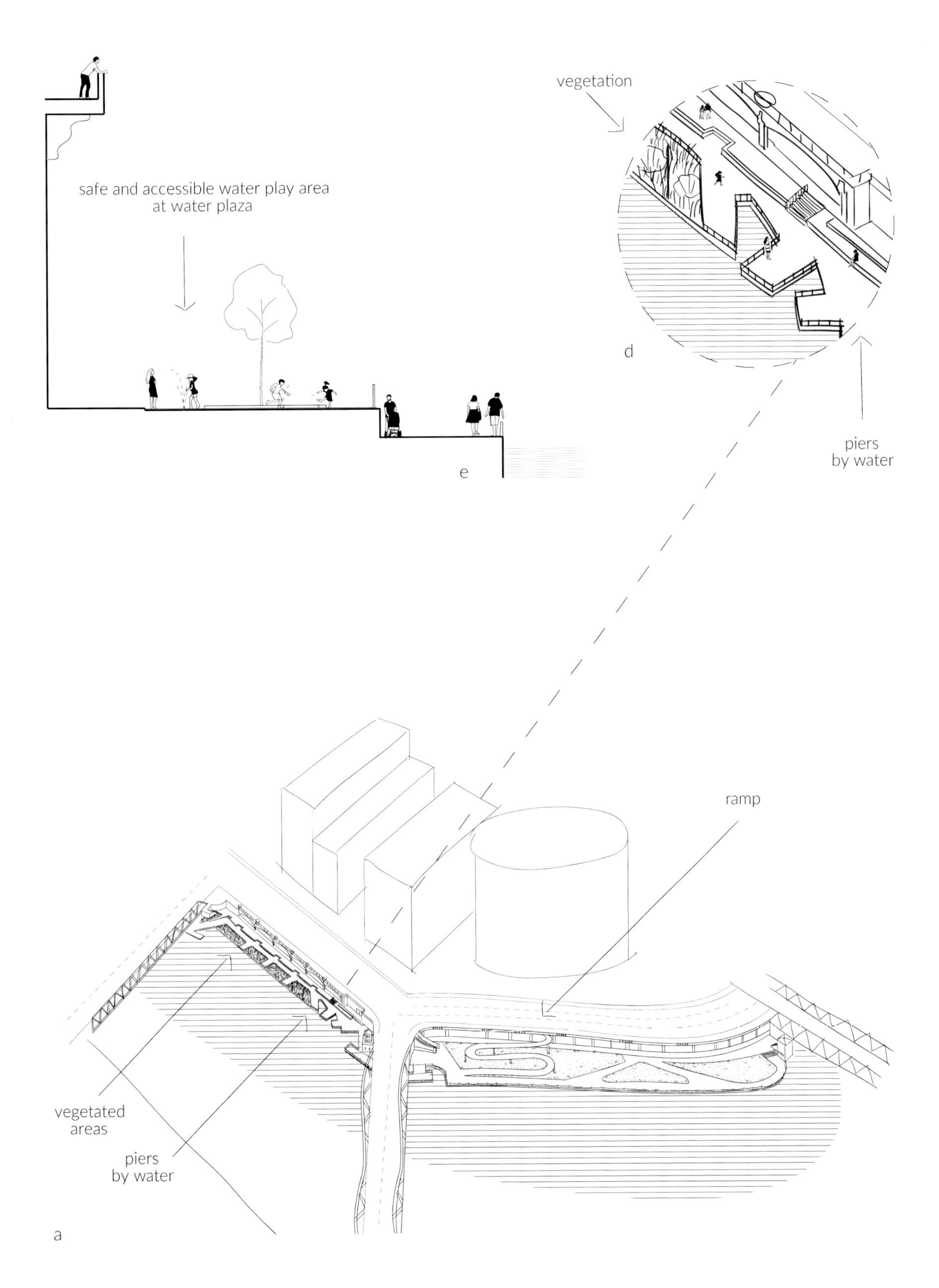

Figure 11.15a–e (continued)

Cheonggyecheon River revitalisation, Seoul, South Korea

The Cheonggyecheon River revitalisation in Seoul is a well-known and ambitious river recovery project. It was designed by Hyundon Shin, Wonman Hoi, Juhyun Chug and Yangkyo Chin and initiated by the Seoul Metropolitan Government in 2005. It is one of the most important recent projects for urban renewal and was created by demolishing a run-down expressway and revitalising a buried river and its immediate neighbourhood at the same time. The Cheonggyecheon central area now hosts a green waterfront park accompanied by an improved public transport system as its main attraction.

The Cheonggyecheon area is the largest commercial centre in Seoul. It was once an important river in the history of Seoul, but pollution levels became a concern. To resolve this, the river was covered with concrete and turned into a highway in 1960 to host the increasing traffic. By the end of the century, the highway became outdated, as costs for its maintenance increased and the volume of transport posed health concerns for the surrounding neighbourhood. It also separated local communities. Noise pollution and safety hazards contributed to an unfavourable living environment around this central district, where even company headquarters moved away because of the overall experience of stagnation.

Instead of investing a huge budget to upgrade the highway, the municipality decided to demolish it in 2003. As the elevated highway provided traffic access, its removal while restoring the river was seen as quite a radical idea that many residents, businesses and traffic experts initially opposed. The city government therefore engaged stakeholders through consultations before carrying out the work. The aim was to clarify the benefits of restoring the Cheonggyecheon stream over reconstruction, how it addressed safety problems and mobility demands and how it could revitalise community life.

After removing the expressway and opening the river park in 2005, the air quality and noise levels improved. This was further enhanced by upgrading public transport and giving it priority over cars, thus promoting walkability along the new corridor. The almost 6-km-long re-discovered Cheonggyecheon stream has enhanced the quality of

Figure 11.16
A view on the revitalised Cheonggyecheon River
(*Source*: Hana Shin)

life in this part of Seoul, and the river has become an attractive element of the city, inviting not only locals but tens of thousands of daily visitors. One might call it an extensive park in the sense of a linear playground combining history, urban culture and urban nature. The project also reduced the urban heat island effect along the waterfront, reducing the local temperature by 5°C and increasing wind speeds. It also introduced biodiversity into the dense urban landscape, even introducing new animal species. The main pedestrian passage along the water edge on both riverbanks is located on lower-level terraces with natural recreational areas and even willow wetlands along its banks (Figure 11.16). It provides access to the water with steps, timber decks or stepping stones, offering quite a sense of being away.

Project quality rating assessment

This project, due to its location, shows some limitations in different aspects. It mostly performs well for accessibility, though it is a little weak in visibility and inclusive access. The design quality is also excellent, although the project may be a bit costly to maintain. It is well endowed with facilities, although for such an extensive linear space, the amount of seating seems to be rather low, and it lacks the necessary accessibility to the promenade. Health and well-being issues are generally rated quite high, apart from being away in such an artificial urban environment and for contact with nature. Again, water accessibility is also rated highly, apart from the range of possible activities as well as the lack of water safety equipment. Physical activity opportunities are weak, although children's play and logical zoning are well provided for. This is a great example of an urban revitalisation project which overcomes huge challenges and offers outstanding solutions to provide something special in the urban landscape of Seoul. Figure 11.17 shows the analysis of the project in sketches.

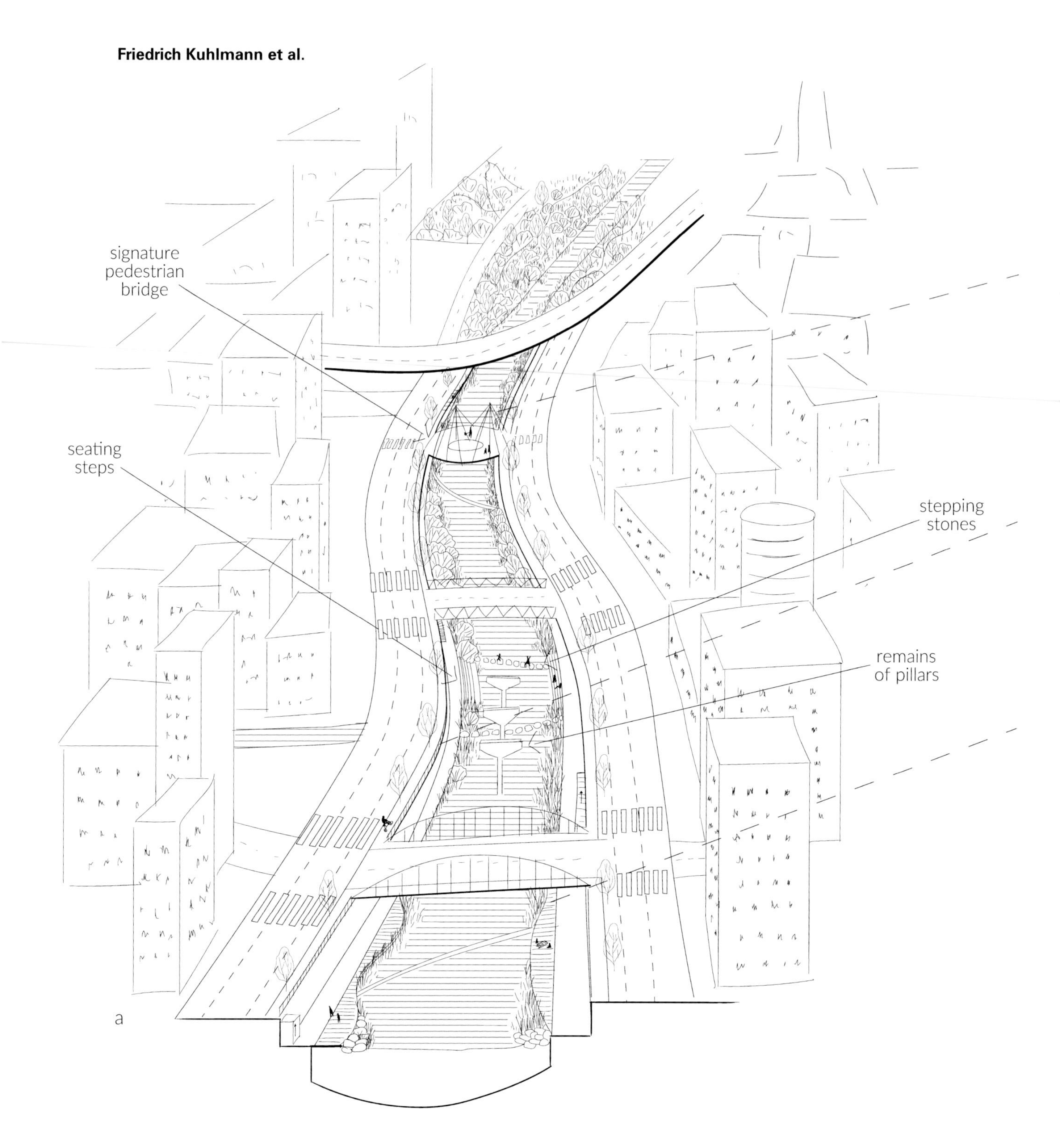

Figure 11.17a–e

a) The concept for the Cheonggyecheon River offers thematic and functional zoning; b) detail of the eastern part of the project, highlighting the extensive use of lush vegetation at the river; c) the central part with the remaining viaduct pillars and access to water by stepping stones and seating terraces; d) access to the water is provided under the bridge; e) section across the central part, depicting the seating terraces

(*Source*: Anna Wilczyńska and Jekaterina Balicka)

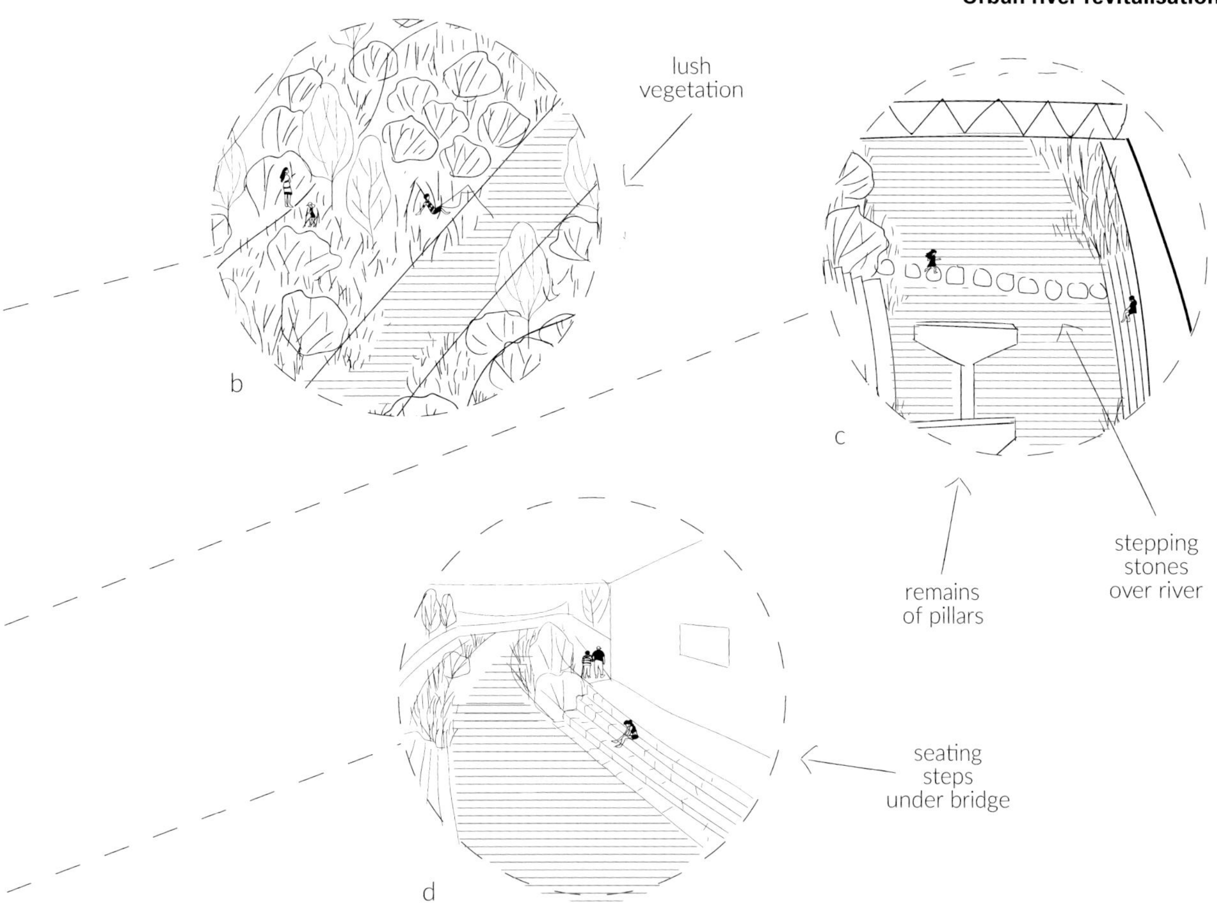

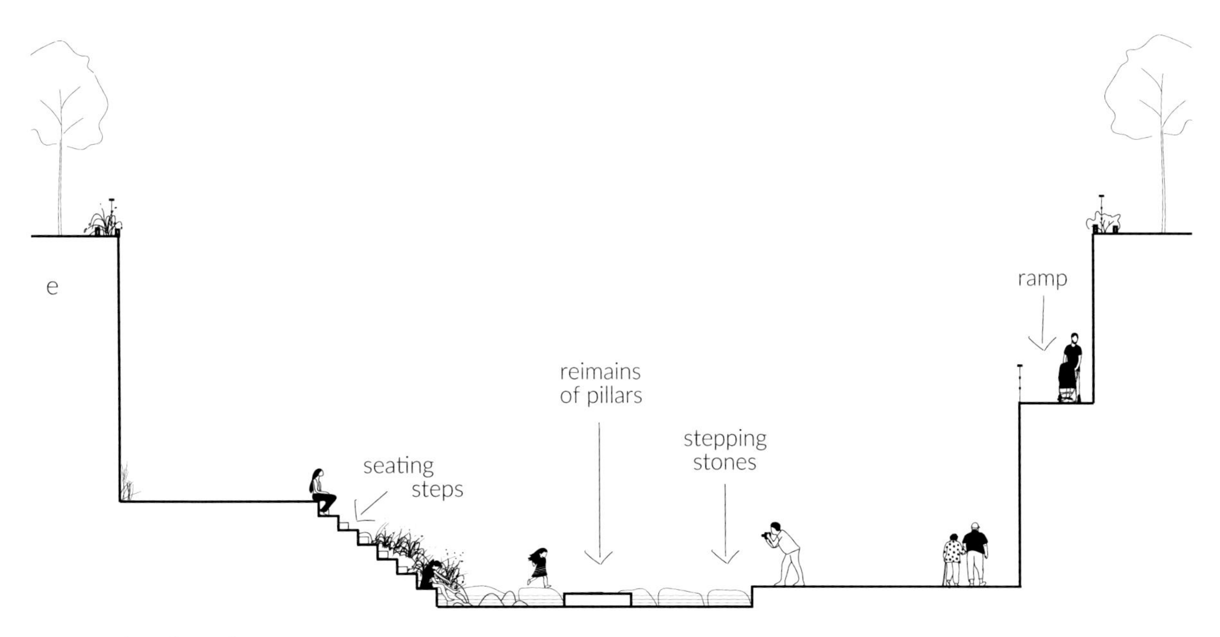

Figure 11.17a–e (continued)

Aalborg's new waterfront, Aalborg, Denmark

The new Aalborg waterfront was designed and built in two phases in 2004 and 2013 by C.F. Møller Architects together with Vibeke Rønnow Landscape Architects. Aalborg always had a dense functional connection to its fjord river; however, in the past decades, it has changed from an industrial city into a university and cultural centre, where new cultural activities have moved into the former factory area at the adjacent fjord. In this context, the conversion of this area into the new waterfront not only functionally links the centre with the fjord by filling voids in the post-industrial urban fabric but also creates a new relationship between the city and the fjord. It has become a new unifying landscape element, giving the use of the port back to the city.

The first phase of the new waterfront was opened in late 2011, and the second stage continued with the same approach, where the promenade acts as a unifying component. Other variations of spaces close to the concert hall were added, highlighted by a rectangular platform with marked surfaces, called an *urban plinth*. The idea of this phase was to extend the waterfront promenade to resemble a marsh connected to the plinth, as in a dune landscape. This plinth also provides necessary flood and wind protection for the area with a sequence of spatial gaps providing different elements such as wooden piers, pontoon terraces, seating steps and an outdoor public swimming pool. This interplay of linear spaces and rolling topography is inspired by the intersection of dune and beach, common in Danish fjord landscapes.

Figure 11.18
The pool at the Aalborg waterfront
(*Source*: Visit Aalborg. Photographer: Adam Lehn)

The new promenade consists of varied squares and gardens which host markets, sports or play facilities and spaces for different seasonal recreation activities connected to water. These are integrated into the promenade sequence, creating green spaces with dense groves of native trees and shrubs, while the overall surfaces are reminiscent of the industrial past, asphalt, concrete and wood being the main materials. An emphasis was put on lighting for marking the waterfront at night to encourage visitors after dark.

In general, the new Aalborg waterfront provides an important upgrading of the city's living quality since the historical centre lacked green and public spaces for the city's inhabitants and users of the immediate neighbourhood. The whole area along the fjord now has a different character, offering a new aesthetic experience.

Project quality rating assessment

This project performs well for accessibility due to the layout and location, apart from public transport connections, surprisingly for Denmark. Design quality is good, apart from the cultural heritage aspects, which do not feature much in the project. The extent of facilities is limited, since it is exposed to wind and sun, but offers a new quality of nature connected to features of urban character. Also, the health and well-being potential is rather limited in terms of being away, genius loci and contact with nature. Water connections are limited, except for connectivity and access from the water, while physical activity opportunities are generally good but less so for informal ones and water sports. The project is excellent at achieving formal quality given the location and spatial limitations. Figure 11.19 shows the interpretation of the design using drawings.

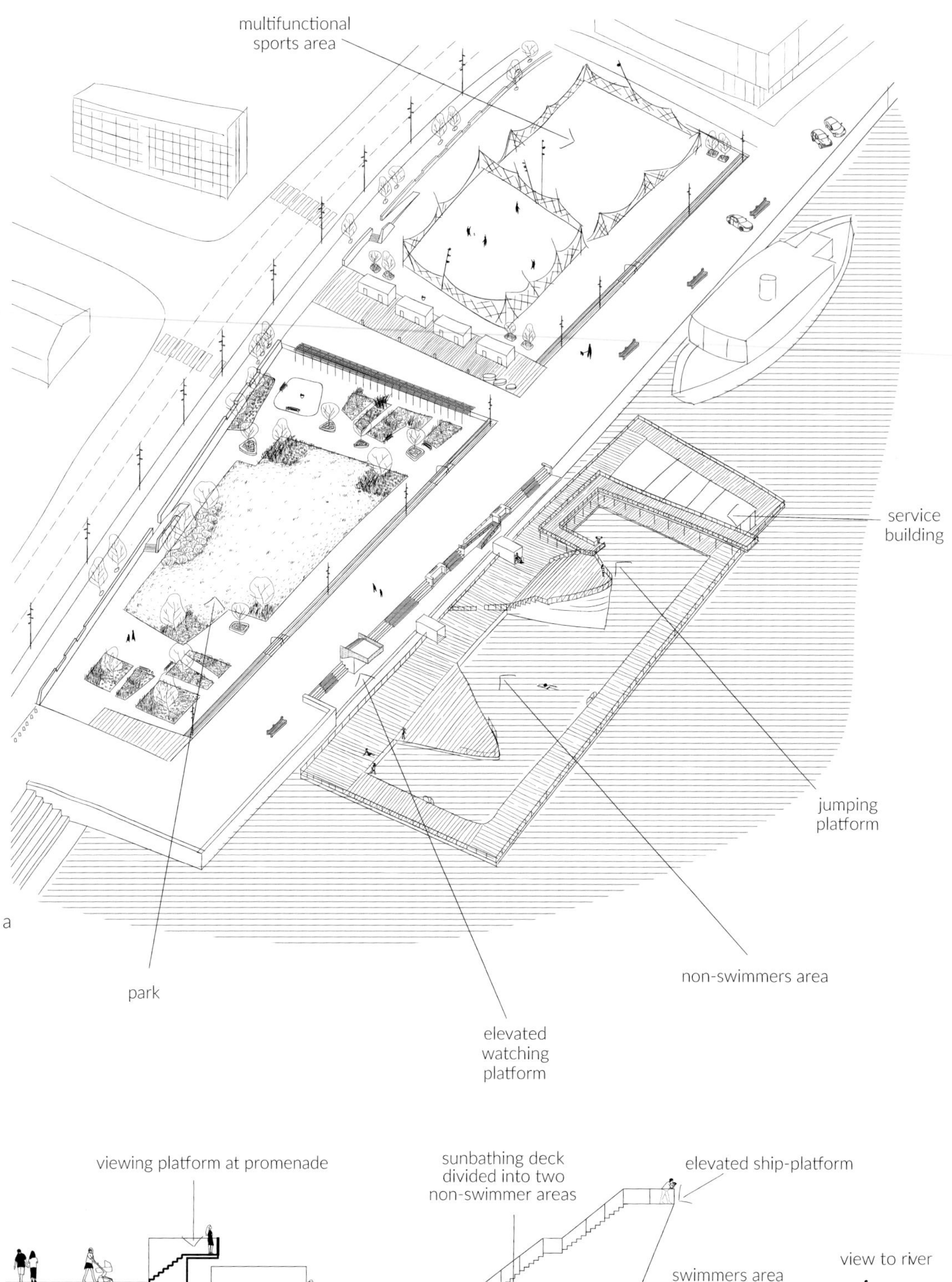

Figure 11.19a and b

a) Design concept of the Aalborg waterfront with accessible bathing and diving possibilities; b) cross-section through the elevated viewing platform and the pool

(*Source*: Anna Wilczyńska and Jekaterina Balicka)

Being away at the river: Banks of the Sâone, Rochetaillée, France

The banks of the Saône River at Rochetaillée sur Saône were planned and constructed in 2014 by an interdisciplinary team under the leadership of IN SITU Paysages & Urbanisme landscape architects. The team consisted of vegetation engineers, lighting designers and civil engineers. Following an international competition three years earlier, the project regenerated the old lost waterfront for the community. The landscape architects also collaborated with four contemporary artists, who created several installations on a route called the "river movie". This is similar to a cinematic shot that continues into other sequences along the river. The artworks blend into the river landscape and are a reference to the local history and surrounding landscapes, creating places where visitors can stop to admire the Saône area.

Rochetaillée is a small commune located north of Lyon on the left bank of the Sâone river. The area of the River Sâone banks project is part of the strategic "Rive de Sâone project" initiated by the Lyon urban community. It is a 15-kilometre-long pedestrian promenade that has been developed in different stages between Lyon and the Saône Valley. This bigger project highlights and preserves the region's ecological heritage, such as the façades of historical buildings built along the Saône, and relates to activities such as rowing, fishing, walking and children's play. It alternates between the urban and pastoral atmospheres. Eventually the long pedestrian promenade changes into a more pastoral route where the local meadow vegetation forms the setting and the banks are widened to form wide beaches. This particular project is located along a 2-kilometre section and set in a 6-hectare expanse.

Originally, a towpath followed the banks of the Saône, where small barges were towed by horses. This was bordered by regularly flooded islands, which served as a grazing place for the village herds. These islands formed so-called *lônes*, diverse ecosystems formed by oxbow lakes or meanders separate from the main river. With the appearance of the Lyon tramway, visitors came to the Saône waterfront on summer holidays and weekends for activities. Simple rustic taverns known as *guinguettes* were built to offer fried foods and entertainment. Later, the river was canalised and the *lônes* were infilled to create land for roads. The swimmers left the banks, but the taverns stayed.

Due to recent sanitation efforts, the river was revitalised, although swimming is still prohibited. The *guinguettes* are now popular restaurants, which line the new promenade along the former towpath. The promenade is divided into two lanes, one for light traffic and one for walking. This allows people to enjoy the connection to the river in different ways and at different speeds. The spaces provide a place for picnic tables and large lounging benches for relaxing and leisure (Figure 11.20). The design reinforced the damaged riverbanks and created a large meadow with natural views, punctuated by pebble and sandy beaches that gently descend towards the river. Furthermore, it accommodates events, such as music concerts or movie screenings. An observation platform located at the floodgate was opened to the public in 2018 to observe the passage of boats.

Figure 11.20
Seating elements facing the Saône
(*Source*: Guillaume Robert-Famy/La Voie Bleue)

Project quality rating assessment
The project is assessed well for accessibility in all aspects because of its linear character, as it is both connected to the river and the main traffic lines. It offers overall good design quality, and it rates highly for all aspects regarding facilities. It has a strong genius loci and sufficient water connections, although there is less direct contact with the water since swimming is prohibited. The focus on physical activities is directed towards informal activities and children's play. It is a good example to showcase the high status of French landscape architecture, and Figure 11.21 shows how it has been analysed using sketches.

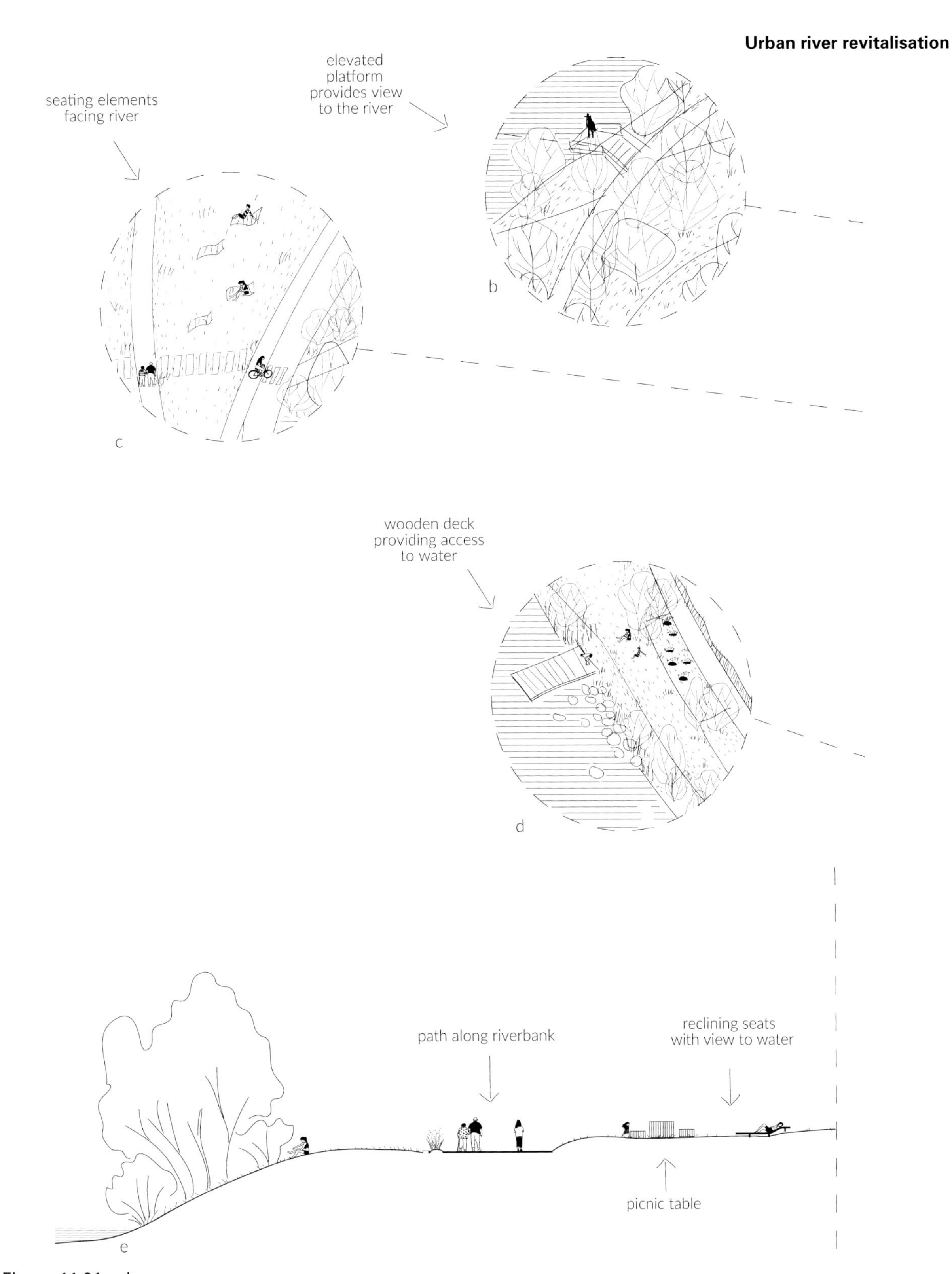

Figure 11.21a–d

a) Design concept of the Banks of the Saône. The sketch depicts how the project efficiently creates space in the narrow strip of land between river and road; b) the terraced lawn containing seating elements and a path from concrete slabs connecting park and street; c) a *guinguette* and the deck to access the water; d) a section across the terraced lawn with seating adapting to the landform, through the path to the water edge

(*Source*: Anna Wilczyńska and Jekaterina Balicka)

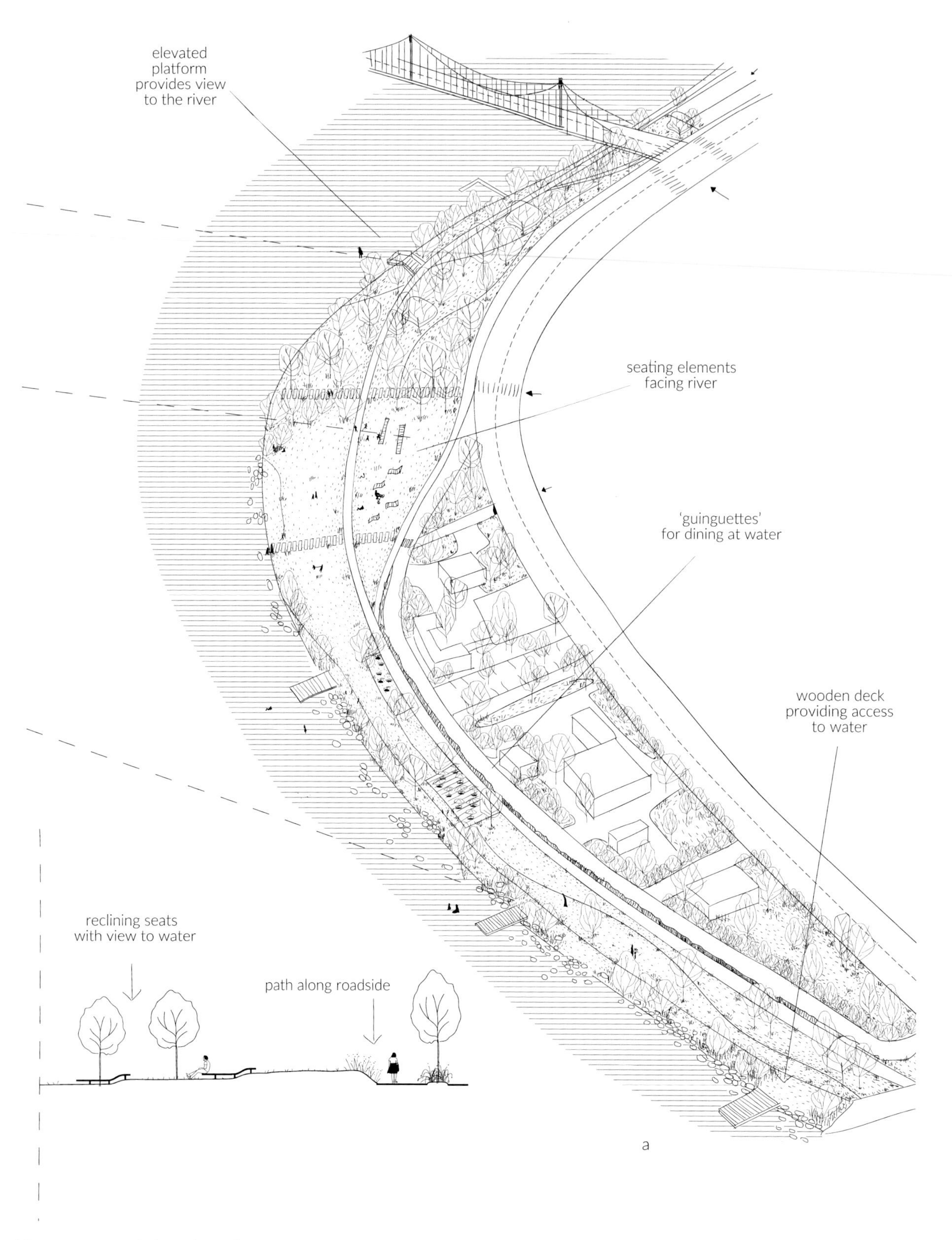

Figure 11.21a–d (continued)

River banks in Perreux-sur-Marne, France

The city of Perreux-sur-Marne has re-established the relationship to its river, considering it one of the main features of the city's attention in terms of improving its environmental qualities to tackle while combining that with the desire of the community to bring locals and visitors back to the banks of the Marne. The project, initiated by the city, was planned and built by BASE landscape designers + Champalbert hydrologic engineering in 2013. It was designed with an extended boardwalk to allow different uses and crossings on a quite limited site. It is connected by a sequence of meeting places equipped with pontoons and benches along the Marne and includes a playful garden in the centre.

Initially a holiday resort, Perreux became a mid-size city at the beginning of the 20th century, welcoming crowds of day-trippers from Paris to appreciate the bucolic setting of the banks of the Marne. Up to the 18th century, small houses were built on the slope of the undeveloped banks. Only a few laundry boats, public baths or fishing pontoons were installed, but the channelling of the watercourse to facilitate trade traffic led to the conversion of the riverbanks to hard surfaces.

The new appearance of the place was reinforced by emphasising the bucolic setting of the riverbanks. The design thus incorporated the atmosphere of a grove. Due to the almost village-like character of the neighbouring settlement, accessibility was enhanced for pedestrians and light traffic. The pathway is not immediately noticed when entering the area, and the materials used fit the ambience of the surrounding. This approach also allows a layering of the vegetation by combining contemporary urban planting practices with sustainable water ecology.

The project has brought back the people, flora and fauna to the banks of the river. The water and urban edges have been softened by converting former concrete flood defences into vegetated engineered slopes. This has been achieved by removing the masonry blocks and accepting seasonal flooding to widen the variety of different environments. People are attracted to the water when the riverbanks become accessible, especially when new aquatic and terrestrial plants, different surfaces, lighting and furniture were added to allow people to spend time near the water. The types of seating provided are made of wood and constructed for different user needs; it offers an outdoor gym and children's play areas and can be accessed from the river by the jetty (Figure 11.22).

Figure 11.22
A boardwalk facing the Marne
(*Source*: ©BASE)

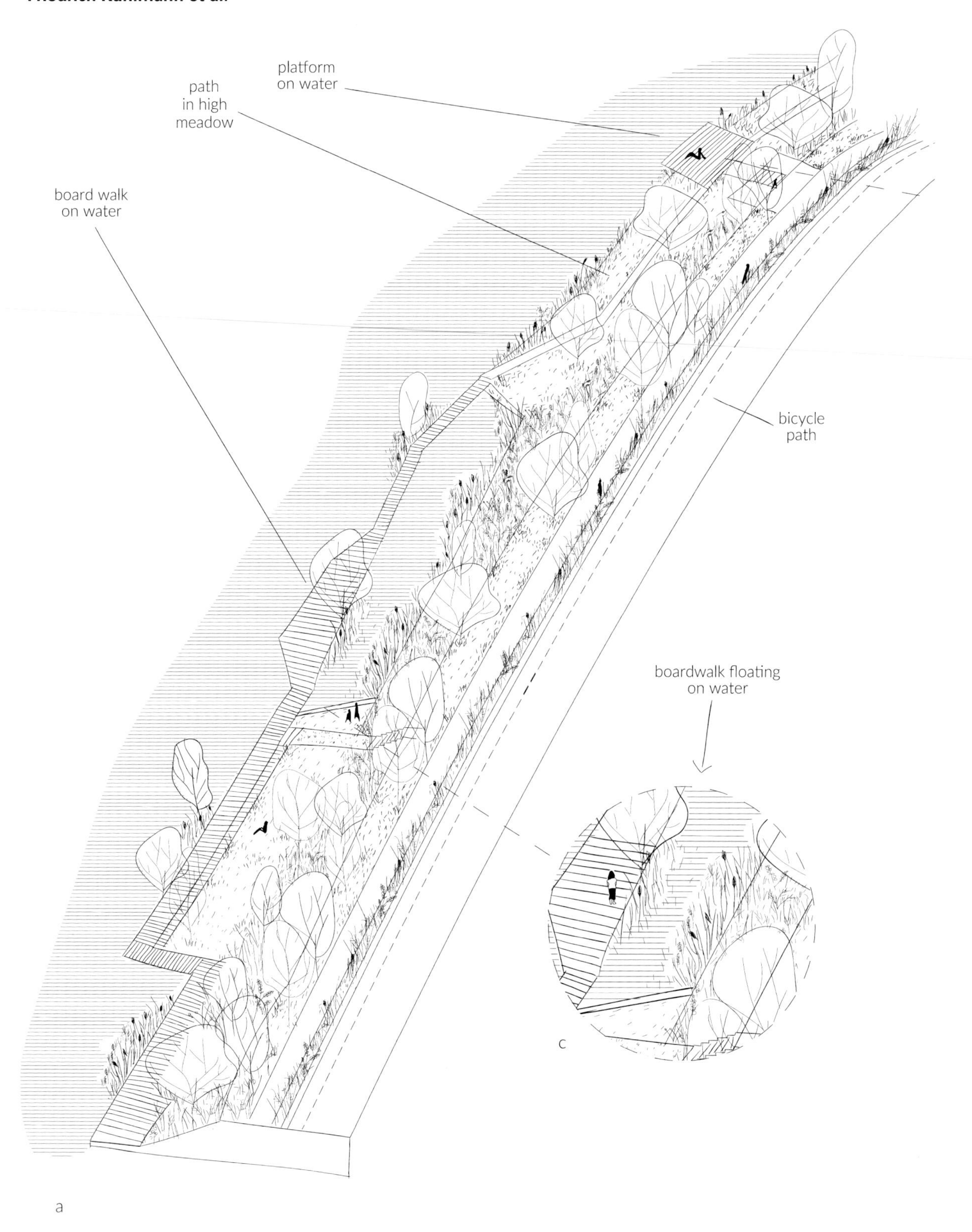

Figure 11.23a–d

a) The Marne boardwalk project uses the narrow space between river and road resourcefully, including the creation of additional space by providing a boardwalk on the water; b) the entrance and platform are connected; c) the boardwalk on the water, providing a new site for riparian vegetation; d) a section from the street down to the platform

(*Source*: Anna Wilczyńska and Jekaterina Balicka)

Project quality rating assessment

The accessibility of this site as a recreation area was improved by the rediscovery of the Marne riverbank to provide a promenade. The design quality is good, although it performs lower for cultural heritage aspects, due to the fact that there is not much historical material to consider, just a symbolic connection. Facilities are quite well provided, although the site is exposed to wind and lacks shade in places. For health and well-being, it shows weakness in the sense of being away due to the very built-up environment. Thus, it supports health and well-being benefits for local inhabitants, allowing people to embrace the beauty of this environment. Water connections are generally good, apart from direct access into the water or water activities as well as lacking safety equipment. Children's play is very well provided for, but the range of possible water sports activities is somewhat limited by the given terrain and nature of the design. A good project making excellent use of limited space in a peri-urban context. Figure 11.23 shows how it has been analysed using sketches.

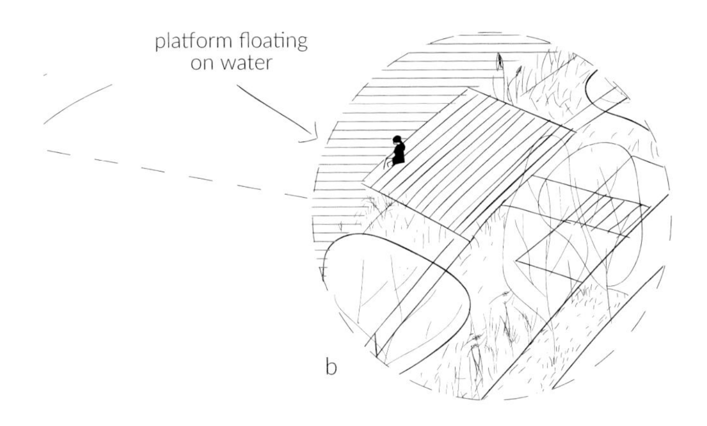

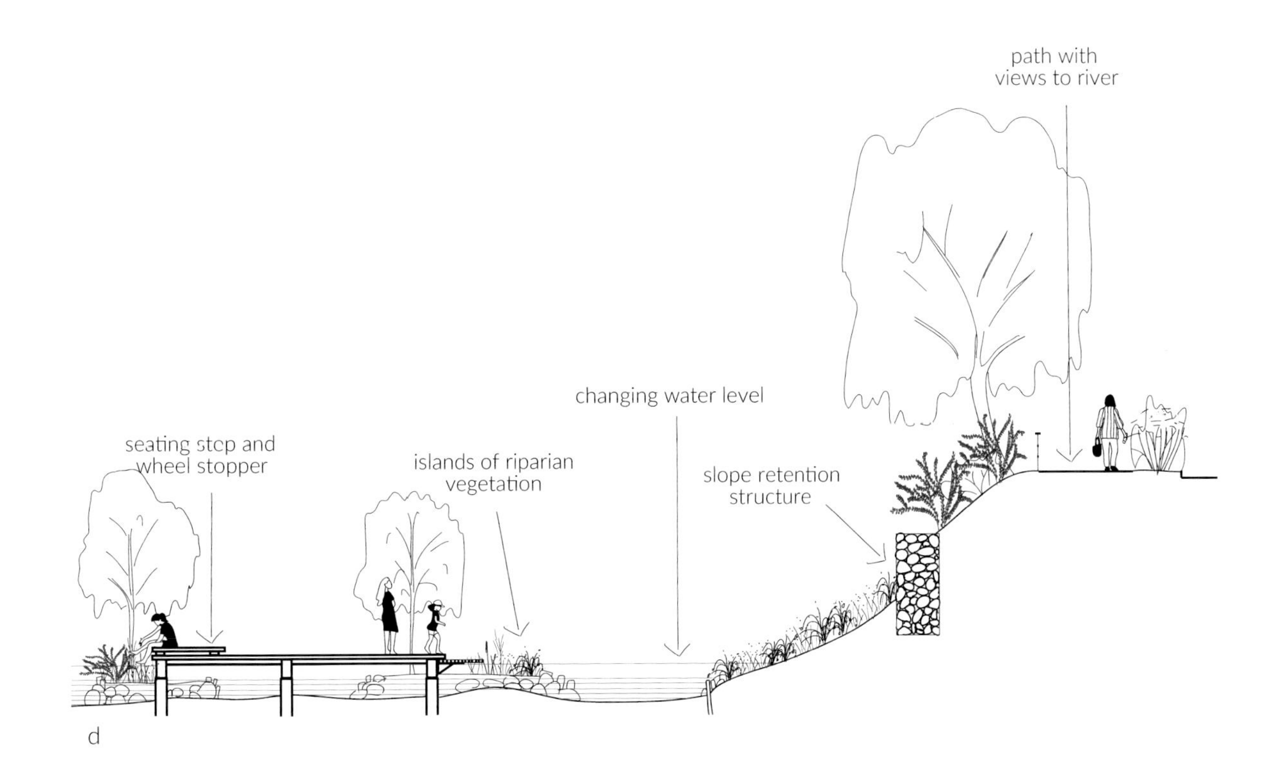

Figure 11.23a–d (continued)

Red Ribbon Tanghe River Park, Qinhuangdao City, China

The Red Ribbon Tanghe River Park in Qinhuangdao City, China, is a river landscape project integrating decidedly artistic elements into an almost-forgotten natural terrain with overgrown vegetation. It was initiated by the municipality and planned and constructed in 2006 by an interdisciplinary design team assembled under the lead of TurenScape landscape architects. This red ribbon follows a linear corridor for 500 metres in an area of about 20 hectares, integrating lighting, seating and orientation signs. It shows how a minimal but distinctive design solution improves the surrounding river landscape. It preserves as much of the natural river as possible, while a process of urbanisation happens nearby.

Despite the urbanisation process, the project keeps the ecological processes of the site intact by inventing an urban river that goes beyond the traditional way of presenting a landscape image under human control that completely restrains natural processes. The project is located on the Tanghe River at the growing urban fringe of Qinhuangdao, and the site is covered with lush native vegetation that provides diverse habitats. It was a rubbish dump with deserted sheds, huts and irrigation facilities, once used for farming. Although the site offered some recreational uses such as fishing or jogging in the past, it was virtually inaccessible for most visitors. Thus, the site conditions presented opportunities as well as challenges for the design solution.

The major design challenge was how to preserve the natural habitats along the river while reacting to new affordances evolving from the increasing population. So instead of replacing lush nature with hard pavement and ornamental flower beds, the new red ribbon design was implemented. The ribbon itself is a long, red-coloured bench covering a former irrigation ditch wall, integrating a boardwalk made of fibre steel, which is lit from inside, with plants growing in well-placed holes in the ribbon. Along the path, cloud-shaped steel pergolas located at strategic meeting points provide shade, accompanied by a patchwork of perennial flower gardens (Figure 11.24). The red ribbon links the natural vegetation and the new flower gardens, providing a structural instrument to reorganise the former unkempt and inaccessible site.

Figure 11.24
A cloud pavilion at the Red Ribbon River Park
(*Source*: Turenscape)

This minimal intervention turned the formerly inaccessible waterfront into a recreational area. The Red Ribbon is a central element weaving the site together, while the park maintains the natural state of the vegetation that changes depending on the water level. The intervention creates spaces for people to rediscover their nearby urban wilderness.

Project quality rating assessment

This project appears to perform unequally when compared to others in this chapter. Accessibility is good, apart from its visibility from a distance and for car parking. The design quality is also rated highly, apart from the lack of reference to cultural heritage which, given its origins as quite a new landscape, is obvious. Facilities are generally good, though the wind shelter and the range of facilities could be higher in this respect. The health and well-being potential is outstanding, mainly since the area is set within a lush woody landscape with few signs of human activity. Water access, apart from visual access, is impossible given the terrain, so naturally it is assessed as rather low. Physical activity is clearly limited to children's play while providing good activity zoning. A very iconic and original design creates a new image and strong genius loci. Figure 11.25 shows how it has been analysed with sketches.

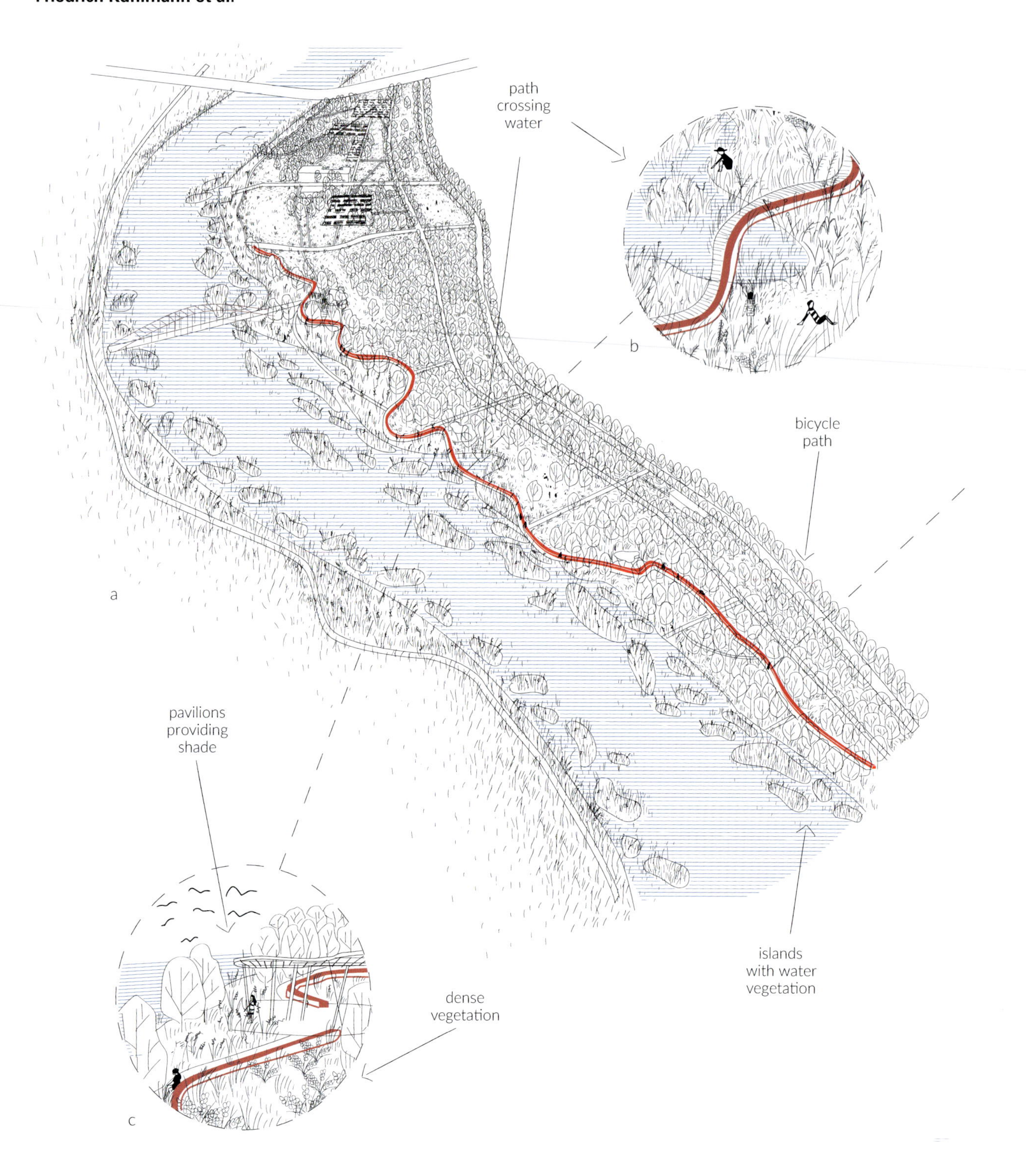

Figure 11.25a–f

a) Overview of the design concept for the Red Ribbon River Park embedded into the existing environment; b) the boardwalk crosses water and wetland; c) detail of the educational platform; d) the boardwalk weaves through dense vegetation; e) a section showing the relationship of the Red Ribbon and the boardwalk near the river; f) a cross-section through the recreational platform with the pavilion

(*Source*: Anna Wilczyńska and Jekaterina Balicka)

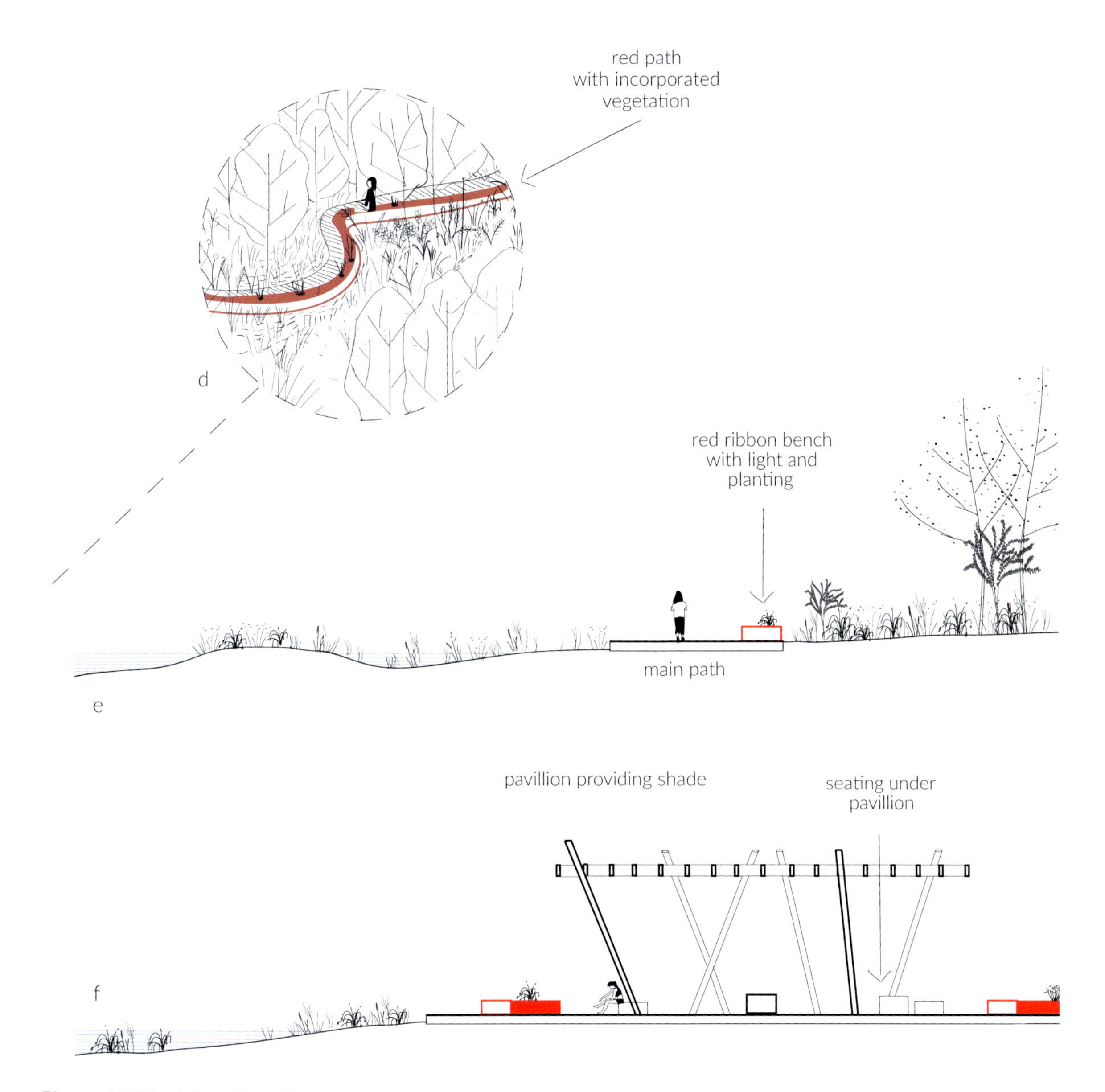

Figure 11.25a–f (continued)

Tagus Linear Park, Vila Franca de Xira, Portugal

The Tagus Linear Park is a15-ha area designed and completed in 2013 by the team of Topiaris landscape architecture for the Municipality of Vila Franca De Xira in Portugal. It connects neighbouring, growing urban communities with the riverside close to both water and industrial enterprises. The challenge was to develop an urban public space located in a complex urban industrial, agricultural and natural landscape while protecting and developing the existing fragile natural system and maintaining the ecological regeneration of damaged former industrial areas. This part of the river is close to its mouth, so it is dominated by industrial purposes, being easily accessed by shipping. It separated residents from the water and paid no any attention to the natural marsh ecology, public access or recreational opportunities.

The park consists of two different sectors: a square connected to the river and a network of trails (Figure 11.26). The square was designed to keep its sense of place and is the area where most of the park facilities are placed and

Figure 11.26
Birds-eye view of the Tagus Linear Park
(*Source*: Photographer Joao Morgado)

most recreational activities happen. The other sector is the connection of cultural, recreational and natural aspects by a network of trails. These provide the main spatial structure, consisting of both elevated and ground-level paths which bring people to the riverfront. In a sense, they act as a threshold to the river, giving the visitor a feeling of an arrival at the water and a sense of being away.

The marshland was protected and developed along the riverfront to restore ecological functioning after the impacts of industrial use. The existing vegetation in the square was preserved and extended in a formal pattern of compact protected clusters of native sand-connected species on mounds, which contrast with the extensive sandy area. Together with existing and newly planted trees, these clusters create a green environment. The park contains a diverse arrangement of facilities that provides attractions catering to the active visitor and calm spaces for watching birds or wildlife. Other structures include the educational Centre for Environmental and Landscape Interpretation, built from reused containers; a volleyball court; a children's playground; a bird observatory; and wooden shade structures parallel to the paths that provide opportunities for relaxation.

Project quality rating assessment

This project shows good accessibility, apart from public transport, as well as its visibility from a distance. The overall design quality is good, apart from potentially high costs of maintenance and views. It generally does well for facilities, especially offering a wide range of facilities. The health and well-being aspects are also generally well provided for, and this place also has a strong genius loci and opportunities for contemplation. Overall, it is a fine example of a project in this context making good use of a place to enhance the natural qualities with great design features and sensitivity to the site. Figure 11.27 presents the sketched analysis of the project.

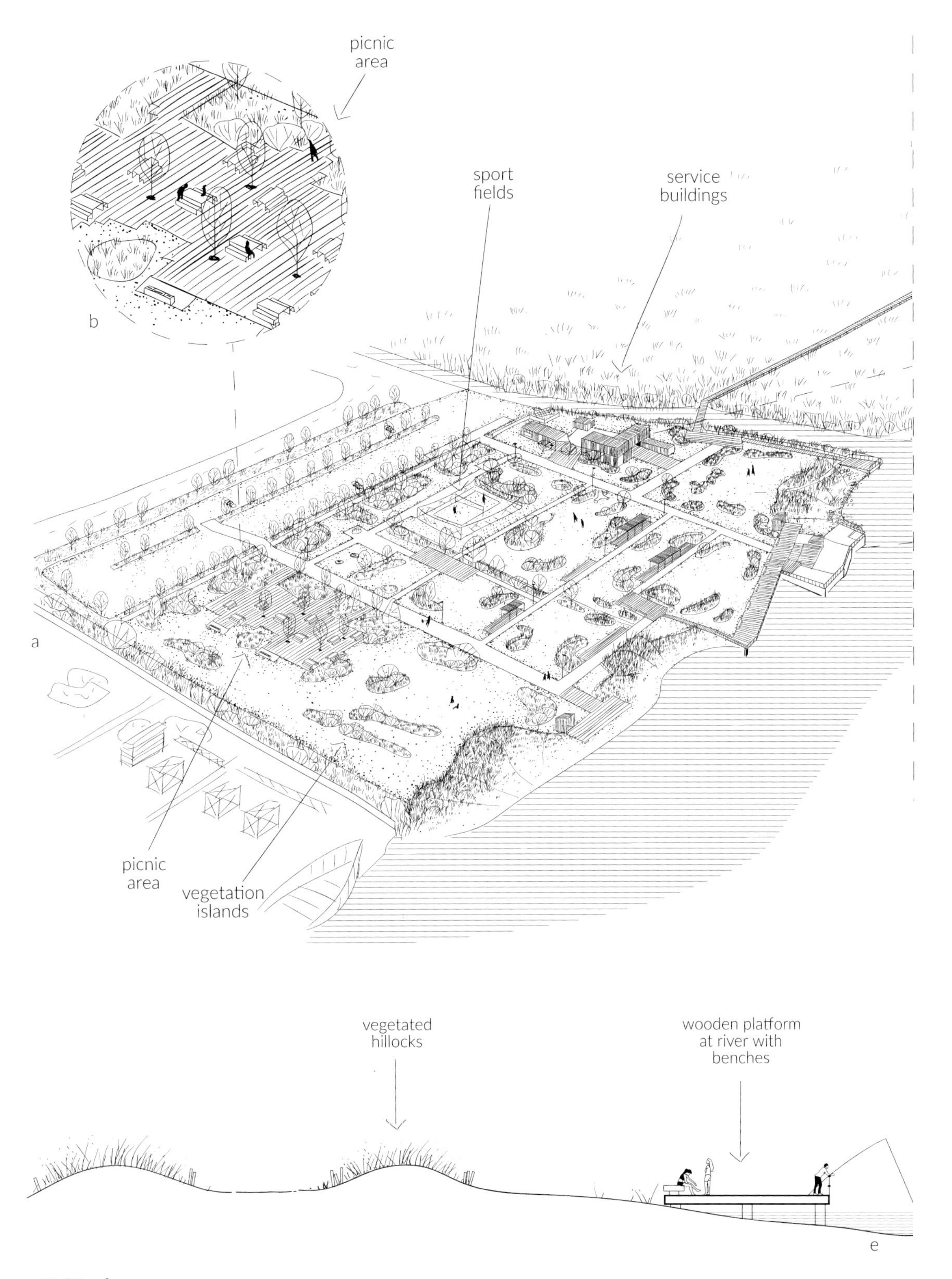

Figure 11.27a–f

a) Design concept of Tagus Linear Park with the main recreational area, boardwalk and bird-watching platform; b) detail of the decked picnic area; c) the service area with old industrial remains; d) the deck and platforms at the Tagus River; e) cross-section through the wooden deck at the water; f) detail of the bird-watching platform and hide

(*Source*: Anna Wilczyńska and Jekaterina Balicka)

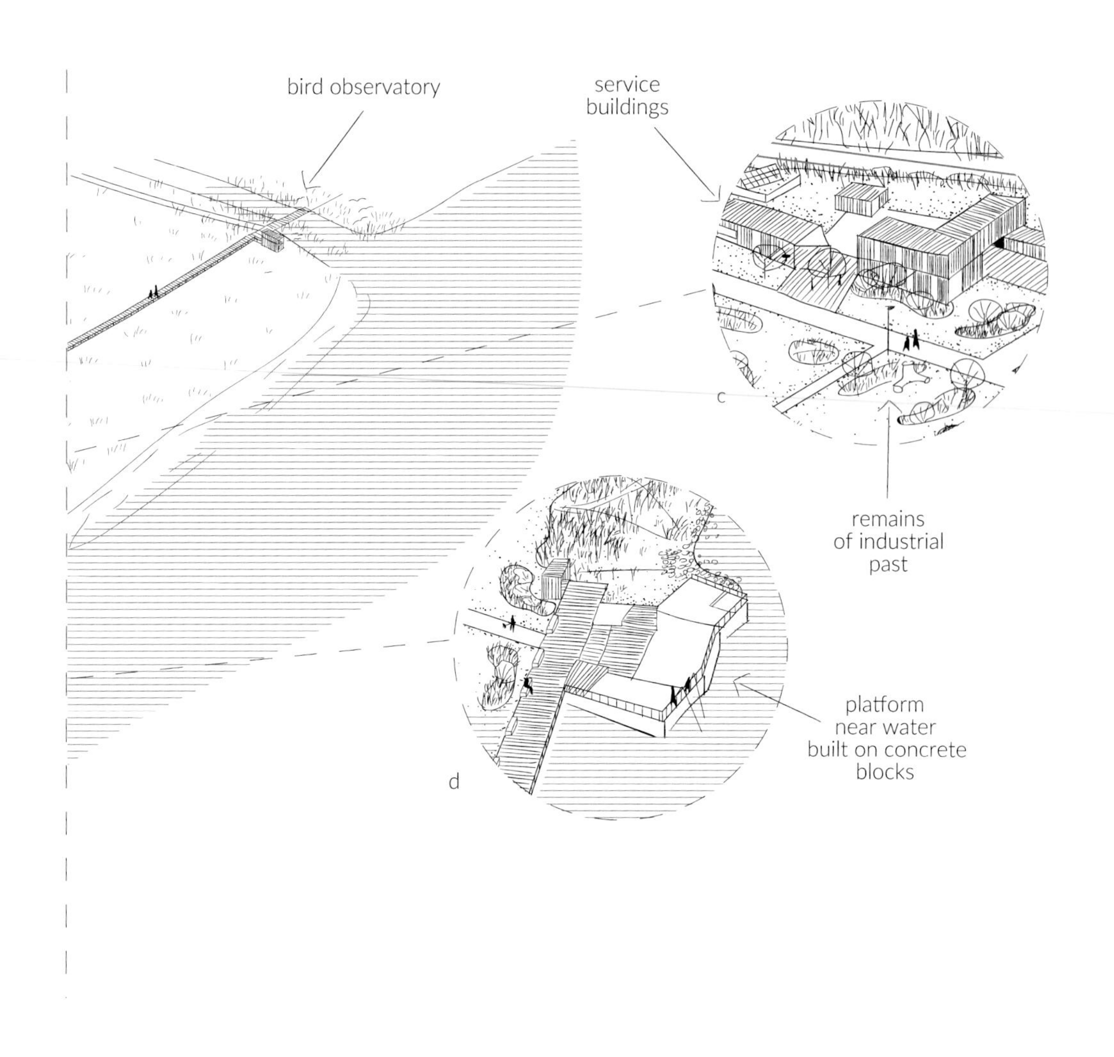

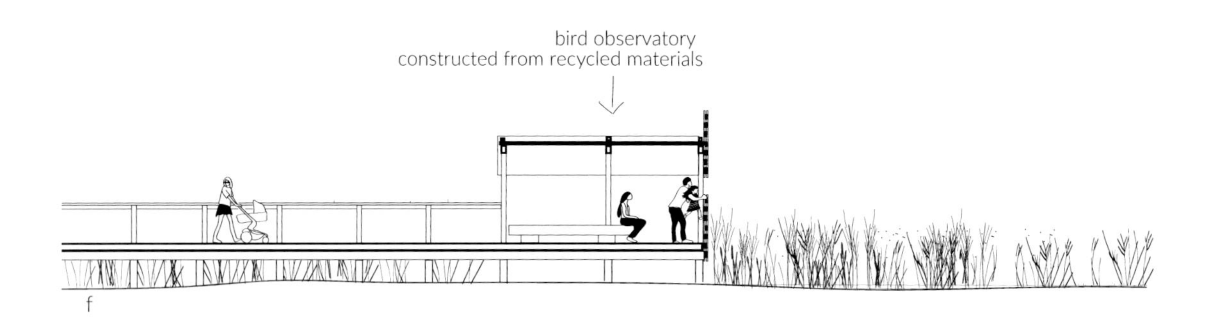

Figure 11.27a–f (continued)

Comparison of projects in terms of different aspects

General design aspects

The projects presented in this chapter were chosen for their versatility, originality and contextual fitting. They exhibit quite a lot of similar qualities connected to linear water bodies. The projects are often connected with the sense of place aspects and introduce creative solutions to the respective situations according to the project objectives. Many have been competition winners and demonstrate that provocative and innovative solutions are possible even in congested linear spaces such as the Rhône riverbank or the Chicago Riverwalk. References to cultural history are an aspect which is only a feature of some of the designs, such as the Rochetaillée banks of the Sâone or the revitalisation of the River Aire, while many projects appear in places where none were present before, as in Norges or the where the architects found little to refer to, as in Aalborg.

Potential for enhancing health and well-being

Almost all projects display several opportunities to improve health and well-being. Physical activities near the water are provided in most, and the projects generally aim to attract and facilitate these as an integral part of the design, as at the Tagus Linear Park. De-stressing, getting closer to nature or simple contemplation may have more potential in some places such as the Norges Boardwalk or the Red Ribbon Park. However, most river edges are quite exposed to sun and wind; therefore, the presence of shade and shelter provided by the projects is not always sufficient.

Accessibility

All the sites are very accessible, even though, because of their spatial context and design idea, they sometimes only have two or three entrances, as at Norges Boardwalk, Red Ribbon and Tagus Linear Park, or are separated from their surroundings by infrastructure, as at the Rochetaillée banks of the Sâone. While the Cheonggyecheon project has an issue with only offering steps and elevators to access its famous lowered promenade, in most projects, an accessible design for all projects by ramps and wide paths is provided.

Interaction with water

River waterfronts are in general connected to the water, with good access as a consequence of their history, as shown in the introduction to this chapter. All projects have demonstrated a design approach which enables direct, visual and symbolic access to the water and an overall connection to the river. The cases of Soestbach and Cheonggyecheon demonstrate how the historical water body was reopened and brought back into the city space after it was inaccessible due to previous canalisation. In the case of the Chicago Riverwalk, the water was not hidden but definitely lacked possibilities to socialise or to be near the water; now users are taken almost to the edge. A similar approach was applied in Perreux-sur-Marne and in Velenje, where besides recreational opportunities in the latter project, the steps to the water also provide a place for social events. In the case of the Rochetaillée banks, the visual connection to the river is mostly created by dramatically changing views while walking on the elevated promenade. Sometimes water is not directly accessible, and at the Rhône riverbanks in Lyon, this problem was approached by adding a safe means of playing with water on the promenade itself. Another approach has been used in Aalborg, where a safeguarded lido was arranged as a seasonal extension to the promenade. These approaches can also be found in projects described in Chapters 12, 14 and 15. Finally, contact with water can be enabled through the perception of related ecosystems and plant communities, as demonstrated in the cases at Soestbach, Perreux-sur-Marne, Red Ribbon, Cheonggyecheon and Tagus Linear Park.

Seating and opportunities for socialising

All projects offer seating, often in conjunction with large decks or terraces, as at the Alborg waterfront; linear benches along riverbanks, as at the Rhône riverbank or the Chicago Riverwalk; or hybrid seating and strolling solutions, as in Velenje city centre. Of course, at many riversides, informal seating on the ground is also an option, and it is possible for users to bring their own blanket, as at the Rochetaillée banks of the Sâone or Tagus Linear Park.

Use of materials

The narrow variety of materials and their discreet constructive appearance in most projects reviewed here are important features, since the local atmosphere and the flowing water are the main components. Concrete is used in Velenje and at the Rhône riverbank, but timber is also extensively used in decking, such as at Aalborg or the Aire, as well as the boardwalks at Norges and Perreux-sur-Marne. Rocks and stone are also used to some extent for walls and directing the water, as at Soest. The use of these materials, such as concrete or raw wood, is clearly connected with the aim to reduce maintenance costs.

Use of vegetation and ecological aspects

In many projects, the planting of new vegetation plays only a minor role, but at many sites, there are plenty of existing trees and shrubs, and some sites, such as Norges, have an existing high ecological value and corresponding sensitivities. Some rows of trees and ornamental plants were planted in the Cheonggyecheon project, while in Tagus Linear Park and Aire, the design introduced newly sown grassed areas. Groups of trees as small groves were occasionally established in Lyon or clusters of shrubs, such as the artificial dune vegetation in Aalborg. Water plants and reeds were used at Red Ribbon and the riverbank at Perreux-sur-Marne, where the boardwalks traverse a humid, sometimes boggy environment.

Site management and maintenance

All projects seem to be well maintained, and many have been in use for over five years and are relatively crowded during favourable seasons so that renovation and further maintenance would already be necessary. If the construction followed a high standard and used appropriate durable materials as well as good surveillance against vandalism, this usually leads to a reduced need for extensive maintenance. Nevertheless, the use of wooden elements and surfaces for seating, as in Aalborg, or boardwalks, as in Norges and Tagus, leads to a need for constant renovation, since it alters due to effects of the seasonality in Nordic climates and humid environments. Since these sites are also quite publicly exposed, they need to be kept clean, which helps to maintain them as socialising open spaces.

Conclusions and implications for practice

This chapter has reviewed the history and importance of riverbanks and connected linear public spaces as places for the benefit of health and well-being. The familiar spare-time promenading along specially constructed banks and the collective gazing at the flowing river continues, but the activities of the projects presented here make historical references while also introducing innovative and provocative responses following design competitions.

The projects presented here have their strengths and weaknesses according to a number of factors such as the local setting, the terrain, its respective history or climatic conditions. Nevertheless, each design team has endeavoured to boost the feasible opportunities and diminish the given constraints. At the same time, they have also produced solutions which provide improved opportunities to interact with water and to infuse a novel or even reimagined sense of place. These projects also have a significant impact on the local gastronomy and hospitality along the rivers, as well as on the advertised representations of the places they tackle.

Following the comparisons made, certain aspects stand out: the projects retain a context-specific design, so the differences in approaches of interacting with the water are based on each context. They demonstrate a wide range of design approaches to enhance this connection to the water by bringing people physically closer to the water, enabling direct contact to the water or safe access within the project area. Also, a wide range of activities near the water is presented by providing places for meetings and events, for looking and being looked at. The useful application of riparian vegetation helps to consolidate the riverbanks and establishes a near-natural environment, while the projects uncover the rich history of the urban river landscape and its cultural heritage to celebrate the pleasure of living, staying or just relaxing at the river.

References

Aversano-Schreiber, D. (2007) *Victor Hugos Rheinreise [Victor Hugo's Rhine journey]*, Scientia Nova. Das interdisziplinäre Wissenschaftsmagazin, Reinhold Kolb Verlag, Mannheim, Vol. 8, pp. 63–73

Hugo, V. (1842) *Le Rhin [the Rhine]*, Société d'éditions littéraires et artistique, Paris

Prominski, M., et al. (2012) *River Space Design: Planning Strategies Methods and Projects for Urban Rivers*, Birkhäuser, Basel

Rosenberg, E. (2019) *Before and After. Both. The Revitalization of the Aire River*, Landscape Architecture, Switzerland, pp. 122–133

Twain, M. (1883) *Life on the Mississippi*, James R. Osgood & Co., Boston. www.rijkswaterstaat.nl/water/waterbeheer/bescherming-tegen-het-water/maatregelen-om-overstromingen-te-voorkomen/ruimte-voor-de-rivieren/index.aspx (last visited 25.02.2021)

Chapter 12: Seafronts, beaches, lakesides and promenades

Simon Bell, Himansu S. Mishra, Anna Wilczyńska and Jekaterina Balicka

Introduction

When we think of obtaining the health benefits of blue spaces, we cannot help but think of the role that visiting the seaside and spending time on the beach or strolling along a promenade has had over several centuries. Visiting the seaside and sea-bathing has a history stretching back to the 18th century, when the wealthy upper and growing new upper-middle classes of the time began their obsession with health which had begun with the idea of taking water at spas. These had been set up by medical doctors on the basis of the claimed medical benefits of mineral water and hot springs (of course, visiting spas and drinking mineral water are still important sectors of the wellness industry today), which themselves went back to Roman times at least (with *Aquae Sulis* or Bath in England being one famous example). There were also older sea-bathing traditions in parts of Europe where the August tides were thought to have prophylactic properties.

The first examples of polite society taking up sea-bathing can be found in Yorkshire, at the fishing town of Whitby and then the spa town of Scarborough, today still popular holiday resorts (Walton, 1983). The year 1720 seems to be the start date for this transformation, but until the advent of the railways, travel to the seaside from London became synonymous with the south coast of England. Bath and its waters remained popular, but once the Prince Regent (the future King George IV) took up the habit, it was inevitable that Brighton would become the focus, together with lesser resorts to its east and west. This fashionable resort became the centre for a hedonistic lifestyle. The prince built the famous Moorish-style Pavilion, and the town expanded dramatically – between 1821 and 1831, it was one of the fastest-growing towns in England (the other being Bradford). The fashionable ladies and gentlemen spent their summer days strolling along the edge of the beach (promenading) and entering huts on wheels (bathing machines) which were drawn into the sea so that they could immerse themselves in the water for their health. The town also featured stylish houses, ballrooms and shops. In the same period, the idea of the picturesque and the sublime in landscape became popular trends, with mountains becoming popular places to visit (on the Grand Tour crossing the Alps) and the dramatic seascape also taking on a role.

By the 1840s, railway mania had taken hold in Britain, and this led to several social changes. First, travel to more distant places became much quicker, so that other towns on the extensive British coast could find a market as resorts. The second aspect was the possibility for the middle and then the working classes to travel by train to the seaside. The middle classes could afford to spend a week or so at a boarding house or hotel, while at first, the working classes could only make a day trip. This developed so that Blackpool became the first resort with a predominantly working-class clientele, accompanied by beach activities, fish and chips, amusement arcades and the Tower ballroom (Barton, 2005). Numerous other towns also became larger or smaller resorts, catering to holidays right through until the 1960s, when Spanish beach resorts became more affordable. Promenades to facilitate strolling, social interaction,

DOI: 10.4324/9780429056161-16

Figure 12.1
"Brighton: the front and the chain pier seen in the distance," by Frederick William Woledge (active 1840)
(*Source*: Public domain image courtesy of the Paul Mellon Collection, Yale Center for British Art, Yale University, New Haven, Connecticut)

Figure 12.2
Brighton beach with a view to the promenade and then the buildings lining it
(*Source*: Public domain photograph)

being seen and as a place to sit and enjoy the sunshine were one of the main investments, together with the pier, whose technical solution came with the development of cast-iron structures (Walton, 2000).

From its British origins in the 18th century, the modern seaside resort gradually assumed a global character. The concept has undergone many developments and reinventions over time and has generated stiff competition for the British market, a competition intensified in recent years as a result of cheaper travel on budget airlines.

Surprisingly, however, despite is highs and lows, it has remained a popular and valued feature of tourism, and during the crash of the late 2000s, it was to some extent reinvented for "staycations". Some notable reinvestments in promenades and other infrastructure can also be seen, rebranding and upgrading some once-tired towns.

Seaside resorts also began to appear on the French Channel coast and in the Low Countries (now Belgium and the Netherlands) by the late 18th century. From the early 19th century, Normandy and southwest France – centred on Biarritz – but also northern Germany and even parts of Scandinavia became developed for the national markets as the bourgeoisie of those countries increased in number and wealth and wanted to emulate the British middle classes (Corbin, 1995). Later on, the Spanish Atlantic coast also saw the introduction of seaside resorts. The Mediterranean, now synonymous with beach holidays, developed rather later. The French and Italian Riviera first saw developments based on the restoration of health through climate – especially in the wake of epidemics of tuberculosis, where warm climates could slow the progress of the disease – rather than sea-bathing. However, by the mid-19th century, some important Italian resorts had grown up on the Adriatic coast, where German and especially Austrian visitors formed the key market, since these territories were, at the time, part of the Austro-Hungarian Empire and newly accessibly by train. Rimini was one among several such resorts established by the end of the 19th century. Up to this time, the seaside resort was for healthy air, taking the waters, immersion in the sea for health and other social activities.

The Mediterranean as the premier maritime tourist playground of today – the French Riviera and Côte d'Azur in particular – was established by the fashionable sets of the 1920s and 1930s with the new vogue for sunbathing and personal display on warm and languid beaches (Boyer, 2002). While the benefits of sunshine for health were identified in the early 20th century, it was the 1920s when fashion designer Coco Chanel accidentally got sunburnt while visiting the French Riviera. When she arrived back in Paris, she sported a suntan; her friends liked the look and started to adopt darker skin tones themselves. Tanned skin also became a trend because of Coco's status and the longing for her lifestyle by other members of society. In addition, Parisians also fell in love with Josephine Baker, a "caramel-skinned" singer in Paris in the 1920s, and idolised her dark skin. These two women were leading figures of the transformation that tanned skin underwent, in which it became perceived as fashionable, healthy and luxurious. Jean Patou capitalised on the new tanning fad, launching the first suntan oil, "Huile de Chaldee", in 1927. From this, the modern beach holiday developed (Cross and Walton, 2005). European resorts also developed features to distinguish them from their British origins. There were more relaxed attitudes to bathing (including issues surrounding modesty and the mingling of the sexes on the beach), casino gambling, drinking, Sunday observance and public dancing than were to be found in Britain. The popularity of Spanish beaches and the development of the Costas was delayed by the Civil War until the 1950s and 1960s. Greece also followed a little later, and Turkey has become the latest Mediterranean coastline to be developed, especially attracting tourists from Russia and Eastern Europe.

Promenades or esplanades have for a long time been the typical structure marking the division between beach and urban area in most sea coastal resorts. As a general rule, there is a long row of beachfront hotels, guest houses, restaurants and bars separated from the promenade by a road, then a long, continuous wide walking path with steps and ramps leading down to the beach. A very good example of this can be found in Tel Aviv, where the entire Mediterranean frontage of the city comprises a well-provisioned promenade. In tidal seas, the extent of sand varies through the day, and the esplanade may increasingly function as a flood defence and to hold back storms. There are other types of promenade with a backdrop of parks or more natural landscapes, and in cities with cliffs instead of beaches, access to the sea is facilitated with more engineered structures. Countries with dangerous waters – for example, due to currents or the presence of sharks – have also developed methods of enabling visitors to get in contact with the sea through indirect means.

Figure 12.3
Part of the promenade at Tel Aviv, Israel
(*Source*: Simon Bell)

Why the cases were chosen

For the selection of cases to present in this chapter and to show the range of recent examples of the interface between the sea or lakes and different types of urban coastline or seaside, we looked for originality in concept and design, variety of location and type and something extra which makes them stand out. We also looked for examples which to some extent offer continuity in the tradition of the beachfront or seaside promenade, as well as unique solutions to specific problems. We consider that water bodies such as the ocean, sea or lakes often provide similar features – beaches (whether sandy, shingly or rocky) and cliffs which may be linked directly to the urban fabric or connected to a park or more natural area yet still within the urban context. The ocean or sea may at times present significant dangers through strong currents, waves, tides or storms or possibly risks from sharks. Thus, the cases present a set of different ways in which problems and opportunities have been combined in unique solutions. We have three main categories of projects: beaches, water access in the absence of safe beaches and a small category of solutions to gain access under difficult physical constraints.

Beaches

We start with the most traditional of seaside experiences, the sandy beach used for sunbathing and sea or lake swimming. These are perennially attractive, but it is often the junction between the beach and the edge of the city or other landscape which needs most attention. This may be the archetypal promenade, as discussed in the introduction, or it may be backed by a busy road or even a railway. Accessibility is often, therefore, the main issue to be solved. Protection of vulnerable habitats may also be necessary and the provision of facilities to mediate between people and landscape, to relieve pressure of numbers of people on sites with limited capacity. The projects included in this section are as follows:

- Dover Esplanade, Dover, England, United Kingdom
- Playa de Poniente, Benidorm, Spain
- Vinaròs promenade, Vinaròs, Spain
- Amager Beach, Copenhagen, Denmark
- Sea Park, Saulkrasti, Latvia
- Myrtle Edwards Park, Seattle, United States

Projects providing access, safe swimming and artificial beaches

The next set of projects use a lot of construction to create safe, accessible places where people can enjoy proximity to the sea or lake without facing a range of risks. They also provide unique ways of experiencing the blue spaces. These projects supply opportunities and solutions to problems which need imagination and creativity. They also include cultural and historical connections. The projects included in this section are as follows:

- Veules-les-Roses, France
- Sugar Beach, Toronto, Canada
- Cairns Esplanade-Swimming Lagoon, Cairns, Australia
- Paprocany Waterfront, Tychy, Poland
- Sjövikstorget, Stockholm, Sweden
- Sea Organ, Zadar, Croatia

Visual and physical access to the water landscape

The last and smallest category of projects includes cases where obtaining direct access to the water – the sea or lake – is especially challenging, mainly due to steep terrain. The solutions may not be able to overcome all the challenges for all possible users as a result, but they provide some spectacular opportunities for views out over the water. The projects included in this section are as follows:

- Bondi Bronte coastal walk, Sydney Australia
- Concordia University lakeshore, Concordia University, Wisconsin

Each project is briefly described (based on information from a range of sources, often the designer or articles, as well as what the authors have seen). It is then illustrated with a photograph of a typical view, assessed for project quality based on the factors presented in Chapter 10 and illustrated using a set of sketches designed to bring out the key aspects which make the project special and inspirational. These are presented as annotated images, and they aim to complement the text visually, so there is no additional description in the text, only the captions.

Beaches: Dover Esplanade, Dover, Kent, England

This project is essentially a reworking of a traditional seaside promenade concept to provide a clear edge between the beach of the English Channel and Dover town as well as to enable universal access and shelter and, above all, to create a new sense of identity and place through the use of sculptural elements integral to the design – in fact, combining design and art through the exploration of the wave form. The project was designed by Tonkin Liu for a group of clients including the Dover Harbour Board, Dover District Council, Kent County Council, SEEDA and English Heritage. It was completed and opened in 2010. The project was conceived as three artworks known as the Lifting Wave, the Resting Wave and the Lighting Wave and was the winner of a design competition. The project consists

Figure 12.4
A view along the Dover promenade showing the different waves which form the design
(*Source*: Courtesy of Tonkin Liu)

of a new 3,500-m^2 promenade to connect Dover's eastern and western docks and includes a Sea Sports Centre and a crossing linked to a tunnel connecting the seafront to the central town square. The designers used a method they call "asking, looking, playing, making" to investigate the character and potential of the place, the three sculpture/promenade elements being the result.

The Lifting Wave is a repeated set of pre-cast white concrete ramps and steps to connect the Esplanade to the lower shingle beach. It includes a surface that catches the light as well as being universally accessible. Plants and a rainwater collector follow the ramps downwards. The Resting Wave is a retaining wall that runs the length of the Esplanade. It is notable for providing bays with seating, giving shelter and sun together. The surface of the wall creates shadows and prevents glare. The Lighting Wave is a line of white columns with artwork to follow the form of the sea wall and terrace as well as to improve lighting. The designers claim that the three waves each refer to place, respond to the seafront and fulfil social functions.

Project quality rating assessment

This project is particularly strong in accessibility, except for the visibility of the site (and therefore its visual accessibility), which is a little hidden due to its lower elevation. The design quality is also excellent, although the project may be a little costly to maintain. The range of facilities is good, although shade and especially shelter are weaker due to the exposed south-facing location. For health and well-being, it shows weakness in the sense of being away (it is backed by the urban setting and has views of ferry terminals) and contact with nature, being in a very built environment. It also rates generally highly for accessibility and connection to water but lacks safety equipment. Physical activity opportunities are generally good for most informal types but not for formal ones. Overall, it is a very good project. Figure 12.5a–c shows the interpretation of the design using drawings.

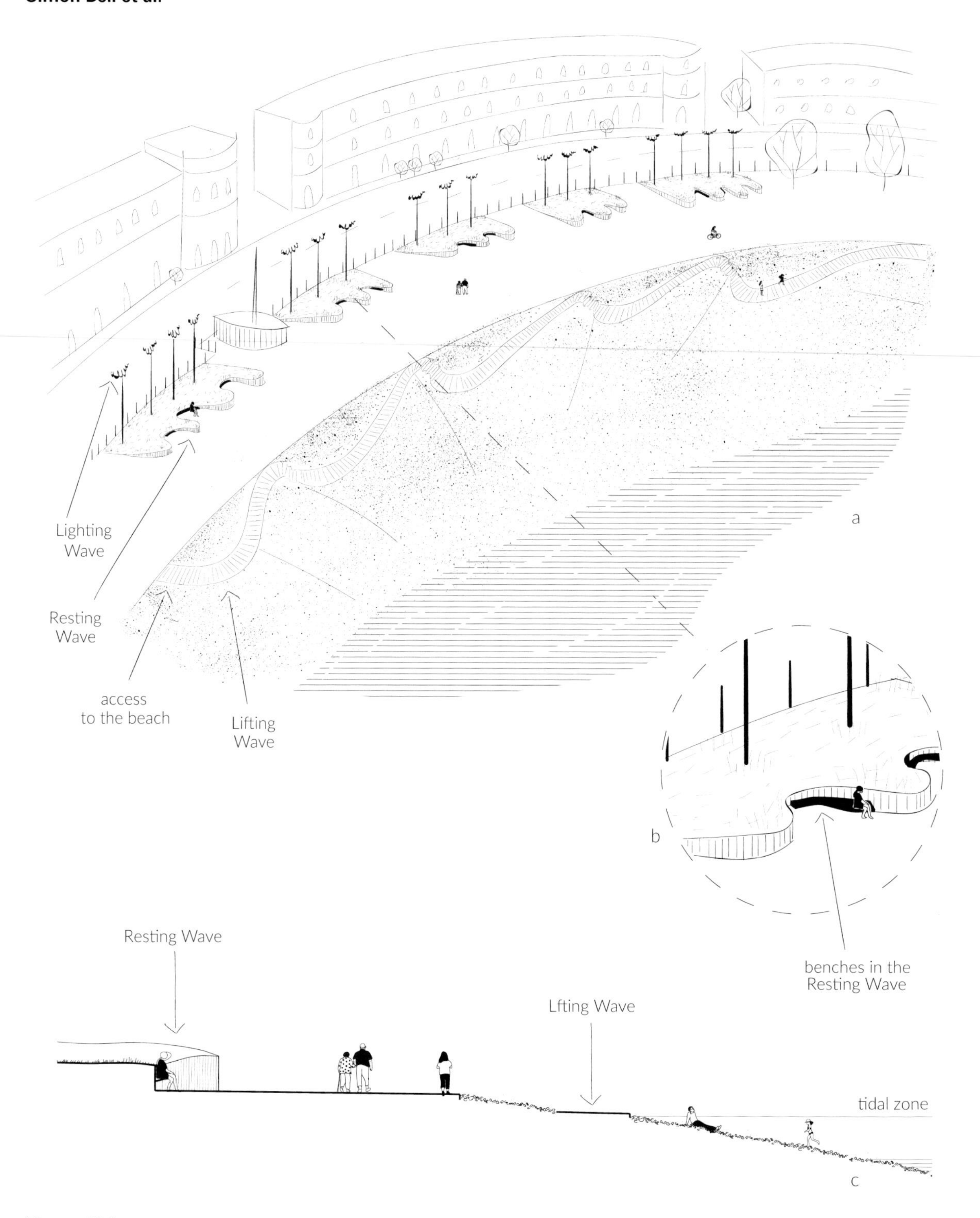

Figure 12.5a–c

a) The design concept of the Dover promenade wave construction not only reflects the idea of the sea but also forms very effective benches providing shelter. The sketch brings out the design of the marine-themed lighting and also the beach path with its wavy shape, providing a strong sense of unity; b) the three-dimensional form of the wave wall with the integral benches offering sheltered, sociable seating; c) a section across the promenade from the street to the beach demonstrating how it accommodates changes in level and tidal variation

Playa de Poniente, Benidorm, Spain

This project is another reworking of a promenade along the extremely busy beach at the bustling resort of Benidorm, designed by Carlos Ferrater at the Office of Architecture Barcelona and completed in 2009. A four-lane highway and lots of car parks with only limited access points down to the beach has been transformed by constructing a wave-like promenade with better access and also shade while reducing the traffic. Benidorm has long since been a resort which has recently wished to improve its image and to move upmarket. Improving the beachfront and esplanade has been central to this.

The promenade therefore forms a new transitional space between the built city and the natural sea and beach (Figure 12.6). The architect designed it not as a frontier/borderline but as an intermediary space for a permeable transition. It is designed to be a dynamic space for strolling and observing the sea and includes different stopping and relaxing points. The promenade functions by channelling longitudinal and transverse circulations and allows easy access to the beach. In ways similar to the design at Dover, a series of sinuous interwoven lines is used to

Figure 12.6

A typical view along the Playa de Poniente showing the distinctive colour themes, waving profile and overhanging walls, with the dense urban fabric immediately behind

(*Source*: Carlos Ferrater and Xavier Martí, OAB)

create a form which evokes natural and organic shapes similar to the motion of waves and tides and also the fractal structure of a cliff. The promenade follows a three-layer structure: the first uses white concrete to establish the perimeter line, the second uses paving in different colours and the third layer comprises the street furniture and the water and vegetation. All these contribute to a unified and harmonious whole. The place is also functional, as explained by the designer and clearly visible in the design: all aspects being brought together: the promenade, rest and relaxation area, vantage points, transition to the beach, architectural barriers, direct access to parking, rainwater collectors, beach lighting, road communication, integration of street furniture, services infrastructure and so on.

Project quality rating assessment

This project has excellent accessibility, apart from its visibility from a distance and for car parking – deliberately reduced as one of the main design aims, so not a negative aspect here. The design quality is good, although it includes few cultural heritage aspects due to the fact that there are none to take into account. It may also be rather costly to maintain. It is well endowed with facilities, although for such an extensive promenade, the amount of seating seems to be rather low, it lacks shade in such a sun-exposed area and some areas may not be well lit at night. For health and well-being, being a very busy and urban place, it has limitations in a sense of being away and may be a place with some risk to safety, such as from crime, due to the large numbers of relaxed visitors there. Water accessibility is very good, except for access from the water (no jetties) and activities in the water – swimming, of course, but not a lot else. The amount of safety equipment appears to be rather limited for such a busy beach. There are plenty of physical activities possible on the beach and also walking and jogging and so on along the promenade itself. A very iconic and original design which creates a new image and strong genius loci. Figure 12.7a–d shows the interpretation of the design using drawings.

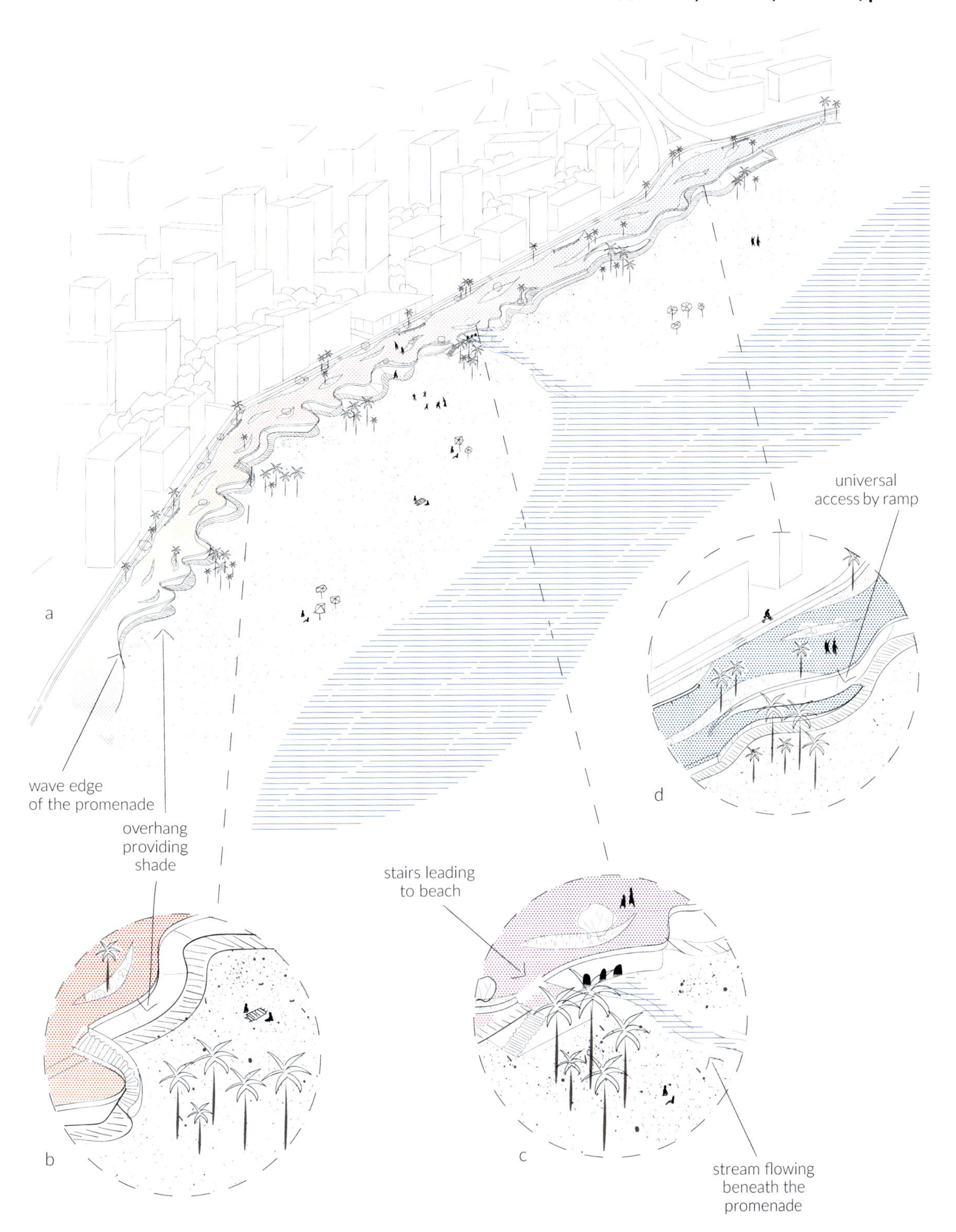

Figure 12.7a–d

a) General overview of the Playa de Poniente showing how the promenade acts as a connector, viewing deck and shelter simultaneously. It also depicts the spectral gradient of the colours used in the surfacing; b) the access points showing how the stairs are integrated into the structure; c) the watercourse flows beneath the promenade and across the beach to the sea; d) detail of the ramp providing universal access down to the beach

Vinaròs promenade, Vinaròs, Spain

This project dates to 2007 and was designed for the town of Vinaròs, the most northerly town in the Valencia region in Spain, by Guallart Architects, following the design winning first prize in a national competition. During the 20th century, urban growth led to the construction of a seafront promenade that was a focus of attraction for the 1960s Spanish tourist boom. By avoiding the huge developments of the 1980s onwards, it was possible to revitalise the area without having to demolish such developments. Rejuvenating the promenade presented an opportunity to define the desired standards of urban quality in the town. The main objective was to convert the promenade for pedestrian use and to maximise the tourist and civic potential. It was possible, at the planning stage, to reroute the traffic to exclude it from the promenade for part of the way and to provide a tunnel for the rest together with an underground car park. Removing the concrete wall separating the beach from the promenade allows the whole area to be seen as a continuous space (Figure 12.8). Compared to the Dover and Benidorm examples, the promenade here runs in a dead straight line. The promenade was also levelled, and a series of tiers are used to change the level from the top down to the beach. The design combines paving in stone, decking and the beach, with some ramps leading down from the upper parts for easy access to the beach. The steps also incorporate planted trees – palms – and the decking includes a series of wooden sculptural forms. Metal elements such as railings, lighting standards and ramps are painted red. Cafes spread their tables out onto the upper paved area.

Figure 12.8
A typical view of the Vinaròs promenade showing the decking, steps and wooden "rocks"
(*Source*: Guallart Architects)

Project quality rating assessment

This project can be judged extremely well for accessibility in all aspects. Design quality is good, apart from the cultural heritage aspects, which do not feature in the project. Facilities are reasonably well provided, although the site is quite exposed to wind and lacks shade. Health and well-being aspects are also generally well provided for, and the place functions very well for access and interaction with the water and for physical activity. An excellent project with great imagination and sensitivity to site. Figure 12.9a–e shows the interpretation of the design using drawings.

Amager Beach, Copenhagen, Denmark

This project was completed in 2005 and designed by the firm of Haslov and Kjaersgaard Planners and Architects on an artificial island next to the coastline in the Copenhagen district of Amager. The site is a large-scale landscape which provides a contrast to the density of the rest of the Copenhagen waterfront, where an open sky and wide horizon offer special experiences. The first ideas for this project emerged in the early 1980s from local grassroots organisations and other stakeholders. People involved in promoting the project wanted to ensure that openness would be the main quality in the area, and the edge of the existing beach was to be moved further out to form a better one. This was achieved by creating a 2-km-long artificial island which is separated from the original beach by a lagoon which is crossed by three bridges. The beach is organised into two sections. The northern section comprises a natural beach environment of winding paths, broad sandy beaches and low dunes. The southern section is the so-called *city beach*, where there is a wide promenade and areas for playing games or picnicking (Figure 12.10). At the southern end, there is a small marina and car parking. The lagoon has shallow, sheltered areas safe for children and a 1000-m swimming course. The architectural structure focuses on the meeting between the linear coastal road and the building lines in the flat landscape of the island of Amager and the new coastline. Long sight lines run through the beach park. The coastline is laid out to take account of the dynamics of wind, waves and currents. There are focal points: the point at the extreme east (that governs the main orientation of the two beaches) and the two jetties to the north and the south. The "beach stations" have a special character to help to create the sense of place. They follow the lines of the landscape and form artificial cliffs for people to walk on and around.

Project quality rating assessment

This project is rated very highly for accessibility in all aspects. The design quality is also very good, apart from the lack of reference to cultural heritage, which, given its origins as a new landscape, is no surprise. It provides many facilities, apart from the lack of shade across the site. It also has potential for promoting health and well-being while performing very well for water connection and activities, less so for formal sports. An all-round excellent example which showcases the high reputation of Scandinavian landscape architecture. Figure 12.11a–i shows the interpretation of the design using drawings.

Sea Park, Saulkrasti, Latvia

This is in many ways the most natural of the projects in this section, completed in 2014 and designed by Substance SIA, architect Arnis Dimiņš. The small Latvian town of Saulkrasti, a little way up the Baltic Sea coast from Riga, is popular for summer activities. The town was looking for its place among Latvian seaside towns and decided to focus on tourism, recreation and various annual events. The idea to improve the central part of the beach and to create the Sea Park emerged as a result. The project area consists of primary and secondary dune ramparts with flatter dune slacks between the dunes. The key design element is the network of wooden footbridges and boardwalks right across the area – allowing access while protecting the fragile dunes (Figure 12.12). The wooden deck planks are reinforced vertically with slits corresponding to the thickness of the boards. As a result, the wooden decking becomes a unifying theme which can integrate all of the small elements such as benches, loungers, bicycle racks and waste

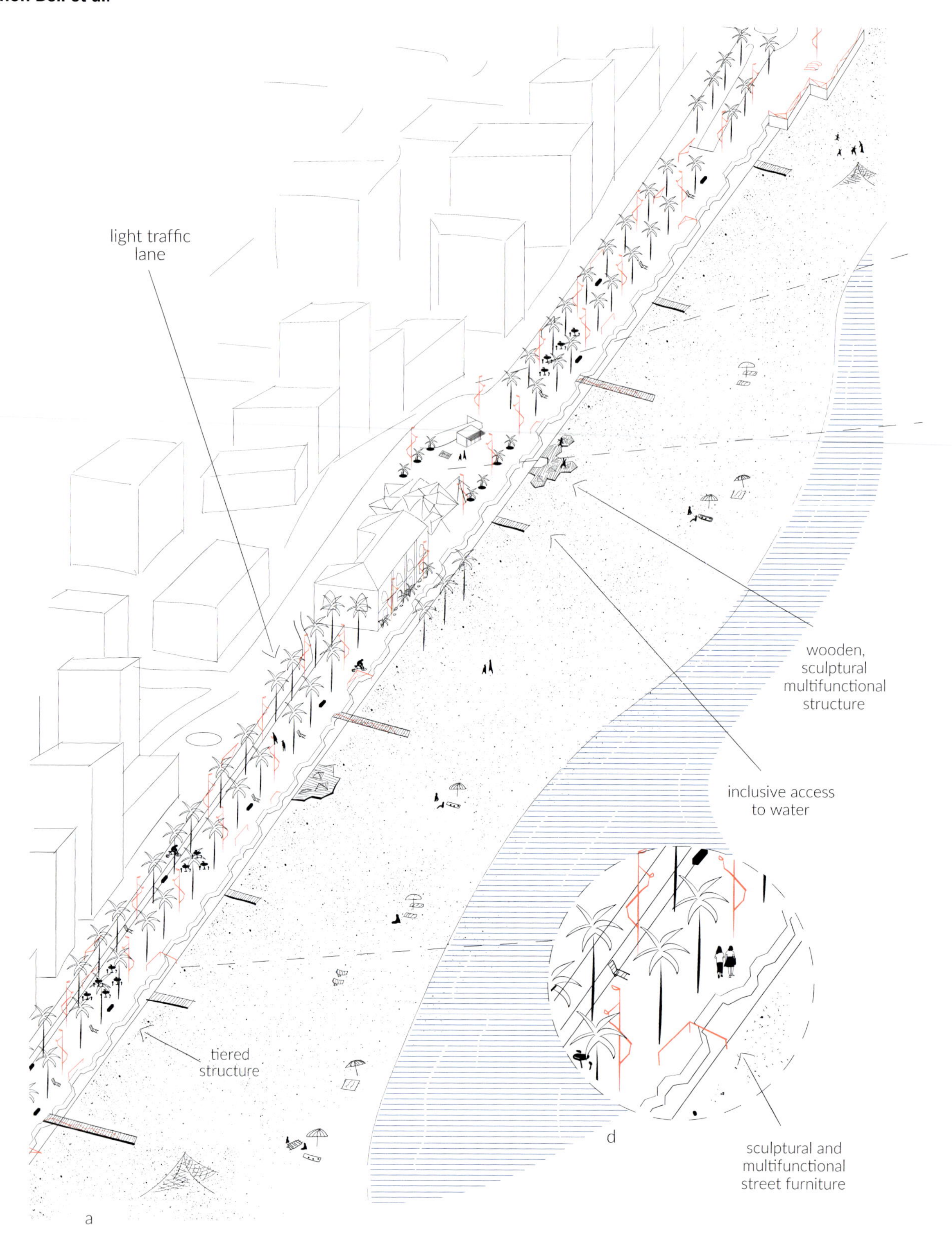

Figure 12.9a–e

a) The entire Vinaròs promenade has a rich diversity of elements, offering many affordances yet at the same time possessing a strong sense of design unity; b) the ramp providing inclusive access to the beach; c) the multi-functional wooden "rocks"; d) the use of the red colour and same materials is a feature of the promenade furniture; e) a section providing a detail of how the promenade links the street to the beach

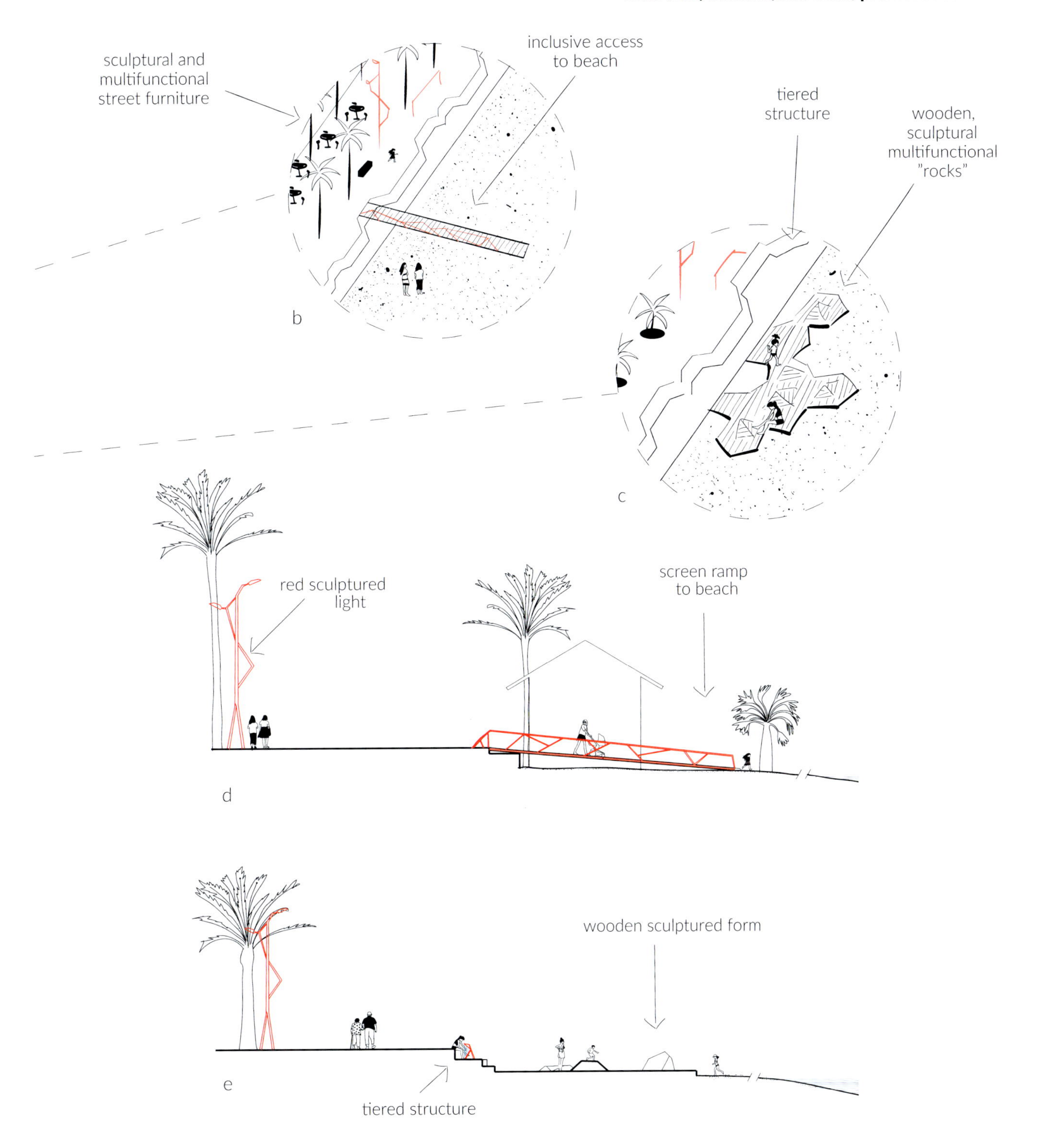

Figure 12.9a–e (continued)

Figure 12.10
A view along the promenade section at Amager Beach with one of the raised building platforms in the background
(*Source*: Mads Farsö)

bins, also made entirely out of wood. As the sea character varies according to the weather and seasons, ranging from completely peaceful and quiet to loud and billowing, the exit points of the wooden footbridges on the beach were designed to form wedges to break the waves. The triangular form thus became a key element as the best geometric form for stability against external forces. Only wooden surfacing is used in the park, while metal elements are only used for lighting and fitness equipment. The sea park includes two beach volleyball courts with small, two-level terraces/podiums, outdoor fitness area, beach showers, gymnastic equipment and children's playgrounds.

Project quality rating assessment

Accessibility is generally excellent, apart from car parking, which is less satisfactory. The site visibility is low, as it is hidden behind tees – this gives screening and segregation from the rest of the nearby landscape, however. For design quality, it also rates well, except for its likely maintenance costs – due to the fact that a lot of wood has been used which will need replacement and also the risk of sand covering surfaces and needing to be removed. References to cultural heritage are low, since there are none to be made. Facilities also rate highly, although the site is rather exposed to the sun, with little shade available, except along the edges, where there are trees. For all aspects of health and well-being, it is also very good. Water access and activities are mixed – access from the water and water sports are not really very possible, and there is a lack of water safety equipment. Figure 12.13 shows the analysis of the project in sketches.

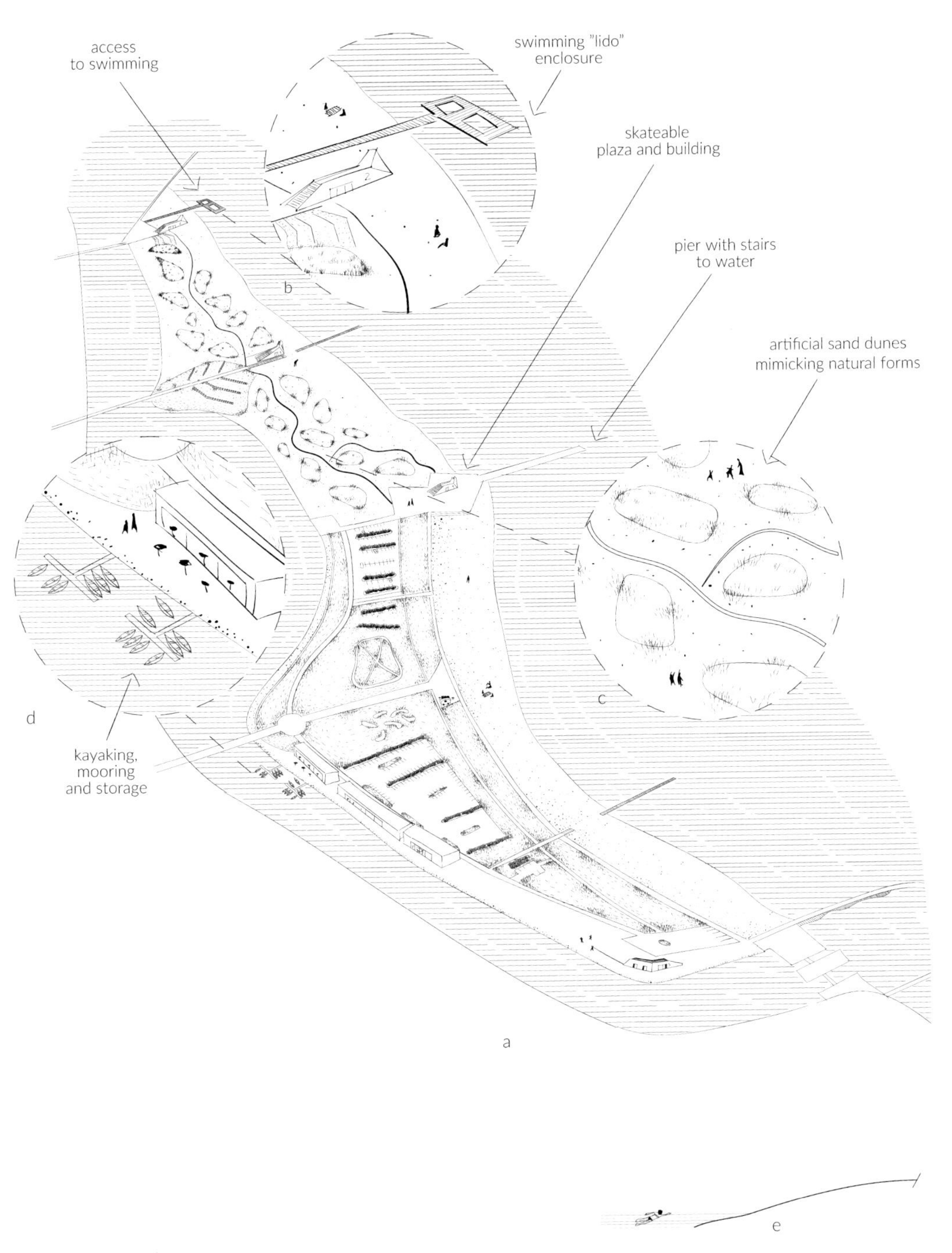

Figure 12.11a–i

a) Overview of the extensive Amager Beach highlighting the division of the extensive site into a series of different zones with a variety of functions and affordances; b) the lido located in the sea, providing safe bathing and swimming opportunities together with one of the buildings which acts as a viewing platform; c) the artificial dunes, which are designed to mimic natural forms; d) the small kayak rental and anchoring site in the lagoon; e) a section across the island showing the artificial dunes and exposure to both sea and lagoon; f) the concrete jetty section of the promenade, with the elevated elements providing views over the otherwise flat site and ending in a small lighthouse; g) a section of the steps with access down to the sea at the end of the jetty; h) the cross-section of the jetty with riprap protection against wave action; i) the access to the kayak rental centre and marina

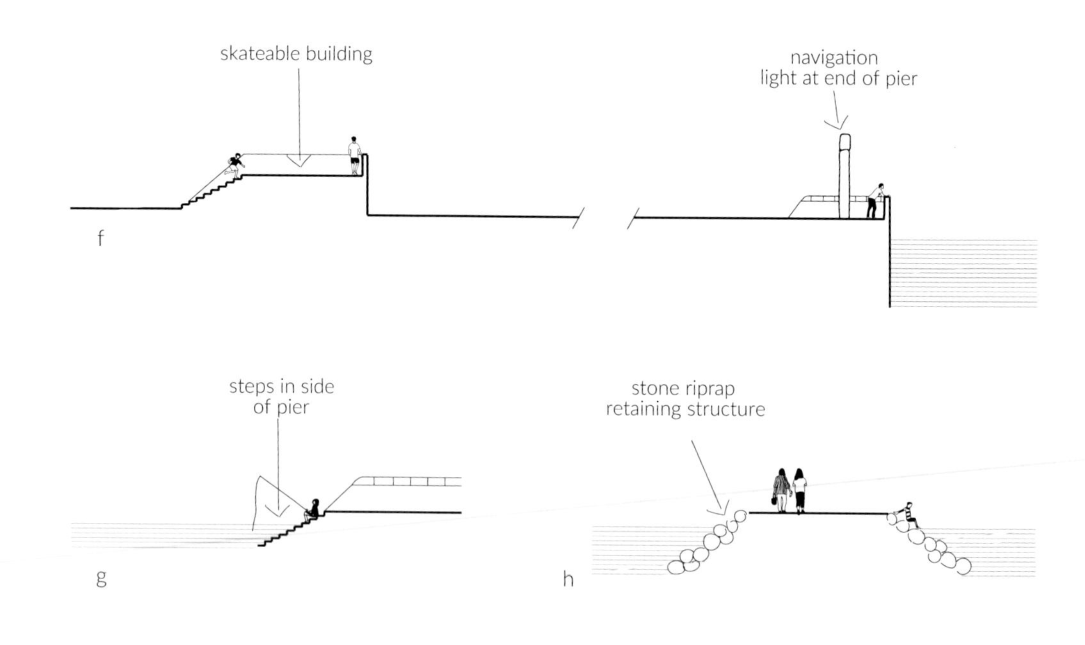

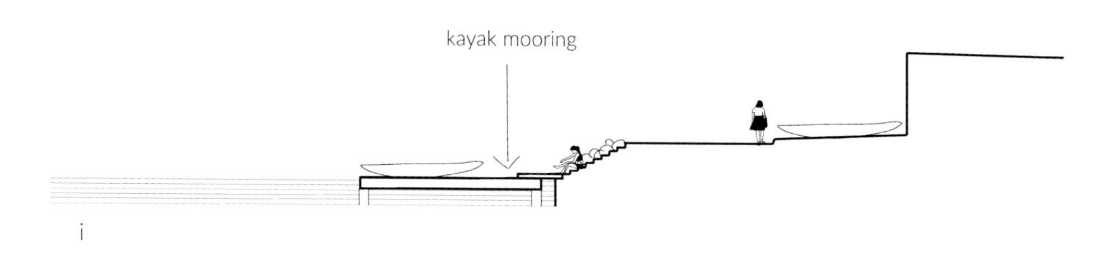

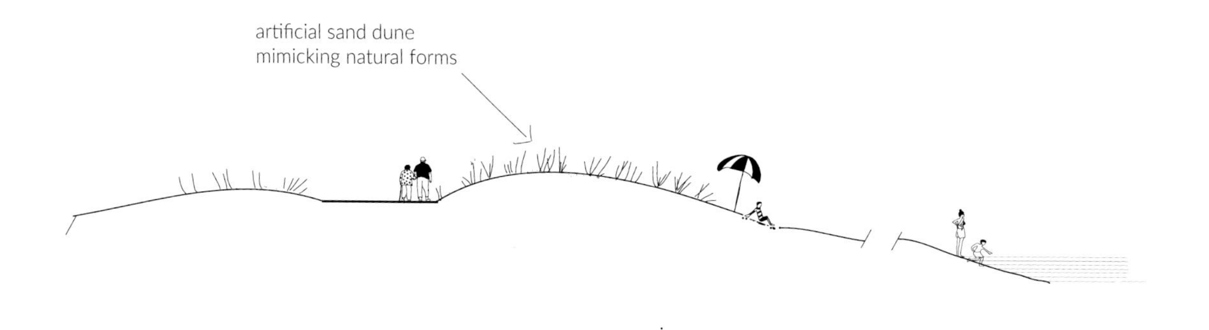

Figure 12.11a–i (continued)

Figure 12.12
A view of Saulkrasti Sea Park showing the decking, seating and equipment
(*Source*: Jekaterina Balicka)

Myrtle Edwards Park, Seattle, United States

This extensive park system in Seattle, Washington, United States, comprises the Olympic Sculpture Park, Elliott Bay Trail, Myrtle Edwards Park, Centennial Park and Elliott Bay Park and was constructed between 2001 and 2007. The designs were created by Charles Anderson Landscape Architects and Architecture Design Team for the consortium of Seattle Art Museum, Seattle Parks and Recreation and the Port of Seattle. A series of sub-parks starts at the Olympic Sculpture Park and ends with the Elliott Bay Park. This connected park system connects with the dense urban fabric at the northern and southern ends but is (or was) completely cut off from the city itself by railway tracks that run parallel to it. The connection has been improved since the original completion by the construction of the Olympic Sculpture Park. This is the main point where the park connects with the city structure to allow pedestrians and cyclists access over a bridge across the railway tracks. The layout of the park, which is generally narrow and linear, consists of a separate, winding asphalt pedestrian and cycle path, equipped with resting and viewing points, lawns, sculptures and benches (Figure 12.14). The water edge consists of riprap forming small bays with gravel or shingle beaches between which driftwood was placed to create a habitat for fish and invertebrates at high tide. The terrestrial part includes viewing points, a rose garden, groups of trees, a cafeteria and shelters good for bird watching. The various points of attraction provide opportunities to linger, obtain direct contact with water and relax. There are unobstructed distant views of the bay. The main activities the site promotes are walking by the bay, jogging, cycling, picnicking, photography, fishing, dog walking and exercising.

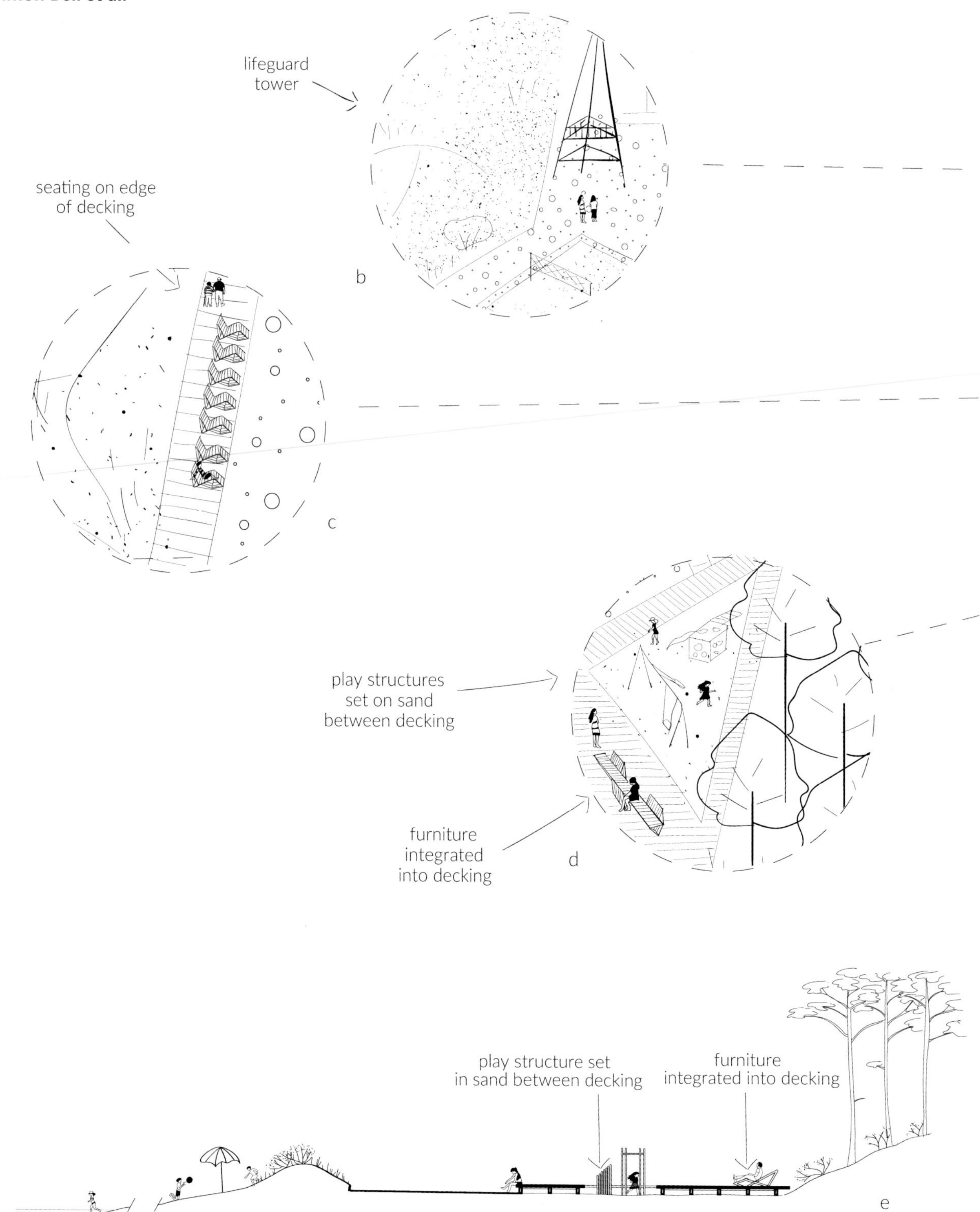

Figure 12.13a–e

a) Overview of Saulkrasti showing the relationship of all the elements according to different functional zones and their relationship to the forest, sand dunes and sea; b) the wooden paving using logs set into the sand;

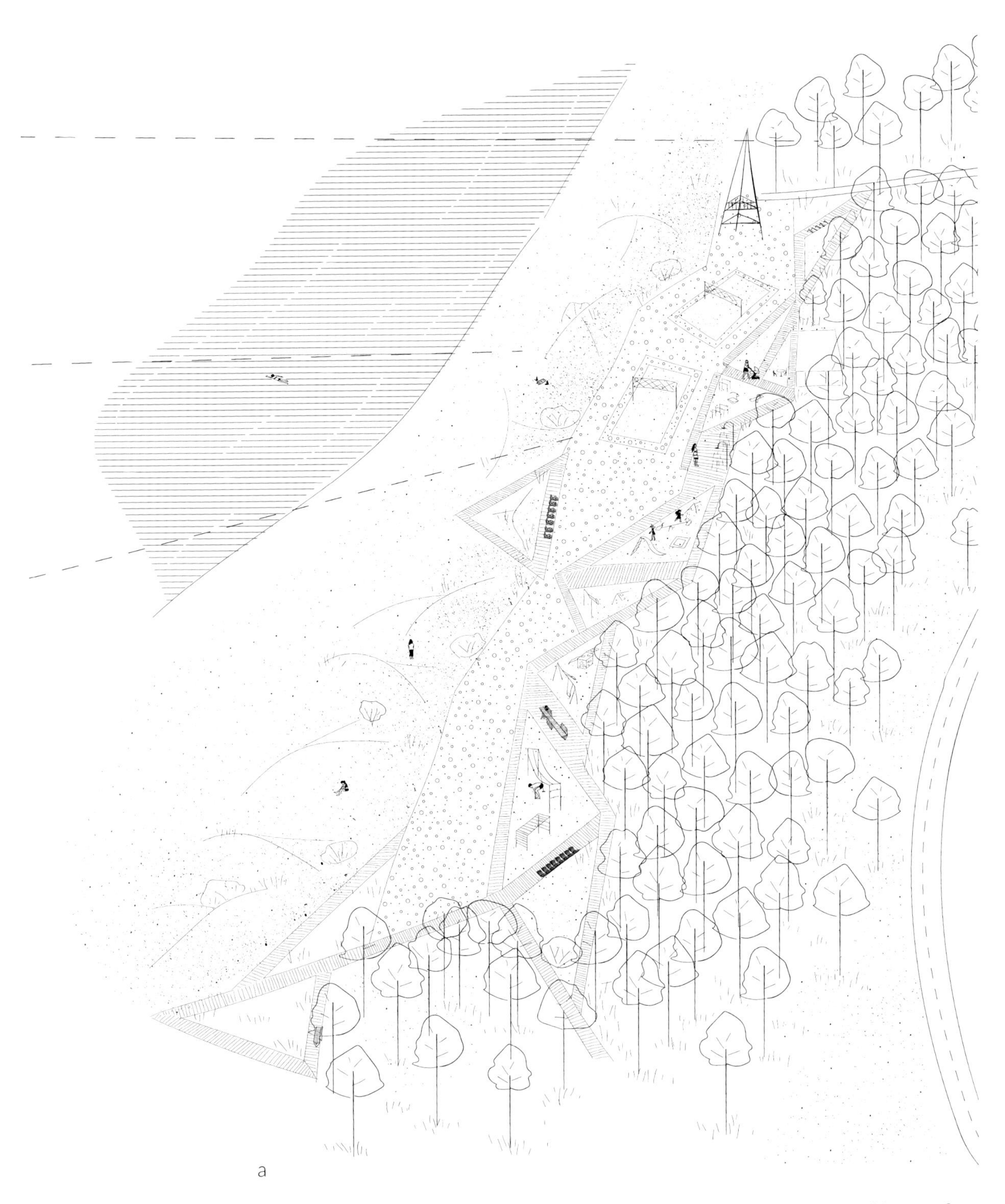

c) the reclining seats are integrated into the decking; d) one of the functional zones – the play area – with one of the variations of the seating design, also integrated into the decking; e) a section across the site from sea to forest showing the spatial relationships

Figure 12.14
An evening view along the shore at Myrtle Edwards Park showing the grassy slopes, large rocks on plinths as sitting spots, the natural vegetation and the views back to the industrial remains
(*Source*: Courtesy of Seattle Parks)

Project quality rating assessment

The assessment of this project shows that access to the park has limitations due to the railway line immediately behind it, and it is not very visible from the city side. The design quality does not have the kind of unique originality of some examples we have looked at but is fine otherwise. The cultural heritage aspects are rated less due to the lack of any elements to include which would make such a connection. The park is not especially full of facilities but does not need them to be successful given its location. It has little lighting and is rather exposed. It performs very well for health and well-being potential, apart from the sense of being away, given its industrial location. The water connection is mainly visual, as the sea is not suitable for activities, and access to and from the water is limited. It has plenty of opportunities for physical activity but not formal sports or water sports. Overall, it is a fine example of an informal park making good use of a place to enhance the natural qualities but does not have the cachet of the other promenades featured here, which is why in some respects it is lower rated. Figure 12.15 shows how it has been analysed using sketches.

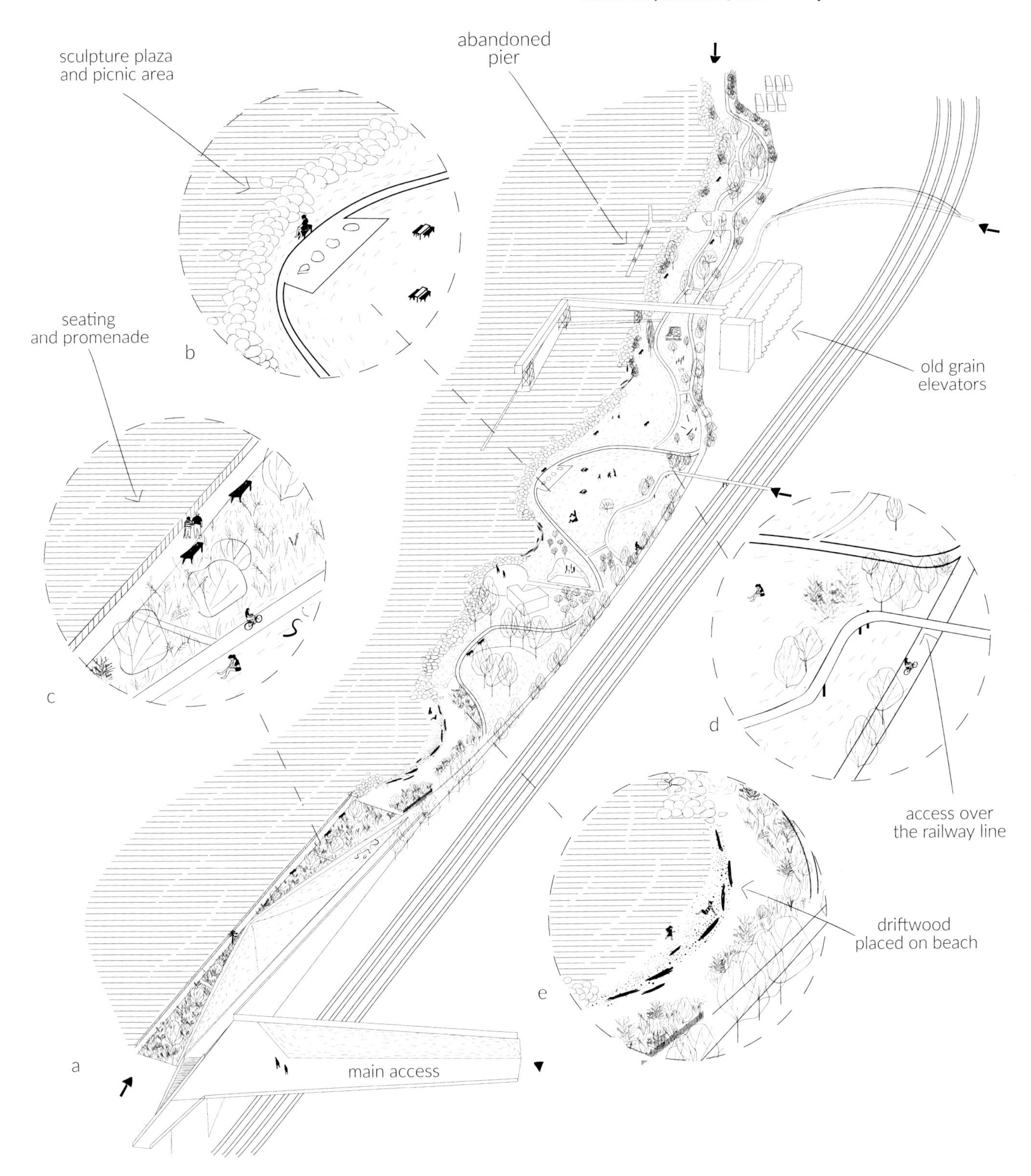

Figure 12.15 a–h

a) Overview of the entire Myrtle Edwards Park site highlighting its location and relationship between the railway line and the water as well as the different character areas; b) the sculpture plaza with seating and riprap edging to the water; c) the promenade along the water and also some dense natural vegetation contrasting with the managed

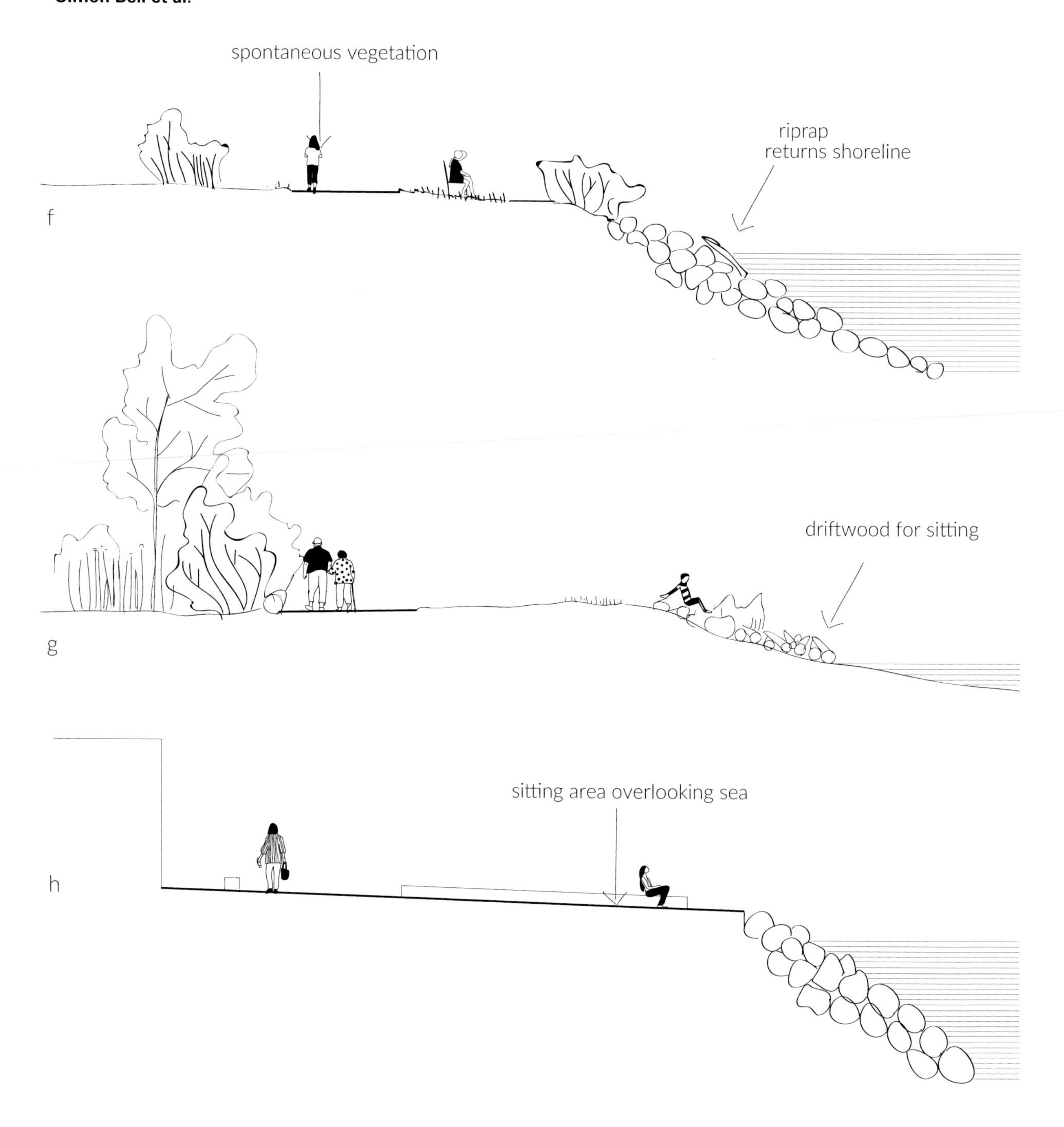

Figure 12.15 a–h (continued)
grass areas; d) the pedestrian bridge across the railway enabling access to the park; e) the driftwood placed on the beach to offer informal seating, a reference to nature and also the spontaneous vegetation around the beach; f) the situation along the path where riprap is used to protect the shoreline, with benches on the grassy areas behind; g) a section across the beach with driftwood along it parallel to the path, providing informal seating; h) a platform next to the building, with seating along the water providing opportunities for contemplation of the water

Figure 12.16
A view of Veules-les-Roses showing the structures above the beach
(*Source*: Jekaterina Balicka)

Projects providing access, safe swimming and artificial beaches: Veules-les-Roses, France

This project, constructed sequentially between 2001 and 2013 and designed by Atelier Ruelle for the City of Veules-les-Roses and Communauté de Commune de la Côte d'Albâtre, restores some seaside activities and presence in an unusual way. This small resort of Veules-les-Roses suffered from bomb damage during the Second World War and then from the post-war reconstruction, which included channelling the river and covering it with car parking. The small-scale opening to the sea descends down the narrow valley of the small river and is squeezed between chalk cliffs. The project comprises two main sections. The first, the main part of the design, consists of a large wooden deck, designed to be evocative of an ocean liner, constructed on top of the sea wall. This has two elements inserted into it – an open-air paddling pool and a sand-covered children's play area – needed due to the steep shingle beach and strong waves, which make the sea rather dangerous (Figure 12.16). Behind the decking and between it and the town is the re-exposed river with a small park on either bank, before it flows beneath the decking and through the sea wall into the sea. The decking overlooks the beach, which is also used for many activities in and out of the water. This decking then continues across a concrete promenade, which also projects over the seawall. There are numerous benches, a viewpoint on a pier which extends from the decking into the sea, playgrounds and paddling pool for children. The last phase of the project uncovered the river.

Project quality rating assessment

This project performs very highly for accessibility; design, especially for circulation; views; and cultural heritage. The facilities are also very good, apart from the site being exposed to wind and sun. It is assessed very highly for all aspects of health and well-being and has excellent water connections. For physical activity, is it especially good for children's play – the paddling pool being a special feature here. It is not so strong for water-sports other than some sailing due to the nature of the sea. Figure 12.17 shows how it has been analysed using sketches.

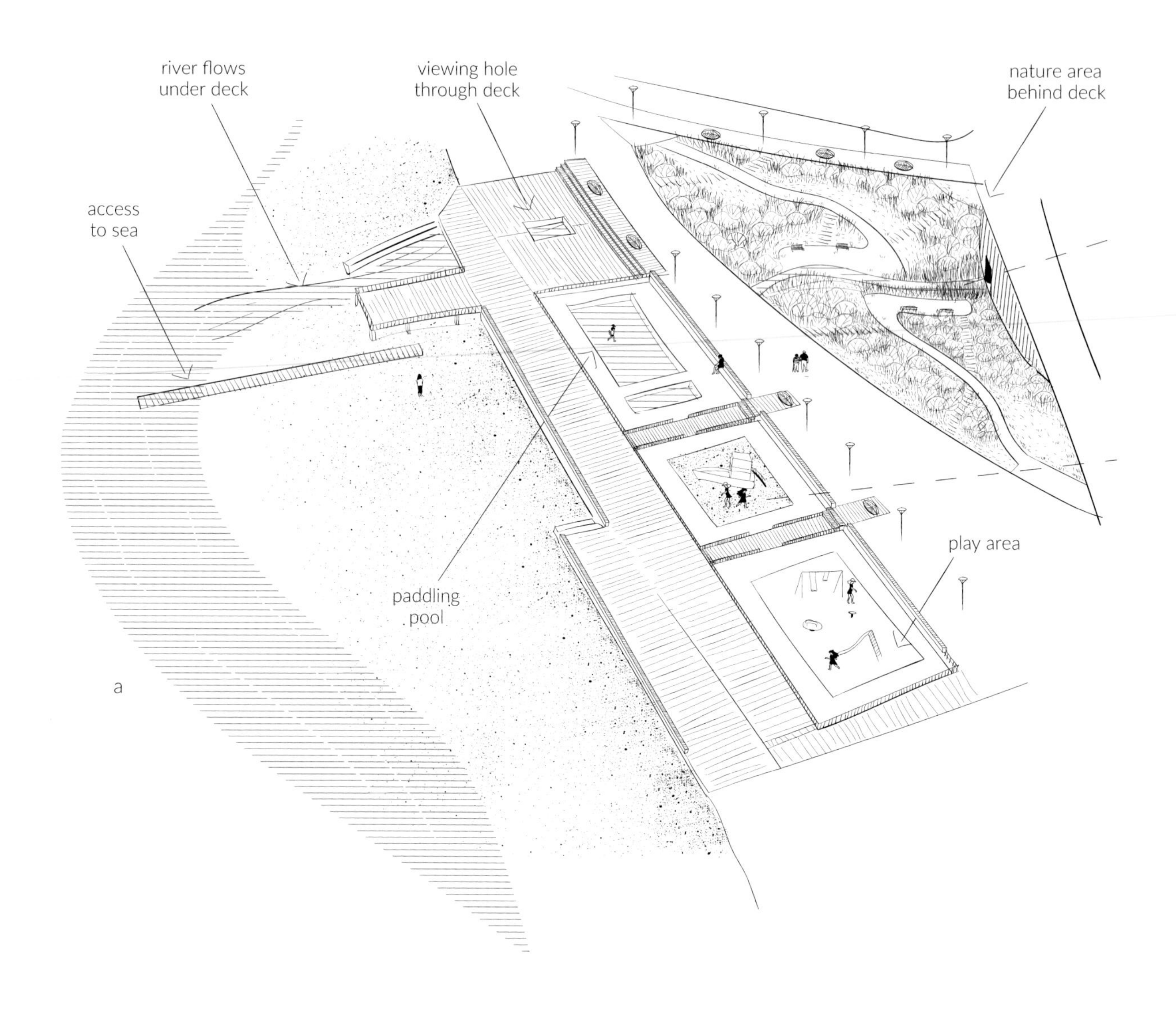

Figure 12.17a–e

a) Overview of the whole Veules-les-Roses site as well as the division into two main zones – the elevated play and recreational area on the deck, with a view over the water, and the small estuary of the river, with lush vegetation, as it flows beneath the deck to the sea; b) the green area on the estuary; c) detail of one of the play areas and the bathing pool for small children within the play and recreational zone; d) the relationship between the raised deck and the stream flowing beneath, where the water is visible in three places: over the edge to the vegetated estuary, through a hole in the deck and from the deck down to the beach and final outflow; e) the previously inaccessible or dangerous water has been made safer for small children through the provision of the shallow pool

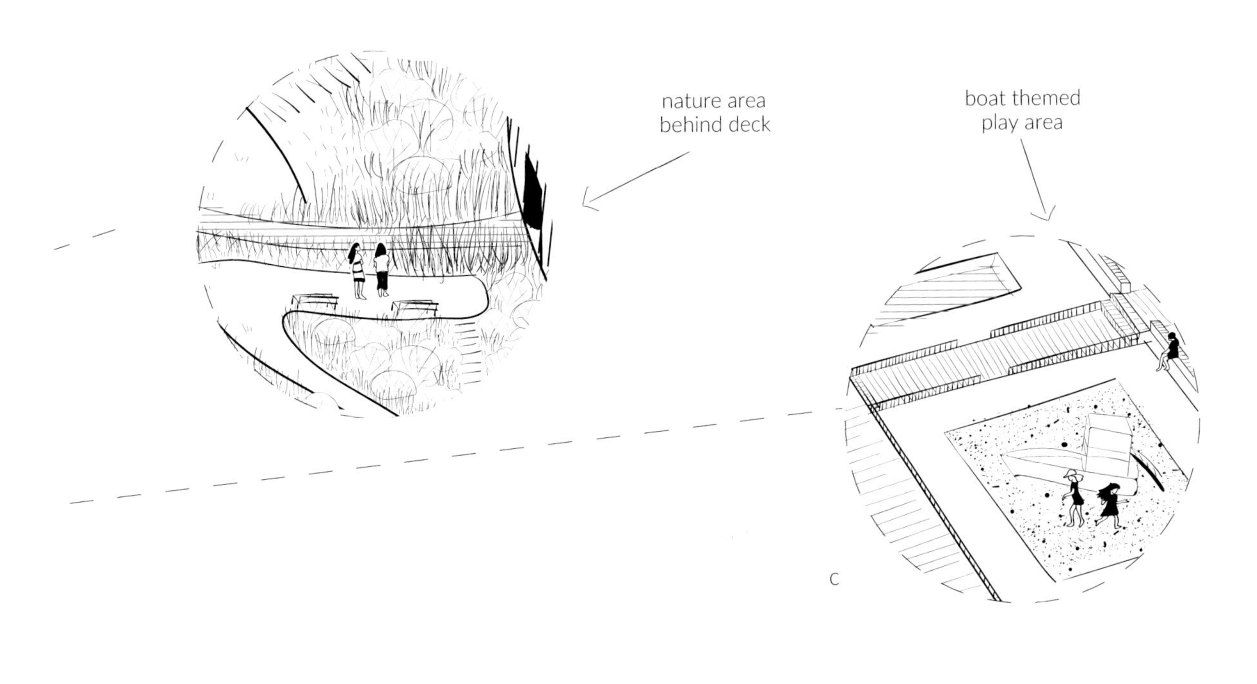

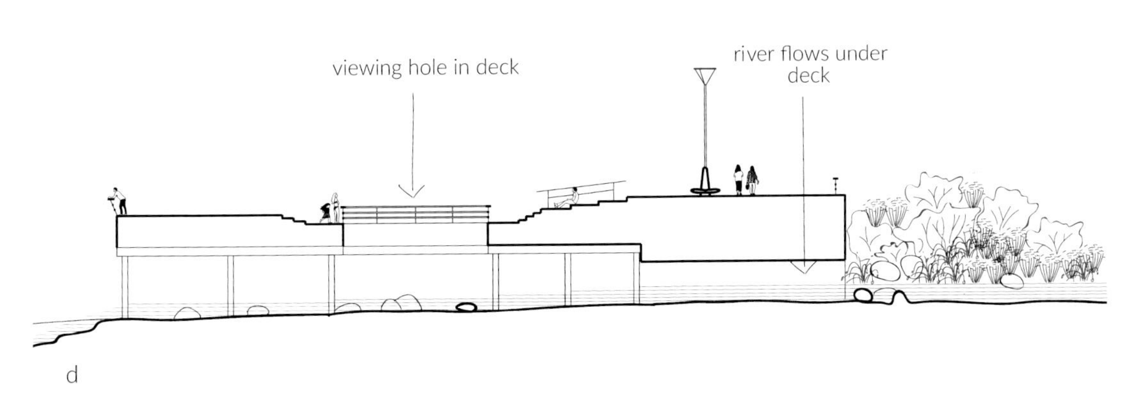

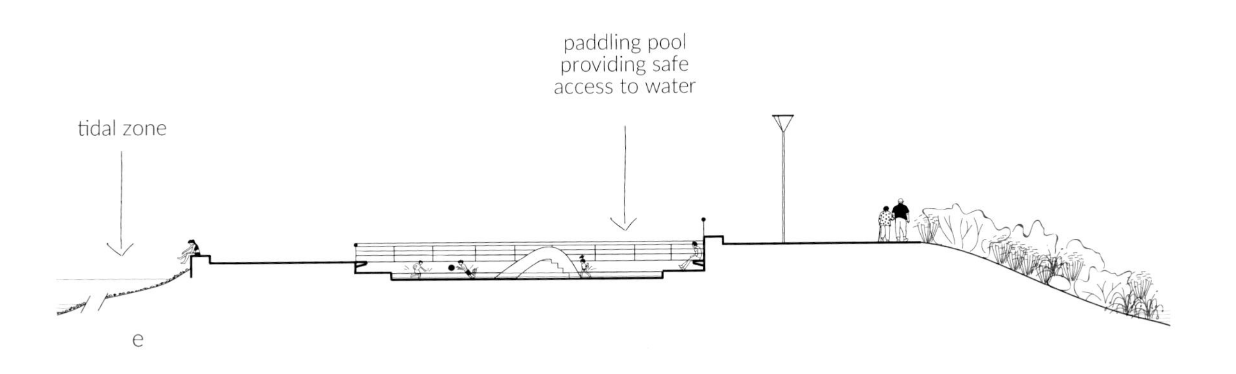

Figure 12.17a–e (continued)

Sugar Beach, Toronto, Canada

This popular project, located on Toronto's East Bayfront on Lake Ontario, was constructed in 2010 from designs by Claude Cormier Landscape Architecture. Sugar Beach is an imaginatively designed park of some 8500 m^2 that transformed a surface car park in a former industrial area into a contemporary urban beachfront – the first public space visitors see if they travel along Queens Quay from the central waterfront. The design reflects and gained inspiration from the industrial heritage of the area, especially its relationship to the neighbouring Redpath Sugar factory. The layout of the park comprises three distinct sections: an artificial urban beach created from imported sand; an open multi-functional plaza space; and a tree-lined promenade which is aligned diagonally through the park and provides a shady route to the water's edge, providing visitors with many opportunities to sit and enjoy views to the lake, beach or plaza. It also contains a dynamic water feature for playing in, in the shape of the Canadian maple leaf. Grass-covered earth mounds and the tree grove will eventually hide the view of the beach from the main street. The most iconic and identifiable features of the park are the bright pink beach umbrellas, which double as lighting at nighttime, and candy-striped rock outcrops (Figure 12.18). The main activities which take place are typical of a beach: sunbathing, playing, walking, relaxing, socialising and public events. People stroll through the park along a granite cobblestone with a maple leaf mosaic pattern. Access to the beach is provided by an extended wooden boardwalk to the beach.

Project quality rating assessment

This project performs very well for accessibility. It has a limited relationship to cultural heritage. It is generally well provided with facilities, apart from the exposed nature of the site. It is assessed well for health and well-being potential, apart from contact with nature – it being an artificial landscape down at the docks, while water connection is good – due to the presence of a play fountain, apart from the activities on or in the water, which are limited here (no

Figure 12.18

A view of Sugar Beach showing the dock edge, sand, trees and pink umbrellas – the trademark of the project

(*Source*: Raysonho Creative Commons CC0 1.0 Universal Public Domain Dedication)

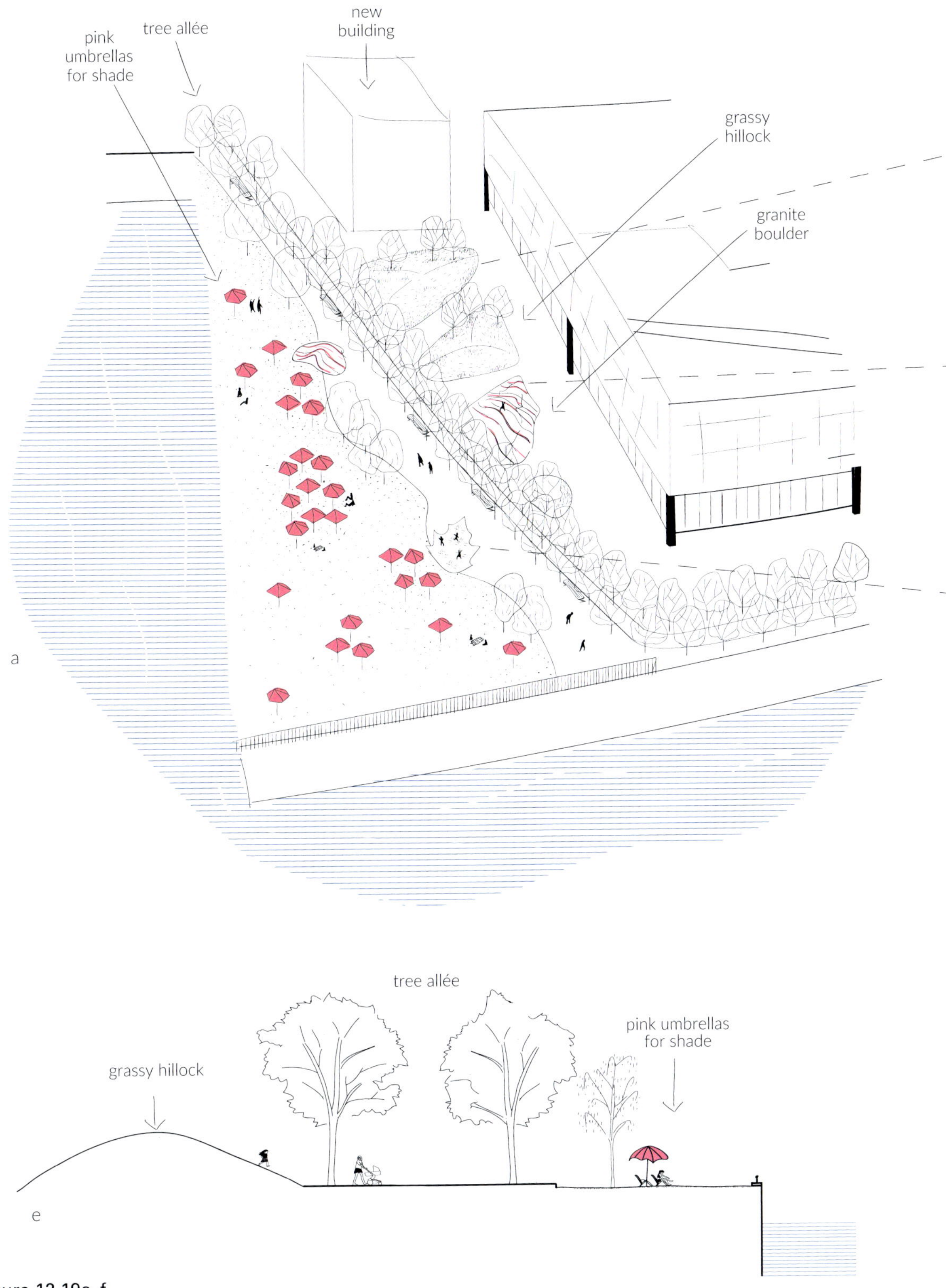

Figure 12.19a–f

a) Overview of the Sugar Beach site, where it is divided into two main zones – the sand-covered artificial beach and the grass-covered hillocks, separated by a path and tree alleé; b) one of the grassy hillocks used for sunbathing; c) the large granite boulder, which provides a range of affordances, including children's play; d) the otherwise inaccessible water is brought to people in the form of the maple-leaf fountain; e) a cross-section from the larger hillock, over the path and on to the water; f) the beach extending from the path to the dock edge and featuring the iconic pink umbrellas

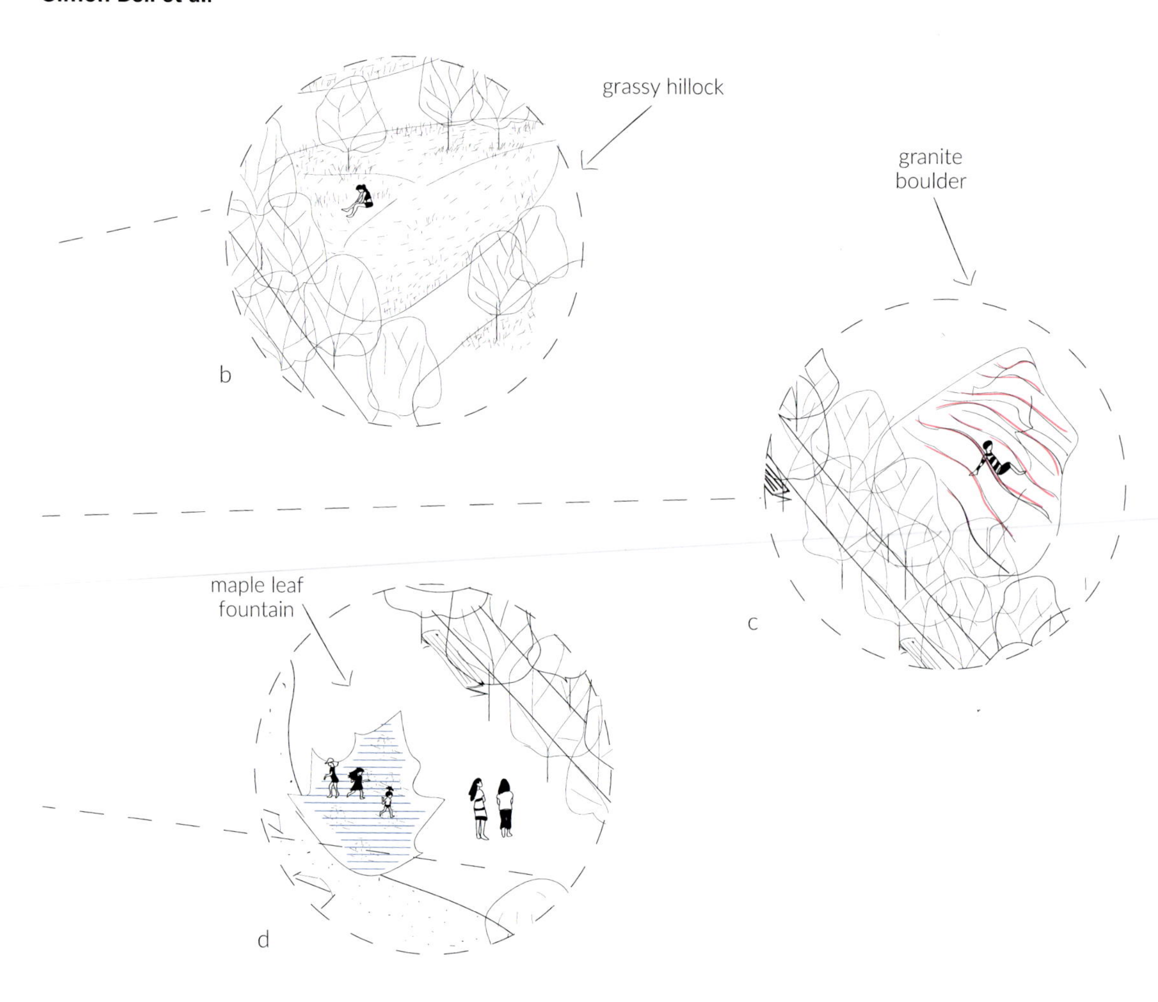

Figure 12.19a–f (continued)

swimming allowed). Physical activity opportunities are more averagely rated due to the location and size of the site. Overall, a very good project which has captured the imagination of many people, making it an iconic contemporary landscape. Figure 12.19 shows how it has been analysed using sketches.

Cairns Esplanade-Swimming Lagoon, Cairns, Australia

This ambitious project was completed in 2003 to designs by landscape architects Tract Consultants following a national design competition. Cairns is located on the northern coast of Australia and between the Great Barrier Reef and lush rainforest. The site as a public space reflects the activity and character of the two types of landscape. The project links blue space with green space and provides swimming facilities by the creation of an artificial lagoon on the former tidal mud flats. The shallow lagoon is flanked by shady gardens, trees and shade structures, necessary in a tropical climate, and provides safe swimming free from the risk of crocodiles or marine stingers (Figure 12.20). There is a range of swimming spaces varying in water depth from 30 cm to 1.6 m. A wooden promenade connects this project with other spaces and observation decks that project into the sea at intervals to give extensive views to the sea, island and reefs beyond. The lagoon can accommodate hundreds of swimmers at a time. There is also a sand beach for families as well as pockets of wet seating areas for couples and groups. Floating timber sunning decks also offer shelter and picnic spaces. The sea wall that contains the lagoon functions as a walking and jogging track, but not for cycling. This is an interesting example of a project where serious risks of venturing into the sea have been avoided, yet the atmosphere and the views allow users to maintain a strong connection with the sea. It is a project that has put Cairns on the map.

Figure 12.20
A view over the Cairns Esplanade artificial lagoon out to the urban area beyond
(*Source*: Alex Monckton, Creative Commons Attribution-Share Alike 3.0 Unported license)

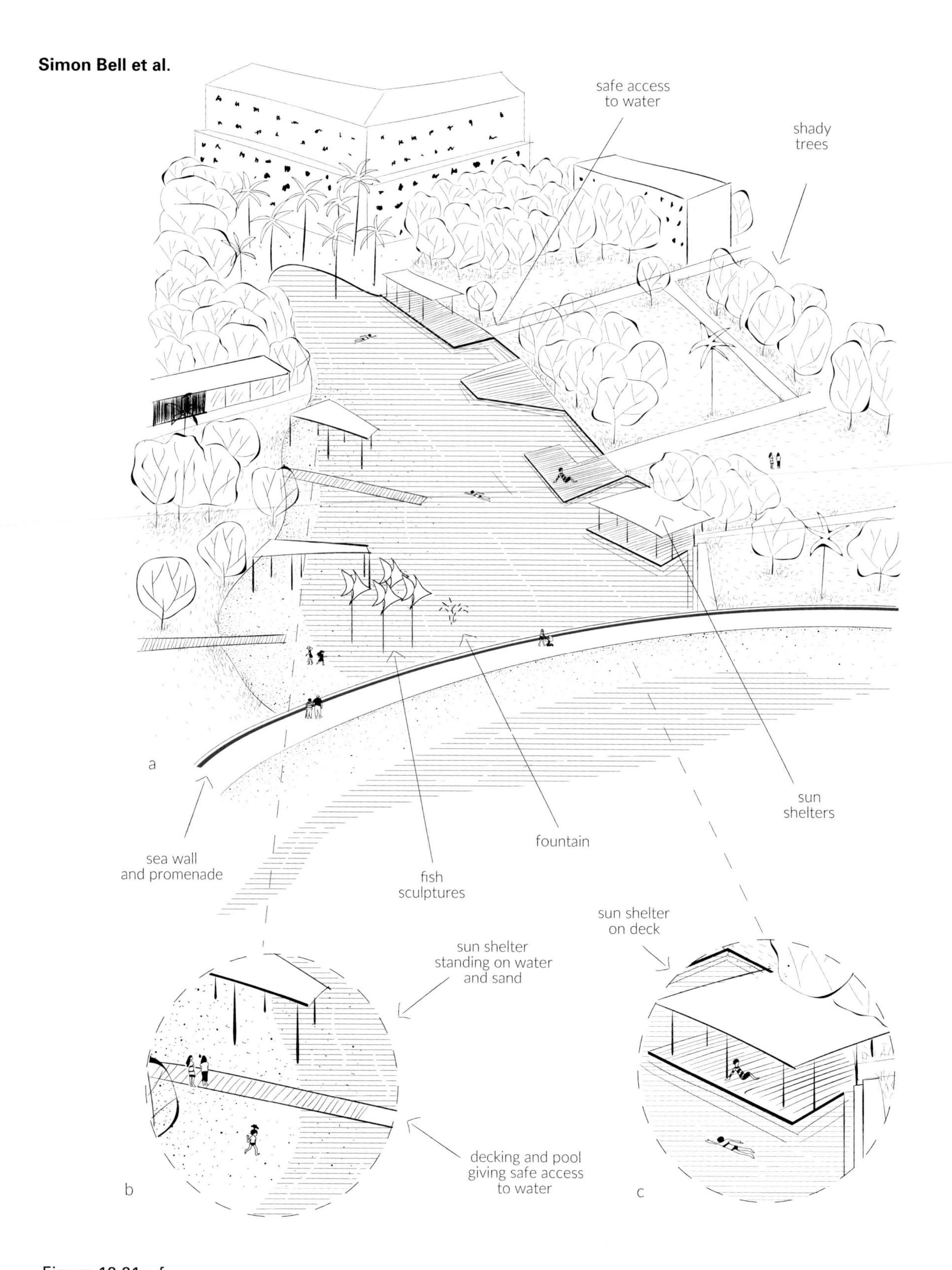

Figure 12.21a–f

a) An overview of the Cairns Esplanade to show the relationship of the plaza, pool and promenade which separates the site from the ocean, demonstrating the gradient from urban to ocean and the gradient in pool depth; b) the wooden decks and roof structures extend over the pool, shading both land and water; c) the shady wooden deck; d) a section from the grassy lawn with tall, shady trees and a shade structure to the pool; e) a cross-section

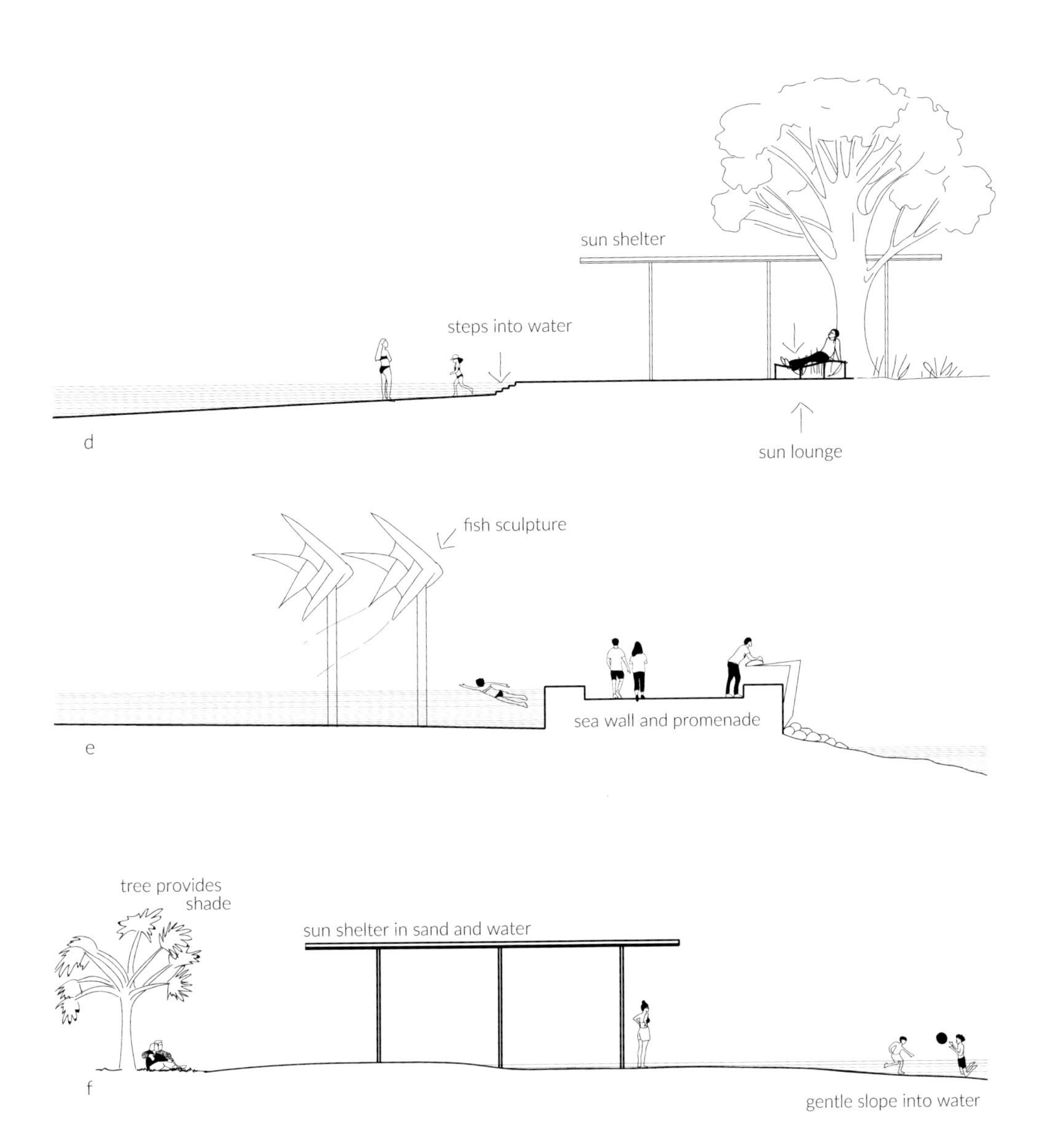

Figure 12.21a–f (continued)

through the pool and across the promenade separating it from the ocean, highlighting how bathing is safe for everyone in terms of water depth and protection from crocodiles; f) a section showing the transformation from tree shade and shade structure to the gently sloping pool

Project quality rating assessment

This project is assessed highly for accessibility, apart from its visibility from a distance due to the layout and location. The design quality has no specific cultural-historical aspects, but then, none are relevant; otherwise, it performs well, apart from probably high costs of maintenance. The facilities are very good, apart from wind exposure and quality of nature – mainly due to the artificial character of the project and the open views to the ocean. Health and well-being potential is generally quite high but less so for the sense of being away and for contact with nature due to the artificial environment. Water connections are good, except for water activities and access from the water – not surprising, given it is isolated from the ocean for safety reasons. All kinds of physical activity related to the water are also possible. This is clearly an excellent project which provides a lot of enjoyment and protects people from some serious water-associated risks. Figure 12.21 analyses the project using sketches.

Paprocany Waterfront, Tychy, Poland

The town of Tychy in Poland sits directly on an extensive lake, separated from it by some forest. In this project, realised in 2014 by Robert Skitek, a promenade formed from wooden decking runs along a stretch of the shoreline, facing out to the lake, which appears to be completely natural, while the town is behind and out of sight. According to the designers, the concept is based on the wooden promenade along the lake shore, which alternately meanders out over the lake and back to the shore. This design permits different views and feelings of space to be obtained from various points along the promenade. The pedestrian/bicycle path mainly runs parallel with the shore, but where it runs over the water, the path dips to almost touch the lake. On the promenade, there are several unique elements, such as an opening in the decking with a net stretched over the water, where people recline, and specially designed benches (Figure 12.23). In addition, there is a new sandy beach and outdoor gym. The materials were selected to emphasise the natural character of the site and landscape, using mainly natural ones. Part of the site was covered with specially shaped landforms planted with grass. The promenade, benches and railings are all made of softwood. Hard surfaces such as bike parking and areas under the gym equipment were constructed from water-permeable mineral aggregates. The sections of the promenade over the lake are constructed on steel beams fixed to reinforced concrete piles driven into the lake floor. All illumination is by energy-saving LED lights.

Project quality rating assessment

This project is very accessible, although it is not visible from a distance due to the forest behind the waterfront screening views. Design quality is good for the context. As a very natural area, the absence of references to cultural heritage is to be expected; there are no landmarks, and the project is considered expensive to maintain (lots of timber). It performs well for provision of facilities, although some could be more accessible to disabled people. The health and well-being potential is excellent, mainly since the area is set within a forest with no signs of human activity. Water accessibility and connections are also excellent, although water safety equipment is not very evident. Physical activity opportunities are good; however, children's play is not obviously well provided for, nor are formal sports – although this is probably not a part of the project brief. Overall, an interesting and novel project which has some unusual features but which also requires a lot of maintenance. Figure 12.22 shows the analysis of the project using sketches.

Figure 12.22
Part of the Paprocany Waterfront showing the wooden structures and canvas shading umbrellas
(*Source*: courtesy of Tomasz Zakrzewski/archifolio.pl)

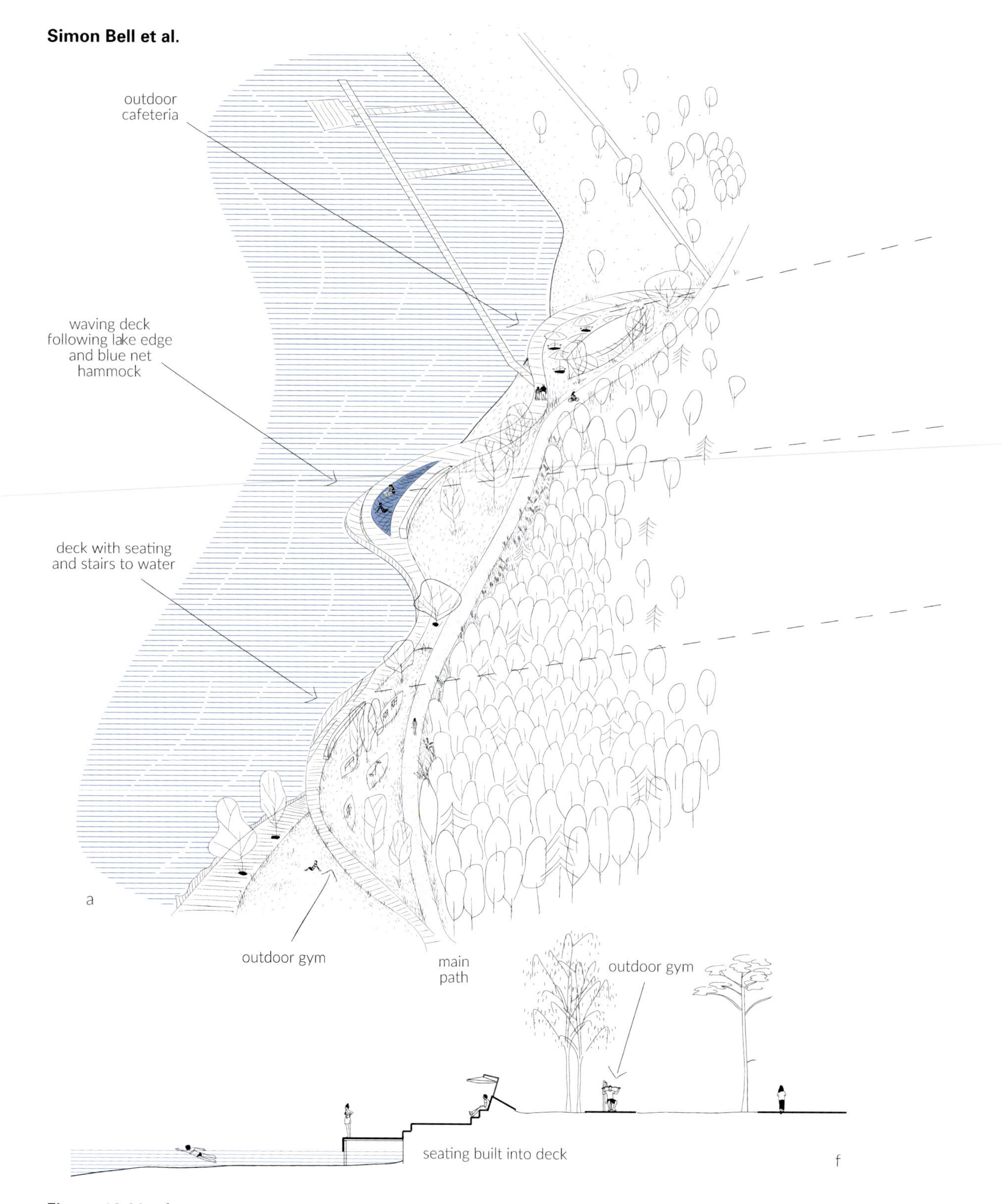

Figure 12.23a–f

a) Overview of the Paprocany project concentrating on the wooden deck and the path between the forest and the lake. Note how each wave in the path divides the site into separate functional zones; b) detail showing the outdoor cafeteria with a view to the lake and the way the wooden structure blends into the landscape; c) the blue hammock net set into the deck, which also provides open views across the lake – one of the elements which gives the project its identity and introduces playfulness into the design; d) the outdoor gym, terrace and steps, where all the design language of the structures creates unity; e) a cross-section through the deck with the net hammock; f) a section through the outdoor gym to the deck and steps leading to the water

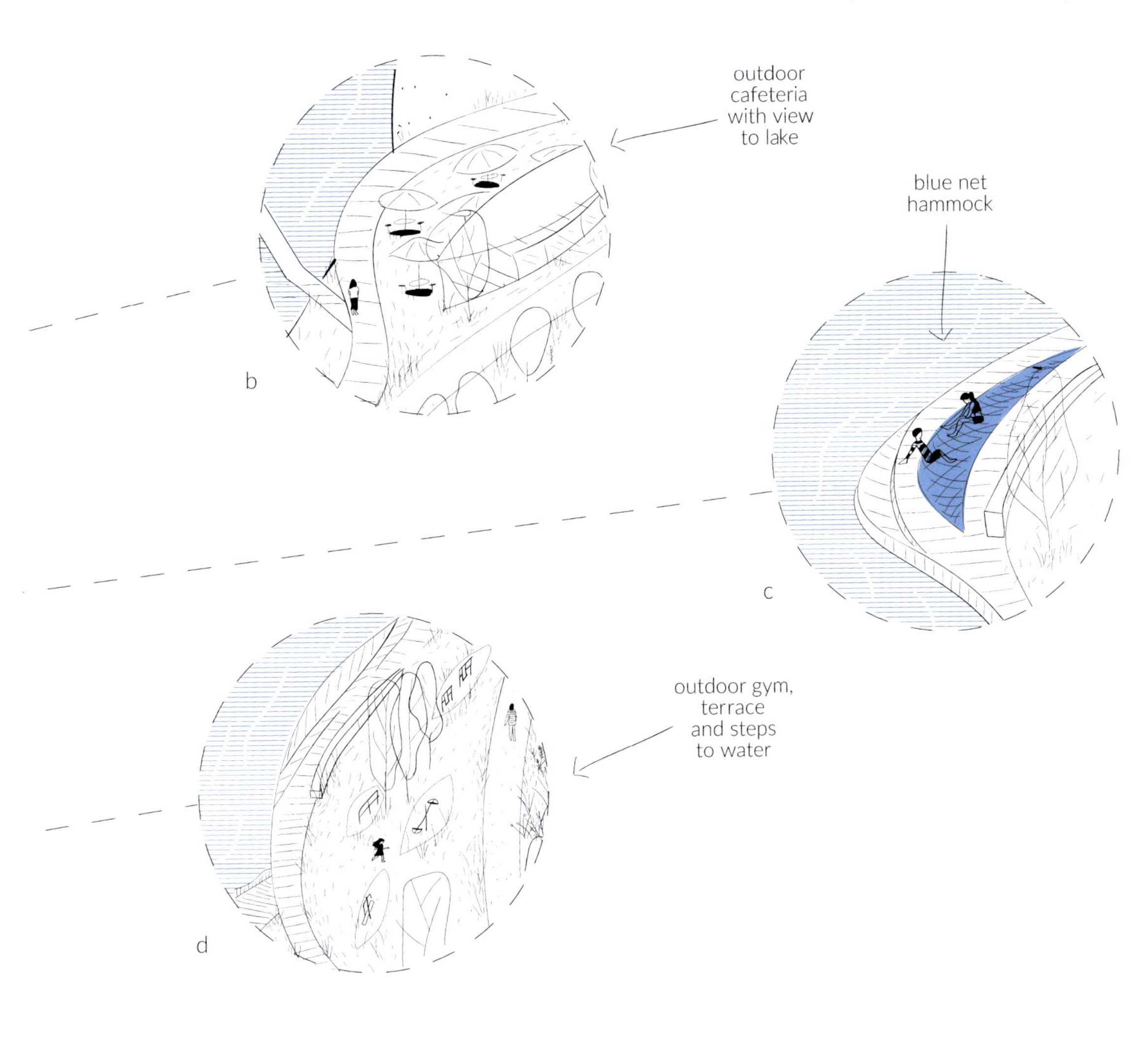

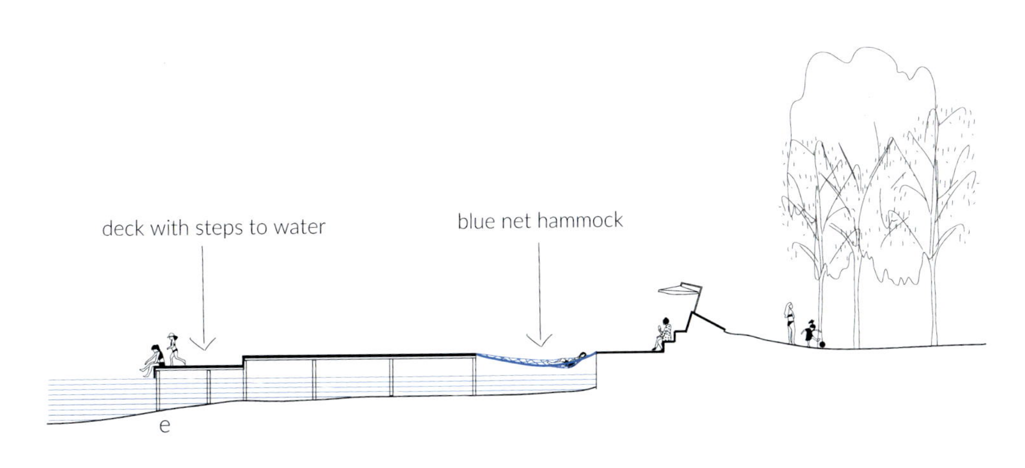

Figure 12.23a–f (continued)

Sjövikstorget, Stockholm, Sweden

This project, located in central Stockholm, was completed in 2010 from the designs of Thorbjörn Andersson and Sweco Architects. Stockholm is a city on the water within an archipelago of hilly islands, and the designers of Sjövikstorget wanted to express this quality on the water body where it is sited. This is achieved by using the fact that the rhomboidal space among the buildings opens up towards the water and "borrows" the wider landscape. To emphasise this, the square is formed of a wedge-shaped flat plane which has then been tilted towards the view at an angle of 3° from the horizontal. The design comprises three segments. The upper terrace consists of two horizontal lawns set within an open tilted and paved surface for walking supplied with benches formed from the granite edges which become higher as the plane descends relative to the lawns (Figure 12.24). This defines the space as a square and frames the views to the lake. The middle space along one of the sides extending out along the water forms a sunken platform, with benches facing towards the water. The lower section consists of a promenade and a pier parallel to the bottom of the sloping square. A grove of trees fills part of the void between the wedge and the space formed by the buildings, mirrored by a line of trees down the opposite side. Finally, there is a pier and deck continuing the line of the edge of the square and the line of trees, letting the form extend out over the water as if the space becomes submerged. The square allows for contact with the water and is well used in summer for sunbathing, though not for direct access into the water. The gentle slope allows for very easy accessibility to the water edge.

Project quality rating assessment

This project has good accessibility, apart from the views of it from a distance. The design quality is excellent, although it lacks reference to cultural heritage – not surprising given the context. It is expensive to maintain – all the wooden decking needs a lot of upkeep. The extent of facilities is limited – it is exposed to wind and sun and has no contact with nature – again, features of its urban character. Health and well-being potential varies a lot – sense of being away and contact with nature are not possible in such a setting. Water connections are generally good, apart from direct access into the water or water activities. It is not a place where there is much scope for physical activity. A good project making great use of limited space in a very urban context. Figure 12.25 shows sketches analysing the project.

Figure 12.24

A view of the Sjövikstorget showing the stepped and tilted paving and the enclosed nature of the space with the views out beyond

(*Source*: Courtesy of Thorbjörn Andersson/SWECO)

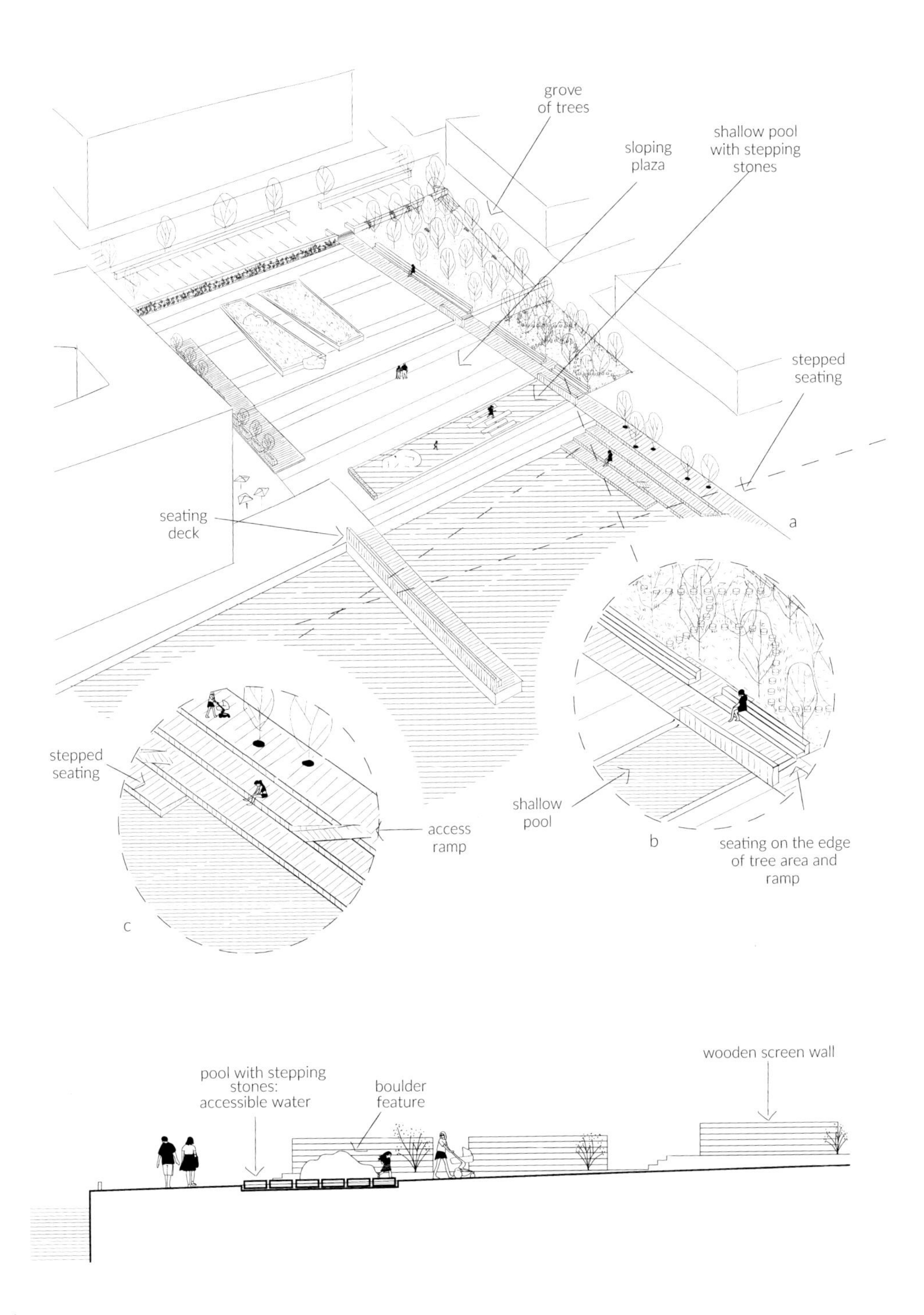

Figure 12.25a–d

a) Overview of the Sjövikstorget project emphasising the layout – the narrow tree belt, the sloping plaza with water feature and the wooden seating along or projecting into the water; b) the seating along the tree line overlooking the open plaza; c) the wooden stepped seating along the water's edge; d) a section over the whole area showing the descent from the urban edge through the plaza to the water

Sea Organ, Zadar, Croatia

This project, designed by Nikola Bašić, was constructed in 2005 and is a unique feature set on the shores of the Adriatic Sea at Zadar, a resort in Croatia. The Sea Organ (*morske orgulje*) is a form of natural musical instrument modelled on the ancient Greek *hydraulis*. The new stepped embankment constructed by master stonemasons is 70 m long, and the instrument consists of 35 organ pipes linked to a resonating chamber laid under the concrete substructure of the new sea wall, itself constructed to restore poor post-war reconstruction (Figure 12.26). The musical pipes are located so that the sea water pushes in with the movement of the waves, and then the air so displaced resonates to produces sounds of different pitch. The designer claims that it achieves a communication with nature and promotes a unity of architecture and environment. As wave movements are unpredictable, the range of sounds produced is infinitely variable. Besides the sea organ, the embankment with its steps and ramps provides places to sit, to sunbathe and to access the warm seawater, all the while hearing the sounds continually produced. It is a very evocative way of experiencing blue space through different senses.

Project quality rating assessment

The project has good access, apart from public transport, and the design quality is high, although such a complex feature is expected to be expensive and complex to maintain. It is limited in terms of facilities – it is a small and specialised element, so this is understandable – but it is very exposed to sun and wind and, due to its character, has little in the way of nature associated with it. Its unique quality gives potential for health and well-being, although not a sense of being away or contact with nature, due to its location (although the sounds from the organ also convey a special form of contact with nature). Water connections are very good, although it does not feature many water activities – not part of the design brief – and likewise, it is not designed for promoting or offering physical activities. Figure 12.27 shows how it has been analysed by sketching.

Figure 12.26

A view of the Sea Organ showing the steps and the holes along the top step where the sound emerges

(*Source*: Creative Commons Attribution-Share Alike 2.0 Generic Licence)

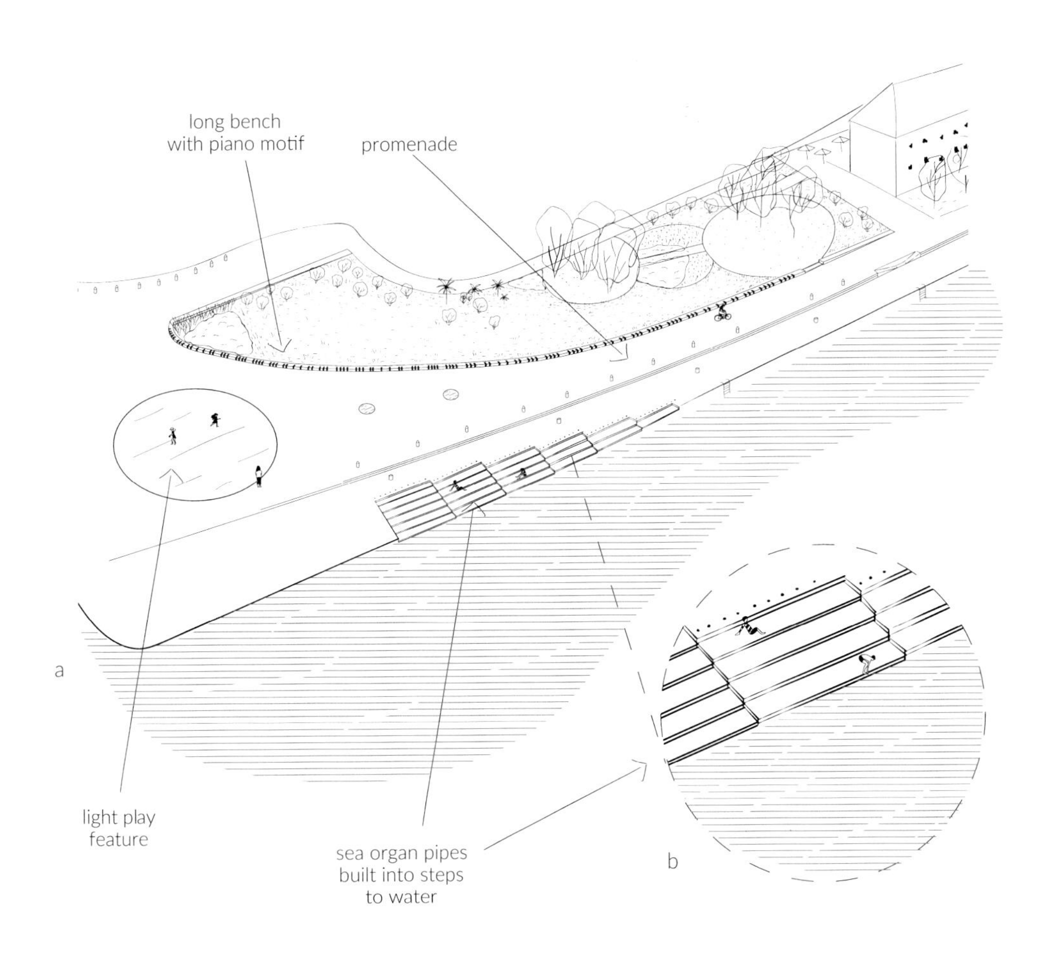

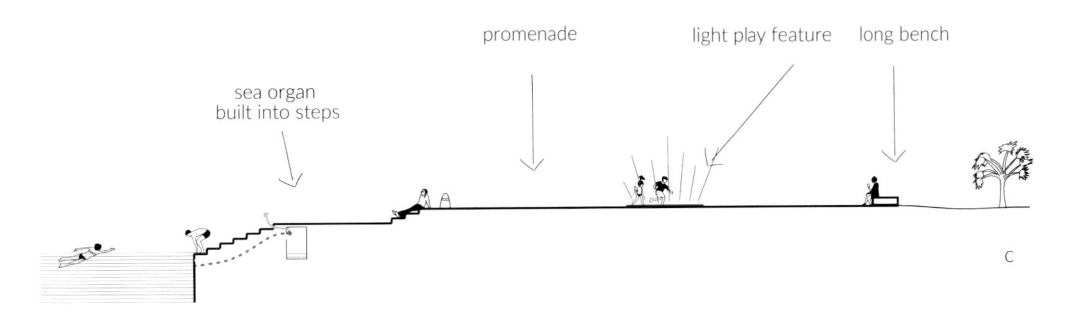

Figure 12.27a–c

a) Overview of the Sea Organ project showing how the steps extend along the shore, which contain the sea organ components, with the broader plaza behind featuring lighting which is interactive with the wave movement, connecting light and sound; b) the steps containing the sound-generating pipes; c) a section through the steps down into the water

Visual and physical access to the water landscape: Bondi-Bronte coastal walk, Sydney Australia

This project was completed in 2009 from designs by Aspect Studios of Sydney. It is a 515-m extension of the 9-km-long coastal walk stretching from South Head to Marouba. This section, the Bondi-Bronte walk, is located in eastern Sydney. From here it is possible to obtain amazing panoramic vistas, and it is a heavily visited location. The site is a series of sandstone escarpments and cliffs, which posed severe challenges for engineering and construction. It is also very sensitive, and so the project needed to take this into account. It is an example of a constructed facility which enables access while protecting the landscape, although due to the terrain and constructional challenges, universal access could not be achieved. The elevated boardwalk is constructed from stainless steel with wooden decking, steel grill or mesh steps surfaces, wooden seating and handrails. It resolves complex geotechnical, structural and historical conditions (Figure 12.28). The walk highlights the sublime qualities of the land and sea interface. As well as the walkway, there are a number of observation points, each focusing on a different aspect of the geology and landscape. The structure appears quite delicate and minimal and sits lightly on the fragile cliffs. The route also presents different vistas, as one is hidden and another one revealed as the walker proceeds along it.

Project quality rating assessment

This project, due to its location and the terrain, was always going to show some limitations against different aspects. In terms of accessibility, it suffers in several aspects, especially universal access, as well as its visibility from a distance. The design does well for some but not all aspects – cultural heritage is weaker given its location – but the quality of materials suggests it should be low maintenance. The number of facilities is necessarily limited, and the whole site is very exposed to the elements. The health and well-being potential is very good, apart from direct contact with nature over most of its length. Water access – apart from visual access – is impossible given the terrain, so naturally it is rated low. Physical activity is clearly limited to walking. The project is excellent at maximising potential given the location and terrain limitations. It makes the most of the challenging design environment and engineering requirements and manages to remain modest, allowing the spectacular scenery and ocean views to dominate, which is as it should be. Figure 12.29 expresses the character of the site using sketches.

Figure 12.28

A view of the walkway and steps on the Bondi-Bronte coastal walk, showing how it perches above the cliffs and ocean

(*Source*: jipe7 via Flickr)

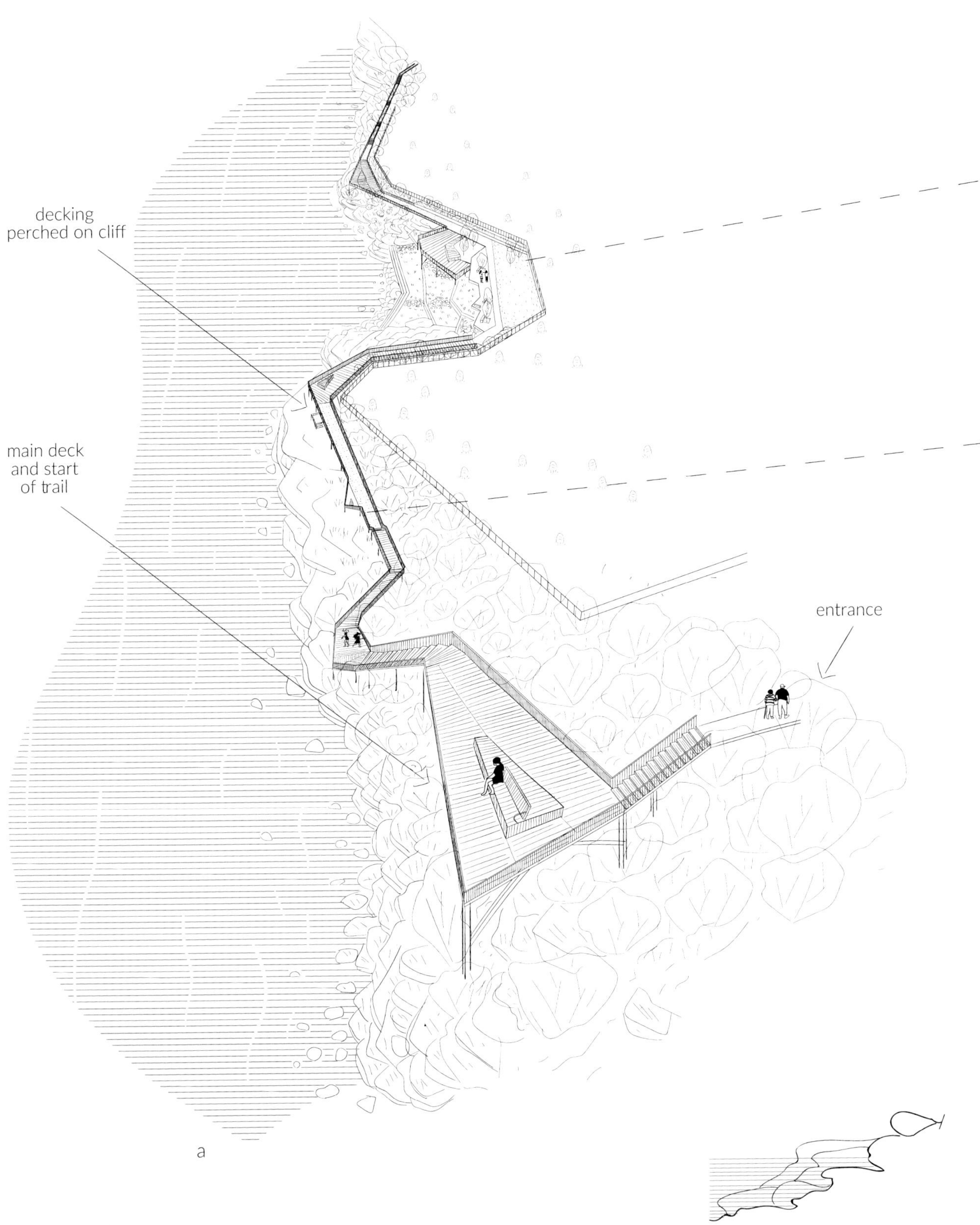

Figure 12.29a–e

a) The Bondi-Bronte pathway clings to the shore and winds across the rocks, emphasising how it provides access to a challenging stretch of coastline; b) detail of wooden decking connecting to a path with steps leading down a terraced section and ending close to the sea; c) one of the seating pockets which provide a great place for resting and admiring the view; d) cross-section of the terraced, grassed spaces in the central portion; e) a section through the elevated deck, stairs and seating pocket with bench

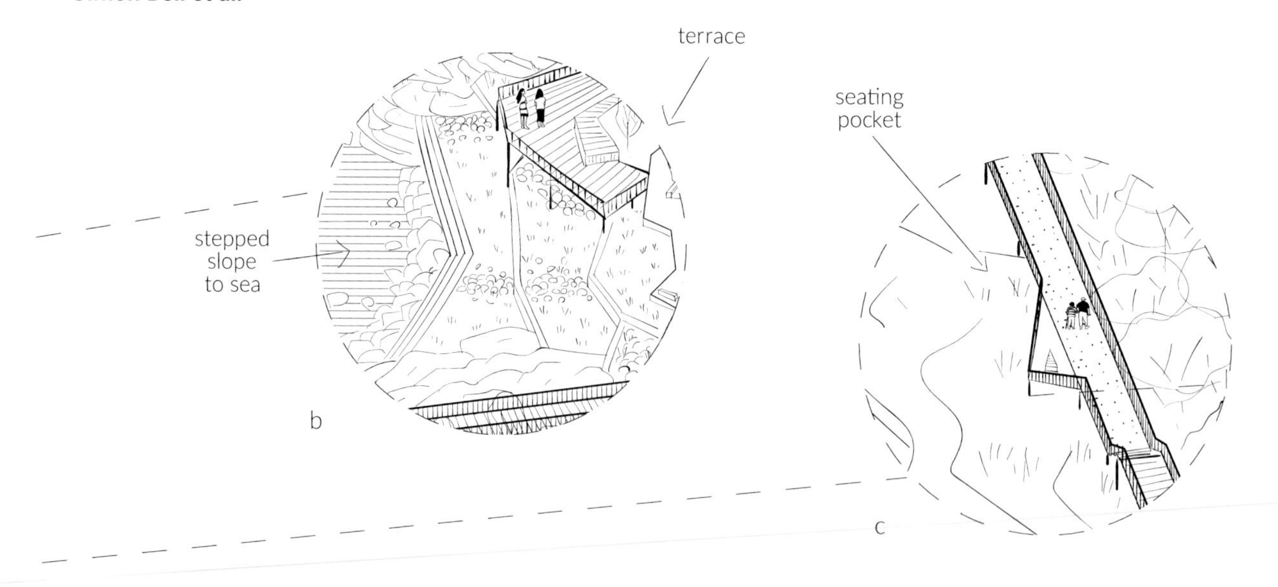

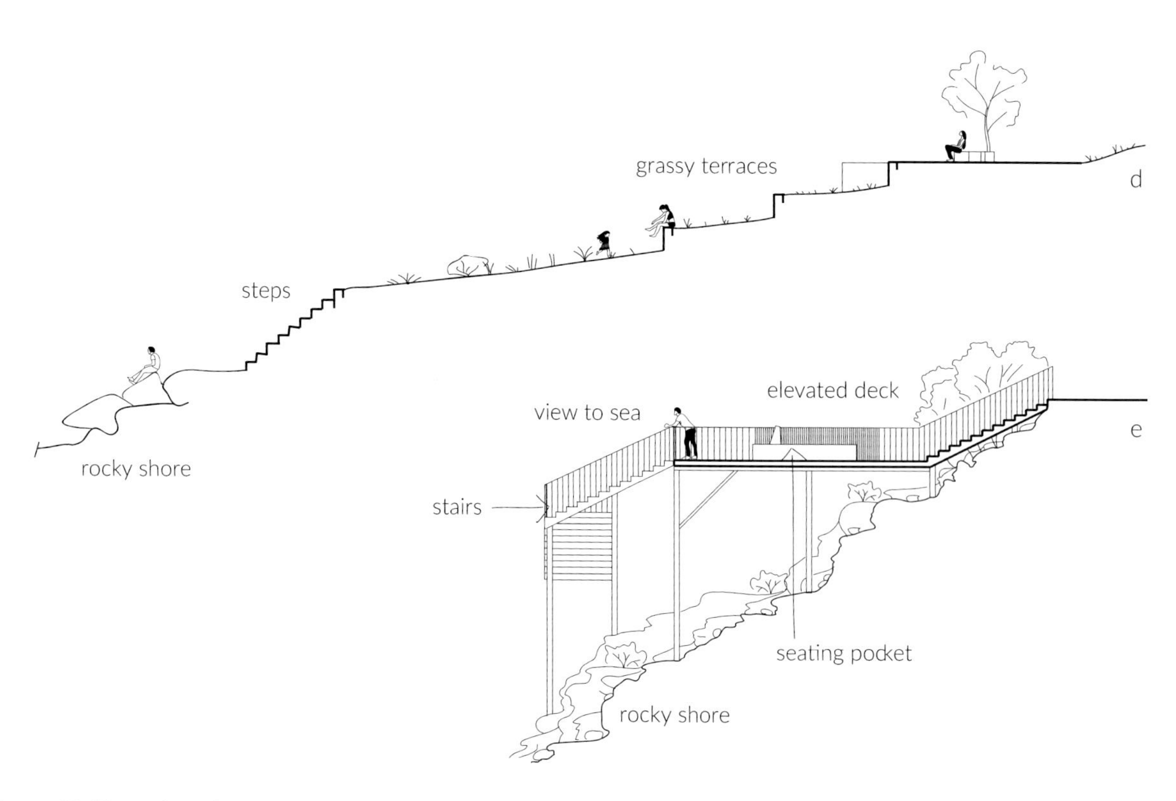

Figure 12.29a–e (continued)

Concordia University lakeshore, Concordia University, Wisconsin, United States

This project, completed in 2010, was designed by Smith Group for Concordia University. The site comprises the top, slopes and bottom of a high, steep bluff lying above Lake Michigan. The height of the bluff is 40 m, which made accessibility down to the lakeshore from the university campus a major challenge. In fact, the project started for the purpose of slope stabilisation but became a more complex design project with inclusive access, landscape restoration, wetland and coastal area designs, storm water management and use of slope-stabilising native plants. The project connects the university with its main natural asset, the lakefront, for the university staff and students as well as the general public. The project provides beaches, hiking, fishing, swimming, wildlife observation, landscape viewing and educational resources. The open-air theatre built into the design is used as an outdoor classroom. The design features a series of zig-zag ramps traversed with a more direct access via steps (Figure 12.30). The theatre overlooks the lake and is located at the top. The paths incorporate drainage channels to collect the runoff and are lit at night. The beach at the bottom is flanked by stone riprap stabilisation structures.

Project quality rating assessment

This project provides excellent accessibility, except for its visibility from a distance (given the large lake). It is also an excellent design, apart from the lack of reference to cultural historical aspects – which, given its location, is no surprise. The facilities are somewhat limited by the terrain and gradients, and it lacks seating on the climb (despite seating at the top as part of the open-air theatre). It is also exposed and lacks any shade or shelter. It has excellent

Figure 12.30
A view of the Concordia University Lakeshore slope with the paths and steps leading down to the lakeshore
(*Source*: Smith Group)

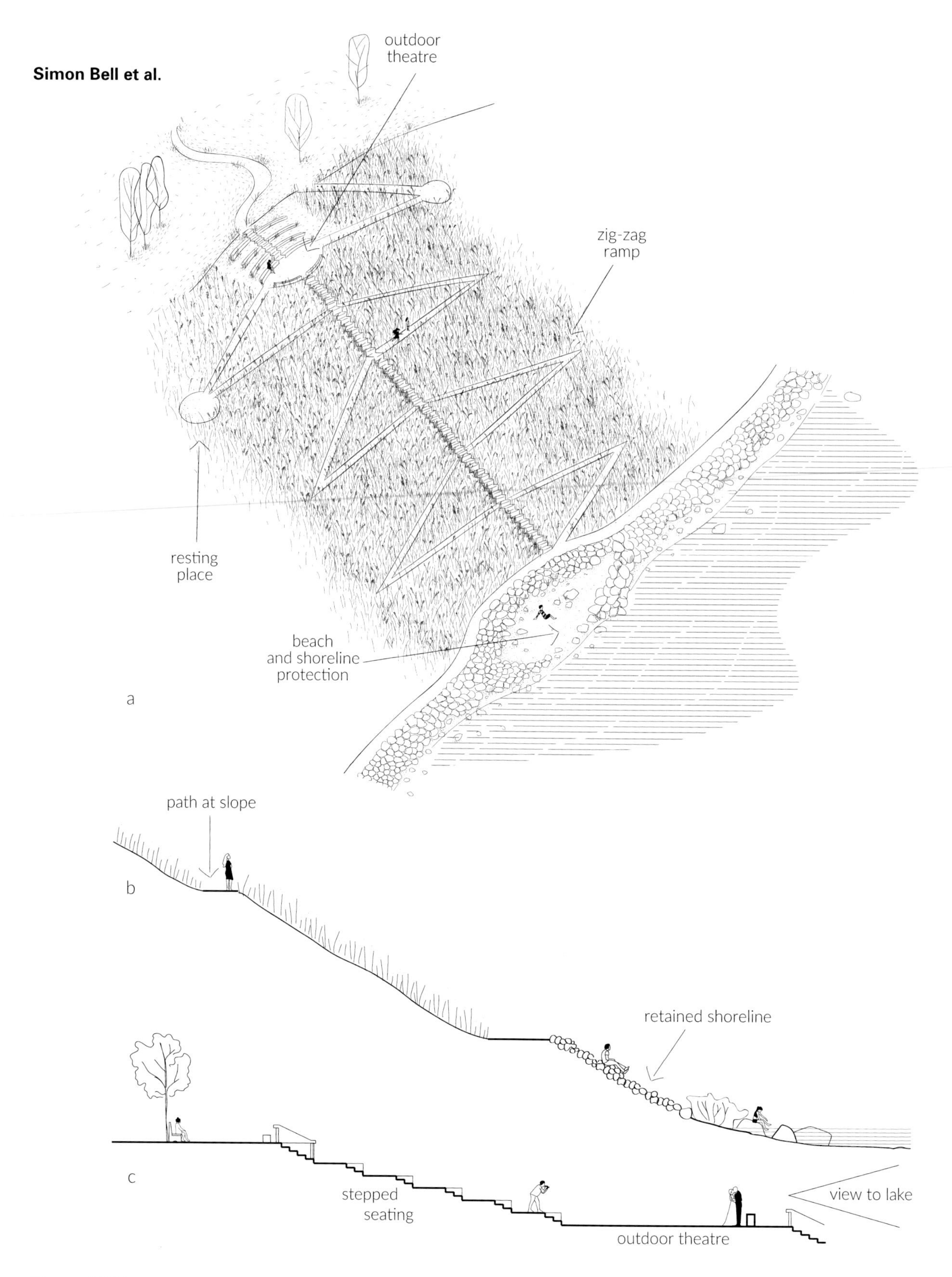

Figure 12.31a–c

a) Overview of the Concordia University Lakeshore project showing the three main sections – the platform and theatre at the top of the slope, the zig-zag ramp and step sequence leading down to the lake and finally the lake-shore and lake access; b) a section highlighting the bottom of the slope showing how the ramps are incorporated into it and how they finish at the beach and retained shoreline; c) section focusing on the upper part with the theatre and steps leading downwards

potential for health and well-being. Water accessibility is also very good, apart from accessibility from the water – no jetties – and the range of possible activities in or on the water – due to the poor accessibility, it is assumed. The range of possible physical activities is also necessarily limited by the terrain and nature of the design. This is a really good example of a project which overcomes huge challenges and results in a unique and sensitive solution that provides something special in an otherwise rather bland landscape. Figure 12.31 presents the sketched analysis of the project.

Comparison of projects in terms of different aspects

General design aspects

The projects presented in this chapter were chosen for their diversity and originality, and they each display many interesting and exceptional qualities in this regard. They each combine a sensitivity to sense of place and place creation with a high degree of creative solutions to the specific contexts and project briefs. That many were competition winners also demonstrates that new and innovative solutions are possible even in traditional or familiar places such as at the seaside or on the beach. One aspect which has only been a feature of the designs in a few cases is the reference to cultural history – many are in places with little of this present, or else the designers did not find much to which to make reference. Even the regenerated promenades such as at Dover or Benidorm tend to refer to inspiration such as the movement of waves rather than historical elements.

Potential for enhancing health and well-being

Almost all the projects display many opportunities to improve health and well-being. Onshore and in-water physical activities are possible, and the projects generally aim to attract and facilitate more of this as an integral part of the design. De-stressing, getting closer to nature and contemplation may have more potential in some places, but busy tourist beaches can be noisy and full of stimulation, which limit this. All beaches tend to be very exposed to the sun and wind, and the presence of shade provided by the projects varied, many having none at all, which could pose risks for skin cancer, sunburn and so on.

Accessibility

All the sites except for one (Bondi-Bronte walkway) are very accessible – even the Concordia lake shore. Some sites have local issues with steps, such as Zadar, and it seems that public transport is not always ideal. Some sites are isolated, others well connected outside the boundaries.

Interaction with water

Beaches, promenades and sea/lake fronts are in general all constructed with water access in mind – as a result of the history of sea-bathing summarised in the introduction to this chapter. With some exceptions, such as Sugar Beach or Sjövikstorget, all the beaches and promenades featured here promote direct access to the water. It is the Bondi-Bronte walkway, which provides a promenade but no direct access, that is the only one not directly connected with the water.

Seating and opportunities for socialising

Most of the projects make plenty of provision for seating, often in conjunction with viewpoints, as at Bondi-Bronte and Myrtle Edwards Park; sheltered nooks along promenades, as at Dover; or beneath umbrellas, as at Sugar Beach. However, some do not provide much or any formal seating, and so steps and other structures take the role, for example, at Zadar or Sjövikstorget. Some projects lack sufficient seating, such as the Concordia University Lakeshore, where the long ramps look daunting. Of course, at many beaches, seating is optional, and it is possible for users to bring their own or to rent it, so it is unnecessary to provide it as part of the design.

Microclimate amelioration

Almost all the beaches and promenades presented here, for obvious reasons of their location and purpose, are very exposed to the sun and wind – usually both. This can present a risk to health, especially in locations where the sun is strong, such as the Mediterranean Sea resorts of Benidorm or Vinaros or in Australia – especially at tropical Cairns. It is a factor which designers could consider more when working on such projects (see final recommendations in the following). The shading structures at Benidorm, cast in concrete as part of the promenade, help to some degree, but there are other potential solutions available, such as stretched fabric, which could be used more, as could vegetation.

Use of materials

There is a relatively narrow range of materials used in the construction of the projects reviewed here. Concrete is popular – it is more resistant to waves and storms – as in Dover, Benidorm and Veules-les-Roses, but timber is also extensively employed in decking, boardwalks, buildings and other structures, such as at Saulkrasti, as well as at Paprocany. Stone is also used to some extent, often for high-quality specialist paving or for walls and seating as at Zadar or Sjövikstorget. In coastal climates with salt in the air, steel is less sustainable unless stainless or galvanised and is not used so much (except at Bondi-Bronte). The use of certain materials, such as concrete, is clearly with the aim of reducing maintenance costs (see the following). Artificial beaches, such as Amager, also require a lot of sand, which, in the conditions of natural water movement, may be washed away and need to be replaced.

Use of vegetation and ecological aspects

In many projects, planting plays only a small role – some rows of trees (sometimes palms which do not provide shade or shelter), grassed areas (where wear and tear may be less of an issue) and occasional ornamental flowers. This seems to be a missed opportunity, especially when there is a need for shade and shelter in many locations and there are plenty of suitable trees available. Some sites clearly have ecological values and sensitivities – such as Saulkrasti in Latvia or the cliffs at Bondi-Bronte and the bluff at Concordia University – where the boardwalks protect the ground surface and encourage people to stay on the paths.

Site management and maintenance

All the projects are well maintained – and many have been in use for over 10 years so that repair and maintenance would be expected to be necessary by now. If the construction has been to a high standard and good-quality materials have been used, then this should lead to a reduced need for extensive maintenance. However, the widespread use of timber for decking leads to a need for constant checking and repair, since it can react to different weather conditions even if it does not rot. The sites also appear to be free from vandalism and are kept very clean, which helps to maintain them as welcoming places.

Conclusions and implications for practice

This chapter has reviewed the history and importance of the seaside, lakesides, beaches and promenades as places to visit with enduring attraction for local residents and tourists alike. The heydays of promenading along specially constructed "proms" and esplanades in the 19th and 20th centuries continues, but new and reconstructed projects range from references back to the classical models of yesteryear to innovative and highly creative responses following national or international design competitions. The selection presented here all have their strengths and weaknesses according to a number of factors such as the setting, terrain, history or climate. Each designer has attempted to maximise the opportunities and minimise the constraints while also producing solutions which provide better opportunities to interact with water and to imbue a new or reimagined sense of place. These projects have often also had significant impacts on the local economies and on the image and brand of the places where they are located.

There are a few specific aspects we wish to draw attention to:

- Increasing the availability of shade and shelter as we move into times of more extreme weather events, heat-waves, storms and so on and in order to reduce the risks of skin cancer.
- Making more use of sustainable materials which balance longevity and low maintenance with local origin and flexibility of application for different functions.
- Including more vegetation in projects which offer the potential for it – both ornamental, functional (shade or shelter) and ecological (to reduce the need for hard materials and to restore damaged habitats).
- To celebrate and maintain continuity with the long traditions of being at the seaside – sun, sea and sand; strolling along the prom; and keeping cars away from families relaxing and enjoying themselves.

Finally, in this chapter, we have highlighted the enduring value and importance of beaches and promenades, seeing how they have been re-invented in recent years to provide facilities which satisfy current social requirements. From their origins over 200 years ago and through the highs and lows of popularity as holiday destinations, together within the current contexts of environmental and social change, it is gratifying to see creative approaches taking account of these challenges. It shows how adaptability is at the heart of successful design in these conditions.

References

Barton, S. (2005) *Working-Class Organisations and Popular Tourism, 1840–1970*, Victorian Manchester University Press, Manchester

Boyer, M. (2002) *L'Invention de la Côte d'Azur: l'hiver dans le Midi (The Invention of the Côte d'Azur: Winter in the Midi)*, Édition de l'Aube, Paris

Corbin, A. (1995) *The Lure of the Sea*, Penguin Books, London

Cross, G. and Walton, J. K. (2005) *The Playful Crowd: Pleasure Places in the Twentieth Century*, Columbia University Press, Chichester

Walton, J. K. (1983) *The English Seaside Resort: A Social History 1750–1914*, Manchester University Press, Manchester

Walton J. K. (2000) *The British Seaside: Holidays and Resorts in the Twentieth Century*, Manchester University Press, Manchester

Chapter 13: Urban wetlands and storm water management

Himansu S. Mishra, Simon Bell, Anna Wilczyńska and Jekaterina Balicka

Introduction

Increasing risks of flood damage to life and property combined with wider health and socioeconomic and environmental issues are perceived as a major threat in both developed and developing societies. Many global cities have built grey infrastructure to provide efficient urban services (e.g. road infrastructure, drainage), which has marginalised natural hydrological systems and concealed them underground. A high proportion of grey infrastructure and techno-sols in urban areas results in a huge amount of polluted urban storm water following significant rainfall events and has been acknowledged as a so-called "wicked problem" with widespread public health implications. Due to increases in urban land sealing, impervious surfaces and the interruption of natural infiltration of runoff coupled with urban activities (e.g. ground water extraction and domestic, commercial, agricultural and industrial wastewater discharge), high volumes of peak runoff discharge can be produced, which alters the natural hydrological pattern and cycle and causes localised flooding. An excessive runoff load event puts pressure on the existing and conventional storm water drainage infrastructure that forces storm water to mix with sewage and disgorge into natural stream and river systems. In response to the growing prevalence of urban flooding and storm water-induced socioeconomic and health issues, urban planners have shifted their focus towards adopting nature-based solutions (NBS) (see Chapter 2) and low-impact development (LID), water-sensitive urban design (WSUD) and integrated storm water management (ISWM) approaches and practices (Fletcher et al., 2015). Cities have been re-inventing, reinstating and liberating forgotten and modified natural hydrological systems, such as rivers (see Chapter 11), natural drains and wetlands, for environmental and societal benefits.

Historical accounts of ancient civilisations (e.g. Indus and Minoan) show how they developed sophisticated systems to collect rainwater, prevent nuisance flooding and convey waste, based on many trial-and-error modifications (Burian and Edwards, 2015). In mediaeval Europe, urban drainage practices were non-existent, and urban storm water runoff and industrial wastewater were discharged into local streams and rivers – a practice that continued until relatively recently. Over the last century, there has been an evolution in management of urban storm water. Especially in the United States, the establishment of local and federal regulations requiring storm water control measures (SCMs) explains the early developments of single-service engineering solutions, such as sediment traps or drywells, which proved efficient and effective SCMs to detain or retain storm water (McPhillips and Matsler, 2018).

The inclusion of ecological components that changed the paradigm of storm water management can be traced back to Boston's renowned "Emerald Necklace" park system. Designed by landscape architect Frederick Law Olmsted in 1895, the park demonstrates a well-established concept of blue-green infrastructure (Marks et al., 2015). It encompasses a hydrological network that resolves the functional issues of urban storm water management and contributes to providing aesthetic, functional and cultural values as Boston's largest public park (Figure 13.1). The

DOI: 10.4324/9780429056161-17

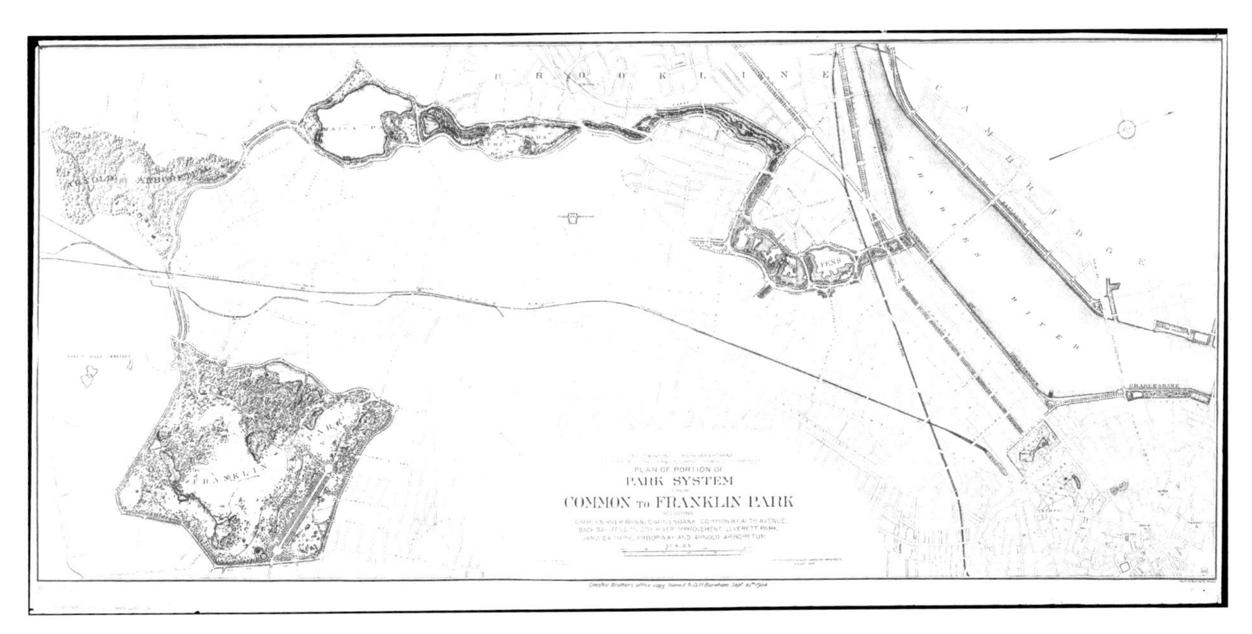

Figure 13.1

A late plan of the Boston Park System by Olmsted in 1894, which shows an integrated network of blue-green infrastructure

(*Source*: Wikipedia Creative Commons)

Clean Water Act (CWA), established, reorganised and expanded in 1972, formed the basic legal structure for regulating discharges of pollutants into the waters of the United States and regulating quality standards for surface waters. Also in the United States, the low-impact development concept emerged from the approach of "design with nature" (a term coined by Ian McHarg in 1969) and aimed to minimise the cost of storm water management and its adverse impact on nature.

The integrated urban water management concept in the 1980s broadened the practices of urban drainage and combined with water supply, ground water, wastewater and storm water (Fletcher et al., 2015). Similarly, in the 1980s, the sustainable urban drainage system (SUDS) was developed in the United Kingdom and defined the scope for controlling urban runoff. The concept of water-sensitive urban design began to be applied in the 1990s in Australia, with the objectives of managing the water balance to enhance water quality, encourage water conservation and maintain aquatic environments.

The concept of green infrastructure emerged in the United States in the 1990s to promote storm water management practices by using a network of green spaces (Benedict and McMahon, 2006). However, this goes beyond storm water and encompasses the role of vegetated systems in enhancing urban amenity and human health (Tzoulas et al., 2007). The European Union Water Framework Directive (Directive 2000/60/EC of the European Parliament and of the Council) establishes a framework for the protection of inland surface waters, transitional waters, coastal waters and groundwater. It aims to prevent and reduce pollution, promote sustainable water use, protect and improve the aquatic environment and mitigate the effects of floods and droughts.

Urban green storm water infrastructures (UGSWIs) can help to mitigate urban flooding by introducing a sustainable and resilient water cycle in the city. Innovative storm water management approaches have been widely accepted and used compared to conventional grey infrastructures (Li et al., 2019). These systems operate at different spatial scales, and, especially at the city scale, they deal with domestic and conventional water flow and the local atmospheric water cycle. Most cities adopt combined sewer and storm water discharge systems, which have shown many flaws over time in managing and treating wastewater, especially during wet weather conditions.

Storm water infrastructure can be directly connected to the landscape either through landscape application of ecological principles, landscape features supporting ecological principles or both. These spatial structures formed of natural or semi-natural areas are claimed to accomplish three main objectives: water quantity, water quality and amenity and biodiversity (Perales-Momparler et al., 2015). Moreover, they can contribute to Sustainable Development Goals (SDGs) by providing flood resilience (e.g. flood mitigation), natural resources management (e.g. protected water quality, quantity and biodiversity), increasing liveability for people (e.g. improved microclimate and enhanced social cohesion, etc.) and transition and innovation (e.g. stakeholder participation, improved economy, built knowledge, etc.) (Sørup et al., 2019).

The term 'storm water management system' refers to the ability to control the quantity (e.g. reduction of runoff and velocity) and improve the quality (e.g. reduction of pollutants) of urban storm water. To elaborate further, the function of an effective storm water management system depends on the environmental processes it involves and bio-physical features it uses to support various functions and services (Dover, 2015) and to promote human health and well-being. For example, the Active Beautiful Clean (ABC) water programme in Singapore demonstrates the popularity of using storm water management projects for outdoor recreation and nature experience (Lim and Lu, 2016).

Green storm water management infrastructure projects utilise natural processes to infiltrate, retain, transport and treat storm water using different biophysical elements. There are different kinds of sustainable drainage system techniques available for different functions. For runoff reduction at the source, landscape structures such as rain gardens, rainwater harvesting, vegetated roofs, bio-retention cells and infiltration structures such as permeable paving are proven effective. For the purpose of reducing peak flow of storm water, vegetated detention basins or dry and wet ponds are designed to hold temporarily and pre-treat the first flush of storm water before regulating discharge to a receiving water body, from where the water is slowly released over 24–72 hours into the stream or river system. For sediment removal and water quality improvement, bio-swales, filter strips and wetlands are effective measures. Besides cleaning and filtering water, a large number of urban wetland projects support citizens' needs for cultural, social and recreational activities. Thus they have emerged as popular places for obtaining nature experiences and have been found to be frequented by large numbers of visitors annually. The important design aspects that promote the health and well-being potential provided by green storm water management systems are an increase in accessibility that facilitates activities and minimises the risks (since the water in these parks may be rather polluted).

Semi-natural and constructed wetlands are flood plains inundated or saturated by shallow water, seasonally or annually, sufficient to support plant and animal growth and reproduction. They are formed of and connect with lakes, ponds, rivers or streams and create a transition between dry land and open water. Due to rapid urbanisation of rural land, uncoordinated urban management and infrastructure development, agriculture and so on, many natural wetlands have been destroyed and degraded. However, in recent years, cities around the world have recognised and begun to understand the importance of ecosystem services provided by wetlands and the benefits of restoring and, wherever necessary, creating new wetlands (McInnes, 2014; Jia et al., 2011). Wetland functions and benefits depend on the hydrological regime, soil conditions, local vegetation types and the size and location of the wetland in the landscape. Wetlands, irrespective of whether they are natural, semi-natural or constructed, provide benefits and contribute to wildlife habitat, flood control, pollutant filtration, storm and wind protection, agricultural land fertility, recreation and tourism, carbon storage, education and jobs and enhance property prices, climate change mitigation and so on. Wetlands, depending on their size, shape and location, adjust the urban micro-climate by increasing urban cooling, an effect found to be important in mitigating the urban heat island effect (Sun and Chen, 2017). Wetlands purify water naturally by trapping, removing and settling or detoxifying pollutants such as chemicals (nitrates, ammonium, phosphorus); sediment loads or soil particles; fertilisers; pesticides; and grease and oil from vehicles, roads or parking areas. Despite the fact that they provide conventional water treatment replacement cost benefits, recent research and design has focused on their additional recreational values and economic benefits.

Urban wetlands may attract large numbers of people to perform a range of outdoor activities such as bird watching, recreation and sightseeing and, when close to settlements, they promote nature connectedness. With the increasing risk of destroying or degrading wetlands as a result of ill-thought-out urban growth, we may permanently lose these important recreational, health and well-being and economic benefits. Therefore, when planning the design and management of wetlands in and around urban areas, it is important to maintain the complex socioeconomic and natural ecosystem to help create liveable cities. While urban wetland planning processes set out tasks for the determination of wetland function, type of wetland, spatial distribution and water requirements for the maintenance of ecological function (Jia et al., 2011), there is a need to explore the social, cultural and experiential paradigm of wetlands as landscape settings, and research on this aspect has been lagging. There has been an increase in wetland creation and restoration projects, and many of these have been monitored to see how the different benefits accrue and to demonstrate their role as scenic, recreational and cultural hotspots. Modern public and institutional campuses also incorporate wetland landscapes and, with careful site planning, integrate them with everyday site functions and recreation.

Why the cases were chosen

For the selection of cases, this chapter covers categories of blue space projects based on their success at combining storm and other water treatment measures and solutions with recreational aspects in green storm water management infrastructures, wetland and urban parks and open space demands and functions. We selected a range of projects that were successful in restoring existing natural waterways which fell victim to urban development and the processes of controlling water environments within urban environments. We also looked for examples that are multifunctional public urban spaces that function within the urban context and offer extended ecosystem services. We consider that these engineered blue spaces have the potential to serve communities in a similar way to conventional parks and plazas yet also offer more possibilities for interacting with the natural environment in different ways. Thus, we present cases with a combination of development themes and an array of unique solutions pertaining to the particular problem and a specific context. We have four categories of projects: restoration of natural streams as green infrastructure, public space and urban waterfront green spaces, green infrastructure and storm water management and natural and semi-natural wetland parks.

Restoration of natural water bodies as blue-green infrastructure

Projects that completely restructure the urban fabric are unconventional and require strong motivation, justification and budgetary requirements. They are large-scale projects involving either the reinvention of lost blue and green natural environments or re-establishing natural processes within an urban environment. They represent the concept of adapting to the forces of nature and making urban living more resilient to those forces as opposed to trying to control or tame the environment for societal purposes. They may serve urban communities at different scales through the adoption of different nature-based solutions. Therefore, the access to and use of such environments created within societies are fundamental to human activities that connect social systems and the ecosystem. The projects included in this section are as follows:

- Bishan-Ang Mo Kio Park, Singapore
- Mill River Park and Greenway, Connecticut, United States
- West Seoul Lake Park: Seoul Urban Renewal, Seoul, South Korea

Blue infrastructure as public space

The next set of projects focus on public spaces at different scales that are predominantly built environments and designed spaces for urban functions and also provide unique ways to experience blue space. They have predominantly evolved as architecturally inspired spaces juxtaposed with engineering functions. However, they indirectly engage users with an environment that retains, infiltrates and treats storm water. They are valuable projects that respect the urban context, whether historical, sociocultural or economic, as well as urban planning and construction practices. The projects included in this section are as follows:

- City Park, Bradford, United Kingdom
- Sherbourne Commons, Toronto, Canada
- Witangi Park, Wellington, New Zealand

Blue infrastructure and storm water management creating community spaces

These projects demonstrate the current trends of sustainable environmental practices with urban developments that produce low-management and resilient localised solutions for storm water management that combine with the requirements of community blue-green spaces. The projects included in this section are as follows:

- Welland Canal Park & Civic Square, Welland, Canada
- Anchor Park, Malmo, Sweden
- Nansen Park, Oslo, Norway

Wetland parks

The last category of projects represents recent attempts to restore natural wetlands or create constructed wetlands as recreation destinations. They are very useful biotopes to support a deteriorating urban ecology and support innumerable urban ecosystem services yet depend on their size, location and carrying capacity. Despite being nature-based solutions specific to water detention, retention and treatment, they also create safe and enjoyable environments with very high cultural ecosystem services. They are multifunctional environments that provide both urban and rural experiences; however, they also require large areas and a longer time to be realised and conceivable. Wetlands are found to be very popular destinations for outdoor recreation, as they provide spectacular opportunities to interact and be immersed in the natural setting, which promotes a high sense of being-away.

- Tianjin Qiaoyuan Wetland Park, Tianjin, China
- Magnuson Park, Seattle, United States
- Sydney Park Water Reuse Project, Sydney, Australia

Each project is briefly described (based on information from a range of sources, often the designer or articles, as well as what the authors have seen). It is then illustrated with a photograph of a typical view, assessed for project quality based on the factors presented in Chapter 10 and illustrated using a set of sketches designed to bring out the key aspects which make the project special and inspirational. These are presented as annotated images, and they aim to complement the text visually, so there is no additional description in the text, only the captions.

Restoration of natural water bodies as blue-green infrastructure: Bishan-Ang Mo Kio Park, Singapore

Bishan-Ang Mo Kio Park was developed as one of the largest urban parks in central Singapore that was realised under the Public Utility Board's Active, Beautiful and Clean Waters scheme. The project was initiated in 2009 and designed by Ramboll Studio Dreiseitl for the Public Utilities Board/National Parks Board, Singapore. The project transformed an old concrete canal into a 3-km-long meandering river with natural banks offering different types of blue and green infrastructure and public spaces for different recreational and social activities. The project is located between two housing estates and first opened in 1988 (and is thus an early example of such a project) on a 62-hectare site. It attracts millions of visitors annually and hosts many organised events. The aim was to create cleansing biotopes using bio-remediation, which provides many benefits through creating inclusive playgrounds, diverse habitats, community allotment gardens and places for nature play and recreation. Dealing with the wicked problem of urban hydrology by applying principles of landscape ecology, the project helps to break away from civil-engineering solutions to a more nature-based bio-engineering approach that increases the carrying capacity of the river. Coupled with re-engineering of the cross-section of the river using a nature-based approach, the project transformed community perceptions towards water in the city and promotes close interaction with nature and biodiversity.

The design of the park with the river offered a balanced functional, ecological and sociocultural space. The park, to date, is home to a growing number of species of wildflowers, birds and dragonflies enriching the biodiversity. The site features which promote active and passive interaction with water include bridges, terraced riverside galleries, river platforms, stepping stone paths and a water playground (Figure 13.2). The project incorporates a comprehensive river monitoring and a warning system, signal lights, sirens and audio announcements to provide early warning to the park users in the event of heavy rain or a possible flood.

Figure 13.2
Stepping stones at Bishan-Ang Mo Kio Park used for interaction with water and nature play
(*Source*: Ramboll Studio Dreiseitl Singapore)

Project quality rating assessment

The project demonstrates excellent performance in all aspects of accessibility to the site from the surrounding community and the city. The site is very visible and provides good and sufficient car parking. It was found to have good design quality, though it does not feature conservation or protection of cultural heritage, as there are no elements to take into account; however, it is successful at restoration of the natural heritage within the area. The site is very well provisioned for public amenities and facilities. The site offers good potential for health and well-being benefits through its safe and secure condition, opportunities for relaxation and contemplation, sensory affordances and some sense of being away. The aspect of contact with nature is limited to certain activities and limited compared with other aspects. Water accessibility and connectedness in terms of direct tactile experience is limited to a few areas. The site provides very good opportunities for nature play, different recreational activities and places to organise events and informal sports. The site is less suitable for water sports, as swimming and other immersive water activities are prohibited due to temporal changes of water level and water quality, though people like to paddle in it. The design is unique and an exemplar of a multi-functional nature-based solution that is iconic and a popular destination for recreation. Figure 13.3 presents the sketch analysis of the park.

Mill River Park and Greenway, Connecticut, United States

Mill River Park and Greenway in Stamford, Connecticut, is a long greenway design; the 11.33-hectare (28-acre) park is spread over 4.8 kilometres (3 miles). It was initiated in 2007 by OLIN for the Mill River Collaborative that is located along the Rippowam River in downtown Stamford, Connecticut, United States. This river landscape project, finished in 2013, was conceived to revitalise aquatic and terrestrial habitats, reduce flooding, restore the canalised river's edge and promote native planting. The project involved extensive community participation and was funded by a community collaborative of the city, state and federal government, along with local corporations and private citizens.

The riverbank within the project area has dramatically evolved over the years from its intense industrial past of mill and manufacturing activities. In the 20th century, it fell into disrepair, becoming an abandoned and unused green space; the river with the imposing concrete walls turned into an eyesore and a barrier between communities. The derelict and polluted riverfront had accumulated decades of debris, and an unmanaged riparian edge choked the river, leading to flooding. In 2005, a master plan was developed to remove the concrete dam and restore the meandering river and to offer the community a maintainable and implementable public space for recreation, with a rich natural habitat of native flora and fauna.

Besides regulatory ecosystem services such as flood management, the renewed riverbank offered places for active and passive recreation and active interaction with river's edge. The large flexible green space is suitable for events, which makes the place popular for waterfront entertainment. There is also the opportunity for contemplation and relaxation, and using native planting in the landscape design promotes regionalism.

The project revitalised the aquatic and terrestrial habitat and reduced flooding by introducing native plants and restoring the natural meandering form of the river (Figure 13.4). By implementing green infrastructure principles, the project provided habitat rehabilitation and community public green space. It also accomplished an ecological

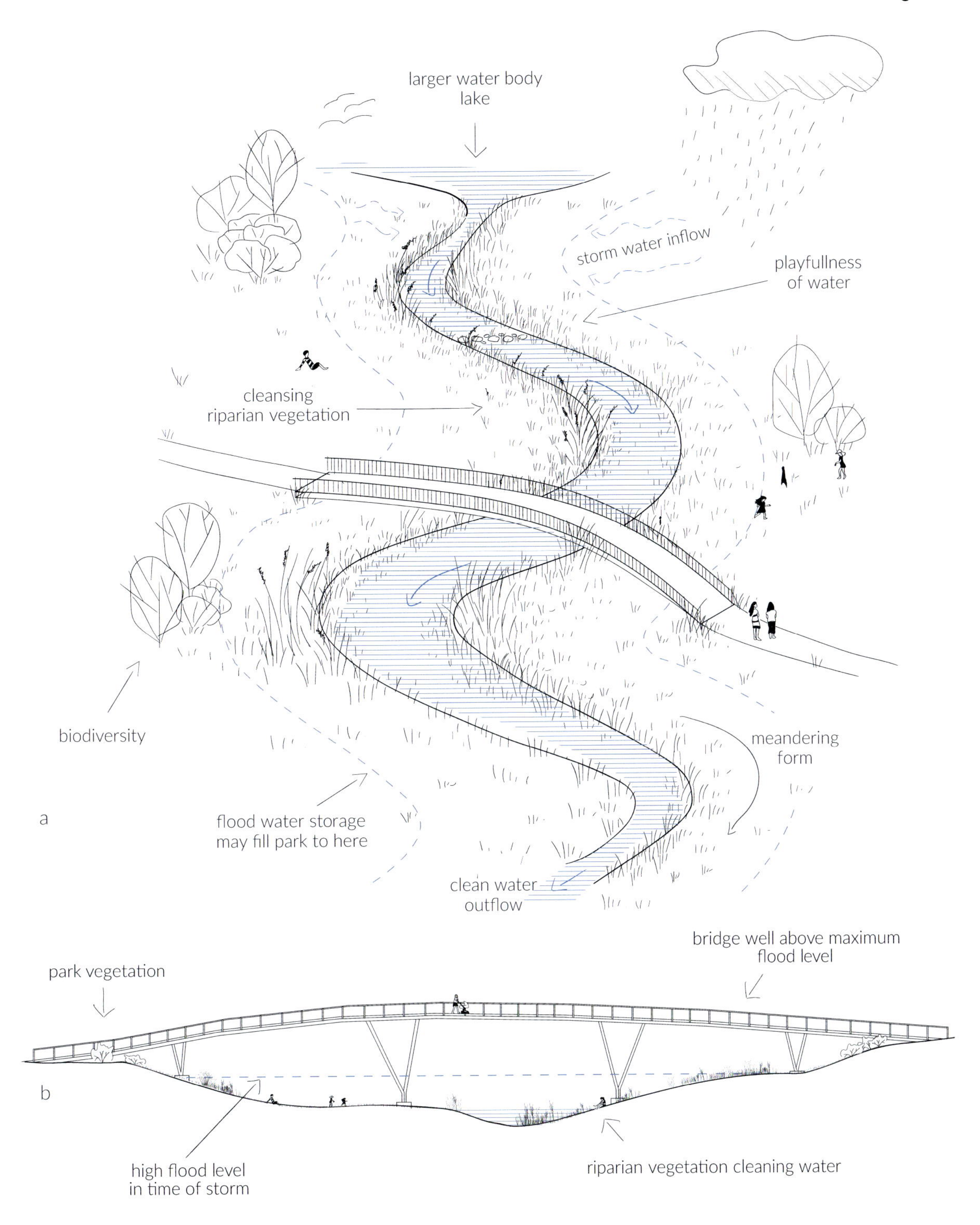

Figure 13.3a and b

a) A simplified water flow scheme at Bishan-Ang Mo Kio Park, explaining how the water enters the park, flows along the restored meanders through different vegetation types criss-crossed by paths and bridges and then exits as clean water; b) a cross-section showing the water channel with the vegetated flood terraces to hold and filter water during heavy rain events, with a bridge at its widest point so that people can cross over it even during a flood

(*Source*: Anna Wilczyńska and Jekaterina Balicka)

Figure 13.4
The restored meandering profile of Rippowam River within an upgraded park setting that provides opportunity for activity and water connection
(*Source*: OLIN)

revitalisation by bringing together a natural, protective flood plain, preventing flooding and managing the peak flow of water during a heavy storm event. The project was envisioned and developed in phases.

Project quality rating assessment

The project is rated very well for aspects of accessibility, design and facilities. In terms of health and well-being, the site can be perceived as highly restorative, except for the sense of being away. As the site is highly accessible and frequented by visitors, it is perceived to be safe and secure. Water connectedness and water safety are limited, however. Except for water sports, the project supports physical activities for formal, informal sports and children's play. Figure 13.5 presents sketches analysing the site.

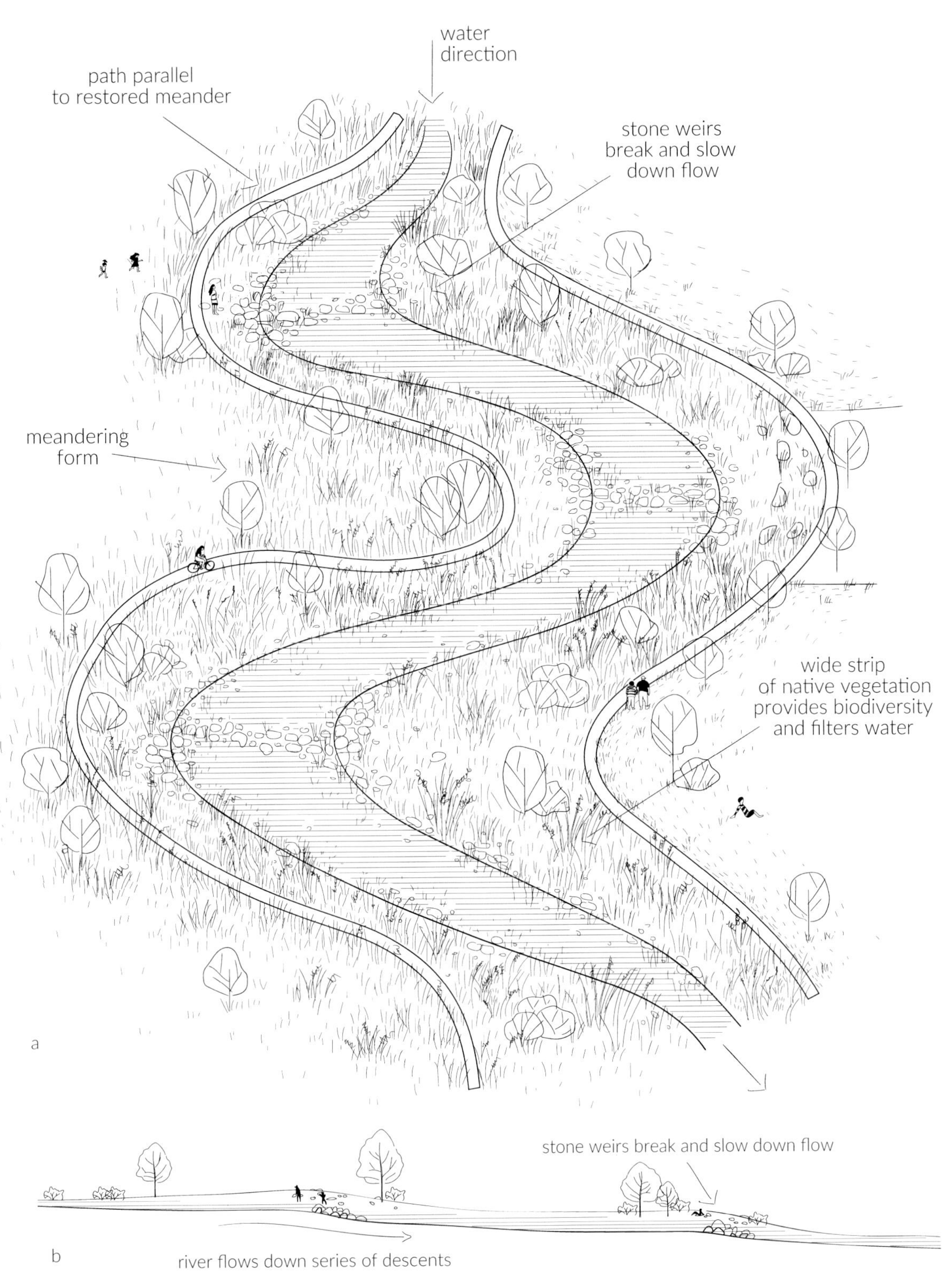

Figure 13.5a and b

a) Schematic overview of the Rippowam River describing the essential character of the project – the restored meander with stone weirs to break the flow and to manage the level changes, the vegetated slopes and the parallel path along the edge of the restored valley; b) longitudinal section showing a typical part where the stone weirs break and slow down the flow

(*Source*: Anna Wilczyńska and Jekaterina Balicka)

West Seoul Lake Park: Seoul urban renewal, Seoul, South Korea

West Seoul Lake Park is an urban renewal project that was developed in an old and abandoned water treatment plant and industrial facility and reclaimed as a zone for public recreation and community park. The park design was initiated with collaboration between landscape architecture firm CTOPOS Design and architecture firm JIAN Architects for the Seoul Metropolitan City and was opened to the public in 2009.

The project adopted the concept of an ecological park because the place was considered inappropriate for residential development due to the constant noise coming from the nearby international airport. The design embraces the old and dilapidated industrial fragments, and its core design concepts are regeneration, ecology and communication. The function of the new park is an "open cultural art space" that fosters community interaction and diversifies areas of identity and urban culture. It integrates nature, culture and urbanity and promotes education about urban nature and urban ecology.

The park embodies environmental sensitivity and sustainability and is also welcoming and environmentally friendly. As the central theme of the park is water purification, the spatial organisation considered the horizontal and vertical arrangement of old water pipes that dominated the space. The design highlights water by retaining the natural appearance of the old water treatment plant, lake views and recreational spaces and facilities located between the lake and the old water treatment building (Figure 13.6). Demolition of high walls opened up lake views, and water jets reduce overhead aircraft noise, making the place popular. A central plaza was created by opening up old structures (with a few left in place to reflect the heritage); a square garden introduces a variety of scales and produces a harmonious effect. The new water circulation and purification system replaces the existing one by creating a constant loop that feeds water into the series of landscape features and biotopes, for example, a water purification

Figure 13.6

A view of the West Seoul Lake Park showing the pattern of paving and planting, the pools and the old industrial structures retained in the design

(*Source*: Hana Shin)

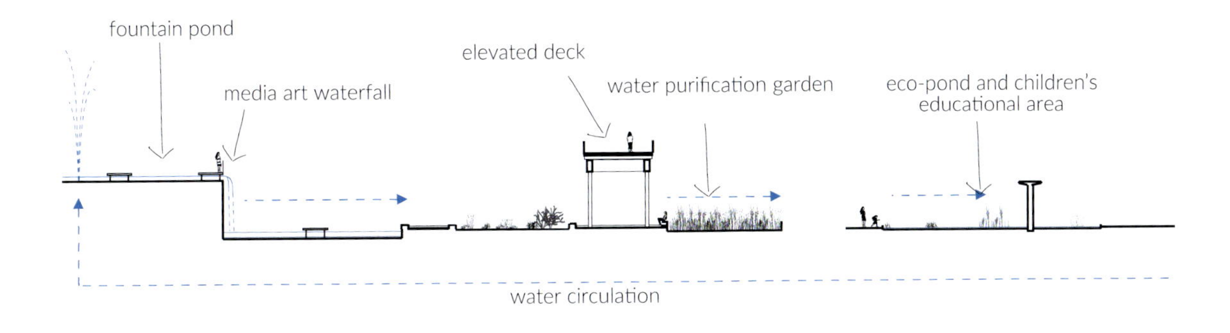

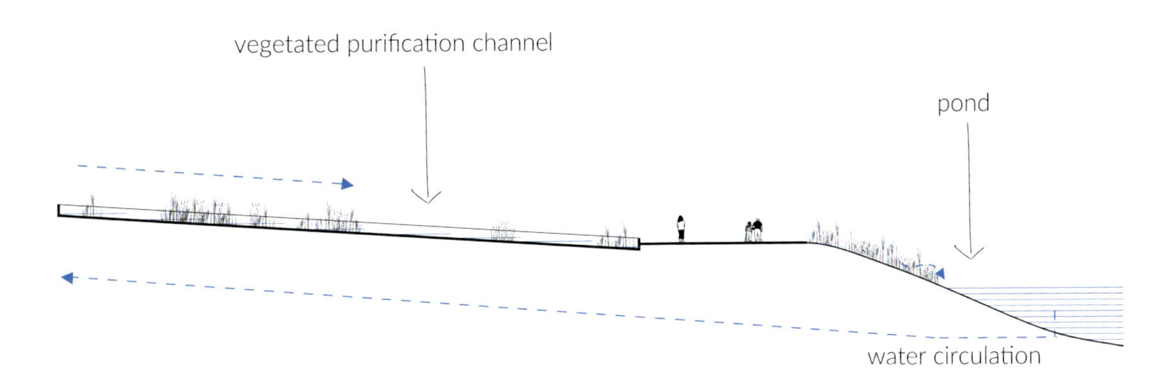

Figure 13.7

Schematic section of the West Seoul Lake Park water purification system using the different basins, some with aeration features (waterfall); the water purification garden; and then provision for user activities such as ecological play or a botanical garden, with higher-level paved areas among it. There is also re-circulation of the water to increase the purification process

(*Source*: Jekaterina Balicka)

garden, ecological waterway, aqua botanic garden and ecological water playground. A large fountain illuminated by LED lights using renewable energy makes the place enjoyable at night. This project is a good example of restoration of old city infrastructure as well as use of water and nature to successfully create public space to improve community health and well-being. Its contribution to integration of urban renewal and landscaping is an exemplar.

Project quality rating assessment

The project is highly accessible and displays excellent design quality. Cultural heritage value is included, and the place has been designed as a cultural melting pot. This ecological park offers flexible spaces for different activities and facilities, performing well for quality of nature, amount of seating, arrangement and accessibility of facilities compared to other aspects. The project also has potential for health and well-being and is safe and secure. The water connectedness in terms of water visibility, access to water and land-water connectivity is all positive. The water safety issue is of less importance, as the water body is shallow. It is good for informal sport activities and possibilities for children to play with water. However, the project also offers formal play facilities nearby. The site divides the space very well in terms of zoning. Figure 13.7 shows sketches analysing the site.

Figure 13.8
A view of City Park Bradford showing the flooding and fountains in action
(*Source*: City of Bradford)

Blue infrastructure as public space: City Park, Bradford, United Kingdom

City Park, Bradford, was opened in 2012, designed by Gillespies Landscape Architects, United Kingdom, for the Bradford city council. In the masterplan for the city centre drawn up in 2003, a signature project as a focal point in the city was envisaged through regeneration and the creation of a public space. The resulting project created a destination for informal recreation, altered public perception of the area and supported the local economy and businesses by drawing people to it and increasing foot traffic. The project involves water features, planting and public amenities. The water feature is the central, unique element consisting of a 4000-m^2 mirror pool and 100 fountains with a complete drain-down provision so that water can appear or disappear (Figure 13.8). This multi-functional 2.4-ha public space is capable of holding large-scale events, as sections function as causeways when the water level is lower. Crucially for the purposes of this chapter, it also acts as a rainwater retention pond, collecting storm water from the immediate area while maintaining the overall visual quality of the place. The tailor-made lighting design is an innovative feature of the place that provides a playful, night-time setting, making the place unique and attractive. The public realm design offers flexible space to be adapted over the years and offers longevity of the life cost of material in use.

Project quality rating assessment

The space is highly accessible, except for car access and parking (which is controlled to ensure the area is pedestrianised). The design quality of the place is unique, providing a perfect juxtaposition of functionality and aesthetics. However, the cost-effectiveness of maintenance is an issue due to the expensive lighting design and technology for storm water treatment, as well as floor surface treatment – although high-quality materials and construction are essential here. The park offers flexible spaces for different activities and facilities, performing well for lighting and seating facilities. It also provides an excellent sense of place and sensory experiences. It is also very safe and secure. The water

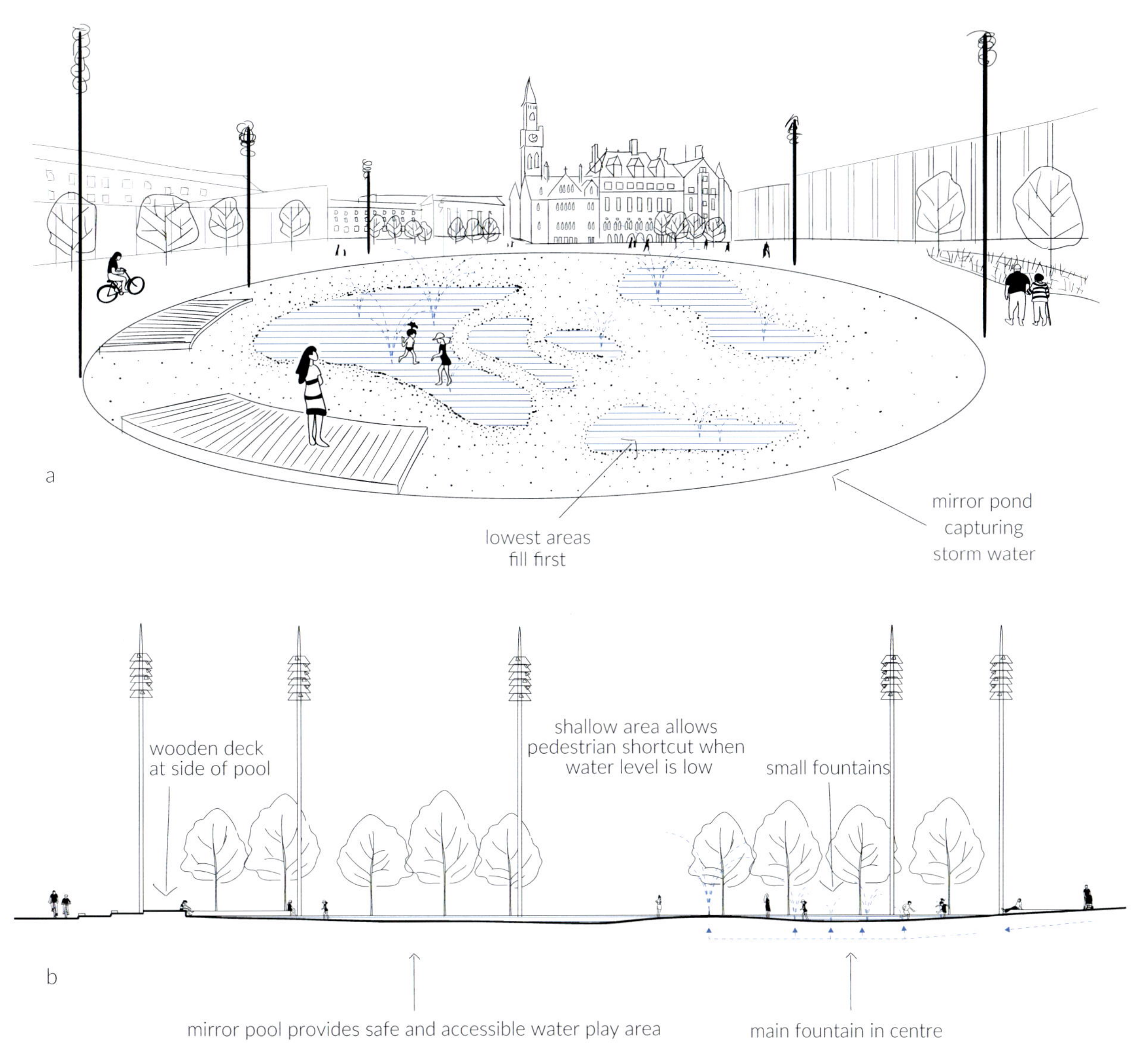

Figure 13.9a and b

a) Overview of the Sherbourne Commons sketch of the City Park circular basin, which, when full, becomes a mirror pool and otherwise has a slightly higher centre and several lower sections with fountains; wooden decking for walking and seating is placed around two sides; b) cross-section showing the gradual variation in levels for holding and draining the water and associated fountains, lights and decks

(*Source*: Anna Wilczyńska and Jekaterina Balicka)

connectedness within the place is excellent for water visibility and direct access to water. Water safety is of less importance, as the water body is shallow or has no water present during dry periods. It is also a good place for informal sport activities and children's play possibilities with water. Figure 13.9 demonstrates how the site works through sketches.

Sherbourne Commons, Toronto, Canada

The Sherbourne Commons is a brownfield regeneration project located on 1.47 hectares (3.63 acres) of land along a neglected area of Toronto's waterfront with a post-industrial heritage. The project was designed by landscape architects PFS Studio and Associates for the Waterfront Toronto and made open to the public in 2010 before completion

Figure 13.10

View of the Sherbourne Commons storm water treatment and purification facilities that provide space for water interaction and water showers improve the aesthetics of the place – here seen illuminated at night

(*Source*: Tom Arban)

in 2011. The public space has been created by developing a connecting park equipped with storm water treatment facilities. The park presents a concept interweaving landscape design, architecture, engineering and public art. The place caters to a large, mixed-use waterfront community and has become a popular flexible waterfront park, with the essential facilities for a diverse community. The park offers places for tranquillity and for recreation and active socialising. For children, the park provides many opportunities for play, information gathering and relaxation that also includes children's playgrounds.

The main landscape and sculptural features installed in the park form a composition of storm water collection and purification before discharge into Lake Ontario. The water treatment system consists of a UV treatment unit, a water cascade with a series of light showers and a bio-filtration plant bed and aquatic grass beds. The civic amenities, green space, lawn, splash, plaza and pavilions complement and are integrated with the nature-based solutions (Figure 13.10). The park provides an opportunity for activities in all seasons and different times of the day. The water treatment units, especially the water showers, create visual interest as well as active water interaction opportunities. It is a good example of reconnecting and re-engaging people with the old and forgotten waterfront.

The park exemplifies landscape design for public engagement with nature, community integration and increased opportunities for socialisation, sustainability and innovation. The sustainability features incorporated in the park include easy access to public transport, bicycle storage and reduction of light pollution, as well as water efficient planting. The project saves a huge amount of potable water by treating and reusing storm water. Overall, the park offers a destination for recreation and relaxation in a dense and busy urban environment while preserving the *genius loci*.

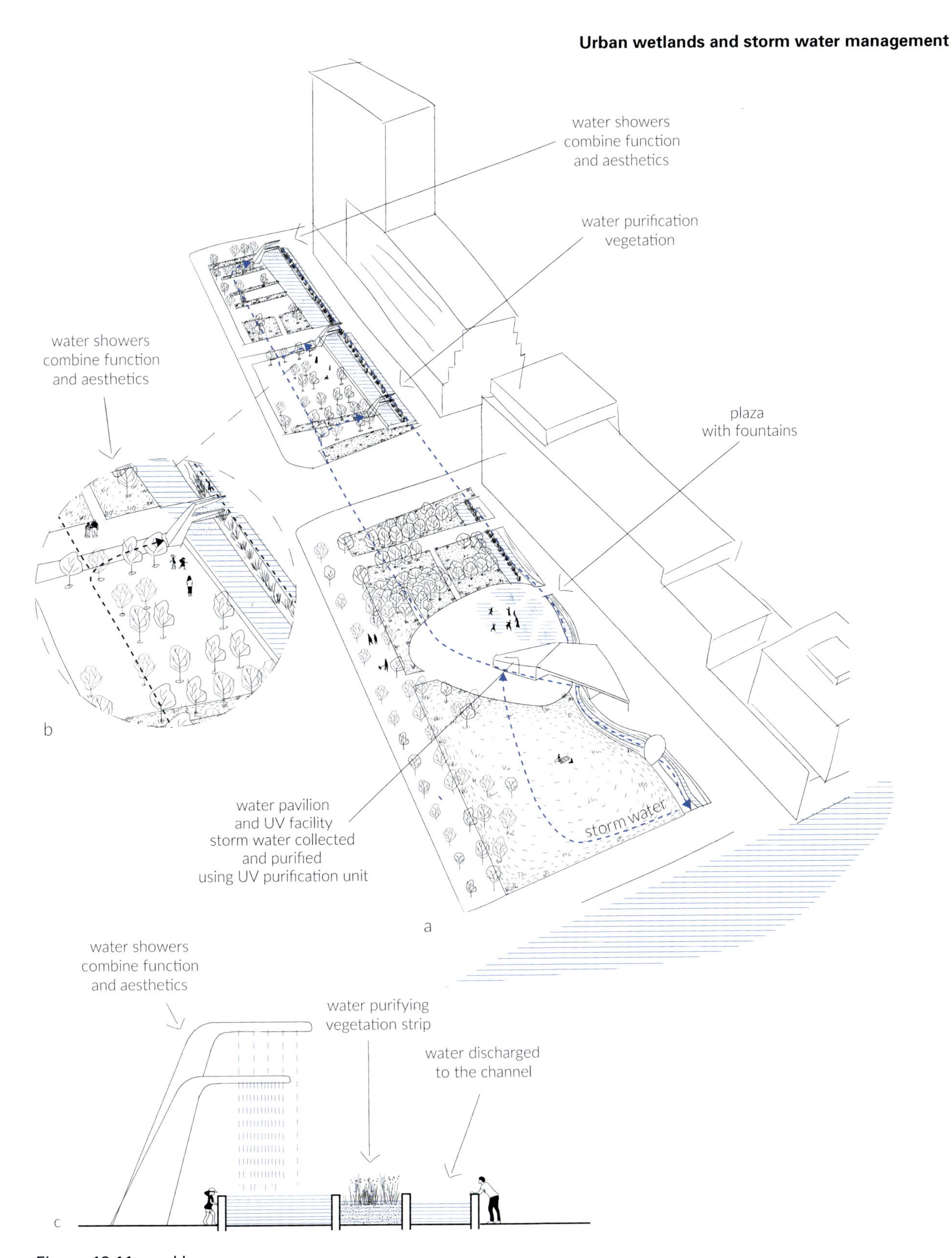

Figure 13.11a and b

a) Overview of the Sherbourne Commons showing the water movement between the different elements – inflow, ultraviolet purification, use of water showers and flow of water through the area to the channel from where it is discharged; b) cross-section focusing on the water movement from the water showers, through the vegetated strip and into the channel from where it flows out

(*Source*: Anna Wilczyńska and Jekaterina Balicka)

Project quality rating assessment

This project is highly accessible. Design quality and site planning and circulation perform very well, although the project is considered expensive to maintain because of all the pumps and other technical equipment. In terms of facilities and amenities, the site has good lighting and a wide range of facilities which are very accessible. It is rather wind exposed. The site provides plenty of seating and a good quality of nature experience. In terms of health and well-being, the project is very good for safety and sense of place, especially the opportunity for sensory stimulation. Water connectivity is also good, promoting water visibility and access. For physical activities, children's play has the greatest potential, followed by informal sports opportunities. The site design divides it very well into zones for different activities. Water sports do not, of course, feature here, nor does access from the water, and so water safety equipment is not needed. Figure 13.11 sketches present the site analysis.

Waitangi Park, Wellington, New Zealand

Waitangi Park is a brownfield regeneration in Wellington. This multifunctional park integrates an urban park and waterfront destination with a water treatment landscape that also supports public amenities and many diverse activities. The waterfront park was designed by Wraight Athfield landscape architecture and built in 2006 on a total area of 5.8 hectares (39.04 acres) for the Wellington Waterfront Limited. It features an environmentally sustainable design

Figure 13.12

A view of Waitangi Park, Wellington, showing access paths and some of the planting used as part of the water treatment system

(*Source*: Bruno Marques)

that implements water-sensitive urban design for treating and harvesting storm water, interwoven with recreational uses for a diverse range of users (Figure 13.12). The park is divided into five zones: a promenade, informal sports and recreation area, spaces with cultural and ecological promotion, the field and blue-green infrastructure. The operational blue-green infrastructure contributes to improved water quality and enhances the aesthetic quality. The storm water filtration system designed at Waitangi Park includes the main elements of filtration of storm water road runoff, bio-retention along the Waitangi Stream, recycling of the harvested water for irrigation of plants and use of ecologically sourced native plants from the Wellington region.

Project quality rating assessment

The project appears to perform poorly for water connectivity when compared to other aspects. The site accessibility is good, except for inclusive access. The overall design quality is very good, except for cost-effective maintenance (always a feature of such parks where this is especially important) and cultural heritage values (none to be taken into account). The facilities and amenities perform well, except for measures for protection from sun and wind, this being in part due to the design strategy of providing open views to the water wherever possible. The health and well-being aspect has high potential, except for the sense of being away, this being partly due to the high popularity of the place and to its being predominantly an urban setting. Water connections are limited due to the past industrial use of the place, although the storm water system provides ample opportunities to view and experience passive water-related activities such as spending time in and around the re-created wetland designed to filter and cleanse the Waitangi Stream. The site supports many physical activities, except for water sports – not being relevant given the context. Figure 13.13 presents the sketched analysis of the site.

Blue infrastructure and storm water management create public spaces: Welland Canal Park and Civic Square, Welland, Canada

Welland Canal Park is a civic square in front of the city hall building designed by Janet Rosenberg & Studio and constructed in 2005 on a 0.6-hectare (1.5-acre) site. The project comprises a series of gardens, ramps, bridges and viewing platforms that also retain the former historic walls of the canal. The space was built into the existing recreation network of the city and enhances the experience of using the existing scenic and historic canal walk. The place is perceived as a very welcoming destination for obtaining an outdoor nature experience and relaxation and provides all the necessary civic amenities such lighting, signage, walkways, seating, artworks and planting (Figure 13.14). The project also aimed to reinforce Welland's urban core. The project is very accessible to local transport and also provides car access and parking. It is also well connected to pedestrian and cycle paths and provides opportunities for walking, running, sitting and relaxing, together with spaces to organise small concerts and events. The design has improved the aesthetic quality by adding viewing points, selecting a unified palette of vegetation, introducing the plaza and tree planting. The water treatment aspect of the park comprises a series of pockets of artificially created biotopes, and the plaza itself helps to infiltrate storm water before its release into the canal.

Project quality rating assessment

The project appears to perform well or very well for almost all aspects, except for possible physical activities. It has high accessibility. The design quality is good, especially for views and landmarks and cultural heritage values. In terms of facilities and amenities, it performs well for lighting and quality of nature. Health and well-being potential is also very high for safety and security, opportunities for contemplation and sensory experiences. The site has good water visibility and water safety equipment but no real direct access (although the canal is next to the site). The Figure 13.15 sketches analyse the site.

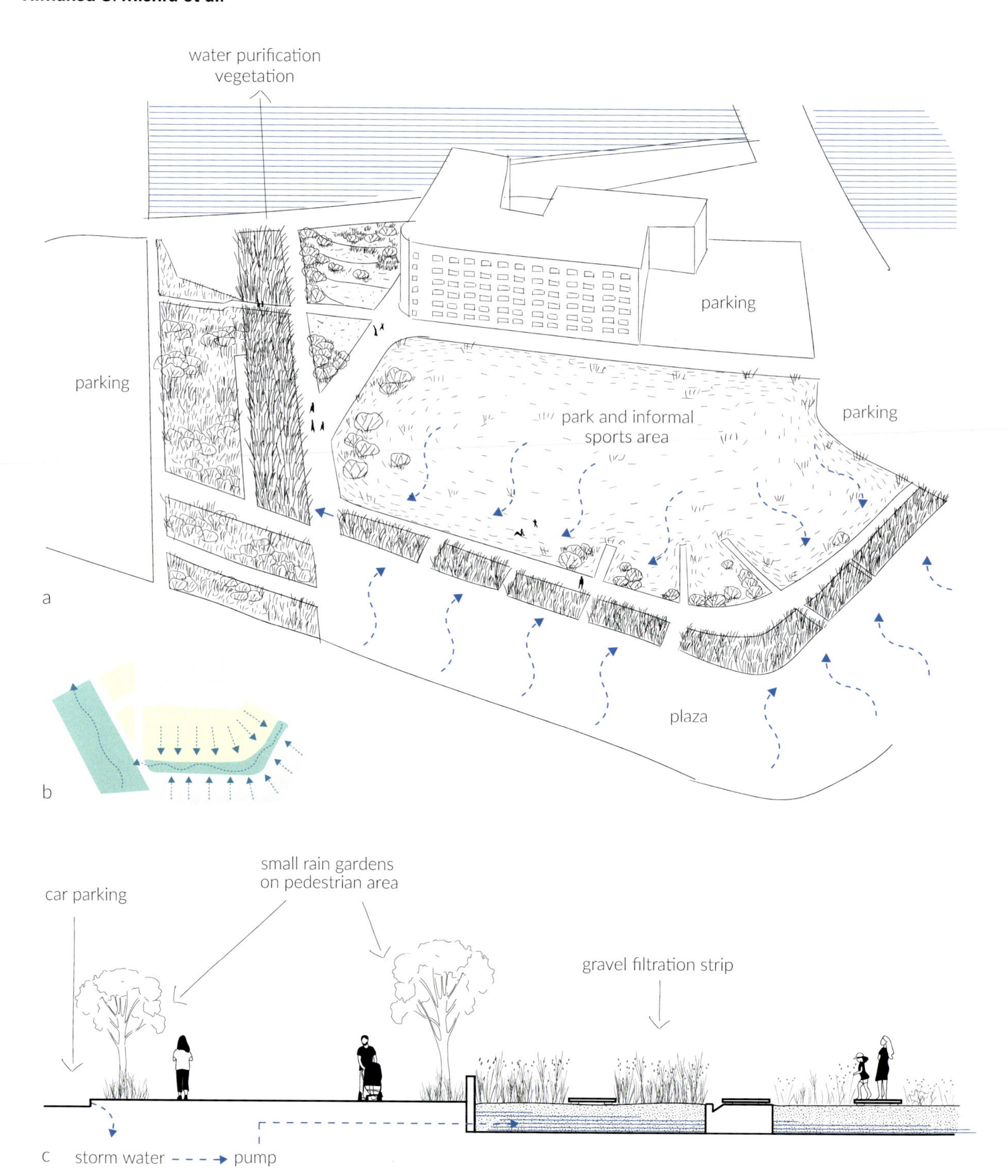

Figure 13.13a-c

a) Layout of the main elements of Waitangi Park and scheme of the water flow using the storm water run-off onto the planted area for irrigation and filtration; b) scheme showing how the water moves across the site; c) section from parking across the planted areas, showing how the storm water is pumped from the sealed surfaces (roads and parking) into the gravelled and planted filtration beds, which also incorporate paths for pedestrian access

(*Source*: Anna Wilczyńska and Jekaterina Balicka)

Figure 13.14
View of Welland Canal Park wooden decks within series of filter strips increase the provision of access to view water and provide a place for relaxing and contemplation
(*Source*: Landscape Architecture by Janet Rosenberg & Studio, photography by Jeff McNeill)

Anchor Park, Malmö, Sweden

The site under review was designed by Stig L. Andersson (SLA) in 2000–2001 as a central open space within the new urban development at the Västra Hamnen, or Western Harbour, in Malmö. This was an area of docklands on land artificially reclaimed from the sea in the period between 1948 and 1987 when the economic downturn led to it being abandoned as a harbour. After a period lying unused, a new set of economic opportunities emerged following the opening of the Öresund Bridge in 2000. The Västra Hamnen then became the site for the development of a new urban residential quarter, whose iconic symbol is the tower block known as the Turning Torso (which stands overlooking the park). The area is divided into different architectural zones with a range of styles and models. The focus is on safe and pedestrian-friendly streets, with vehicular traffic limited in its entry and a human scale. The seafront retains the harbour walls and features an esplanade park. In the centre of the district lies the Anchor Park, which forms the main public space for the district and is well connected to the rest of the residential areas and to the esplanade via a number of paths. It follows the line of an original channel through the area, now a shallower linear lake, with one side having a straight edge formed of concrete and a promenade next to residential buildings. On the opposite side, the channel takes a more serpentine form, still formed from concrete but backed by extensive grassy areas and groups

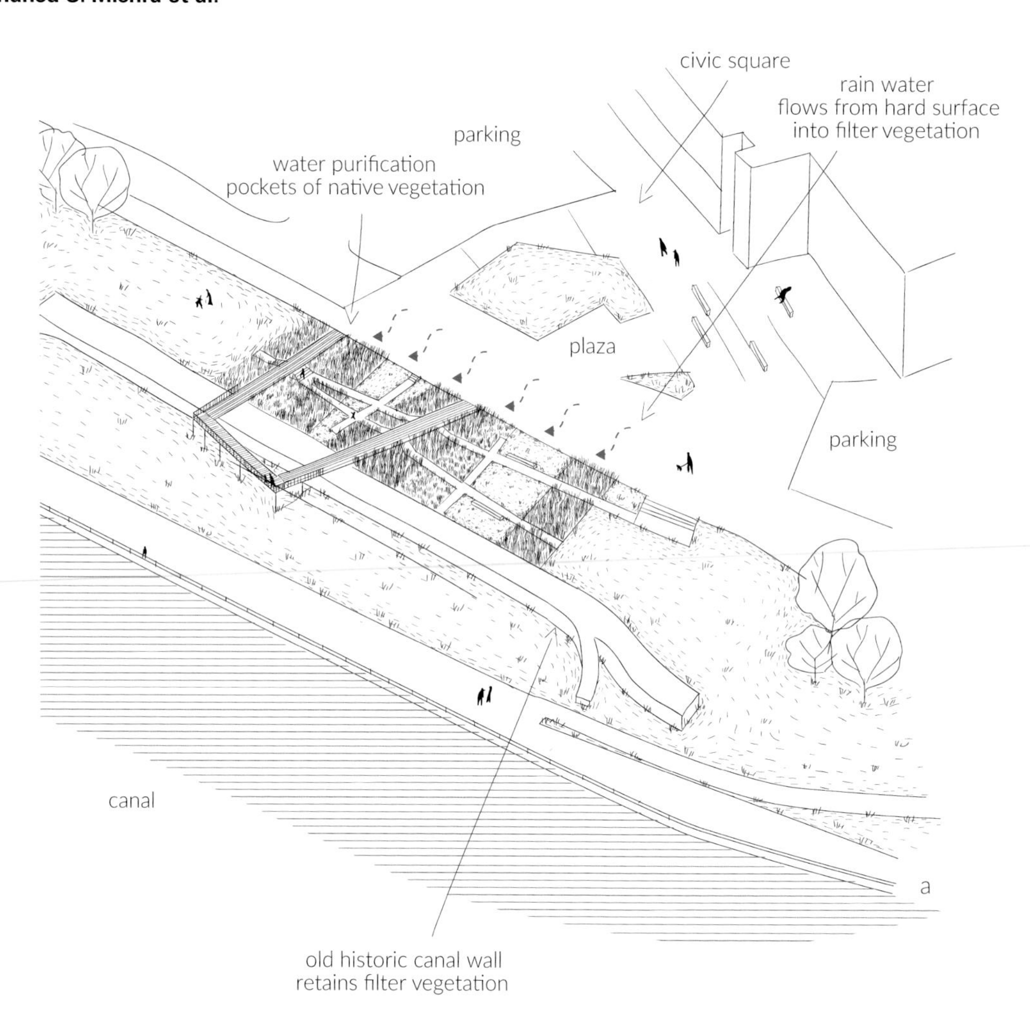

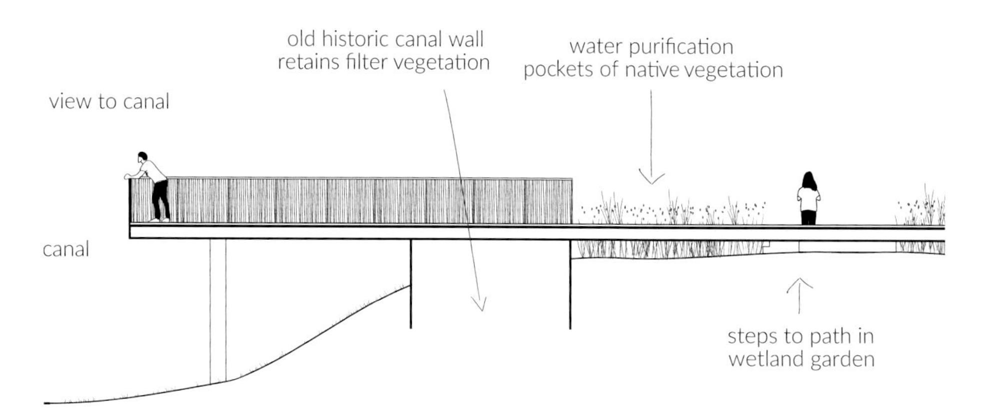

Figure 13.15a and b

a) Overview of the Welland Canal Park site showing the different site components and the vegetated areas used for filtration; b) section depicting the level changes across the site and the location of the vegetated filter strip

(*Source*: Anna Wilczyńska and Jekaterina Balicka)

Figure 13.16
A view of Anchor Park showing the different water edges and the wetland vegetation, overlooked by the Turning Torso
(*Source*: Lisa Rizell)

of trees surrounding some wetlands to help deal with storm water (Figure 13.16). The site is furnished with wooden decks and bridges, and the water area connects with the rest of the water system by canals leading to and from it, acting as water retention.

Project quality rating assessment

This project rates highly for accessibility – although not so much for cars, since these are deliberately designed out of the project, while little reference to cultural heritage can be found in the park itself owing to the complete redevelopment of the original site. The facilities lack shade and shelter, and there is a low degree of lighting within the park. The health and well-being aspects are good, although there can be no sense of being away, given the fact it is overlooked by housing, and the lack of lighting may lower the sense of safety and security in places (although it is overlooked). The water body is not designed for recreation, nor is it equipped for formal sports, although other physical activities can be pursued. Figure 3.17 shows the site analysis through sketches.

Nansen Park, Oslo, Norway

Nansen Park and the new community in Oslo, Norway, is one of the largest industrial wasteland reclamation projects and serves as an active and attractive meeting place for the community. It also reflects a strong identity, simplicity

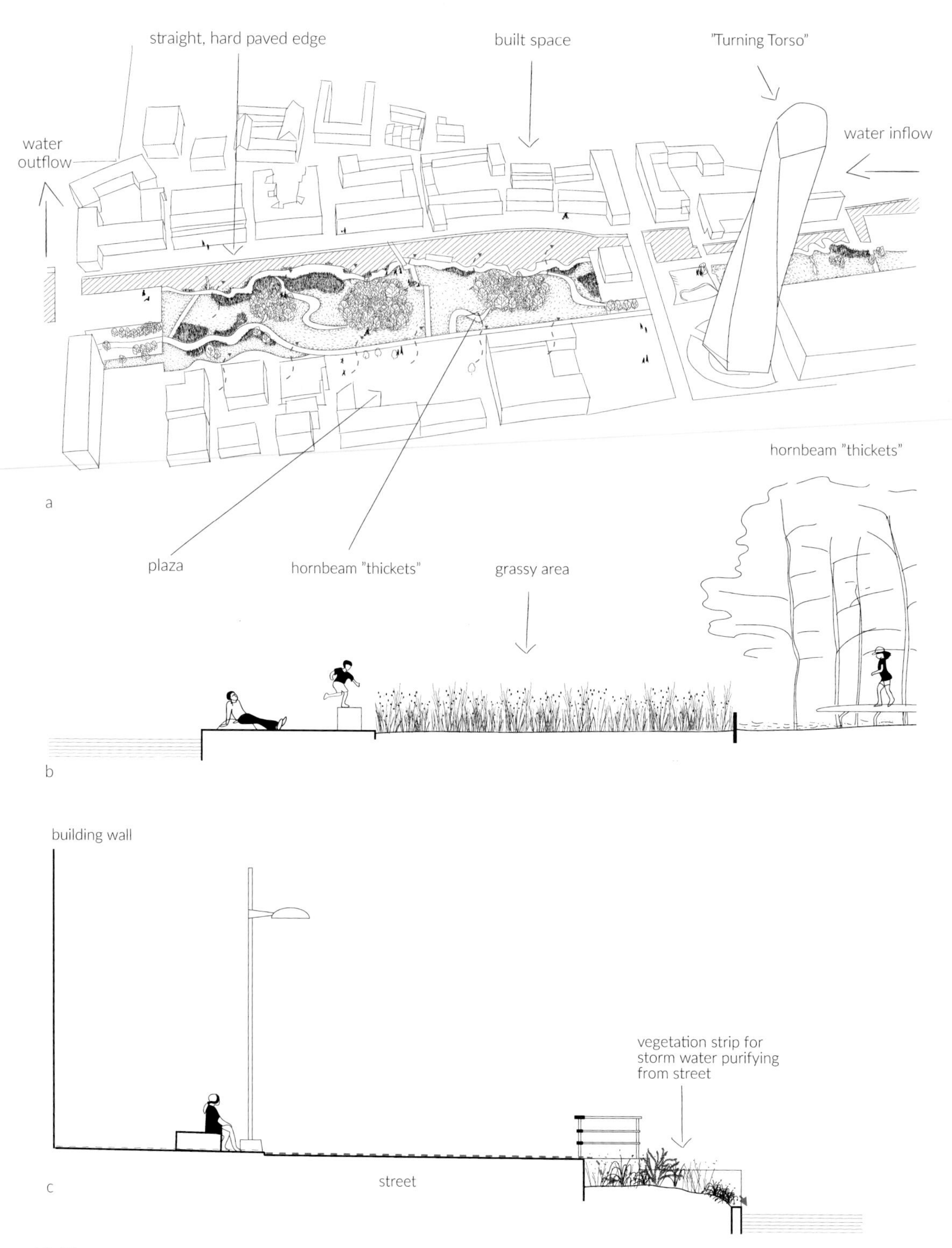

Figure 13.17a–c

a) Overview sketch of Anchor Park showing the main features – the contrast between the straight section with paving and the meandering water's edge; the patches of planting each function as filtration beds, and the sloping site allows water to flow into the water body; b) a general section across the site showing the location of the water body between buildings, part paved and part park; c) the different sections – water edge, grass and tree thickets

(*Source*: Anna Wilczyńska and Jekaterina Balicka)

Figure 13.18
View of Nansen Park, Oslo, showing one of the water collector swales with the parallel path and vegetation elements
(*Source*: Blørbekk and Lindheim)

and endurance. The park was designed on 20 hectares of land by Bjørbekk & Lindheim landscape architects and was completed in 2008. The design of the new community and the park, which transformed the central part of the old airfield, maintained its original linearity and dynamism and fragments of the original cultural landscape. The public space consists of an open plaza for holding festivals and events and has made artistic use of stone and water. The place offers different types and scales of recreational possibilities. The master plan of the area conceptualised the space as a bowl-shaped landscape with a centrally located park and seven green arms reaching out towards the sea in all directions. The water feature forms the central landscape element and is constantly changing, with playful variation between geometric and organic forms for the pool, stream, falling water and so on (Figure 13.18). The central lake collects all the water, which is cleaned using biological and mechanical filters to ensure good water quality. The surplus water is allowed to overflow into an infiltration area before it is released into the fjord. The storm water management system also efficiently caters to the drainage from the nearby housing area areas and roads. Most of the water is recycled and used in the park for park activities and aesthetics. The project thus presents a strong ecological profile that supports the whole transformation process. Polluted grounds and materials have been cleaned, retrieved and reused in a landscape of different spatial qualities.

Project quality rating assessment

The project is very accessible. It has very high design quality, with a good range of facilities and amenities, as well as health and well-being aspects. The water connection is limited to some degree, and some of the aspects are less well provided for, such as water safety equipment and water activities (to be expected, as the site is not designed for this). The site also provides many physical activity opportunities. The sketches in Figure 13.19 present the site analysis.

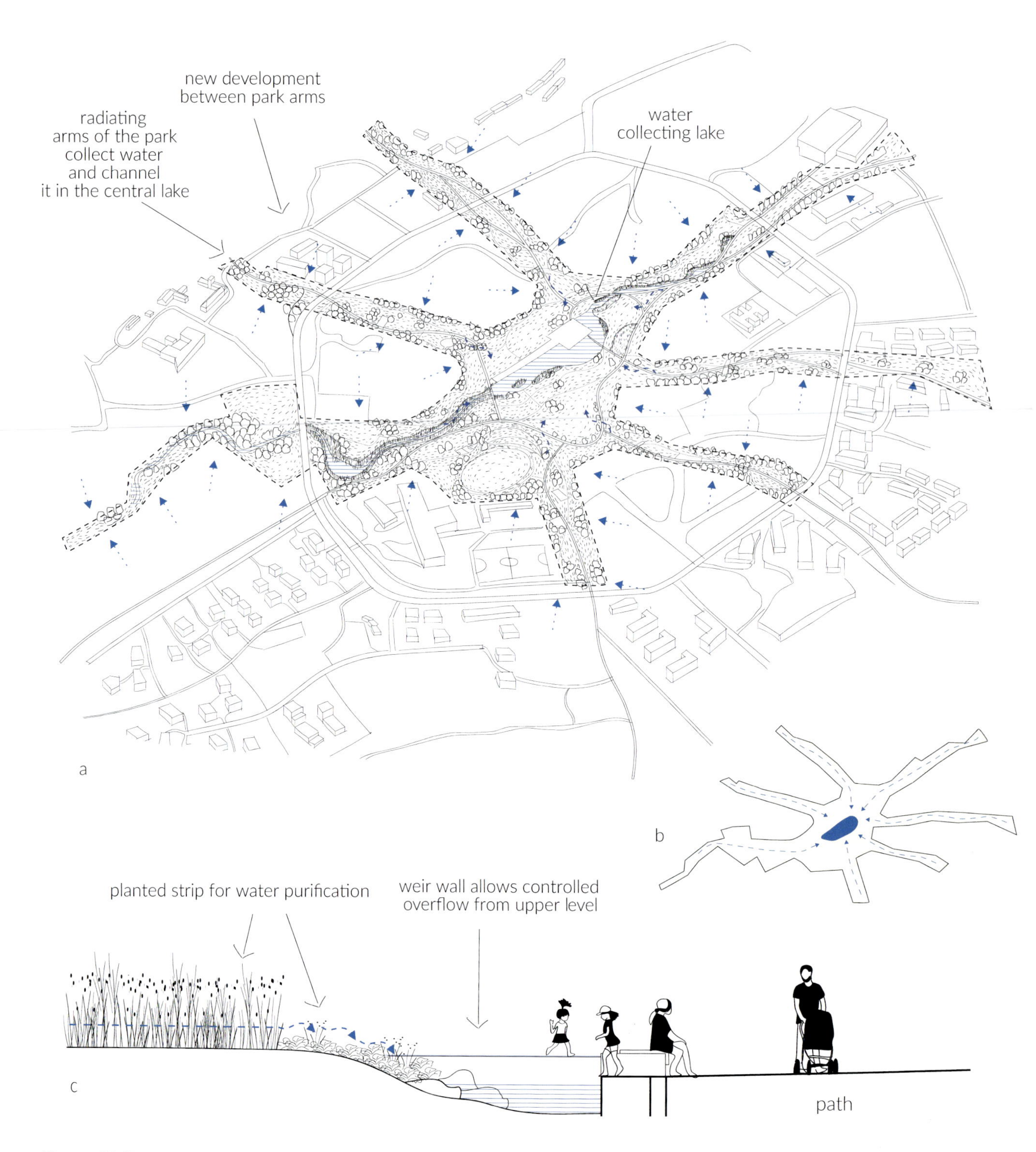

Figure 13.19a–c

a) Overview of Nansen Park showing the radiating arms lying between the developed area collecting storm water, which flows down to the central lake, being cleaned as it does; b) schematic plan showing how water is allowed to run down the swales with water features and planting which follows all the paths down towards the centre, where the water collects in the detention/retention pond from which it infiltrates, is recycled or allowed to flow into the fjord; c) section showing how the water can flow over the ground surface to the water features, through vegetation and into the swales edged by the paths and by rocks

(*Source*: Anna Wilczyńska and Jekaterina Balicka)

Wetland parks: Tianjin Qiaoyuan Wetland Park, Tianjin, China

The Qiaoyuan Wetland Park project in the Chinese city of Tianjin was designed by Turenscape and completed in 2008. The wetland park was built on a 22-hectare site based on an adaptive strategy to deal with storm water by creating a series of biologically diverse ecosystems that also help decontaminate the soil. Once a polluted and contaminated industrial and landfill site, it has been transformed into a place rich in habitat diversity and a destination for recreation and nature experience. The design reclaimed the brownfield site by integrating regenerative ecological functions and provided a high-quality public space for the surrounding dense residential community. This regenerative process involved changing the landform to create a series of pools, promoting the natural process of plant adaptation and community evolution to create a low-maintenance urban park that contains and purifies storm water, improved soil chemistry (reducing alkalinity) and a rich aesthetic experience.

The project was initiated with the aim of resolving issues related to storm water management, including minor flooding within the area and to create a multi-functional public space to meet community needs. The wetland park has been designed as a series of wet and dry ponds with local materials and plants, creating a framework for nature

Figure 13.20

View of the water retention ponds at Qiaoyuan wetland park and the different wetland habitats that provide opportunities to connect with nature and recreation

(*Source*: Yu Kongjian)

to rejuvenate ecological processes. The ponds are laid out like a series of cells within a structure of recreational spaces and a network of footpaths and linkages (Figure 13.20). The layout thus created rainwater catchment facilities with both retention and detention functions. Platforms and bridges provide different visitor experiences and park views. The key objectives of the project include the creation of habitats, selection and design of plant communities and provision of cultural services. The overlapping and intertwined concepts that supported the wetland park design objectives have resulted in a powerful and successful landscape that is resilient and regenerative and provides a myriad of ecological services. The project has become a major destination park and attracts large number of visitors each year, as well as providing educational opportunities for children from nearby schools.

Project quality rating assessment

This project has excellent accessibility, although it is not so visible from outside, which could be due to the large site area and dense vegetation that occupies much of the land area. The design quality is excellent but lacks cultural heritage references (no relevant here) and views and landmarks (as an enclosed and large site). The facilities and amenities are somewhat limited – partly due to its function as a wetland park, although it does well for quality of nature and lighting conditions. The health and well-being potential for all aspects suggests the site can be perceived as being highly restorative. Despite good health-promoting qualities, the water connection aspects are limited (except for access to water and water visibility) – to be expected for a water-purifying park when some of the water bodies are still polluted. Except for zoning of activities, the site has limited opportunities for physical activity – again, it is not designed for this, so it would not be expected. Figure 13.21 shows how the site has been analysed by sketching.

Magnuson Park, Seattle, United States

Magnuson Park in Seattle, United States, is located along the shore of Lake Washington. It has rejuvenated an old wetland that was converted into industrial land and which changed dramatically under the land ownership of the US Navy. The park was designed by the Berger Partnership PS and was built in three phases. The park was partly completed and open to use in 2006, and the development then continued until 2012. As the second-largest park in the city of Seattle, the park covers an area of 62.32 hectares (154 acres) and has a 1.6-kilometre-long stretch of shoreline. The park offers a variety of recreational uses, social events, play opportunities, nature experiences, wildlife interaction and wetland habitats.

The park design established a hydrological regime formed by a grid of ponds on a slope to create a cascading effect as the storm water fills the upper ponds and overflows to the lower ponds and so on. The wetland system collects water running off the playing fields and parking lots. The ecological function of the wetland concept is manifested through leaky berms, log weirs, rice paddies, willow-wattles and peaty sponges as water flows through the system of 63 connected ponds which vary in depth (Figure 13.22). The site layout provides a framework that allows nature to reclaim the land and provide an abundance of wildlife in the wetlands. Native species were planted on the berms, in the ponds and in the forest to provide shelter for insects, amphibians and birds. The wetland also provides clean water for amphibian habitats and a freshwater lagoon. The constructed wetland treats storm water runoff by reducing suspended solid particles and bacteria and increasing dissolved oxygen. The project has successfully and substantially increased biodiversity and reduced carbon dioxide emission by recycling old techno-sol from the site. The park attracts a large volume of visitors and local school and university students, while local communities are engaged in activities such as tree planting, nature experience, research, invasive species removal and establishing native planting.

Project quality rating assessment

The project is very accessible, although access via public transport is limited and site visibility is not so good due to it being a large area with high forest cover that screens views. Design quality is moderate overall, although the site

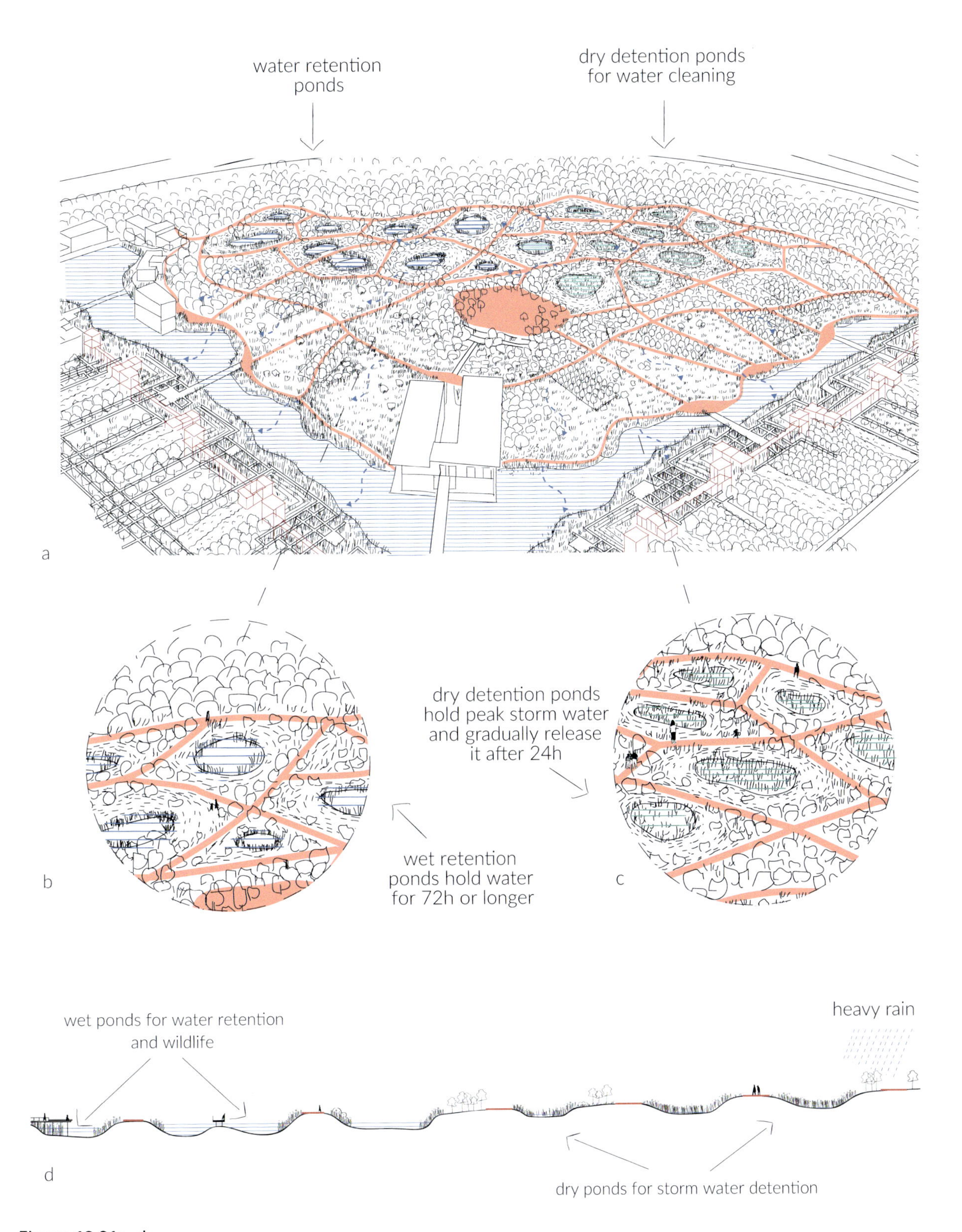

Figure 13.21a–d

a) Broad overview of the entire Qiaoyuan park in its wider setting, with the pattern of pools (wet for retention to dry for detention) which treat the water; b) detail of the pattern of paths and wet retention ponds; c) some of the movement of the water across the site from detention ponds which fill during storm events; d) a typical section showing the transition across the site from the upper dry detention to the lower retention ponds and on to the larger lake

(*Source*: Anna Wilczyńska and Jekaterina Balicka)

Figure 13.22
View of Magnuson Park, Seattle, showing the series of descending ponds with access paths between them and the natural vegetation
(*Source*: Seattle Parks)

circulation, the cost effectiveness and the design of furniture to the context are highly rated design attributes. Other facilities and amenities are limited, although quality of nature, range of and accessibility to facilities perform well. The health and well-being potential is moderate, but within this, there are good possibilities for contemplation, a sense of being away, sensory stimulation and contact with nature. Similarly, the water connection is supported by conditions that provide opportunities for access to and viewing water, less so for the opportunity for water activities or for the availability and condition of safety and security equipment. The site provides good opportunities for formal and informal activities. Figure 3.23 presents the sketches of the site analysis.

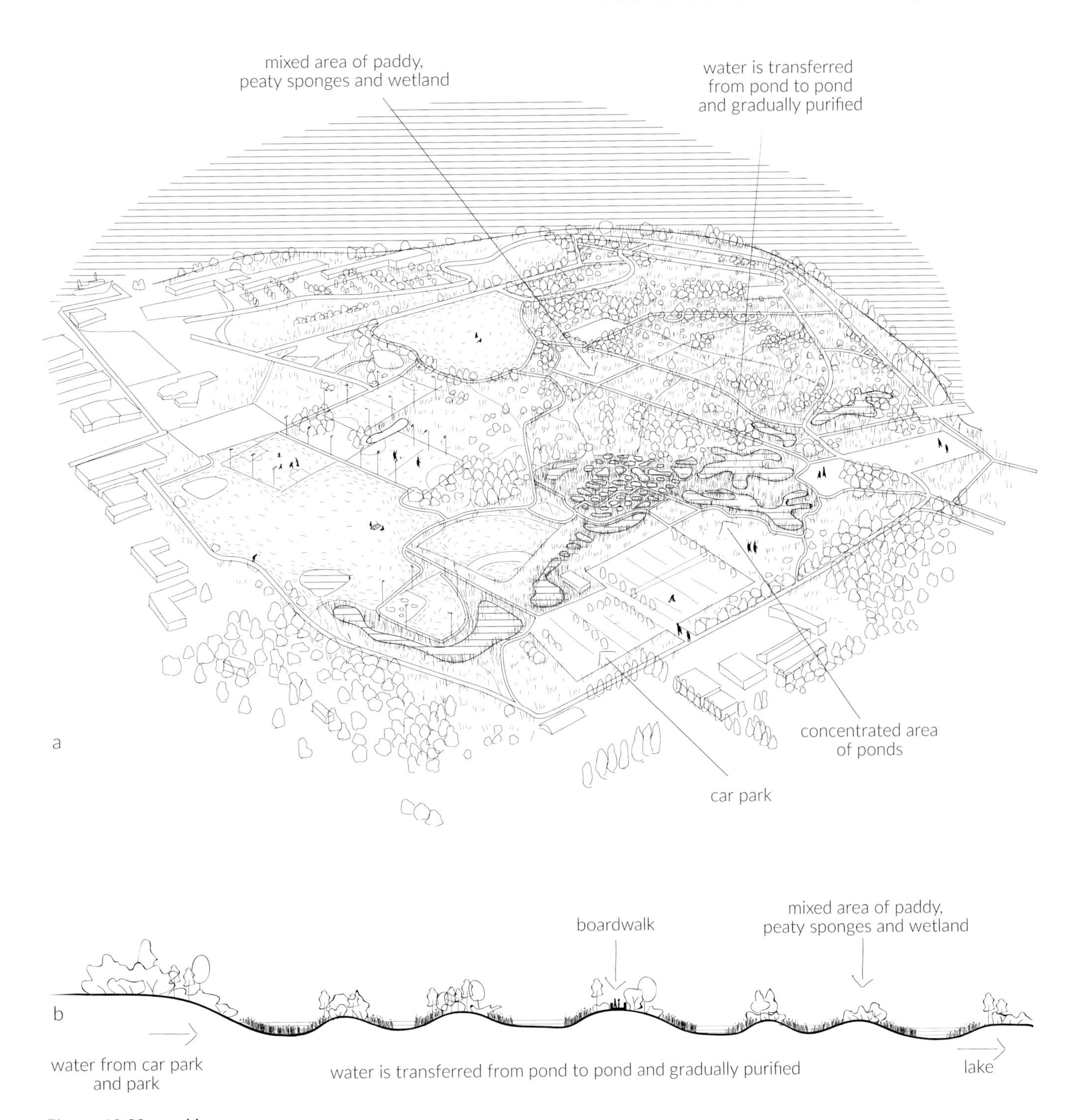

Figure 13.23a and b

a) Overview sketch of Magnuson Park showing the relationship of the natural wetland areas lying between the car parking and the rest of the restored wetland, providing a rich biodiversity area; b) section through the park showing the typical level changes and the way the water passes gradually from level to level through each set of ponds

(*Source*: Anna Wilczyńska and Jekaterina Balicka)

Sydney park water reuse project, Sydney, Australia

The Sydney park water re-use project was designed by Turf Design Studio, together with Environmental Partnership, Alluvium, Turpin+Crawford, Dragonfly and Partridge and was completed in 2015 on a 44-hectare area with 1.6 hectares dedicated to water reuse facilities. The project implemented a green infrastructure strategy and upgraded an industrial and landfill site to a public park in an inner city suburb of Sydney. It incorporates storm water treatment infrastructure, thereby creating a vital asset for the growing communities of southeast Sydney. The project demonstrates an overlapping of art, design and science and highlights the intrinsic relationship between water and urban life, topography, people, flora and fauna. The story about water within the project is carefully narrated through the functions and processes involved from collecting/harvesting water through to cleaning and reusing it within the park.

The project in part rejuvenated an existing park wetland and transformed it into a sustainable park that reuses its own water with little need for precious water from external sources. The project enhanced the circulation of water through ponds and wetlands and renewed the ecosystem into a greener and more functioning public amenity space. The system of blue infrastructure harvests a large amount of water annually and uses it for maintaining park functions and the ecological health of the ponds and wetlands. The water treatment within the park is carried out through water pollutant traps, bio-retention systems, vegetated swales, aeration devices and a series of wetlands (Figure 13.24). The park, while offering a thriving wildlife habitat, also improved the cultural use of the site by promoting increased nature connectedness and connecting people to the concepts of blue infrastructure in terms of capturing, circulating and

Figure 13.24
The view of water harvesting in Sydney park water reuse project
(*Source*: Turf Design, Sydney/Ethan Rohloff Photography)

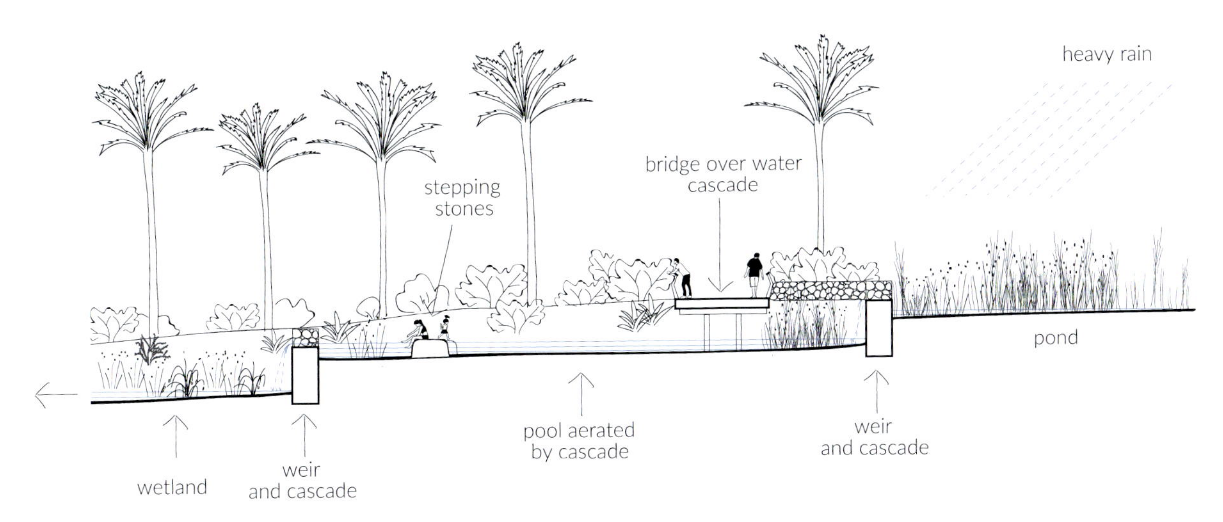

Figure 13.25a and b

a) Diagrammatic overview of the Sydney park water reuse project system showing how the water enters and passes from lake to lake; b) section showing the terraces and cascade from which water flows into the pond and aerates it at the same time

(*Source*: Anna Wilczyńska and Jekaterina Balicka)

cleaning water. The wetlands have been attracting new wildlife to the park and recorded a high population of native bird species in the local area. The park offers numerous opportunities for activities and relaxation for the local Sydney community. The cascading wetland system and stepping stones especially offer play opportunities for children.

Project quality rating assessment

In this wetland restoration project, all variables of accessibility perform very well. The design took a very balanced approach dealing with important design criteria and does very well in all sections. In terms of facilities and amenities, it performs very well for lighting, the range of facilities present, accessibility to these facilities and the amount of seating and quality of nature it offers to the users, although it is rather wind exposed and not especially well shaded. The site offers very good access to water and has high water visibility that promotes water-related activities, although not for formal or water-based sports. The site can be considered highly restorative, as it is rated very well for health and well-being potential. The site offers an excellent opportunity for nature contact and experience. Figure13.25 presents the analytical sketches of the site.

Comparison of projects in terms of different aspects

General design aspects

The projects presented in this chapter were chosen for their diversity and creativity in dealing with storm water using different nature-based solutions in different built environments. Each project displays many interesting and exceptional design qualities and demonstrates multi-functional landscapes that integrate technical concepts and detailing for storm water management. They also demonstrate how projects can create a sense of place along with high-quality, aesthetically attractive places for recreation and relaxation. Many of the projects selected in this chapter are highly acclaimed, demonstrating how imitative and technical solutions to deal with the wicked problems of storm water are possible within more traditional landscape design approaches. All these projects that adopted different nature-based solutions which have demonstrated high-quality design solutions both in the organisation of space and detailing they contain. All projects have given consideration to an efficient site circulation of water along with designs of furniture that fit the context. Cost effectiveness of projects may vary, considering that they belong to different socioeconomic conditions and planning practices and in many cases they are technically complicated. The variation in cost effectiveness also depends on the objective of the project and whether the built structures or vegetation material used for it fit the context and improve aesthetic quality of the space. All projects have created new landmarks as design elements to attract more users and to improve the sense of legibility with the site.

Potential for enhancing health and well-being

Almost all projects display many opportunities to improve health and well-being. All projects have considered safety and security as one of the common and important attributes to ensure health and well-being of visitors (and to reduce risks – especially if the parks include access to actual or potentially polluted water). Most projects also either maintained the existing or created a new sense of place by using water creatively. The sense of being away can only be felt prominently in large-scale projects rather than small ones rooted within an urban setting. The selection of design elements and construction materials can play a role here. For example, wetland projects have shown a higher sense of being away compared to the public spaces which are blue infrastructure projects. Despite all projects representing different environmental qualities, features and characteristics, they promote high mental health through opportunities for contemplation, sensory stimulation and, especially, contact with nature. These health benefits were found to be higher for large-scale, more natural projects within an urban environment, such as the West Seoul Lake Park, Nansen Park or Tianjin Qiaoyuan Wetland Park restoration project.

Accessibility

All the sites evaluated are very accessible for most. Variability in access conditions is observed mainly due to varying disabled access provisions (although this is sometimes hard to determine exactly) and car access and parking provisions – where car access was restricted in favour of better pedestrian or cycle access. The extent of visibility of these sites is less important due to most of the sites being large in size and visually disconnected by dense vegetation in and around the perimeter. However, this contrasts with public plaza-type environments, which are designed as open, connected and legible systems that are meant to support urban functions and need to be visible.

Interaction with water

Water has been the key feature in all projects evaluated, contributing to ecosystem services and sustainable water management in an urban environment. Interaction with water as a tactile experience is a key predictor of nature connectedness, and the success of each project depends on the degree to which it supports the concept of human ecology. All the projects assessed successfully promote physical and mental accessibility to water, although to varying degrees. It is important to understand that nature-based solutions create opportunities for nature play and active interaction with water and associated natural biotopes, as well as providing knowledge about biodiversity that promotes pro-environmental behaviour. Efforts to restore natural settings (e.g. urban stream and wetland restoration projects) within highly built environments could benefit inhabitants and users the most. These projects have dealt with the challenge of reusing polluted storm water for recreational purposes through creating adaptive, sustainable and resilient systems of blue infrastructure that benefit both people and the environment.

Physical activities and opportunities for socialising

Physical activity and opportunities for socialising depend on the space organisation, zoning, design and availability of recreational facilities and seating as well as good accessibility to spaces and facilities. Most of the projects provide space and opportunity for children's play, although playing in water greatly depends on the quality of water available for reuse. In this context, natural stream or river restoration projects, such as Bishan-Ang Mo Kio Park and large-scale community park projects, such as Nansen Park, Oslo; West Seoul Lake Park, Seoul; and wetland park projects have demonstrated higher-quality water environments that are safer for nature play. Most of the projects provide plenty of opportunities for informal sport activities, primarily due to the design of multifunctional, flexible and adaptive spaces. Almost all sites demonstrate good zoning of activities, despite the fact that these landscapes are primarily designed to harvest, retain, contain and purify water. After completion, all have become popular destinations for communities and attract large numbers of visitors annually and encourage recreation, nature contact and social cohesion.

Microclimate amelioration

Almost all projects contribute to local climate amelioration and improve microclimate within the area of intervention, although it depends on the size, scale and type of project. Water as the most common and prominent landscape feature produces a cooling effect, so river or stream restoration and wetland projects that retain large areas of water with vegetation improve the cooling effect, such as the Sydney Park water reuse project. Similarly, reduction of noise coming from the nearby airport operation has been successfully accomplished in West Seoul Lake Park. Moreover, creation of urban plazas and use of water features always provides microclimatic benefits in hot weather. The presence of both still and moving water in highly built urban environments, such as Bradford City Park and Toronto's Sherbourne Commons, provide numerous health benefits to users through microclimate improvement and high-quality sensory experiences.

Use of water, vegetation and ecological aspects

All the projects have used water to create functional and aesthetic landscapes that support different ecosystems and provide many ecosystem services. Most used native plants and restored natural forms and functions of water bodies either through mimicking nature or providing support frameworks for nature to reclaim and restore the poor health of an existing natural ecosystem. River, stream and wetland restoration projects also strongly demonstrate the role of landscape ecology and bio-engineering in solutions that substantially improve the environmental quality and increase biodiversity within the projects. The biotopes created within the projects to deal with storm water management and cleansing also support other functions such as an increase in aesthetic value, providing places for activities and increased opportunities for biodiversity interaction.

Sustainable storm water management

The main focus of this chapter is of course storm water management, systems for which the blue infrastructure components are manifested in both static and dynamic hydrological structures. These structures are embedded within landscapes that promote ecosystem functions and services, as demonstrated for the most of the projects. When we recognise the multifunctional role of storm water management systems, using similar projects becomes vital to urban areas where both a lack of nature and continuing or increasing storm water problems are prevalent.

The idea of integrating engineering solutions to improve environmental quality, to create social functions and to regulate storm water efficiently are unique aspects of these projects. Incorporation of sustainable urban drainage systems to manage storm water is technically complex and takes up street space. While mostly working in the everyday landscape, landscape architects and designers should be able to work freely and innovatively with SUDS so as to improve the overall quality, character and identity of the neighbourhood. Moreover, the symbiotic relationship between green and blue allows wildlife habitats to thrive, protects water quality, recharges groundwater, provides soil stability, enhances water supply and improves quality of life, health and well-being. Sustainability and energy efficiency is the main focus among landscape architects and engineers involved in such practices for creating flexible, beautiful, functional and regenerative projects. Most of the reviewed projects adopted tools and techniques to reduce water demand, filter and reduce storm water runoff, promote and protect wildlife habitats, improve environmental quality and human health and increase opportunities for outdoor recreation. These have demonstrated different ways of adopting storm water management tools and techniques within different levels starting from master planning down to the details of landscape design and construction.

Conclusions and implications for practice

This chapter has reviewed the history and importance of stream and wetland restoration projects, urban plaza projects that used water as prominent features, large- to medium-scale community projects that demonstrate the application of landscape ecology concepts and bio-engineering techniques to create multi-functional landscapes. These places have become successful recreational spaces to visit and engage with nature, which was not otherwise possible. They promote high educational benefits for children, students, researchers and local residents alike. These projects demonstrated ways of dealing with storm water as a wicked problem within urban areas. Some projects involve low cost and simple interventions, while some demanded high investment and complex, overlapping concepts and methods of landscape architecture, landscape ecology and engineering. However, all projects have demonstrated high levels of public participation and community involvement, thus proving that projects of such a complex nature can be successfully implemented using an active integration of the community through the process of place-making. The selections presented here all have their strengths and weaknesses according to a number of factors such as the setting, terrain, history or climate. Despite the fact that these projects are primarily designed to deal with harvesting and cleaning storm water, they often also have had significant impacts on the local economy and aided the process of regeneration of places where they are located.

There are a few specific aspects of the projects we wish to draw attention to:

- The projects used and respected the local environmental setting and context of the development; they adopted sustainable and innovative approaches to co-create spaces both for the environment and the community to co-exist and flourish;
- They used the terrain and intelligently blended the presence, quality, flow and importance of water in landscape design;
- They efficiently used the static and dynamic values of water;
- They encouraged native planting and native biodiversity;
- They involved communities in the project development process and used community knowledge to create multi-functional landscapes;
- They applied landscape architecture and landscape ecology concepts combined with bio-engineering techniques; and
- They promoted high health and well-being values through creating high-quality landscapes, flexible spaces that promote a myriad of opportunities to become active and relax within these blue spaces.

Finally, we can observe that the selection of parks here represents a very important category of blue space design. It is not always certain how effective they are at treating water, and combining public access and recreation may also pose threats or risks of water-borne diseases, perhaps at certain times of year or in certain climatic regions, which need to be monitored. Nevertheless, in terms of combining functions of water treatment, storm water management, ecological restoration and public recreation, they are truly inspirational as multi-purpose landscapes.

References

Benedict, M. A., & McMahon, E. T. (2006). *Green Infrastructure: Smart Conservation for the 21st Century.* Sprawl Watch Clearinghouse Monograph Series. Washington, DC.

Burian, S. J., & Edwards, F. G. (2015). *Historical Perspectives of Urban Drainage*. Department of Civil Engineering, University of Arkansas. www.researchgate.net/publication/228877768.

Directive 2000/60/EC of the European Parliament and of the Council of 23 October 2000 establishing a framework for community action in the field of water policy Official Journal L 327, 22/12/2000, pp. 0001–0073.

Dover, J. W. (2015). *Green Infrastructure: Incorporating Plants and Enhancing Biodiversity in Buildings and Urban Environments*. London: Routledge.

Fletcher, T. D., Shuster, W., Hunt, W. F., Ashley, R., Butler, D., Arthur, S., . . . Mikkelsen, P. S. (2015). SUDS, LID, BMPs, WSUD and more – The evolution and application of terminology surrounding urban drainage. *Urban Water Journal*, 12(7), 525–542.

Jia, H., Ma, H., & Wei, M. (2011). Urban wetland planning: A case study in the Beijing central region. *Ecological Complexity*, 8(2), 213–221.

McHarg, I. L., & American Museum of Natural History. (1969). *Design with Nature*. New York: American Museum of Natural History.

Lim, H. S., & Lu, X. X. (2016). Sustainable urban storm water management in the tropics: An evaluation of Singapore's ABC waters program. *Journal of Hydrology*, 538, 842–862.

Li, C., Peng, C., Chiang, P. C., Cai, Y., Wang, X., & Yang, Z. (2019). Mechanisms and applications of green infrastructure practices for stormwater control: A review. *Journal of Hydrology*, 568, 626–637.

Marks, A., Wescoat Jr. J. L., Noiva, K., & Rawoot, S. (2015). Boston "Emerald Necklace" Case Study Product of research on "Enhancing Blue-Green Environmental and Social Performance in High Density Urban Environments", Sponsored by the Ramboll Foundation, Massachusetts Institute of Technology.

McInnes, R. J. (2014). Recognising wetland ecosystem services within urban case studies. *Marine and Freshwater Research*, 65(7), 575–588.

McPhillips, L. E., & Matsler, A. M. (2018). Temporal evolution of green stormwater infrastructure strategies in three US cities. *Frontiers in Built Environment*, 4, 26.

Perales-Momparler, S., Andrés-Doménech, I., Andreu, J., & Escuder-Bueno, I. (2015). A regenerative urban stormwater management methodology: The journey of a Mediterranean city. *Journal of Cleaner Production*, 109, 174–189.

Sørup, H. J. D., Fryd, O., Liu, L., Arnbjerg-Nielsen, K., & Jensen, M. B. (2019). An SDG-based framework for assessing urban stormwater management systems. *Blue-Green Systems*, 1(1), 102–118.

Sun, R., & Chen, L. (2017). Effects of green space dynamics on urban heat islands: Mitigation and diversification. *Ecosystem Services*, 23, 38–46.

Tzoulas, K., Korpela, K., Venn, S., Yli-Pelkonen, V., Kaźmierczak, A., Niemela, J., & James, P. (2007). Promoting ecosystem and human health in urban areas using green infrastructure: A literature review. *Landscape and Urban Planning*, 81(3), 167–178.

Chapter 14: Docklands, harbours and post-industrial sites

Simon Bell, Anna Wilczyńska and Jekaterina Balicka

Introduction

Many cities around the world have long functioned as ports of one sort or another – sometimes incorporating huge areas with excavated docks controlled by lock gate warehouses and transport infrastructure, sometimes comprising smaller harbours or quaysides along rivers for more limited exchange of goods. Many of these, such as the London Docks, evolved and developed over the centuries until changes in shipping technology – principally the shift to containers – rendered them obsolete. This was in part because the huge container ships could not use the docks, which were too small, and in part due to the need for extensive storage spaces and a different form of transport and loading/unloading system. This change came about following developments in the 1950s to the1970s and largely replaced existing ports in the 1980s. The result of this was the creation of huge areas of abandoned and derelict land and water bodies, as well as de-industrialisation, unemployment and social problems among the original dockworker communities and local economic recessions. As well as container shipping, bulk carriers and enormous oil tankers led to further changes in other types of ports which handled oil or grain and where deep water and large areas suitable for manoeuvring such ships was possible.

The question of what do with these areas – large parts of the London Docklands, Hamburg port or the Port of New York, to name but three, took some time to find answers. Once a formula was identified, many cities have now adopted a waterfront renaissance in their former dock or harbour areas (Hoyle et al., 1988; Marshall, 2001). One of the major projects of the 1980s was the redevelopment of the London Docklands into a new urban district with housing, businesses (especially the creation of a new financial district), new transport links and the re-use of the dock basins as part of the setting of these new gentrified neighbourhoods. Figure 14.1 is a map of the London Docklands in 1882 – more or less the area which has been redeveloped today.

The London Docklands had evolved over many centuries and wove a dense fabric of local communities into the busiest port in the world at the time (Rule, 2009). Once the area was abandoned following the move of the main dock activity to Tilbury further down the river, a new function had to be found for this substantial area located next to the historic heart of the City of London. The central area within the large meander of the River Thames is the Isle of Dogs (see Figure 14.1), and this is the heart of the area, now featuring the O2 Arena. While attracting mixed opinions about its direction at the time, the development has matured, and the key feature of the area from a residential point of view is the presence of and access to water – to most of the old dock basins, which are now marinas or water sports centres (apart from Surrey Dock, which is partly filled in) and to the River Thames (d'Arcy, 2012). Figure 14.2 shows a view over the Royal Victoria Dock basin towards two of the iconic – and controversial – elements: the O2 Arena to the left (formerly the Millennium Dome) and the new financial district with the then-tallest tower in the United Kingdom, Canary Wharf.

DOI: 10.4324/9780429056161-18

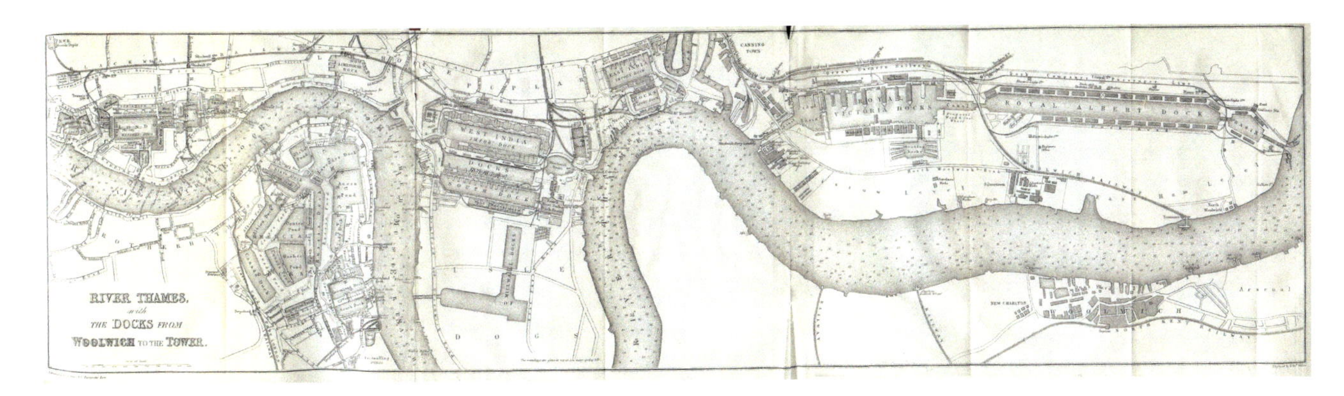

Figure 14.1
Map of the London Docklands in 1882 by Edward Weller
(*Source*: A Dictionary Practical, Theoretical, and Historical of Commerce and Commercial Navigation by J.R. McCulloch – Longmans, Green and Co. London, 1882, Public Domain)

Figure 14.2
A night-time view of the O2 Arena and Canary Wharf from the Royal Victoria Dock
(*Source*: Michael Pead: Photos of the Docklands, Creative Commons CC BY-SA 2.0)

Some of the challenges of redeveloping the territories of docklands into new city districts include polluted land; old warehouses and dock structures which may or may not have potential for renovation and re-use, for example, into apartments of offices; and retaining something of the cultural and architectural heritage, as well as social memories associated with places that often had close-knit communities. We will see later in the chapter how some of these aspects have been taken into account in projects.

Water access is also a particular challenge. Harbours, wharves and dock basins are all designed so that access to boats or ships from the land surface is several metres above the water level, allowing for vessels to tie up and also to account for changes in water level in tidal conditions. They are also constructed with walls or other structures allowing for vessels to be moored close alongside; such walls are therefore vertical. This means that there are numerous risks to people using such spaces for recreational use – there are obvious dangers of drowning if anyone falls in, so that safety aspects are crucial when designing public spaces. Adding lower-level floating platforms can mean that access down into dock basins is possible and allows for use of boats and water craft.

In this book, we are featuring projects which are quite recent, but it is also worth looking at some other examples of dock or harbour redevelopment which have stood the test of time and are not at the same scale as the London Docklands redevelopment. The Inner Harbor in Baltimore, Maryland, United States, is an example that started life in the 1950s, with the Charles Center project (offices, hotels and shops) starting the process in 1958 onwards, and from then, the area was converted into a mixed use series of parks, cultural attractions and water use (Breen and Rigby, 1994). In the 1950s, economic changes led to the end of cargo and passenger use. The derelict old piers were demolished over time to be replaced by parkland used for recreation purposes and some events. The waterfront itself then gradually saw a number of parks and plazas set amongst new offices, hotels and leisure attractions. Further developments were added over time, including corporate headquarters and a public park and waterfront promenade, and following a gathering of tall ships in 1976 for the US Bicentennial, further attractions such as the National Aquarium, Maryland Science Center and Harborplace, which functions as a festival marketplace, were added up to the 1980s.

The Baltimore Inner Harbour was seen as a model of urban planning and waterfront development. It was cited by the American Institute of Architects in 1984 as "one of the supreme achievements of large-scale urban design and development in U.S. history". Figure 14.3 shows the current appearance of the Baltimore Inner Harbour.

Figure 14.3
Baltimore Inner Harbour
(*Source*: Chris6d – Own work, Creative Commons CC BY-SA 4.0.)

The scale of redevelopment can also be much more modest, but many of the same aspects apply – managing risks, dealing with water pollution, maximising the use of cultural heritage and providing attractive and accessible waterfronts to attract people to live, work and play.

Why the cases were chosen

For the selection of cases to present in this chapter and to show the range of recent examples of the regeneration of former docklands (with post-industrial remains) and harbours, we looked for originality in concept and design, variety of location and type and something extra which makes them stand out. We also looked for examples which to some extent offer some continuity with or reflection of the culture and tradition of the port and related industrial design and material heritage, as well as unique solutions to specific problems. We consider that ports and harbours may be linked directly to the urban fabric from when they formed a central and often pivotal role in the economic life of the city, which often turned its back on the water itself. The water bodies of ports and harbours may present significant dangers through polluted, often deep water and as a result of high and vertical harbour walls. Thus, the cases present a set of different ways in which problems and opportunities have been combined in unique solutions. We have two main categories of projects: larger port and harbour complexes with associated post-industrial elements and smaller developments along old harbour-sides which are often from an earlier generation of ports but which retain the same contact with the water and some of the same challenges for planning and design.

Larger port and harbour complexes

We start with a sample of the larger sites where, as a result of new technology such as containers, the port activities moved out of central urban locations and were relocated at a distance where the huge container ships can dock and there is adequate space for handling and storing containers and suitable road and rail access. These have often formed major elements of urban renewal in a number of cities, and the examples we have selected here show particular creativity in the design of the parks and access facilities which have replaced them – sometimes a result of major reconstruction, sometimes in very imaginative solutions for technical challenges at the sites.

- The Magellan and Marco Polo Terraces in the HafenCity in Hamburg, Germany
- Carradah Park, Sydney, Australia
- Erie Basin Park, Red Hook, Brooklyn, New York, United States
- Barangaroo Reserve, Sydney, Australia
- Brooklyn Bridge Park, New York, United States

Smaller developments along harbour-sides

These projects are more modest development in terms of scale but also form a group of highly creative solutions to making old harbour edges – generally in smaller or simpler harbours or dock edges in city centres. They provide great opportunities for summer activities and socialising but do not have the larger scale of more comprehensive development that characterises the larger port redevelopment projects.

- Taranaki Wharf, Wellington, New Zealand
- Aker Brygge Stranden/Waterfront, Oslo, Norway
- Kalvebrod Waves, Copenhagen, Denmark
- Harbour Bath, Copenhagen, Denmark
- Spruce Street Harbour, Philadelphia, United States
- City Deck, Green Bay, Wisconsin

Each project is briefly described (based on information from a range of sources, often the designer or articles, as well as what the authors have seen). It is then illustrated with a photograph of a typical view, assessed for project quality based on the factors presented in Chapter 10 and illustrated using a set of sketches designed to bring out the key aspects which make the project special and inspirational. These are presented as annotated images, and they aim to complement the text visually, so there is no additional description in the text, only the captions.

Larger port and harbour complexes

The Magellan and Marco Polo Terraces

These two linked projects, completed in 2007 from the designs of the Barcelona architecture firm of EMBT for the HafenCity authority, are part of the extensive redevelopment of the old harbour and free trade zone – the "Grosser Grasbrook" area – in Hamburg, a historic port city located on the River Elbe in northern Germany which suffered heavily from Allied bombing in the Second World War. The project replaced the port structures with an extensive new complex of residential, commercial and cultural buildings set around the various harbour basins. The overall project has been several decades in the making and has provided 6000 homes, 40,000 workplaces and an open space structure based around the open water areas of the dock basins. For these, the planning included artistic content to give a clear sense of identity to the place which reflects the old industrial character while including new elements. The River Elbe has a large tidal range which was accommodated through different levels and the use of piers and pontoons to allow visitors access down to the water; ramps, stairways and terraces are used to link the water to the land and the different levels with each other. The Magellan Terraces features stairs arranged like a theatre, which focuses views down to the harbour, at the bottom of which is a 400-m-long floating promenade (Figure 14.4). The influence of the Spanish (Catalan) architects is evident in the use of Mediterranean idioms and

Figure 14.4
The Magellan Terraces at HafenCity, Hamburg
(*Source*: Jeroen de Vries)

elements such as large fish bas-reliefs on the walls. Free-form paving patterns and sculptural elements break the visual monotony of extensive surfaces, and the space connects with the main street running at right angles, separated by low bollards. At the Marco Polo Terraces, while the design vocabulary remains the same, there are also differences. Limited numbers of trees and patches of lawn were introduced on each terrace, although these are somewhat small for the scale of the spaces and are dominated by the buildings. The Marco Polo Terraces incorporate wooden raised platforms placed irregularly on the grass. They permit a range of informal uses and also allow good views of the water.

Project quality rating assessment

For accessibility, car parking is deliberately excluded from the project area, and due to the low level of the water compared to the dock, the interior spaces are hidden from the view of the casual observer (Figure 14.5). Design quality is generally high, although the site is expensive to maintain, due in part to its popularity but also some of the elements such as the trees set in lots of hard surfacing. The site is open to the elements and lacks shelter and shade, and there is little nature present. As a busy urban site, it does not permit much of a sense of being away or contact with nature, and the other health and well-being aspects are limited due to the inherent site character. The water connections are mainly visual due to the fact that it is a former dock, with all the challenges that creates, although access down to the water and some boat access is provided successfully. The site is not designed with lots of physical activities and is not suitable for sports of any type.

Carradah Park, Sydney, Australia

This site, close to central Sydney and with spectacular views to the Harbour Bridge and Opera House, was completed in 2004 from the designs of landscape architects McGregor Coxall for West Sydney Council. The site started life in 1920 as a set of huge tanks for the storage and distribution of oil and petroleum piped from tankers docking at the nearby wharf. These tanks were set into the rocky sandstone terrain by blasting cylindrical forms to accommodate them. In the 1980s, the site was recognised as being contaminated, and redundant structures were removed and the site cleaned up, after it closed in 1993, and a restoration project started in 1997. The voids which resulted from removal of the tanks, together with other concrete industrial remains, provided the inspiration for the design, defining space and structure (Figure 14.6). The site is surrounded by suburban development yet has a hidden, sublime quality. The park in part balances the provision of public waterfront access and also reserves part of the waterfront (0.9 ha) for future maritime use. The park is mainly used by people from the nearby residential areas and features walking trails, stairways and interpretive signs. As well as providing views across the bay, the forms and spaces of the park and the use of industrial materials for access decking across the uneven sandstone surfaces at the upper levels of the park give the site a unique character, reflecting its industrial past. The circular galvanised steel viewing deck over the cliff blasted to accommodate the biggest tank is especially spectacular. The lower levels in the former tank bases make stages and also provide views across the bay. As well as the set of walkways, there are other structures made of brick or concrete, for instance, at the entrances and in smaller spaces. Finally, native plants were used to restore the unique cliff habitats.

Project quality rating assessment

This project shows some limitations in access, mainly due to the difficult nature of the cliffs and former constructions – it is impressive how these have been overcome (Figure 14.7). The design quality is high in all dimensions. The range of facilities is limited, partly due to the nature of the site and the challenges that presents, as well as its location. It performs well for health and well-being potential, although the sense of being away and contact with nature are understandably a little weaker. Direct water connections are not part of the site design, but visual connections

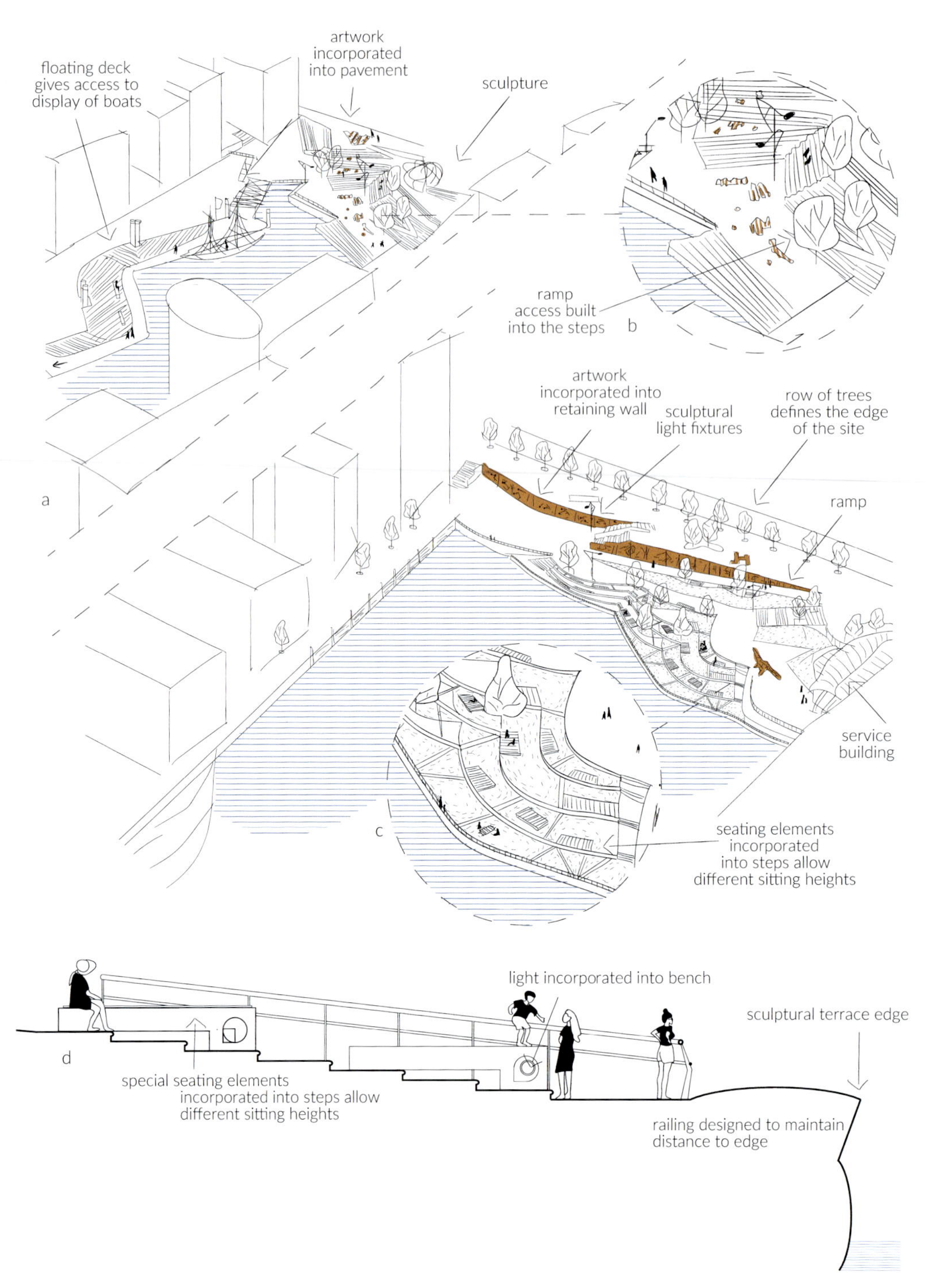

Figure 14.5a–c

a) Overview of the Magellan and Marco Polo Terraces – looking into the two dock basins and showing how the two terraces provide access down into the docks and floating piers providing closer contact with the water (although nowhere is water directly accessible); b) the Marco Polo Terrace, showing the organisation of different levels and different types of seats providing views into the dock basin; c) a section through the Magellan Terrace from the dock level down to the water, showing how the changes in level are achieved

(*Source*: Anna Wilczyńska and Jekaterina Balicka)

Figure 14.6
A view of the Carradah Park space and steel deck in the largest void where a huge tank once stood
(*Source*: McGregor Coxall)

are good. It is not specifically designed with lots of physical activities in mind. This park is another example of how it is not possible to provide for everything, given the physical limitations of terrain and former use, but also how such challenges have been changed into opportunities for creating a dramatic solution with a very powerful sense of genius loci.

Erie Basin Park, Red Hook, Brooklyn, New York, United States

This project is a park on a former dockland area uniquely developed and completed in 2008 by a private company from designs by Lee Weintraub Landscape Architecture as part of a large IKEA retail store complex. Following the decline of the ports along the waterfronts of New York, many areas became neglected. Red Hook is the neighbourhood next to the formerly busy Erie Basin and once had a substantial community of dock workers nearby. Following the closure of the dock and general abandonment by industry, there was high unemployment, and people moved away, leaving the Erie Basin derelict. This has been redeveloped into a combined retail development (IKEA), public park and waterfront. The park has a strong concept based on the stories and artefacts associated with the history of use of the site, featuring dock cranes, dry docks and piers as well as smaller objects (Figure 14.8). A key feature of the park is its views across the water to New York City – especially to the Manhattan skyline and the Statue of Liberty. Normally, regenerated waterfronts act as catalysts for redevelopment of the surrounding areas, and in this case it was not local authorities but the private sector who was responsible. The project landscape architects developed the layout and design of the site furniture by studying New York public park seating with the aim of introducing a new way of socialising while experiencing public open spaces. The park is open to the public, and vegetation and

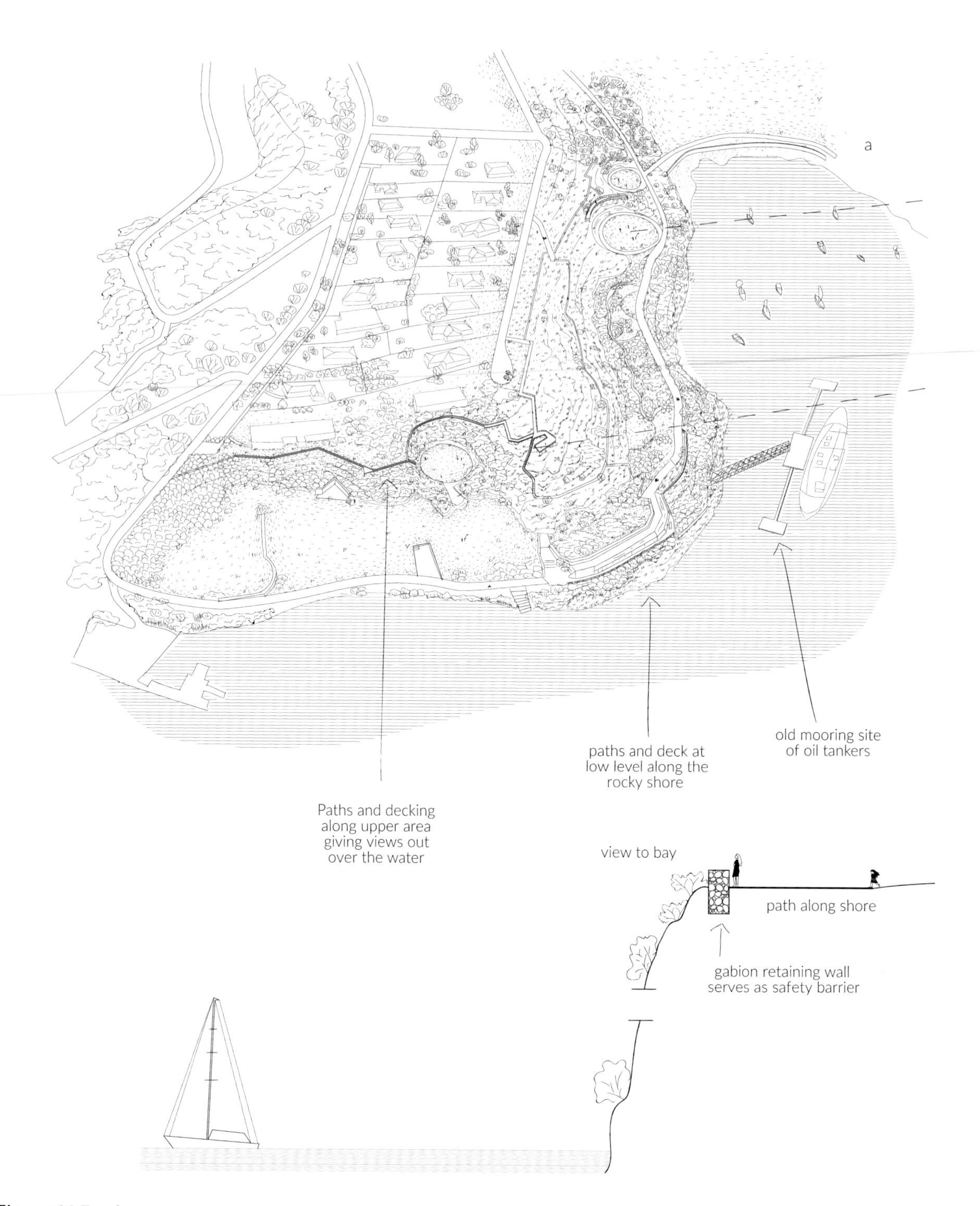

Figure 14.7a–d

a) General layout of Carradah Park located on the cliff and former oil tank bases, showing how the industrial origins are clearly integrated into the project; b) detail of one of the oil storage tank sites with a circular lawn area beneath the cliff and a viewing platform on the top of the cliff providing views over the park and bay; c) detail of the main path passing along the lower part and connected, via stairs, with the upper sections; d) cross-section through the site of one of the oil tanks, showing the viewing platform at the top of the cliff and the levelled oil tank base with lawn, which also provides views to the bay, and the path

(*Source*: Anna Wilczyńska and Jekaterina Balicka)

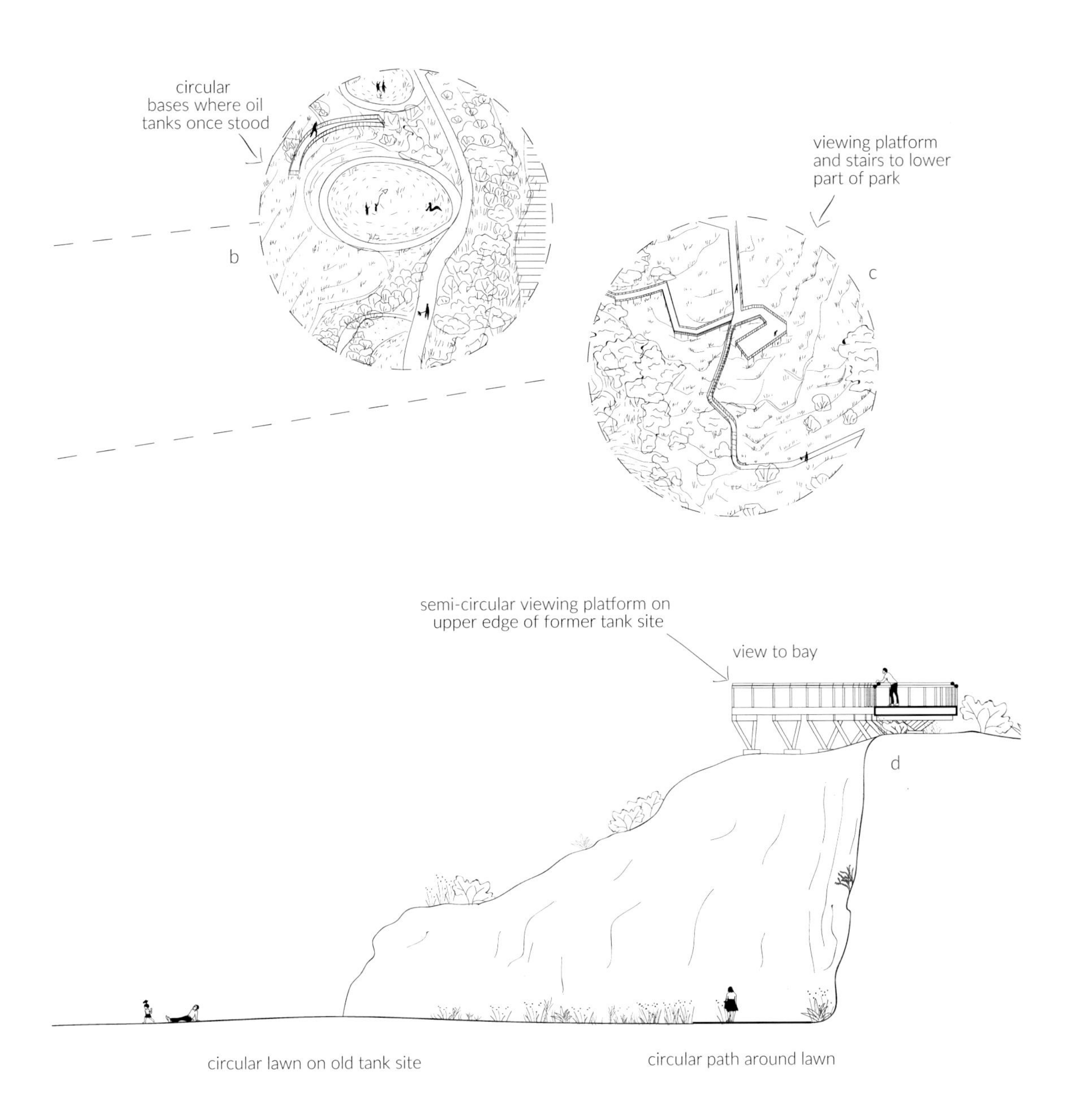

Figure 14.7a–d (continued)

Figure 14.8
Part of the Erie Basin park at night showing some of the main features and the use of lighting to emphasise elements such as the dockside crane
(*Source*: Colin Cooke)

elements such as colourful corrugated sheets visually separate the store from the park, although entry to it is also via the store. A huge gantry crane marks the entrance. The designers salvaged many industrial elements, and those which provide seating, shelter, and edge protection were inspired by the industrial heritage, while long wave-shaped benches take inspiration from water movement. Lots of found objects, such as metal sheets folded to create seats, were also used. Likewise, blue lights used under the circular tables mirror those typically used along the water edge for safety.

Project quality rating assessment

The park has very good accessibility, especially by car (given it is next to the IKEA store with a huge parking lot) (Figure 14.9). The design quality is high across all aspects, although site maintenance is considered expensive. The facilities are well provided for although the site is exposed to sun and wind and there is not so much nature present (for obvious reasons). It offers some good opportunities for promoting health and well-being – apart from the sense of being away or contact with nature – due to its setting. As a former dock, direct contact with water is a problem, and there is no direct recreational access to or from the water (there is some access by waterbus). There is no provision for formal sports on land or water – this is not relevant for the site due to its location.

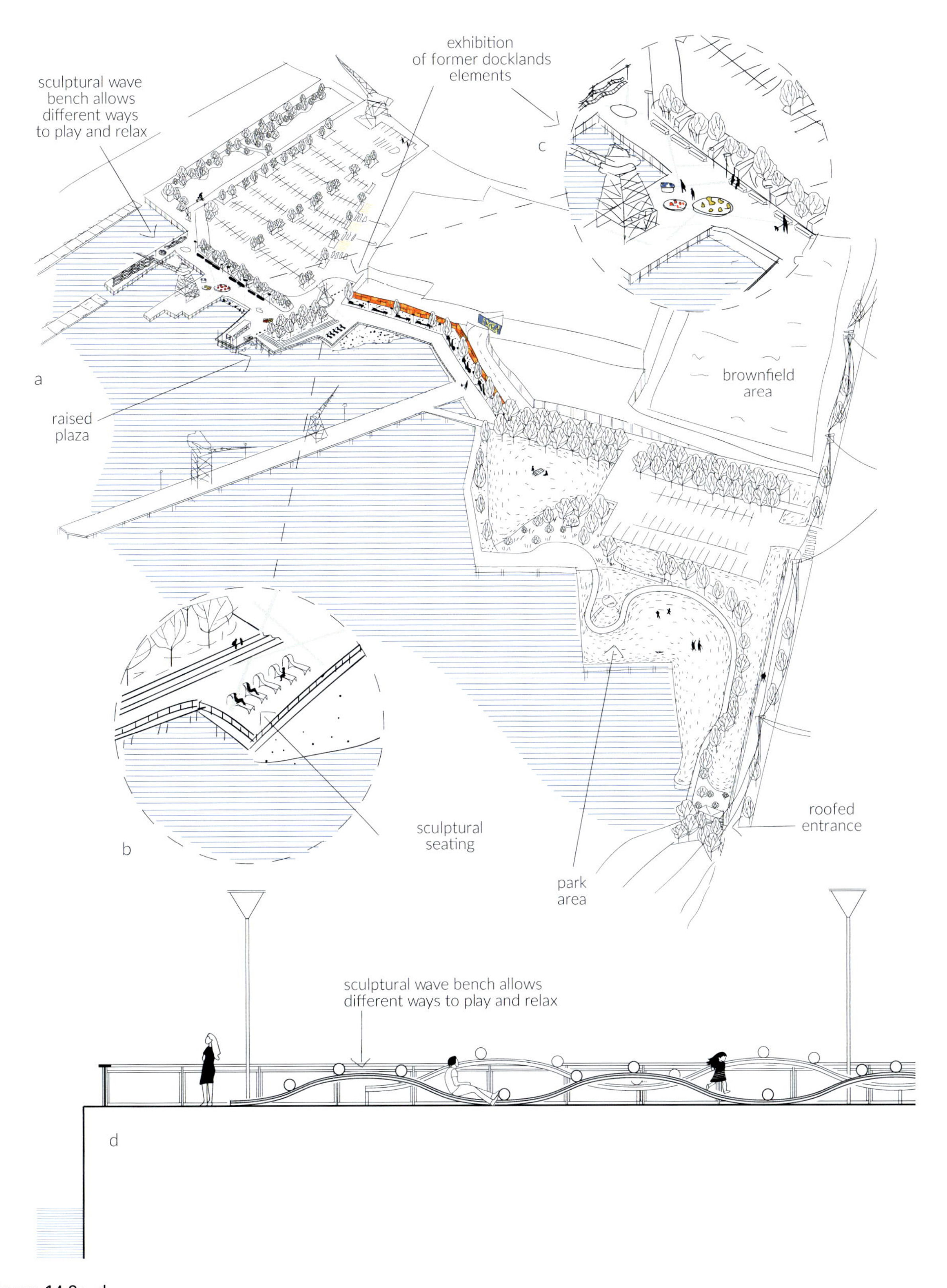

Figure 14.9a–d

a) General layout of the Erie Basin park containing three main sections arranged around the IKEA store and its car park and storage yard; b) detail of the lounge seating area; c) detail of the exhibition of the old dock elements; d) cross-section showing the wave benches in more detail

(*Source*: Anna Wilczyńska and Jekaterina Balicka)

Barangaroo Reserve, Sydney, Australia

Barangaroo Reserve is a multi-award-winning new park completed in 2015 from designs by PWP (Peter Walker and Partners) together with Johnson Pilton Walker for the Barangaroo Delivery Authority. The 6-hectare abandoned industrial dock and shipyard area in Sydney Harbour was a flat, rectangular area created by levelling the rocky headland and filling in a small bay in the 1830s and 40s onwards The site was originally known as Miller's Point before it was flattened to make room for wharves, containers and maritime industrialisation, which formed its function until the 1960s, when it was closed and became inaccessible. The new name is in honour of an aboriginal woman who lived and traded there in the 1830s. The project design eliminated this flat area and rebuilt the form of the headland in both plan and profile, with its lower levels covered using specially formed and laid sandstone blocks in what is called a tessellated pavement, inspired by the natural bedding and joints of sedimentary sandstone. This was used to clad the new landform, taking quarried stone (sourced from within the site when constructing underground parking) and laying it according to the natural rock bedding in the area. The result is a stepped stone surface arising out of the water (including artificial rock pools exposed at low tide) to a headland summit 18 metres above the water level offering spectacular views over the rest of Sydney Harbour. The paving does not emulate natural variability but is more formal in order to emphasise the fact that it is artificial. The use of sawn stone is the main feature of most of the elements used besides the terraces to maintain the design unity. There is also extensive planting of native species in an introduced artificial soil. Alongside the stone terraces and the public road is a promenade, which gives the form for the parallel alignment of the terraces from which access to the site is obtained down steps and along ramps (Figure 14.10). The site has also established a connection with a longer coastal walk.

Figure 14.10
A view of Barangaroo Reserve showing the stone tessellated rocky foreshore and the promenade hugging the line of the shore, as well as some of the extensive native planting
(*Source*: Courtesy PWP)

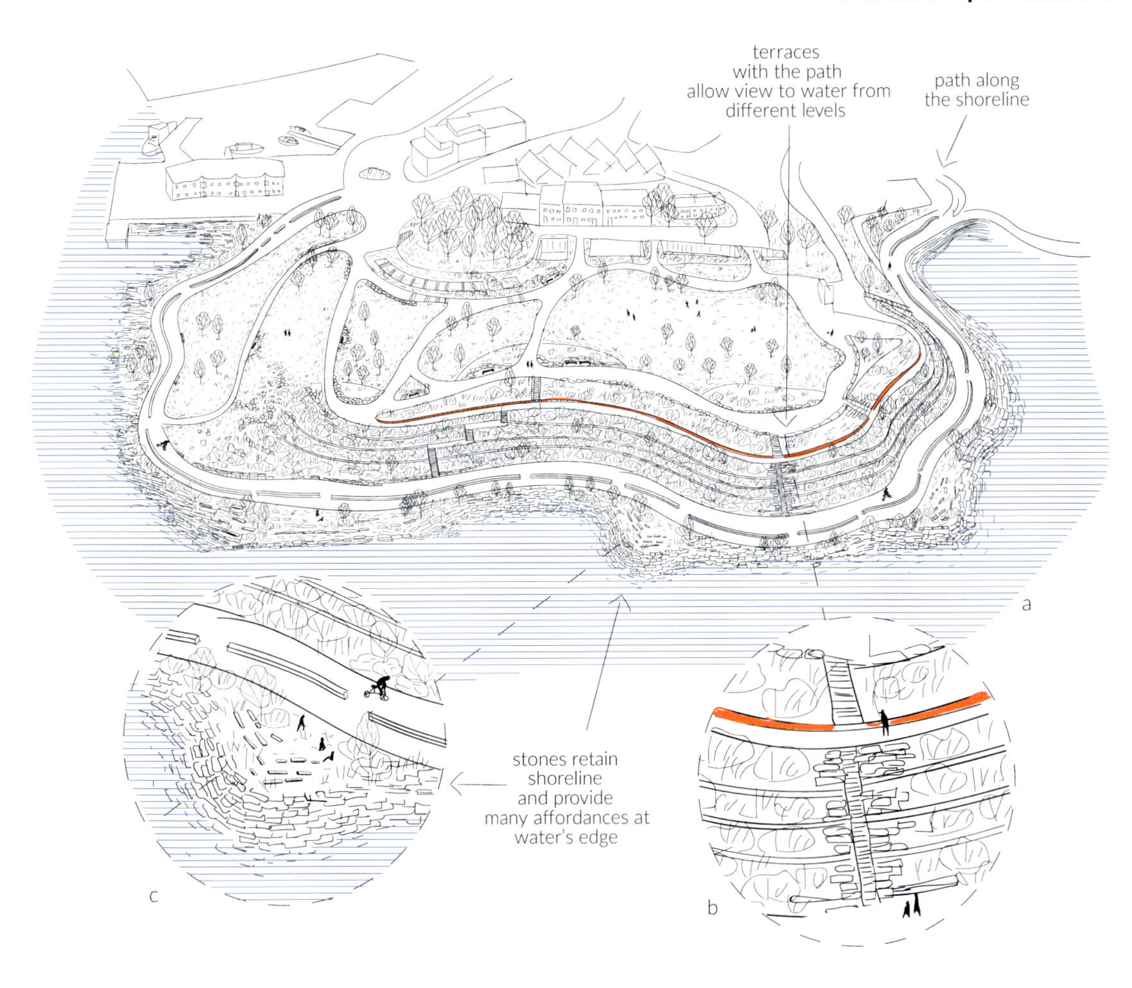

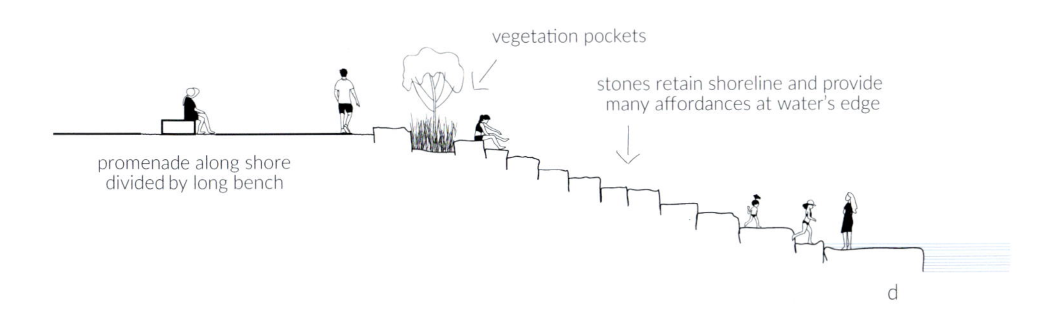

Figure 14.11a–d

a) General layout of the Barangaroo Reserve, which has created a new landform and as a result has provided access to a new green public space on the water; b) detail of the lower part of the park where the slope is covered with stepped rockwork providing informal seating next to the water; c) detail of the steps leading down through the rock terraces from the upper to lower paths; d) cross-section through the lower part of the park with the path and rocky shore giving access to the water

(*Source*: Anna Wilczyńska and Jekaterina Balicka)

Project quality rating assessment

The site has excellent accessibility, very high design quality – albeit with some expensive maintenance – and a wide range of facilities – although rather exposed to sun and wind, at least until the trees grow to a reasonable height. It also performs very well for health and well-being aspects. Direct water connections and activities are limited, but, of course, the site is strongly linked visually to the water (Figure 14.11). The physical activities possible are many and varied, apart from formal sports on land or water, these being impractical or inappropriate for the site.

Brooklyn Bridge Park, Brooklyn, New York, United States

This project occupies a substantial site along the East River in New York. The park was designed by Michael Van Valkenburgh and Associates for the Brooklyn Bridge Park Development Corporation. The land for the park was formerly an industrial stretch of waterfront owned by the Port Authority of New York and New Jersey. The objective was to transform what had been a break-bulk cargo shipping and storage complex which had become obsolete once shipping containers took over the maritime cargo trade. After the city and state signed a joint agreement in 2002, site planning and project funding went ahead. The first phase in 2007 included the demolition of a warehouse under the Brooklyn Bridge itself. Since the opening of the first phase at Pier 1, more and more sections of the park have been completed (Figure 14.12). However, there have been disputes and lawsuits over several aspects, including the construction of residential developments to help pay for the project. The site covers 85 acres/35.4 hectares and runs

Figure 14.12

Looking southeast to Pier 1 of Brooklyn Bridge Park, showing the waterside promenade and the vegetated slopes rising behind

(*Source*: Jim Henderson, Creative Commons CC0 1.0 Universal Public Domain Dedication)

along the waterfront for 1.3 miles/2.2 km, incorporating six old piers and two pre-existing parks (Empire–Fulton Ferry and Main Street Parks) into the whole project. The site comprises two stretches at an angle to each other, dominated at the apex by the huge tower of the Brooklyn Bridge itself. The design made use of the different dock edge conditions to create a range of settings for people to enjoy and to view the iconic cityscape of lower Manhattan to be seen across the river along a continuous promenade linking the different piers. The facilities provided include playgrounds, basketball courts, sports fields and a roller skating rink. There are also lots of food concessions on the site. In places, the park descends to the water, with rock edges and green slopes with trees behind. Each of the piers can be considered a mini-park with different designs and innovative approaches to creating spaces and adding vegetation to the elevated structures. The design made use of recycled materials, such as old beams for park benches.

Project quality rating assessment

This is a very accessible park, although less so for car access due to limited parking opportunities. It demonstrates excellent design quality and a wide range of facilities – albeit exposed to sun and wind – and provides good settings for health and well-being, apart from being able to obtain a sense of being away and close to nature, due to the site context (Figure 14.13). Water connectivity is limited, and the dock walls prevent physical contact. The site is very well equipped for land-based formal sports but not for water sports.

Smaller developments along harboursides: Taranaki Wharf, Wellington, New Zealand

This project was designed by Wraight + Associates Ltd for Wellington Waterfront Ltd and completed in 2005. The site was a wharf used by ships bringing cargoes from Tasmania from the early 20th century to the 1990s. The designers aimed to establish a strong city to sea connection and to create a new role for the dock edges as a public promenade. The idea was to maximise the interactions at the water edge to generate a rich waterfront experience for visitors. The site also strengthens the connections along the Wellington waterfront, linking Frank Kitts Park in the north to Waitangi Park in the south and at the same time establishing connections to the city centre. There are a number of old and new buildings around the site, which itself uses the wharf structures and refers to the natural and cultural heritage of the place. The surfaced areas are balanced with wet and dry gardens, and the details refer to industrial and nautical materials and finish in a palette of elements. The main focal feature which lends a unique character and animates the site is the jump platform, a twisting staircase up which people climb and then jump down into the sea, which is below the level of the wharf in a cut section of the surface, meaning that the water is hidden from the casual viewer (Figure 14.14).

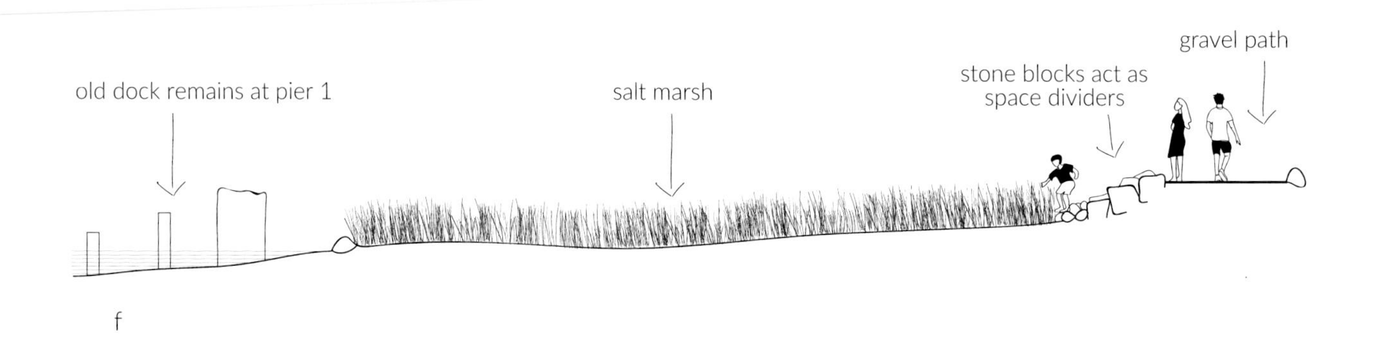

Figure 14.13a–h

a) Overview of the huge Brooklyn Bridge Park, which has provided a major additional public green and blue space on this former dockland, with a focus on sport activities; b) detail of a children's playground on Pier 5, where a hole through the dock floor gives a glimpse down into the structure; c) detail of the Pier 1 park showing the access paths and start of the artificial wetland created there; d) detail of the artificial beach providing swimming and bathing as well as access for kayaking on the site of the former Pier 4; e) detail of the water ply area; f) cross-section through the artificial salt-marsh next to old Pier 1; g) cross-section showing relationship of path and beach to water at Pier 4; h) cross-section through the sunbathing and sitting area with riprap edge and then the elevated section of Pier 5 providing access to the marina

(*Source*: Anna Wilczyńska and Jekaterina Balicka)

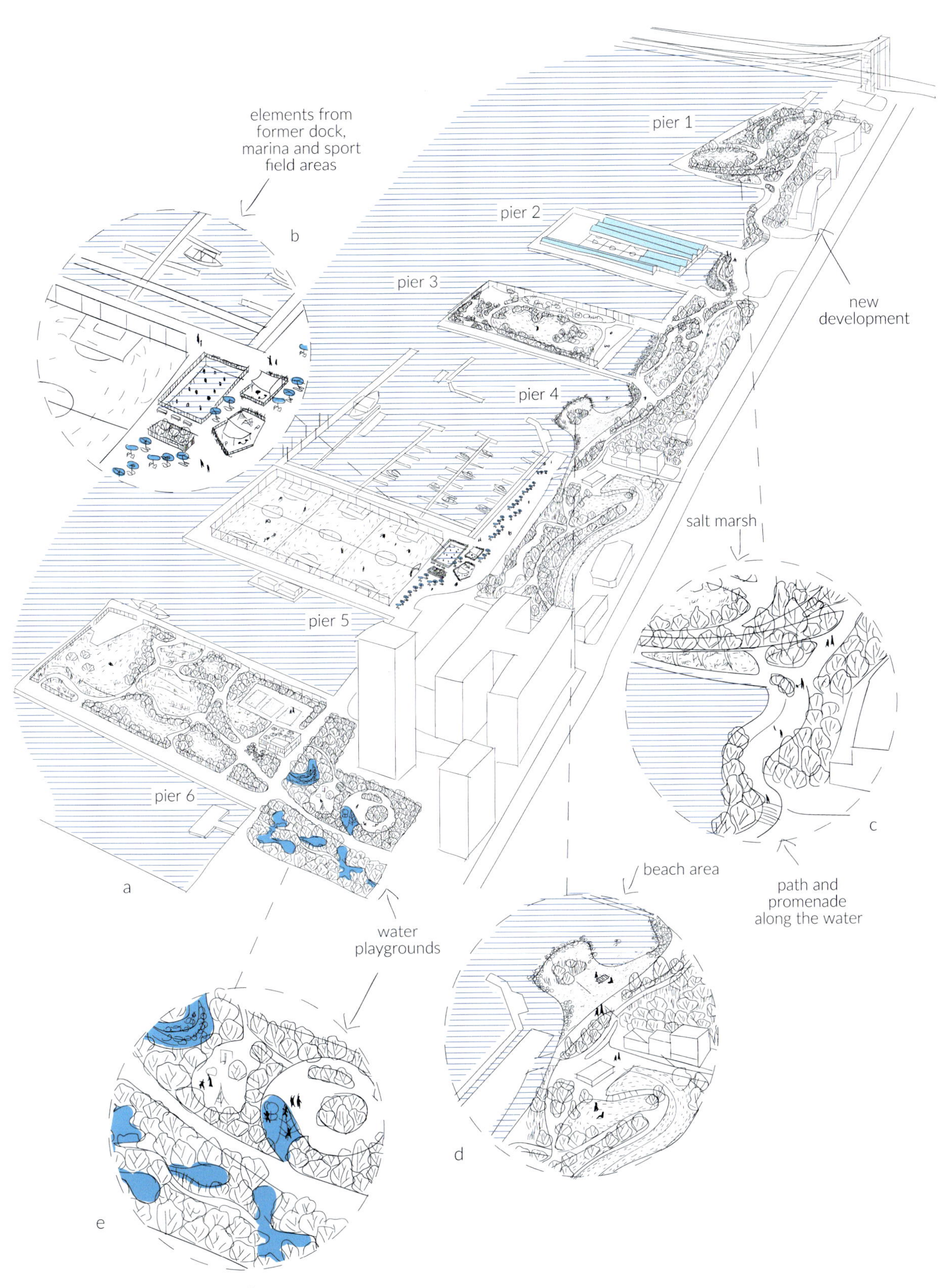

Figure 14.13 a–h (continued)

Figure 14.14
The jump platform, the central unique feature at Taranaki Wharf
(*Source*: Bruno Marques)

Project quality rating assessment

There is excellent accessibility to the site, which generally exhibits high design quality and a good range of facilities although it is rather exposed to the wind and seems a little short on seating. Health and well-being opportunities are good, apart from the sense of being away and in contact with nature (Figure 4.15). Water connections are also good, and there is quite a lot of activity on the water – although limited in scope. The range of physical activities is also good.

Aker Brygge Stranden/Waterfront, Oslo, Norway

This project, completed in 2016 from the designs of LINK Landskap Aker Brygge, is part of the rejuvenation of the Aker Brygge, a very popular area of central Oslo situated along the western side of the Pipervika, an arm of the Oslo Fjord. It was the shipyard of the Akers Mekaniske Verksted, set up in 1854, which functioned until 1982, after which the area was gradually regenerated. The aim is to provide public access to the waterfront along a 12-km stretch from the east to the west of the city. The developer, Norwegian Property (NPRO), as well as building new residential and commercial buildings, also focused on the refurbishment of the outdoor spaces, especially along the waterfront. This first phase of the Stranden was completed in 2014. Additional phases in 2015/2016 included the new main

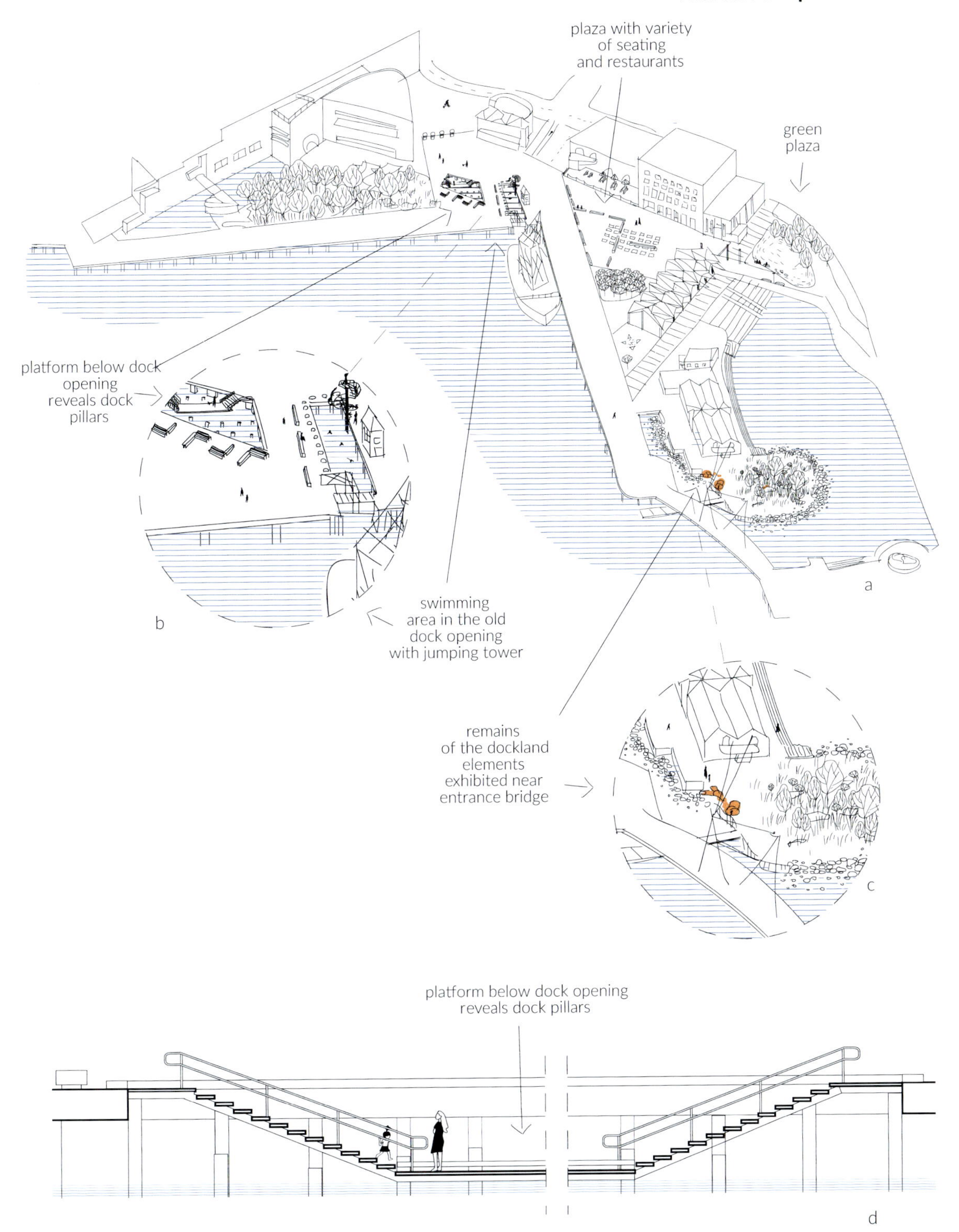

Figure 14.15a–d

a) General layout of Taranaki Wharf and how the project is divided into different functional and thematic zones; b) the opening through the dock surface revealing the supporting structure as well as the genius loci, featuring the jump platform; c) closer view of the section planted with trees and shrubs and displaying old dock heritage objects; d) cross-section through the steps leading down to the water, enabling both a view to the dock basin and direct contact with the water

(*Source*: Anna Wilczyńska and Jekaterina Balicka)

Figure 14.16
A view along the Stranden at Akerbrygge showing the granite paving, orange benches and timber decking
(*Source*: Aker Brygge)

square, Bryggetorget, and improved access between the waterfront and the city. The plan for Stranden was aimed to increase both visual and physical contact with Oslo's characteristic and dramatic fjord landscape setting while also encouraging a range of appropriate activities – promenading, sitting, social interactions and of course linkages with restaurants and shops located in the Aker Brygge development as a whole (Figure 14.16). The project achieved a simpler and cleaner cross-sectional reconfiguration by reorganising and consolidating the promenade, making it wider and roomier so as to cope with increased use while achieving a strong sense of design unity. The resulting space is very flexible for promenading and socialising activities as well as providing more opportunities for spontaneous and generally un-planned activities. This has resulted in more possibilities to experience the fjord landscape in different ways. The surfacing of Stranden uses granite paving throughout, with some stepped timber decking in places, especially where boats can tie up. The designers aimed to create a robust and non-directional surface, which resulted in a restrained unified surface directing the visual focus inwards to the new and historical facades and outwards to the fjord. It is complemented by a series of orange benches permitting sitting and reclining and looking at the view across the fjord.

Project quality rating assessment

The project shows some limits on accessibility due to its location in relation to the city in general. Design quality is high for all aspects (Figure 14.17). Compared to other sites, this one lacks some facilities – but this is due to the

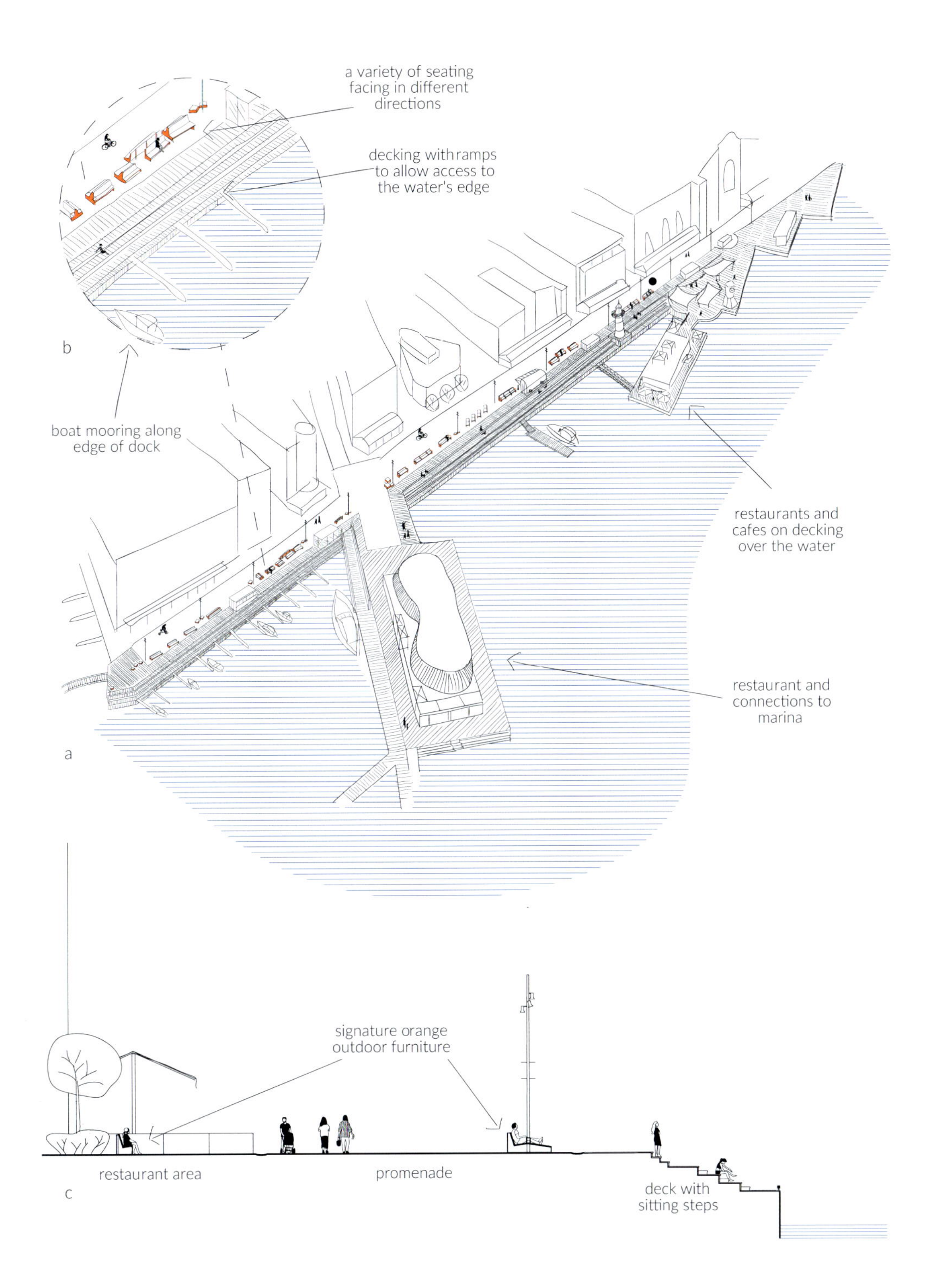

Figure 14.17a–c

a) General layout of the Stranden promenade showing the division of the site into several zones; b) closer view of the main recreational zone featuring the sitting terraces with the wooden decking and original quayside furniture which adds to the sense of identity of the new promenade; c) cross-section through the promenade from the restaurant level to the water, showing how the design deals with the changes in level

(*Source*: Anna Wilczyńska and Jekaterina Balicka)

location and project brief. It is also exposed to wind and sun. Health and well-being potentials are very good, apart from being able to gain a sense of being away – this is the city centre – and contact with nature. Direct water connections are not part of the design brief so are understandably absent, nor is there any provision for formal sports for the same reasons.

Kalvebod Waves, Copenhagen, Denmark

The Kalvebod Wave project was designed by JDS/Julien De Smedt Architects and Klar and completed in 2013. It is a special project forming part of the larger Kalvebro Brygge redevelopment, which commenced in the 1990s. Sited opposite the popular summer meeting place of Islands Brygge, it is located on reclaimed land in the Vesterbro district of the city, which was used for various industries such as a timber yard, railway and gas production. This new addition to the waterfront provides opportunities for a larger range of activities. Being close to the central train station and the Tivoli amusement park, the Kalvebod Bølge, or Kalvebod Waves, provides a new connection for the inner city with the harbour. The project consists of two main differently sized three-dimensional decked areas floating on pontoons and extending directly from the water edge in front of two new buildings which dominate the area. These are connected by decking which rises and falls in its level – hence the waves used in the name (Figure 14.18). This decking extends across the water, encloses the water available for swimming and boating and is positioned to capture sunlight and provide shelter from the wind. The southern pier allows for a flexible public space on the water and includes facilities to enable events, especially those related to the creative industry, to take place. Thus an active water enclave has been created for various water-related activities. A flow of boats to

Figure 14.18
The Kalvebod Waves, showing the characteristic flowing, undulating decks and the enclosed water area as well as the accessible water's edge, with central Copenhagen behind
(*Source*: Naotake Murayama, licensed under the Creative Commons Attribution 2.0 Generic Licence)

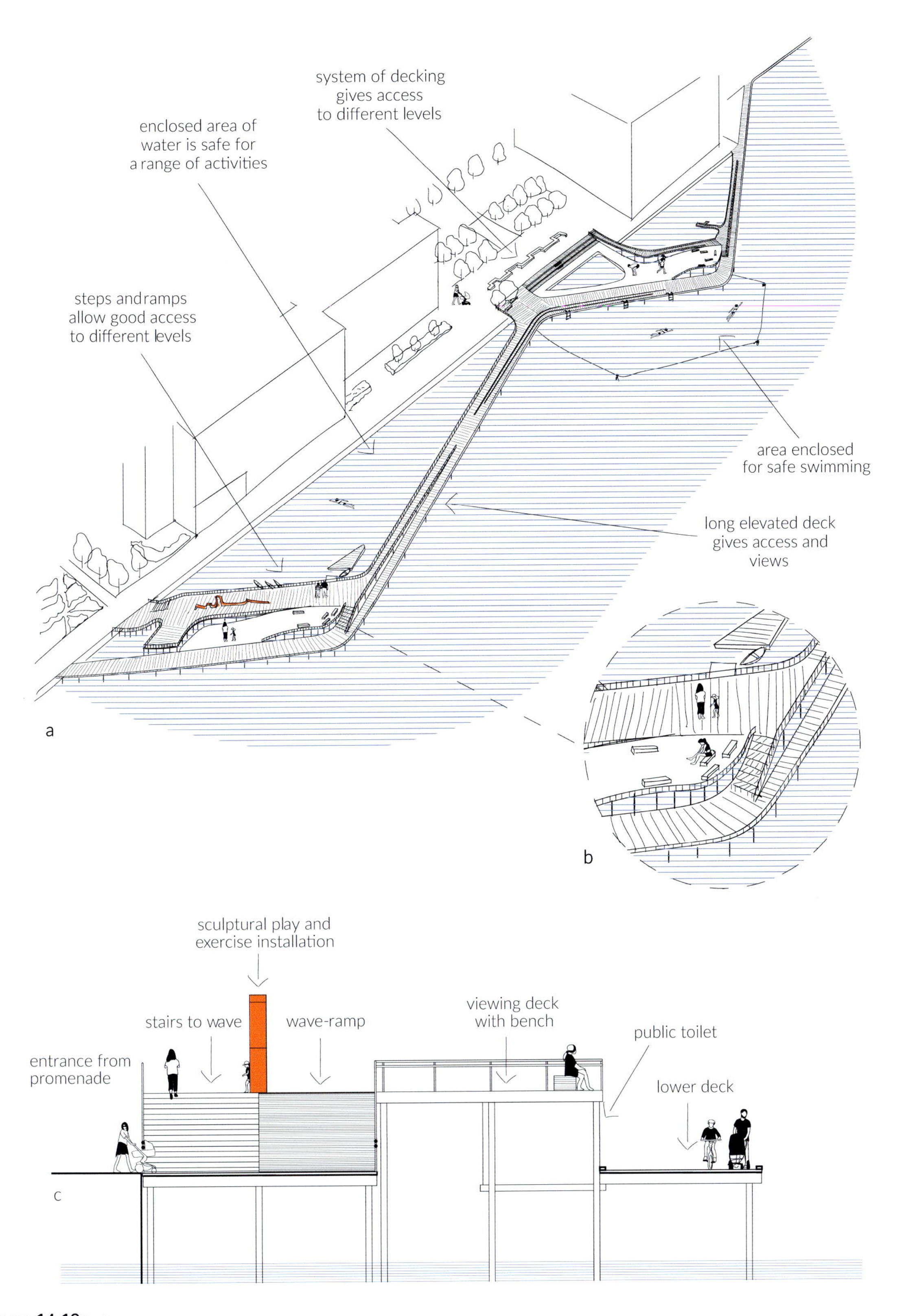

Figure 14.19a–c

a) General composition of the Kalvebod Waves project with the two main sections; b) detail showing the south-western part of the site with a multifunctional play and fitness area on the top of one of the wave structures; c) cross-section through the promenade, showing the internal basin and the height differences of the wooden deck

(*Source*: Anna Wilczyńska and Jekaterina Balicka)

and from the water hub of the southern segment also creates an active maritime atmosphere and maximises the connectivity of the project with the rest of the city. The northern unit provides a kind of oasis on the water, close to and accessible from the land but also somewhat away from it, which, as it includes a beach, allows people a break from hectic urban life.

Project quality rating assessment

The site has excellent accessibility and very high design quality – although it is somewhat weaker in cultural heritage values (it is an entirely new structure) and is expensive to maintain. The range of facilities is somewhat limited, mainly due to the design content, and it is exposed to wind and sun with no cover. Health and well-being opportunities are also good, apart from a sense of being away and closeness to nature. Access to and from the water and activities on it are good, although in limited ways due to the design (Figure 14.19). There is little formal physical activity but plenty of opportunities for various informal sports.

Figure 14.20

A view of the Copenhagen Harbour Baths showing the diving tower, the main pool, the lighthouse and the popularity of the project

(*Source*: Milsgrammer, licensed under the Creative Commons Attribution 2.0 Generic Licence)

Harbour Baths, Copenhagen, Denmark

This project, lying directly opposite the Kalvebod Waves project described previously, is another part of the Copenhagen harbour redevelopment, this time on Islands Brygge, another former industrial area. Designed by BIG/Bjarke Ingels Group, JDS/Julien De Smedt Architects and PLOT, it was completed in 2003 and has been an exceptionally popular place to go for sunbathing and swimming, among other activities, every summer since then. It extends the adjacent park and promenade over the water by incorporating the practical needs and demands for water accessibility, safety and programmatic flexibility. People use it in the same way they would use the beach rather than indoor swimming baths – not just to exercise but mainly to socialise, play and enjoy the sun. The design consists of a large floating timber-clad series of decks raised above the water (Figure 14.20). It is divided into three separate water pools equipped with ladders for access. The smallest one has a sloping floor for gradual access and shallow water, and the biggest has a diving tower shaped like the prow of a ship and is much deeper, linked to the harbour water. A red-and-white striped building resembles a lighthouse used for storage. The whole complex can be secured and closed. It is also fenced off along the outer waterfront sides to prevent access by boat – it is therefore a completely enclosed type of floating lido. Next to the baths is the park noted previously, with grassy areas used for sunbathing, and the promenade, thus offering easy access and a range of activities linked to the baths, making them part of a larger recreational complex. Generally, the water in the Copenhagen canals is clean, thus permitting the harbour baths to function as a

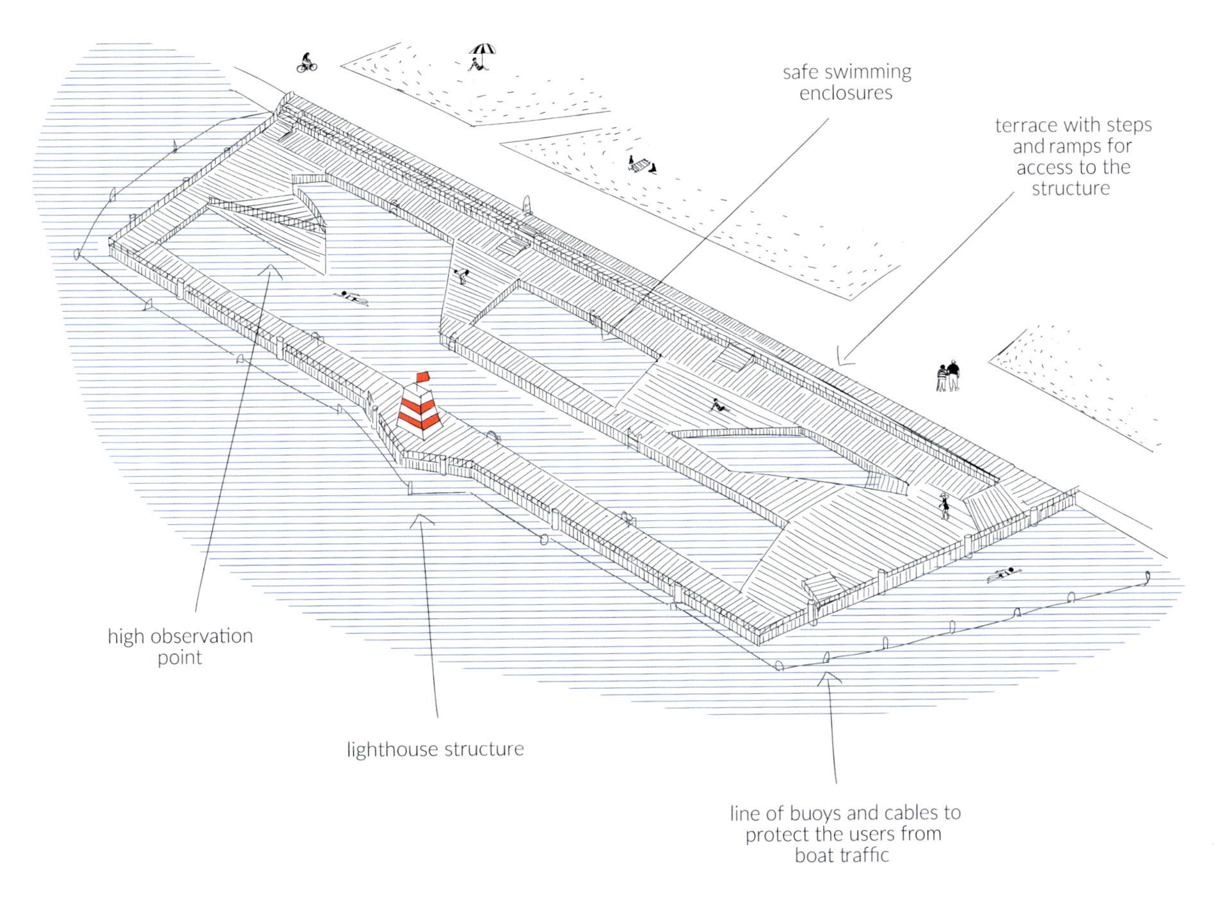

Figure 14.21
The design of the Copenhagen Harbour Baths project provides opportunities for bathing and swimming where it was not possible before
(*Source*: Anna Wilczyńska)

safe bathing area (it also applies to the Kalvebod Waves). Occasionally, however, as a result of strong rains, sewage may spill into the harbour and cause *E. coli* bacteria pollution, closing the harbour baths temporarily.

Project quality rating assessment

The site has excellent accessibility – apart from car parking – and very good design quality, although it is expensive to maintain (Figure 14.21). The range of facilities is limited (compared to other sites) due to the fact that is has a primary function as swimming baths (it is also exposed to sun and wind), and the health and well-being aspects are lacking a sense of being away or being in contact with nature, also due to its location and design. Water connections and physical activities are also strong, though limited due to its main swimming function.

Spruce Street Harbour, Philadelphia, United States

This project by the Groundswell Design Group was commissioned by the Delaware River Waterfront Corporation to create a new summer attraction at a tired and underused riverfront park located between the edge of the Delaware River and a four-lane highway in Philadelphia, Pennsylvania. The resulting park, set within an enclosed marina where pleasure boats and some museum ships are moored, is small and open seasonally – not quite a pop-up park, as it is

Figure 14.22

A view from the Spruce Street Harbour promenade out over the enclosed water garden at Spruce Street Harbour Park, surrounded by the three moored barges populated by trees, containers and seating

(*Source*: Mike Barone)

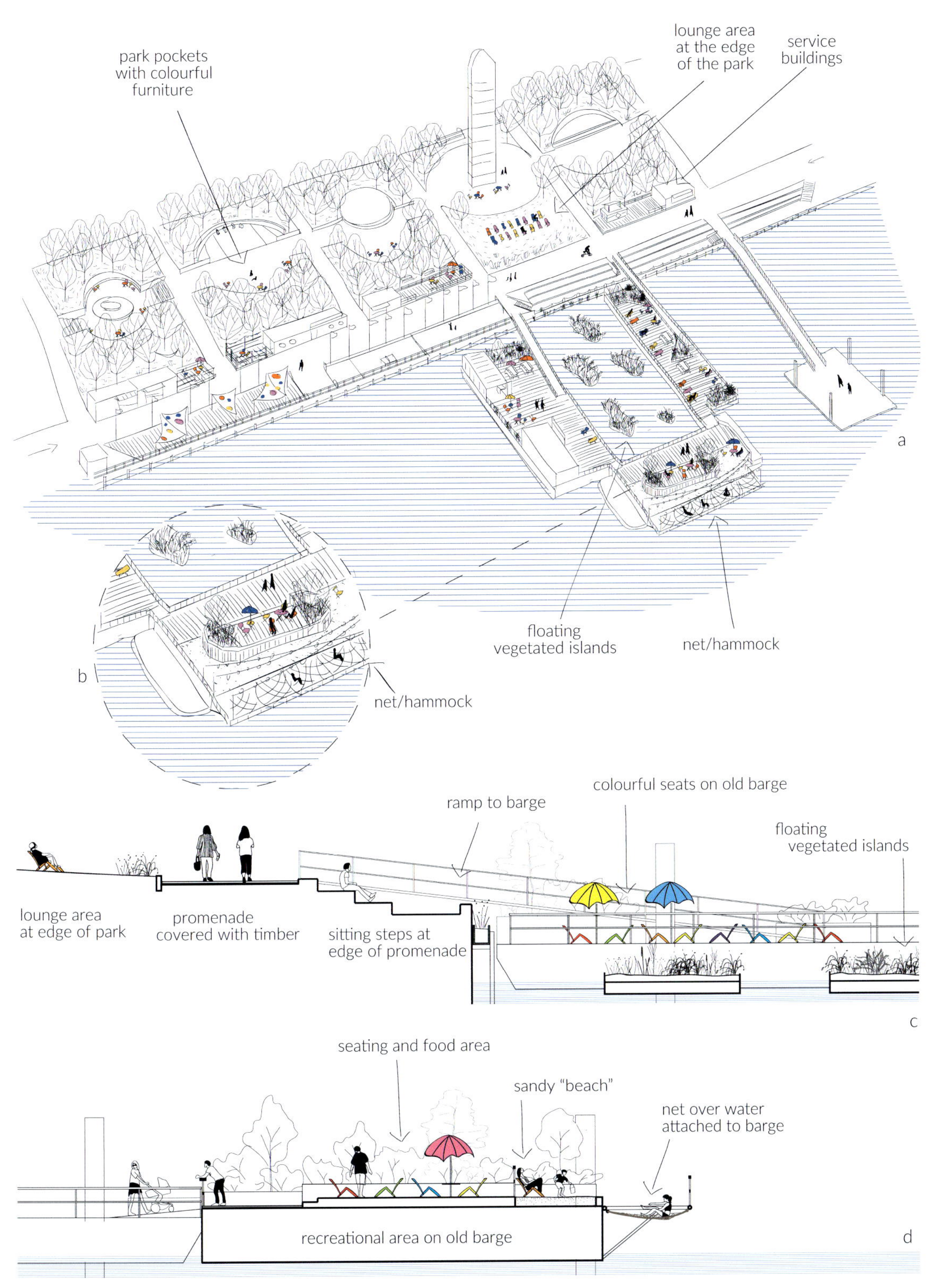

Figure 14.23a–d

a) General layout of the Spruce Street Harbour project showing its vivid, multi-functional character with many opportunities for family recreation close to the water; b) closer view of the platforms constructed on top of the old barges with decking, seating and net hammocks suspended over the water; c) cross-section from the recreational part on the upper levels through the steps to the water area enclosed by the barges; d) section across one of the barges with seating, beach and net hammocks

(*Source*: Anna Wilczyńska and Jekaterina Balicka)

sometimes described, because it is permanently there – but it becomes very busy in the summer period. The main element of the park is an enclosed floating garden which replicates a natural wetland (Figure 14.22). This has been formed by connecting three old barges which were towed 20 miles up the river from Chester, Pennsylvania, and six shipping containers. Within the space formed from the barges, which makes up three sides of a square, the other side being the river edge promenade, there are seven islands made of recycled plastic that draw water and nutrients to the wetland plants – which are also very colourful and ornamental. Two of the shipping containers are used as a bar and restaurant, continuing the incorporation of elements of the working waterfront into the design. Quite large trees have been planted on the barges, which are illuminated at night. The park is provided with many elements to allow people to congregate and enjoy the summer weather – as well as to make it comfortable in the heat or in the evenings, such as a cantilevered "net lounge" out over the river, a hammock garden and a fire pit. There is also a boardwalk along the water's edge with pipe-fitted trees designed by local artists, which are equipped with LED lights and misters to create a Mist Walk that leads to an urban beach. Facilities for recreation, relaxation and food and drink consumption are also integrated into the spaces, including painted wooden Adirondack chairs and umbrellas. Many activities, events and performances take place in the park hosted by local artists, vendors, face-painters and musicians. The site also benefits from its marina location, permitting access and activities on the water nearby, which can be considered part of the whole experience.

Project quality rating assessment

The site has excellent accessibility and great design quality – although it is somewhat expensive to maintain. The facilities are good, and the structures provide shade and shelter, which not many sites of the type reviewed in this chapter seem to do (Figure 14.23). There is good health and well-being potential, apart from the sense of being away. Water connections are strong – in part due to facilities nearby which give access – and physical activities are also good, also due in part to the possibilities of the setting within which the park is located.

CityDeck, Green Bay, Wisconsin, United States

This project was completed in 2012 from the designs of Chris Reed, Stoss Landscape Urbanism, and Ed Weisner for the City of Green Bay, Wisconsin, United States. The project transformed a brownfield site on the city centre riverfront into a focus of civic life. This included the restoration of an old harbour site. The surrounding area had, in common with many places, turned its back on the river. Before the project, neighbouring areas consisted of many empty spaces often used for car parking and frequently only used during business hours. The elevated walk running along the existing river retaining walls prevented direct access to or from the river. The contaminated site presented various challenges, as it had a high groundwater table, and in winter, ice floated down the river. The design includes a number of different elements organised spatially along the site. These take into account the different heights of the embankment wall and unify them using a folded wooden surface which also created spaces for dramatic views at the northern end (Figure 14.24). Other elements include an open space for vendors and festivals and an informal outdoor theatre. A play fountain marks the southern end. The CityDeck has many events programmed there, such as "Fridays on the Fox" during the summer and "Dine on the Deck" Wednesday lunches. The project has been a catalyst for the further construction of residential and retail units and a bank headquarters and has much mixed-use development nearby, which has brought this part of the city back to life. The design of the main deck starts as a simple boardwalk following the edge of the city and river, which later changes its form by undulating to meet different spatial requirements. The benches incorporated into the deck are designed to take into consideration the scale of the human body; folds in the deck structure create a range of different seats, benches, and *chaises longue* permitting a choice and flexibility for users. This varied seating was arranged in different configurations: some were placed in close proximity to the water's edge; some further away, which commanded a view of the river; some close to the water, others further back but overlooking it; some were grouped together, providing points for socialisation; and some in rows or on their own for opportunities more suited to quiet reflection. Lower-level decks and jetties connected by ramps allow access to and from boats.

Figure 14.24
A view along the CityDeck at night showing how the connections to the river are made and how lighting complements the design
(*Source*: City of Green Bay)

Project quality rating assessment
The site is in a generally highly accessible location – though not so well served by public transport. The design quality is high, apart from inclusion of cultural heritage values in the project. The overall design quality and number of facilities are very good, apart from the site being exposed to sun and wind (Figure 14.25). The health and well-being potential is good, apart from the sense of being away and for contact with nature. Water access is good, as are general water connections, though activities on the water, apart from boating, are limited; nor are there any formal sports activities and only limited informal sports, due to its location and primary function.

Comparison of projects in terms of different aspects

General design aspects
The projects presented in this chapter were chosen because they represent two major divisions of the subject – the larger port or dock developments, where significant territories have been re-developed following industrial decline, and the move of ports away from inner cities and the smaller-scale addition of functions and features into generally smaller-scale harbour locations. As in the other chapters, in this section, projects were chosen to show the diverse range and originality of concepts among the best projects, and they also display many unique qualities. Owing to the specific context, the larger-scale sites, especially, contain the remains of major engineering structures – some intact, such as docksides, others removed, such as oil storage tanks or cranes. Thus they each contain, to different degrees,

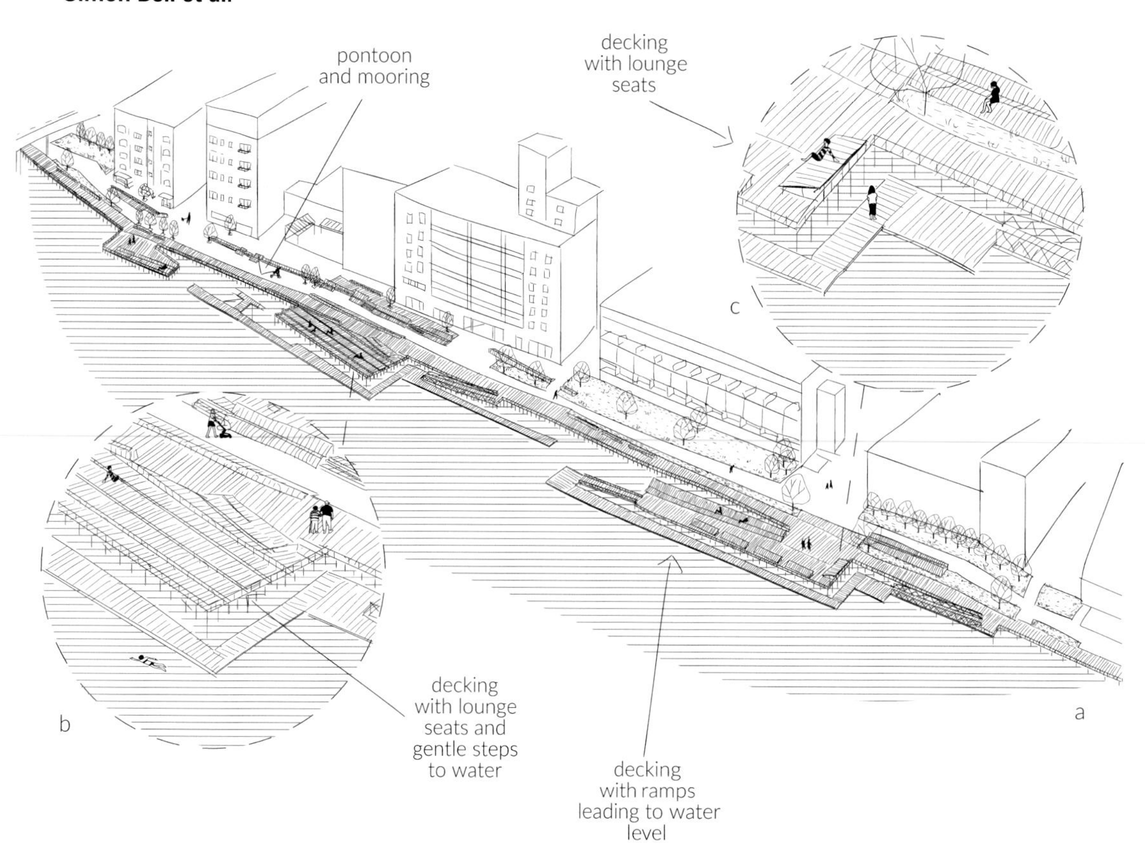

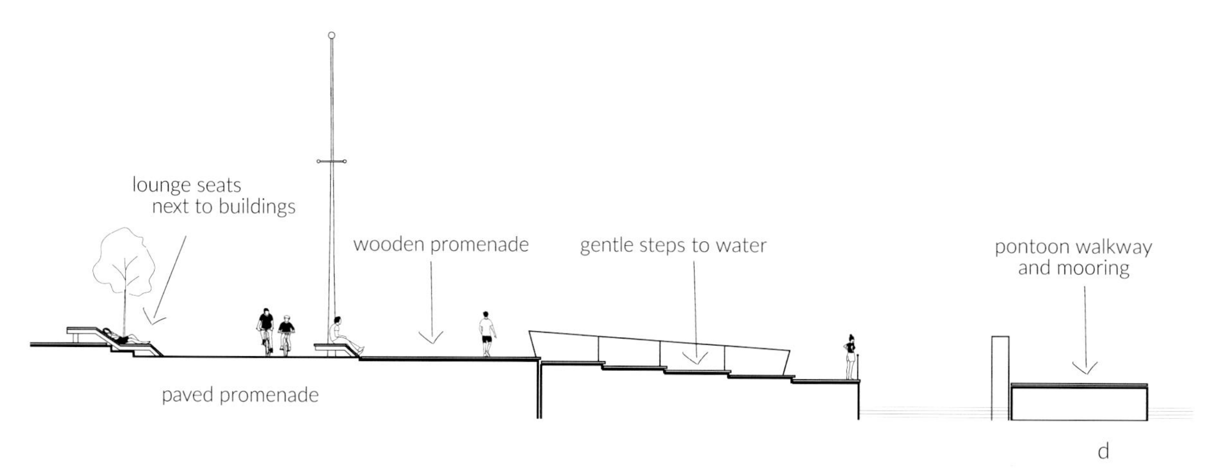

Figure 14.25a–c

a) The CityDeck project as a whole, emphasising the different platforms enabling closer contact with the water; b) close-up of one of the platforms featuring different seating elements on the promenade, the sitting terraces and access to the small dock; c) detail of the decking with lounge seating and lower level access to the water; d) cross-section through the whole promenade showing the means of descent to the water

(*Source*: Anna Wilczyńska and Jekaterina Balicka)

impressive built heritage, necessitating a sensitivity to context combining much imagination in terms of dealing with the challenges such sites present in order to meet the various project briefs. That many were competition winners also demonstrates that new and innovative solutions are not only possible but positively invited by the challenges of such sites. These have provided some of the biggest and most exciting challenges to designers in recent years. One aspect which tends to stand out from all projects is the importance of referring to the historical and cultural heritage. This may be quite direct – such as using artefacts within the structure or displaying different engineering elements – or indirect such as referring to forms of demolished structures in the design.

Potential for enhancing health and well-being

Almost all projects display many opportunities to improve health and well-being but within certain limitations and challenges. Owing to problems of water pollution, while in-water physical activities are possible in some locations, new solutions have had to be introduced in others – such as providing special pools for bathing and swimming such as in Copenhagen (see the following). Owing to the very urban character of many of the projects, it is understandably difficult to obtain a sense of getting away from the stresses of city life, but some of the larger projects, especially, offer plenty of opportunities for physical exercise on land, with promenades for running, walking and cycling. A key aspect of many projects is also the chance for relaxing and sunbathing in inner-city locations, although, in many cases, due to the very urban and built form with limitations on planting large trees, the sites tend to be very exposed to the sun and wind, with little shade provided by many of the projects, which could pose risks for skin cancer, sunburn and so on. Where projects such as Hafen City incorporate a lot of housing and businesses, then well-being can come about through the proximity to water and views of it.

Accessibility

Given that all these projects are former ports and harbours, then clearly use of water by boats is a major possibility, with many of the projects incorporating marinas or places to moor boats. This is not always as easy as it sounds due to the height of some of the dock walls, meaning that special structures can be needed to make them practical for smaller pleasure craft.

Accessibility to the dock edges and quaysides is usually very straightforward, and the majority lead directly from streets. Then they may require ramps in order to descend down to be closer to the water. In one or two specific cases, the terrain is more of a challenge – such as Carradah Park in Sydney, Australia – where the cliffs are then used for elevated decks giving spectacular views. Floating structures are also used in places – such as Spruce Street Harbour Park – to provide easy access.

Interaction with water

Given that the projects reviewed here mainly involved ships and transfer of cargo or passengers, it would seem ironic that interaction with water can prove very challenging. In part it is because the dock edges or walls can be very high, since they were designed with large ships in mind – especially the more recent larger ports as opposed to the older, smaller harbours. So, for many projects, the main interaction with water is visual. Nevertheless, ways to interact have been developed in several projects – whether the floating harbour baths, the ramps leading down to the water at Copenhagen or even the jump platform in Wellington at Taranaki Quay. Boats can tie up at many projects once the problem of the dock level has been solved. Pollution remains an issue in many settings, restricting what is possible.

Seating and opportunities for socialising

Owing to the inner-city context of all of these projects, one of their main goals has been to create places for people to meet and socialise. There is often a connection between the quay edges, seating and local cafes and restaurants – especially at the Spruce Street Harbour and Oslo's Aker Brygge or Green Bay City Deck. Decking, steps and ramps are often used in multi-functional ways to provide both access and seating. The larger projects such as Brooklyn Bridge Park include mini-parks on different piers, each with different opportunities for forms of socialising and participating in group activities. The Magellan and Marco Polo terraces in Hafen City also incorporate combinations of elements with different affordances for socialising.

Microclimate amelioration

Many of the projects are in quite exposed places, while others are set amongst built forms. If the harbour is wide and exposed, then shelter is a problem, and even where there are nearby buildings, the wind can gust around them, making it uncomfortable. Given the inner-city locations and engineered structures, it may be that heat collects and is radiated from the many hard surfaces, although the water bodies should ameliorate the urban heat island effect. Nevertheless, sun exposure and lack of shade is something that designers have tried to deal with using tree planting where possible, such as at Erie Basin. Buildings probably also offer shade in some places. However, this is an aspect worth further consideration. With many references to ships at most sites, materials and forms inspired by sails could be used more to provide both shelter and shade.

Use of materials

The materiality of many of the projects is dictated by the presence of dock walls, harbour surfacing, steel decking and timber piling or decks and concrete in recent docks. Dressed stone edges are commonly a distinctive feature, such as at Hafen City and Erie Basin. The projects are often dominated by the use of hard materials, and this is continued as part of the design language. At Barangaroo, stone is used extensively to restore the landform, and at Carradah Park, the remains of excavated cliffs where the oil storage tanks were located also features heavily. Timber decking was also a feature of many harbours or docks and is also used widely, notably at Kalvebod Waves and the CityDeck. At Spruce Street Harbour, old barges are used as floating decks, which is very innovative. The craftsmanship of the stonework of the older dock walls was often of a very high order, and this attention to detail is key for ensuring design unity between old and new elements in most projects.

Use of vegetation and ecological aspects

Given the former uses of most of the sites, the opportunities for increasing vegetation can be extremely limited, requiring imaginative solutions for establishing trees on hard surfaces, using raised planting sites, for example, or even floating artificial islands for aquatic plants such as at Spruce Street Harbour. A number of sites have no vegetation – such as Kalvebod Waves, Copenhagen City Baths or Aker Brygge – and are none the worse for that. On some larger sites, there is scope, and restoration of vegetation at Barangaroo, Carradah Park and Brooklyn Bridge Park has been successful. In some places, such as at Marco Polo Terraces in Hafen City, the trees appear to be struggling in difficult conditions.

Site management and maintenance

All the projects are well maintained – and in many, the fact that original materials and particularly robust construction have been used has made it easier for maintenance generally. However, the widespread use of timber for decking in a number of projects leads to a need for constant checking and repair, since it can react to different weather conditions even if it does not rot. The sites also appear to be free from vandalism and are kept very clean, which helps to maintain them as welcoming places.

Conclusions and implications for practice

This chapter has reviewed the history and importance of former harbours, docks and post-industrial waterfront sites which have been reimagined and redeveloped to provide either mixed-use development with some recreational public spaces or else parks and public attractions. The opportunity to use the extensive inventory of such brownfield sites has been a major feature of urban planning and landscape design and has provided tremendous possibilities to designers to apply their imagination in challenging locations. The selection presented here all have their strengths and weaknesses according to a number of factors such as scale, previous uses, physical limitations, site conditions and water quality. Each designer has taken something unique from the historical conditions, material remains and significant site constraints while producing multi-purpose solutions which not only often celebrate the cultural history but also rehabilitate the difficult sites and provide many opportunities for use by people. Achieving direct interaction with water is one challenge that is not always solvable under the circumstances, but otherwise, there are many rich opportunities for obtaining health and well-being benefits.

There are several specific aspects we wish to draw attention to:

- Increasing the availability of shade and shelter in urbanised and exposed locations also dominated by built forms and hard surfaces in order to ameliorate wind exposure and turbulence and to reduce the risks of skin cancer.
- Making use of original structures and materials which balance longevity and low maintenance with cultural historical associations.
- Including more vegetation in projects where this can be achieved, perhaps using more innovative approaches to overcome the problems of hard surfaces, poor or polluted soil and lack of water infiltration into the soil. However, there are places which do not need vegetation just for the sake of it, so this fact should not be ignored.
- To celebrate the maritime and mercantile heritage usually associated with ports and harbours by examining the history – economic and cultural – and building it into the project as much as possible.
- To ensure that connections to the sites from nearby residential areas are strong and that links to the water are also maximised, subject to the limitations noted previously.

Finally, we can note that the selection of projects presented here reflects the variety of types and scales of site which have been developed. The largest sites, in particular, represent significant public or private investments and, if the latter, expect a reasonable return on capital, perhaps in the form of enhanced property values. Nor are they cheap to maintain, with significant safety aspects to manage and infrastructure which can suffer from immersion in salt water. The challenge of providing the best access possible to water that may be polluted, if not all the time then certainly at some times, must also be recognised. Nevertheless, as major polluted brownfield sites, the scale of improvement and re-development as well as the ambitions shown in many of the projects deserve to be celebrated as one of the major achievements of urban planning of recent decades.

References

Breen, A. and Rigby, D. (1994) *Waterfronts: Cities reclaim their edge*. McGraw-Hill, New York.

d'Arcy, K. (2012) *London's 2nd city: Creating Canary Wharf*. Rajah Books, London.

Hoyle, B. S., Pinder, D. and Husain, M. S. (Eds.) (1988) *Revitalising the waterfront: international dimensions of dockland redevelopment*. Belhaven, London.

Marshall, R. (2001) *Waterfronts in post-industrial cities*. Taylor and Francis, London.

Rule, F. (2009) *London's docklands: A history of the lost quarter*. The History Press, London.

Chapter 15: Tactical urbanism, urban acupuncture and small-scale projects

Jekaterina Balicka, Joanna Tamar Storie, Friedrich Kuhlmann, Anna Wilczyńska and Simon Bell

Introduction

In each of the previous four chapters, we have mainly focused on projects of a significant scale – long river banks and coastline redevelopment projects, wetland parks and extensive projects on ports and former docklands sites. While there has been some variation in scale in those examples, what has characterised them in general is that they are complete designs of the spaces they occupy, planned and designed to change almost the entire area. The budgetary demands on both capital funding to construct them and revenue funding to maintain them are also generally rather large. As projects, they take a lot of effort to achieve final success – from initial organisation of architectural competitions (where these are used), developing plans and design ideas, to final design, construction and on into post-completion management and maintenance. Do improvements made to places with the aim of promoting health and well-being always have to occupy extensive areas and be expensive projects? In this chapter, we explore other ways of approaching such problems, through designs that apply much more minimal solutions. These solutions can easily be tested and modified, can be flexible and even temporary and can cost a mere fraction of the sums spent on some of the projects reviewed in Chapters 11–14. We have demonstrated in the cases presented in the previous chapters that formal open public spaces near water can offer benefits for health and well-being. This chapter illustrates to what extent informal, possibly underused, urban blue spaces can be used by people for recreational purposes without any significant infrastructure and little or no management.

Many cities today contain significant areas of post-industrial or waste land near water (Unt and Bell, 2014; Pearsall and Lucas, 2014), often former abandoned industrial or harbour areas which, despite the safety and other risks involved, may be popular with local people for various types of activities. This land may be reserved in urban plans for development at some time in the future as a new public space or a residential, commercial or industrial area, but what of the potential between now and that often distant time in the future?

As well as these vacant, "unused" spaces, there are also many existing public spaces which lack up-to-date infrastructure to satisfy local demands. There are numerous examples of such situations: a river promenade designed some decades ago and still waiting for funds or ideas before it can be revitalised; a historical city core where the existing urban context must be protected and where major redesign or adding a new function could be difficult or impossible because of heritage conservation regulations; the run-down park where there are no resources for revitalisation and where vandalism or anti-social activities deter some types of users, such as women, parents with children or older people. There may also be various natural areas which have never been developed or made officially accessible to the public, although they also may provide health benefits to people who use them. In these cases, visitors may spontaneously use the site or existing elements on the site for recreation (Unt and Bell, 2014; Mathey et al., 2018), such as old concrete blocks for sitting, or they provide their own informal infrastructure, such as self-made seating

DOI: 10.4324/9780429056161-19

around a fireplace, thus manifesting their attachment to and appropriation of the space (Lara-Hernandez and Melis, 2018). Such places allow people, often from deprived areas, to escape from their stresses (Rupprecht et al., 2015). These places are often used in a number of different ways, such as walking, sport activities, being alone, contemplation, sunbathing and swimming (Unt and Bell, 2014). These are places waiting for change, for the future, which is still undefined, yet in need of some degree of improvement to uncover their potential for promoting different activities and health and well-being.

In order to provide an up-to-date function for such places, different approaches may be used. These include concepts based on bottom-up, sometimes "guerrilla", methods (Marletto and Sillig, 2019); they may involve very temporary solutions aimed at providing space for activities over a weekend ("pop-up landscapes"). Both may be considered unofficial or even illegal, and authorities may respond by either demolishing or subsequently adopting them. In this chapter, we consider several approaches which have become popular practices in recent years as means of creating places on a small budget, often for specific purposes. In this chapter, we identify and describe three such approaches that are superficially similar and which sometimes overlap: *tactical urbanism*, *urban acupuncture* and *small-scale projects*.

Tactical urbanism

Tactical urbanism unites a range of planning and design approaches to address a problem of a lack of infrastructure with low-cost, often small-size, sometimes even temporary or non-spatial means. Tactical urbanism is often also referred to as guerrilla urbanism, pop-up urbanism, city repair or DIY (do-it-yourself) urbanism. The term was coined in 1984 in a translation of a book by Michel Certeau, *The Practice of Everyday Life*, where he used the term to distinguish the scale of practices he was describing from "strategic urbanism". Its current usage was broadly popularised by Mike Lydon, an American urban planner, who has written the seminal book on the subject together with Tony Garcia (2015). Another set of actions which helped to establish the credibility of the approach and application came through the activities of the New Urbanist "CNU NextGen" group, who adopted it at a meeting in New Orleans in the United States in 2010 as one means to help to deal with the aftermath of Hurricane Katrina, which saw many sections of the city still abandoned several years later. The method was also used in Christchurch in New Zealand following the earthquake there.

Tactical urbanism includes interventions or actions ranging from temporary appropriation (Lara-Hernandez and Melis, 2018), including the use of spaces for street food or events, to the construction of small-scale, low-cost or temporary interventions. These types of interventions can also be placed on a scale of bottom-up to top-down planning approaches. The bottom-up or guerrilla types of interventions typically originate in urban environments with no or little planning interest and lack of control: archetypical bottom-up examples where tactical urbanism has been a powerful agent in urban renewal can be found in cities like Detroit in the United States and Berlin in Germany.

One of the projects described in this chapter is the Paris Plages – a widely known European example of a long-running tactical urbanism intervention. A similar summer project was initiated in Saint-Quentin in the Aisne region of France some years earlier, in 1996, before the actual term 'tactical urbanism' was widely adopted. This intervention made Saint-Quentin the pioneer European city for organising what has become a popular practice: the seasonal beach in the "normal" public space. The demands placed on public spaces in parts of the city of 60,000 people encouraged the municipality to transform the Place de l'Hotel de Ville (Town Hall Square) into a sandy beach, with an orchestrated programme of, for example, sports competitions, cultural events and temporary pools (Figure 15.1). This event has continued every year since 1996, and many cities and communities in France and Europe have also taken up this idea. For more than a decade, these approaches, once they demonstrated their success as catalysts for urban renewal, have also been appropriated by city authorities and applied in an official way as top-down planning instruments.

The approach of tactical urbanism is now applied widely in practice (Lydon and Garcia, 2015). Reason for such success might include the complexity of urban space and urban processes. The development of an urban place is,

Figure 15.1
The temporary beach in the Place de l'Hotel de Ville, St Quentin, France
(*Source*: Sandra Cohen-Rose, Creative Commons Attribution 2.0 Generic (CC BY 2.0))

nowadays, no longer a simple linear and top-down process controlled solely by the city authority and its planning department. There are usually many different stakeholders, often with competing views and diverse demands in urban development processes, and the pathway to a common vision and agreement can be long and difficult. Landowners, users, city government elected and appointed officials, planners and businesses might not have the same goals, interests or ideas about what a good urban public space is. Therefore, there is a growing need for careful, low-cost and experimental planning instruments, which might convince other sectors by demonstrating effective results or raise a discussion among the involved parties.

Research into how a tactical intervention might affect the use of a space and the short-term health and well-being of users has been carried out to a limited extent; one such research example is an experiment which was conducted in an urban blue space (Roe et al., 2019) by a group from the University of Virginia in the United States. They tested a temporary intervention in the context of a waterfront in West Palm Beach in Florida. A small day-long intervention was installed, and users were tested on the state of their mental well-being (using well-established instruments) before, during and after the installation, over three days. The results showed reduced stress levels among users during the intervention as opposed to the control (pre- and post-intervention) times, although the levels of statistical significance were low.

Urban acupuncture

Urban acupuncture is a term applied to a socioenvironmental theory that combines contemporary urban design approaches, which are not dissimilar to tactical urbanism, with the concept behind the traditional Chinese medicine practice of acupuncture. Like tactical urbanism, urban acupuncture applies small-scale or even point design interventions to affect or catalyse the transformation of the larger-scale urban fabric.

First coined by Spanish architect Manuel De Solà-Morales (1999, 2004), the concept encompasses projects with a high degree of reversibility, allowing for corrective measures and improvements (a problem with large projects, where correcting mistakes is very costly). The tactic has the advantage of being a fast-tracked planning method and thus being implemented swiftly and often with modest means. With fewer bureaucratic requirements, these localised gestures are aimed to trigger a chain reaction of improvement in the quality of the adjacent urban environment, ranging from an increase in social cohesion to an improvement in public safety. The architect and urban planner Jaime Lerner, who was also three times mayor of the city of Curitiba in Brazil, is one of the leading advocates of urban acupuncture, seeing it as a means to bring immediate improvements to the urban environment, bypassing long decision-making processes and surpassing economic impediments. As Lerner says: "the lack of resources is no longer an excuse not to act. The idea that action should only be taken after all the answers and the resources have been found is a sure recipe for paralysis" (2014), and this helps to explain the idea of urban acupuncture as an experimental urban planning tool.

Another key advocate of the approach is the Finnish Architect Marco Casagrande (2015), who describes urban acupuncture as a "cross-over architectural manipulation of the collective sensuous intellect of a city". He views the city as a "multi-dimensional sensitive energy-organism, a living environment". According to Casagrande, sensitivity is needed to understand the energy which flows beneath the visual city, and then it is possible to react to the hot spots revealed by this analysis as target locations for an intervention. Casagrande thus applies the tenets of acupuncture by identifying and treating the points of blockage (or stress) in the urban fabric and claims that by releasing this, relief can ripple throughout the urban body. The idea is also that the approach is more immediate and sensitive to community needs than the more traditional and institutionalised forms of large-scale urban renewal planning. This means that interventions not only respond to localised needs but do so from a deep knowledge base of how urban systems operate and why they converge at that specific point. This, according to Casagrande, releases pressure at strategic points and subsequently releases pressure for the whole city.

Intervention target sites are not selected randomly or opportunistically, as may be the case in tactical urbanism, but involve the analysis of a range of spatial, social, economic and ecological factors (similarly to conventional design methods), and designs are developed through dialogue between designers and the community in a co-design process. So, conceptually, as the Chinese practice of acupuncture claims to relieve stress in the complete human body by acting at specific pressure points, urban acupuncture aims to relieve equivalent stresses in the built environment. As noted, urban acupuncture is not a synonym for tactical urbanism but implies a similar range of practices, and the two terms may be confused.

Small-scale interventions

Small-scale projects are not always specifically built as an urban acupuncture or tactical urbanism exercise. However, small projects may sometimes achieve a high degree of success in terms of design or social or environmental impacts. A number of these may be temporary, which can mean that they are designed and constructed for a few days, weeks or months, during a festival, for example, or for a longer duration until a site is developed, in which case the term "temporary" may be of long duration (several years). In addition, small-scale interventions can be easily built, dismantled, stored and moved according to the seasons. For example, wintertime in northern climates may mean temporary shelters or structures for winter sports, while in summer, seasonal swimming places might be established. Waterside structures may be damaged in winter storms or by ice, which also argues for their being easily moved and only used when safe to do so.

While urban acupuncture is rather theory driven, there is some research evidence for the impact of what may be counted by some as urban acupuncture or otherwise just as small scale. Small projects also offer the potential to test design ideas before implementation using modelling techniques. One such project was undertaken within the BlueHealth project based on the intervention site in Tallinn described in Chapter 3 (Vassiljev et al., 2020). A series of virtual small-scale interventions were designed using a combination of the evidence gained from observations of the site (see the demonstration of the BlueHealth Behaviour Assessment Tool in Chapter 6), site analysis and inspirations from various projects – some of which feature in this chapter. Three-dimensional models were constructed for each using a virtual landscape setting and experiential videos created to present the designs (Figure 15.2). An extensive questionnaire survey was carried out to determine people's preferences and the potential for enhancing the health and well-being of each design option.

One approach that is key to all designs – but which is especially useful in the case of small-scale interventions, whether following the principles of tactical urbanism or urban acupuncture – is to respond to the potential to provide

Figure 15.2

Temporary, small-scale interventions in Kalarand, Tallinn, constructed in 2011 during the Cultural Capital year, supported the existing use of an informal public space. Decks built along the shore and on old concrete blocks enabled recreation near water

(*Source*: Anna-Liisa Unt and Reio Avaste)

affordances which may be lacking in a particular space. Affordances are the properties of the environment which offer various opportunities to people (Gibson, 1979). At the very smallest scale, an intervention can be a bench to afford resting by, for example, older people; this affordance then makes it possible for someone who cannot walk without resting to visit and experience the waterside and so obtain other benefits. Close observation of a space may reveal missing opportunities which can be tested using the method described in the previous section and in Chapter 6.

All the planning approaches described previously aim either to support already existing uses or to uncover the potential of the area. Affordances may be needed to make the existing use of space more comfortable, such as sitting on a bench instead of on a rock, or enabling uses of the area in new ways, such as by providing access to the water where there was none before or other small-scale and relatively low-cost infrastructure for relaxation, bathing or swimming.

Another typical feature of such a design and planning approach is the careful and respectful way in which the intervention is fitted into the existing landscape, therefore highlighting its character – its *genius loci*. The small-scale and often temporary nature of the intervention enables or even demands more careful construction methods. The existing built or urban nature surrounding the intervention therefore stays untouched.

Finally, interventions of this type usually signify that care is now being taken of the place, particularly where some of these areas were previously neglected. This is where such interventions may be temporary and serve as a first step in the development cycle of the area in need of change. As already noted, such places are often considered marginal or are associated with decay and might have perceived or real safety and vandalism problems (Nassauer and Raskin, 2014; Pearsall and Lucas, 2014; Newman et al., 2018). Gentrification is an issue which can also result from larger developments, leading to a change of user profile and often leading to the exclusion of "marginal" groups who formerly used the site. This may be less the case when tactical urbanism or urban acupuncture is the approach adopted. Public space redevelopment also has scale effects which need to be considered carefully and which may be positive if the tactical urbanism or urban acupuncture models are applied, so that such small-scale construction may serve as a cure to "environmental decay" (Branas et al., 2011), which has negative effects on the perception of the area by people and the well-being of the community living in proximity to the site.

In Chapter 3, we introduced readers to the experimental interventions undertaken in the BlueHealth project which were used to test the impact of design on attracting people to use blue spaces. Each of these was small scale and inexpensive relative to the budgets needed on the larger projects, yet it seemed that they had in many cases an impact far larger than the scale might suggest. Two projects – Can Moritz in Rubi near Barcelona and Teats Hill at Plymouth – were incorporated into schemes already underway and funded, although the budgets were still modest; they were still small-scale new or refurbished elements inserted into a run-down setting. Others, such as those in Tallinn, Tartu and Guimarães, were even more modest, with small budgets (in the 20–30,000 Euros range), and represented small elements in larger spaces, where they acted as new focal points added into the landscape, intended to support the existing use of the space, to stimulate new types of use or to invite users to discover fresh areas as well as to give signals about welcome or safety. All of these interventions were designed with great respect for each existing urban environment. Moreover, the sites were in some cases rather neglected or unmanaged, while, according to the comments during the public involvement process, this wild character would allow users to enjoy urban nature in solitude. The design fit into the place, supporting its particular values. The development process of these designs was driven by the rich knowledge gained during the BlueHealth project: evidence of blue space health and well-being benefits, the results of on-site enquiries, the public involvement process and, finally, the theories and design approaches described in this chapter.

Why the cases were chosen

This chapter presents a selection of different small-scale/urban acupuncture/tactical urbanism projects representing different scales, purposes and design approaches. While some small-scale projects were built to be temporary, others are a permanent type of construction. All the intervention examples described in this chapter provide and strengthen the connection to the water: physically, visually, mentally, socially or educationally. The selected examples represent a variety of the most creative and versatile approaches to such types of design, and since they do not demand large investments, they provide an opportunity for an experimental and playful approach, much in keeping with tactical urbanism and urban acupuncture. Small-scale/temporary projects are interesting not just from the point of view of exemplifying appealing and effective urban planning phenomena but also because they can be used to experiment, to analyse their impact, to learn from and to transfer the experiences gained to planning and design principles at a bigger scale.

Contrary to the other chapters in this part of the book, owing to their small size and local impact, the project review and critique of the various factors affecting project success as presented in Chapter 10 is not appropriate. In addition, since the photographs often show all there is to know about a project, we only use sketches in particular cases.

Temporary interventions

The following projects have been selected to represent temporary interventions. They were built and taken away, and the photographs and reviews help to reconstruct the impact of these projects which otherwise only exist in memory.

- Micro-installations on stairs near Piaskowy bridge in Wrocław, Poland
- Two canal installations for the Bruges Triennial, Bruges, Belgium
    - Canal Swimmer's Club
    - The floating island
- "Between waters" art installation and community garden in Emscher Park, Germany
- Skaters' shelters, Winnipeg, Canada

Seasonal interventions

The next projects are seasonal installations: projects constructed for the summer. They are dismantled at the end of the season and constructed again the following year.

- Paris Plages, Paris, France
- Olive Beach, Moscow, Russia

Permanent interventions

The final set of projects are permanent installations of different scales and with different design foci:

- Kastrup sea-bath, Copenhagen, Denmark
- Steveraue platform, Steveraue, Germany
- Public space and sauna, Gothenburg, Sweden
- River Ljubljanica platform, Ljubljana, Slovenia
- Vinaròs microcistas, Vinaròs, Spain

Temporary interventions

Micro-installations on stairs near Piaskowy bridge in Wrocław

This temporary installation was designed and constructed to provide a recreational function to a run-down space near the river. The stairs to the water, built some decades ago, provide a potential to a view and proximity of the

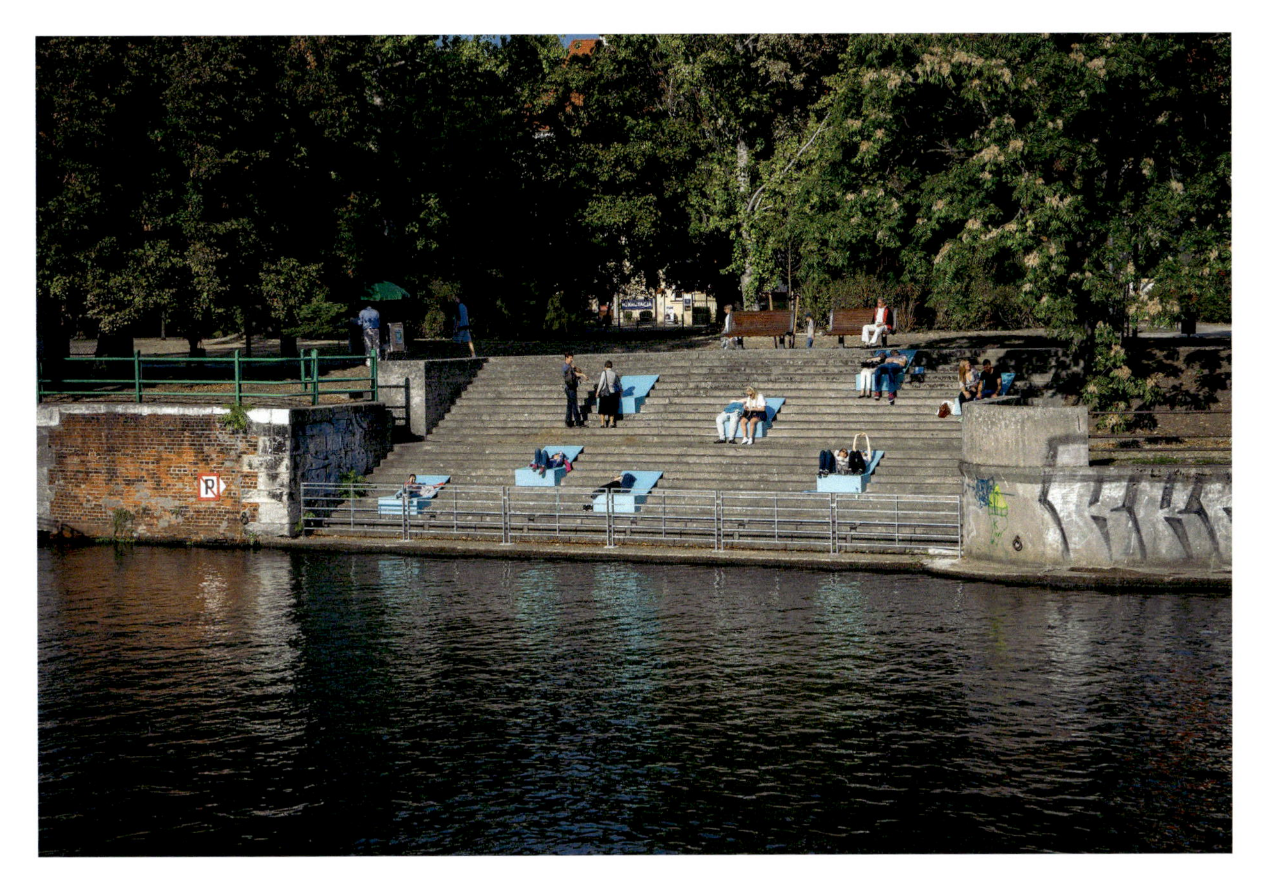

Figure 15.3
The seating on the steps near Piaskowy bridge viewed from the river
(*Source*: Studio NO)

water but none of the infrastructure needed for a longer stay: no seats or benches. The intervention was designed and constructed by No studio based in Wrocław in 2016 as a part of DOFA, the Lower Silesian Festival of Architecture, as part of activities organised in Wrocław as European Capital of Culture 2016; after the festival, these seating installations were expanded to other places as well. With very little investment and minimal design (almost no design, according to the authors), the previously neglected and underused space near the river became functional. The installations were constructed from simple plywood and were easy to build on site.

The design provided simple seating and sunbathing places for one or two persons built into the existing concrete steps; therefore, these simple constructions provided a function which was only potentially possible beforehand due to the lack of functional infrastructure. Seen from the other river side, the colourful benches attract attention and invite the users explore the stairs near the river. This installation was site specific and revealed the hidden potential (affordances) of a place. The design offered a possibility to stay, relax and socialise near the water while enjoying the view of the river.

Canal installations for the Bruges Triennial

The Bruges Triennial provides a place for contemporary art and architecture in the urban space of Bruges historical centre. For this chapter, we selected two temporary installations designed for the Bruges Triennial in 2015 and 2018, which provided better access and connection to water.

Figure 15.4
The Bruges canal swimmers' club installation, showing its immense popularity
(*Source*: Dertien12, photographer Stef Declerck)

Canal Swimmer's Club

This installation was designed and constructed by Japanese Atelier Bow-Bow together with local architects Dertien 12 for Bruges Triennial 2015 at the confluence of the Spinolarei-Potterierei and Sint-Annarei canals in Bruges. The installation consisted of a wooden deck leading to a floating lounge with a sun shelter. Access from the embankment was enabled with a ramp from both ends. The intervention provided numerous opportunities of recreation by the water and in the water, such as relaxation, visiting the events and swimming. The design offered a different perspective of Bruges' canals. Usually, getting on-the-water experience is possible only from a boat, and swimming in the canal is not a usual practice in the centre of Bruges. According to the authors, the installation extended the public space, which was usually crowded during the high tourist season in the city. It also drew attention to the fact that the water quality has been improved in recent years, and nowadays the canals are swimmable. This temporary intervention also communicated that the direct connection to the water in Bruges, although is a city permeated by canals and known for it worldwide, is still a missed opportunity.

The Floating Island

This temporary intervention was also created for Bruges Triennial in 2018 by the Korean architecture office OBBA together with Dertien12. The wave-formed platform was constructed near the Snaggaardbrug in the historical centre of Bruges. Access from the canal embankment was enabled with stairs and a ramp at each end of the structure. The

Figure 15.5
The Bruges Floating Island as viewed from across the canal, seen in its setting with the city behind
(*Source*: OBBA, photo Matthias Desmedt. Creative Commons Attribution-Share Alike 4.0 International license)

wooden platform floated just above the water level. A long screen made of cloth ropes in the middle of the platform created a visual border and enhanced the closeness to the water on the one hand, on the other hand providing a playful and creative way to use the installation, such as through ropes attached vertically, offering hammock-like places; a net stretched over the water, providing a resting place; and hanging textile balls for swinging. This intervention is an example of providing a playful environment for recreation and interaction with water where a permanent installation is not possible; it also creates various affordances and offers the visitors various options of interaction with the space.

"Between the Waters" art installation and community garden

"Between the Waters" was an art installation and at the same time functional infrastructure, constructed for the art festival EMSCHERKUNST in 2010. The project was located on a narrow strip of land between the Rhine-Herne Canal and the Emscher River, near Karnap north of Essen in Germany. It was a temporary art installation which addressed the problem of water quality, one of the key issues in the region, due to its industrial past. The project was created by the artist Marjetica Potrč and OOZE studio and was a functional water purification system, a community garden and an art installation all at the same time.

The construction cut across the narrow unused strip of land and united the two waters of the river and the canal through a nature-based water purification system. One part of the construction consisted of two toilets, symbolically

Figure 15.6

A view of the complete Between the Waters project capturing all project elements, allowing water purification and a view as well as symbolic transformation of the water

(*Source*: OOZE. Photographer: hans@blossey.eu)

Figure 15.7

The Winnipeg skaters' shelters forming a group like a herd of bison – note the curving plywood construction giving them the unique form

(*Source*: Patkau Architects)

elevated over the waters of Emscher River, which is very polluted. The water from the river was pumped into the septic tank of the toilets, then ran down and flowed through a series of purification systems: a constructed wetland, a rainwater-harvesting roof and a water storage bag. Finally, the purified water had the same quality as rainwater and could be used for irrigating the community garden or even for drinking and could be enjoyed from the drinking fountain, symbolically located on the platform over the Rhine-Herne Canal waters.

The project was primarily an environmental art intervention, located in an unused area without any public function, and was well visited by the attendees of the Festival. All the facilities provided by the installation were fully functional. The projects offered a new function and addressed the topics of water quality and inaccessible unused urban areas, doing so ironically and playfully.

Skaters' shelters, Winnipeg, Canada

Winter in Winnipeg, a city in Canada with a population of around 600,000 and a continental climate, is harsh, with extremely cold temperatures, regularly dropping below minus 20–30°C. Over time, local inhabitants developed cultural practices to embrace the winter; thus, skating on the frozen Red and Assiniboine Rivers has been a popular winter sport, providing a different perspective of the city. Skating along the frozen river enjoyed a resurgence due to the establishment of modern river trails. To enhance the use of the ploughed skating trails, each year, the municipality holds a competition to encourage the design of shelters suitable to the exposed wintry trails and providing places of respite from the wind. In the winter season of 2011, Patkau architects designed these cone-shaped shelters. The shelters were huddled together, each providing wind shelter to the other, each with their backs to the wind, like a herd of buffalo that roamed the Canadian prairies of the area in the past. The apparently random arrangement of shelters was designed precisely so that each shelter shielded the entrance of another and created a further protected interior space between the shelters. The shelters were also in a dynamic relationship to the sun position and the wind that altered as the sun moved across the sky during the day. Each shelter varied in the degree of shelter it could provide according to its relationship to the sun and the wind at any one time. Each shelter was constructed from two layers of thin plywood that could bend and deform in response to the wind. A triangular base and wedge-structure provided the rigidity needed to withstand the pressure from the snow, whilst the lightness of the construction allowed the movement generated by the wind to loosen any accumulated snow. The structures swayed and creaked like boats stuck on the frozen surface of the river, yet their warm colour and wooden interiors enveloped the skaters, providing protection from the elements. Seating was also provided inside for the comfort of the skaters.

Seasonal interventions

Paris Plages, Paris, France

Paris Plages is a pop-up summer intervention carried out by the municipality of Paris since 2002 on the banks of the Seine as a public-private partnership in different stages. Each year, between mid-July and the beginning of September, the path on the right bank of the Seine and connected areas host different leisure and sporting activities with sandy beaches, mobile palm trees and resting possibilities on a length of what is now more than 3 kilometres of riverbank, with more than 1 kilometre of fine sandy beach and additional connections to other parts of the city centre, thus changing the morphology of the river banks. Vehicle traffic is interrupted at this segment of the expressway running parallel to the river for the duration of the whole event, from its installation until its final dismantling, to make the riverbank accessible to pedestrians and cyclists. As a capital and a major economic centre, Paris has always had huge parts of its inner city circulation routes connected along the Seine since the decline of harbour activities and the river and city became disconnected. In recent years, discussions about a long-term traffic reduction in Paris have started.

Figure 15.8

A view of a section of the Paris Plages, showing the sandy beach and also the many shade umbrellas provided

(*Source*: Peter Haas/CC BY-SA 3.0 Creative Commons Attribution-Share Alike 3.0 Unported)

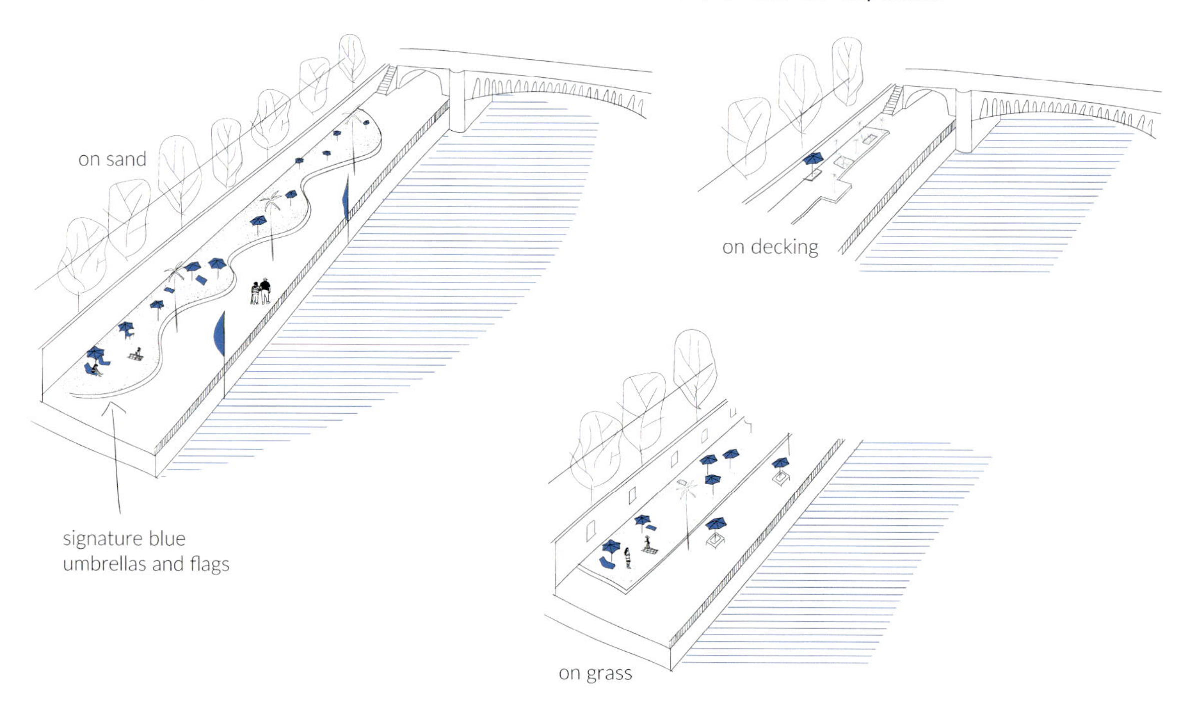

Figure 15.9

A sketch of the Paris Plages project interventions showing how it has developed over the years and in different rivershore sections

(*Source*: Anna Wilczyńska)

Before the Paris Plages event was initiated, a closure of the expressway to traffic took place every Sunday from 1995. Based on these experiences, the municipality decided to extend this operation to the whole summer, because during this period of lower economic activity, the centre of Paris usually experienced less traffic. The main objective was for Paris inhabitants to enjoy an inner-city vacation with all of the activities which are normally practiced on coastal beaches. Since Paris Plages appears during the official summer holidays, the scenography of the event is staged each year by different artists on the theme of, for example, French Polynesia or Brazil for the activities and spaces. In this sense, Paris Plages can be understood as part of the tactical urbanism movement by employing temporary events to raise awareness towards urban problems connected to traffic, pollution or social congestion in cities which would finally materialise into long-lasting infrastructure and elements.

In 2006, together with the opening of the left bank of the Seine, floating basins were also installed on the river, as well as introducing a shuttle to connect the different sections of Paris Plages. As an extension of activities further from the river, a new site at the basin de la Villette was opened in 2007, including nautical activities, children's play, outdoor gyms and large picnic areas. Opening the pools was considered one of the measures to mitigate heat waves, which Paris has experienced several times over the last decades. Furthermore, the entrances were transformed and highlighted to create better visibility of the access to the beaches from the road, as part of a new relationship between city and river. Thus we can see here how a small and temporary project has actually grown and developed – it is still tactical urbanism, but it has outgrown its original small scale.

Olive Beach, Moscow, Russia

Olive Beach is situated next to the Pushkin (Andreevsky) Bridge on the River Moskva and close to Gorky Park. The project was developed by the architectural office Wowhaus in 2011.

Figure 15.10

A view of Olive Beach from the Pushkin Bridge showing the wooden decking structure. In this photo, the site is not fully open, so the decking is clear to see, together with the bases of the parasols and showers projecting over the river

(*Source*: Wowhaus)

The aim of the project, besides providing a recreational area near water, was to create a side entrance to the park that would look "cozier" and less imposing than the austere granite and marble of the official entrance. The timber-decked area provides a welcoming entrance site with a warm and playful atmosphere. This embankment area is close to central Moscow and squeezed in between the wide river and the road running past Gorky Park and turns a dull space into a leisure zone. The facilities include a spacious multi-functional lounge and sunbathing deck, called the "Solarium"; showers; and a bar. The Solarium area is constructed from different angled wooden decking that slopes down towards the river edge. This surface provides a space-saving multiplicity of comfortable options for lounging in the sun and has proved a popular spot in summer. Owing to the poor water quality, swimming in the river is not an option, so instead, visitors can use showers to cool themselves throughout the summer months. The showers are located on piers jutting out over the river linked to the solarium. The water from the showers is collected on trays beneath the piers and is drained into the sewage system. Shade is offered by a pergola constructed from a complex wooden frame that is also designed as a space for music. In front of the canopy are olive trees in tubs that give their name to the area and offer some shade. Bars and wooden terraces are located under the bridge to provide additional facilities. After the summer season, the whole structure is dismantled and removed, stored and then reassembled the following summer. This intervention provides comfortable and playful recreation near the river, where a use of this type wasn't imaginable before.

Permanent installations

Kastrup Sea Bath, Copenhagen, Denmark

This structure, which provides sheltered access to the sea at Kastrup Beach, Copenhagen, was completed in 2005 from the designs of White Arketekter of Sweden. It has become affectionately known as 'The Snail' and consists of a circular raised enclosed platform and a pier leading out to it, a new beach and a service building containing toilets and accessible changing facilities set into the circular structure. All functions provided are therefore incorporated into

Figure 15.11

A view of the Kastrup Sea Baths from the shore showing the curving structure with sheltering walls at the end of the deck

(*Source*: Mads Farsö)

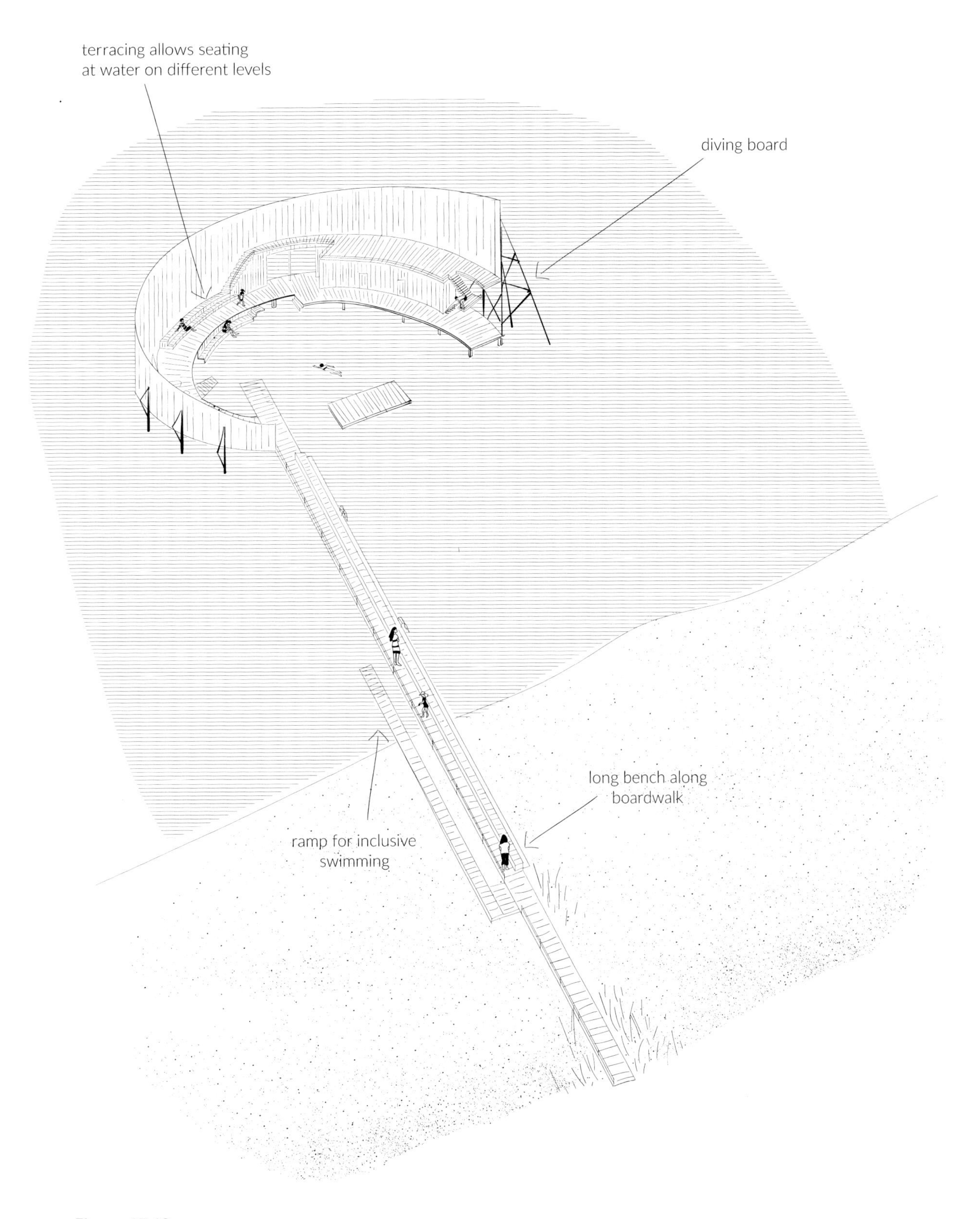

Figure 15.12
A sketch of the Kastrup Sea Baths which reveals the form and function of the sea bath – which is not visible from a ground-level view
(*Source*: Anna Wilczyńska)

the one structure. The idea of the form was a response to the exposed north-facing beach where shelter is needed; the wooden pier meets the bathing structure and continues into the south-facing circular enclosure, gradually rising above sea level and ending in a 5-m-high diving platform. The circular shape creates a focused interior that provides shelter from the wind and the perfect protected retreat for swimming and sunbathing. A continuous bench runs along the inner pier wall, providing lots of seating for resting and relaxation. It was designed to be fully accessible and inclusive, open at all times (it is illuminated at night and free of charge). It is constructed of an extremely durable African hardwood called azobé. For disabled users, it is possible to make use of special wheelchairs to go into the water for a swim. The site was a former brownfield and lies close to the Amager Beach park described in Chapter 14.

The main approach to the design of this intervention was to "bring the land into the sea", and the intervention does this by providing access to deeper water away from shallow beaches. It therefore enables many ways to enjoy water in a controlled and overlooked site and at the same time creating an environment fully surrounded by the sea.

Steveraue Platform, Germany

Steveraue is a nature reserve sited in a former coal mining area near the town of Olfen in the North Rhine-Westphalia region of Germany. The aim of this project, developed by Bureau Baubotanik in 2010 and still continuing in its development, was to build an observation platform for viewing the wildlife of the reserve without entering and disturbing

Figure 15.13
The Steveraue platform set within the living structure of the *Salix* trees and the view to the meadow and the river
(*Source*: Jonas Büchel)

it, since it is a protected area. From the platform, it is possible to see a stork's nest and the semi-wild herds of Heck cattle and Konik ponies. The observation platform and the recreational areas around it are separated from the nature reserve but made to observe the wildlife in Steveraue, are connected to local hiking and provide access to the river.

The platform is built on a natural floodplain area next to the River Stever, so it is also possible to view the wildlife within this natural riparian environment. One of the most interesting aspects of the project is that it uses an innovative construction method. The platform is constructed around an internal metal structure, and live willow trees (*Salix viminalis*), which commonly grow in this wet area, have been planted around it. This botanical structure will develop over time as the trees grow around and through the metalwork, creating a self-sustaining living structure. Landscape changes are slow and not often perceptible to the human eye, so the aim of the structure is to make the long-term growing processes of the renaturation of the Steveraue reserve visible and tangible. The ingrowing structure has also an educational purpose to showcase the actual construction method – a growing botanical structure. As well as being able to observe nature, it is possible to enjoy the river environment, as there is an opportunity for picnics on the benches provided, and there is a floating pontoon that allows access to the river itself.

Public space and sauna in Gothenburg Harbour, Sweden

The creation of the sauna in Gothenburg Harbour in Sweden is part of the Bathing Culture Project. The project was developed by Raumlabor Berlin in 2014 with a substantial amount of public involvement. The aim was to develop a public space as part of a step-by-step urban regeneration process for the redevelopment of the old derelict harbour.

Figure 15.14
The approach decking and glimpsed view of the elevated sauna in Gothenburg
(*Source*: Raumlabor)

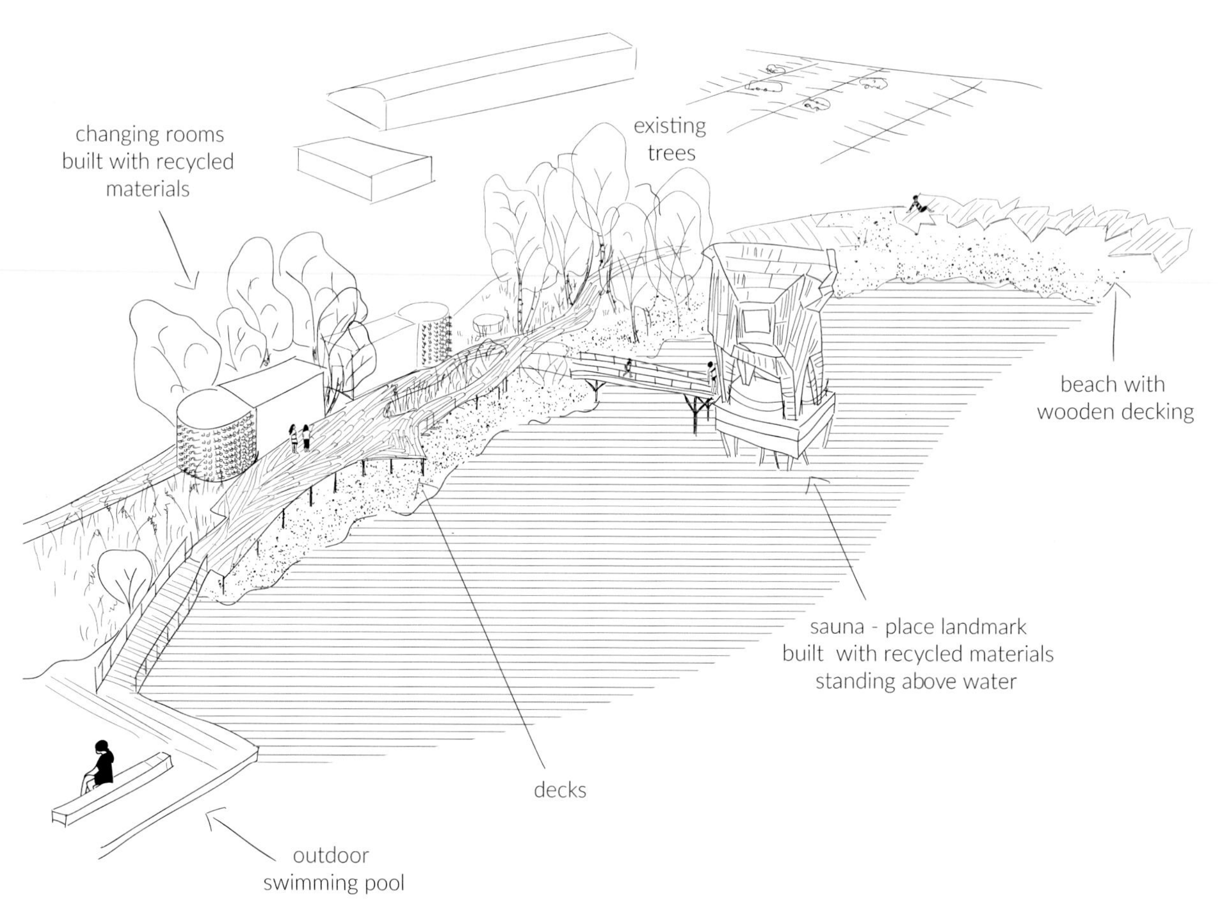

Figure 15.15

A sketch showing the Gothenburg intervention complex: the sauna building built on the deck above water, changing rooms and showers, beach with wooden decks, boardwalks and part of the lido

(*Source* Jekaterina Balicka, Anna Wilczyńska)

The project demonstrates a process initiated by the city in subsequent developments of design and construction of a site-specific recreational area that would lead to a cultural transformation of the site. The public space regeneration involved an agglomeration of small-scale interventions to foster a long-term creative development vision. In this case, the plans for the area and the aim of this intervention were to spur an exploration of what constitutes a park in the 21st century. The project investigated relevant criteria through community involvement.

The project contains several interventions, with a focus on recreation, leisure and education and community needs. In this section, we mostly concentrate on the sauna building, constructed above the harbour waters together with functional buildings (dressing rooms and showers), and the outdoor space with decks and paths for bathing and recreation near the water. The sauna and the functional buildings were built from reclaimed building materials found on-site – relics from its industrial heritage. The unusual structure, crafted with care with the aid of the local community, has imbued new life and a vision for the future, which spills over into the town and stretches the conventions of park design, giving it a new aesthetic expression. The site also meets the social needs of the people of Gothenburg and provides a site for swimming, sauna, bathing, relaxing and walking, strongly supporting both the existing cultural practices in Sweden and the needs of the local community.

River Ljubljanica platform, Slovenia

Ljubljana is a city renowned for its bridges, beautiful tree-lined riverside pathways and embankments, largely designed in the late 18th and early 19th centuries. The city, however, lost its connections to the river, and the old city fell into decline. In an effort to revitalise the once-thriving riverside area and bring the city back into harmony with the parallel riverside streets, the city authorities decided to revitalise the public space along the river. A series of small interventions were planned by BB arhitekti 2009–2011 The new interventions sought to bring a different perspective to the city by integrating the river back into the fabric of the townscape. The interventions made the river more present to the community and visible in the everyday functioning of the city. The pier featured here, located near the new Zitni Bridge, or Grain Bridge, is one of 20 interventions planned for the river that flows through the heart of Ljubljana. Each intervention is unique. The Zitni Bridge intervention is constructed of several elements. A prefabricated concrete stairway and seating area leads to a platform built over the water. The pier itself is built on a steel pontoon and paved with wood. The pontoon moves up and down in response to the changing level of the water in the river. The pier is connected to the concrete platform by an adjustable wooden and steel stairway. The intervention provides a connection from the city to the water level, enabling visitors to perceive the townscape from an unusual perspective and providing a space to view the river or a platform for fishing. The

Figure 15.16

The Ljubljanica platform showing its relationship to the retained riverside wall and the steps leading down to the deck

(*Source*: Breda Bizjak, BB arhitekti; photographer Jani Peternelj)

concrete seating area on the embankment allows for sitting and contemplating the life of the river, including the boats that frequent it.

Microcostas Vinaròs decks, Spain

Vinaròs is situated on the east coast of Spain, approximately halfway between Valencia to the south and Barcelona to the north. This Castellón seaside town has undergone rapid development, with a proliferation of single-family dwellings that dominate the landscape, particularly near the seafront, sometimes obscuring the view of the sea. The aim of the project, developed by Guallart Architects, was to provide public access to the sea from this fragile and rocky landscape. The installations had a demanding brief to withstand the rough sea waters and reduce erosion whilst maintaining the integrity of the habitat and the sea views. The size of the installations reflects the small size of the coves and peninsulas that form these miniature jagged coastlines squeezed between the sea and the urban infrastructure. Modular hexagonal platforms constructed from steel and wood were assembled using dry construction techniques in order to leave as little impact as possible on the rocks below. These geometric shapes in combination create little islands of variable sizes with micro-topographical details forming various convex and concave profiles that echo the angular geometry of rock. They provide a more comfortable surface than the jagged rocks below, as well as providing protection to the fragile rocks from human activities. The varying sizes make them suitable for different-sized groups, ranging from single people to couples and families. The

Figure 15.17

A view along the Vinaròs rocky shore showing a selection of the different platform designs

(*Source*: Guallart Architects)

multifunctional outdoor furniture elements offer various affordances: visitors can relax, sit or lie down close to the sea edge. The interventions allow people access to the wild places at the urban edge while making little impact on the landscape. They provide space to view the sea, to contemplate, sunbathe or just lounge. They also allow space for picnicking or a place to put things in a dry place while swimming. A previously overlooked landscape has now become now accessible.

Comparison of projects in terms of different aspects

General design aspects

In all the projects, we can see a lot of imagination and creativity – ranging from the very simplest, like the seats in Wrocław, to the ingenious solution at Vineròs (which responds to a very challenging location). There are also interesting and unique forms which have considerable artistic content, such as the sauna in Gothenburg, the skating shelters in Winnipeg or the sea-bath at Kastrup, an expression enabled in part due to the small scale and use of materials in an almost craftsmanlike way.

Potential for enhancing health and well-being

The projects chosen in this chapter have a specific focus, and the health and well-being opportunities may not be obvious at first. However, they all encourage and permit people to spend time close to water more safely or more easily (as at Vineròs), and they add special qualities attracting people to them or addressing water-related topics (such as "Between Waters"). Clearly, they do not have the kind of potential offered by the larger projects explored in previous chapters, but when considered in relation to their scale, they do generally exhibit that key aspect of urban acupuncture in their impact on the wider surroundings.

Accessibility

Improved access to blue spaces is a key objective of all projects, although realised in different ways. For example, the Vineròs microcostas are clearly important for giving access across a rugged shore; the platform on the Ljubljanica River provides access down to the river itself; the Kastrup sea-bath provides excellent access for everyone out to the swimming structure where the water is deep enough; the canal swimmers' club also provided excellent access to the canal, which was clearly used by many people during its existence, as did the floating island.

Interaction with water

All of the projects, in their own way, provide or provided (in the case of the temporary structures) access to water, be it visual or physical. Several projects promote bathing and swimming; decks provide access to the water surface and opportunities to touch it. In places where swimming and bathing are not options, such as at Olive Beach, the public sauna in Gothenburg or the "Between Waters" project, water is still made accessible but in different ways: there are showers at Olive Beach, the possibility to use water as part of a sauna routine and outdoor pool in Gothenburg and drinking and irrigating purified water in Essen, Germany.

In places where the water is completely inaccessible, such as the Seine in Paris, beaches at least give as close a connection as possible, in attractive surroundings encouraging people to stay and spend time there.

It is noteworthy how different designers approached the objective of connecting people and water using such small devices. In some cases, people were brought closer to water just in order to enjoy its proximity (e.g. Vinaròs, Ljubljanica river platforms, Wroclaw steps). In cases where direct access to natural water is or was not possible, the water was still available, albeit in a different form (Olive Beach showers, Gothenburg sauna). A more powerful approach is to bring the "land" into the water in order to provide swimming facilities where it was not possible before

(Kastrup sea bath, "swimming club" in Bruges and la Villette pools as part of the Paris Plages project). Also worth mentioning are the designs supporting winter use near water and traditional cultural practices (Gothenburg sauna, Winnipeg shelters).

Seating and opportunities for socialising

Some projects, such as the steps in Wrocław, focus (or focused) on providing seating – a basic affordance in that specific case which was perhaps not so obvious without the seats on the steps. Welcoming people to use the steps for sitting, as signalled in this way, encourages people to linger and so to socialise. Seating is also crucial to allow some user groups, for example, older or less able people, to walk along the river, providing possibilities to rest. The Kastrup sea bath has many terraces and relaxing areas for socialising during swimming, and the decking or beach structures such as at Paris Plages, Olive Beach and Vineròs also provide excellent affordances for staying ("hanging out") and socialising. The installation on the Ljubljanica River provides more of both, a solitary and social style of seating, where people sitting at the river are divided from the passing people on the promenade. This type of seating is also suitable for small-scale outdoor performances with a small audience.

Microclimate amelioration

Owing to the fact that these are small interventions, their location in an existing landscape as well as some aspects of design have been taken into account with respect to the microclimate in several examples. Shade structures at Olive Beach and Paris Plages are important in hot weather, and sheltering structures such as the planking walls at the Kastrup sea bath protect swimmers from the cold wind, while, uniquely, the skaters' shelters at Winnipeg, where the temperature can be very cold indeed, enabled skaters to stay out and exercise for longer.

Use of materials

From a design perspective, there are some very interesting uses of materials and associated craftsmanship in several structures – such as the plywood curved to form the skaters' shelters, the timber structures of the Kastrup sea bath or the decking at Vinaròs and Olive Beach. The sauna structure at Gothenburg is the only permanent project to use recycled materials. All are very careful in the attention to detail in the construction. The use of materials – their selection for the purpose, durability, recycling or upcycling – is an aspect which is very relevant in terms of sustainability and material justice and for showcasing construction. This aspect is more prominent in the design of a single small object than over a larger site and where sculptural qualities are an integral part of the design.

Use of vegetation and ecological aspects

With the exception of the temporary garden at Emscher, few of the projects include any planting or ecological aspects. One interesting example is the Severaue platform, which incorporates *Salix* trees as a part of its actual construction. The sauna project in Gothenburg is built around and highlights the existing ruderal vegetation on the site. The Steveraue project, as well as the platforms at Vinaròs, are located in natural places, where the impact on the natural environment was considered in their design.

Site management and maintenance

The site management of the projects depends a lot on their character; for example, if they are temporary, this is not usually an issue. If they are seasonal, then they need to be erected, maintained and dismantled, with the disassembled sections moved, stored, repaired and modified as necessary. Permanent structures are managed as part of the overall sites and locations, such as the river banks in Ljubljana, the nature park at Severaue and the Vinaròs coastline.

Maintenance of seasonal structures can be carried out in the off season wherever they are stored, while others which are exposed to the elements need more regular and careful maintenance.

Conclusions and implications for practice

This chapter has provided a contrast from the other chapters in this part of the book, highlighting the positive benefits of less being more and small being more impactful. The lessons we can learn are also connected to the extensive discussion of theory which we set out at the beginning of the chapter.

There are several aspects we draw attention to:

- Temporary interventions can have a very valuable role, whether for very short-term animation of spaces within, for example, a festival, or in places where the signals of welcome and safety help to catalyse the blue space improvement process.
- In specific cases and contexts, modest, cheap and community-led interventions can provide space and time for experimentation and testing, for creativity and flexibility. This can help to ensure that the end product is not only functional but also socially acceptable to the local community and more sustainable. It is particularly easy to ensure this in this context as opposed to larger projects.
- Just because projects are small in scale and less costly than average landscape design or architectural projects does not mean that they cannot reach high standards in construction. Attention to detail and robust construction are very important, especially if the intervention is located in an exposed place – exposed to the elements or to potential damage or vandalism. In several cases, the construction goes hand in hand with artistic creativity in the generation of the forms and the way materials are used.
- Seasonal structures can also have a major role to play – activating spaces to provide different affordances according to the seasons, since winter and mid-season use is often overlooked in terms of human-water interaction. This approach is worthy of greater consideration more generally in design projects at the land-water interface.

Finally, we can note that the range of projects presented here, although not extensive, represent a diversity of approaches and solutions within the scope of tactical urbanism, urban acupuncture or just small in scale because that is appropriate. They show the range of creativity and the potential for real experimentation with few of the risks associated with much larger capital-intensive projects.

References

Branas, C. C., Cheney, R. A., McDonald, J. M., Tam, V. W., Jackson, T. D., Havey, T. R. T. (2011) A difference-in-differences analysis of health, safety, and greening vacant urban space. *American Journal of Epidemiology* 174–181, 1296–1306.

Casagrande, M. (2015) From urban acupuncture to the third generation city. In J. Revedin (ed.) *La ville rebelle. Démocratiser le projet urbain.* Gallimard, Paris.

Certeau, M. (1984) *The Practice of Everyday Life.* University of California Press, Berkeley.

De Solà-Morales, M. (1999) Progettare città [Designing the City]. *Electa* 23.

De Solà-Morales, M. (2004) The strategy of urban acupuncture. In *Structure Fabric and Topography Conference.* Nanjing University, Nanjing.

Gibson, J. J. (1979) *The Ecological Theory of Perception.* Houghton Mifflin, Boston.

Lara-Hernandez, J. A., Melis, A. (2018) Understanding the temporary appropriation in relationship to social sustainability. *Sustainable Cities and Society* 39, 366–374.

Lerner, J. (2014) *Urban Acupuncture*. Island Press, Washington, DC.

Lydon, M., Garcia, A. (2015) *Tactical Urbanism: Short-Term Action for Long-Term Change*. Island Press, Washington, DC.

Marletto, G., Sillig, C. (2019). Lost in mainstreaming? Agrifood and urban mobility grassroots innovations with multiple pathways and outcomes. *Ecological Economics* 158, 88–100.

Mathey, J., Arndt, T., Banse, J., Rink, D. (2018) Public perception of spontaneous vegetation on brownfields in urban areas – Results from surveys in Dresden and Leipzig (Germany). *Urban Forestry and Urban Greening* 29, 384–392.

Nassauer, J. I., Raskin, J. (2014) Urban vacancy and land use legacies: A frontier for urban ecological research, design, and planning. *Landscape and Urban Planning* 125, 245–253.

Newman, G., Park, Y., Bowman, A. O. M., Lee, R. J. (2018) Vacant urban areas: Causes and interconnected factors. *Cities* 72, 421–429.

Pearsall, H., Lucas, S. (2014) Vacant land: The new urban green? *Cities* 40, 121–123.

Roe, J., Barnes, L., Napoli, N. J., Thibodeaux, J. (2019) The restorative health benefits of a tactical urban intervention: An urban waterfront study. *Frontiers in Built Environment* 5, 71.

Rupprecht, C. D. D., Byrne, J. A., Garden, J. G., Hero, J. M. (2015) Informal urban green space: A trilingual systematic review of it's role for biodiversity and trends in the literature. *Urban Forestry & Urban Greening* 14, 883–908.

Unt, A.-L., Bell, S. (2014) The impact of small-scale design interventions on the behaviour patterns of the users of an urban wasteland. *Urban Forestry & Urban Greening* 13–14, 121–135.

Vassiljev, P., Bell, S., Balicka, J., Ali, A. U. A. (2020). Urban blue acupuncture: An experiment on preferences for design options using virtual models. *Sustainability* 12, no. 24, 10656.

Chapter 16: Future outlook studies

The use of scenarios to create healthy blue cities

Judith Hin and Susanne Wuijts

Introduction

So far in this book, a lot of material has been presented outlining the evidence base for blue health, presenting methods and tools for stakeholder involvement, assessing spaces and populations and also presenting inspiring examples and learning lessons from practice. In this final chapter, we turn to the future and consider what kinds of possibilities may emerge as a result of a range of drivers of change.

The challenges facing urban areas are complex. In urban settings, space is scarce and is subjected to multiple demands and complex interactions, while population density is high. Urbanisation and other future trends in demography, economy, technology, ecology and climate ostensibly unrelated to urbanisation can have large and unforeseen impacts on the environment and human populations (UN-Habitat, 2016), depending on the local context (Ebi et al., 2018). In order to create resilient, liveable and healthy blue cities, we need to understand the impact of these trends, their character and the forces which drive them. Furthermore, we need to identify which of these are most relevant and how they could interact at this local scale.

Future outlook studies are used to develop scenarios to enable politicians, local planners, public health practitioners and ordinary citizens to gain insights into the possible future impacts of (interacting) global and national trends in the specific local context, thereby supporting the development of effective policy strategies. Understanding the impact of global and national trends helps to prepare for the 'likely future' but, combined with the analysis of 'desired futures' in a local context (local pressures and priorities), gives insight into the broader scope of 'possible futures' and is input for these 'scenarios' that can be used for local policy decisions (see Figure 16.1). This chapter presents the approach in which scenarios were developed for five European cities, focusing on their particular opportunities and challenges around water and the marine environment and their impact on health and well-being.

After this introduction, we briefly explain the concept of future outlook studies, followed by a section summarising the major issues facing urban areas in Europe related to or driven by global and national trends. Then we outline a step-by-step method of building a normative or value-driven trend scenario from the local perspective. Next we summarise and present the outcomes of scenario building on the topic of creating healthy blue cities in five European examples which offer the opportunity to explore the role of blue spaces in very different geographical and sociopolitical contexts: Amsterdam (the Netherlands), Barcelona (Spain), Plymouth (United Kingdom), Tallinn (Estonia) and Thessaloniki (Greece). This reveals the way which the same trends may have different impact at the local level and lead to different potential options for appropriate policies and interventions. Finally, we compare the five cities we studied in order to reveal the dominant trends for blue health in Europe and the range of interventions possible. In order to obtain an idea of what a trend scenario for a city looks like, in the appendix to the chapter, we present a more detailed overview of the scenarios for the city of Plymouth (for more information

DOI: 10.4324/9780429056161-20

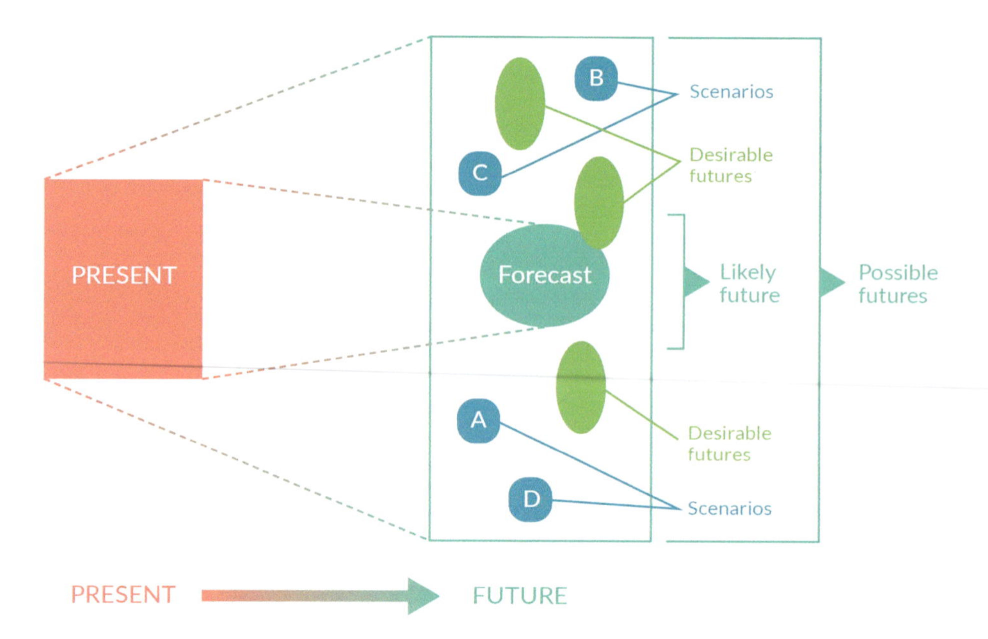

Figure 16.1
Different ways of looking at possible futures
(*Source*: Hilderink et al., 2018)

on the other four cities and on future outlook studies on blue health, see the website https://bluehealth2020.eu/projects/scenarios/).

Urban blue health and the concept of future outlook studies

Future outlook studies aim at identifying emerging opportunities and challenges in light of long-term trends. With regard to our theme, a future outlook study can reveal the particular connections between global, national and local driving forces in a city and their impacts on the blue environment and blue health – see Figure 16.2. Understanding these connections paves the way for integrated thinking about effective policies around water and the marine environment that could improve the health and well-being of urban dwellers, taking into account local differences in both pressures and priorities.

Global trends, such as climate change, suggest not only an increase in the number of warm days but also sea level rise; a higher frequency of extreme weather events, such as storms and heavy rainfall; and increased perceived temperature (a combination of temperature and humidity) (Scoccimarro et al., 2017), all of which have implications for quality of life in urban settings. Ageing, migration and increasing prevalence of chronic disease among urban populations all imply different demands for the design of urban spaces. Economic developments, such as changes in income distribution, may result in increased social inequalities, for example, in inner-city areas where contrasts between rich and poor are most pronounced. The knock-on effects on society may be considerable, for example, when it leads to social unrest or when income inequalities negatively impact environmental quality and access to high-quality and affordable healthcare (e.g. Drabo, 2011), all of which constitute threats to maintaining public health. Ecological degradation results in less green and blue space and decreasing biodiversity in urban areas, which in turn increases the impact of temperature rise in the urban environment (exacerbating the urban health island effect) (Koop and Van Leeuwen, 2017).

Figure 16.2

A concept sketch of a future outlook study of urban blue health

(*Source*: Dutch National Institute of Public Health, 2020; illustration: BlueHealth Scenarios, 2020: https://bluehealth2020.eu/projects/scenarios/)

The future challenges for urban areas are many and varied. Moreover, the trends driving these challenges interact. For instance, the urban heat island effect exacerbates risks from extreme heat among vulnerable groups and relatively more so for those living in deprived neighbourhoods (Filho et al., 2017; Macintyre et al., 2017). Many cities are situated in environments prominently featuring water, and since their infrastructure relies heavily on their water resources, such cities are especially vulnerable to certain impacts of climate change, such as flooding, drought, sea level rise and the consequent effects on society, such as risks to health from infectious diseases and death by drowning.

Future scenarios can be used to identify future challenges and possible strategies within the complexities of an urban area. They are based on possible future developments while acknowledging the inevitable uncertainties that come with them – not only uncertainties as a result of limited knowledge about future developments – but also as a result of deviating ideas, ambitions and visions about the desired future expressed by residents, stakeholders or authorities. They are, thus, not attempts to predict the future but explicitly to describe the kinds of futures desired by particular groups and the possible impacts of autonomous trends that might be anticipated by policymakers (in the case of anticipation, these future scenarios themselves influence and change future outcomes).

It is crucial to view urban water themes in a future scenario not only in a negative manner – as a risk or a resource under threat – such as infectious diseases, lower well-being or drowning. The urban water environment can also play an important role in the process of realising a sustainable and healthy urban environment (UN-Habitat, 2016), as demonstrated by the evidence presented in Chapter 2. For example, water infrastructure can be designed not only to be climate resilient but also to maximise co-benefits through mitigation of urban heat island effects and promotion of physical activity (see many of the examples presented in Chapters 11–15).

The way in which these different opportunities and challenges in relation to water infrastructure are apparent in the five European cities studied in this scenario project will be presented after we provide some insight into the major issues facing Europe and a brief explanation of the various steps in the future outlook method to develop a future scenario with policy options to improve the blue health of cities in Europe.

Major issues facing urban areas in Europe: global and national trends

Although the extent to which a global or national trend may be relevant on a local scale may vary, some general trends can be identified as potentially very relevant on the scale of Europe for the establishment of healthy blue cities by 2040 (20 years after the work which contributes to this book was completed).

Both urbanisation and climate change are regarded as trends with a major impact on blue spaces in terms of both risks and benefits. Rising temperatures may lead to an increase of water use for recreation and sport. High-precipitation events may, however, result in flooding and sewage overflow and thus affect water quality. Water availability for human consumption and recreation, as well as for industrial use and agriculture, may be threatened through extended periods of drought; this may also negatively affect water quality due to the reduced dilution of point sources of pollution in the water system. Urbanisation and related demographic and economic trends impose greater demands on the availability of good-quality water but also offer a window of opportunity to improve the health and well-being of urban residents through the design of attractive blue spaces.

Economic inequalities, increased recreational use of blue spaces and climate change can be regarded as trends with important potential effects on health. Economic inequalities could lead to an increased disease burden and social unrest (impacting well-being) (Camilio Cardenas et al., 2002; Drabo, 2011). Increased recreational use of blue spaces could result in both increased health risks (drowning, waterborne diseases) and benefits (physical exercise, mental health and well-being) (WHO, 2005, 2014; White et al., 2020). The projected effects of climate change on water availability and quality may also have an effect on health due to increased exposure to pathogens and risks of drowning in the case of flooding; however, climate change adaptation measures in blue spaces, such as the development of wetland parks to deal with flood water, as demonstrated in Chapter 13, could also have beneficial effects on stress reduction and physical exercise. The loss of biodiversity could also make blue spaces less attractive to visit. Older people and those with chronic illness are more vulnerable to the consequences of heat waves. The combination of this with social deprivation could worsen the health consequences of these types of events, as these groups may have less access to adequate information or care.

The development of technology is a global trend that will have significant impact on the possibilities for domestic water management and urban water systems, making them more efficient and smarter using data and algorithms. Moreover, development of user-friendly interfaces for data and information related to urban biodiversity and healthy environment can boost available information, especially regarding water-related health risks and benefits. Such data will presumably have a big impact on the ability of people to make more individual choices in terms of healthcare and to create possibilities for personalised healthcare, for instance, with regard to blue health opportunities.

Figure 16.3
Future outlook dependent on local developments and perception
(*Source*: BlueHealth Scenarios, 2020: https://bluehealth2020.eu/projects/scenarios/)

Impact and challenges of global trends

The impact of these global trends can be assessed differently from one European city to another, since local stakeholders often have different preferences, perceptions and priorities for the societal challenges that arise from the business-as-usual-scenario (Francis and Lorimer, 2011; Van Broekhoven et al., 2014). For this reason, the scenario-building process starts with stakeholders identifying the values they perceive to be important for water and health in the local context – as visualised in Figure 16.3. While stakeholders in some European cities perceive climate resilience to be the most important aspect, stakeholders in other cities prioritise access to blue spaces for all or preserving biodiversity instead.

Moreover, the various trends pose different local challenges. Some European cities appear to be magnets for attracting highly educated employees from both inside and outside the country. The presence of companies and technology together with a favourable social and cultural living environment attracts such people, while other cities struggle with economically less favourable conditions, partly due to the disappearance of traditional industries and the fact that well-educated people prefer to go to other, more attractive cities. Tourism is also a subject that is considered a challenge in some urban areas, while others describe it as an opportunity. The inhabitants of Barcelona, for example, have reduced access to the beach during the summer months, as this is a hotspot for the huge number of tourists who visit the city. In both Amsterdam and Barcelona, affordable housing for all population groups has been under increasing pressure as the prices for accommodation are strongly affected by high tourist rental rates. Conversely, other cities, such as Plymouth or Thessaloniki, would like to attract more tourists in order to strengthen the local economy. They would like to use the opportunity of creating healthy blue spaces to set this development in motion. For many cities, the presence of water is an important opportunity, since it is attractive for people to both live and recreate at or on the water. However, a pressing question for these cities is how to guarantee access for all to these healthy blue spaces.

Towards scenarios for healthy blue cities in Europe – a step-by-step method

Before going into more detail on the specific trends in the five European pilot cities, we present an overview of the step-by-step method for constructing blue health future outlooks.

To set the scope for future healthy blue cities, the scenario development process starts by framing the issue around the main question: "What policy interventions on urban blue infrastructure can be beneficial to public health and well-being?" Urban blue infrastructure is defined in these scenarios as the physical structures and facilities built in, on and around blue spaces (such as those presented in the projects evaluated in previous Chapters 11 to 15. The scenarios use a time horizon of 2040, as this seems to accommodate the different time horizons of various trends the best.

Step 1: Local values and ambitions for water and health

The scaling down from the general trends to identify their impact at a local scale and to attach possible policy interventions is carried out in an interactive, multidisciplinary stakeholder workshop with experts and local professionals

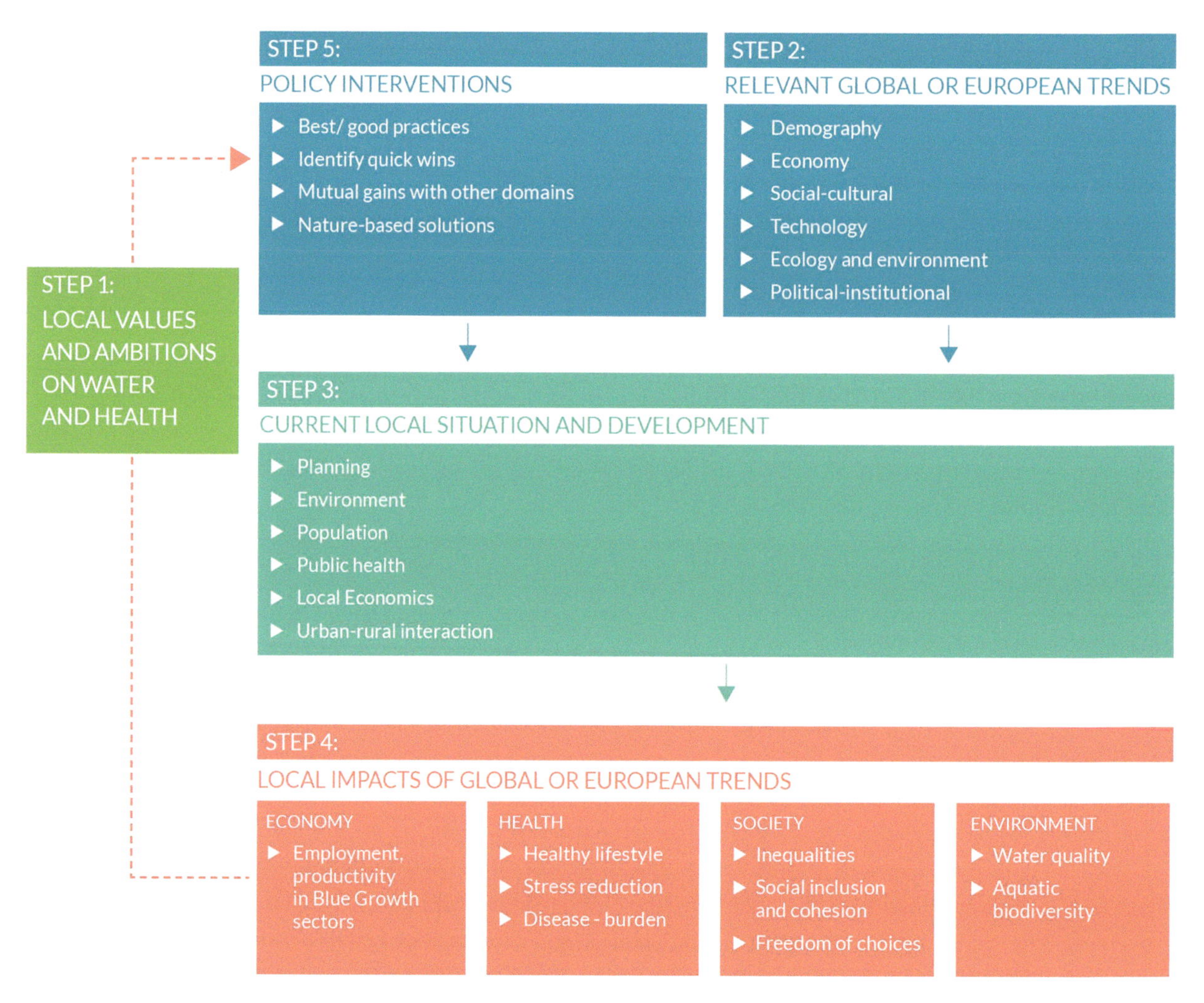

Figure 16.4

The step-by-step method of future outlook studies for blue health in European cities

(*Source*: Anna Wilczyńska, based on Wuijts, S. et al., 2021)

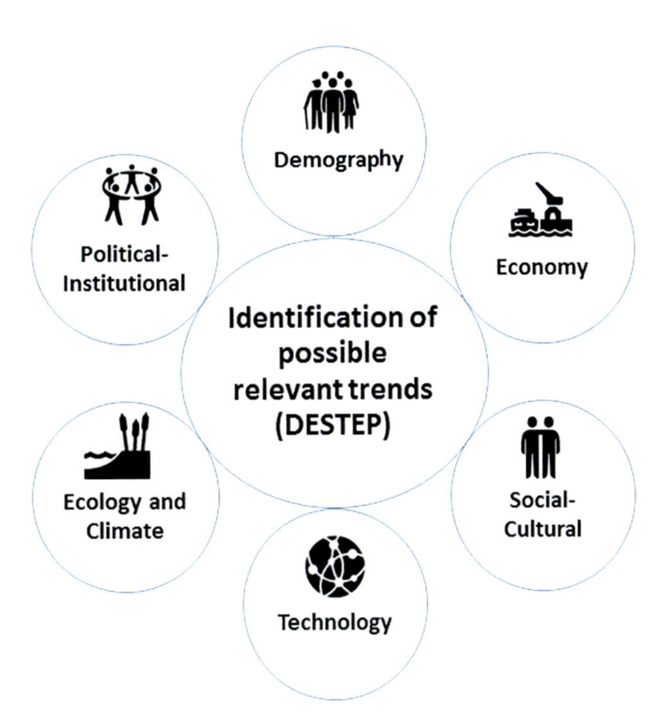

Figure 16.5
DESTEP trends
(*Source*: Wuijts et al., 2019)

from various backgrounds (such as water quality management, public health, spatial planning, landscape architecture, policy and governance, social science, technology, climate and environment). Besides cognitive uncertainties concerning the development of trends in these future outlooks, normative uncertainties of values and ambitions are addressed by commencing the local workshops with an analysis of the local values/perspectives related to water and health in the future. These values/perspectives are gathered at the start but only used in the final step in order to interpret the prioritisation of trends by the stakeholders and to assess the local impact of these trends, which is a prerequisite for identifying suitable policy options and strategies.

Step 2: Relevant global or European trends

The identification of global or European trends and their interactions is regarded as the second step of the scenario-building process. The broad identification of global trends, including their interaction, that drive changes in the field of water and health/well-being were established by researchers with different disciplinary expertise reviewing information on indicators and relevant literature (Wuijts et al., 2019). These trends are structured by using the DESTEP categories: demography, economy, social-cultural, technology, ecology and environment, political-institutional (see Figure 16.5).

Step 3: Current local situation and developments

The trends identified at Step 2 are prioritised by stakeholders, based on local data for the six DESTEP categories. The stakeholders then select the five most relevant and five most uncertain trends, as they perceive them, looking at the future of the urban area and population/city level. The results are subsequently reflected upon by the group of stakeholders as a whole in order to understand the outcomes against the relevant background of the local developments according to six themes: urban planning, environment, population, public health, local economics and urban-rural interaction.

Step 4: Local impacts of global or European trends
After deciding the most relevant and most uncertain trends at the local level, an analysis of the possible impacts of these prioritised trends on the economy, health, society and (the natural and built) environment of the local situation is established by discussion in the stakeholder group. To compile the trends scenario, these results are complemented and supported in the report (that is produced as an output of the scenario workshop) by any available data on relevant issues (e.g. population development, climate change). Where possible, these data should be quantitative. However, not all relevant issues can be included in (quantitative) models, and therefore semi-quantitative and more qualitative descriptive methods can also be used. The draft narratives are then validated by the involved stakeholders and other interested parties in order to identify quick wins in urban policy and to facilitate mutual learning. The result is a so-called *trend scenario*, describing trends for an urban area without taking into account any interventions.

Step 5: Policy interventions
The final step is to identify possible policy options around the most relevant values/perspectives identified by the stakeholders that were gathered in step 1. The result of combining the local impacts of trends with this 'desired future' based on values/perspectives is a so-called *normative* or *value-driven scenario*, which reflects the ambitions of different local stakeholders. This provides insight into the challenges local stakeholders face regarding their ambitions as well as a window of opportunity for local action: best/good practices, identifying quick wins, mutual gains with other domains and nature-based solutions.

Blue health future outlook in Europe: trend scenarios for five pilot cities

BlueHealth scenarios were compiled for five cities located across Europe: Amsterdam (the Netherlands), Barcelona (Spain), Plymouth (United Kingdom), Tallinn (Estonia) and Thessaloniki (Greece) (Figure 16.6). The cities were selected for their diversity of climate zones, the availability and type of urban blue spaces (coast, lake, river, canal, basin), socioeconomic conditions and governance regimes. It was envisaged that this would provide a variety of results that would facilitate a discussion of the added value of this approach for policy planning. In these five European cities, interactive workshops with local (professional) stakeholders from a range of relevant disciplines were organised. With the results of these workshops, trend scenarios were developed stating the local impact of global trends, based on local values/perceptions, with possible interventions attached to improve local blue health conditions.

This section first presents summaries of the situation of each of the five cities in relation to the DESTEP categories (Wuijts et al, 2021). Then, the results of local stakeholders prioritising global and European trends for their impact at the local level (*trend scenarios*) are presented, combined with local values and ambitions, giving an insight into different opportunities and challenges (*normative scenarios*) for interventions around water and the water environment to improve health and well-being. To illustrate in more detail the way in which these scenarios were compiled, an overview of the complete trend and normative scenario for Plymouth is presented in the appendix to this chapter. An overview of the methodology applied can be found on the BlueHealth website (https://bluehealth2020.eu/projects/scenarios/).

- **Amsterdam**, the capital of the Netherlands, is a densely populated urban area (5,042 inhabitants/km^2), including a port complex and adjacent industrial zones characterised by high economic value. It is situated in the delta

Figure 16.6

The pilot cities of BlueHealth: Amsterdam, Barcelona, Plymouth, Tallinn and Thessaloniki

(*Source*: BlueHealth Scenarios, 2020: https://bluehealth2020.eu/projects/scenarios/)

of several major international river basins (Rhine, Meuse, Scheldt and Ems) and is sited below sea level. The main risk of flooding in the future is posed by heavy rainfall in the city itself, as the dykes in the Netherlands provide a high level of protection. Amsterdam has a mild maritime climate, with rainfall throughout the year. The population of Amsterdam is projected to age progressively in the coming decades, and ethnic diversity will further increase; currently 70% of the population has a (mixed) ethnic background. The continuing development of social inequalities is a major challenge for the city.

- **Barcelona**, the second most populous city in Spain and capital of the autonomous region of Catalonia, is situated on the Mediterranean Sea. The city has a very high population density (16,000 inhabitants/km^2), is characterised by its rich cultural heritage and is a major tourist destination. It has a large port that consists of a commercial, logistics and historical zone and also has a number of beaches along the southeastern edge of the city. Barcelona has a Mediterranean climate with mild winters, warm/hot summers and infrequent rainfall, including long periods without rain. Droughts are a recurring concern but also intense and high volumes of rainfall when it does rain. The hilly terrain, the largely impermeable surfaces due to urbanisation and extensive canalisation of rivers all contribute to the risk of flooding. Income inequality in Barcelona is large, and there is a strong spatial concentration of poverty in a number of neighbourhoods. By 2030, almost a third of Barcelona's residents will be aged 60 years or older. Access to affordable housing is likely to decrease, with rents in the city continuously rising and reduced availability of suitable housing for residents due to tourism.
- **Plymouth**, termed Britain's Ocean City, is a medium-sized city located on the coast of the southwest of England. It has moderate population density (3,300 inhabitants/km^2) and a remarkably rich heritage and a maritime community with international recognition in trade, emigration, exploration and ocean science. The coastal infrastructure in Plymouth is partly classed as 'artificial', with sea walls and rock armour revetment. The city has many pockets of socioeconomic deprivation, a reality in contrast to the extensive recreational redevelopment of many of the city's waterfront areas to attract tourists and second-home owners. The Plymouth population is growing and ageing, and life expectancy in some neighbourhoods is among the lowest in the United Kingdom. Plymouth has a temperate oceanic climate which is generally wetter and milder than the rest of England.
- **Tallinn**, the capital of Estonia, is an historic Hanseatic city on the shore of the Gulf of Finland of the Baltic Sea, with close ties to Helsinki in Finland and Saint Petersburg in Russia. It was a major satellite city of the Soviet Union for decades, when many Soviet migrants were housed in new residential districts comprising extensive developments of multi-storey blocks of flats added to the city. Currently, slightly more than half of the population of Estonia lives in Tallinn, of which about one third is of Russian descent. The city has a below-average population density (2730 inhabitants/km^2) and is the country's major financial, industrial, cultural, educational and research centre. Tallinn has the highest number of start-up companies per person among European countries, is the birthplace of many international high-technology companies and platforms and is listed among the top ten digital cities in the world. The city has a humid continental climate with warm or mild summers and cold, snowy winters.
- **Thessaloniki** is a Greek city on the Thermaic Gulf, at the northeastern corner of the Aegean Sea, alongside the delta of the Axios River. It is a medium-sized city with an average population density (7100 inhabitants/km^2). The city has an extensive sea front and hosts the second-largest container port in Greece that functions as a major transportation hub for southeastern Europe. A major section of the waterfront has been renovated and many areas redeveloped, making efforts to attract more international tourists to visit its rich and unique cultural heritage (for example, as a destination for cruise ships) alongside domestic tourists. Unemployment rates are high as result of the Greek economic crisis, especially among young people. The city has a Mediterranean climate, with cold and wet winters and hot and dry summers, with urban heat island effect and sea level rise being the main climate change concerns.

These local (DESTEP) characteristics reveal the broad range of interacting factors that affect the impact of possible interventions in the marine environment for making the cities more resilient, liveable and healthy. Using the step-by-step method for constructing a blue health scenario, local stakeholders in each of the five cities prioritised these global and European trends for their city as well as their dominant values – see the results in Table 16.1. Local stakeholders were invited from a broad range of organisations with local knowledge, different fields of expertise related

Table 16.1 **Relevant trends and dominant values identified during the interactive stakeholder workshops in the five pilot cities**

Prioritised trends:	*D = demography* *E = economy* *S = society and culture* *T= technology* *E = ecology and environment* **P = politics and institutions**	*Amsterdam*	*Barcelona*	*Plymouth*	*Tallinn*	*Thessaloniki*
D	Increasing life expectancy		■	■	■	
	Changing population composition				■	
	Migration					■
E	Changes in income distribution	■	■	■	■	
	Changes in labour conditions					■
S	More recreational use of blue spaces			■		■
	More waterfront development for urban regeneration			■	■	
	Increasing individualisation	■				
T	Digitalisation of society				■	
	Towards healthy urban living		■			■
E	Climate change		■		■	■
	Higher risks of flooding	■				
	Higher risks of water scarcity	■	■			
	Further loss of biodiversity and other ecological impacts			■	■	
P	Changing institutional and governance structures	■	■			
	More healthy urban living in EU policies and strategies					

Dominant values		Amsterdam	Barcelona	Plymouth	Tallinn	Thessaloniki
	Climate resilience	■	■			
	Promoting social equity	■	■			■
	Access to blue spaces			■	■	
	Improving identity/pride in the city			■		
	Preserving biodiversity				■	
	Sustainable urban design					■

(*Source*: Wuijts et al., 2021)

to one or more of the DESTEP driving forces and different roles and responsibilities but all related to blue spaces and health. In addition to their thorough local knowledge of different aspects relevant to urban blue health, different stakeholders also expressed different values and ambitions for the future.

The results of the stakeholder workshops revealed that in a future outlook scenario of urban blue health in Amsterdam, *climate change and social inequality are interlinked challenges and opportunities for the city*. Some of the more deprived neighbourhoods in Amsterdam are prone to flooding, making them more vulnerable to pollution and infectious disease risk if heavy rainfall causes an overflow of the sewage system. Stakeholders pointed out that the vast diversity of citizens could make it challenging to reach out and communicate these risks to all the different groups,

Figure 16.7
Climate change and social equity themes in Amsterdam
(*Source*: BlueHealth Scenarios, 2020: https://bluehealth2020.eu/projects/scenarios/)

as well as the risks in using blue spaces – for example, for bathing, of which many of the citizens of Amsterdam are unaware (Municipality of Amsterdam, 2016). On the other hand, open water bathing sites may be cheaper and more accessible, and climate change is an opportunity to improve outdoor spaces.

Promising strategies to act upon this future outlook scenario for Amsterdam could be to increase *cross-sectoral spatial planning and citizen engagement*. Both health and climate resilience need to be accounted for in the spatial planning processes, such as when introducing waterfront protection zones to secure access for all and creating safe bathing sites. Engagement of local groups could add information on usage and satisfaction of blue spaces and increase awareness of risks of blue spaces (e.g. Assmuth et al., 2017). The ambitions towards healthy environments stated in the upcoming national Environmental and Planning Act (due 2022) could support this.

In Barcelona, the future outlook scenario of urban blue health based on stakeholder input also focused on *climate resilience and social equality*, with emphasis on *balancing sociocultural inequalities*. Vulnerable groups (e.g. lower income, elderly) often have fewer resources to adapt to the expected effects of climate change on the availability of drinking water, heat stress and bathing water quality. According to stakeholders, the access to blue spaces is unevenly distributed in Barcelona and generally better for high-income groups. Investments to improve blue spaces could result in more gentrification and worsen social inequalities if not taken into account in urban planning processes.

To act upon this future scenario a promising strategy could be to *raise the awareness for climate resilience in other policy domains* (e.g. related to work, income, housing, transport) *and among citizens and companies*, especially in neighbourhoods with a high density of activities, use of space and complex social interaction. Implementation of so-called Superblocks, where greening and traffic-calming measures in a cluster of several blocks are applied, could be a promising strategy to improve health and liveability if implemented on a city-wide scale (Mueller et al., 2020). Increasing blue and green spaces in the city could help to store water and form a source of cooling and shade during warm periods in summer, especially in deprived neighbourhoods. Stakeholders also stated that more awareness could be raised among the citizens of the need to use water more efficiently.

In the future outlook scenario of urban blue health for Plymouth – which is presented in more detail step by step in the appendix – stakeholders prioritised *the redevelopment of accessible waterfronts*, stated *as an impactful opportunity and challenge*. Economic investment to this end may lead to increasing employment opportunities in the service industry. It could also improve health, as increasing recreational opportunities stimulate physical activity, and a stronger identity of the city enhances social cohesion. Yet stakeholders emphasised that if redeveloping accessible

Figure 16.8
Accessibility and inclusiveness themes in Barcelona
(*Source*: BlueHealth Scenarios, 2020: https://bluehealth2020.eu/projects/scenarios/)

waterfronts leads to gentrification, which in turn can be enhanced by changing income distribution, it might 'price out' poorer residents.

Promising strategies for inclusive waterfront heritage in Plymouth for all groups include *public participation to ensure space meets the health needs of the population purported to benefit from it, in the face of greater vested interests* from other waterfront redevelopments (such as the highest probable economic return). Another significant factor to be included to foster recreation and identification is *the valuing (and preserving) of the city's identity in its natural and cultural heritage*, which could function as an asset to diversify the local economy with the importance of the marine and naval industry declining and pressure from sea-level rise.

In Tallinn, the central themes in the future outlook scenario of blue health prioritised by stakeholders are *loss of biodiversity, climate change and urban regeneration as intricate challenges*. The water bodies of Tallinn suffer from the negative effects of pollution, depletion and loss of biodiversity, while climate change relates to risks of moderate flooding and heat stress. Tallinn has several beaches open to the public, but there is a risk that they are built on and could become private areas without public access to the sea being retained. The relatively young population of Tallinn requires access for different age groups with different private/work/care balances.

In response to this future outlook, promising strategies in Tallinn are *to link spatial planning, demographics, economy and IT in the development of waterfront access*. The Environmental Strategy 2030 could be an important vehicle, as it recognises the essential role of water bodies, including the sea, in the internal structure of the city. It aims to increase links between green and blue spaces and residential areas, of which the development of new public waterfronts could be part. The advanced technological/digital infrastructure could be used to establish domestic water management and smarter urban water systems as well as user-friendly interfaces for data and information related to blue health – such as water-related health benefits and risks.

The future outlook scenario of blue health in Thessaloniki aims, according to stakeholders, at *balancing challenges set by climate change and social cohesion*. Climate change poses the challenge of increasing flooding of waterfronts, but increasing rainfall also creates the opportunity for more water flow in the Gallikos River and Aliakmon delta serving both the urban population, as well as biodiversity. Climate change also leads to increasing heat waves that

Figure 16.9
Accessibility and city's identity themes in Plymouth
(*Source*: BlueHealth Scenarios, 2020: https://bluehealth2020.eu/projects/scenarios/)

impact especially vulnerable groups (e.g. low income, the elderly) who do not have the resources to adapt to this effect. Stakeholders identified gentrification as a potential challenge for urban cohesion, as it pushes lower-income groups out of their traditional neighbourhoods.

Possible strategies to act upon this future outlook for blue health in Thessaloniki are that *climate change can be used as a catalyst for developing more healthy blue spaces with sustainable urban design*. For cooling, the wind off the sea could be used as a ventilation system in the streets, more trees could enlarge the amount of shaded surface and more free drinking water points for all citizens could be created. Water activities, such as swimming, could be stimulated, keeping in mind that this also requires more lifeguards and lessons at school to keep swimming safe. Increased accessibility of blue spaces – for which there is great potential on the long waterfront of Thessaloniki – could make the city more attractive to tourist and thus generate economic benefits. As beaches are far from the city centre, free transport could improve access for everyone. Stakeholder engagement as well as big data management could give insights into needs and ideas. The Internet of Things concerning urban transport, water and energy resources, waste and weather information – such as a heat map, including alerts for vulnerable groups – could enhance the development of blue health spaces for residents and tourists.

Insight into opportunities for blue health through future outlook studies – the city cases compared

The future scenarios for the five cities were established separately to identify the local opportunities and challenges. The examples of Amsterdam, Barcelona, Plymouth, Tallinn and Thessaloniki show how future scenarios can assemble contributing and interacting causes and priorities into a coherent picture. Thereby, the scope of the 'likely future' in a city is broadened to 'possible futures', giving ways to think about 'desirable futures' within this wider perspective – as shown in Figure 16.1. Combining these 'desirable futures' in a city based on local values and ambitions, within the context of the impact of global and European trends, provides a route to the development of concrete scenarios for each of these five cities. These scenarios resulted in (a first overview of) suitable interventions tailored

Figure 16.10
Waterfront access theme in Tallinn
(*Source*: BlueHealth Scenarios, 2020: https://bluehealth2020.eu/projects/scenarios/)

to local opportunities and challenges to enhance blue health not only for the present moment but in the light of global and European trends for the next 20 years.

Comparison of the separate scenarios for these five cities gives insight into predominant trends and the different ways in which similar trends work out differently in the local context. This chapter, therefore, concludes with a comparison of the five future outlook scenarios for Amsterdam, Barcelona, Plymouth, Tallinn and Thessaloniki.

The future outlook studies in the five cities in this research show that climate change and income inequality appear to be the most often mentioned trends with most impact on urban blue health. Moreover, it reveals that local interventions not only vary in subject but also in their focus on different groups, places, processes and/or institutions, depending on the opportunities and challenges of the local context (see Figure 16.7).

In almost all the cities, increasing income inequalities were regarded by the local stakeholders as having a negative effect on the accessibility and inclusiveness of blue spaces. In Amsterdam and Barcelona, these problems were perceived as being exacerbated by the negative consequences of (global) mass tourism. For example, local residents have to compete for housing with international and private investors (e.g. AirBnB) who want to rent out properties to tourists and for the use of urban blue spaces. In Plymouth and Tallinn, other, more local issues were raised by the participants, such as affordability of houses for local residents due to gentrification of the seafront. Global factors were considered of less relevance, such as the global housing market and the increase of mass tourism. In general, water-based mass tourism and restrictions to public waterfront access were among the top issues for all cities. In the case of Tallinn, the connection to the waterfront was also blocked by a fast road and railway, thus hampering accessibility. In Thessaloniki, local stakeholders were more concerned about trends of migration and changes in labour conditions, and they focused on more sustainable urban design to create healthier urban living conditions and to combat the impact of climate change.

Figure 16.11
Sustainable urban design theme in Thessaloniki
(*Source*: BlueHealth Scenarios, 2020: https://bluehealth2020.eu/projects/scenarios/)

Climate change appeared to be a significant trend in both Amsterdam and Barcelona, but while in the former, the issue of flooding was seen as more relevant, in the latter, the focus was more on water scarcity, especially for uses other than drinking water. In Tallinn, the loss of biodiversity was prioritised over climate change, but moderate flooding was also mentioned as a blue health challenge, as was the case in both Plymouth and Thessaloniki.

Interventions with regard to these predominant trends in these five European cities varied in their focus on groups, places, processes and institutions. Climate-proof interventions, for instance, could be implemented to benefit the growing group of vulnerable older people in the city the most (such as low-income neighbourhoods in Amsterdam) or be used to strengthen the local economy (such as innovation and tourist attractions in Thessaloniki). In other

Figure 16.12
Narrative of prioritised trends in the five pilot cities of the BlueHealth scenarios – follow-up from Table 16.1
(*Source*: BlueHealth Scenarios, 2020: https://bluehealth2020.eu/projects/scenarios/)

cases, the scenarios reveal that an important factor in improving the blue health of a city is not only about specific places and/or target groups but also on improved governance structures (for example, better urban planning in Tallinn, more citizen participation in Plymouth). Scenarios can also support the decision-making process by providing insights into the opposing effects of certain developments, such as the fact that tourism might be an important economic engine of the city but significantly reduces the equality of access to blue places for the citizens (as found in the gentrification in Barcelona).

The conclusion is that blue health scenarios are not a recipe for the future resulting in a list of ready-made solutions but rather stimulate interventions that prepare for the future in a specific local context and have the most win-win effect for the urban blue health in a city as it includes the effects of inevitable global and European trends.

Appendix: a more detailed scenario for Plymouth

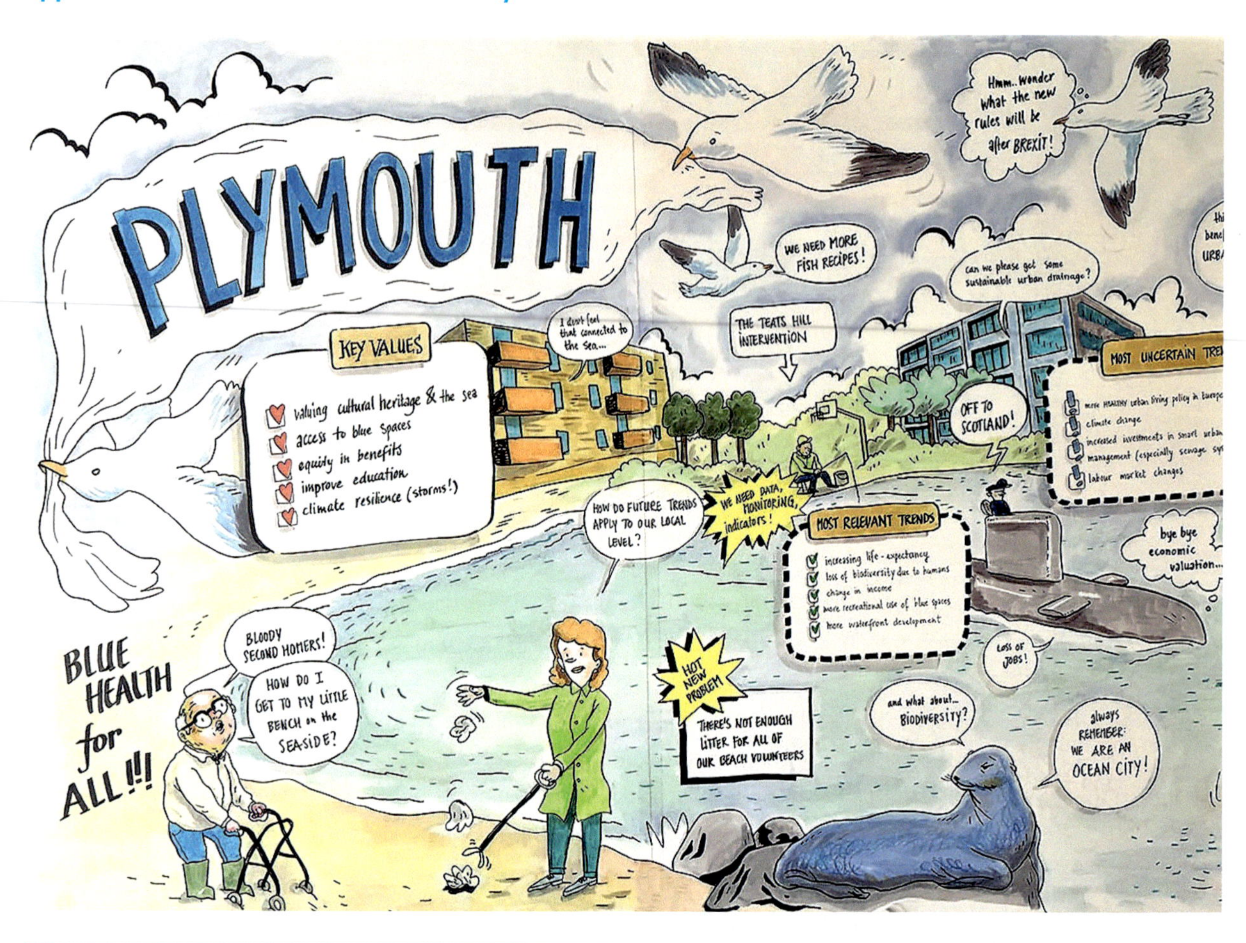

BACKGROUND PLYMOUTH

Plymouth, coined "Britain's Ocean City" in 2013, has a remarkable rich heritage beginning as a fishing village with a population of about 3,500 in the 16th century. The city is situated at the south-west coast of England, in the county of Devon. Plymouth is famous for its associations with Sir Francis Drake and the defeat of the Spanish Armada in 1588, the departure point for the Pilgrim Fathers on board the Mayflower to North America in 1620 and a major base for the Royal Navy, the largest in western Europe, which still generates around 10% of the city's income and employs around 2,500 service personnel and civilians. However, it was also heavily bombed in the Second World War and has a number of areas categories as highly deprived.

As of 2016, it had 264,000 inhabitants and under the unitary authority of the Plymouth City Council it covers a total surface area of 30.82 sq mi (79.83 km2) with a population density of about 8,500/sq mi (3,300/km2). As a maritime community with an international recognition in trade, emigration, exploration, and ocean science, it is located right on the sea coast in the south-west of England with 33% of its coastal infrastructure classed as 'artificial' (i.e. sea walls and rock armor revetment) .

TRENDSCENARIO PLYMOUTH

(more information: https://bluehealth2020.eu/projects/scenarios/)

Relevant trends in Plymouth

Increasing life-expectancy

- Proportion of the population aged 65 and over increases
- Variation between city districts in life-expectancy

More waterfront development and blue recreation, but concern about income inequalities

- Waterfront regeneration to become 'one of Europe's most vibrant waterfront cities'
- Popularity of water related activities is growing as result of technology (e.g. wetsuits) and ease of travel
- Increasing income inequalities enhancing differences in health and well-being

Increase of ecological impact due to human activities

- Deterioration of water ecosystems leading to a loss of biodiversity

Impacts of these relevant trends in Plymouth

- **Growing impact of water-related infectious diseases, risk of drowning and heat stress** due to environmental changes, use of water that is not designated for recreational purposes, but especially as result of the progressively aging and thus vulnerability of the population – though life expectancy differs substantially between neighborhoods
- **Different urban water use** as the shift in age groups, changing frequency of age-related diseases and increased use of nature conservation and water retention areas as playgrounds and parks
- **Increasing sense of pride to be Plymouthian** (or 'janner') as waterfront is arguably the city's most valuable asset and is central to its identity as Britain's Ocean City
- **Increasing inequity in access to and gains from blue space** due to increasing income inequalities and gentrification that pronounce differences between neighborhoods
- **Increasing public awareness** of ecological quality, marine issues and sustainable recreational water activities by developing a National Marine Park and of sustainability in surface drainage by implementing a reduction in household water bills
- **Significant economic cost and less attractive blue spaces** due to decreasing water body ecological status – which could be countered by well-executed waterfront regenerations that have **a positive effect on biodiversity and create healthier blue space and economic advantages**

References

Assmuth, T., et al. (2017). "Fair blue urbanism: demands, obstacles, opportunities and knowledge needs for just recreation beside Helsinki metropolitan area waters." *International Journal of Urban Sustainable Development* **9**(3): 253–273.

BlueHealth Scenarios, European Union Horizon 2020 project BlueHealth, see: https://bluehealth2020.eu/projects/scenarios/

Camilio Cardenas, J., et al. (2002). "Economic inequality and burden-sharing in the provision of local environmental quality." *Ecological Economics* **40**(3): 379–395.

Drabo, A. (2011). "Impact of income inequality on health: Does environment quality matter?" Environment and Planning A **43**(1): 146–165.

Ebi, K., et al. (2018). "Monitoring and evaluation indicators for climate change-related health impacts, risks, adaptation, and resilience." *International Journal of Environmental Research and Public Health* **15**(1943).

Filho, W., et al. (2017). "An evidence-based review of impacts, strategies and tools to mitigate urban heat Islands." *International Journal of Environmental Research and Public Health* **14**(1600).

Francis, R. and Lorimer, J. (2011). "Urban reconciliation ecology: The potential of living roofs and walls." *Journal of Environmental Management* **92**(6): 1429–1437.

Hilderink, H.B.M. et al. (2018). "Public health future outlook [in Dutch]." In: Van der Duin P. and Snijders D., editors. *Met de Kennis van morgen: Toekomstverkennen voor de Nederlandse overheid.* Amsterdam, Amsterdam University Press: 127–159.

Koop, S. and C. Van Leeuwen (2017). "The challenges of water, waste and climate change in cities." *Environment, Development and Sustainability* **19**: 385–418.

Macintyre, H., et al. (2017). "Assessing urban populations vulnerability and environmental risks across an urban area during heatwaves – Implications for health protection." *Science of the Total Environment* **610**(61): 678–690.

Mueller, N., et al. (2020). "Changing the urban design of cities for health: The superblock model." *Environment International* **134**.

Municipality of Amsterdam (2016). *Water Vision Amsterdam 2040 [In Dutch].* Amsterdam, Municipality of Amsterdam: 112.

Scoccimarro, E., et al. (2017). "The role of humidity in determining perceived temperature extremes scenarios in Europe." *Environmental Research Letters* **12**: 11

UN-Habitat (2016). *World Cities Report 2016 – Urbanization and Development: Emerging Futures.* Nairobi, Kenya, United Nations Human Settlements Programme.

Van Broekhoven, S., et al. (2014). "Boundaries in action: A framework to analyse boundary actions in multifunctional land-use developments." *Environment and Planning C: Government and Policy* **32**.

White, M., Elliott, L., Gascon, M., Roberts, B. and Fleming, L. (2020). "Blue space, health and well-being: A narrative overview and synthesis of potential benefits." *Environmental Research* **191**: 110169. https://doi.org/10.1016/j.envres.2020.110169

WHO (2005). *Water Recreation and Disease Plausibility of Associated Infections: Acute Effects, Sequelae and Mortality.* Geneva, World Health Organization.

WHO (2014). *Global Report on Drowning: Preventing a Leading Killer.* Geneva, World Health Organization.

Wuijts, S., et al. (2019). *Conceptual Framework and Trend analysis for BlueHealth Future Scenarios (D6.1).* European Union's Horizon 2020 Research and Innovation Programme. www.bluehealth.eu

Wuijts, S., et al. (2021). "The health potential of urban water: A future outlook on local risks and opportunities." *Cities Under Review.*

Appendix 1: The blue space typology

Here we present for the first time a comprehensive typology of blue space categories and sub-types, describing the main characteristics and features of each. In the BlueHealth project, we were rather pragmatic and kept it quite simple because the typology was to be used in a number of public surveys and we needed the descriptions to be simple and easily understood by survey respondents, as well as being easily translatable into several languages. Thus, while there are other, more formalised approaches to creating a typology, such as Brand's typological matrix for port cities (Brand, 2007), and we took some of the ideas proposed by her, we wanted to keep it the same as in the other Blue-Health research, which is described and summarised, at least methodologically, in other chapters in this book. We believe that such a typology is necessary in order to fill out the typologies which already exist for green and public spaces but where water is often treated as an afterthought.

In the rest of this section, we present sets of tables which summarise the typology and the characteristics of each type as well as the kinds of blue infrastructure found there, the possible health and well-being benefits, associated risks and some ecological aspects and sensitivities.

Coastlines

The first set of types is coastlines. These are determined in part by the geological and geographical structure, the location within the urban-rural gradient and the constructed blue infrastructure found there. For examples of design projects on coastal landscapes, see Chapter 12.

Type	*Main characteristics*	*Blue infrastructure*	*Recreational, health and well-being benefits*	*Risks*	*Ecological aspects and sensitivities*
Constructed coastal spaces					
Promenade	A constructed terrace running behind the beach (of whatever type) both protecting the urban structure behind and providing many amenities for visitors.	The main terraced walkway, shelters from wind and rain, lighting, access ramps and steps down to the beach or sea, shade structures, sometimes trees.	Ideal places for walking, cycling or jogging, obtaining fresh sea air, enjoying the view, sunbathing.	In some locations, storms break over the promenade and may risk washing people away. If too exposed to the sun, there is a risk of sunburn.	Usually no natural ecological values present. The structure may alter natural beach processes.

(*continued*)

Appendix 1: The blue space typology

Type	*Main characteristics*	*Blue infrastructure*	*Recreational, health and well-being benefits*	*Risks*	*Ecological aspects and sensitivities*
Pier	A constructed deck extending out into the sea, made of cast iron, steel, timber or concrete.	Traditionally, piers have amusements, cafés and even theatres; seating and shelters from wind and rain.	Walking, sitting, enjoying leisure activities, looking at the view, breathing in the sea air, fishing.	Some risk in storms and sun exposure.	May be some effect on the local beach and sea processes due to the structure. Seaweed and shellfish may colonise the structure, and birds may nest on it.
Natural coastal spaces					
Sandy beach	A beach, tidal or non-tidal, composed of sand deposited by longshore drift. If tidal, covered by the sea twice a day and washed clean, or detritus is washed up. Sloping to flat in profile.	The beach may be contained by sand dunes, a promenade, cliffs or other structures. The sand may be retained by groynes or other structures.	Sunbathing, sea bathing, relaxing, playing beach sports, horse riding, swimming, fishing, surfing, wind surfing and other action sports.	Some risk of drowning if the water off the beach is deep, if there are currents or an undertow; risk of sunburn. If there is sewage pollution in the sea, there is a risk of disease, and spray from polluted water may cause diseases if breathed in by people some distance from the sea.	If a pure sand beach, the ecological values may be limited. Some sea life down at the strand line in tidal beaches.
Stony beach	A similar profile to the sandy beach, tidal or non-tidal, with a promenade, cliffs or other structures behind it.	As such beaches are not so attractive for recreational use, there are fewer structures present.	Walking (if the stones are not too big), enjoying the view, breathing in the sea air, fishing.	Some risk of drowning or from storms. If there is sewage pollution in the sea, there is a risk of disease, and spray from polluted water may cause diseases if breathed in by people some distance from the sea.	A stony beach may be less disturbed by people but still formed of dynamic materials altered by the water and not a very attractive habitat.
Sand dunes	A series of ridges and hollows parallel to the beach/ perpendicular to the wind direction. The dunes are dry	As the dunes are erodible, there may be wooden boardwalks to make it easy to	Walking, sitting, picnicking, bird watching.	Blown sand may get in people's eyes. If there is sewage pollution in the sea, there is a	A very valuable habitat and very sensitive to physical disturbance and erosion,

Type	Main characteristics	Blue infrastructure	Recreational, health and well-being benefits	Risks	Ecological aspects and sensitivities
	and covered in, for example, grasses; the slacks (the low valleys in between) are moist and have salt marsh vegetation.	walk over them to the beach area (usually between the fore-dune and the sea).		risk of disease and, spray from polluted water may cause diseases if breathed in by people some distance from the sea.	also risk of disturbance to wildlife such as nesting birds.
Sea cliffs	Steeply sloping, up to vertical and may be low or extremely high, made of different types of bedrock and sometimes softer sediments. If bedrock, then likely to be accompanied by wave-cut platforms, caves, arches, stacks and other geological features, including rock pools in the intertidal zone.	May be provided with steps down to the beach, if present, or intertidal zone; may be safety barriers along the top of the cliff, walkway along the top.	Viewing the sea, observing wildlife, beach activities (if there is a beach), breathing in the sea air, gaining a sense of perspective in the face of the forces of nature (the sublime).	Falling off the cliff, material falling from the cliff, being cut off by the sea at high tide if people use the wave-cut platform or beach down below the cliff. If there is sewage pollution in the sea, there is a risk of disease, and spray from polluted water may cause diseases if breathed in by people some distance from the sea.	Cliffs provide seabird nesting, adapted plant habitats (especially for salt tolerant species); rock pools and the intertidal zone are very rich in sea life, especially shellfish.
Salt marsh	Low-lying areas behind the sea and sand dunes or shingle bars which are generally wetter and saline, colonised by vegetation adapted to the conditions.	May be wooden boardwalks to allow hiking through the salt marshes.	Walking (if paths provided) bird watching.	Few risks unless deep mud/quicksand present.	Very important habitats for specially adapted plants and invertebrate species; used by migrating birds and sensitive to disturbance at nesting times.
Estuary	The point where a river disgorges into the sea and where mud and other silty materials are deposited. If tidal, then mudflats are commonly found, exposed at low tide.	Very difficult to place infrastructure, apart for some boardwalks, due to the dynamic nature.	Bird watching, enjoying the view and sea air.	Can be dangerous when the tide comes in, cutting people off if they are not heedful of the tidal patterns.	Very dynamic habitats, important for wading birds.

Appendix 1: The blue space typology

Lakes and other still water bodies

This set of water bodies are characterised as mainly freshwater and have only small low rates of circulation, fed either by inflowing rivers, streams or ground water or, in the case of reservoirs, artificially dammed or contained. Some feature open water, while others may have started as shallow lakes but have become infilled by vegetation over many years, decades or centuries to become fens, mires or bogs. They may be characterised by different pH values and possess many different ecological values. For examples, see Chapters 12 and 13.

Type	*Main characteristics*	*Blue infrastructure*	*Recreational, health and well-being benefits*	*Risks*	*Ecological aspects and sensitivities*
Natural lake	A fresh water body with edges which are usually vegetated, the vegetation depending on the gradient and depth of the water. May have sandy beaches, stony edges or vegetation such as reed beds and emergent plants.	At beaches, there may be toilets, changing rooms, swimming platforms and jetties, boat launching facilities, picnic sites, trails and boardwalks	Depending on the context, there will be possibilities for water-based physical activities in summer such as boating, swimming and fishing and winter (if in the north); frozen lakes offer skiing, ice-fishing, skating. Being close to nature, sunbathing, fresh air, solitude.	Lakes can be affected by nitrate pollution, water can be cold at depth even if warm on the surface, ice can break in winter, algal blooms or risk of water-borne disease vectors. Risk of drowning; sunburn.	Natural lakes usually have high ecological values, although these depend on the water quality and degree of oligotrophism or eutrophism. Fish, invertebrates, birds, mammals and plant species can be sensitive to human activities.
Artificial lake	Usually either excavated for recreational purposes or restored after mineral working, such as sand and gravel extraction or stone quarries. Usually shallow (except in the case of some rock quarries) and, if sand and gravel origin, colonised by natural vegetation.	May be provided with artificial beaches, swimming platforms and jetties, play areas, picnic sites and boat launching.	Water-based physical activities such as swimming, boating, fishing in summer, with, if the lake freezes, ice fishing, skiing, skating in winter. Socialising, fresh air, being closer to nature.	Pollution from human activities (faecal matter, industrial pollution), eutrophication, drowning, sunburn.	Depending on the origin of the lake and the substrate, they may be colonised by fish, invertebrates, birds and mammals. Fish may also be introduced stock. Not usually as sensitive ecologically as natural lakes.
Reservoir	Usually created by damming a stream or river to create a water body for human water supply purposes or electricity generation. May be steep slopes	Some reservoirs are not accessible for recreation or direct use because of water purification	May only permit waking along the edges and views and experience of being close to water and	Deep cold water can be very dangerous, with increased risk of drowning. Risk of ice breaking in winter.	Reservoirs can be rich habitats for many species – fish, invertebrates, birds, mammals, but

Type	*Main characteristics*	*Blue infrastructure*	*Recreational, health and well-being benefits*	*Risks*	*Ecological aspects and sensitivities*
	leading into the water if a deep valley was dammed. Water levels tend to fluctuate as water is drawn down at certain times of the year.	restrictions. Others may be opened to recreation such as water sports or, in safe places, swimming and informal recreation on the shores. Swimming platforms and jetties, boating facilities, beaches, picnic sites.	nature. If accessible, then physical activity of water sports such as sailing, kayaking, canoeing and fishing in summer or, if frozen, ice fishing, skiing, skating.		the effect of the drawdown has an impact on the quality of the water-margin ecosystems. If impounded for drinking water, there is no pollution.
Pond	A water body smaller than a lake, may be natural (such as a former river meander or kettle-hole) but mainly artificial, created for a variety of purposes depending on their age – fish ponds, flax retting ponds, animal drinking water supply or purely ornamental. Usually shallow and either ground water-fed or dammed and fed by streams. Vegetated naturally or maintained as grassy edges in, for example, urban parks.	Depending on size and depth may be used for swimming and boating, fishing and ice fishing (if frozen in winter). May have swimming decks, benches, paths and lighting if in urban parks.	Viewing as part of the scenery (ornamental ponds), physical activity such as swimming or boating in summer; skating, ice hockey, curling and sauna-dipping if frozen in winter.	Drowning, water-borne disease if affected by pollution and water is not circulated and changed naturally.	Ponds can be extremely valuable habitats depending on their age, size, origin and vegetation. In urban areas, ducks are the main species. These remove many other species which may otherwise live there.
Wetland	These can be areas which contain shallow water and are affected seasonally by rainfall, being wetter or drier at different times of the year. May be smaller or larger in size. New wetlands are created in order to help storm water to infiltrate the urban ground water and to assist in capturing pollutants. They may comprise a mosaic of open water areas, saturated soils and	These are difficult to access so usually are provided with boardwalks to enable visitors to walk in them.	Wildlife viewing, birdwatching, getting close to nature, solitude.	May be polluted if the function is bio-remediation. Insect bites and insect-borne diseases in summer.	Wetlands are usually rich habitats for fish, birds, amphibians, invertebrates, mammals and a range of specialised plants. Pollution by, for example, heavy metals, may affect some species. They are usually eutrophic. If artificial, then

Appendix 1: The blue space typology

Type	*Main characteristics*	*Blue infrastructure*	*Recreational, health and well-being benefits*	*Risks*	*Ecological aspects and sensitivities*
	vegetation such as reed beds or willows and other woody vegetation suited to waterlogged sites.				they are not so sensitive to changes or impacts as natural ones.
Fen	These are the result of shallow ponds or lakes becoming filled over time with peat, retaining a basic pH. Usually partly open water and partly covered in emergent vegetation such as reeds, sedges and pioneer woody species.	Not very accessible, although some may be possible to use for boating. Boardwalks may be provided around the perimeter to offer some access.	Viewing nature, wildlife, birds, getting close to nature, solitude.	Risk of drowning if someone strays into the fen off proper paths. Insect bites and insect-borne diseases in summer.	Extremely rich habitats and valuable for fish, amphibians, invertebrates, birds and mammals. Plant species may also be rare. Sensitive to changes in water level and nitrates from adjacent farm land.
Marsh	Areas of mud which are inundated by tidal flows – salty, brackish or fresh in composition, usually associated with river estuaries.	Access is difficult, so boardwalks may be provided to allow people to experience them or to use them for obtaining worms for fishing.	Experiencing nature wildlife viewing, solitude.	Little risk unless people stray into them and get cut off by the tide. Insect bites and insect-borne diseases in summer.	Very rich habitats, especially for migratory birds feeding on invertebrates living in the mud. May also feature rare plants. Sensitive to sea level rise, pollution from incoming water or nitrates from nearby agricultural land.
Bog	A waterlogged area that started as a shallow lake or pond, went through the fen stage and then, as the peat accumulated, became more acidic and raised above the land surface. Dominated by acid-tolerant plants – mosses, low shrubs, some stunted trees.	Very difficult to access, so usually limited to boardwalks floating on the surface.	Berry picking, bog-shoeing, bog swimming (in pools inside the bogs) wildlife viewing, experiencing nature. In winter, possible skiing and snowshoeing if snowy.	Some risk of drowning if straying off paths or in bog pools, which are very cold. Insect bites and insect-borne diseases in summer.	One of the most important habitats in the areas where these occur (northern latitudes). Impacted by peat extraction but now considered extremely important. Locally sensitive to human activity on the surface vegetation.

Rivers, streams and canals

This set of blue spaces comprise linear bodies, usually flowing so that the water is ever changing (even canals which appear to be still have slow flow rates). Some may be tidal, and their character depends on their place in the hydrological and riverine regimes, including gradient, valley form and degree of modification and regulation for, for example, flood control or ease of water transport. For some examples, see Chapter 11.

Type	*Main characteristics*	*Blue infrastructure*	*Recreational, health and well-being benefits*	*Risks*	*Ecological aspects and sensitivities*
Large river with artificial banks	Large rivers usually run through the centre of a city and are the reason the city was founded. Many are canalised or regulated for flood control and to enable ships to pass. The rivers may be tidal, so their levels rise and fall daily. The main features are retaining walls made of stone or concrete and/ or embankments with steep slopes. The top of the embankment may be lined with trees.	There are usually walkways or promenades along the top of the retaining walls or embankments, although in some cities, roads follow them as well, making it noisy and disturbed. There may also be lower-level terraces with steps and/or ramps leading down to them, enabling closer contact with the water – these are usually submerged during floods. Bridges may offer spectacular views.	Wider rivers help to give a sense of openness and views, mainly to other parts of the city. The upper embankment and lower terrace walkways provide opportunities for walking and running, cycling, sitting, sunbathing, and the lower ones may feel less busy and quieter, enabling some escape from crowds. Fishing may be possible if the water is clean. Boating of various sorts allows a different perspective of the city.	Depending on the presence of safety rails and barriers, there are risks of drowning. Floods may pose a threat depending on the height of the water reached during severe flood events. Polluted water spray may cause diseases if blown into surrounding areas.	The water may be too polluted to permit much aquatic life, but if it is clean enough, there will be fish and invertebrates, but such rivers are not very ecologically sensitive.
Large river with natural banks	Urban rivers with natural banks are quite rare. It may be that part of the river bank is natural, while other sections are embanked. If the river is in a deeper valley compared with the city and if it is relatively straight, then less engineering may have been	Within the sections of river bank that are less steeply sloping, there may be footpaths or cycle paths which can be flooded at certain times. Steps or ramps lead down from the upper to lower sections. Roads or paths usually follow	The natural character provides access to nature in the city, closer contact with water, opportunities for walking, running, cycling. If the water is clean, then fishing is possible. Resting and enjoying the view. Boating of various sorts also allows different perspectives of the city to be obtained.	Usually along the edges of natural rivers, there are no barriers or railings, so there are risks of drowning. Floods may pose a threat depending on the height of the water reached during severe flood events. Polluted water spray may cause diseases if blown into surrounding areas.	The presence of natural and dynamic vegetation along an urban river makes the ecology very valuable. The different types of vegetation offer habitats for many animals and plants, especially birds and

(*continued*)

Appendix 1: The blue space typology

Type	*Main characteristics*	*Blue infrastructure*	*Recreational, health and well-being benefits*	*Risks*	*Ecological aspects and sensitivities*
	required in the past and the flood risk may be lower. Riverbanks are usually vegetated with trees which are suited to the dynamic conditions of flowing water and changing levels. The banks may be steep or shallow depending on the topography.	the edges of the river. Bridges may offer spectacular views.			mammals. The ecology is sensitive to changes in the river dynamics.
Medium-sized river with artificial banks	The characteristics of medium-sized rivers are similar to those of larger rivers, except that they are usually less wide and less deep, have less shipping and do not give such a grand scale of urban landscape. They have retaining walls and/or embankments but may not have the type of lower terrace, since they are not so deep. There may be trees planted along the edges.	The infrastructure associated with medium-sized rivers may be similar to that for larger rivers but on a smaller scale. Paths along the banks and possibly lower down nearer the water, places to sit, bridges offering views.	If there are no lower terraces, then all activities take place along the banks, which may be mixed with traffic, noise, pollution and so on. Normally walking, running, sitting, sunbathing and fishing. If clean and not so swift flowing, then water-based activities may be more common than on bigger rivers.	Depending on the presence of safety rails and barriers, there are risks of drowning. Floods may pose a threat depending on the height of the water reached during severe flood events. Polluted water spray may cause diseases if blown into surrounding areas.	Similar to larger rivers, the water may be too polluted to permit much aquatic life, but if it is clean enough, there will be fish and invertebrates, but such rivers are not very ecologically sensitive.
Medium-sized river with natural banks	As with larger rivers, examples with natural banks are quite rare but may be found in smaller cities which are less developed. Riverbanks are usually vegetated with trees which are suited to the dynamic conditions of flowing water and changing levels.	The infrastructure associated with medium-sized rivers may be similar to that for larger rivers but on a smaller scale. Paths along the banks, places to sit, bridges offering views.	Similar to larger rivers, the natural character provides access to nature in the city; closer contact with water; opportunities for walking, running, cycling. If the water is clean, then fishing is possible. Resting and enjoying the view. Boating of various sorts also	Usually along the edges of natural rivers, there are no barriers or railings, so there are risks of drowning. Floods may pose a threat depending on the height of the water reached during severe flood events. Polluted water spray may cause diseases if blown into surrounding areas.	Similar to larger rivers, the presence of natural and dynamic vegetation along an urban river makes the ecology very valuable. The different types of vegetation offer habitats for many animals

Type	*Main characteristics*	*Blue infrastructure*	*Recreational, health and well-being benefits*	*Risks*	*Ecological aspects and sensitivities*
	The banks may be steep or shallow depending on the topography.		allows different perspectives of the city to be obtained.		and plants, especially birds and mammals. The ecology is sensitive to changes in the river dynamics.
Stream with a mix of artificial or natural banks	A small, relatively narrow and shallow stream, if not piped underground as has been the case in many urban areas, is likely to be enclosed by built structures or possibly running through a park, where it may have more natural character.	There is usually little or no infrastructure giving direct access to the water, but paths running alongside, places to sit and bridges are provided.	The size of urban streams usually precludes any water-based activities, but walking, sitting, running and cycling along the paths, socialising, enjoying the water atmosphere are all possible.	Even if shallow and narrow, there is a risk of drowning. Localised flooding may occur, and if the water is polluted, there can be a risk of disease.	Similar to larger rivers, the presence of natural and dynamic vegetation along natural sections of an urban stream makes the ecology very valuable. The different types of vegetation offer habitats for many animals and plants, especially birds and mammals.
Urban canal	A linear artificial water body created by excavation and the installation of edge-retaining structures. Running between built-up areas and active or former industrial/ commercial areas. Water flows very slowly, as the canal levels are kept topped up. Originally used for industrial transport, nowadays mainly for recreational traffic.	Canals were originally equipped with locks for controlling water levels, docks/piers for loading/ unloading boats, bridges and towpaths running alongside. These provide access to and along the canals. May be places to sit.	Pleasure craft use the canals, but usually few activities in the water are possible (occasional swimming in some places). Walking running, cycling along towpaths.	Canals are not normally very deep, but with steep edges and no safety rails (for practical purposes), there may be risks of drowning. Water may be polluted.	Very urban canals with artificial edges have little ecological value, but where edges are softer there can be lots of aquatic vegetation, invertebrates, birds and fish, as well as mammals and amphibians.

Type	*Main characteristics*	*Blue infrastructure*	*Recreational, health and well-being benefits*	*Risks*	*Ecological aspects and sensitivities*
Rural canal	Similar to urban canals but running through less built-up areas, between fields or through woodland. Usually with softer edges.	Equipped as for urban canals but lacking docks and piers. Equipped with a towpath giving access.	Pleasure craft use the canals; limited if any other water-based activities. Walking, running, cycling along towpaths.	Canals are not normally very deep, but with steep edges and no safety rails (for practical purposes), there may be risks of drowning. Water may be polluted.	Canals in rural areas usually have softer edges with lots of aquatic vegetation, invertebrates, birds and fish, as well as mammals and amphibians. More natural terrestrial vegetation may come close to the canal, offering additional ecological benefits.
Waterfall or rapids	A steep section of a river or a place where a sudden change in level – perhaps due to geological conditions such as a cliff – results in water flowing more quickly or crashing over an edge. May have been controlled in order to harness power in urban areas.	Viewing platforms, safety railings, places to sit.	Rapids may be used for extreme water sports, but usually these are dramatic and exciting places to observe water, experience spray and noise and obtain a feeling of closeness to nature.	Risk of falling and injury if no safety railing and slippery, wet surfaces. Risk of drowning in the plunge pool or getting trapped in rocks. In flood conditions, the water may be more powerful and cause physical damage to structures, depending on how much water flows.	Cliffs and water-spray-covered, moist rocks may be habitats for specially adapted plants and animals.

Docks, ports and marinas

These types are all artificially created or modified places on the sea or rivers which are used for mooring boats or ships and for transfer of cargo, whether from fishing boats, cargo boats or container ships, as well as pleasure craft. Many have been released from their commercial use and have been redeveloped. For examples of some of these, see Chapter 14.

Type	*Main characteristics*	*Blue infrastructure*	*Recreational, health and well-being benefits*	*Risks*	*Ecological aspects and sensitivities*
Docks	Excavated or artificially built-up combination of water spaces suitable for ships to dock and tie up, hard surfaces for transferring cargoes and containers from ships, storage buildings, roads, cranes. Water edges are retained using stone or concrete to form high vertical walls. If the docks have ceased operation, many objects may have been removed or demolished leaving the water areas, hard surfaces and dock walls.	If the docks are in active use, there will be no public access and no possibilities for recreation. If under redevelopment, then the water edge areas may be equipped with safety rails, seating, shelters and possibly cafes, restaurants and other facilities, while the larger spaces may be given over to housing and commercial development. Direct water access may be achieved and boating or marina facilities added with steps and ramps leading down from the dock edges to floating pontoons.	Redeveloped docks provide opportunities to gain access to water after periods when there was none. Residential development and recreational infrastructure can allow for people to live close to or on the water and to gain the benefits of such proximity.	Docks often present high vertical walls descending into deep and polluted water. There is a risk of drowning. If tidal, the water levels fluctuate, and flooding can also be an issue unless the docks were equipped with infrastructure to control water levels (such as lock gates). Water may be polluted, so some risk of disease.	As very artificial areas, often in a combination of excavated and built-up land, large areas of sealed surfaces and pollution, the ecological values are usually very low. Post-redevelopment sites may have more greenery added, and water may become cleaner and offer more aquatic life.
Harbour	Areas of water enclosed by artificial walls and breakwaters to enable ships and boats to tie up and exchange cargoes, as well as to provide havens in the event of storms. If commercially active, they may be accessible to the public and may be shared with pleasure craft.	Harbour walls, docks, sea defences, storage buildings. Usually lack safety railings due to practical constraints. If of mixed use, may have cafés and kiosks, seating and services for pleasure craft.	Recreational sailing and boating, fishing (off the harbour walls or using boats). Watching activities, being by the sea, experiencing the seaside landscape, breathing in the sea air, gaining a sense of perspective in the face of the forces of nature (the sublime).	Risk of drowning, accidents with boats and equipment, water may be polluted, with some risk of disease.	If the harbour connects with the sea, then fish and marine mammals may use the water (with food coming from fishing boats). Seabirds may nest or use the harbour for food scavenging. Rocks and old sea walls may be colonised by specialist vegetation.

(*continued*)

Appendix 1: The blue space typology

Type	*Main characteristics*	*Blue infrastructure*	*Recreational, health and well-being benefits*	*Risks*	*Ecological aspects and sensitivities*
Marina	An arrangement of floating pontoons and decks used to tie up pleasure craft of various types and sizes, together with services for boat owners. May be located in sheltered parts of former docks, harbours or lakes or backwaters of rivers from where boats can move out to open water.	Pontoons, decking, service facilities such as fuel tanks, onshore boat storage areas, car parking, onshore seating, shelters, cafés and possibly restaurants depending on the scale of the development.	Main opportunities to go sailing, using motor boats and yachts of varying sizes and types, as well as enjoying the proximity of boats and the social activities which go with them.	Accidents associated with sailing and boating, drowning, storms and flooding.	If the water is clean, then marine or aquatic biodiversity should be present. Birds may be attracted by food. Otherwise, not much nature in a constructed area. Oil pollution may cause problems to aquatic life.

Other blue infrastructure

These types are a set of miscellaneous examples which may be significant and important for a range of purposes – ornamental, therapeutic or recreational.

Type	*Main characteristics*	*Blue infrastructure*	*Recreational, health and well-being benefits*	*Risks*	*Ecological aspects and sensitivities*
Ornamental water feature or fountain	Individually designed exciting and dynamic features which use the varying characteristics of water movement and hydraulic equipment to create attractive focal features.	Depending on the location and scale, these may be traditional fountains with a basin, some form of sculpture and jets or water emerging to fall into the basin. May also be more interactive features, with jets coming up from paving, allowing people to splash and play. May also be jet features placed into and floating on larger water bodies.	Aesthetic benefits of seeing dynamics of water, cooling in hot weather, play for children and adults.	Low risk of drowning in fountain basins; if water is not clean, there may be a risk of disease; slipping and physical injury on wet surfaces.	Not usually any ecological features associated with these.

Type	*Main characteristics*	*Blue infrastructure*	*Recreational, health and well-being benefits*	*Risks*	*Ecological aspects and sensitivities*
Mineral spring	A source of water containing various minerals associated with health-promoting properties. May be a small local feature or a large spa where the water is available for drinking in a special building. Whole towns have developed based on the promotion of the properties of the water.	Infrastructure ranges from enclosed pools with access to a spring where water can be collected, maybe with a shelter and some seating, to large buildings with special taps and places to sit, talk and stroll.	Direct benefits of drinking the water containing minerals (as long as these have scientifically accepted therapeutic values).	Overconsumption or some degree of poisoning if the chemicals are not really salutogenic; slipping on wet surfaces.	Usually none, except in places with natural undeveloped springs where the minerals may favour unique plants and animals.
Thermal spring	Sources of naturally occurring warm or hot water, usually but not always associated with volcanically active areas.	Infrastructure ranges from small rudimentary enclosed pools for people to immerse themselves in the hot water to elaborate complexes of indoor and outdoor pools of different temperatures with changing rooms and cafes.	Direct health benefits such as relieving muscle pain to pleasure or relaxation in warm or hot water, socialising, de-stressing.	Drowning, shock from moving from hot to cold water, slipping on wet surfaces.	
Outdoor skating, curling or ice hockey rink	A natural or artificial shallow pond which is allowed to freeze in winter, where conditions allow, and then used for ice skating or playing ice hockey or curling.	May be a simple pond used informally without any specific facilities or may be equipped with markings and special equipment such as goal posts, benches and shelters.	Physical activity in winter – skating, curling, ice hockey.	Potential risks if the ice breaks, falling and injury on the ice.	A natural pond may have good ecological conditions during the non-icebound periods of the year.

Appendix 1: The blue space typology

Type	*Main characteristics*	*Blue infrastructure*	*Recreational, health and well-being benefits*	*Risks*	*Ecological aspects and sensitivities*
Lido/open-air swimming pool	An artificial pool filled with either natural (e.g. sea-water) water or treated freshwater, heated only by natural sunshine.	May be a pool formed by stone and concrete which is built into natural rocks or cliffs; may also be a completely artificial outdoor pool, such as in a city with water treatment. Usually equipped with changing facilities, sitting areas and possibly cafes.	Swimming, sun bathing, enjoying sea air.	Drowning, sunburn, slipping on wet surfaces.	No ecological associations.

Bibliography

Brand, D. (2007). Bluespace: A typological matrix for port cities. *Urban Design International, 12*(2–3), 69–85. https://doi.org/10.1057/palgrave.udi.9000195Table 0.1 Summary of the blue space typology used in BlueHealth

Index

Note: Page numbers in *italic* indicate a figure, and page numbers in **bold** indicate a table on the corresponding page.

Index